Simona Montanari and Suzanne Quay (Eds.)
Multidisciplinary Perspectives on Multilingualism

Language Contact
and Bilingualism

Editor
Yaron Matras

Volume 19

Multidisciplinary Perspectives on Multilingualism

The Fundamentals

Edited by
Simona Montanari and Suzanne Quay

DE GRUYTER
MOUTON

ISBN 978-1-5015-2538-4
e-ISBN (PDF) 978-1-5015-0798-4
e-ISBN (EPUB) 978-1-5015-0790-8
ISSN 2190-698X

Library of Congress Control Number: 2019944934

Bibliographic information published by the Deutsche Nationalbibliothek
The Deutsche Nationalbibliothek lists this publication in the Deutsche Nationalbibliografie;
detailed bibliographic data are available on the Internet at http://dnb.dnb.de.

© 2021 Walter de Gruyter Inc., Boston/Berlin
This volume is text- and page-identical with the hardback published in 2019.
Typesetting: Integra Software Services Pvt. Ltd.
Printing and binding: CPI books GmbH, Leck
Cover image: Anette Linnea Rasmus/Fotolia

www.degruyter.com

Contents

Suzanne Quay and Simona Montanari
1   Multilingualism from Multidisciplinary Perspectives:
    Introduction and Overview —— 1

Part I: Societal Multilingualism: Historical, Political, Economic and Educational Forces in Different World Regions

Ahmed Ech-Charfi
2   Multilingualism, Language Varieties and Ideology in North Africa —— 7

Bee Chin Ng and Francesco Cavallaro
3   Multilingualism in Southeast Asia: The Post-Colonial Language Stories of Hong Kong, Malaysia and Singapore —— 27

Lennart Bartelheimer, Britta Hufeisen and Simona Montanari
4   Multilingualism in Europe —— 51

Wayne E. Wright and Virak Chan
5   Multilingualism in North America —— 77

Part II: Language Use in Multilingual Communities

John Maher
6   Diglossia in Multilingual Communities —— 103

Anat Stavans and Ronit Porat
7   Codeswitching in Multilingual Communities —— 123

Charlotte Gooskens
8   Receptive Multilingualism —— 149

Deborah Chen Pichler, Wanette Reynolds and Jeffrey Levi Palmer
9   Multilingualism in Signing Communities —— 175

Part III: Individual Multilingualism: From Development to Loss

Suzanne Quay and Sarah Chevalier
10 Fostering Multilingualism in Childhood —— 205

Elizabeth Lanza and Kristin Vold Lexander
11 Family Language Practices in Multilingual Transcultural Families —— 229

Xiao-lei Wang
12 Multilingualism through Schooling —— 253

Ulrike Jessner and Manon Megens
13 Language Attrition in Multilinguals —— 275

Part IV: Differences between Bilingualism and Multilingualism

Simona Montanari
14 Facilitated Language Learning in Multilinguals —— 299

Elisabeth Allgäuer-Hackl and Ulrike Jessner
15 Cross-linguistic Interaction and Multilingual Awareness —— 325

Dorit Segal, Gitit Kavé, Mira Goral and Tamar H. Gollan
16 Multilingualism and Cognitive Benefits in Aging —— 351

Iris M. Strangmann, Stanley Chen and Loraine K. Obler
17 Multilingual Language Processing and the Multilingual Brain —— 375

Simona Montanari and Suzanne Quay
18 Conclusion and Directions for Future Research —— 397

Index of Key Words —— 409

Index of Languages / Language Families —— 417

Index of Countries and Continents —— 421

Suzanne Quay and Simona Montanari
1 Multilingualism from Multidisciplinary Perspectives: Introduction and Overview

> [M]ultilingualism should not be seen as a variant of bilingualism but rather be studied in its own right as further evidence of human potential and capacity for language. The research done so far on multilingualism, both as individual and social phenomena, has shown that stimulating insights into the acquisition and attrition processes can arise from a focus on learning three or more languages from multidisciplinary areas such as psycholinguistics and linguistics, applied linguistics, second language acquisition, sociolinguistics, neurolinguistics and education. As discussed, research on many of the issues raised in this chapter is limited and many more studies are needed to understand what makes multilingualism unique or rather similar with respect to bilingualism
> (Quay and Montanari 2019: 560).

Thus ends not only our chapter giving an overview on "Bilingualism and Multilingualism" where we made a distinction between using, learning and unlearning two versus more than two languages but also *The Cambridge Handbook on Bilingualism* edited by Annick De Houwer and Lourdes Ortega. That chapter inspired our journey in this volume towards understanding issues in multilingualism that are beyond studies of bilingualism. The purpose of this volume is to show through research evidence that multilingualism is a typical aspect of everyday life for most of the world's population. It is present among individuals of all backgrounds – from the educated to the poor and in all geographical areas – and is a complex phenomenon that involves a myriad of linguistic and extra-linguistic forces.

This volume, consisting of four parts, attempts to disentangle the linguistic and extra-linguistic forces that can explain the complexity of multilingualism through the multidisciplinary lenses mentioned in the above quote. The chapters in this volume explore multilingualism in different contexts and provide new and wider perspectives of this phenomenon as a result. The first part provides the setting for the contributions in Parts 2, 3 and 4. In particular, it focuses on societal multilingualism in four different geographical areas: North Africa (Ech-Charfi, Chapter 2), Southeast Asia (Ng and Cavallaro, Chapter 3), Europe (Bartelheimer, Hufeisen, and Montanari, Chapter 4) and North America, in particular the United States and Canada (Wright and Chan, Chapter 5). While

---

Suzanne Quay, International Christian University, Tokyo, Japan
Simona Montanari, California State University, Los Angeles (CA), U.S.A.

https://doi.org/10.1515/9781501507984-001

this section is certainly not exhaustive of all the world regions where multilingualism is practiced, it gives examples of communities in the Global North and the Global South with a long-established tradition of linguistic diversity, where the use of more than two languages is an everyday experience. This part sets the stage for the contributions in Parts 2, 3 and 4, which provide new methods and wider perspectives in the study of multilingualism. Indeed, the second part of the volume examines novel concepts and practices in the use of more than two languages in multilingual communities: in diglossic domains (Maher, Chapter 6), through code-switching practices (Stavans and Porat, Chapter 7), and receptively in communities where multilingual speakers share closely-related mutually intelligible languages (Gooskens, Chapter 8). The final chapter of this section discusses bimodal language use in signing communities (Chen Pichler, Reynolds, and Palmer, Chapter 9), highlighting a new and exciting area of investigation that provides unique insights into the human capacity for multilingualism. The third part focuses on multilingualism in individuals: how it is fostered in childhood (Quay and Chevalier, Chapter 10), the language practices of transcultural families (Lanza and Lexander, Chapter 11), the effects of schooling (Wang, Chapter 12), and the consequences of changes in linguistic dominance, proficiencies and skills in multilinguals (Jessner and Megens, Chapter 13). This section underscores new perspectives in the study of the effects that families and educational systems have on children's multilingualism. The final section of this volume addresses differences between bilingualism and multilingualism in terms of additional language learning (Montanari, Chapter 14), cross-linguistic interaction and multilingual awareness (Allgäuer-Hackl and Jessner, Chapter 15), cognitive benefits in aging (Segal et al., Chapter 16), and language processing in the brain (Strangmann, Chen, and Obler, Chapter 17), highlighting the unique nature of multilingualism with respect to bilingualism.

As we envisioned in Quay and Montanari (2019), this volume adds to current knowledge about the use, acquisition, and loss of multiple languages from a multidisciplinary perspective ranging from sociolinguistics, psycholinguistics, linguistics, applied linguistics, and education to neurolinguistics. The chapters in this volume reflect the academic styles of authors from different disciplines who have provided us with reviews of the literature in their areas of expertise. This was a challenging task for those in areas where scant research has been done on multilinguals who, for example, can sign and speak – at times simultaneously – in more than two signed and spoken languages (bimodal signers in Chen Pichler, Reynolds, and Palmer, Chapter 9), are being educated in a language other than their home languages (Wang, Chapter 12), are elderly with comparable language backgrounds, education and experiences (Segal et al., Chapter 16), or have participated in neuroimaging studies (Strangmann, Chen, and Obler, Chapter 17). To supplement the dearth of literature in their area, Segal et al. in Chapter 16 introduce a preliminary study they have conducted themselves on the effects of multilingualism on cognitive performance in aging.

Due to length constraints for each chapter, the contributors to Part 1 could only focus on some countries within the regions they were asked to write about. Thus, Ech-Charfi (Chapter 2) focuses on North Africa, Ng and Cavallaro (Chapter 3) on Hong Kong, Malaysia and Singapore, Bartelheimer, Hufeisen, and Montanari, (Chapter 4) on countries mostly in northwestern Europe, and Wright and Chan (Chapter 5) on Canada and the United States. Colonialism (Ech-Charfi, Chapter 2; Ng and Cavallaro, Chapter 3) and migration (Bartelheimer, Hufeisen, and Montanari, Chapter 4; Wright and Chan, Chapter 5) are discussed as reasons for linguistic pluralism and/or individual multilingualism in those regions. Thus the volume starts with macro-level structural features that regulate the use of languages in culturally diverse settings. Sociopolitical and sociolinguistic forces along with educational policies encourage the development of multilingualism in the populations described in all four chapters. In Chapter 6, Maher situates contemporary examples of diglossic practices in Ireland, Finland, India, and especially in Japan, along with a historic discussion of the phenomenon. By doing so, he broadens the global perspective of multilingualism started in Part 1. In Chapter 8, Gooskens also expands on the region covered by Bartelheimer, Hufeisen, and Montanari (Chapter 4) with her discussion of receptive multilingualism in Scandinavian countries and elsewhere in Europe.

Some of the chapters present "models" to aid in our understanding of how multilinguals process languages while code-switching (Stavans and Porat, Chapter 7) or blending signed and spoken languages (Chen Pichler, Reynolds, and Palmer, Chapter 9), lose their language abilities (Jessner and Megens, Chapter 13), transfer skills from earlier acquired languages to learn new languages (Montanari, Chapter 14), and use their languages in a complex and dynamic way (Allgäuer-Hackl and Jessner, Chapter 15). Other chapters deal with actual cases of multilingual children and their families. While Quay and Chevalier (Chapter 10) look at how childhood multilingualism can be nurtured in the home and external community, Lanza and Lexander (Chapter 11) explore this issue from the perspective of transcultural families providing their own community of practice and fostering multilingualism through digitally-mediated language practices. Wang (Chapter 12) then addresses how schooling can have positive and negative outcomes. That is, new languages can be added and developed further in the educational setting, but linguistic and cultural distances between languages may make it easier or harder to achieve academic success when developing literacy in the school language. The school context may also lead to the loss of previous languages acquired in the home.

Montanari and Quay (Chapter 18) conclude this volume with a synthesis of the common threads that run through the chapters: from historical and political perspectives that affect not only multilingualism at the societal level but also at the individual one to economic and educational perspectives related to migration and family language practices and policies. The complexities that arise in multilingual language use surpass – internally and externally – bilingual use and result in much more variability as discussed throughout this volume. This concluding chapter also provides new insights and trends in research that we foresee will be valuable for stimulating further research to increase our limited understanding of multilingualism in the 21st century.

Acknowledgments: For their time and expertise, we are indebted not only to all the contributors who helped us with the internal reviewing process but also to Katja Cantone, Jean-Marc Dewaele and Robert Mayr.

Reference

Quay, Suzanne & Simona Montanari. 2019. Bilingualism and multilingualism. In Annick De Houwer & Lourdes Ortega (eds.), *The Cambridge handbook of bilingualism*, 544–560. Cambridge, UK: Cambridge University Press.

Part I: **Societal Multilingualism: Historical, Political, Economic and Educational Forces in Different World Regions**

Ahmed Ech-Charfi
2 Multilingualism, Language Varieties and Ideology in North Africa

2.1 Introduction

The notion of multilingualism rests on a tacit assumption that languages (and related concepts such as varieties, dialects, accents, etc.) can be identified, delimitated and enumerated. Without this assumption, there would be no sense in distinguishing multilingual from monolingual communities. Indeed, there would be no sense in speaking even of individual languages or in doing linguistic analysis of the sort we have inherited from Saussurian structuralism. Saussure (1972: 86) conceived of human languages as systems "in which all the parts can and must be considered synchronically interdependent". One of the implications of this conception is that only linguistic analysis can reveal the number of varieties in use in any given society, region or country. The problem, however, is that this implication has so far been more of an assumption than a verified fact. There is ample evidence, as will be explained further, that what individuals and communities identify as distinct languages or dialects are in fact social constructs contingent on specific socio-historical factors. So, many of the languages catalogued today are the outcome of such factors, including the European colonization and, more importantly, the European discourse about language and nation.

The objective of this chapter is to build on the extant literature – which attempts to reconsider the notion of multilingualism and to advance a critique of the foundations of structural linguistics – in order to approach multilingualism in North Africa (NA). The next section will provide a brief review of this literature while the remaining sections will be devoted to the analysis of the major components of the NA linguistic scene. In particular, Section 2.3 will deal with French and other foreign languages; Section 2.4 with Arabic; and Section 2.5 with Berber.

2.2 Language as a socio-political construct

Scholars from various disciplines have long noted that languages usually emerge as a corollary to the emergence of socio-political entities. In fact, language provides some of the useful resources that a community needs to distinguish itself

---

Ahmed Ech-Charfi, Mohammed V University, Rabat, Morocco

https://doi.org/10.1515/9781501507984-002

from neighboring groups. If this observation is true of all languages, it is even more true of standard languages. In his classic paper, Haugen (1966) identifies four steps in the process of constructing a standard language: (a) selection of a variety; (b) codification of its form; (c) elaboration of its functions; and (d) acceptance by the community. That languages characteristically exhibit some variation is considered as a fundamental tenet of sociolinguistics, but state-builders tend to favor linguistic homogeneity by reducing variation in standard languages to the minimum, an aspect that made these languages appear to many linguists as artificial.

Another work that is more relevant to the purposes of this chapter is Kloss (1967). Kloss notes that, when enumerating and classifying varieties in preliterate societies, a linguist is forced to treat linguistically distant varieties as belonging to different languages. He calls these *abstand* ('distant') languages. But when varieties are related with varying degrees of mutual intelligibility, a linguist's classification may differ, to a lesser or a greater extent, from that adopted by communities. Oftentimes, what a linguist tends to treat technically as a single language may be fragmented into various languages, with different communities claiming to speak a different language than those of their neighbors. Kloss calls these *ausbau* ('developed') languages, classic examples of which are the Scandinavian languages and the languages born in the aftermath of the disintegration of Yugoslavia. Kloss's insight indicates that *ausbau* languages are sociological phenomena that should be approached not only through linguistic analysis, but also through the methods of other social sciences, if an adequate understanding of them is to be achieved.

But languages are not always invented by their own communities for ethnic, political or whatever reasons; they may also be created by foreigners (e.g. colonial administrators, missionaries, etc.) and imposed on the local population. Recent literature (cf. Makoni 1998; Makoni and Pennycook 2007, 2012, among others) revisits some of the languages of Africa, Asia and America to highlight the circumstances in which they were identified, labeled and catalogued. What these studies conclude is that, in many of the cases revisited, the languages were simply not recognized as separate entities by the local populations. For example, in their attempt to translate the scriptures in local varieties, missionaries often classified those varieties according to their own conception of what a language is or should be, usually along Western principles, without considering the indigenous worldviews.

One of the interesting facts that these non-Western conceptions uncover is that "not all people have 'a language/languages' in the sense in which the term is currently used in English" (Heryanto 1990: 41). That of course does not mean that these people do not communicate through linguistic means, but only that they do not recognize any classification of their linguistic resources into entities called languages, each with its own name, as is the case in other cultures. The mere existence of such cultures, no matter how exotic they may be, should call for a reconsideration of the prevalent essentialist view that reifies language. As pointed out earlier, the notion of multilingualism rests on this essentialist view endorsed by structural linguistics since its inception a century ago. But in situations where either no languages are recognized or where the languages are too broad to allow for a structuralist analysis as generally practiced, the very notions of language variety or linguistic system – and that of multilingualism they give birth to – simply break down. Any attempt to impose them on such situations would be a Procrustean endeavor that misses more about language than it highlights.

Therefore, if we cannot determine how many languages are spoken in an area on the basis of linguistic analysis only, we should opt for a sociological approach to uncover the ideologies behind the construction of different language varieties. As formulated by Makoni and Pennycook (2012: 440), the main questions we will be concerned with are:

- [U]nder what sociohistorical contexts did [these languages] emerge, what are the philosophical strategies used in their construction and how does invention impact the linguistic practices of the users, and our understanding of multilingualism?
- What are the metadiscursive regimes [...] used in the construction of "languages"?

With these questions in mind, we will turn to the discussion of the main languages spoken in NA.

2.3 French, English and other foreign languages

Foreign languages were brought to NA by the colonial powers. Following an agreement between these powers, Egypt went to Britain; Libya to Italy; Tunisia, Algeria, Mauritania and parts of Morocco went to France, while the north and the south of Morocco were relegated to Spain. As a consequence, English, Italian, French and Spanish are spoken in these countries, with varying degrees. The variation depends on a number of factors, most important of which are: (a) the linguistic policy of the colonizer, with France giving importance to imposing its language and culture more than the others; (b) the importance given by post-independence elites to the promotion of their national languages; and (c) the continuing presence of economic interests of the former colonizer.

In Morocco, for example, where the elite has maintained common interests with the French, the French language is still omnipresent in the private sector, education and the media, and enjoys a lot of prestige among the upper and the middle classes. In comparison, Italian is less visible in Libya; the nationalist ideology of the Gaddafi regime stressed the promotion of Arabic and was less tolerant toward the presence of foreign languages.

The present chapter, however, is less concerned with the domains of use of the foreign languages than with the ideologies and representations that support their existence as independent languages. The obvious fact that these languages are learned and used with varying degrees of proficiency should not be undervalued as a natural aspect of language learning in general. Instead, it should be taken as indication of a cleavage between linguistic reality and the discourse about that reality, especially when we know that many interlanguage features have fossilized in the local forms of the foreign languages. In the case of French in Morocco, for instance, Ennaji (2005: 98–101) distinguishes three different varieties that he calls: (1) Highly Educated French, (2) Standard Educated French, and (3) Uneducated French. But although this classification is based on a set of features, the three varieties are not recognized either by other linguists or by the general population. French in NA, just like English, Italian and Spanish, continues to exist in the imaginary as a unified language, and systematic divergences from standard usage are not considered good reason to believe that what is spoken is anything other than French, albeit in what is considered as imperfect forms (cf. the papers in Pleines 1990 for example).

The question as to why these local varieties of these languages are not recognized as distinct varieties is not a trivial one. In some parts of the world such as India and Nigeria, varieties of English are treated as full-fledged varieties in the growing discourse on World Englishes (Kachru, Kachru, and Nelson 2009). In comparison, there seems to be no similar discourse in NA, particularly with French, no matter how omnipresent it is in the region. The unity of this language is created and maintained by a political discourse about Self and Other that puts more emphasis on memories of the past than on facts of the present. French is still viewed as the language of the colonizer, especially in Algeria, where the war for independence was rather bloody. Memories of that period are now used to legitimize the rule of the military in the country. But even in Morocco and Tunisia, where independence was earned at a less costly price, objections against the integration of French in national culture have gained strength to the extent that they are now part of the legitimate discourse. Consequently, those who are favorable to French among the upper and the middle classes are forced to express their position in covert terms. One manifestation of the legitimate discourse against French is reflected in law, as in the case of Morocco, where legal texts avoid any explicit mention of French and use instead the rather general expression "foreign language" (Ruiter 2001). In brief, the discourse about foreign languages in NA associates these languages with colonial powers and, for that reason, rejects the adoption of the local versions of these languages.

There is also another deeper factor behind the rejection of such versions that has to do with the conception of standard languages (Milroy 2001). According to this conception, standard usage is the only correct usage. Moreover, incorrect forms produced by non-native speakers, no matter how stable they may be, cannot be considered as part of a distinct variety. Ortega (2018: 10) calls this conception "the teleological view". She is referring to a general assumption about linguistic development in Second Language Acquisition research according to which "native speakers serve [...] as the unquestioned golden benchmark against which to adjudicate gain, progress, learning, and proficiency". In essential conceptions of language, "the idealized notion of a native speaker in possession of a complete, bounded, and perfectly uniform language is deeply rooted" (Ortega 2018: 10), and the same conception has somehow found its way to lay culture as well. In NA, the view that standard languages belong to their competent native speakers is widespread among learners and their parents, who would like to see their children speak these languages the way native speakers do, e.g. French like French people. This view is inculcated in their minds by all sorts of prescription agents such as teachers, grammar books, newspaper columnists, etc. who were influenced in turn by theories about language. It is true that this view has been boosted by modern schooling, which has been heavily influenced by Western culture, but its presence in the local culture goes back to Arabic grammarians. Being part of the Arab world, NA inherited what Milroy (2001: 531) calls "standard language culture" from early Arabic linguistic theorizing, which put much emphasis on correct usage, as will be explained in the following section.

In brief, the status of French, English, Spanish and Italian as colonial languages, together with the teleological view of linguistic development, continues to hinder the emergence of local varieties of these languages in NA. So far, there is no indication that something like Algerian French or Egyptian English will be recognized in the same way that Indian or Nigerian English are recognized in India and Nigeria, respectively.

2.4 Arabic

What is known as "the Arabic language" presents a very complex situation in which linguistic reality is shaped and reshaped by different ideologies, each contesting the views of the others. The number of varieties recognized even by linguists themselves seems to reflect different views about the language, not as dictated by an allegedly objective analysis, but also as an expression of views of the past and the present situation of society and its future aspirations. But this unstable situation provides us with a good opportunity to reconsider the structural linguistics' general practice of taking the existence of language varieties as a given. The notion of diglossia will be discussed first before the standard and the colloquial varieties of Arabic are considered in some detail.

2.4.1 Diglossia

Among all the works on Arabic, Ferguson's (1959) paper was probably the most influential. The paper considers Arabic as the epitome of what its author calls *diglossia*, a situation in which two varieties of the same language exist side by side, but each is used for a different set of communicative purposes. Ferguson also mentions Greece, German Switzerland and Haiti as similar cases of diglossic communities. Since the publication of this seminal paper, studies on diglossia have arisen exponentially. Most of these researchers, however, tend to be more interested in how the social functions of the High (H) and Low (L) varieties reinforce and are reinforced by attitudes – and how stable and changing social factors contribute to the maintenance of diglossia or its subsequent development into a situation of standard-with-dialects – than in the linguistic aspects of the H-L interaction. This sociological interest is best exemplified by Fishman's (1967) conception of diglossia as not limited to historically related varieties only, as Ferguson's definition requires, but also extended to non-related languages when these stand in an H-L relationship (see also Chapter 6, this volume).

There is good reason, however, to suspect that Ferguson built his analysis on folk notions which were – and still are – prevalent in the societies he considered in his 1959 paper. In relation with Arabic, he does mention that H corresponds to what Arabs call *fuṣḥā* (a most eloquent version of 'language') and that L corresponds to their *ʕāmmiyya* ('language of common people') or *dariʒa* ('colloquial language'). There is not much research on how these concepts made their way into modern Arabic culture, but researchers suspect that they were inventions of the 19th century when Arabs came into contact with Western civilization (Brustad 2017; Ech-Charfi 2017). Traditional Arabic writings do not seem to adopt the equivalent of the opposition between "language" and "dialect". The term *lahʒa* ('dialect') is most probably an invention of the same period as well; before that, it used to mean "tongue" or "tip of the tongue", but it was very infrequent. The term *luya*, which used to mean both 'language' and 'variety of language', was reinterpreted to stand as an equivalent of the Western "standard language".

The term *fuṣḥā* itself had probably never been used as an attribute for H Arabic before the 19th century, when the opposition between "language" and "dialect" was borrowed into the Arabic culture. That of course should not mean that speakers of Arabic had not been until then aware of the differences between the varieties they spoke and that of the Quran, for example. It is only that they did not feel any need to classify the two into different categories. After all, differences did not exist only between the varieties they spoke and that of the literate culture, but also between their spoken varieties and those of their close and distant neighbors. Therefore, what could be concluded from these remarks is that the distinction between *fuṣḥā* and *ʕāmmiyya/dariʒa*, which Ferguson assumes to be a defining criterion of Arabic diglossia, is in fact a borrowing from European linguistic culture in which this distinction developed in different circumstances (Haugen 1966).

It may be claimed that diglossia is real and that H and L have an independent existence, irrespective of whether local culture recognizes it or not. Such a view is not supported by linguistic facts, however. Immediately after the publication of Ferguson's (1959) paper, studies on Arabic started to doubt the possibility of drawing a clear boundary between H and L and, indirectly, their very existence as distinct varieties. Blanc (1960) and Palva (1969) were among the earliest works to note that native speakers of Arabic tend to mix features generally considered as standard or colloquial in such a way that any attempt to classify their speech as either *fuṣḥā* or *ʕāmmiyya/dariʒa* would be random. Today, there seems to be a consensus, among Western scholars at least, that Arabic constitutes one language with various stylistic levels, and each level is appropriate to a set of contexts, though it may be exploited for various pragmatic purposes in other contexts as well. We owe this sociolinguistic approach to Badawi (1973), who conceived of Arabic as forming a continuum. He does identify five major levels corresponding to usages of the major social classes in Egypt, but he denies that each level constitutes a distinct variety. In other words, Arabic is like a color spectrum in which shades of one color (corresponding to Badawi's level) fade gradually into those of another. Therefore, as Brustad (2017: 41) notes, "diglossia does not serve us well as a tool of linguistic analysis."

2.4.2 Standard Arabic

The question that ensues immediately from the claim above is: how are H and L constructed in Arabic diglossia, and what purposes do they serve? What constitutes an H text or an L text from the point of view of different speakers is an empirical issue but, unfortunately, not much research has been done along these lines. Parkinson (1993) raises this question and tries to answer it indirectly by testing the *Fuṣḥā* proficiency of a sample of Cairene inhabitants. His findings indicate that only individuals with a college degree in Arabic approach what can be considered an acceptable proficiency level. Those without such a degree, even with a high education, can fail to get a reasonable understanding of literary texts even from the modern era, let alone the classical texts. By implication, it seems that Arabs' judgments vary considerably on what constitutes an H or an L text. Many researchers have remarked that the boundaries between *Fuṣḥā* and *ʕāmmiyya* are variable (Hary 1996; Mejdell 2006 among others). In turn, this remark implies that different individuals or groups may have different representations of the two varieties, and that these representations manifest in their linguistic behavior. In other words, it is very likely that speakers with limited knowledge of *Fuṣḥā* would judge a text as *Fuṣḥā*-like even when the number of colloquial features it exhibits is relatively high; e.g. the spoken texts on cultural issues broadcasted on radio or television programs. In comparison, those with a better knowledge of *Fuṣḥā* would downgrade even written texts meant to be standard literary productions. Naguib Mahfouz, the Nobel Prize winner, for example, is criticized for transgressing many rules of grammar as handed down by the tradition (cf. Holes 1995).

In the face of this great disparity between linguistic reality and its dichotomization into *Fuṣḥā* and *ʕāmmiyya/dariʒa*, Brustad (2017) argues that the notion of diglossia is an ideology. Her argument is based mainly on a well-documented shift in attitudes toward the classical usage after the so-called *Nahda* ('Renaissance') period, which started in the mid-19th century when the Arab elite developed a new discourse about the backwardness of their societies relative to the West and how to achieve a new revival of the Arab-Islamic civilization. Before this period, attitudes toward the classical usage of *Fuṣḥā* were rather lax, as testified by the large number of writings in what Western scholars classify as "middle" Arabic (Zack and Schippers 2012). Although some of these writings were produced by authors who undoubtedly had a good mastery of Arabic grammar, they exhibited many colloquial features that were ruled out by the grammatical tradition (for examples of such authors, see Brustad 2017). Scholars note that such texts were common throughout the Arab world since the 16th century, indicating that a new standard variety was probably developing as a means of written communication. But the development was halted by the *Nahda* discourse which, by setting the classical usage as the ideal standard, denigrated the colloquial varieties. Consequently, throughout much of the 20th century, the language academies tried to develop a standard language that would enable its users to express modern scientific and technological concepts while at the same time remaining faithful to the styles and the phraseology of the classical variety. So far, however, this variety has survived more as an ideal than a reality. Arabs continue to feel that writings in modern *Fuṣḥā* are unsatisfactory and fail to attain the ideal usage in many respects. The idealization of *Fuṣḥā* is opposed by a total rejection of the local varieties such as Moroccan or Egyptian Arabic, and between the two was caught the soul of the *Nahda* Arab, unsatisfied by its stark reality but unable to realize its own ideal.

A similar discourse was also adopted by pan-Arabists during the first half of the 20th century. Faced with the decision of the colonial powers to create small states in the Middle East, the Arab elite saw their dream of a great Arab nation vanishing, despite all the promises they had received from those powers. Instead of accepting the new reality, the elite chose to reject the new polities and the borders artificially drawn by the colonizers (Hourani 1967). Language was their solid ground to express this rejection and on which they tried to build their ideal nation. Arab nationalists sought inspiration in the writings of the 19th century German nationalists because these also put much emphasis on a common language as a defining criterion of a nation (Suleiman 2003). For them, the Arab nation should include all those for whom Arabic is the means of communication, irrespective of whether or not they were originally Arabs. Obviously, what they meant by "Arabic" was *Fuṣḥā* since the colloquial varieties differed from one region to another. Like their predecessors of the *Nahda*, pan-Arab ideologists also rejected the use of *ʕāmmiyya/dariʒa* because that would imply acceptance of the divisions enforced by the colonizers on Arab people. Husari, one of the pan-Arab prolific writers, argues that, just like the borders between the Arab polities, so-called "Iraqi Arabic" or "Egyptian Arabic", for example, are artificial constructs since Arabic dialects form a continuum (Suleiman 2003), a remark that is undoubtedly true. On the other hand, he held *Fuṣḥā* to be both a unified and a unifying language in the sense that all Arabs adhere to the same standards, namely those set by the grammatical and literary traditions. According to him, *Fuṣḥā* also brings together the present and the past, thus unifying the Arab nation in time as well (Suleiman 2003). Obviously, this argument is ideological in the sense that it minimizes the variation in Arabic texts produced in different periods of history: for the classicist elite, the Arabic of the 20th century is identical with that of the pre-Islamic era.

In comparison, Western Arabists tend to identify more varieties of *Fuṣḥā* than are recognized by Arabs themselves. For these scholars, at least three different varieties should be distinguished corresponding to different stages in the development of the language. The first includes the pre-Islamic dialects spoken in Arabia, which are generically referred to as "Old Arabic". Apart from the pre-Islamic poetry which was recorded by early Arab and Muslim philologists, only a few texts have survived in the form of inscriptions from that period. The rise of the Arab-Islamic Empire in the 8th century created a need for a linguistic norm to serve as a means of written communication, including literate culture, for all those who embraced the new civilization. That norm is commonly referred to as ʕarabiyya, which coincides to a large extent with the ideal *Fuṣḥā* of modern Arabs. But since the *Nahda* period and, later on, the establishment of language academies starting from the second decade of the 20th century, this ʕarabiyya underwent substantial modernization, with a significant influence from the major Western languages. The outcome of such a process is what Western linguists call "Modern Standard Arabic". In addition to these three varieties, a fourth one, known as "Middle Arabic", is also added to refer to the less standard variety(ies) in which some texts were produced from a very early period of the language, but especially in the 16th century and after. Since these varieties are not standardized, modern Arab authors may produce texts exhibiting characteristics of any of these varieties. In other words, the Western categorization is not diachronic only. For the ideological reasons already sketched out, however, only Arab linguists writing in foreign languages are likely to accept this categorization while the others continue to recognize only one *Fuṣḥā*, a fact which indicates that the unifying force of ideology is still strong.

2.4.3 Colloquial Arabic

Unlike H, L in the Arab world is undergoing fragmentation. As was noted earlier, Arabic dialects form a continuum from the Atlantic coast in the west to the Gulf in the east, and from southern Turkey in the north to Yemen in the south. In this continuum, political borders have so far not been barriers to communication that could give rise to bundles of isoglosses and, thus, hinder mutual intelligibility. But feelings of belonging to nation-states have been growing in strength, continuously boosted by common experiences and future expectations. Unsurprisingly, linguistic differences, no matter how insignificant they may be, become resources for the expression of national identity that legitimize the creation of national varieties of Arabic; e.g. Moroccan Arabic, Algerian Arabic, etc. Evidently, no such varieties were recognized before the creation of the nation-states to which the colonial powers contributed to various degrees. Unlike the classicist elite, who continue to stress the unity of *Fuṣḥā* as a symbol of the unity of the Arab-Islamic culture, those who are less influenced by the classicist tradition are more and more conscious of the differences that distinguish them from other Arabs. In a sense, these are more directed toward the construction of national identity than the educated classicist.

The emergence of Moroccan Arabic (MA) in metalinguistic discourse is a case in point. Ech-Charfi (2016: 134) identifies two processes through which "MA is raised to consciousness and, thus, crystallizes into a distinct concept in the metalinguistic discourse developed by Moroccans": (1) similarity between Arabic dialects spoken in Morocco, and (2) contrast between these dialects and those spoken in other Arab countries. Although French dialectologists coined the expression *l'arabe marocain* ('Moroccan Arabic') to refer to Arabic dialects spoken in Morocco, it is probable that only a small minority of educated people were aware of its existence. The majority, however, used to refer to these dialects simply as ʕərbiyya ('Arabic'). This appellation serves to distinguish Arabic dialects from other languages spoken in the country, mainly Berber. The need to distinguish the Moroccan variety of Arabic was created by contact through media with other varieties of the Middle East, particularly Egyptian, Levantine and Gulf Arabic, whose cultural influence has been noticeable. These varieties are used in songs, movies and series that Moroccans have been consuming since the introduction of modern media technologies about a century ago. The Egyptian art production in particular is widely consumed throughout the Arab world to the extent that Egyptian Arabic is now understood by large sectors of Arab populations. Moroccans refer to it simply as *l-misriyya* ('Egyptian'), unlike Moroccan, Algerian or Tunisian varieties, which are identified by phrases like *l-ləhʒa l-* ... .*yya* ('the x dialect'). *l-ləhʒa l-məyribiyya* ('the Moroccan dialect') is a relatively recent coinage dictated by the need to distinguish this variety (or group of varieties) spoken in Morocco from similar varieties spoken in other countries. As pointed out earlier, it is obvious that without the existence of these national identities, there would have been no need for such concepts as "Moroccan" or "Egyptian" Arabic.

It should be pointed out that North Africans in general have a feeling of cultural inferiority relative to the Middle East. The division of the Arab world into a *Mashreq* ('East') and a *Maghreb* ('West') is centuries old; the *Mashreq* always considered itself as the center of Arab-Islamic culture, and a similar tendency continues in the present. But the young generations in the *Maghreb* are becoming more and more self-conscious. An aspect of this self-consciousness manifests in reactions to accommodation to Middle Eastern speakers by local artists on pan-Arab channels like MBC or LBC. The reaction is generally one of rejection since the accommodation is perceived as harmful to self-esteem and national pride. Hachimi (2017) has studied a blog by young Moroccans blacklisting Moroccan artists who switch to some Middle Eastern variety of Arabic by dint of accommodation. She notes the development of a community discourse promoting the use of MA as an expression of national pride. Such a discourse will certainly boost Moroccans' awareness of this variety, which is gradually named simply as *Darija* (the standard French spelling of *dariʒa*). It seems that this label is no longer understood as a modifier of ʕərbiyya to refer to colloquial Arabic, as explained above, but rather as a proper name.

The growing tendency to treat *Darija* as a distinct language is more discernible in the recent call for its use in education. The call was first made in 2003 in a few newspaper articles, but it soon developed into a movement which involved intellectuals, businessmen and, unsurprisingly, linguists. Quite expectedly, a strong counter-attack was launched by classicists who refused categorically such a proposal. What is of more interest to our purposes here is that even these classicists, while defending the maintenance of *Fuṣħā*, tend to treat *Darija* as a danger allegedly backed by external (mainly French) intrigues and, thus, perhaps unintentionally consider it as a distinct language rather than as an Arabic dialect heteronomous on *Fuṣħā*. In reaction to the use of a few colloquial words in a primary school textbook, the classicists launched their most recent attack in September 2018. This time, they advanced a legal argument according to which the Moroccan constitution specified *Fuṣħā* as the official language of the country and, therefore, any use of *Darija* in education in present time should be deemed unconstitutional (see the Islamists' reaction at: http://mondepress.net/news.php?extend.6242.1). In fact, the constitution mentions "Arabic" as the official language without specifying whether or not *Darija* is included under the term. The pro-*Darija* activists could have used this ambiguity to assert that *Darija* is part of "Arabic" and claim that they were calling merely for the use of the colloquial variety in the early stages of education. But so far, they seem to accept the validity of the legal argument, preferring instead to stress the importance of the mother tongue in primary education (see an example at: https://www.hespress.com/writers/405791.html).Whether this acceptance is an intelligent maneuvering on their part or a mere unquestioned assumption is hard to tell. In any case, as *Darija* emerges slowly as a distinct linguistic entity, the interpretation of "Arabic" as referring to *Fuṣħā* only will become of no significant value since it is hard to imagine the state institutions operating exclusively in *Fuṣħā* because most people are not fluent in it.

A final note concerning the discourse about language is in order. It was already mentioned that pan-Arab nationalists had been very much under the influence of German writers who considered language as an essential criterion of nationhood. Since the dream of a unified Arab nation has proved to be chimerical, a similar discourse is manifesting again in relation to nation-states. But instead of creating a state that would coincide with the borders of the language, the language is being tailored to fit the borders of the state. So, we are apparently witnessing the birth of a Moroccan, Algerian, Tunisian, etc. language out of the Arabic continuum as a result of the Western discourse about language and nation. Consequently, speakers in border areas (e.g. between Morocco and Algeria) claim to speak different varieties although their varieties may have more features in common than they have with other varieties spoken in the same country. The conclusion that should be obvious by now is that language varieties emerge as a consequence of ideologies rather than real linguistic processes.

A similar disparity between linguistic reality and ideology exists also in the case of Berber. As will be shown in the following section, a different reality is structured by more or less the same discourse.

2.5 Berber

Chaker (2006: 138) remarks that Berber is "un champ de mythes, dominé par l'ideologie" [a field of myths that is dominated by ideology]. Chaker (2006: 137) summarizes his point as follows:

> On montrera la puissance et la permanence de certaines thèses de nature essentiellement idéologique et leur capacité à impulser et à porter des dynamiques sociales, à reconstruire/produire le réel et/ou à peser lourdement et durablement sur la perception scientifique.
>
> [We will show the power and permanence of certain theses of an essentially ideological nature and their capacity to boost and give rise to social dynamics, to reconstruct/produce reality and/or to weigh heavily and durably on scientific perception].

To be sure, what the term "Berber" stands for is a complex and heterogeneous reality. How this heterogeneous reality ended up as a single concept not only in the minds of those who formulated the discourse about Berbers, but also for Berbers themselves, is an intricate matter involving present and past conflicts as well as external and internal interests.

The invention of Berber as an ethnolinguistic and a historical entity is often blamed on/credited to the French colonizers. These colonizers of NA must have noticed early that the local populations spoke different dialects belonging to two *abstand* languages. But NA is a vast region, and the Berber dialects must have seemed to the observer, in the 19th century as in the present, as different languages. Besides, neither Arab nor Berber populations had a single term to refer to Berber ethnicity in its totality or to the Berber language as a whole; only concepts of regional groups and their languages were available. In Morocco, as in Algeria, each group of dialects constituted a distinct language, e.g. *Tashlhyt, Tamazight, Tarifit, Takbaylite,* etc. In brief, from an internal point of view, Berbers did not form a single ethnicity or the Berber varieties a single language. For the colonizers, however, the separation between Berbers and Arabs as two distinct blocks could be used in their favor.

But to be fair, the French were not the real instigator. Because of its strategic position, NA was colonized by different powers since ancient times: Greeks, Phoenicians, Romans, Byzantines and Arabs. When the Arab conquerors arrived in the 9th century, they were faced by different Berber nations, some showing resistance, others favoring alliance. But the conquerors must have encountered in current usage the term "Berber" or some equivalent form – probably ultimately derived from the Greek or the Latin *barbarus*. It is unlikely that they took it from the Berbers themselves since the term is not attested in any of the Berber dialects known today. In any case, the conquerors soon realized that the use of such a concept enabled them to treat their new subjects as a single entity, as an "Other" for the Arab "Self" in these new territories. In brief, the "Berber" category was more an invention of the colonizers than an expression/reflection of a socio-political reality: Berbers never had a unified cultural center of their own (Chaker 1987).

But the reinvention of the Berber myth by the French was undoubtedly more effective and had more far-reaching outcomes than the previous versions. Studies in the domains of history, anthropology, dialectology and other disciplines all claimed to investigate aspects of what was for them one people, one culture and one language. The creation of Berber departments in Algerian and Moroccan universities during the colonial period and, later on, in French universities produced a sense of self-consciousness in the local elites, who gradually rediscovered their "lost" identity (Chaker 2006). It is very difficult to reconstruct how this feeling developed and what repercussions it had on the life of different individuals and groups. What is certain is that small elitist movements started to proclaim their right to preserve and practice their culture and language as a way of resisting the dominant Arab-Islamic culture. Such movements started in the 1930s in Algerian *Kabylia* (a region that is part of the Tell Atlas mountain range in the north) and, a few decades later, in Morocco. The common objective of all these movements was to establish a Berber nation with its Berber language. Since the term "Berber" was considered an alien and a pejorative term (because it was believed to be a cognate of the Latin "barbarus"), these movements replaced it with the native term *Amazigh*, meaning "free person". Thus, the proclaimed nation is now called *Tamazgha* and the language *Tamazight* or *Amazigh* (Tilmatine 2015).

Now, let's consider in what sense the Berber language is a myth. In Morocco, for example, Berber dialects form a continuum from the south to the north. Just like in any language continuum, a traveler from one village to the next would not notice any abrupt break in communication between the inhabitants of neighboring villages. But the same traveler would notice some salient dialectal differences as s/he moves from one region to the other, though those differences would not constitute a major problem to mutual intelligibility as long as contact between people of the two regions is frequent enough. The salient dialectal variants usually serve to index tribal or some other social differentiation. But as the distance between villages increases, the linguistic differences accumulate and speakers become unable to translate dialectal forms into the equivalent forms in their dialects, especially if they have no previous experience with these dialects. This happens when there is no urban, economic or cultural center in which speakers of the different dialects come into contact with each other. The result is that mutual intelligibility between such speakers becomes difficult and sometimes impossible. In such situations, MA often serves as the lingua franca for Berber speakers.

Yet, Berbers in Morocco have always divided themselves into three categories, each using a different name for their language. Those of the north call themselves *Irifin* and their language *Tarifit;* those of the center call themselves *Imazighen* and their language *Tamazight,* while the *Chleuhs* of the south say that they speak *Tashlhyt*. The origin of this tripartite division is unknown, but it must have served some socio-political goal in the past. Even today, when speakers of the three varieties do not have any common institution to represent them, each group has a sense that it is different from the other two groups. Local cultures, social networks, regional histories and similar factors have contributed to the maintenance of these divisions, and further divisions are likely to exist even within each of the three groups. For example, in the *Tamazight* area, from which I come, Berbers of the Middle Atlas and those of the High Atlas tend to treat each other as different sub-groups; those of the northeastern plains can also be singled out as another sub-group. For the reasons outlined above, these sub-groupings usually correlate with some salient dialectal differences. Yet, a similar language label continues to unify the speakers at some abstract sociolinguistic level.

In Algeria as well, which has the second largest Berber population, Berbers form different groups both at the social and the linguistic levels. Where these groups are separated by Arab populations or by natural barriers, bundles of isoglosses are formed on the borders of each group, thus providing an additional linguistic dimension to the social definition of the group. Indeed, Berbers in Algeria show some degree of discontinuity that becomes even higher in other countries to the east and to the south. *Kabylia,* for instance, forms a natural region in the Tell Atlas mountains on the Mediterranean coast, while the *Chaouia,* another major Berber area, forms a different natural region in the Aures mountains. This geographical isolation, together with relatively different histories and other social factors, made these major areas distinct cultural regions as well. Towards the south of Algeria, just like in the other neighboring countries,

Berbers usually live in isolated oases. In such cases, it is not hard to imagine the consequences that this isolation will have in the long run on mutual intelligibility with other Berber varieties. Given that this situation has probably lasted for centuries, what are treated by the ideological discourse as dialects of the same Berber language could easily be treated as different languages.

Given this diverse and heterogeneous reality, one can only wonder how the ideal of a Berber language could be realized. As long as the existing nation-states continued to ignore or oppose the demands of Berber militancy, the ideal survived as a myth fueling resistance against the establishments. But since the 1990s, some concessions have been made resulting in the promotion of Berber to the level of a national language in Algeria in 2002 and a second official language in Morocco in 2011. Special institutions were also set up with the objective of promoting the Berber culture, including the codification and the standardization of the language. Consequently, what had been a mere diachronic relation between Berber varieties had to be turned into a sociolinguistic reality. These legal and political achievements, however, could not have been made without concessions. In particular, the dream of a pan-Berber nation had to be sacrificed because it meant a radical geopolitical change. Pan-Berberism not only threatened the status of the dominant Arab-Islamic culture, which legitimized the existing ruling elites, but also augured internal strife between Berberphones and Arabophones. In short, the *Tamazgha* dream was judged too radical and, therefore, unrealistic.

Let's consider some influential proposals on the Berber language today. Chaker (2010: 78), both a well-established researcher and an activist, asserts the following:

> Comme il ne peut y avoir d'aménagement "pan-berbère" sans un espace institutionnel «pan-berbère», on ne voit pas par quelle opération miraculeuse une «normalisation pan-berbère» serait possible.
>
> [As there can be no "pan-Berber" planning without "pan-Berber" institutions, we do not see by what miraculous operation a "pan-Berber normalization" would be possible].

A few lines after that, he asserts categorically that "il ne peut y avoir de standard berbère unique parcequ'il n'y a pas d'espace politique berbère unique" [there can be no unified Berber standard because there is no unified Berber political space] (Chaker 2010: 78). The same view is expressed by another researcher and rector of the Royal Institute of the Amazigh Culture (IRCAM) in Morocco, Ahmed Boukous (2011: 232), who asserts that:

> [I]t seems that the standardization which would aim ultimately at creating the linguistic foundation of the Amazigh [koiné] might lead to generating a "stateless monster language" without anchoring [it] in the sociolinguistic and cultural reality.

Given the influence that these two researchers and their circles have had on the Berber movements, we could safely conclude that this view represents the mainstream trend that will prevail. In that case, we will no more be dealing with one Berber, but with different Berber languages, partially coinciding with the existing nation-states.

As a matter of fact, the state ideology in either Morocco or Algeria has been shaping the Berber language, sometimes in accordance with the expectations of Berber activists, but sometimes not. The ruling elites in both countries have distrusted these movements, perhaps because of the memories of the so-called Berber policy of the French colonizers, which attempted to divide Berbers and Arabs (cf. Ageron 1971). As they rejected pan-Berberism, these elites also rejected regional standard varieties, but for different reasons. For them, Berber in each country should be treated as a single language to prevent potential territorial claims in the future. For this reason, both the Moroccan and the Algerian constitutions refer to a single national Berber language (Chaker 2017). This state policy agrees with the aspirations of those activists who militate to unify the language at least at the national level. But for those who prefer the promotion of regional varieties, the policy could be yet another obstacle to surmount.

In Morocco, there seems to be a consensus about the adoption of a national Berber standard. Therefore, what the Moroccan constitution refers to as "Berber" is just a potentiality waiting to be actualized through the efforts of IRCAM. In contrast, there is no such consensus in Algeria and, consequently, the use of the same term in the Algerian constitution is apparently an attempt by the state to deal with the thorny issue of Kabylia by treating all the Berber varieties in the country as a single language. More specifically, Kabylians have always expressed regional aspirations mainly through the call to promote their language, and the Algerian state's attempt to treat this variety as a Berber dialect among others is perhaps an attempt to cloud the issue. As Tilmatine (2015) explains, the Kabylian activists have been using *Amazigh* and *Tamazight* rather ambiguously, sometimes with a broad sense to refer to the pan-Berber language and sometimes with a narrow sense to refer to the Kabyle language/culture. In reaction to the rulers' attempt to consider Berber the language of all Algerians, Kabylian militants proclaimed the promotion of *Kabyle*, their regional language. Politically, they have even proclaimed the right to self-determination. Thus, regionalism reinforces and is reinforced by the creation of a regional standard. If this trend stays in force, other Berber languages in Algeria will appear in the future, and that will certainly have repercussions on Berbers in the neighboring countries.

To conclude, whether one or more Berber languages are recognized is not a technical issue to be resolved by trained linguists. Rather, it is the outcome of a long socio-political process in which actors make use of linguistic and other knowledge available to them to formulate projects and rally supporters behind them. In the case of Berber, the process is still ongoing.

2.6 Conclusion

In this chapter, the focus was on the ideological factors that underlie the classification of linguistic resources available to NA speakers into different language varieties. Ordinary speakers are usually influenced by non-linguistic factors when they develop a folk discourse about the language(s) they speak. On their part, linguists, both native and foreigner, contribute to this discourse and are affected by it at the same time. In other words, they often act as observers and social actors, which is paradoxical. This seems to be the cost of ignoring the social nature of language, which cannot be studied satisfactorily if the ideological processes involved in its construction are ignored.

Acknowledgements: I would like to thank Lourdes Ortega for her comments and suggestions on an earlier version of this chapter.

References

Ageron, Charles-Robert. 1971. La politique berbère du protectorat marocain de 1913 à 1934. *Revue d'Histoire Moderne et Contemporaine* 18(1). 50–90.
Badawi, El-Said. 1973. *Mustawayāt al-ʕarabiyya al-muʕāṣirafīmiṣr* [Levels of Modern Standard Arabic in Egypt]. Cairo: Dār al-Maʕārif.
Blanc, Haim. 1960. Style variations in Spoken Arabic: A sample of interdialectal educated conversation. In Charles A. Ferguson (ed.), *Contributions to Arabic linguistics*, 81–161. Harvard: Harvard University Press.
Boukous, Ahmed. 2011. *Revitalizing the Amazigh language* [Translated into English by Karim Bensoukas]. Rabat: IRCAM.
Brustad, Kristen. 2017. Diglossia as ideology. In Jacob Høigilt & Gunvor Mejdell (eds.), *The politics of written language in the Arab world*, 41–67. Leiden & Boston: Brill. https://brill.com/abstract/book/edcoll/9789004346178/B9789004346178-s004.xml (accessed 12 July 2018).
Chaker, Salim. 1987. *Berbères aujourd'hui*. Paris: L'Harmattan.
Chaker, Salim. 2006. Berbères/langue berbère: Les mythes (souvent) plus forts que la réalité. In Hélène Claudot-Hawad (ed.), *Berbères ou Arabes? Le tango des spécialistes*, 137–153. Paris: Éditions Non-Lieu. https://hal.archives-ouvertes.fr/hal-01779742/document (accessed 23 September 2018).

Chaker, Salim. 2010. Un standard berbère est-il possible? Entre réalités linguistiques et fictions sociolinguistiques. *Revue des Études Berbères* 5. 77–89.
Chaker, Salim. 2017. Berbérité/Amazighité (Algérie/Maroc): La 'nouvelle politique berbère'. *Studi magrebini, Università degli studi di Napoli 'L'Orientale'*, 129–153. https://hal-amu.archives-ouvertes.fr/hal-01770548/document (accessed 23 September 2018).
De Ruiter, Jan Jaap. 2001. Analyse (socio)-linguistique de la Charte Nationale. *Languages and Linguistics* 8. 29–47.
Ech-Charfi, Ahmed. 2016. *Standardization of a diglossic low variety: The case of Moroccan Arabic*. Saarbrücken, Germany: Scholar's Press.
Ech-Charfi, Ahmed. 2017. *Al-lugha wa al-lahja: Madxal li al-sosyulisāniyāt al-Ṣarabiyya* [Language and dialect: An introduction to Arabic sociolinguistics]. Rabat: Faculté des Sciences de l'Education.
Ennaji, Moha. 2005. *Multilingualism, cultural identity, and education in Morocco*. New York: Springer.
Ferguson, Charles A. 1959. Diglossia. *Word* 15. 325–340.
Fishman, Joshua. 1967. Bilingualism with and without diglossia; diglossia with and without bilingualism. *Journal of Social Issues* 23(2). 29–38.
Hachimi, Atiqa. 2017. Moralizing stances. In Jacob Høigilt & Gunvor Mejdell (eds.), *The politics of written language in the Arab world*, 239–265. Leiden & Boston: Brill. https://brill.com/abstract/book/edcoll/9789004346178/B9789004346178-s004.xml (accessed 12 July 2018).
Hary, Benjamin. 1996. The importance of the language continuum in Arabic multiglossia. In Alaa Elgibali (ed.), *Understanding Arabic*, 69–90. Cairo: The American University in Cairo Press.
Haugen, Einar. 1966. Dialect, language, nation. *American Anthropologist* 68. 922–35.
Heryanto, Ariel. 1990. The making of language: Developmentalism in Indonesia. *Prisma* 50. 40–53.
Holes, Clive. 1995. *Modern Arabic: Structures, functions and varieties*. London & New York: Longman.
Hourani, Albert. 1967. *Arabic thought in the liberal age, 1789–1939*. Oxford: Oxford University Press.
Kachru, Braj, Yamina Kachru & Cecil L. Nelson. 2009. *The handbook of world Englishes*. Malden, MA & Oxford: Wiley-Blackwell.
Kloss, Heinz. 1967. Abstand languages and ausbau languages. *Anthropological Linguistics* 9(7). 29–41.
Makoni, Sinfree. 1998. African languages as European scripts: The shaping of communal memory. In Sarah Nuttall & Carli Coetzee (eds.), *Negotiating the past: The making of memory in South Africa*, 242–248. Oxford: Oxford University Press.
Makoni, Sinfree & Alastair Pennycook (eds.). 2007. *Disinventing and reconstituting languages*. Clevedon: Multilingual Matters.
Makoni, Sinfree & Alastair Pennycook. 2012. Disinventing multilingualism: From monological multilingualism to multilingua francas. In Marilyn Martin-Jones, Adrian Blackledge & Angela Creese (eds.), *The Routledge handbook of multilingualism*, 439–453. London & New York: Routledge.
Mejdell, Gunvor. 2006. *Mixed styles in spoken Arabic in Egypt*. Leiden & Boston: Brill.

Milroy, James. 2001. Language ideologies and the consequences of standardization. *Journal of Sociolinguistics* 5(4). 530–555.
Ortega, Lourdes. 2018. SLA in uncertain times: Disciplinary constraints, transdisciplinary hopes. *Working Papers in Educational Linguistics* 33. 1–30.
Palva, Heikki. 1969. Notes on classicization in modern colloquial Arabic. *Studia Orientalia* XL, 3. 1–41.
Parkinson, Dilworth B. 1993. Knowing standard Arabic: Testing Egyptians' MSA abilities. In Mushira Eid & Clive Holes (eds.), *Perspectives on Arabic Linguistics V*, 47–73. Amsterdam & Philadelphia: John Benjamins.
Pleines, Jochen (ed.). 1990. *Mahgreb linguistics*. Rabat: Editions Okad.
Ruiter, Jan Jaap de. 2001. Analyse (socio)-linguistique de la Charte Nationale. *Languages and Linguistics* 8. 29–47.
Saussure, de Ferdinand. 1972. *Course in general linguistics* [Translated & annotated by Roy Harris]. London: Duckworth.
Suleiman, Yaser. 2003. *The Arabic language and national identity: A study in ideology*. Edinburgh: Edinburgh University Press.
Tilmatine, Mohand. 2015. Berbère/Amazigh ou Kabyle? Évolution et fluctuation d'une dénomination en contexte d'idéologies dominantes. *Studi Africanistici* 4. 378–412.
Zack, Liesbeth & Arie Schippers (eds.). 2012. *Middle Arabic and mixed Arabic*. Amsterdam: Brill.

Bee Chin Ng and Francesco Cavallaro
3 Multilingualism in Southeast Asia: The Post-Colonial Language Stories of Hong Kong, Malaysia and Singapore

3.1 Introduction

Much of Asia's modern history is influenced and shaped by contact with some forms of exploitative colonialism: the English in India, Malaysia, Hong Kong and Singapore; the French in Vietnam; the Dutch in Indonesia; the Spaniards and the Americans in the Philippines; and the Japanese in Korea and Taiwan. Each colonial contact has left various degrees of unique traces in the cultural and linguistic make-up of the places affected. At the same time, many of these traces were transformed and assimilated in ways which are often unexpected. An example of such transformations is seen in linguistic practices and in particular, the use and survival of the English language. This chapter focuses on the impact of colonialism on the linguistic landscapes of Hong Kong, Malaysia and Singapore. These three States[1] make compelling case studies as they share very similar colonial histories and demographic compositions but experienced very different trajectories in language planning and development in the post war decolonization process. As aptly pointed out by Mccloud ([1995] 2018), the diversity in the post-colonial experience is testimony to the agency by which the different "colonized worlds" have selectively absorbed and adapted ideas and practices that are culturally and politically relevant to the local contexts.

All three States were colonized by the British empire in the 19th century and all for around 130–150 years. The Chinese ethnic group makes up a significant part of the three States' population. Hong Kong's population is more homogenous with the Chinese as the dominant group. Malaysia and Singapore, on the other hand, are multi-ethnic, multi-lingual and multi-religious. The decolonization process for Malaysia and Singapore began after WWII in an accelerated manner with both declaring self-government in the 1950s and 1960s. The British remained in

---

[1] In the interest of consistency and ease of reference, the term "State" will be used in reference to Hong Kong post 1997 as a Special Administrative Region of the People's Republic of China. "State" will also be used in reference to Singapore and Malaysia and denotes their status as independent countries.

Bee Chin Ng and Francesco Cavallaro, Nanyang Technological University, Singapore

https://doi.org/10.1515/9781501507984-003

Hong Kong until 1997 when it was reassigned as a Special Administrative Region of the People's Republic of China. In all three cases, the decolonization process calls forth a consolidation of identity which is often keenly negotiated through language use.

These three States today display very different linguistic practices and also different attitudes towards the official languages that are in place. Hong Kong is evolving from monolingualism to trilingualism with Cantonese strongly entrenched as the language of identity and English as the language of commerce. Malaysia has Malay as the national language. Attempts to make it the language of national unity have had mixed success. Although each ethnic group still holds on to their own individual language(s), Malay is also a lingua franca among the different ethnic groups. English, on the other hand, enjoys a position of prestige in Malaysia despite the lack of official support over the years. Finally, Singapore has moved from multilingualism to an English-plus bilingualism with English firmly and securely ensconced as the inter-ethnic lingua franca. It is even the language most used at home by a third of the population.

In the following sections, we will review how language policies and practices in these different States evolved and how each state embarked on different pathways resulting in these diverse practices. At the same time, the pressure of English as a global language is also exerting a homogenizing force from another end. This pressure means that English occupies a unique position as the language of economics and trade in all three States. So, while internal policies and politics are driving linguistic practices in these three places in different directions on the one hand, there is also a common thrust to adapt to the English push. This chapter will specifically focus on this tug-of-war, the push and pull of these different forces. But first we will provide an overview and summary of language practices in each State.

3.2 Hong Kong

Hong Kong was colonialized by Britain from 1841 to 1997, and during this period, English was the official language until 1974 and was used in sectors such as international trade as well as government administration. Mandarin Chinese was relatively insignificant in the 1960s and was not given strong support by the government, but was made a co-official language after 1974 under the Official Languages Ordinance (Hong Kong Government 1974). Alongside English, Mandarin Chinese was also used in various sectors such as government business and higher education. In addition to these two languages, Cantonese had a dominant position as the spoken language in the

1960s and 1970s and is spoken by approximately 95% of the population as a first language (Sung 2015). However, Cantonese was not accepted as one of the official languages for the purported reason that it lacked a standardized written form (Simpson 2007).

3.2.1 Hong Kong before 1997

Hong Kong is a densely populated city state with a population of approximately 7 million. This is remarkable when one considers that in 1841, the population of Hong Kong was under 10,000. Hence, the bulk of the settlement in Hong Kong took place during British rule. There were two significant waves of immigration where the population increased by more than 20% – the first after WWII and the second in 1951. The Chinese ethnic group dominating the population demography constitutes 92% of the population. Due to its proximity to Guangzhou, a major proportion of residents in Hong Kong are Cantonese speaking and Cantonese is the first language spoken by approximately 95% of the Chinese population in Hong Kong.

Compared to Singapore and Malaysia with their largely multi-ethnic population, the majority of residents in Hong Kong during this period were Chinese monolinguals. Therefore, while language policy decisions in Singapore and Malaysia were largely influenced by their multi-ethnic population, the evolution of language use in pre-1997 Hong Kong appears to be organic. The common colonial history in these three states naturally saw an emphasis placed on English during British rule. In Hong Kong, there was a shift towards English-medium schooling because of the economic benefits that learning English brought.

During the initial phase of colonial rule (1842–1941), the educational system was split into a Western style education stream at the primary and secondary levels, as well as a Chinese-medium stream[2] at the primary level. Post 1941, the English secondary stream expanded rapidly and almost 90% of students were studying in secondary schools with English as the medium of instruction (Evans 2000). Even so, the Chinese-medium schools retained their dominance at the primary level, and for most part of the post-war period, children received primary education with Chinese as the medium of instruction. Since being

---

[2] The term "Chinese" is used here instead of Cantonese because, although the language spoken in the classroom was Cantonese, the written form was Mandarin Chinese. There is similarity between the two scripts but written Cantonese is substantially different from written Mandarin Chinese. For a discussion of the distinction between Cantonese and standard written Chinese, see Bauer (1988) and Snow (2004).

competent in English was a factor in economic mobility and advancement, the post-war generation of parents and students chose to pursue secondary education in English-medium schools. However, due to the lack of proficiency of English-speaking staff, mixed-language teaching, where teachers alternate between English and Cantonese, was a common practice (Johnson 1998).

During the first half of the 20th century, the degree of multilingualism was substantial, and Cantonese continued to be spoken by the vast majority. Cantonese enjoyed high levels of vitality and functioned as a language of solidarity and as a symbol of Hong Kong identity during British rule (So 1998). In 2001, the percentage of males and females in Hong Kong speaking Cantonese was 87.3% and 91.3%, respectively. The increasing use of Cantonese also gave rise to English and Cantonese code mixing, where English words are inserted into Cantonese (Bacon-Shone and Bolton 2008).[3]

3.2.2 Hong Kong after 1997

The latest demographics and census data show that Cantonese continues to be the most widely spoken language by both males and females. Its use has remained relatively stable throughout the years, with 93.0% female and 96.5 % male speakers in 2016. This is compared to English, with 46.6% female and 51.8% male speakers, and Mandarin Chinese,[4] with 44.8% female and 48.9% male speakers (Census and Statistics Department, Hong Kong 2017).

Even though there was a concern that the change of sovereignty in 1997 would result in the dominance of Mandarin Chinese over English, English remains the language of international trade due to shifts in Hong Kong's economy. Prior to 1997, attitudes towards English were more negative because it was perceived as a colonial imposition. However, as Hong Kong's economy boomed, the status of English shifted from being a colonial language to being a major lingua franca of intercultural communication (Poon 2010). Despite this shift in mindset, English is still spoken as a second language by most Hong Kong people to varying degrees of ability (Setter, Wong and Chan 2010).

---

[3] Interestingly, there was less occurrence of Cantonese-Putonghua mixing two decades post-1997.
[4] Mandarin Chinese is the general term used to refer to *Putonghua* ("common language"). Putonghua is the term used in Hong Kong and the PRC to denote the Chinese variety spoken in Mainland China. In Taiwan, the same language is referred to as *Guo Yu* ("National Language"). In Singapore and Malaysia, it is referred to as *Huayu* ("Chinese language"). For the purpose of consistency, the term "Mandarin Chinese" will be used in this chapter. See Cavallaro et al. (2018) for a discussion of these different terms and what they signify.

Without sovereignty, Hong Kong had more discussions and input from the People's Republic of China (PRC) about decolonialization than in Malaysia and Singapore. In 1995, a new language policy was put in place to promote a "biliterate" (Mandarin Chinese and English) and "trilingual" (Cantonese, Mandarin Chinese [*Putonghua*] and English) society (Lau 1995). Commonly known as the *liangwensanyu* 两文三语, "biliterate and trilingual" policy, in Hong Kong, it promotes Mandarin Chinese as a medium of instruction in schools and as a compulsory school subject (Bolton 2011). Thus Mandarin Chinese has become a compulsory subject in both primary and secondary schools after 1998, while Cantonese has been used as the medium of instruction for content subjects in Chinese-medium primary and secondary schools (Wang and Kirkpatrick 2015). Under this policy, Chinese and English are taken to be the official languages, while Cantonese is acknowledged as Hong Kong's official spoken language.

As a result, almost 70% of English-medium secondary schools were converted into Chinese-medium schools (Zeng 2007). The aim of the new policy is to facilitate communication with the PRC, and this was perceived to increase the status of Mandarin Chinese (Tan 1997). The policy of compulsory Chinese-medium instruction has been criticized because many felt that it has led to a decline in English standards (Poon, Lau, and Chu 2013). In addition, Evans (2002) reports that English and Chinese-medium schooling creates a social divide between the "elite" English stream and an "inferior" Chinese medium stream. A call was made to remove the separate categorizations of the two models (Education Bureau 2010).

In the current situation, English still seems to be a language of high prestige and continues to remain a co-official language of the government administration and law institutes. It is also the language of higher education and economic development. With 95% of the population speaking Cantonese, it is used in many different domains, including in the government and media. Although Mandarin Chinese is the national language, it has not been heavily imposed as the national language, mainly because of the promise of the "One country, two systems" policy, allowing Hong Kong to be different (Bolton 2011).

In the 2015 census data (Census and Statistics Department, Hong Kong 2015), 54.9% of the population rated themselves as *Very Good* and 31.7% as *Good* when asked about their perceived language competence in Cantonese. On the use of spoken English, 41.8% of participants rated themselves as *Average* and only 23.2% rated themselves as either *Very Good* or *Good*. Lastly, with Mandarin Chinese, 41.1% rated themselves as *Average* while 24.6% rated themselves as *Very Good/Good*, while 34.1% rated themselves as *Not so good/No knowledge*. The survey results suggest that even in recent years, Cantonese is still widely spoken and people are most comfortable with speaking in Cantonese. On the use of written Chinese, more than 70% of participants rated themselves as being *Very Good* or *Good* but only 23.3% rated themselves as being *Very Good* or *Good* in written English, with 41.6% of participants rating their proficiency as *Average*. According to the 2016 census, approximately 36.6% of the population is trilingual, and a vast majority (92%) of those between 15–34 are biliterate. This is evidence of increased levels of trilingualism and also rising biliteracy among Hong Kong speakers.

In 2017 (Census and Statistics Department, Hong Kong 2017), the language used for communication and for entertainment remained unchanged, with 90% to 96% reporting the use of Cantonese as the main language of communication. In addition, 88% to 94% of Hong Kongers aged 6 to 65 years old consumed media mostly in Cantonese. This points to the undiminished vitality of Cantonese as the home language.

3.2.3 Hong Kong now

The rising influence of Mandarin Chinese and English is visible. This is evident in the language attitudes towards the different languages as seen from the survey data, where 69% and 58% of persons aged 6 to 65+ in educational institutions were willing to spend spare time studying English or Chinese, respectively.

Li (2017) shows that there has been a gradual positive shift in the attitudes towards English. Before the 1980s, students were not as concerned about the need to speak English, limiting its use to the professional workplace or in the academic domain. However, from 1980 onwards, people became more aware of the instrumental value of English as more students felt proud of being able to speak better English than their peers. On the other hand, students were rather indifferent towards Mandarin Chinese, even though it is the most commonly spoken language in Mainland China. Most students also considered themselves as "Hong Kongers" rather than Chinese or "Chinese Hong Kongers".

Li (2002) described the relationship between Hong Kong residents and English as a "love-hate" complex in post-colonial Hong Kong. Li (2018) also pointed out that English is clearly seen as an international language and the language of economic mobility. Therefore, many parents were more inclined to send their children to English-medium schools. Yet, almost 90% of the population speaks Cantonese with family, friends and peers and consumes electronic media in Cantonese. There is little to no motivation to use English completely for intra-ethnic communication. Also, the lack of English use in non-formal domains has resulted in a lot of discomfort and reluctance for Hong Kongers learning English to use the language actively. In this sense, Li's (1999) evaluation of the status of

English in post-colonial Hong Kong as a "value-added" language instead of an "auxiliary" language still holds.

Bolton and Kwok (1992) point to an evolving tension between English, Cantonese, and Mandarin Chinese in Hong Kong, where English has retained its importance and prestige in the 21st century, serving as the language of the government, law, education, business and international trade. In their analysis, Cantonese will continue to serve as the vernacular lingua franca for most of Hong Kong's Chinese. However, as pointed out by Simpson (2007), the years ahead may see Mandarin Chinese surpassing English and Cantonese in certain domains such as politics and administration due to the increasing influence the PRC has in Hong Kong, world affairs and the world economy. Yet others like Li (2018) argue that while the vitality of Cantonese may not be threatened by English, it may be replaced by Mandarin Chinese in the educational domain. In a series of studies using both matched-guise, surveys and interviews, Lai (2009, 2010, 2012, 2013) found further robust support for the strong vitality of Cantonese and the positive orientation towards English. In addition, although Mandarin Chinese was ranked below Cantonese and English in affective and pragmatic measures, it was still ranked generally positive and, after 12 years, her findings indicate an upward trend for positive orientation towards Mandarin Chinese. Her prognosis is a levelling of influence of all three languages in Hong Kong. The outcome could be a highly polyglossic situation with Mandarin Chinese and English being the languages used in many formal domains and Cantonese serving as the home language used within the family (Pierson 1988).

3.3 Malaysia

The history of colonization of Malaysia is a more complex one than Hong Kong's and involves other colonial interests (Portuguese and Dutch) in the region since the 1500s. Malaysia as we know it today is a modern concept as prior to 1946, it was a collection of small kingdoms each with its own Sultanates known as Malaya. The Anglo-Dutch treaty in 1824 saw the Dutch ceding control of Malacca to the British, ushering in the presence of the English in the Peninsula. British influence only covered a set of states commonly referred to as British Malaya. These were Singapore, Malacca, Penang and the Labuan islands. However, due to the strategic location of Penang and Malacca, the influence of the British extended beyond the territories they had direct control over. At the same time, a large segment of Malaya belonged to various princely states which coexisted outside the influence of British rule. The British stay in Malaya lasted from the early 18th century until 1957, and the large-scale movements of Chinese and Indian laborers during this period formed the basis of Malaysia's multicultural makeup that exists till today.

In terms of geographical span and linguistic diversity, Malaysia is the largest and the most linguistically diverse in the group discussed in this chapter. Apart from the 11 states in the Malay Peninsula, its jurisdiction includes the Borneo states of Sabah and Sarawak. The population of Malaysia is approximately 32.4 million with Malays, Chinese and Indians forming the major ethnic groups. Malay has the greatest number of speakers and is the national language. The *bumiputeras*, "sons of the soil", comprising Malays (50.1%) and non-Malays indigenous to the Malaysian peninsula and Malaysian Borneo (11.8%), form 69.1% of the population and the *non-bumiputras*, that is, the Chinese[5] and the Indians constitute 22.6% and 6.7% of the population, respectively (Department of Statistics Malaysia 2018).

In total, 134 languages are spoken in Malaysia, 112 are indigenous languages and 22 are non-indigenous languages (Simons and Fennig 2018). *Bahasa Melayu* ("Malay") is the official language with Mandarin Chinese and other Chinese languages (e.g. Cantonese, Hokkien, Hakka, Foochow and Teochew) commonly spoken by the Chinese population. The Indian languages spoken in the community are Tamil, Malayalam, Telugu, Bengali, Punjabi, Hindi and Gujarati. The indigenous population speaks languages that are vastly linguistically diverse ranging from Mon-Khmer to Austronesian languages.

3.3.1 Malaysia before 1957

Under British rule, English was the official language and was the medium of instruction in most schools located in urban areas. Malay, Chinese and Tamil were classified as vernacular languages. These languages served as the medium of instruction in vernacular schools (Hashim 2009), which were mostly found in rural areas (Azmi 2013). The colonial government only provided funding to English-medium schools and since these schools were located in urban areas, most of the students were Chinese (Puteh 2010). If students were able to attend English medium schools, they were more likely to have opportunities for further education and employment. A dual system was also implemented for the Malays, one for Malay peasantry and another for Malay nobility, which served different purposes for the British, and only those of nobility were provided with

---

[5] In 1957, the Chinese population was 38% of the total Malayan population of 6.3 million (Hirschman 1980).

an English education (Tan 2013). Before Malaysia's independence, a committee was set up to study the education system in Malaysia. Its findings, published in the Barnes report (Central Advisory Committee on Education 1951), proposed a single inter-racial school, which would provide six years of free bilingual (Malay-English) education for all 6- to 12-year-olds. The committee recommended that the Chinese and Indians give up their vernacular education to study in schools that used Malay as the medium of instruction so that ethnic minority groups studied Malay at the primary level and English at higher levels (Yang 1998). Malay was chosen because the British preferred the Malay language since it was the mother tongue of the dominant ethnic group (Gill 2005).

During this period, English education was reserved for the elites and people of higher status among the local indigenous population. These were typically wealthy Chinese traders, Eurasians or Malay aristocrats (Stephen 2013). English became the language of prestige and power, even after Malaysia's independence (Lowenberg 1991). In contrast, Malay was the low status language. This created a social divide which fermented through the post-war years fueling the emphatic determination to redress the situation by those who did not have access to English.

3.3.2 Post-1957 Malaysia

After gaining independence in 1957, language policies were largely driven by various concerns during different periods: the 1960s to 1980s, the 1990s, and the 21st century. In the post-independence period, English was an official language alongside Malay from 1957 to 1967. One of the most immediate post-war concerns was to build national unity and identity. A resulting language push was to make *Bahasa Melayu* the national and official language, cementing its status as the language of the government (Gill 2005). This was possible because Malays were the dominant ethnic group, and they considered themselves to be *bumiputera*s in comparison to the *non-bumiputras* who were immigrants. Another reason for this choice was that the government saw Malay as the language that would build national unity and identity. As indicated earlier, this decision was also fueled by the resentment the Malays felt towards the increasingly economically successful Chinese and South Asians (Thirusanku and Yunus 2012). During this time, support for English was seen as a remnant of colonial times where English was only taught to the elites and was associated with economic opportunity and professional mobility.

The move to make Malay the national and official language was enshrined in the Malaysian Education Policy of 1961 and the National Language Act of 1967 where Malay was officially made the national language and English became a second language in the education system. School children were required to study but not required to pass English (Gill 2006). Meanwhile, there was a proliferation of independent vernacular schools in Mandarin Chinese and Tamil. Children studying in vernacular schools were allowed to remain in those schools but were required to attend one year of special transitional classes in Malay and English, known as "remove classes", to easily transition into Malay-medium secondary schools (Dumaniga, David, and Symaco 2012). During this period, the anti-colonialist sentiments displaced English and there was a resistance to anything associated with English (Asmah 1992), leading to the conversion of many English-medium schools into Malay-medium schools. Ironically, these changes drew more pronounced boundaries around the three ethnic groups. The following description by Stephen (2013: 5) succinctly captures these divisions:

> As a result, at the time of Independence, Malaya had a divided education system which separated the bumiputera Malays and the non-bumiputera Chinese and Indian communities. The schools were located based on ethnic group locations, i.e. in the kampungs, or rural villages (Malay-medium alongside religious education in Arabic), in towns (English-medium and Chinese-medium), and in the plantations (Tamil-medium). Education was available in the different languages and each type of school followed its own curriculum, which served different purposes from the curricula in the other schools.

Even though English was retained as a co-official national language alongside Malay, the National Language Act of 1967 removed the official status of English in the Peninsula. The status and role of English was significantly reduced, from being the only language taught during the colonial time, to being taught in schools as a second language. From 1969 onwards, Malay became the medium of instruction at all levels in the education system.

In 1993, the Prime Minister announced that English would once again be introduced as a medium of instruction for science and technology courses (Zaaba et al. 2011). In 1996, the Education Act and the Private Higher Education Institution Act were introduced. The Education Act allowed English to be used as the medium of instruction in technical areas while the latter allowed the use of English in overseas institutions that had campuses in Malaysia. Malay was made a compulsory subject in private institutions (Puteh 2010). However, the use of Malay as the main medium of instruction in higher education resulted in a decline in English proficiency with graduates having difficulty finding jobs. Due to globalization pressures, in 2003, English was re-instated as the medium of instruction for mathematics and science in primary and secondary schools (Azmi 2013).

Malay originally replaced English in the hope of removing the inequality present among the different ethnic groups. This was a problem because much of the scientific and technological knowledge was in English. Translation capabilities were not advanced enough to keep up with the proliferation of information (Gill 2005). Meanwhile, in the wider world, English grew to be the major lingua franca for business and international trade and the demand for English proficiency grew even in Malaysia itself. This is what led to a partial reversal of the policy in 2003.

One reason was the lack of suitably qualified staff to teach mathematics and science subjects in English. With the general election in 2008, there was a change in political leadership and the government decided that this policy would be phased out by 2012 (Zaaba et al. 2011). In 2011, a new policy was introduced called *Memartabatkan Bahasa Malaysia dan Memperkukuhkan Penguasaan Bahasa Inggeris* (MBMMBI), "To Uphold Bahasa Malaysia and to Strengthen the English Language" (Tharmalingam 2012). Here, the political message was to develop English but not at the expense of Malay. The English Language Standards and Quality Council (2015: 26) proposed that the target for Malaysia's English education system would be "the production of school leavers and graduates with the level of English proficiency they need to make themselves employable in the modern globalized world", thereby, aligning Malaysia with the world's standards in terms of English proficiency (Kaur and Shapii 2018). Yet, this has been seen by many as the further strengthening of the position of the Malay language parallel to a decline of English (Darmi and Albion 2013).

3.3.3 Small languages in Malaysia

Lost in this debate are the numerous smaller languages as Malaysia is also home to 134 other indigenous languages that face extinction because of the small marginalized populations that speak these languages. Since Bahasa Melayu and English are such dominant languages, Malaysians perceive that knowledge of indigenous languages is an obstacle to development and upward mobility. Despite the threat of extinction of these minority languages, their speakers are still advocating for their preservation, for example, the Bidayuh community in Sarawak where a variety of the language is being taught in certain preschools (Ting and Campbell 2017). It is also evident that proactive approaches can help in language preservation. Coluzzi, Riget, and Wang (2013) report that there is a high degree of vitality of Mah Meri on Carey Island because of the positive attitudes that the native speakers have of the language as well as the high degree of language maintenance in the community, although there are also signs of language shift.

The general prognosis for small indigenous languages in Malaysia is grim (David, Cavallaro, and Coluzzi 2009). The spread of Malay and English is pervasive and these pose severe dangers to minority languages. The researchers call for "functional bilingualism" – that is, acquiring the languages that are more beneficial for education and economic purposes without forgetting the native language. The issue is that "functional" here is used in a one-sided sense. For bilingualism to be functional, both languages have to be significant and meaningful in bilinguals' life. Even the descriptor here sounds the death knell for these minority languages as these languages are clearly not required in education and economy. Hence, unless they retain a strong cultural role, erosion of their use seems inevitable.

3.3.4 Malaysia now

Today, there are three mediums of instruction in Malaysia. Malay is the medium of instruction in both primary and secondary schools, while languages such as Mandarin Chinese and Tamil are used in vernacular schools. English is learned as a second language in both vernacular and Malay schools. How, Chan, and Abdullah (2015) conducted a study with students from vernacular Tamil and Chinese schools and found that 81.6% of Chinese and 74.58% of Tamil school students used Mandarin and Tamil at home, respectively. These students did not consider Bahasa Malay to be a dominant or a preferred language. More significantly, Malay ranked the lowest in vitality; it is used infrequently and is clearly not a preferred language. The participants were also accepting of English as a language to form a hybrid Malaysian identity, highlighting how the international language is emphasized more than the national language despite the educational policies favoring Malay since 1957.

Even though Malay is not used as a lingua franca among the Chinese and the Indians, it is the most commonly used inter-ethnic lingua franca among the different ethnic groups in Malaysia. This contrasts with Singapore where English is the main inter-ethnic language. There is not much research on language attitudes in Malaysia but the little there is suggests a keen desire for English proficiency and a recognition that English is the language of trade and diplomacy (Crismore, Ngeow, and Soo 1996; Ting 2003). However, as pointed out by Muniandy et al. (2010), English is gaining more importance and relevance in the country. Presently, English is used in various domains such as in business as well as academic settings; and the growth of English in the wider community may change the current status of language use. Albury (2017) drew attention to an interesting trend in recent years where Chinese, Malay and

Indian students have been fostering inter-ethnic inclusiveness through the use of *Bahasa Rojak*, or Manglish. Manglish, as described by students, is a phenomenon of language contact and is essentially code-mixing of Malay and English to facilitate inter-ethnic cohesiveness.

3.4 Singapore

As indicated in section 3.3, Singapore was part of British Malaya and the beginning of British rule in Singapore can be dated to 1819 with the arrival in Singapore of its founder, Sir Thomas Stamford Raffles. The sociolinguistics of Singapore has been chronicled in various places (Bolton and Ng 2014; Cavallaro and Ng 2014; Cavallaro, Ng, and Tan in press) and the following will be a summary of the above research. In surface area, Singapore is roughly one-third the size of Hong Kong. Geographically, it sits in close proximity to Malaysia, a giant in terms of land size and resources. Apart from sharing a similar colonial past with Malaysia, Singapore also shares the same ethnic demography as Malaysia (albeit in different proportions) with a more limited indigenous population.

Like Hong Kong, Singapore is a densely populated metropolis of 5.5 million and growing, but unlike Hong Kong and similar to Malaysia, it is multilingual and multicultural. In terms of population growth, Singapore followed the same trajectory as Hong Kong beginning with 13,750 in 1826 to the 5.5 million in the 2015 census. While the acceleration of Hong Kong's population growth was fueled by political upheavals in the PRC prior to 1960, Singapore's population growth has been gradual, only rising precipitously post-1960. However, 20% of this is accounted for by a foreign work force. Singapore is also more similar to Hong Kong in the higher number of ethnically Chinese in its population make up. As can be seen in Table 3.1, throughout the last 60 or so years, the Chinese have remained as the majority at approximately 75% of the population, the Malays at 14% and the Indians at about 8–9%.

3.4.1 Singapore before independence (1965)

As early as the 1200s, Singapore was a major trade stop between the Indian Ocean and the South China Sea. From all historical accounts, prior to the arrival of Raffles, Singapore was a sleepy fishing village already highly linguistically diversified in its tiny population. There are, however, very definite historical records since the arrival of the British to the island. Raffles' own words described Singapore as multi-ethnic in the composition of its inhabitants. The list of

Table 3.1: Ethnic composition of Singapore residents (%).
Source: Department of Statistics (2001, 2006, 2010, 2015); Kuo (1980).

	Chinese	Malay	Indian	Others
1957	75.4	13.6	8.6	2.4
1990	77.8	14.0	7.1	1.1
2000	76.8	13.9	7.9	1.4
2010	74.1	13.4	9.2	3.3
2015	74.3	13.3	9.1	3.2

speakers/inhabitants included Malay, Bugis, Javanese, Siam, Burmese, Arabic, Pali, Madurese, Chinese, etc. (Raffles 1819). This marked the beginning of a long relationship between the British and Singapore, and the rise of Singapore as a booming seaport. In 1826, Singapore became part of the Straits Settlements along with Penang and Malacca as an outlying residency of the British East India Company. From around 10,683 people living on the island in the first census of 1824, more than 200,000 called Singapore their home by the turn of the century. The ethnic makeup also changed in that time from 60% Malays in the 1820s to 56.2% Chinese as early as the 1880s (Lim 2008).

Under the British rule starting in 1824, there was minimal involvement of the colonial government in the education system, and the British mostly adopted a laissez-faire policy where each language community took care of their own needs. The British only gave funding to English and Malay schools because they saw the Malay Language as the vernacular of Singapore (Doraisamy 1969). However, the first goverment school in Singapore was set up to educate the children of local chiefs and acted as a premier learning institution to facilitate research in various aspects such as the history and resources of other countries (Buckley 1984). Raffles applied to the East Indian Company to set up a school with the specific purpose of "civilizing" the natives and propagating European ideas. As in Malaysia, the main aim of the school was to educate the sons of the elite and the privileged. This school was founded in 1823 and evolved to the present-day Raffles Institution.

On the other hand, missionary groups and clan associations formed schools for Chinese, Malay and Tamil children, and no support was given to these schools by the colonial government. There was no common national syllabus in Singapore and schools mainly taught in their own languages and with their own curricula. This meant that children were largely exposed to their own languages in the school system. Before WWII, 5,800 students were enrolled in Malay schools, while 38,000 were in Chinese schools and 1,000 in Tamil schools (Doraisamy 1969). Therefore, there was a very compartmentalized form of education which segregated the different ethnic groups. This is reminiscent of post-independence Malaysia. As in Malaysia, this system created a divide between the wealthier English-educated class who was rewarded with better job prospects and the rest (Kwan 2000).

Although English was already the working language in Singapore, there were debates over the medium of instruction in government primary schools in the 1930s. Many were in favor of an English education, as English would mean better job prospects. The fact that English-educated Singaporeans were drawing higher incomes created an economic schism in the community between the English and Chinese educated. In the years before 1945, enrollment in vernacular schools plummeted (Abshire 2011). Being pragmatic, parents were sending their children to English schools due to the promise of better job opportunities with English as a first language (Ho 2016).

In 1963, Singapore was briefly merged with Malaya in a bid to form a political alliance. During the merger with Malaya, Malay was adopted as the national language in Singapore. During this period, Malay gained unprecedented importance. Civil servants were sent to learn Malay, and Malay was made a compulsory second language in all schools. In 1956, Lee Kuan Yew spoke of his shared regret with Nehru that he could not speak his own mother tongue as well as he could speak English and emphasized, as Josey (1968: 64) put it: "that an age was passing, an age in Malaya and Singapore in which the English and the English-educated ruled the roost". At that time, Malay was poised to become the main language in Singapore as it did in Malaysia. However, history took a different course leading to Malaysia's and Singapore's divergent language routes.

3.4.2 Singapore after independence

After the failed merger and Singapore's independence in 1965, the government implemented a number of reforms, including a new common syllabus for all school subjects and reinstated all four major languages – English, Chinese, Malay and Tamil – as the four official languages of Singapore. Children were given free primary education in any of the four languages, depending on the parents' choices (Tan 1997). Amongst the four languages, English was taken to be the language of the workplace and an important lingua franca because it was thought to be important for commercial development and international trade. However, the increasing emphasis on English as a tool for social and economic mobility led to the dominance of English and, in turn, to many undesirable cultural influences termed as "Westernization" (Chua 1995). Also, English was seen as a colonial language, and it was felt that the adoption of a monolingual English policy would have detrimental effects on Singapore's cultural identity (Lee 2000).

So, in 1966, a bilingual policy was implemented and was made compulsory in schools. In its original form, the language policy stated that the four official languages were the medium of instruction. The majority of schools at that time were English-medium. However, there were also a number of Tamil-, Malay- and Mandarin-medium schools. By 1987, nonetheless, all of these were closed because of decreasing enrollment (Cavallaro and Ng 2014; Tan 2007). Therefore, most students were instructed in English but were also required to study a "mother tongue",[6] depending on their ethnicity.

In 1979, the government implemented the "Speak Mandarin Campaign", which aimed at uniting the different Chinese vernacular groups and to facilitate communication in Mandarin among the Chinese (Gopinathan 1998, 2004). It is important to note that the Chinese community spoke various Chinese vernaculars, referred to as "dialects". It is also worth noting that in 1957, 80% of the population in Singapore spoke Hokkien at home (Kuo 1980). However, with the Speak Mandarin Campaign, the use of Chinese dialects fell drastically and is still declining today: census data show indeed that it has fallen from 76.2% in 1980 to 12.2% in 2015 (Department of Statistics 2015). In the then Prime Minister Lee Kuan Yew's words (Lee 1980: 9): "In fact, dialects have no economic value in Singapore. Their cultural value is also very low. English has cultural value. Mandarin has cultural value and will also have economic value 20 years later".

Another concern that arose was the use of the colloquial English variety, Singlish. This is a variety of English born due to language contact between the different languages in Singapore and is mostly used in home domains and for everyday communication among people from different backgrounds. In 2000, the government initiated the Speak Good English Movement (SGEM) to discourage the use of Singlish and to promote the use of Standard English. Even so, Singlish is widely used among Singaporeans and is seen as a symbol of Singaporean identity (Rubdy 2003).

3.4.3 Singapore now

The series of language policies and relentless campaigns left an indelible mark on current language use. At present, the percentages of languages spoken at home are shown in Table 3.2.

---

[6] In the Singapore context, "mother tongue" does not refer to the language one first learned during childhood, but instead refers to the language Singaporeans are assigned to learn in school, usually based on their father's ethnicity. This may or may not be one's ancestral family language.

Table 3.2: Speakers of the main languages in Singapore (%).
Source: Department of Statistics, 2010, 2015.

	English	Mandarin	Chinese Vernaculars	Tamil	Malay
1957	1.8	0.1	74.4	1.4	13.5
1980	11.6	10.2	59.5	3.1	13.9
1990	18.8	23.7	39.6	2.9	14.3
2000	23.0	35.0	23.8	3.2	14.1
2010	32.3	35.6	14.3	3.2	12.2
2015	36.9	34.9	12.2	3.3	10.7

What is clear from Table 3.2 is the dramatic rise in the use of English and Mandarin since independence. Table 3.3 shows the changes in language use across the ethnic groups. What we can see is an increase in the use of English at home by all groups, with a more rapid rise among the Chinese. What is also significant is the decline in the use of Chinese vernaculars in Singapore. Essentially, the country has a post 1975 population likely to be made up of English dominant bilinguals. It is not uncommon now to find that the younger generations feel more comfortable speaking English as compared to their "mother tongue", while Chinese vernaculars are slowly disappearing from the language repertoire of younger Singaporeans. Over the last 10 years or so, there seems to have been a stabilization in the use of Mandarin and Tamil.

Table 3.3: Languages spoken in Singapore across 35 years by ethnic group (%).

Ethnic Group	Language Spoken at home	1980	1990	2000	2010	2015
Chinese	English	10.2	21.4	23.9	32.6	37.4
	Mandarin	13.1	30	45.1	47.7	46.1
	Chinese vernaculars	76.2	48.2	30.7	19.2	16.1
Malays	English	2.3	5.7	7.9	17	21.5
	Malay	96.7	94.1	91.6	82.6	78.4
Indians	English	24.3	34.3	35.6	41.6	44.3
	Tamil	52.2	43.5	42.9	36.6	37.7
	Malay	8.6	14.1	11.6	7.9	5.6
	Other Indian languages	14.9	8.1	9.2	13.2	12

What is fascinating about Singapore is that the more heated debate is about the validity and solidarity of Singapore English. As discussed in Cavallaro, Ng, and Tan (in press), despite some linguistic insecurity on the part of the State, Singaporeans do feel they have ownership of English and identify with English more than they do with other languages. It is the language they are schooled in and it has also now become the language that they bond with. The majority of Singaporeans is functionally bilingual and can speak at least English plus one other language. Although there is still some strong tendency for Singaporeans to show covert denigration of their more distinctive local variety (see Cavallaro and Ng 2009; Cavallaro, Seilhamer, and Ng 2014), overtly, Singlish is celebrated as a distinctive Singaporean variety. Mandarin Chinese is also used amongst the Singaporean Chinese; yet, it has not become the default intra-ethnic lingua franca. Instead, English is used among bilinguals. Typically, Singaporeans will only use Mandarin Chinese to older speakers who do not speak English. Malay Singaporeans are possibly the most bilingual of the three ethnic groups. But as indicated by Cavallaro and Serwe (2010), this may well change in the next decade with language shift also creeping up on them.

3.5 Conclusion

In these three cases, we argue that while colonial history laid the foundation for the introduction of English, it is the demographic features of each State that have determined the language ecology of each country at the initial point of decolonization. The British neglect of the vernaculars and the privileging of English no doubt led to the emergence of English as the language of the elite. However, Hong Kong's change from a predominantly Cantonese speaking population to one characterized by trilingualism is clearly due to local and/or internal language decisions. In particular, the rise of Mandarin Chinese was artificially introduced through the classroom and the media. In the case of Malaysia, the postcolonial political will to supplant English with Malay in an attempt to forge national identity and address inequality was partially successful as Malay is now the intra-ethnic lingua franca. One could speculate that had the merger between Malaysia and Singapore been successful, this might well have been the outcome for Singapore. Given that the importance of English was felt keenly in Singapore as far back as 1930 and vernacular schools had already started dwindling by 1945, this scenario was unlikely in this state. However, had the momentum to introduce Malay classes as part of the curriculum in Singapore continued, most Singaporeans might have been trilingual. What is interesting is that despite active suppression of English in the school system in Malaysia during the decolonization process, English was still the preferred language of prestige, just as it still is today. In Singapore, the active promotion of Mandarin Chinese to replace other Chinese languages as the intra-ethnic language promoted English as the pan-Chinese intra-ethnic language instead. So, it seems that the survival force of English is strong, not because of the colonial past but because of the global and instrumental growth of English in the new economy. This is supported by the status of English in countries which were not colonized by England, for example Indonesia and Vietnam. In these countries, English has also enjoyed unprecedented rise that far outstrips Dutch or French (their respective colonial languages). The homogenizing force of the global market will continue to propel the use of English in these three cases. However, in all three cases, the capacity of agencies like governments and, through them, schools to transform language use and language ecology of a community is profound. To use a taste analogy, colonialism may have given Hong Kong, Malaysia and Singapore a specific flavor which they each have actively adapted and modulated to produce their own distinctive and unmistakable taste.

In conclusion, we must point out the common bias made by Western scholars who take colonialism as the starting point of historical narratives and fail to see that these "colonies" have a rich and diverse history before them. Eventually what takes root is not what the colonial past dictated but what the locals wish to nourish:

> The colonial experience did not erase the past for Southeast Asians; the colonial period did introduce new structures and practices, but although this experience may have obscured their past and temporarily deflected Southeast Asians, it did not stop them from evolving a modern system based on their indigenous cultural and political heritage. Anything Southeast Asians may have absorbed from the colonial experience or from the West in general has been conditioned and legitimized by their own cultural and historical perceptions and experiences (Mccloud 2018: 19).

References

Abshire. Jean E. 2011. *The history of Singapore.* Santa Barbara: ABC-CLIO/Greenwood.
Albury, Nathan J. 2017. Mother tongues and languaging in Malaysia: Critical linguistics under critical examination. *Language in Society* 46(4). 567–589.
Asmah, Haji Omar. 1992. *The linguistic scenery in Malaysia.* Kuala Lumpur, Malaysia: Dewan Bahasa dan Pustaka, Ministry of Education.
Azmi, Mohd Nazri Latiff. 2013. National language policy and its impacts on second language reading culture. *Journal of International Education and Leadership* 3(1). 1–11.

Bacon-Shone, John & Kingsley Bolton. 2008. Bilingualism and multilingualism in the HKSAR: Language surveys and Hong Kong's changing linguistic profile. In Kingsley Bolton and Han Yang (eds.), *Language and Society in Hong Kong*, 25–51. Hong Kong: Open University of Hong Kong Press.

Bauer, Robert. 1988 Written Cantonese of Hong Kong. *Cahiers de Linguistique Asie Orientale* 17(2). 245–293.

Bolton, Kingsley. 2011. Language policy and planning in Hong Kong: Colonial and post-colonial perspectives. *Applied Linguistics Review* 2. 51–74.

Bolton, Kingsley & Helen Kwok. (eds.). 1992. *Sociolinguistics today* London: Routledge.

Bolton, Kingsley & Bee Chin Ng. 2014. The dynamics of multilingualism in contemporary Singapore. In Kingsley Bolton & Ng Bee Chin (eds.), Language and identity in Singapore. [Special issue]. *World Englishes* 33(3). 307–318.

Buckley, Charles B. 1984. *An anecdotal history of old times in Singapore 1819–1867.* Singapore: Oxford University Press.

Cavallaro, Francesco & Bee Chin Ng. 2009. Between status and solidarity in Singapore. *World Englishes* 28(2). 143–159.

Cavallaro, Francesco & Bee Chin Ng. 2014. Language in Singapore: From multilingualism to English plus. In Yvette Slaughter & John Hajek (eds.), *Challenging the monolingual mindset. A book in memory of Michael Clyne*, 33–48. Bristol: Multilingual Matters.

Cavallaro, Francesco, Bee Chin Ng & Ying Ying Tan. In press. Singapore English. In Kingsley Bolton & Andy Kirkpatrick (eds.), *Handbook of Asian Englishes*. New Jersey: Blackwell-Wiley.

Cavallaro Francesco, Mark Seilhame & Bee Chin Ng. 2014. Singapore Colloquial English: Issues of prestige and identity. *World Englishes* 33(3). 378–397.

Cavallaro, Francesco, Mark Seilhamer, Yen Yee Ho & Bee Chin Ng. 2018. Attitudes to Mandarin Chinese varieties in Singapore. *Journal of Asian Pacific Communication* 28(2). 195–225.

Cavallaro, Francesco & Stefan Serwe. 2010. Language use and shift among the Malays in Singapore. *Applied Linguistics Review* 1(1). 129–170.

Census and Statistics Department. 2015. *Thematic household survey report – Report no. 59.* The Government of the Hong Kong Administrative Region. https://www.censtatd.gov.hk/hkstat/sub/sp370.jsp?productCode=C0000086 (accessed 9 November 2018).

Census and Statistics Department. 2016. *The government of the Hong Kong administrative region. Population by-census.* https://www.bycensus2016.gov.hk/en/bc-index.html (accessed 9 November 2018).

Census and Statistics Department. 2017. *Proportion of population aged 5 and over able to speak selected languages/dialects by sex.* The Government of the Hong Kong Administrative Region. https://www.censtatd.gov.hk/hkstat/sub/gender/demographic/index.jsp (accessed 9 November 2018).

Central Advisory Committee on Education. 1951. *Report on the Barnes report on Malay education and the Fenn-Wu report on Chinese education.* Kuala Lumpur, Federation of Malaya: Government Press. https://satusekolahuntuksemua.files.wordpress.com/2009/07/021_report-on-barnes-report-on-malay-education-and-fenn-wu-report-on-chinese-education-1951.pdf (accessed 18 November 2018).

Chua, Beng-Huat. 1995. *Communitarian ideology and democracy in Singapore.* London: Routledge.

Coluzzi, Paolo, Patricia N. Riget & Xiaomei Wang. 2013. Language vitality among the Bidayuh of Sarawak (East Malaysia). *Oceanic Linguistics* 52(2). 375–395.

Crismore, Avon, Karen Y-H. Ngeow & Keng-soon Soo. 1996. Attitudes toward English in Malaysia. *World Englishes* 15(3). 319–335.

Darmi, Ramiza & Peter Albion. 2013. English language in Malaysian education system: Its existence and implication. Paper presented at the 3rd Malaysian Postgraduate Conference (MPC2013), Sydney, New South Wales, Australia, 4–5 July. Proceedings, pp. 175–183. https://eprints.usq.edu.au/23984/13/Noor_Rahman_MPC2013_Full%20Proceedings_PV.pdf (accessed 9 November 2018).

David, Maya K., Francesco Cavallaro & Paolo Coluzzi. 2009. Language policies – Impact on language maintenance and teaching: Focus on Malaysia, Singapore, Brunei and the Philippines. In Francesco Cavallaro, Andrea Milde & Peter Sercombe (eds.), Language, culture and identity in Asia. [Special Issue]. *The Linguistics Journal*, 155–191. British Virgin Islands: Time Taylor.

Department of Statistics. 2001. *Census of population 2000, Statistical release 2: Education, language and religion*. Singapore: Department of Statistics, Ministry of Trade and Industry. https://www.singstat.gov.sg/publications/cop2000/cop2000r2 (accessed 17 November 2018).

Department of Statistics. 2005. *General household survey 2005*. Singapore: Department of Statistics, Ministry of Trade and Industry. https://www.singstat.gov.sg/publications/ghs/ghrs2 (accessed 17 November 2018).

Department of Statistics. 2006. General household survey statistical release 1: Sociodemographic and economic characteristics. Singapore: Department of Statistics, Ministry of Trade and Industry.https://www.singstat.gov.sg/publications/ghs/ghrs1 (accessed 17 November 2018).

Department of Statistics. 2015. *General household survey 2015*. Singapore: Department of Statistics, Ministry of Trade and Industry. https://www.singstat.gov.sg/publications/ghs/ghs2015 (accessed 17 November 2018).

Department of Statistics Malaysia. 2018. *Current population estimates, Malaysia, 2017–2018*. https://www.dosm.gov.my/v1/index.php?r=column/cthemeByCat&cat=155&bul_id=c1pqTnFjb29HSnNYNUpiTmNWZHArdz09&menu_id=L0pheU43NWJwRWVSZklWdzQ4TlhUUT09 (accessed 19 November 2018).

Doraisamy, Theodore R. 1969. *150 years of education in Singapore*. Singapore: TTC Publications Board, Teachers Training College. http://ezlibproxy1.ntu.edu.sg/login?url=http://search.ebscohost.com/login.aspx?direct=true&db=cat05206a&AN=ntu.17139&site=eds-live&scope=site (accessed 17 November 2018).

Dumaniga, Francisco P., Maya K. David & Lorraine Symaco. 2012. Competing roles of the national language and English in Malaysia and the Philippines: Planning, policy and use. *Journal of International and Comparative Education* 1(2). 104–115.

Education Bureau. 2010. *Enriching our language environment, realising our vision*. Hong Kong: Education Bureau, the Government of the Hong Kong Special Administrative Region. https://www.edb.gov.hk/attachment/sc/student-parents/ncs-students/about-ncs-students/moi%20booklet-eng-17apr2010.pdf (accessed 17 November 2018).

English Language Standards and Quality Council. 2015. *English language education reform in Malaysia: The roadmap 2015–2025*. Ministry of Education Malaysia. http://anyflip.com/detl/zspi/basic (accessed 17 November 2018).

Evans, Stephen. 2000. Hong Kong's new English language policy in education. *World Englishes* 19(2). 185–204.

Evans, Stephen. 2002. The medium of instruction in Hong Kong: Policy and practice in the English and Chinese streams. *Research Papers in Education* 17(1). 97–120.

Gill, Saran K. 2005. Language policy in Malaysia: Reversing direction. *Language Policy* 4(3). 241–260.

Gill, Saran K. 2006. Change in language policy in Malaysia: The reality of implementation in public universities. *Current Issues in Language Planning* 7(1). 82–94.

Gopinathan, Saravanan. 1998. Language policy changes 1979–1997: Politics and pedagogy. In Saravanan Gopinathan, Anne Pakir, Wah Kam Ho & Saravanan Vanithamani (eds.), *Language, Society and Education in Singapore: Issues and Trends*, 2nd edn., 19–44. Singapore: Times Academic Press.

Gopinathan, Saravanan. 2004. Language planning in education in Singapore: History, transitions, futures. *ASCD (Singapore) Review* 12(2). 14–23.

Hashim, Azirah. 2009. Not plain sailing: Malaysia's language choice in policy and education. *AILA Review* 22(1). 36–51.

Hirschman, Charles. 1980. Demographic trends in peninsular Malaysia 1947–1975. *Population and Development Review* 6(1). 103–125.

Ho, Stephanie. 2016. *Vernacular education*. Singapore: Eresources.nlb.gov.sg. http://eresources.nlb.gov.sg/infopedia/articles/SIP_2016-10-03_094744.html (accessed 9 November 2018).

Hong Kong Government. 1974. *Official languages ordinance [no. 10/74]*. Hong Kong: Government Printer.

How, Soo Ying, Swee Heng Chan & Ain Nadzimah Abdullah. 2015. Language vitality of Malaysian languages and its relation to identity. *GEMA Online Journal of Language Studies* 15(2). 119–139.

Johnson, Robert K. 1998 Language and education in Hong Kong. In Martha Pennington (ed.), *Language in Hong Kong at century's end*, 265–276. Hong Kong: Hong Kong University Press.

Josey, Alex. 1968. *Lee Kuan Yew: The crucial years*. Singapore: Donald Moore Press.

Kaur, Paramjit & Aspalila Shapii. 2018. Language and nationalism in Malaysia: A language policy perspective. *International Journal of Law, Government and Communication* 3(7). 1–10.

Kuo, Eddie C. Y. 1980. The sociolinguistic situation in Singapore: Unity in diversity. In Evangelos A. Afendras & Eddie C. Y. Kuo (eds.), *Language and society in Singapore*, 39–62. Singapore: National University of Singapore Press.

Kwan, Anna. 2000. Language shift, mother tongue, and identity in Singapore. *International Journal of the Sociology of Language* 143. 85–106.

Lai, Mee Ling. 2009. 'I love Cantonese but I want English' – A qualitative account of Hong Kong students' language attitudes. *The Asia–Pacific Education Researcher* 18(1). 79–92.

Lai, Mee Ling. 2010. Social class and language attitudes in Hong Kong. *International Multilingual Research Journal* 4(2). 83–106.

Lai, Mee Ling. 2012. Tracking language attitudes in postcolonial Hong Kong: An interplay of localization, mainlandization and internationalization. *Multilingua* 31(1). 1–29.

Lai, Mee Ling. 2013. The linguistic landscape of Hong Kong after the change of sovereignty. *International Journal of Multilingualism* 10(3). 251–272.

Lau, Chi-kuen 1995. Language of the future. *South China Morning Post*, 18 September.

Lee, Kuan Yew. 1980. Drop dialects at home and help your child do better in school. *Straits Times*, 17 November 1980. http://eresources.nlb.gov.sg/newspapers/Digitised/Article/straitstimes19801117-1.2.39?ST=1&AT=filter&K=lee+kuan+yew+and+mandarin&KA=lee+kuan+yew+and+mandarin&DF=&DT=&Display=0&AO=false&NPT=&L=&CTA=&NID=straitstimes&CT=ARTICLE&WC=&YR=1980&QT=lee,kuan,yew,and,mandarin&oref=article (Accessed 30 May 2018).

Lee, Kuan Yew. 2000. *From third world to first: The Singapore story: 1965–2000*, 1st edn. New York: Harper Collins.

Li, David C. S. 1999. The functions and status of English in Hong Kong: A post-1997 update. *English World-Wide* 20(1). 67–110.

Li, David C. S. 2002. Hong Kong parents' preference for English-medium education: Passive victims of imperialism or active agents of pragmatism? In Andy Kirkpatrick (ed.), *Englishes in Asia. Communication, identity, power & education*, 29–62. Melbourne: Language Australia.

Li, David C. S. 2017. The Hong Kong language context. In David C. S. Li (ed.), *Multilingual Hong Kong: Languages, literacies and identities* (Multilingual Education), 1–19. Cham, Switzerland: Springer.

Li, David C. S. 2018. Two decades of decolonization and renationalization: The evolutionary dynamics of Hong Kong English and an update of its functions and status pass. *Asian Englishes* 20(1). 2–14.

Lim, Peng Han. 2008. English schools and school libraries before the Second World War: A Singapore perspective. *Singapore Journal of Library & Information Management* 37. 61–80.

Lowenberg, Peter H. 1991. Variation in Malaysian English. The pragmatics of languages in contact. In Jenny Cheshire (ed.), *English around the world: Sociolinguistic perspectives*, 363–375. Cambridge: Cambridge University Press.

Luke, Kang Kwong & Jack Richards. 1982. English in Hong Kong: Functions and status. *English World-Wide* 3(1). 47–64.

Mccloud, Donald. 2018 [1995]. *Southeast Asia: Tradition and modernity in the contemporary world*, 2ndedn. New York: Routledge.

Muniandy, Mohan K., Gopala K. S. Nair, Shashi K. K. Shanmugam, Irma Ahmad & Norashikin B. M. Noor. 2010. Sociolinguistic competence and Malaysian students' English language proficiency. *English Language Teaching* 3(3). 145–151.

Pierson, Herbert D. 1988. Language attitudes and use in Hong Kong: A case for Putonghua. Paper presented at the First Hong Kong Conference on Language and Society. Hong Kong, 24–28 April.

Poon, Anita Y. K. 2010. Language use, language policy and planning in Hong Kong. *Current Issues in Language Planning* 11(1). 1–66.

Poon, Anita Y. K, Connie Lau & David Chu. 2013. Impact of the fine-tuning medium-of-instruction policy on learning: Some preliminary findings. *Literacy Information and Computer Education Journal* 4(1). 946–954.

Puteh, Ales. 2010. The language medium policy in Malaysia: A plural society model? *Review of European Studies* 2(2). 192–200.

Raffles, Thomas S. 1819. *Minute by Sir T.S. Raffles on the establishment of a Malay college at Singapore*. [No publisher or place stated on the manuscript].

Rubdy, Rani. 2003. Creative destruction: Singapore's Speak Good English movement. *World Englishes* 20. 341–355.

Setter, Jane, Cathy S. P. Wong & Brian H. S. Chan. 2010. *Hong Kong English*. Edinburgh: Edinburgh University Press.

Simons, Gary F. & Charles D. Fennig (eds.). 2018. *Ethnologue: Languages of the world*, 21st edn. Dallas, Texas: SIL International. Online http://www.ethnologue.com.

Simpson, Andrew. 2007. Hong Kong. In Andrew Simpson (ed.), *Language and national identity in Asia*, 168–185. Oxford: Oxford University.

Snow, Don. 2004. *Cantonese as written language: The growth of a written Chinese vernacular*. Hong Kong: Hong Kong University Press.

So, Daniel W.C. 1998. One country, two cultures and three languages: Sociolinguistic conditions and language education in Hong Kong. In Barry Asker (ed.), *Teaching language and culture: Building Hong Kong on education*, 152–175. Hong Kong: Longman.

Stephen, Jeannet. 2013 English in Malaysia: A case of the past that never really went away? *English Today* 29(2). 3–8.

Sung, Chit Cheung Matthew. 2015. Hong Kong English: Linguistic and sociolinguistic perspectives. *Language and Linguistics Compass* 9(6). 256–270.

Tan, Jason. 1997. Education and colonial transition in Singapore and Hong Kong: Comparisons and contrasts. *Comparative Education* 33(2). 303–312.

Tan, Jason. 2007. Schooling in Singapore. In Gerard A. Postiglione & Jason Tan (eds.), *Going to school in East Asia*, 301–319. Westport: Greenwood Publishing Group.

Tan, Yao Sua. 2013. The British educational policy for the indigenous community in Malaya 1870–1957: Dualistic structure, colonial interests and Malay radical nationalism. *International Journal of Educational Development* 33(4). 337–347.

Tharmalingam, S. 2012. Language policy changes in Malaysia: Progressive or regressive? Paper presented at the International Conference on Linguistics, Literature, and Culture 2012 (ICLLIC 2012), Park Royal Hotel Penang, 7–9 November http://irep.iium.edu.my/26806/1/Language_policy_changes.pdf (accessed 17 November 2018).

Thirusanku, Jantmary & Melor Md. Yunus. 2012. The many faces of Malaysian English. *ISRN Education* 2012. 1–14.

Ting, Su-Hie. 2003 Impact of language planning on language attitudes: A case study in Sarawak. *Journal of Multilingual and Multicultural Development* 24(3). 195–210.

Ting, Su-Hie & Yvonne M. Campbell. 2017. The role of indigenous languages in schools: The case of Sarawak. In Moses Samuel, Meng Yew Tee & Lorraine P. Symaco (eds.), *Education in Malaysia: Developments and Challenges*, 119–136. Singapore: Springer Singapore.

Wang, Lixun & Andy Kirkpatrick. 2015. Trilingual education in Hong Kong primary schools: An overview. *Multilingual Education* 5(3). 1–26.

Yang, Pei Keng. 1998. Constitutional & legal provision for mother tongue education in Malaysia. In Kia Soong Kua (ed.), *Mother tongue education of Malaysian ethnic minorities: Papers presented at the seminar on Mother Tongue Education of Malaysian Ethnic Minorities organised by Dong Jiao Zong Higher Learning Centre at its Kajang campus on 1 & 2 November 1997, 26–71*. Kajang, Selangor, Malaysia: Dong Jiao Zong Higher Learning Centre.

Zaaba, Zuraidah, Farida Ibrahim Ramadan, Anthony I. N. Aning, Haijon Gunggut & Katsuhiro Umemoto. 2011. Language-in-education policy: A study of policy adjustment strategy in Malaysia. *International Journal of Education and Information Technologies* 2(5). 157–165.

Zeng, Wei. 2007. Medium of instruction in secondary education in post-colonial Hong Kong: Why Chinese? Why English? *Working Papers in Educational Linguistics* 22(1). 42–56. https://repository.upenn.edu/wpel/vol22/iss1/3 (accessed 9 November 2018).

Lennart Bartelheimer, Britta Hufeisen and Simona Montanari
4 Multilingualism in Europe

4.1 Introduction

4.1.1 Multilingualism in Europe: A relevant topic?

Months of protests, riots, a national assembly paralyzed by obstructionism, and even a pistol duel between a member of parliament and a prime minister – these were the consequences of the Badeni Language Ordinances issued in 1897 during the Austro-Hungarian Dual Monarchy. The ordinances aimed to give the German and Czech languages equal status in the Austrian crown lands of Bohemia and Moravia, which were inhabited by Germans and Czechs alike. Instead, they gave rise to the monarchy's gravest crisis, fueling nationalism and turning political disputes in the Imperial and Royal Monarchy into violent conflicts (see e.g., Burger 1994; Krzoska 2005).

Fast-forward 120 years to 2017, where in the German federal state of Baden-Württemberg the curtain was brought down (at least for the time being) on a debate that had raged bitterly for years regarding foreign language instruction in the state's primary schools. The fifteen-year-long practice of introducing foreign language instruction in the first grade (French in the areas bordering France and English in the rest of the state) was eliminated. The responses to the decision were controversial, as were the discussions leading up to it (on the arguments in favor, see Philologenverband Baden-Württemberg 2017; on those against, see Maldacker 2017). Over the years, lawsuits had already been filed again and again against the state of Baden-Württemberg and its decades-long practice of starting with French rather than English as the first foreign language in schools in areas along the Rhine River (bordering France) (see Hans 2007).

While these two examples are rooted in two fundamentally unrelated historical contexts, they make a very clear point: language matters. Languages, language policy, and multilingualism are deeply relevant topics in Europe today and always have been. This significance is reinforced by the fact that Europe's societies are in a state of upheaval owing to the ongoing processes of inner-European unification – and in some places unfortunately also estrangement – as well as to migration and advancing globalization at the international level. This

---

Lennart Bartelheimer, Britta Hufeisen, Technische Universitaet Darmstadt, Darmstadt, Germany
Simona Montanari, California State University, Los Angeles (CA), U.S.A.

https://doi.org/10.1515/9781501507984-004

shows that languages are, just as in the past, nearly always used as a defining factor for national and cultural identities.

The aims of this chapter are twofold: firstly, we intend to provide an overview of the status, origins, and various manifestations of multilingualism – some of which are very diverse, such as regional multilingualism, national multilingualism, regional minority and immigrant languages – that exist in different European countries. Secondly, we offer an overview of (foreign) language policy, language programs, and institutions at the European level and explain how research, teaching, and work are conducted in this area in different contexts.

In this chapter, we make a distinction between multilingualism and multilingual learning on the one hand (Festman, Poarch, and Dewaele 2017), and bilingualism and learning a (first) foreign language on the other (Jessner 2006; ten Thije and Zeevaert 2007). In particular, we refer to "multilingualism" as the ability to interact in more than two languages, whether an individual grows up with three or more languages or whether he/she has learned at least two languages in addition to his or her first. Indeed, linguistic research investigating multilingualism always involves at least three languages. It assumes that learning a second foreign language is by various standards substantially different than learning a first foreign language and is not simply repeated second language acquisition.

4.1.2 What is Europe?

Europe can be defined in different ways: Europe as a geographical entity, i.e., as a continent, from Ireland to the Ural Mountains; Europe as a political entity, i.e., the European Union; or Europe as an object of language policy, debated by institutions such as the Council of Europe. In this chapter, we deal with the perspective of the Council of Europe, one of whose important aims is the preservation of Europe's linguistic diversity. In Europe, a wide range of different languages is spoken, independent of nations and national territories. There are a large number of official languages, as well as languages in the sense of dialects or language varieties, along with regional minority languages and immigrant languages. In this regard, Europe is a plurilingual continent with a number of officially monolingual but also bilingual and multilingual countries. For example, while France and Germany are officially monolingual countries (with French and German, respectively), there are more or less recognized regional minority languages (such as Basque or Breton in France, or Danish or Sorbian in Germany) as well as widely spoken immigrant languages (Arabic in France and Turkish in Germany). Most inhabitants of both national territories speak a number of different languages, making both countries in fact plurilingual. Belgium is a trilingual country in which Dutch, French, and German are spoken, although this does not mean that all of Belgium's inhabitants are trilingual. In Norway, in contrast, there are two varieties of Norwegian, Nynorsk and Bokmål, which all Norwegians understand. Switzerland, with four official languages (German, French, Italian, and Rhaeto-Romance) and Luxembourg, with the languages French, German, and Luxembourgish, are also multilingual countries.

Because of the diversity of Europe's linguistic landscape, plurilingualism and multilingualism are social phenomena and objects of sociolinguistic research. At the same time, these phenomena are also studied at the individual level from the perspectives of psycholinguistics and applied linguistics. For example, research conducted from applied or psycholinguistic perspectives tends to study English as a language of wider communication, as the most widely learned foreign language, as the foreign language learned first, or as a teaching language ("English-medium instruction") (Lasagabaster 2016). Studies test, for example, the extent to which the acquisition of English as the first foreign language draws on learners' existing multilingualism, or how it can prepare for subsequent foreign language learning (Jessner 2006). Another line of research investigating the acquisition of typical second foreign languages – in other words, those learned subsequent to the first foreign language (usually English) – tends to focus on questions about how learners draw on previously learned languages in order to make novel language learning more effective, efficient, challenging, and more routine (Meißner 2010).

In this chapter, we focus on the various manifestations of multilingualism and the (foreign) language policy, language programs, and institutions that support it at the European level. Since Europe is a construct that can be defined in so many ways and is characterized by plurilingualism, multilingualism, and great cultural diversity, in the sections below we use specific examples from one or more countries or regions to illustrate the particular aspects discussed. In the context of this chapter, it will not be possible to present the entire spectrum of extraordinarily vital linguistic research into multilingualism without being selective. For this reason, our observations are primarily based on language-policy sources and on a limited number of representative research sources.

4.2 Multilingualism in different countries in Europe

Europe may be the cradle of the notion of the nation-state, and language has always played a central role as a significant sign of an individual's affiliation with a *nation*. This may, however, belie the fact that even in Europe, multilingualism has always been and continues to be a given, although the extent of multilingualism varies. As already mentioned in the introduction and as the examples below repeatedly make clear, the status of multilingualism today is frequently the result of long historical processes, and the topic of language or languages and the relationship of different languages to each other has often been the object of political controversy and heated debates. Political changes continue to influence language development and use – which is visible, for example, in Southeast Europe with the (re-)separation of the Serbo-Croatian language into Bosnian, Croatian, and Serbian after the disintegration of Yugoslavia. Catalan aspirations for independence from Spain show another example of political and linguistic pluralism in an otherwise relatively stable country.

However, it is often difficult to find appropriate ways to describe the phenomena involved. The term "official language" is only of limited use in describing the language that is used within a country, since it suggests a state of clarity and unambiguity that frequently does not exist in reality. For instance, there are countries with a single official language, countries in which several languages are valid as official languages at the national level, countries in which certain languages are valid as official languages in certain regions, and those in which several languages are used in different areas of the political administration. Ammon (2015: 202–203) proposed the terms "solo-official" for languages that are the only official language in their respective countries and "co-official" for those that are official languages alongside one or more others. In general, forms of regional and national multilingualism can be distinguished from forms that constitute a blend of the two. Regional multilingualism means that there are different languages used in different geographical areas in one country, while national multilingualism means that different languages are used in the country as a whole. Furthermore, a myriad of other languages that have no official status (e.g., immigrant and some regional languages) can be widely spoken within and across countries. Below we present several examples of multilingualism in different regions of Europe.

4.2.1 Regional multilingualism: Belgium and Switzerland

Belgian society is divided into French-speaking Wallonia, in the southern part of the country, and Flanders in the north, where Dutch is spoken. The division of the Netherlands in the seventeenth century into a Protestant region in the north and a Catholic area in the south gave rise to this situation. Today, the national border between the Netherlands and Belgium still tends to follow denominational rather than linguistic lines. The language border bisects the Belgian country, dividing Belgium into Dutch-speaking Flanders and French-speaking Wallonia. The social and political developments of the subsequent centuries gave rise to a dualism between the two groups. Unlike in Ireland, for example, where religious denomination became the main marker of division between different groups, in Belgium, it is language. French gained the status as the language of the higher society and education. The growing wealth in Wallonia, rooted in the rise of heavy industry, led to Walloon self-confidence that the Flemish did not appreciate so much (which inverted somewhat after the decline of heavy industry in the late twentieth century). This dualism persisted even after Belgium achieved independence in the nineteenth century, leading to a highly complex structure of languages (Witte and Van Velthofen 1999).

Today's Belgium is a federation with three official languages: Dutch, French, and German. At the national level, however, only Dutch and French are used but with equal status. All laws are published in both Dutch and French, for example. At the federal level, there is a complex relationship between various authorities: the *regions* and the *communities*, each having their own parliaments, governments, and political competencies. Brussels, as the capital of the country, has over decades turned into a French-speaking island in a Flemish-speaking environment, as it is geographically located in Flanders. Today, the city is officially bilingual, and conflicts with the monolingual neighboring towns are always present. Multiple constitutional reforms in the 1970s and 1980s greatly expanded the communities' competencies, thus granting them extensive autonomy in the areas of culture, language, teaching, and administration. The German-speaking community, whose administration is conducted in both German and French, has a special status in this structure because it is geographically located in French-speaking Wallonia, but has some special legislation concerning the official use of German. The school system is particularly noteworthy. While the language of instruction in this region is German, from third grade on, French is part of the curriculum, and in secondary school, it is the language of instruction in some cases (Ammon 2015: 236–237). Most parents in this part of Belgium support this educational policy based on German-French bilingualism, in stark contrast with the situation in the German federal state of Baden-Württemberg as described in the introduction. School policy differs between the communities, but the introduction of other foreign languages in the curriculum occurs later than in most other countries in Europe: even English is studied by only 46.3% of the students at the high school level (see Eurostat 2016: 3).

A similar territorially determined form of multilingualism exists in Switzerland. The Confederatio Helvetica is one of the most federally structured countries in the world, with four official languages at the national level, spoken in relatively clearly delineated language regions. However, the political authority to determine the official language(s) is delegated to the cantonal level. Of twenty-six cantons, fourteen are German-speaking, four are French-speaking, and one is Italian-speaking. In addition, three cantons are German- and French-speaking and one canton (Grisons) has three official languages: German, Italian and Rhaeto-Romance (Ammon 2015: 219). As in Belgium, Switzerland's language regions are relatively clearly delineated. In other words, few individuals in Switzerland are multilingual from birth. Rather, they learn the first language(s) of their fellow citizens in foreign language instruction at school, which is also regulated at the cantonal level. At present, this foreign language instruction is hotly debated. While for a long time there was consensus that one of the official languages of Switzerland should be the first foreign language to be taught in school, English is now increasingly being taught as the first foreign language, especially in the German-speaking parts of Switzerland. In 2009, the HarmoS Concordat took effect with the aim of harmonizing most of the cantons' school systems. Article 4.1 of the Concordat stipulates the latest point at which foreign languages are to be introduced (fifth grade for the first foreign language and seventh grade for the second) but does not define which language should be learned first. Since then, many German-speaking cantons have introduced English as the first foreign language and French as the second (Swiss Academies of Arts and Sciences 2015: 2).

4.2.2 National multilingualism: Luxembourg

The tiny Duchy of Luxembourg has three official national languages. However, the relationship of the three languages to each other is fundamentally different than in Belgium or Switzerland (Berg 1993). While the former constitution of Luxembourg of 1848 declared German and French official languages with equal status and the amended constitution of 1948 delegated the question of an official language to a language law that was yet to be written, most of Luxembourg's citizens consider Luxembourgish (*Letzeburgisch*) to be their real first language. While nearly all Luxembourg's citizens speak the other two languages fluently, Luxembourgish is still the key feature in the constitution of Luxembourgish identity (Ammon 2015: 224–225). The relationship between the three languages used at the official level was not formally regulated until the Languages Law of 1984 was adopted. All three languages are "administrative languages," with Luxembourgish, which previously was not accorded official status, now declared a national language. French has, for the most part, established itself as the language of legislation and internal administration. While German is permitted in administrative and judicial contexts, in actuality, it plays a minor role, and its status is likely to diminish in the future (Ammon 2015: 227–228). Unlike in Belgium, trilingualism in Luxembourg is not territorially bound. In principle, all three languages are present throughout the country. This comes to bear particularly in the school system, where all three languages are equally mandatory for all children enrolled in school, both as teaching languages and for language instruction. While the classroom language for preschool and primary school is primarily Luxembourgish/*Letzeburgisch*, reading proficiency is taught in German, which is closer to *Letzeburgisch* than French. Starting in second grade, French is introduced as an additional language of instruction and, by the secondary level, it is the main one (Ammon 2015: 228–229).

4.2.3 Mixed forms of regional and national multilingualism: The Norwegian example

Norway provides an example of mixed forms of regional and national multilingualism. Norwegian has two official languages, or two separate written standards: *Bokmål* ('book language') and *Nynorsk* ('New Norwegian,' 'new' in the sense of contemporary or modern). *Bokmål* derives from *Riksmål* ('national language'), the Norwegian variety heavily influenced by Danish from the fourteenth century until 1814, when Norway was part of the Kingdom of Denmark. Despite the strong influence of Danish, the older Faroe Island-influenced dialects (referred to as *Landmål* ['country language']) have remained alive across the centuries, especially in the rural areas of western Norway. After the separation from Denmark and influenced by the nationalist and Romantic zeitgeist that took all of Europe by storm in the nineteenth century, the social status of *Landmål* was elevated, with the Norwegian philologist and linguist Ivar Aasen normalizing it to produce a standard variety – today's *Nynorsk* and Norway's second national language. Since the two languages *Bokmål* and *Nynorsk* are closely related and Norwegian is still strongly characterized by dialects, the differences between the two languages are mainly in the written form. Today *Nynorsk* is still mainly used in western Norway (see Vikør 2015), while *Bokmål* is used in the rest of the country. Both varieties are mutually intelligible and there are no communication problems when people use any of them. Concerning communication with foreigners, English is understood all over the country and is taught to all children beginning in primary school (see Eurostat 2016: 2).

4.2.4 Regional minority languages: The European Charter for Regional or Minority Languages and the debate in France as an example

In several other European countries, regional minority languages exist with different official statuses, including in Spain, Italy, Estonia, and Romania. For example, in Spain, Spanish is in official use throughout the country and spoken by 99% of the population. Yet other languages have legal and co-official status in some of the seventeen autonomous communities (*comunidades autónomas*): Basque in the Basque Country, Catalan in Catalonia and the Balearic Islands, Galician in Galicia, and the Valencian dialect of Catalan in the community of Valencia (Dirección de Documentación del Senado 2013). Some of these languages have daily newspapers and significant book publishing and media presence in those communities, and in the cases of Catalan and Galician, they are the main languages used by the Catalan and Galician regional governments and local administrations. In addition, a number of citizens in these areas consider their regional language as their primary language and Spanish as secondary.

While it is beyond the scope of this chapter to list all of the regional languages used in Europe, it is still important to acknowledge the overall European policy on these languages. In 1992, the Council of Europe adopted the European Charter for Regional or Minority Languages (ECRML). The goal was not only to protect and promote regional minority languages as part of Europe's cultural wealth, but also to establish the use of regional minority languages in both the private and public spheres as a human right (see the preamble to the European Charter). To this end, in addition to other measures, the charter also calls for classroom instruction and educational opportunities to be offered in regional minority languages (Art. 8). However, only 33 out of 47 Member States have signed the charter and 25 have ratified it (see European Charter).

This particular topic is hotly debated in France. Since the French Revolution, the French language has been a central pillar of the nation's unity. Even today, some people there consider regional minority languages such as Basque, Breton, or Occitan to be more of a nuisance than an asset (Wright 2000). Furthermore, in 1999 the French Constitutional Council decided that part of the charter violated the French Constitution, which defines French as the republic's language (Ministère de la Culture 2013: 23–24). While a constitutional amendment and ratification of the charter were adopted by the National Assembly in 2014 and debated in the Senate in 2015, they have not yet entered into force (Council of Europe, n.d.). Nevertheless, on the level of local politics and civil society, there are efforts to keep the regional languages alive and to integrate them into everyday life, for example in the form of bilingual street signs and language education (Coyos 2016 for Basque; Adam and Calvez 2016 for Breton; Escudé 2016 for Occitan).

4.2.5 Europe's immigrant languages

While multilingualism is intrinsic to Europe's autochthonous population, recent immigration has further increased the continent's linguistic diversity, especially in urban areas. Indeed, as a consequence of the opening of the internal European borders, the political and economic developments of regions near and far from Europe, and the increasing number of political refugees, many industrialized European countries – and in particular their cities – are home to an increasing number of immigrants who differ widely, both culturally and linguistically, from the autochthonous population (Extra 2011). In 2000, about one third of Europe's urban inhabitants under the age of 35 had an immigrant background (Gogolin 2002). In 2013, immigrants constituted 11.6% of the total population in France, 11.9% in Germany, 12.4% in the United Kingdom, and 15.9% in Sweden (United Nations 2013). These data suggest that, due to intensified processes of international migration and intergenerational minoritization, immigrant languages – in particular non-European languages such as Turkish and Arabic – have emerged as community languages spoken and learned on a wide scale in urban Europe.

Several studies have indeed shown that the use of more than one language is a way of life for an increasing number of children in European cities. For instance, the Multilingual Cities Project (see Extra and Yağmur 2008 for a review), which collected data from 160,000 students in Göteborg (Sweden), Hamburg (Germany), The Hague (The Netherlands), Brussels, (Belgium), Lyon (France), Madrid (Spain) and later in Essen (Germany) and Vienna (Austria) documented a wealth of hidden evidence on the distribution and vitality of immigrant languages across European cities and nation states. The students were surveyed on their language proficiency, language choice, language dominance, and language preference. The results showed that the proportion of primary school children who spoke languages other than or in addition to the societal language at home ranged between one third and more than a half in each city. The total number of languages reported beyond the majority language(s) ranged between 50 and 90 per city. The major non-national, non-European languages that were reported in the participating cities were Turkish and Arabic, although different cities had also specific language constellations (for example, Russian was highly reported in Hamburg and Berber in The Hague). The results also revealed that the use of other languages at home in these contexts did not occur at the cost of competence in the majority language. Indeed, as put by Extra and Yağmur (2008: 14), "mainstream and non-mainstream languages should not be conceived in terms of competition. Rather, the data show that these languages are used as alternatives, depending on such factors as type of context and interlocutor". Interestingly, the languages with the highest vitality index were Romani/Sinte, Urdu, Turkish, and Armenian, while European languages had the strongest intergenerational shift. Overall, these findings suggest that the traditional view of European multilingualism should be reconsidered and extended to include the languages spoken in these immigrant, highly vibrant communities.

The results of the Multilingual Cities Project were confirmed by a variety of other investigations in other European cities. For example, research in Manchester, UK (Matras and Robertson 2015; Matras, Robertson, and Jones 2016) shows that the city has experienced large-scale immigration since the industrial era, and even after the decline of the industrial sector in the late twentieth century, the city has continued to see an influx of immigrants – not only British Commonwealth and EU citizens but also migrant workers and refugees – to take part in its service-based economy. Indeed, today, more than 150 languages are spoken in the city and based on School Census data, it is estimated that at least 40% of schoolchildren are multilingual (Matras, Robertson, and Jones 2016). In particular, Matras and colleagues found, in a sample of 531 student surveys/interviews, that 48 different languages were spoken by the children, the top being non-European immigrant languages such as Urdu, Somali, Arabic, Bengali, Panjabi, as well as Romani. In line with the findings from the Multilingual Cities Project, proficiency levels for these languages were high, and language vitality was correlated with the time of immigration; that is, high use of and proficiency in the home language were found in communities with a high proportion of new arrivals, often refugees (for example, from Afghanistan, the Middle East and Somalia). Three quarters of the children also reported that they spoke two or more languages in addition to English with family members on a regular basis, suggesting that multilingualism is the norm for this population.

Immigrant languages are not only part of the Northern European landscape but they are also prevalent in Southern European countries and cities. For instance, Italy, once a country of emigrants, has recently witnessed the entry of large numbers of immigrants who now amount to 3.5 million people (5.6% of the population) with at least 600,000 young people present in the educational system (Barni, Vedovelli, and Bagna 2008). These new immigrants speak at least 130 different languages, which they have implanted in large and small cities across the country, diversifying both national and local linguistic spaces. Barni and Vedovelli (2012), who studied two urban contexts in Italy with a marked and long-documented presence of immigrant communities, Rome and

Prato, found that "foreigners" made up 13.66% of Prato's resident population, and the percentage of immigrants relative to the total number of residents in the Esquilino neighborhood of Rome increased from 20.4% to 29.7% from 2004 to 2010. In Rome, the most numerous immigrant communities included Eritreans, Chinese, Bangladeshis, Romanians, Filipinos, Afghanis, Somalis, Ethiopians, and Indians. In Prato, the Chinese community was the most visible: as a matter of fact, the city has the second largest Chinese immigrant population in Italy (after Milan), which it widely employs in its 3,500 workshops in the garment industry. These statistics highlight how Italy's traditional plurilingualism, based on the presence of dialects and of different Italian varieties, is being increasingly modified and revitalized by the languages that immigrants have brought to Italy in the past thirty years. We argue that the same is occurring throughout all European countries.

4.3 Multilingualism from the perspective of the Council of Europe

4.3.1 Introduction

The countries of Europe (both members and non-members of the European Union) are closely connected to each other through a number of multilateral agreements, organizations, and common goals. Indeed, 47 countries are part of the Council of Europe, the continent's leading human rights organization, which bears, among many other tasks, primary responsibility for European language policy, with recommendations on languages and language learning in Europe drawn up by its Language Policy Unit. For one legislative period (2007–2010), the Council of Europe even had a Commissioner for Multilingualism.

As already described above, the Council of Europe represents a plurilingual and culturally diverse region of the world. While this council has two official working languages (English and French), all the member state languages are considered official languages with equal status. Furthermore, in order to lend this plurilingualism expression and weight, the Council of Europe recommends that all member states belonging to the council should support their inhabitants in becoming and remaining fluent in at least two languages apart from their first language(s) (L1+2). To this end, it advises learning a language of wider communication such as English or Spanish, as well as a regional or immigrant language. For Germany, examples include Danish or Polish as regional languages and Turkish or Farsi as immigrant languages (Council of Europe 2008).

Whether or not the language of wider communication is always English is the subject of constant debate. In many areas of life, English has become the language in which (initial and often superficial) understanding is usually possible, although studies have shown that content, cultural coloring, and pragmatically relevant details are lost when such a language of wider communication is used (Crystal 2003). At the same time, there is a risk that languages other than English will no longer be used, will be learned less often, and will ostensibly become less important (Raasch 2013). The United Kingdom's vote to leave the European Union ("Brexit") has raised concerns about whether English can and should continue to be the EU's language of wider communication. At the time of publication, it seems unlikely that English will lose its status as the language of wider communication, although whether other languages could assume this role in the future cannot be predicted.

Although linguistic diversity is conceived as a constituent characteristic of Europe's identity, some languages play a more important role in the European public and political discourse. As a matter of fact, a distinction is made between official languages (all official European national languages), working languages (EU languages used in political debates, negotiations or publications), regional minority languages (e.g., Basque in Spain), and immigrant languages. Whether a language such as Sorbian in northeastern Germany and western Poland is accorded the status of a regional minority language – or whether Turkish is used as a language of instruction – are political decisions, as is the decision to designate language varieties as languages in their own right or as dialects spoken within certain national territories (e.g., Luxembourgish, which is related to the Moselle Frankish dialect). The fact that such decisions tend to be politically motivated means that some regional and immigrant languages are more or less important than others and their use may be promoted or even restricted to various degrees. For example, political conflicts between population groups that arise out of economic, historical, and political factors are also often manifested as language conflicts (such as the conflict between French and Dutch in Belgium, as discussed above). Furthermore, in the case of immigrant languages, debates arise as to the importance of including these languages in the curriculum and using them as languages of instruction in school. As put by Extra (2011: 2):

> Although IM [immigrant minority] languages are often conceived of and transmitted as core values by IM [immigrant minority] language groups, they are less protected than RM [regional minority] languages by affirmative action and legal measures in, for example, education. In fact, the learning and certainly the teaching of IM languages are often seen by majority language speakers and by policy makers as obstacles to integration and as a

threat to the national identity. At the European level, guidelines and directives regarding IM languages are scant and outdated.

This information suggests that not only is the European linguistic landscape extremely complex, but also that vast contrasts can be observed in Europe in the status of various languages as well as in the language policies that are implemented in education. In the following sections, we survey the variety of (foreign) language learning models in the EU, as well as instruments and institutions created by the Council of Europe to support and foster multilingualism and the use of various languages therein.

4.3.2 Language education in Europe

There is no prescribed school-based, university-based, or advanced foreign language training in Europe. In federally organized countries such as Germany, there is not even standardized national foreign language training because the responsibility for education lies with the states. In centralist countries such as France, school education is regulated at the national level. In most Scandinavian countries, the regions are responsible for language training, so that the languages offered at a school in a given place can differ from those at another school located in the same place.

The above-mentioned European language formula L1+2 is not clearly translated into the curriculum of all member states. In some countries and school types, it is quite common to learn two or more foreign languages in addition to the national language(s) or at least have the opportunity to do so; for example, in Luxembourg, it is common to (learn and) speak French, Standard German, Luxembourgish and English (see Section 4.2.2). These are often countries whose languages are not widely spoken elsewhere, e.g., Sweden. In countries such as the United Kingdom or Spain, whose national languages English and Spanish also serve as languages of wider communication, the pressure to learn foreign languages in order to speak with the rest of the world is not as pronounced as in countries with less widespread languages such as Finnish or Hungarian. In some countries, there is a trend for schools to cut down or even eliminate foreign languages – except English as in Norway where it is regarded as a second and not a foreign language – from the curriculum to accommodate other subjects that appear to be more relevant at the moment, such as IT or business administration. In these contexts, the models discussed in the following section can help increase foreign language instruction without costs to the curriculum.

4.3.3 Securing the status of foreign languages in the school curriculum through specific programs, methods and concepts

In the following, we introduce a few models that promote multilingualism by way of combining the learning of a new language to the learning of other languages or subjects. Not all of these models pertain to the European context but are prominent there.

4.3.3.1 European intercomprehension

Examples of both linguistic and methods-oriented projects on multilingual communication and multiple language acquisition include projects such as Scandinavian Semicommunication (ten Thije and Zeevaert 2007) or projects on European intercomprehension such as EuroComRom (Klein and Stegmann 2000) and EuroComGerm (Hufeisen and Marx 2014), and Slavic intercomprehension (Tafel et al. 2009).

Scandinavian Semicommunication focuses on the accommodation processes that allow speakers of Swedish, Danish, or Norwegian to communicate by using their own languages and simply making minor phonological or lexical adaptations in order for others to be able to understand them (Braunmüller 2002; Chapter 8, this volume). The linguistic affinity between the languages in question and the associated similarities and inferable parallels that can facilitate understanding serve as the basis for this method.

All of the projects on intercomprehension have in common the notion that it is possible to learn to read related languages rapidly with the help of certain linguistic, strategic, and methodological techniques. The main feature is the application of the Seven Sieves, which serve as strategies to decipher texts in yet unknown languages. For example, the strategies outlined below from EuroComGerm (Hufeisen and Marx 2014) can help a German speaker use both German and English as bridge languages towards other Germanic languages:
1. Previous knowledge and context facilitate understanding of the topic of a text through pictures, titles, text type, proper nouns.
2. International and Germanic vocabulary help identify familiar words: *international* → *international* (Danish); *word* → *ord* (Danish).
3. There are sound correspondences in the Germanic languages based on sound shifts: d → t: *cold* – *kalt* (German); f/v → b: *life* – *Leben* (German); *have* – *haben* (German) → *ha* (Norwegian).

4. Graphemes and pronunciation have many parallels in the Germanic languages: i/e → ei: *wide – weit* (German); -y → ie/i: *psychology – Psychologie* (German) → *psykologi* (Norwegian).
5. Syntax and sentence structure are similar in the source and the target languages, such as N–V–N: *he likes math/er mag Mathe* (German) → *han tycker om matematik* (Swedish).
6. Morphology has similar construction principles in most Germanic languages: comparison: *-er + than* / *-er + als* (German) → *-are + som* (Swedish).
7. Prefixes and suffixes seem to occur in parallel forms in most Germanic languages: *anti-, pre-/prä-* (German) → *pre-; -ship/-schaft* → *skap* (Norwegian).

Research shows that especially in the beginning phases, the learning process seems to be accelerated because learners of the new languages consider it exciting and interesting, specifically with respect to the potential of creating affordances (Kordt 2018). However, the intercomprehension method does not work that well with advanced learners because it concentrates on reading comprehension and mainly ignores other skills (see Meissner et al. 2011).

4.3.3.2 Content and Language(s) Integrated Learning (CLIL)

Content and Language(s) Integrated Learning (CLIL) is a linguistically based didactic and methodological concept used to integrate foreign languages into content subjects by teaching such subjects in foreign languages. It was developed in connection with Canadian immersion programs whose goal was the reciprocal learning of the second national language (French, English) (Barik and Swain 1978). However, while classes in immersion programs are held mainly in the target language, in CLIL classes, the source language is used as well as the target language: "CLIL ... is a dual-focussed approach in which an additional language is used for the learning and teaching of both content and language" (Marsh and Langé 2010: 1). In this context, students actively experience the practical applicability of languages, which is sometimes not so readily apparent during isolated foreign language teaching.

The most often used CLIL language is English (EMI = English medium instruction, Lasagabaster 2016), but any other language can be used as well (Allgäuer-Hackl et al. 2018). In general, all subjects could be turned into CLIL classes but the social sciences (e.g. history, geography) seem to be typical CLIL subjects in Europe. However, subjects with strong active learning elements such as sports, music or fine arts also lend themselves to CLIL instruction because much can be done in the beginning without much verbalization.

CLIL research has shown that CLIL learning not only has an enhancing effect on the linguistic and language competencies of the learners, but also on content subject, intercultural, meta-cognitive, as well as emotional-attitudinal effects (Coyle 2007). It has also been shown that content is processed more deeply when it has to be understood through a foreign language, so that in fact learners in a CLIL history class tend to learn the content more thoroughly than learners in a regular history class (Lamsfuß-Schenk 2008). CLIL will no doubt play a major role in preserving a multilingual Europe (e.g., Cots et al. 2010; Hélot and Erfurt 2016).

4.3.3.3 Multilingual whole school policy

As will also be discussed in Section 4.3.3.5, the European Centre for Modern Languages in Graz, Austria, recently sponsored a project entitled *PlurCur®* that trials the new concept of a "multilingual whole language policy" in sixteen schools in several European countries (Austria, Estonia, Finland, Germany, Ireland, and Lithuania to name a few). The project entails a systematic shift of foreign language learning and use towards content-integrated learning with a simultaneous reduction in the amount of pure language instruction in individual languages in order to gain time and curriculum hours for other foreign languages.

The research on this and similar projects demonstrates the success of a multilingual whole language policy based on principles that are project-oriented, decisively intercultural, and extend across both school grade and subject (Hufeisen 2018). Exemplary projects have included multilingual theatre workshops across all grades, common grammar terminology across all languages at a given school, and language cafés open to all pupils, instructors, and parents. It was found that the more parties (pupils, instructors, school boards, parents) were involved, the greater the support was for such multilingual projects (Allgäuer-Hackl et al. 2018). As a result, there are now numerous follow-up projects and individual schools that have shifted to the multilingual whole language policy approach; the latest is at a school in Liechtenstein.

4.3.3.4 Foreign languages at universities

Many European universities incorporate language focuses or offer their students the opportunity to learn or study languages during their education. There are a number of terms for the degree programs available at European universities focusing on literature, linguistics, and cultural and regional studies. German universities, for instance, offer majors in 'language and literature' in a variety of languages and other European countries have adopted the same structure according to the European Bologna Process that was introduced to harmonize European education (Hettiger 2019).

In addition, most European universities offer language courses for all students and staff members. In some cases, students enrolled in a non-linguistic degree are required or have the opportunity to learn a foreign language and earn European Credit Points needed to finish their programs. Facilities such as language centers or international offices sometimes offer these courses.

As part of the European Bologna Process for harmonizing university education, more and more bilingual courses of study are being established and sponsored by two or more universities in different countries. The teaching languages are often those of the participating countries. In addition, many courses of study are now being taught in English in order to become more global and attract more international students. In this context, the following questions still need to be resolved: Are all of the participants able to interact in English at a level at which they can complete their degrees in the language? And will the students' own national languages be sufficiently enhanced in terms of technical and scientific terminology if the teaching language is English? The concept of English-medium instruction is being investigated in a number of studies (Lasagabaster 2016).

4.3.3.5 Instruments and institutions developed by the Council of Europe to support multilingualism

We end this section by providing an overview of the instruments and institutions created by the Council of Europe that have fostered methodological innovations in the teaching and learning of foreign languages and have played a decisive role in the promotion of multilingualism. One such instrument is the Common European Framework of References for Languages (CEFR), which was developed to provide a method of learning and teaching all languages in Europe and assessing language competence. This framework is meant to describe the language skills required for individuals to participate in discourse on certain subjects across European countries. It uses six reference levels (starting with A1, which describes the absolute beginner level, moving through A2, B1, B2, and C1, and culminating at C2 as the level of mastery at which the speaker no longer has difficulty making himself/herself understood) to describe the skills and competences required to cope with certain communication situations. While the CEFR was initially developed as a purely descriptive instrument, it is increasingly also being used as a reference framework for designing teaching materials and as an instrument for testing and evaluating language performance (North 2014). The "can-do" descriptions, which were intended originally to be solely descriptive, have thus evolved into assessment criteria.

Another instrument to describe language competencies in Europe is the Framework of Reference for Pluralistic Approaches to Languages and Cultures (German: REPA, French and English: CARAP 2012). This framework provides descriptors for criteria that can be used to describe plurilingually and culturally oriented instruction and is, like the CEFR, used throughout Europe. As with the CEFR, it includes a table of global competences and micro-competences on the one hand, and three lists of descriptors of resources concerning knowledge (*Wissen, savoir*), attitudes (*Haltungen, savoir-être*), and skills (*Fertigkeiten, savoir-faire*), on the other. The CARAP is not as widespread as the CEFR because the criteria for description are not as precise as the CEFR criteria, but it is a useful instrument for describing multilingual and cultural competencies. However, it does not lend itself as an instrument for assessment as clearly as the CEFR (Daryai-Hansen et al. 2015).

In terms of institutions, the Council of Europe founded the European Centre for Modern Languages (ECML) in Graz, Austria, in 1994 to support and foster multilingualism. The ECML addresses socially relevant issues related to language learning, European multilingualism, and social questions associated with all aspects of language learning Europe-wide (for example, the relevance of sign languages) in limited-term projects. The Council of Europe and the member countries fund these projects, which are always extremely practice-oriented and generally are completed before their outcomes are assessed though research. The five-year-long projects fall under specific thematic focuses for which internationally oriented project teams may apply. For example, as discussed above, the project *PlurCur®* trialed the new concept of a "multilingual whole language policy" in sixteen schools in several European countries with the goal of shifting foreign language instruction to content-integrated learning in the foreign language. Technische Universität Darmstadt has supported *PlurCur* with research dealing with the subjective viewpoints of pupils about their own multilingualism. Since researchers found that language minority speakers do not even consider their home language an addition to their multilingual repertoire, the project required these students to learn to use their home language and value it as an asset in the practice-oriented setting of a multilingual theatre group over a whole school year (Henning 2015). As pointed out above, immigrant languages tend to have limited political status throughout Europe, and there is no common policy for including or excluding these languages in the curriculum. However, research shows that immigrant languages are a very relevant part of learners' identities and language repertoires and should be treated accordingly (Berthele and Lambelet 2017).

4.4 Immigrant and refugee languages and changes in the educational system

We conclude this chapter by addressing the drastic increase in the number of migrants and refugees in Europe in the past years and the educational consequences, particularly in the context of Germany. Such an influx of speakers of new languages has increased the diversity of the European linguistic landscape as discussed in section 4.2.5, creating challenges for the educational system and opportunities for change and the promotion of new forms of multilingualism. Indeed, the recent wave of migrants entering Germany between 2015 and 2017 (BAMF 2018: 3) has resulted in the development of new teaching and learning concepts and the hiring of new teachers in order to stem the tide. In the federal state of Hesse alone, the number of so-called intensive classes at general and vocational schools during this period rose from around 300 to 1370 classes, creating a shortage of teachers (Euen 2015). In response, potential teachers with other academic backgrounds have been trained and some new teachers are volunteers. Various studies have been carried out in the context of this development, including on the role of volunteers (Feike, Neustadt, and Zabel 2017; Großmann et al. 2017). Volunteers often teach German as the target language and also teach children in the language of their country of origin, focusing not only on language skills, but also on conveying intercultural values from both the origin and target culture (e.g., the project entitled *Almanya auf Arabisch* ['Germany in Arabic']). Under the auspices of the Mercator Institute for Literacy and Language Education, Massumi et al. (2015) conducted a study on the integration of pupils who had recently migrated to Germany. Their study focused on the changes in the federal states' education-policy requirements and the number and makeup of the newly arrived learners. One of the study's findings revealed differences with regard to school enrollment among the various federal states (von Dewitz, Massumi, and Grießbach 2016: 25) as well as great differences in teaching models for the migrant children. While in some federal states the "submersion" model is the most common method used in the primary grades, in others the "partially integrative" model, which combines academic, language and civics teaching, is more prevalent (Massumi et al. 2015: 45–46). At secondary levels I and II, the "integrative or partially integrative" model is used. In addition, the "parallel model" is also used, meaning that children and young adults also attend "intensive classes" that focus on teaching German (Massumi et al. 2015: 48–49).

Decker-Ernst (2017), in a study that examined education-policy developments since the 1950s, investigated the enrollment of newly migrated children and adolescents in general schools. She also examined the basic conditions of preparatory classes in the federal state of Baden-Württemberg and explained the requirements and their implementation in the everyday school setting, focusing on how newly arrived children are integrated in these programs. An example of a measure for integrating young refugees is the "SchlaU" project in the federal state of Bavaria. "SchlaU" stands for *Schulanaloger Unterricht für junge Geflüchtete* ("school-like instruction for young refugees"). Young migrants receive targeted and individual support in small groups, which allows them to quickly transition into the regular classroom or training courses (SchlaU 2018). Furthermore, many German universities have set up such special language courses for refugees. To this end, new teaching and learning concepts have been developed to support such heterogeneous groups in their learning process. For example, to test the aptitude of potential university students, Technische Universität Darmstadt offers candidates the option to take the TestAS in Arabic to overcome the language barrier. In sum, the influx of migrants and refugees to the already multilingual countries of Europe is modifying their educational models while at the same time promoting new forms of multilingualism.

4.5 Conclusion

For centuries, languages, the relationships between different languages, and multilingualism have been relevant topics in Europe and in the politics of European countries and are often the subject of very controversial discussions. The European continent is a multifaceted, multicultural, and plurilingual region of the world subject to constant changes. These diverse processes of social development have left their mark on the European language landscape, language policy, and research into multilingualism. English has become the most common foreign language throughout Europe, and it is likely to expand further. Even in countries where, traditionally, other foreign languages have had priority, such as Switzerland, English currently holds the position of the first foreign language. This has turned out to be detrimental to other foreign languages which tend to be learned even more rarely. They may not be learned at all any longer in cases where the school system allows concentration on one foreign language instead of two or more as in Norway. In this way, the language landscape of Europe is about to change fundamentally.

In light of the challenge of integrating immigrants and refugees, among other reasons, this dynamism is unlikely to abate but will be intensified. Therefore, Europe, with committed action at all levels and in the interest of all its people, faces the challenge of positively shaping new approaches to education, be it in the form of curricula, didactic models integrating languages and content, and new methods to include other and more languages than just English. The political and educational priorities described here are intended to help Europeans as individuals, as nationals, and as a society to embrace multilingualism in order to preserve the diversity, richness, and multiplicity of European languages and cultures.

Acknowledgements: We would like to thank Katharina Braunagel and Sandra Sulzer for their support with the section on refugees.

References

Adam, Catherine & Ronan Calvez. 2016. De l'éducation bilingue en Bretagne. Breton et gallo à l'école. In Christine Hélot & Jürgen Erfurt (eds.), *L'éducation bilingue en France: Politiques linguistiques, modèles et pratiques*, 183–198. Paris: Lambert-Lucas.

Allgäuer-Hackl, Elisabeth, Kristin Brogan, Ute Henning, Britta Hufeisen & Joachim Schlabach (eds.). 2018. *More languages? – PlurCur! Research and practice regarding plurilingual whole school curricula*. Strasbourg/Graz: Council of Europe. https://www.ecml.at/Portals/1/documents/ECML-resources/PlurCur-EN-final.pdf?ver=2018-05-31-100118-647 (accessed 18 March 2018).

Ammon, Ulrich. 2015. *Die Stellung der deutschen Sprache in der Welt*. Berlin, München & Boston: De Gruyter.

Barik, Henry C. & Merrill Swain. 1978. Evaluation of a French immersion program: The Ottawa study through grade five. *Canadian Journal of Behavioural Science/Revue canadienne des sciences du comportement* 10(3). 192–201.

Barni, Monica & Massimo Vedovelli. 2012. Linguistic landscapes and language policies. In Christine Hélot, Monica Barni, Rudi Janssens & Carla Bagna (eds.), *Linguistic landscapes, multilingualism and social change*, 27–38. Frankfurt am Mein: Peter Lang.

Barni, Monica, Massimo Vedovelli & Carla Bagna. 2008. How immigrant languages change cities: an Italian case study. Paper presented at the 17th Sociolinguistic Symposium, Amsterdam, 3–5 April.

Berg, Guy. 1993. *Mir wëlle bleiwe, wat mir sin. Soziolinguistische und sprachtypologische Betrachtungen zur luxemburgischen Mehrsprachigkeit* (Reihe Germanistische Linguistik 140). Tübingen: Niemeyer.

Berthele, Raphael & Amelia Lambelet (eds.). 2017. *Heritage and school language literacy development in migrant children: Interdependence or independence?* Clevedon: Multilingual Matters.

Braunmüller, Kurt. 2002. Semicommunication and accommodation: Observations from the linguistic situation in Scandinavia. *International Journal of Applied Linguistics* 12(1). 1–23.

Burger, Hannelore. 1994. Die Badenischen Sprachenverordnungen für Mähren: Ein europäisches Gedankenspiel. *Bohemia* 35(1). 75–89.

Cots, Juan Manuel, Amaia Ibarrán, Montserrat Irún, David Lasagabaster, Enric Llurda & Juan Manuel Sierra Plo. 2010. *Plurilingüismo e interculturalidad en la escuela: Reflexiones y propuestas didácticas*. Barcelona: Horsori.

Coyle, Do. 2007. The CLIL quality challenge. In David Marsh & Dieter Wolff (eds.), *Diverse contexts – Converging Goals. CLIL in Europe*, 47–58. Frankfurt am Main: Lang.

Coyos, Jean-Baptiste. 2016. L'enseignement scolaire bilingue basque-français: Avancées et limites. In Christine Hélot & Jürgen Erfurt (eds.), *L'éducation bilingue en France: Politiques linguistiques, modèles et pratiques*, 168–182. Paris: Lambert-Lucas.

Crystal, David. 2003. *English as a global language*, 2nd edn. Cambridge: Cambridge University Press.

Daryai-Hansen, Petra, Brigitte Gerber, Ildikó Lörincz, Michaela Haller, Olga Ivanova, Hans-Jürgen Krumm & Hans H. Reich. 2015. Pluralistic approaches to languages in the curriculum: The case of French-speaking Switzerland, Spain and Austria. *International Journal of Multilingualism* 12(1). 109–127.

Decker-Ernst, Yvonne. 2017. *Deutsch als Zweitsprache in Vorbereitungsklassen. Eine Bestandsaufnahme in Baden-Württemberg*. Baltmannsweiler: Schneider Hohengehren.

Dewitz, Nora von, Mona Massumi & Johanna Grießbach. 2016. Neu zugewanderte Kinder und Jugendliche und junge Erwachsene. Entwicklungen im Jahr 2015. https://www.mercator-institut-sprachfoerderung.de/fileadmin/Redaktion/PDF/Publikationen/MI_ZfL_Neu_zugewanderte_Kinder_Jugendliche_jungeErwachsene_final_screen.pdf (accessed 6 September 2018).

Escudé, Pierre. 2016. Le bilinguisme scolaire français-occitan, histoire et avenir. In Christine Hélot & Jürgen Erfurt (eds.), *L'éducation bilingue en France: Politiques linguistiques, modèles et pratiques*, 231–246. Paris: Lambert-Lucas.

Euen, Claudia. 2015. *Lange nicht beachtet und jetzt heiß begehrt. Lehrer für Deutsch als Fremdsprache*. http://www.deutschlandfunk.de/lehrer-fuer-deutsch-als-fremdsprache-lange-nicht-beachtet.680.de.html?dram:article_id=331703 (accessed 13 March 2018).

Extra, Guus. 2011. The immigrant minority languages of Europe. In Bernd Kortmann & Johan van der Auwera (eds.), *The languages and linguistics of Europe: A comprehensive guide*, 467–484. Berlin & New York: De Gruyter Mouton.

Extra, Guus & Kutlay Yağmur. 2008. Mapping immigrant minority languages in multicultural cities. In Guus Extra & Kutlay Yağmur (eds.), *Mapping linguistic diversity in multicultural contexts*, 139–162. Berlin & New York: De Gruyter Mouton.

Feike, Julia, Eva Neustadt & Rebecca Zabel. 2017. "Zu sagen: Ich bin Sprachhelfer, da ist für mich ein unheimlicher Druck abgefallen"– Selbstverständnis und Rollenreflexion in Schulungsmaßnahmen für ehrenamtliche Sprachhelferinnen. In Annegret Middeke, Annett Eichstaedt, Matthias Jung & Gabriele Kniffka (eds.), *Wie schaffen wir das? Beiträge zur sprachlichen Integration geflüchteter Menschen* (Materialien Deutsch als Fremd- und Zweitsprache 97), 229–243. Göttingen: Universitätsverlag.

Festman, Julia, Greg Poarch & Jean-Marc Dewaele. 2017 *Raising multilingual children*. Bristol: Multilingual Matters.

Gogolin, Ingrid. 2002. Linguistic and cultural diversity in Europe: A challenge for educational research and practice. *European Educational Research Journal* 1(1). 123–138.

Großmann, Uta, Friederike Hinzmann, Coretta Storz & Winfried Thielmann. 2017. Chancen, Grenzen und Konsequenzen ehrenamtlicher Sprachhilfe: Erfahrungsberichte aus ehrenamtlichen Sprachhilfe-Projekten. In Annegret Middeke, Annett Eichstaedt, Matthias Jung & Gabriele Kniffka (eds.), *Wie schaffen wir das? Beiträge zur sprachlichen*

Integration geflüchteter Menschen (Materialien Deutsch als Fremd- und Zweitsprache 97), 245–260. Göttingen: Universitätsverlag.

Hans, Barbara. 2007. Eltern klagen gegen Französisch-Zwang. *Spiegel-Online* 16 May 2007. http://www.spiegel.de/lebenundlernen/schule/pflichtfach-im-suedwesten-eltern-klagen-gegen-franzoesisch-zwang-a-483126.html (accessed 19 December 2017).

Hélot, Christine & Jürgen Erfurt. 2016. *L'éducation bilingue en France: Politiques linguistiques, modèles et pratiques*. Paris: Lambert-Lucas.

Henning, Ute. 2015. Begleitstudie zu vielsprachigem Theaterspiel. Spracheinstellungen qualitativ erforschen. In Elisabeth Allgäuer-Hackl, Kristin Brogan, Ute Henning, Britta Hufeisen & Joachim Schlabach (eds.), *MehrSprachen? – PlurCur! Berichte aus Forschung und Praxis zu Gesamtsprachencurricula* (Mehrsprachigkeit und multiples Sprachenlernen 11), 107–123. Baltmannsweiler: Schneider Verlag Hohengehren.

Hettiger, Andreas. 2019. *Sprachenpolitik an deutschen Hochschulen. Grundlagen und Perspektiven* (Mehrsprachigkeit und multiples Sprachenlernen 14). Baltmannsweiler: Schneider Verlag Hohengehren.

Hufeisen, Britta. 2018. Institutional education and multilingualism: PlurCur® as a prototype of a multilingual whole school policy. *European Journal of Applied Linguistics* 6(1). 1–32.

Hufeisen, Britta & Nicole Marx (eds.). 2014. *EuroComGerm: Germanische Sprachen lesen lernen*, 2nd edn. Aachen: Shaker.

Jessner, Ulrike. 2006. *Linguistic awareness in multilinguals: English as a third language*. Edinburgh: Edinburgh University Press.

Klein, Horst & Tilbert Stegmann. 2000. *EuroComRom – Die sieben Siebe: Romanische Sprachen sofort lesen können*. Aachen: Shaker.

Kordt, Birgit. 2018. Affordance theory and multiple language learning and teaching. *International Journal of Multilingualism* 15(2). 135–148.

Krzoska, Markus. 2005. Die Peripherie bedrängt das Zentrum: Wien, Prag und Deutschböhmen in den Badeni-Unruhen 1897. In Hans-Christian Maner (ed.), *Grenzregionen der Habsburgermonarchie im 18. und 19. Jahrhundert: Ihre Bedeutung und Funktion aus der Perspektive Wiens* (Mainzer Beiträge zur Geschichte Osteuropas 1), 145–165. Münster: LIT.

Lamsfuß-Schenk, Stefanie. 2008. *Fremdverstehen im bilingualen Geschichtsunterricht*. Frankfurt am Main: Lang.

Lasagabaster, David. 2016. English-medium instruction (EMI). In Andrew Linn (ed.), *Investigating English in Europe: Contexts and agendas*, 98–106. Berlin & New York: De Gruyter.

Maldacker, Anika. 2017. Weniger Französisch in der Grundschule – für viele das falsche Signal. *Badische Zeitung* 12 July 2017. http://www.badische-zeitung.de/suedwest-1/weniger-franzoesisch-in-der-grundschule-fuer-viele-das-falsche-signal–139216775.html (accessed 19 December 2017).

Marsh, David & Gisella Langé. 2010. *Using languages to learn and learning to use languages*. Jyväskylä: University of Jyväskylä UniCOM.

Massumi, Mona, Nora von Dewitz, Johanna Grießbach, Henrike Terhart, Katarina Wagner, Kathrin Hippmann & Lale Altinay. 2015. *Neu zugewanderte Kinder und Jugendliche im deutschen Schulsystem. Bestandsaufnahme und Empfehlungen*. https://www.mercator-institut-sprachfoerderung.de/fileadmin/Redaktion/PDF/Publikationen/MI_ZfL_Studie_Zugewanderte_im_deutschen_Schulsystem_final_screen.pdf (accessed 6 September 2018).

Matras, Yaron & Alex Robertson. 2015. Multilingualism in a post-industrial city: Policy and practice in Manchester. *Current Issues in Language Planning* 16(3). 296–314.

Matras, Yaron, Alex Robertson & Charlotte Jones. 2016. Using the school setting to map community languages: A pilot study in Manchester, England. *International Journal of Multilingualism* 13(3). 353–366.

Meißner, Franz-Joseph. 2010. Grundlagen der Tertiärsprachendidaktik: Inferentielles Sprachenlernen. In Franz-Joseph Meißner & Bernd Tesch (eds.), *Spanisch kompetenzorientiert unterrichten*, 28–46. Seelze: Klett/Kallmeyer.

Meißner, Franz-Joseph, Filomena Capucho, Christian Degache, Adriana Martins, Doina Spiţă & Manuel Tost. 2011. *Learning, teaching, research. Apprentissage, enseignement, recherche. Lernen, Lehren, Forschung.* Tübingen: Narr.

North, Brian. 2014. *The CEFR in practice.* Cambridge: Cambridge University Press.

Philologenverband Baden-Württemberg. 2017. Philologenverband Baden-Württemberg zum Fremdsprachenlernen in der Grundschule. https://bildungsklick.de/schule/meldung/philologenverband-baden-wuerttemberg-zum-fremdsprachenlernen-in-der-grundschule/ (accessed 19 December 2017).

Raasch, Albert. 2013. Verständigung und Verständnis für den anderen [Interview Viktoria Will]. *BEGEGNUNG: Deutsche schulische Arbeit im Ausland* 34(3). 46–47.

SchlaU (n.d.) *Schulanaloger Unterricht für junge Flüchtlinge.* https://www.schlau-schule.de/ (accessed 6 September 2018).

Swiss Academies of Arts and Sciences. 2015. Schulischer Fremdsprachenunterricht in der Schweiz: Argumente zur Debatte. *Swiss Academies Factsheets* 10 (1). http://www.sagw.ch/dms/sagw/schwerpunkte/sprachen_und_kulturen/sk-publis/Factsheet_Fremdsprachenunterricht_low.pdf (accessed 5 April 2018).

Tafel, Karin, Rašid Durić, Radka Lemmen, Anna Olshevska & Agata Przyborowska-Stolz. 2009. *Slavische Interkomprehension: Eine Einführung.* Tübingen: Narr Francke Attempto.

Thije, Jan D. ten & Ludger Zeevaert. 2007. *Receptive multilingualism: Linguistic analyses, language policies, and didactic concepts.* Amsterdam: John Benjamins.

Vikør, Lars. 2015. Norwegian: Bokmål vs. Nynorsk. http://www.sprakradet.no/Vi-og-vart/Om-oss/English-and-other-languages/English/norwegian-bokmal-vs.-nynorsk/ (accessed 5 April 2018).

Witte, Els & Harry Van Velthoven. 1999. *Langue et politique – La situation en Belgique dans une perspective historique.* Bruxelles: VUB University Press.

Wright, Sue. 2000. Jacobins, regionalists and the Council of Europe's Charter for regional and minority languages. *Journal of Multilingual and Multicultural Development* 21(5). 414–424.

Documents

BAMF – Bundesamt für Migration und Flüchtlinge. 2018. Aktuelle Zahlen zu Asyl. http://www.bamf.de/SharedDocs/Anlagen/DE/Downloads/Infothek/Statistik/Asyl/aktuelle-zahlen-zu-asyl-juli-2018.html?nn=1694460 (accessed 6 September 2018).

CARAP: Candelier, Michel (coordinator), Antoinette Camilleri-Grima, Véronique Castellotti, Jean-François de Pietro, Ildikó Lörincz, Franz-Joseph Meissner, Anna Schröder-Sura & Artur Noguerol. 2012. CARAP/FREPA: Framework of Reference for Pluralistic Approaches to Languages and Studies. https://carap.ecml.at/Portals/11/documents/CARAP-version3-EN-28062010.pdf (accessed 26 March 2018).

Common European Framework of Reference for Languages: Learning, Teaching, Assessment (CEFR). https://www.Council of Europe.int/t/dg4/linguistic/source/framework_en.pdf (accessed26 March 2018).

Council of Europe. 2008. White Paper on Intercultural Dialogue. https://www.CouncilofEurope.int/t/dg4/intercultural/source/white%20paper_final_revised_en.pdf (accessed 26 March 2018).

Council of Europe. n.d. Promoting ratification of the European Charter for Regional or Minority Languages in France. https://www.CouncilofEurope.int/en/web/european-charter-regional-or-minority-languages/promoting-ratification-in-france (accessed 5. April 2018).

Dirección de Documentación del Senado – Departamento de Documentación Autonómica. 2013. Regulación de Lenguas Oficiales. http://www.senado.es/web/wcm/idc/groups/public/@cta_rrdc/documents/document/mdaw/mdiz/~edisp/lenguas_oficiales_ccaa.pdf (accessed 29 November 2018).

European Charter for Regional or Minority Languages (ECRML). https://www.CouncilofEurope.int/en/web/conventions/full-list/-/conventions/treaty/148 (accessed 5 April 2018).

Eurostat. 2016. European Day of Languages. More than 80% of primary school pupils in the EU were studying a foreign language in 2014. English clearly dominant. https://ec.europa.eu/eurostat/documents/2995521/7662394/3-23092016-AP-EN.pdf/57d3442c-7250-4aae-8844-c2130eba8e0e (accessed 3 December 2018).

FREPA: A Training Kit. http://carap.ecml.at/Teachertraining/FREPAAtrainingkit/tabid/2962/language/en-GB/Default.aspx (accessed 26 March 2018).

Ministère de la Culture et de la Communication. 2013. Redéfinir une politique publique en faveur des langues régionales et de la pluralité linguistique interne: Rapport présenté à la ministre de la Culture et de la Communication par le Comité consultatif pour la promotion des langues régionales et de la pluralité linguistique interne. http://www.culture.gouv.fr/content/download/146460/1576031/version/2/file/RAPPORT_politique%20publique%20en%20faveur%20des%20langues%20regionales_final.pdf (accessed 5 April 2018).

United Nations. 2013. International migration and development. https://www.un.org/development/desa/en/ (accessed 15 May 2019).

Institutions

Council of Europe, Strasbourg: https://www.CouncilofEurope.int/en/web/portal/home (accessed 26 March 2018).

European Centre for Modern Languages, Graz, Austria: www.ecml.at (accessed 26 March 2018).

Language Policy Unit, Strasbourg: https://www.CouncilofEurope.int/t/dg4/linguistic/default_en.asp (accessed 26 March 2018).

Wayne E. Wright and Virak Chan
5 Multilingualism in North America

Despite common misconceptions, the North American countries of Canada and the United States are, always have been, and will continue to be highly multilingual countries. While Canada is recognized as a bilingual country with English and French as official languages, it is home to over 185 languages, including about 76 indigenous languages (Statistics Canada 2016a). The United States is home to around 350 languages including about 150 indigenous languages (U.S. Census Bureau 2015). Immigration has brought rich cultural and linguistic diversity to these North American countries. In this chapter we explore the geography of plurilingualism, including historical and current demographic trends. Next we discuss the character of multilingual communities focusing on two major North American cities, Toronto in Canada, and Los Angeles in the United States. We select these two multilingual cities as examples given their relatively similar population size, diverse populations, and distinct ethnic enclaves. Finally, we discuss the education, political, and linguistic consequences of such plurilingualism.

5.1 The geography of plurilingualism

5.1.1 Historical and current demographic trends in the United States

The United States had an estimated population of 326 million in 2018. Historically, the United States is a nation of immigrants, and immigration rates remain high. For instance, between 2012 and 2016, 13.2% of the U.S. population was foreign-born (U.S. Census Bureau 2016). The source countries of immigrants to the United States have varied across different periods of time. As shown in Figure 5.1, in 1960 about 75% of immigrants to the United States came from European countries, including Austria, Germany, Hungary, Ireland, Italy, Poland, and the United Kingdom. Between 1960 and 2016, the number of European immigrants declined substantially while the number of immigrants from the Americas (predominantly Latin America) and Asia had significant increased. By 2016, European immigration was less than 11%, while Asian immigrants accounted for about 30%, and immigrants from the Americas accounted for over 52% of the

Wayne E. Wright and Virak Chan, Purdue University, West Lafayette (IN), U.S.A.

https://doi.org/10.1515/9781501507984-005

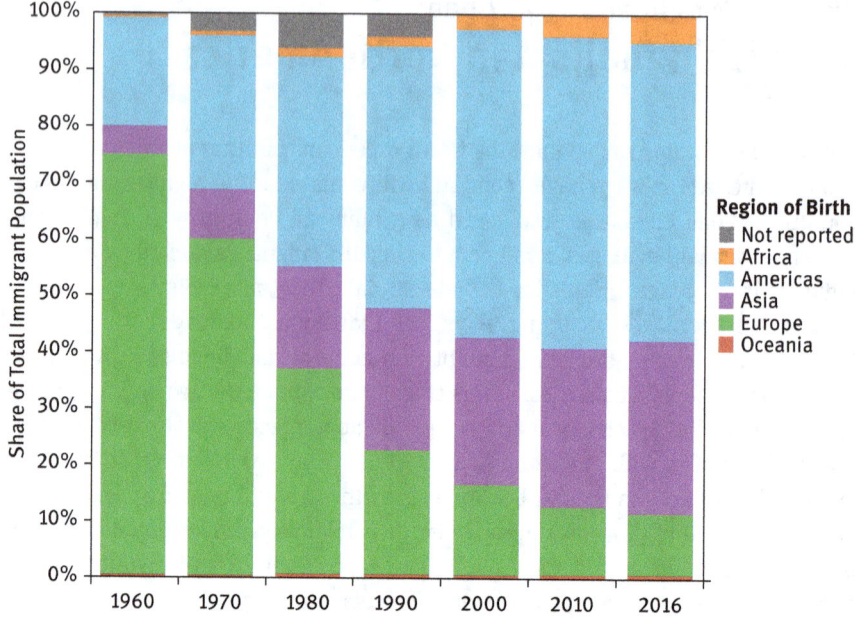

Figure 5.1: U.S. immigrant population by world region of birth, 1960–2016 (Migration Policy Institute, 2018b).

immigrant population. In 2016, Mexico accounted for the largest number of immigrants from the Americas at 26.5%, followed by El Salvador (3.2%), Cuba (2.9%), the Dominican Republic (2.5%), and Guatemala (2.1%); Asian immigrants were predominately from India (5.6%), China (4.9%), the Philippines (4.4%), Vietnam (3.1%), and Korea (2.4%) (Migrant Policy Institute 2018a). Note that the number of African immigrants also increased slightly, and accounts for about 5% of the immigrant population. This dramatic shift from predominantly European to predominantly Latinx and Asian immigrants can be attributed to the Immigration and Nationality Act of 1965. This ended a quota system that had been in place since the 1920s favoring northern European immigrants. While limits were still placed on individual countries, exceptions were made for those with immediate relatives in the United States, and for immigrants with special skills.

5.1.2 Diversity of home languages in the United States

Immigration contributes significantly to the diversity of home languages in the United States. Linguistic diversity has expanded so much that in 2016 the

U.S. Census Bureau increased the number of possible individual language codes from 328 to 1,333. Due to small sample sizes, it collapses them into larger languages and language groups for reporting purposes (U.S. Census Bureau 2017). Following English, Spanish is the second most common language spoken at home, accounting for more than 40 million people. In fact, the United States is one of the largest Spanish-speaking countries in the world. The top 10 languages spoken in U.S. homes include Spanish, Chinese, Tagalog, Vietnamese, Arabic, French, Korean, Russian, German, and Haitian (see Table 5.1).

Table 5.1: Top 10 languages other than English spoken at home for U.S. population 5 years and over. Source: data retrieved from U.S. Census Bureau, 2016 American Community Survey 1-Year Estimates.

Language spoken at home	Population
Spanish	40,489,813
Chinese	3,372,930
Tagalog	1,701,960
Vietnamese	1,509,993
Arabic	1,231,098
French	1,216,668
Korean	1,088,788
Russian	909,374
German	905,691
Haitian	856,009

The U.S. Census Bureau collects limited data on language proficiency, but can provide some evidence of the degree to which individuals reported as speaking a language other than English at home are proficient in English. This can serve as a rough proxy for bilingualism. Among the population 5 years or older who speak a non-English language, 59.7% speak English very well, and only 40.3% reported speaking English less than very well. Even greater rates of bilingualism can be detected when looking at different age and language groups. As shown in Table 5.2, across the major language groups, the school aged population (age 5–17) has the highest rates of English proficiency (74% to 81%), followed by adults ages 18–64 (53% to 70%). Not surprisingly, adults 65 years and older have the lowest levels of English proficiency (29% to 54%).

Table 5.2: Ability to speak English of individuals who speak a language other than English at home in the United States, by age group and language group, 2012–2016 5-year estimates. Source: Adapted from U.S. Census Bureau (2018).

Age Group	% Speak English only or very well	% Speak English less than very well
Spanish		
5–17	80.0	20.0
18–64	54.2	45.8
65 and older	37.7	62.3
Asian & Pacific Islander Languages		
5–17	74.3	25.7
18–64	53.3	46.7
65 and older	29.2	70.8
Other Indo-European Languages		
5–17	81.2	18.8
18–64	69.5	30.5
65 and older	54.0	46.0
Other Languages		
5–17	80.8	19.2
18–64	68.5	31.5
65 and older	52.2	47.5

A telling pattern is that rates of English proficiency are slightly lower for speakers of Spanish and Asian and Pacific Islander languages, given that these groups likely have more recent immigration history than groups speaking Indo-European and other languages.

The U.S. Census Bureau, unfortunately, does not collect data on proficiency in languages other than English. However, these figures suggest that immigrants do learn English and learn it well, and thus become bilingual or maintain some level of bilingualism. However, research within immigrant and language minority communities has long documented patterns of rapid shift towards English (Veltman 1983), especially among school-age children (Rumbaut, Massey, and Bean 2006; Wong Filmore 1991), and has noted concerns from parents and communities' leaders about perceived loss of home languages and cultures among younger first generation (1.5) students (Wright 2004). This is especially true when schools lack bilingual and multilingual education programs.

5.1.3 Historical and current demographic trends in Canada

Canada's total population was estimated by Statistics Canada to be at around 37 million in 2018. Canada has a long history of immigration and has received more than 17 million immigrants since its Confederation in 1867. Immigration to Canada has not always been stable, and the annual number of immigrants varies greatly depending on its changing immigration policies, economic situation, and world events related to migrants and refugees. Figure 5.2 shows the distribution of the foreign-born population of Canada by place of birth between 1871 and 2011. As was the case for the United States, historically, immigrants to Canada were mainly from European countries. In 1871, the foreign-born population were mainly from the British Isles (83.6% or close to half a million people), followed by the United States (10.9%), Germany (4.1%) and France (0.5%). Immigrants from other European countries slowly increased in the late 1800s and early 1900s with the arrival of a new group from Eastern Europe (Russians, Polish, and Ukrainians),

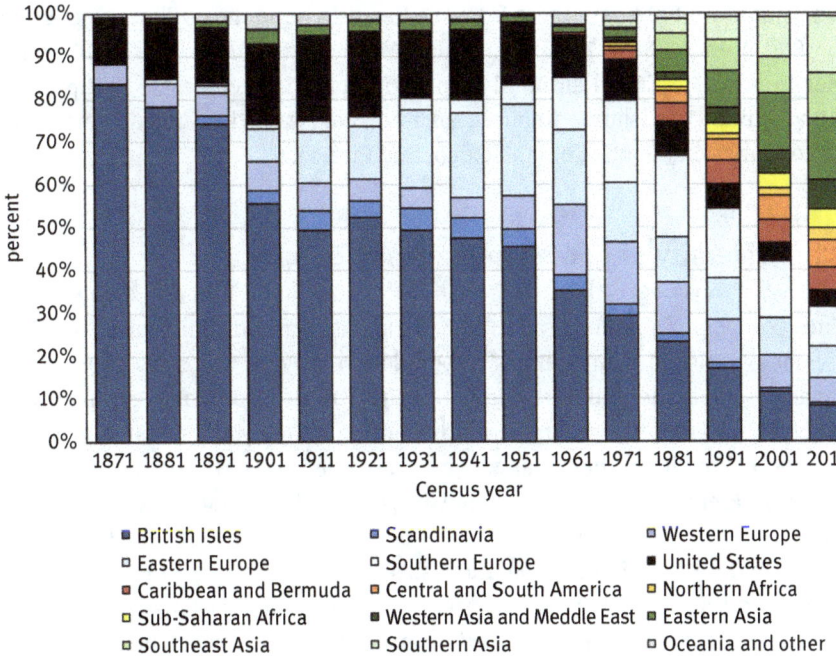

Figure 5.2: Distribution in percentage of the foreign-born population, by place of birth, Canada, 1871 to 2011. Sources: Statistics Canada, censuses of population, 1871 to 2001 (National Household Survey 2011).

Western Europe and Scandinavia, and increased more rapidly after World War II with immigrants from the British Isles, Western Europe (Germany and the Netherlands) and Southern Europe (Italy, Greece, Yugoslavia and Portugal). Immigrants from European countries peaked in the 1970s with 28.3% from the United Kingdom and 51.4% from other European countries (Canada Census 1971). Immigration from Eastern Europe including the Russian Federation and former Soviet republics, Poland, and Romania still continued into the 1980s and 1990s, following the political changes in the Communist bloc countries. Immigrants from Asia (primarily China and Japan) and other parts of the world were also admitted into Canada during the first 100 years after Confederation, and major amendments in its immigration legislation and regulations in the 1960s increased the number of immigrants from these regions. World events also led to movement of refugees and migrants to Canada, including the arrival of 60,000 refugees from Vietnam, Cambodia and Laos in the late 1970s; 85,000 immigrants from the Caribbean and Bermuda (e.g., Jamaica, Haiti, and Trinidad and Tobago) in the 1980s; 225,000 immigrants from Hong Kong over the 10 years leading up to its return to China from the United Kingdom in 1997; and 800,000 immigrants from the People's Republic of China, India and the Philippines in the 2000s (Canadian Megatrends 2016). The top 10 countries from which Canadian immigrants came in 2014 include the Philippines, India, China, the Islamic Republic of Iran, Pakistan, the United States, the United Kingdom, South Korea, Mexico, and France.

5.1.4 Diversity of home languages in Canada

Since Confederation, immigration to Canada has changed significantly and has become one of the main sources of population growth. It has also diversified Canada's population in terms of ethnicity, belief and language. Statistics Canada (2017) reports that English is the more commonly official language with 74.5% speaking it as a home language on a regular basis, while the official language of French is spoken at home by 21.4% of the population. Bilingual English-French speakers make up 17.9% of the population. The 2016 Census reported that 19.4% of the population speak more than one language in the home, and that 7,974,370 people (over 22%) have a mother tongue other than English or French. The top ten of these non-official languages are Mandarin, Cantonese, Punjabi, Spanish, Arabic, Tagalog, Persian, Urdu, Russian, and Italian, as shown in Table 5.3.

Table 5.3: Top ten languages other than English and French spoken most often at home in Canada.
Source: Adapted from Statistics Canada 2016 Census of Population.

Language spoken most often at home	Population
Mandarin	458,795
Cantonese	400,795
Punjabi (Panjabi)	350,015
Spanish	259,345
Arabic	221,815
Tagalog (Pilipino, Filipino)	218,375
Persian (Farsi)	141,480
Urdu	127,740
Russian	115,810
Italian	114,870

5.2 Character of multilingual communities

As large countries both in terms of geography and population, Canada and the United States have many linguistically diverse multilingual towns, cities, and metropolitan areas. Even rural areas that are less known for their diversity are seeing an increase in the number of immigrants speaking a variety of different languages, who often are attracted by jobs in agricultural and manufacturing that do not require high levels of education or proficiency in English. In this section we provide a brief look at the plurilingualism of two major multilingual cities in the U.S. and Canada – Los Angeles and Toronto. Toronto is Canada's largest city, while Los Angeles is the second largest city in the United States (following New York). We select these two cities given their similar population sizes (2.7–3.7 million), their rich cultural and linguistic diversity, and the presence of unique ethnic enclaves.

5.2.1 Los Angeles

Los Angeles is located in the cultural, financial, and commercial center of Southern California, and is the second most populous city in the United States. The U.S. Census Bureau estimated its population at about 3.74 million in 2016. The city is racially and ethnically diverse with Latinx and Asian being the two largest groups, accounting for 48.6% and 11.6% of the population, respectively. Language diversity is also found in the city, with 59.9% of the population reported speaking at least one of 185 different languages other than English at home (U.S. Census Bureau 2016). While Spanish, with 1.6 million speakers, is by far the most commonly spoken language following English, other top 10 languages spoken at home in Los Angeles have between 17 and 91 thousand speakers, including Tagalog, Korean, Armenian, Chinese, Persian, Russian, French, Vietnamese, and Hebrew (see Table 5.4).

Table 5.4: Top 10 languages other than English spoken in Los Angeles, California, 2016. Source: Adapted from U.S. Census Bureau, 2016 American Community Survey 1-Year Estimates.

Languages spoken at home	Los Angeles City, California
Spanish	1,610,733
Tagalog (incl. Filipino)	91,775
Korean	91,758
Armenian	74,691
Chinese (incl. Mandarin, Cantonese)	63,699
Persian (incl. Farsi, Dari)	51,436
Russian	33,258
French (incl. Cajun)	22,543
Vietnamese	19,393
Hebrew	17,294

The city of Los Angeles has several recognized ethnic enclaves that mark concentrations of "Angelenos" who share common heritage and linguistic backgrounds, including Chinatown, Koreatown, Little Tokyo, Little Armenia, Thai Town, Little Ethiopia, Little Persia, and Historic Filipino town. Within the greater Los Angeles area (including Orange County) are other ethnic enclaves, including Cambodia Town in Long Beach, Little India in Artesia, and Little Saigon in Westminster. Olvera Street in downtown Los Angeles, an overly romanticized portrayal of a Mexican enclave, has long been a popular tourist destination (part of El Pueblo de Los Angeles Historic Monument) that was an early settlement site of Mexican families in 1781. However, across Los Angeles County there are several predominantly Latinx neighborhoods such as East Los Angeles, Huntington Park, Boyle Heights, Bell Gardens, and South Gate, just to name a few. Monterey Park and other areas of San Gabriel Valley have large enclaves of more recent Chinese immigrants than historic Chinatown. In these and many smaller unnamed ethnic enclaves, one can find a variety of restaurants, shops, service providers, community organizations, churches, temples, and mosques catering to the local ethnic populations, with signage and other advertising in the corresponding languages adding to the diverse linguistic landscape of Los Angeles. One can easily find newspapers in a variety of languages, including Spanish (e.g., *La Opinion*), Chinese (e.g., *International Daily News*), Vietnamese (e.g., *Nguoi Viet Daily News*), Arabic (e.g., *Beirut Times*), Korean (e.g., *The Korea Times*), Punjabi (e.g. *Quami Ekta*), Japanese (e.g., *Rafu Shimpo*), and Khmer (e.g., *Khmer Post)*. Many of these newspapers are published bilingually with some content in English, and are available in print and online. Likewise, there are local magazines, radio stations, and cable channels available in these and other languages. The Los Angeles Public Library boasts on its website that it has the "largest and finest multi-language resource centers in a North American public library," with a core collection of literature, poetry, drama, history, biography and fiction in 30 different languages. Overall, "its collection is comprised of 260,000 books, audiobooks and DVDs, 250 magazines and newspapers in print and microform, 3,500 language learning CDs and DVDs, and 1,000 travel posters" (https://www.lapl.org/branches/central-library/departments/international-languages).

5.2.2 Toronto

Toronto is the capital of the Canadian province of Ontario and the largest city in Canada, with a total population estimated at almost 2.7 million (Statistics Canada 2016). It is a center for business, finance, arts and culture and is known as one of the most multicultural cities in the world. Toronto is diverse in its racial and ethnic groups with Asians being the largest group, specifically Chinese and Pilipino accounting for 4.88% and 4.41% of the total population respectively. Nationwide, nearly half of Canadians with an immigrant mother tongue live in Ontario (Statistics Canada 2017). Thus, Toronto is diverse in the languages spoken most frequently at home. For the two official languages, English is most commonly spoken at home with 1,739,625 people, while French is only spoken by 17,065 people at home (Statistics Canada 2016). As shown in Table 5.5, the top 10 non-official languages spoken in Toronto homes include Mandarin, Cantonese, Tagalog, Tamil, Spanish, Portuguese, Persian, Italian, Urdu, and Korean. Note that each of these are immigrant languages and are spoken by more people at home than French.

Like Los Angeles, Toronto is also home to several historic and contemporary ethnic enclaves, including Chinatown, Little Italy, Greektown, Little India, Koreatown, Little Portugal, Little Poland, and Little Manila. Its inhabitants are represented by more than 200 ethnic groups, and over 160 languages are

Table 5.5: Top 10 languages spoken other than English and French, Toronto, Canada, 2016. Source: Adapted from Statistics Canada 2016 Census of Population.

Language spoken most often at home	Toronto, Canada
Mandarin	87,760
Cantonese	83,405
Tagalog (Pilipino, Filipino)	42,520
Tamil	42,015
Spanish	41,530
Portuguese	33,425
Persian (Farsi)	33,375
Italian	27,130
Urdu	23,625
Korean	23,625

spoken in this city. Bilingual and multilingual practices are common, particularly in many of the enclaves. These practices are usually reflected in the linguistic landscape and the interactions in shops, restaurants, different community and religious organizations, and service providers that serve these different ethnic communities. For instance, the city's 911 emergency services have interpreter services in 170 languages. In another example, Phan and Luk (2008) studied many business owners in Toronto's Chinatown and pointed to the necessity of multilingual abilities in conducting business and in extending the social networks to benefit businesses there.

5.3 Educational, political and linguistic consequences of such plurilingualism

The U.S. and Canada are two of the largest immigrant destinations in the world. As noted above, they have long histories of immigration and have received large inflows of immigrants from many common sending nations; however, they have pursued strikingly different immigration and language policies which result in the promotion and demotion of plurilingualism at different periods of time. Marcias and Wiley (as cited in Kloss 1998) suggested four orientations in examining policies: promotion-oriented, involving government's active commitment in advancing the official use of minority languages; tolerance-oriented, characterized by government's absence in the linguistic life of the language minority community; restriction-oriented, marked by the government placing conditions on the language minority community's attainment of benefits, rights and opportunities based on its members' ability to use the dominant language; and repression-oriented, involving the state actively seeking the eradication of non-dominant languages. These orientations will be used as a framework for the discussion of the plurilingual promotion and/or demotion in the United States and Canada.

5.3.1 United States

Plurilingualism in the United States has led to a variety of language policies and practices that range from tolerance and occasional promotion to outright restrictions and repression (Kloss 1998). In the early days of U.S. history, repression-oriented policies successfully eradicated most of the African languages of the enslaved, and attempted to eradicate the indigenous languages of Native Americans (Wiley and Wright 2004). In contrast, general tolerance was shown towards most immigrant groups from non-English speaking countries and their descendants. Such linguistic groups typically resided together in neighborhoods or small rural communities where they made up the majority of the local population, and thus could freely use their native language and establish native-language or bilingual schools (Baker and Wright 2017). The Revolutionary War for independence from Britain was a multilingual effort with English and other languages used as the language of command. This is one reason why the founding fathers of the U.S. government never declared an official language, lest they offend their fellow Americans who sacrificed and fought for independence (Crawford 1992). But also, English was so widely spoken by the vast majority of Americans that there was no need to declare English as the official language. It already functioned as if it was, and there was no threat to the continuing status of English as the "de facto" official language. The same remains true today, despite efforts by organizations such as U.S. English to push for official English federal legislation. While over half of the states have passed controversial and divisive official English declarations driven largely by anxiety over immigration, ultimately these declarations have proved to be mostly symbolic (Crawford 2000). These states continue to provide government services in languages other than English such as translations of documents from state agencies and court interpreters due to practical necessity. Indeed, the use of other languages is often as much about accommodating the needs of the government to carry out its work than about accommodating the needs of the multilingual citizens it serves.

High rates of immigration at the turn of the 20th century led to the beginnings of the Americanization Movement that pushed cultural and linguistic assimilation into mainstream "American" society (McClymer 1982). The Nationality Act of 1906 established English proficiency as a requirement for citizenship. World War I intensified anti-German sentiment in the United States which questioned the loyalty of German Americans (Toth 1990; Wiley 1998). Likewise, the loyalty of Japanese Americans was questioned during World War II, which ultimately led to the Japanese internment camps. During these periods, laws were passed in many states that demanded English-only instruction, and sought to restrict the teaching of German, Japanese, and other languages, even in private heritage language classes outside of the public school system (Wiley and Wright 2004). Important U.S. Supreme Court rulings related to these restrictions (e.g., Meyer v. Nebraska 1923; Farrington v. Tokushige 1927) upheld the right of state governments to determine the language of instruction in public schools, but protected the rights of parents to establish private language classes for their children (Del Valle 2003).

Later in the 20th Century, the launch of the Russian Sputnik satellite into space led to cries from the public and politicians to improve U.S. education and ensure students were prepared to help the country compete on a global scale. One result was the passage of the 1958 National Defense Education Act that included promotion of K-12 foreign language education programs. The Civil Rights Movement brought renewed attention to unequal educational opportunities, resulting in the 1964 Civil Rights Act, which prohibited discrimination on the basis of color, race, or national origin. A report by the National Education Association (1966) called for more bilingual programs to address the problem of significant underachievement and high drop-out rates of Latinx students. U.S. Congress passed the 1968 Bilingual Education Act (BEA), which became Title VII of the Elementary and Secondary Education Act. The BEA provides direct financial support to schools through competitive grants to establish bilingual education programs (Leibowitz 1980).

The 1972 U.S. Supreme Court decision in *Lau v. Nichols* established that school districts must provide specialized language programs to identify and address the needs of students who are not yet proficient in English. The Office of Civil Rights established the *Lau Remedies* as a set of guidelines for schools to comply with the court ruling (Wiese and García 2001). These were later codified in part in the Equal Educational Opportunities Act (EEOA) of 1974. The result was a substantial increase in bilingual education and other programs across the country attempting to address the needs of students identified as English language learners (ELLs). Many states passed their own bilingual education policies, in some cases mandating programs when schools had a sufficient number of students from the same language background (Crawford 2004). Despite the push for and rapid increase in the number of bilingual programs, most ELL students were placed in specialized English-medium instruction programs such as English as a second language (ESL) and sheltered (structured) English immersion (SEI). This was due to factors such as a shortage of bilingual teachers and instructional materials (especially in languages other than Spanish), the presence of multiple languages within a single school, a lack of training among administrators on how to start and support bilingual programs, and also due to a lack of commitment and local opposition to bilingual approaches in education.

Around the turn of the 21st century, again during a period of high rates of immigration, restriction-oriented policies were passed by voters in three states with large ELL populations and bilingual programs. The "English for the Children" voter initiative campaigns in California (Proposition 227 in 1998), Arizona (Proposition 203 in 2000) and Massachusetts (Question 2 in 2002) were funded and led by a politically-motivated millionaire entrepreneur who had twice failed to be elected to political office in California (de Jong, Gort, and Cobb 2005; García 2000; Wright 2005a, 2014). These initiatives mandated that ELLs be taught in English through structured English immersion programs. While some allowances for bilingual education programs were available through a stringent waiver process, and interpretation and implementation of the policies varied across the states at different times, the overall result was a substantial reduction in the number of bilingual education programs in these three states. A further blow came in 2001 with the reauthorization of a federal education policy as the No Child Left Behind Act (NCLB), which eliminated the Title VII Bilingual Education Act (Crawford 2002). It was replaced with Title III, the "English Language Acquisition, Language Enhancement, and Academic Achievement Act". Under NCLB, bilingual programs were allowed, but not encouraged or prioritized for federal funding. English was the focus. Furthermore, NCLB mandated annual high-stake standardized English proficiency testing for ELLs, and academic achievement testing for all students, with the expectation that 100% of students would pass these state exams by 2014. Despite some allowances for testing ELLs in their native language, the reality was that the vast majority of ELLs were required to be tested in English (Wright 2005b). With mounting pressure to raise test scores and make "adequate yearly progress" towards ever increasing achievement targets, many school districts felt the need to ensure that the language of instruction closely matched the language of the test (Menken 2008; Palmer and Lynch 2008).

Despite the wave of restriction-oriented policies, many bilingual education programs survived in most states because they were effective and parents wanted them for their children. In the 2010s, the tide began to turn. Models of dual language bilingual education that served both ELLs and English proficient students grew in popularity. This includes two-way models that serve both ELLs and English proficient students in the same classroom, and one-way models that are essentially immersion programs for non-ELL students who wish to learn a world language (Wright 2019). Proposition 58 was approved by California voters in 2016 to essentially rescind Proposition 227 and remove restrictions on bilingual programs (Hopkinson 2017). Likewise, the Massachusetts state legislature overturned restrictions on bilingual education through the passage of the "Language Opportunities for Our Kids" (LOOK) Act in 2017 (Massachusetts Language Opportunity Coalition 2017). By 2018, nearly all states had established or were in the process of developing some form of a "Seal of Biliteracy," which is granted to recognize high school seniors at graduation who can demonstrate proficiency in two or more languages (Wright 2019). Some states, such as Indiana, refer to their seal as a "Certificate of Multilingual Proficiency".

During the Obama Administration, states were provided some flexibility and relief from the unreasonable achievement expectations for NCLB and allowed to negotiate an alternative accountability system based on a set of principles focused on "college and career readiness" (U.S. Department of Education 2012). This laid the foundation for the replacement of NCLB with the Every Student Succeeds Act (ESSA) of 2015. While Title III continues the emphasis on English proficiency and academic achievement testing, ESSA affords greater flexibility to states in setting reasonable expectations for ELL students, and encourages the development and use of tests in students' home languages (Baker and Wright 2017). There is still no specific funding reserved for bilingual education programs, but non-regulatory guidelines issued by the U.S. Department of Education (2016) make specific mention of the research supporting bilingual approaches. ESSA makes special allowances for programs for Native American (including Pacific Islander) children and children in Puerto Rico to learn and study Native American languages and Spanish, but these programs must still ensure that programs lead to an increase in English proficiency (Wright 2019).

Despite the anti-immigration rhetoric of the Trump Administration, the Department of Education's Office of English Language Acquisition (OELA) has funded National Professional Development grants to support the training and certification of teachers working with ELLs, and has prioritized funding for programs that include training and support for dual language bilingual education programs. While current OELA leaders appear to be strong supporters of bilingual education, the future of OELA is uncertain as the Trump administration has proposed the elimination of this office in a restructuring of the Department of Education. This proposal has garnered opposition from language education professional organizations, and it remains to be seen if the restructuring will happen.

As the history above reveals, plurilingualism in the United States has led to political debates and ebbs and flows in the support of bilingual education. Historically, most federal and state support went to weak forms of transitional bilingual education which limited native language instruction to just a few years and focused on moving students into English-only programs as quickly as possible. In contrast, the resurgence of support for bilingual education has tended to favor strong forms, including dual language programs, which typically include instruction throughout elementary school and in some cases through secondary schools. One concern, however, is that the popularity of dual language programs appears to be driven by interests of the more powerful language majority parents who want their children to become bilingual, resulting in many one-way immersion programs that often exclude ELLs. However, even in places such as Utah, whose mostly one-way dual language programs have become somewhat of a model for other states (Freire, Valdez, and Delavan 2017), efforts are underway to increase the number of ELL and heritage language students participating in the program.

The political struggle just to provide quality bilingual programs has prevented attention and efforts to push for multilingual programs that seek to help students gain proficiency in three or more languages. However, many language minoritized students in the United States are truly multilingual. Many immigrants arrived in the United States already bilingual or multilingual, and learn English as a third, fourth, or higher language. Chinese immigrant students often speak a local dialect of Chinese in addition to Mandarin, and have studied English as a foreign language before they arrived in the United States. Duran (2017) describes the accumulated languages and literacies Karenii refugees from Burma picked up on their journey to the United States (e.g., Karenii, Burmese, Thai, and English). Some French heritage language programs are dominated by Haitian-Creole speakers from Haiti and African immigrant students from countries where French was a medium of instruction (Jaumont 2017). Immigrant students from the Middle East may speak one or more varieties of Arabic, and some received instruction in Russian in refugee camps before coming to the United States.

Most American high schools only teach a small number of world languages (e.g., Spanish, French, and German), which are not aligned with the hundreds of different languages heritage language students have exposure to in their homes (Wiley 2007). Thus, high school students with some proficiency in their heritage language often study a third language to add to their existing linguistic repertoire.

The current trend of dual language may be opening some space for multilingual education programs. As one example, Henn-Reinke (2012), in her book *Considering Trilingual Education*, highlights Riverview Elementary School's International Academy in San Diego, California which offers Spanish and

(Mandarin) Chinese immersion programs. Each program includes time for enrichment (about 30 minutes a week) in the non-target language. Thus, students in Spanish-immersion receive about 30 minutes of Chinese language instruction each, while those in Chinese-immersion receive equivalent instruction in Spanish (https://www.lsusd.net/domain/792).

The U.S. is also home to some private international schools that focus on bilingual or multilingual development. For example, at the International School of Indiana, students are in dual language programs in the elementary school grades (e.g., Spanish-English), and then study a third language in the secondary grades (e.g., Mandarin Chinese). At Oasis Trilingual Community School in Temple City, California, instead, students study all three of these languages simultaneously following a 40/40/20 model – 40% of the instruction is in Mandarin Chinese, 40% is in English, and 20% is in Spanish up to 8th grade. (https://oasistrilingualschool.org/curriculum/).

It should also be acknowledged that many students in dual language programs are heritage speakers of languages other than the target language, and there are also many African American students who may speak a non-standard variety of English at home (e.g., African American Vernacular English). Some states are moving away from the English language learner (ELL) label and now refer to students as "emergent bilinguals," in order to draw attention to the fact that they are indeed bilingual and increasing their bilingual skills (García, Kleifgen, and Falchi 2008). Some use this term to refer to both ELLs and non-ELLs in dual language and heritage language programs. Others feel the emergent bilingual label is too narrow and now simply refer to such students as "multilingual learners" (see e.g., Molle et al. 2015). Likewise, recognition of the linguistic repertoires across dialects and languages that students bring into dual language programs, and discussions calling into question the long-standing practice of strict separation of the standardized versions of the two target languages in a bilingual program are contributing to a growing trend to simply use "multilingual education" as an umbrella term for programs that make use of two or more languages for instruction.

5.3.2 Canada

With the current demographic shift in Canada, multilingualism, particularly among the immigrant population, is on the rise, and this happens when official languages are used increasingly alongside immigrant languages. The proportion of the Canadian population speaking more than one language at home increased from 17.5% in 2011 to 19.4% in 2016 (Statistics Canada 2017). However,

Canadian language and educational policies have not always been favorable to the promotion of indigenous and immigrant or heritage languages.

Canadian language policy is the result of an interrelationship among various language communities. Historically, Canada was under British and French colonial rule. In 1867, a single confederation was formed as a result of a compromise between these two immigrant societies. As a result, English and French have been the dominant languages in the country. National language debates have often focused on the use of these two official languages, with little attention to other languages. The use of French and English have never been evenly distributed as the distribution of English-speaking population is more even across Canada, while the French-speaking population is concentrated in Quebec, New Brunswick, Ontario and parts of Manitoba. In response to Quebec separatism and to bolster national unity, the Canadian government made efforts to reconstruct its character through two policy initiatives in the late 1960s: bilingualism and multiculturalism.

The Official Languages Act of 1969 granted equal status to English and French as official languages of Parliament and the federal government. All services of federal institutions were expected to be in both official languages, and provisions were made for all children to learn an official language in school. The right of official language communities was entrenched in the constitution with the Canadian Charter of Rights and Freedoms of 1982, ensuring the right of francophones across the country to French-medium schools, and access to English language education for the anglophones in French-dominant regions (Dicks and Genesee 2017). This has promoted increasing English-French bilingualism among the population in most provinces and territories, particularly in Quebec (Statistics Canada 2017). While federal documents emphasize the rights of the Anglophone and Francophone communities, they classify communities of non-official language speakers as either Aboriginal or multicultural groups. Haque (2012: 18) argues that these references underlie the suppression of distinct indigenous and immigrant languages and "allow[s] the group to be defined only through culture while it stills emerges as a category in opposition to other linguistic groups".

The 2016 Census reported that about 76 Aboriginal languages are spoken in Canada. However, only three – Cree, Inuktitut, and Ojibway – have over 20,000 speakers each and are considered to have chances of long-term survival. Approximately 10 have become extinct over the past 100 years (Ricento 2015). Several others are now endangered with few speakers remaining. Serious language policy intervention needs to be considered for the maintenance of these languages. Unfortunately, as Haque and Patrick (2015: 33) argue, Canada has "a long history of oppressive and discriminatory laws and policies related to 'Indians'". They note several such policies, including the "Gradual Civilization Act (1857), the Gradual Enfranchisement Act (1869), the Indian Act (1876), the Indian Register (1951) and the system of residential schooling (1874–1977)" which are assimilationist in nature and have negatively impacted the efforts of the indigenous communities to preserve their languages and cultures (2015: 33).

The situation is similar with respect to the sustainability of the immigrant or heritage languages in Canada. Language shift data revealed a shift to the use of one of the official languages at home and in the daily life of a heritage language-background speaker in just one or two generations, and this can be attributed to the assimilation pressures, the perceived stigma in using a non-official language, the lack of support for non-official languages in education, and the lack of institutional recognition of the value of heritage languages (Duff and Becker-Zayas 2017).

The Multiculturalism Act of 1988 recognized cultural and racial diversity in Canadian society. One of the objectives of the Multiculturalism Act was to preserve and enhance the use of non-official languages, while strengthening the status and use of French and English in the country. While Canada's version of multiculturalism was praised and adopted internationally, it has been criticized for separating culture and language, and de-emphasizing languages of other cultural groups besides French and English in its Official Languages Act. Haque (2012) argues that multiculturalism within a bilingual framework creates a cultural and linguistic hierarchy and helps maintain white-settler hegemony (see also Guo 2013).

Thus, with the focus on Official English and French, Canadian language policies have been restrictive of the development of Aboriginal and immigrant languages and of innovative educational language programs such as multilingual education (MLE). Immigrant and indigenous students are usually immersed with their English- or French-speaking peers in mainstream classes where content area subjects are taught in English in anglophone dominant provinces, or French in francophone dominant provinces.

However, different forms of bilingual education programs, where the heritage language is also used as a medium of instruction, may be offered depending on the provincial language policies and the needs of the minority-language-speaking communities (Babaee 2014). These programs are available in a variety of different languages, including, for example, the Mandarin/English program in British Columbia (Vancouver School Board 2018), the American Sign Language/English, Arabic/English, Mandarin/English, German/English, and Hebrew/English programs in Alberta (Edmonton Public Schools 2018), the Ukrainian/English program in Saskatchewan (Government of Saskatchewan Education 2018), and the

Ukrainian/English, German/English, Hebrew/English, and Cree/English bilingual education programs in Manitoba (Government of Manitoba Education 2018). Many of these bilingual education programs are transitional in nature, where instruction in the heritage language is provided in the first few years, and beyond that, the heritage language is offered as a separate subject and is taught as an international or foreign language. While different types of bilingual education exist, they are only available in heritage languages that are more common such as Mandarin, Arabic, and Spanish. The less popular languages such as Khmer, Vietnamese, and most indigenous languages are not usually offered. Those heritage bilingual education programs are sometimes initiated and supported by the communities.

The most common form of bilingual education in Canada is French immersion, which features French-medium and later English instruction. However, the country is becoming increasingly diverse culturally and linguistically especially in large cities like Toronto, so many of these immersion programs are also serving students with heritage languages other than French or English. These students usually learn their heritage languages as a subject in addition to French and English based on the needs of the community the school is serving. Heritage languages may also be taught in afterschool and community-based education programs. Dagenais (2013: 292) found that "parents encouraged their children to become multilingual in English, French, and their family languages in the hope that it will help them identify with family and community members nearby and elsewhere, while gaining access to imagined French-English bilingual communities in Canada". Also, effort has been made to integrate innovations in multilingual education into mainstream English or French schools and French immersion programs with students from diverse linguistic backgrounds (Dagenais 2013). These include, for instance, the production of bilingual texts in diverse languages (Cummins and Early 2011) and the use of video making as a powerful form of multimodal and multilingual expression for English learners (Stille 2011).

5.4 Conclusion

As this chapter has shown, the North American countries of Canada and the United States are indeed multilingual countries. The interaction of many different languages in these plurilingual societies is especially apparent in the major cities of Los Angeles and Toronto. Despite some similar patterns of immigration, Canada and the United States have different histories that have resulted in distinct levels of plurilingualism and have had different educational, political and linguistic consequences. Canada's Confederation brought together former British and French Colonies with regions where one language or the other was dominant. Efforts to maintain the Confederation have focused on the use of English and French as official languages and the promotion of English-French immersion education programs, often to the neglect of speakers of indigenous and immigrant languages. For example, one consequence of plurilingualism in Toronto is the reality that there are far more speakers of immigrant languages than of official French language. Yet educational policy promotes French immersion, resulting in fewer opportunities for immigrant students and children of immigrants to develop and maintain their heritage languages. In contrast, the United States never declared an official language, as English was already the dominant language and language of communication across various linguistic communities and groups. Nevertheless, U.S. debates over language, especially in the context of education, often centered around the politics of war and immigration. This resulted in a range of policies throughout U.S. history that ebbed and flowed between more restricted-oriented and more tolerance-oriented policies. In Los Angeles, for example, one consequence of plurilingualism was backlash against bilingual and heritage language programs. During a period when state policies mandated sheltered English immersion programs for ELLs, bilingual programs in several different immigrant languages came to an end. Currently in both countries, there is growing recognition of the need for more tolerance and promotion-oriented policies, programs and supports for a broader range of indigenous, immigrant and heritage language students, in addition to official-language proficient students, to provide them with greater opportunities for bilingual and multilingual development.

References

Babaee, Naghmeh. 2014. Heritage language learning in Canadian public schools: Language rights challenges. https://umanitoba.ca/faculties/education/media/Babaee12.pdf (accessed December 12, 2018).

Baker, Colin & Wright, Wayne E. 2017. *Foundations for bilingual education and bilingualism*, 6th edn. Bristol, UK: Multilingual Matters.

Crawford, James. 1992. *Hold your tongue: Bilingualism and the politics of English-only*. Reading, MA: Addison Wesley.

Crawford, James. 2000. Anatomy of the English-only movement. In James Crawford (ed.), *At war with diversity: US language policy in an age of anxiety*, 4–30. Clevedon, UK: Multilingual Matters.

Crawford, James. 2002. *Obituary: The Bilingual Education Act, 1968–2002*. Tempe, AZ: Language Policy Research Unit, Education Policy Studies Laboratory, Arizona State University.

Crawford, James. 2004. *Educating English learners: Language diversity in the classroom*, 5th edn. Los Angeles: Bilingual Education Services, Inc.

Cummins, Jim & Margaret Early (eds.). 2011. *Identity texts: The collaborative creation of power in multilingual schools*. Stoke on Trent, UK: Trentham Books.

Dagenais, Diane. 2013. Multilingualism in Canada: Policy and education in applied linguistics research. *Annual Review of Applied Linguistics* 33. 286–301.

Del Valle, Sandra. 2003. *Language rights and the law in the United States: Finding our voices*. Clevedon, UK: Multilingual Matters.

Dicks, Joseph & Fred Genesee. 2017. Bilingual education in Canada. In Ofelia García, Angel Lin & Stephen May (eds.), *Bilingual and multilingual education. Encyclopedia of language and education*, 3rd edn., 1–14. Cham: Springer.

Duff, Patricia A. & Ava Becker-Zayas. 2017. Demographics and heritage languages in Canada. In Olga E. Kagan, Maria M. Carreira & Clair H. Chik (eds.), *The Routledge handbook of heritage language education: From innovation to program building*, 57–67. New York, NY: Taylor & Francis.

Duran, Chatwara Suvannamai. 2017. *Language and literacy in refugee families*. London, UK: Palgrave Macmillan.

Edmonton Public Schools. 2018. Languages: Bilingual and immersion programs. https://www.epsb.ca/programs/language/ (accessed 20 November 2018).

Farrington v. Tokushige, 273 U.S. 284 (1927).

Freire, Juan A., Verónica E. Valdez & M. Garrett Delavan. 2017. The (dis)inclusion of Latina/o interests from Utah's dual language education boom. *Journal of Latinos and Education* 16 (4). 276–289.

García, Eugene E. 2000. Editor's introduction: Implementation of California's Proposition 227: 1998–2000. *Bilingual Research Journal* 24(1–2). v–vii.

García, Ofelia, Jo Anne Kleifgen & Lorraine Falchi. 2008. *From English language learners to emergent bilinguals*. New York: The Campaign for Educational Equity, Teachers College, Columbia University.

Government of Saskatchewan Education. 2018. Saskatchewan: Ukrainian education virtual resources portal. https://www.spiritsd.ca/ukrainian/eng_elem_isl.htm (accessed 20 November 2018).

Guo, Yan. 2013. Language policies and programs for adult immigrants in Canada: A critical analysis. *Canadian Ethnic Studies* 45(1–2). 23–41.

Haque, Eve. 2012. *Multiculturalism within a bilingual framework: Language, race, and belonging in Canada*. Toronto, ON: University of Toronto Press.

Haque, Eve & Donna Patrick. 2015. Indigenous languages and the racial hierarchisation of language policy in Canada. *Journal of Multilingual and Multicultural Development* 36(1). 27–41.

Henn-Reinke, Kathryn. 2012. *Considering trilingual education*. New York, NY: Routledge.

Hopkinson, Ashley. 2017. A new era for bilingual education: Explaining California's Proposition 58. *EdSource*. https://edsource.org/2017/a-new-era-for-bilingual-education-explaining-californias-proposition-58/574852 (accessed 20 November 2018).

Jaumont, Fabrice. 2017. *The bilingual revolution: The future of education is in two languages*. Brooklyn, NY: TBR Books.

Jong, Ester de, Mileidis Gort & Casey D. Cobb. 2005. Bilingual education within the context of English-only policies: Three districts' response to Question 2 in Massachusetts. *Educational Policy* 19(4). 595–620.

Kloss, Heinz. 1998. *The American bilingual tradition*. USA: Center for Applied Linguistics and Delta Systems Co., Inc.

Lau v. Nichols, 414 U.S. 563 (US Supreme Court 1974).

Leibowitz, Arnold H. 1980. *The Bilingual Education Act: A legislative analysis*. Washington, DC: National Clearinghouse for Bilingual Education.

Government of Manitoba Education. 2018. Education and training: Bilingual education and programming in Manitoba. https://www.edu.gov.mb.ca/k12/cur/languages/bilingual_qa.html (accessed 20 November 2018).

Massachusetts Language Opportunity Coalition. 2017. LOOK Act. https://languageopportunity.org/look-act/ (accessed 25 November 2018).

McClymer, John. 1982. The Americanization movement and the education of the foreign born adult, 1914–1925. In Bernard J. Weiss (ed.), *Education and the European immigrant: 1840–1940*, 96–116. Urbana, IL: University of Illinois Press.

Menken, Kate. 2008. *English learners left behind: Standardized testing as language policy*. Clevedon, UK: Multilingual Matters.

Meyer v. Nebraska, 262 U.S. 390 (1923).

Migration Policy Institute. 2018a. Largest U.S. immigrant groups over time, 1960–present. Washington, DC: Author. https://www.migrationpolicy.org/programs/data-hub/us-immigration-trends#source (accessed 12 September 2018).

Migration Policy Institute. 2018b. Regions of birth for immigrants in the United States, 1960–present. Washington, DC: Author. https://www.migrationpolicy.org/programs/data-hub/us-immigration-trends#source (accessed 12 September 2018).

Molle, Daniella, Edynn Sato, Timothy Boals & Carol A. Hedgspeth (eds.). 2015. *Multilingual learners and academic literacies: Sociocultural contexts of literacy development in adolescents*. New York, NY: Routledge-Taylor & Francis.

National Education Association. 1966. *The invisible minority . . . pero no vencibles: Report of the NEA-Tucson Survey on the Teaching of Spanish to the Spanish-Speaking*. Washington, DC: Department of Rural Education, National Education Association.

National Household Survey. 2001. Ottawa, Ontario, Canada: Statistics Canada. Retrieved from https://www12.statcan.gc.ca/nhs-enm/2011/dp-pd/prof/details/download-telecharger/comprehensive/comp-ivt-xml-nhs-enm.cfm?Lang=E

Palmer, Deborah & Anissa Lynch. 2008. A bilingual education for a monolingual test? The pressure to prepare for TAKS and its influence on choices for language of instruction in Texas elementary bilingual classrooms. *Language Policy* 7(3). 217–235.

Phan, Mai & Chiu Luk. 2008. 'I don't say I have a business in Chinatown': Chinese sub-ethnic relations in Toronto's Chinatown West. *Ethnic and Racial Studies* 31(2). 294–326.

Ricento, Thomas K. 2015. Global dimensions of bilingual and multilingual education Canada. In Wayne E. Wright, Sovicheth Boun & Ofelia García (eds.), *The handbook of bilingual and multilingual education*, 461–472. Malaysia: Wiley Blackwell.

Rumbaut, Ruben G., Douglas S. Massey & Frank D. Bean. 2006. Linguistic life expectancies: Immigrant language retention in Southern California. *Population and Development Review* 32(3). 447–460.

Statistics Canada. 2016a. Census profile, 2016 Census. Ottawa, Ontario, Canada: Author. https://www12.statcan.gc.ca/census-recensement/2016/dp-pd/prof/details/page.cfm?

Lang=E&Geo1=PR&Code1=01&Geo2=PR&Code2=01&Data=Count&SearchText= Canada&SearchType=Begins&SearchPR=01&B1=Language&TABID=1 (accessed 12 September 2018).

Statistic Canada. 2016b. Ottawa, Ontario, Canada: Author. Census of population. http://www.statcan.gc.ca/eng/subjects/population_and_demography?HPA=1 (accessed 12 September 2018).

Statistics Canada. 2017. An increasingly diverse linguistic profile: Corrected data from the 2016 Census. Ottawa, Ontario, Canada: Author. http://www.statcan.gc.ca/daily-quotidien/170817/dq170817a-eng.htm (accessed 12 September 2018).

Stille, Saskia. 2011. Framing representations: Documentary filmmaking as participatory approach to research inquiry. *Journal of Curriculum and Pedagogy* 8. 101–108.

Toth, Carolyn R. 1990. *German-English bilingual schools in America: The Cincinnati tradition in historical contexts*. New York: Peter Lang.

U.S. Census Bureau. 2015. Census Bureau reports at least 350 languages spoken in U.S. homes. Washington, DC: Author. https://www.census.gov/newsroom/press-releases/2015/cb15-185.html (accessed 12 September 2018).

U.S. Census Bureau. 2016. State and country quick facts. https://www.census.gov/quickfacts/fact/table/US/PST045217 (accessed 12 September 2018).

U.S. Census Bureau. 2017. Language use: Frequently asked questions. Washington, DC: Author. https://www.census.gov/topics/population/language-use/about/faqs.html (accessed12 September 2018).

U.S. Census Bureau. 2018. Language spoken at home. 2012–2016 American Community Survey 5-year estimates. Washington, DC: Author. https://factfinder.census.gov/faces/tableservices/jsf/pages/productview.xhtml?pid=ACS_16_5YR_S1601&prodType=table (accessed 12 September 2018).

U.S. Department of Education. 2012. *ESEA flexibility*. Retrieved from Washington, DC: http://www.ed.gov/esea/flexibility/documents/esea-flexibility-acc.doc (accessed 12 September 2018).

U.S. Department of Education. 2016. *Non-regulatory guidance: English learners and Title III of the Elementary and Secondary Education Act (ESEA), as amended by the Every Student Succeeds Act (ESSA)*. https://www2.ed.gov/policy/elsec/leg/essa/essatitleiiiguidenglishlearners92016.pdf (accessed 15 November 2018).

Vancouver School Boards. 2018. Elementary programs: Mandarin bilingual. https://www.vsb.bc.ca/Student_Learning/Elementary/Mandarin_Bilingual/Pages/Default.aspx (accessed 12 September 2018).

Veltman, Calvin J. 1983. *Language shift in the United States*. Berlin: Mouton.

Wiese, Ann-Marie & Eugene E. García. 2001. The Bilingual Education Act: Language minority students and US federal educational policy. *International Journal of Bilingual Education and Bilingualism* 4(4). 229–248.

Wiley, Terrence G. 1998. The imposition of World War I era English-only policies and the fate of German in North America. In Thomas Ricento & Babara Burnaby (eds.), *Language and politics in the United States and Canada: Myths and realities*, 211–241. Mahwah, NJ: Lawrence Erlbaum Associates, Publishers.

Wiley, Terrence G. 2007. The foreign language "crisis" in the United States: Are heritage and community languages the remedy? *Critical Inquiry in Language Studies* 4(2–3). 179–205.

Wiley, Terrence G. & Wayne E. Wright. 2004. Against the undertow: The politics of language instruction in the United States. *Educational Policy* 18(1). 142–168.

Wong Fillmore, Lily. 1991. When learning a second language means losing the first. *Early Childhood Research Quarterly* 6(3). 323–346.

Wright, Wayne E. 2004. What English-only really means: A study of the implementation of California language policy with Cambodian American students. *International Journal of Bilingual Education and Bilingualism* 7(1). 1–23.

Wright, Wayne E. 2005a. The political spectacle of Arizona's Proposition 203. *Educational Policy* 19(5). 662–700.

Wright, Wayne E. 2005b. *Evolution of federal policy and implications of No Child Left Behind for language minority students* (EPSL-0501-101-LPRU). http://nepc.colorado.edu/publication/evolution-federal-policy-and-implications-no-child-left-behind-for-language-minority-stu (accessed 15 November 2018).

Wright, Wayne E. 2014. Proposition 203 and Arizona's early school reform efforts: The nullification of accommodations. In Sarah C. K. Moore (ed.), *Language policy processes and consequences: Arizona case studies*, 45–72. Bristol, UK: Multilingual Matters.

Wright, Wayne E. 2019. *Foundations for teaching English language learners: Research, theory, policy, and practice*, 3rd edn. Philadelphia, PA: Caslon.

Part II: **Language Use in Multilingual Communities**

John Maher
6 Diglossia in Multilingual Communities

6.1 A day in the life of diglossia

A language is not a unitary entity shared evenly among all members of a community. Its appearance in style and lexico-grammar is not identical in all places and times. Nor is a language separated from "other" languages by a sort of linguistic *cordon sanitaire*. The various languages used in multilingual society are connected through an intricate system of linguistic shapes and networks. They comprise a spectrum of repertoires or "varieties" which invoke, in Bakhtin's felicitous terminology, "heteroglossic utterances", "diverse articulations of speaking subjects", and "multivoicedness" (Bakhtin 1929/1984, 1986).

Speakers inhabit many social worlds and spaces. They dwell in some domains but not others, reflecting and structuring changing social needs and values. A multilingual society recognizes these language varieties and its multilingual people as its own despite the fact that an "underlying monolingual homogenizing logic" (Busch 2014: 23) has shaped the way we organize our communicative practices from our bureaucracy to national history to the school classroom and a child's textbook.

Diglossia in multilingual society has existed since antiquity. It is an existential condition where the indexical order of language and social reality is spread out unevenly; sometimes the relation seems to fragment. Diglossia encapsulates the reality that, in the totality of multilingualism, the functional allocation of the ways and means through which we communicate is heterogeneous.

6.1.1 Agnieszka's story

Agnieszka is a teenager in Galway, Ireland. She "speaks Polish" because her parents speak Kashubian (Pomerian), a distinctive dialect of Polish which is sometimes classified as a language in its own right. Agnieszka is a second generation schoolgirl in multilingual Ireland where one in seven persons below the age of 24 is of minority ethnic background. Standard Polish is the language of her church, her parents' social club and some media outlets that she accesses: websites, cable TV. She reads books, surfs the internet with friends in English and Polish. At home she speaks with her family and skypes

---

John Maher, International Christian University, Tokyo, Japan

https://doi.org/10.1515/9781501507984-006

with her Gdańsk grandparents mixing Kashubian and Standard Polish. During the school day, Agnieszka communicates in Irish (Gaeilge). She attends a Gaelscoil, an Irish-medium school, one of many Gaelscoileanna in which schoolchildren in Ireland study through the medium of Irish (currently about 50,000). The decision to send Agnieszka to a Gaelscoil caused family disagreement. She wanted to go. Her parents thought that Irish – the Republic of Ireland's first official language – was not useful and less prestigious than English. "OK," her father argued, "Irish is 'first,' English 'second' but hey, come on, you know English is higher and Irish lower. Hey. Everyone in the world speaks English". Agnieszka still wanted to go to the local Gaelscoil. She had neighborhood friends there. She argued the opposite: "Dad, it's the other way 'round! Being fluent in Irish as well as English actually increases your life and career prospects in Ireland!"

6.1.2 Describing Agnieszka

How do we classify Agnieszka's situation? Firstly, the empirical terminology of traditional sociolinguistics classifies and situates languages (Kloss 1967; Stewart 1968) in various functional positions in society. *Endoglossic* describes the native local vernacular (Irish). *Exoglossic* (English) refers to the language that was, at some point in history, "imported" to become another official language. Thus, although English is, in fact, the second official (not "national") language of the Republic of Ireland, it is overwhelmingly the most used, the most prevalent language of Ireland in all social domains. This is not a recent linguistic turn. English became a superstratum – the speech of towns, schools and the social elite – from the 17th century.

Secondly, we can describe the how and where and why of Agnieszka's dual operation of Standard Polish and Kashubian Polish. What are their distinctive roles in her family's life? We begin by tracking the different language practices (including her switching and mixing of languages) that occur, in fact quite predictably, in these different contexts. Some of these contexts are more formal – like writing in her journal or reciting prayers in church. Some are informal – like chatting and texting. We can see from observation that Agnieszka's Polish-speaking community in Galway and in the wider Irish nation is not a homogeneous speech community. In fact, in daily life, its members have different competencies in English, and even in Polish. This multilingual situation with a co-existence of different languages and varieties in the speech community and distributed across formal and informal situations is referred to as diglossia.

6.2 Diglossia: Highs and lows

A diglossic situation occurs when two (or more) distinct varieties of a language co-exist in society and are associated with different social functions. One variety is prestigious. It may be the "standard" or "official" language of the community. It is regarded as a so-called "high" (or H) variety codified in grammar books and dictionaries. It has what the term's progenitor, Charles Ferguson, called "specialised functions" (Ferguson 1959). That is to say this variety is the medium of instruction at school and university, religious services in churches and mosques and is used for political discourse, letter writing, the media. The counterpart to the H variety is a "low" (or L) variety that operates less in the above domains but is connected rather to situations such as family, social interactions, shopping, casual talk, folk literature, telling jokes, etc.

Diglossia is the defining feature of multilingual societies throughout history. Consider the language situation of post-invasion Norman England during the early medieval period and early modern period. In practice, following the Norman invasion of 1066, England was in a diglossic situation for about three hundred years where the use of Norman French (H) co-existed with English (L). Code-switching between French and English commonly occurred, as found in the literature of William Langland, Geoffrey Chaucer and the *Gawain* poet (Putter 2012). Indeed, at the time, an increasingly multilingual Britain led to an explosion of bilingual and multilingual texts (Latin, French, English) that involved written code-switching for different purposes (e.g., religious, secular, etc.). This was a case of "diglossic bilingualism" (Fishman 1967), a condition where stable diglossia co-occurs with widespread bilingualism. Another example of diglossic bilingualism was in pre-war 20th century Europe where Jewish males communicated in both Hebrew (H) and Yiddish (L).

Diglossia is the canonical instance of language allocation in a multilingual society. It is important to recognize that the concept is neither new nor unfamiliar in the history of multilingualism. For example, Lipinski (1997: 75) notes that in the sixth century, oral poetry was delivered (only) in proto-Classical Arabic but discussed in Arabic vernaculars, a quite different variety.

The expression diglossia (Greek διγλωσσία *diglōssia*) designates bilingualism itself, as first coined in the 19th century by the illustrious polyglot Greek writer Emmanuel Rhoides. The term entered French as *diglossie* and was in currency among Arabists, in particular William Ambroise Marçais who used the term to characterize the linguistic situation in Arabic-speaking countries, "la concurrence entre une langue savante écrite et une langue vulgaire parfois exclusivement parlée" (Feghali 1928: 59). Dante Alighieri (1265–1321) described the concept pertaining to diglossia in his work on sociolinguistic theory, *De vulgari eloquentia*. In this work, he contrasted the role of global literary Latin, the "grammatical language" of the elite, and the less prestigious vernaculars. Dante's work on this "illustrious vernacular" resulted in the formation of Italian.

The concept began to emerge forcefully in the explication of classical Arabic versus the vulgate (Marçais 1902). Charles Ferguson popularized the English equivalent *diglossia* in 1959. Whilst doing fieldwork on Arabic in the Middle East in the 1950s, he noticed unequivocally that in any community (or "speech community" as he called it), two varieties of a language existed coterminously throughout the community with each having a role to play (Ferguson 1959; see also Chapter 2, this volume). Ferguson was specific about the conditions for diglossia. The two varieties should belong to the same language. The Low (L) form is commonly an individual's mother tongue: in Ferguson's examples, vernacular Arabic or Greek, Haitian Creole or Swiss German. The prestigious High (H) variety is normally acquired – and available – in school education. Thus, the language of formal Arabic is the language of the Koran, which "constitutes the words of God outside the limits of space and time" (Ferguson 1959: 238). In modern Greek, diglossia, Katharévousa (i.e., the H code) and Dhimotikí (i.e., the L code), comprises a continuum of the Greek languages in the same speech community (Gkaragkouni 2009). How different varieties co-exist within bilingual society can be schematized in Table 6.1.

Table 6.1: Diglossia and Bilingualism in Society.

	+Diglossia	−Diglossia
+Bilingualism	Speakers in the community know both H and L. Languages are functionally differentiated (e.g. Haiti)	An unstable, transitional situation. Speakers know H and L though there is a shift to H (e.g., German-speaking Belgium, indigenous language in the former USSR)
−Bilingualism	Speakers of H dominate speakers of L (e.g. Spanish and Guarani in Paraguay or languages geographically located in different areas, as with the different language groups of Switzerland)	A monolingual community which professes a unitary language. No language variation (e.g., The Tower of Babel before Divine intervention, Cuba where Spanish is the only spoken language) (Fishman 1967)

The H and L varieties do not mix. They are stable. They differ in the lexicogrammar, in phonology. They have a different status. The existence of the L variety may be devalued or even denied. The H variety is real language. It may be associated with wealth, prestige, a writing system, with literature, grammar and dictionaries. There are combinations of relation in diglossia. There are situations of both bilingualism and diglossia or neither of them or only one of them. A bilingual community is a community of persons that communicate on a regular basis in two languages. Such a community may operate with (+) two languages in differentiated relation (Haiti) or without (−) diglossia because speakers' choices have become unstable and unpredictable (as in the current shift to French in German-speaking Belgium). In Switzerland's Italian-speaking canton, Italian is spoken mostly in families and informal situations (L) but also as a medium of education (H) whilst French and German (H) are accessed in literary and popular culture, education and media.

Fishman (1967) and Gumperz (1967) insisted on the (Dantean) view that diglossia merely indicates the situation in any society where different varieties are used in different circumstances. Current thinking about diglossia tends towards the "broad" view that diglossia applies to "any degree of linguistic relatedness ... from stylistic differences to separate languages" (Fasold 1990: 53) in the context of a community whose linguistic repertoire is mono- or multilingual. Indeed, when sociolinguists refer to "code-switching", they do not specify whether the "code" is a language or a dialect (see Romaine 1994: 63 for an exemplification of this point). Gumperz (1967) dismissed as linguistically flawed the notion that the gap between two different languages is naturally greater than the gap between two varieties. Gumperz was here deconstructing the problematic classification of two purported languages Hindi and Urdu.

6.2.1 Diglossia and the body politic of multilingual society

In most situations of societal bilingualism, the Low (L) variety loses ground to the superposed High (H) variety and the L language typically loses ground to the H language. This is not always the case, however. H sometimes fails against the onslaught of L.

Over a period of three hundred years from the 5th century, the Low Franconian (Flemish, Dutch) language of the powerful Merovingians during the Salian Frankish dynasty could not supplant Latin. In fact, the barbarians themselves began to learn Latin, which became their *sermo vulgaris* – conversational Merovingian. Not only that, a more formal version of Latin was emerging among the Merovingian bourgeoisie for the purpose of diplomacy and learning, literature and legislation. Thus, in multilingual Merovingian Gaul it was the (Merovingian) Germanic languages that declined. Although Low Franconian still survived as a second language of administration in Austrasia in the 850s, it was obsolete by the 10th century. Likewise, it was at this stage of the development of Latin that its famous diglossic splitting occurred. The speech of social classes became sharply defined. Thus, the emergence of a pagan medium borne by heathens separated itself from Classic Latin with rules of grammar, correctness and stylistic perfection that even the educated classes found hard to follow.

The seeds of the historic decline of Latin as a lingua franca of Europe lie in Latin's diglossic confrontation with surrounding languages. The vernacular form of Latin that had waxed eventually fragmented into regional dialects, and, to the shock of the European elite, classical Latin waned. The arguments at the time were acute and deeply sociolinguistic. *Lingua plebeia* or *lingua rustica* was an emerging (L) vernacular that disgusted writers such as Tertullian who considered it wholly unfit for publication. That variety now moved away from the (H) form of Latin of the Roman church. On the other side of the sociolinguistic argument, the scholar St Caesarius invoked even the sociocultural context of the Christian gospels, which, he noted, were fundamentally "conversational" (Furman 1949). He argued on behalf of the vernacular varieties of Latin, noting that "truth is better than grammar" (i.e. classical Latin) and that the speech of Christ and the fishermen was more real and meaningful than the urbane (classical Latin) usage of scholars and the ruling elite (Furman 1949: 132).

6.3 Fishman's expansion of diglossia

In an expanded diglossic observation, Fishman (1967) noticed the differential use of Spanish and Guarani in Paraguay, thereby extending "diglossia" to refer to unrelated languages that also operate in a diglossic relation in society (see Table 6.1, second row). In this expanded interpretation, "diglossia exists not only in multilingual societies which officially recognize several languages but, also, in societies which are multilingual in the sense that they employ separate dialects, registers or functionally differentiated language varieties of whatever kind" (Fishman 1968: 30). Fishman's description matched the description of language usage and preference among Mexican-American bilinguals in the 1940s (Barker 1975). In Tucson, Arizona, a local variety of Spanish was used in informal and intimate contexts, and English was used in formal situations because Spanish speakers had not, in fact, learned the formal standard Spanish appropriate to such circumstances. Barker noted that English was used for Mexican-mainstream American interactions.

6.3.1 Diglossia in rock 'n' roll and slums

Consider two further examples of diglossia in multilingual situations involving popular culture and neighborhood communities. They illustrate the complexity of diglossic relations which do not fit neatly into the classic H and L categories but which overlap, going back and forth, depending on the cultural context, social pressure, and even the personal selections of speakers at a particular time and place.

In a late-night basement in Helsinki, a German band comes off stage. The music is loud, sung in German and sometimes English, with some greetings in Finnish. It sounded macaronic. Jan, the lead singer, talks to the audience in American-accented English between songs. She knows that English penetrates every vernacular language in popular music. In a study of the impact of the high status "American accent" that characterized all postwar British pop music, Trudgill (1997) noted the seismic jolt that occurred when the Beatles chose to sing in British (aka Liverpool) English. The paradigm shift occurred somewhere along a street called Penny Lane. There is a folklinguistic view that English is somehow "well-suited" to pop music (Trudgill 1997). English is not a tonal language and possibly adapted well to melody composition with its simple prosody (compare French, with definitive stress on every first syllable, or Swedish with its information-bearing double stresses). More significant, however, is the simple fact of status. (American) English is the common language of world pop culture. The unmarked functional variety of the genre, therefore, is American English. This is an example of diglossia at the international level. Sometimes one language variety becomes a symbolic battleground in multilingual Europe with implications for language preference in particular and sociolinguistic status in general. In 2008, French lawmakers lodged an official complaint in the French Parliament when the song "Divine" representing France in the Eurovision Song Contest was delivered in English. Likewise, the Royal Spanish Academy criticized the Spanish singer Ruth Lorenzo for including English lyrics in her entry "Dancing in the Rain". In the above-mentioned Helsinki basement, the lyrics seemed to involve a lexico-grammatical trick – the insertion of English prosody, inflection and lexical mixing of English and German. In other words, the vocals sound like they are English even when they are in German.

Six thousand kilometers away in Mumbai, India, the day is starting in the Dharavi, the largest slum in Asia (population 700,000). Celebrated in Danny Boyle's 2008 film *Slumdog Millionaire*, this sprawling slum is where the potters speak Gujarati and the fishermen Koli Marathi, the Jains speak Punjabi and, irrespective of mother tongue background, the Muslims speak Urdu. The Kalakilla neighbourhood is dominated by Hindi speakers; Ayyappan is occupied by Malayalam speakers and in the Makadawalas Chawl, inhabitants speak a pidgin. Language is the key criterion for the formation of a *chawl* or residential unit (Rajyashree 1989; Sharma 2000). Each *chawl* is dominated by one language that, in turn, is linked to a particular industry or religion. Every *chawl* has its own name board signs – written in different scripts: the Devanagari script in the Marathi-speaking New Municipal Chawl, Tamil and Perso-Arabic in the Gulmuhammad Chawl. Such complex use of bilingual literacy in a multilingual situation means that language mixing is *de rigueur*. The celebrated novel *The Ground Beneath Her Feet* by Salman Rushdie (2000) is the backdrop for a discussion of the multilingualism of its characters who could "prattle on" in HUGME, "Bombay's garbage argot, *Mumbai ki kachrapati baat-cheet,* in which a sentence could begin in one language, swoop through a second and even a third and then swing back round to the first. Our acronymic name for it was Hug-me. Hindi Urdu Gujarati Marathi English" (2000: 43).

6.4 Diglossia, competing varieties/languages and language shift

Diglossia's hierarchical framework is important in explaining the phenomenon of language shift in multilingual society. First of all, there seem to be straightforward contradictions in the Fergusonian categories. It is a simple two-way formula: H and L. The formula looks more complex when we notice competing H varieties, as in Tunisia where French and Classical Arabic, or in Wales where Standard Welsh and Standard English, exist alongside in schools. There is a continuum between bilingualism and diglossia. A transition may occur from one to another as in Quebec in the 1960s where there was partial diglossia until the later shift to partial bilingualism.

The retention/loss of linguistic usage in a situation of language contact has two straightforward explanations, the first being demographic, the second involving diglossic relation. In many cases, the simple formula of "numerical superiority" in bilingual communities is crucial if the speakers of a minority language are to prevail. Thus, Saxon replaced French in bilingual England but was profoundly modified by it; i.e., French remained in the substratum. English established authority in Ireland relatively slowly. It was a minority language until 1850 but speeded up dramatically in the 19th century following the devastating economic policy of the British rulers leading to mass migration of the population. There were simply not enough speakers to maintain Irish

Gaelic as a living language. Nor could the language survive as an unmarked substratum in Irish English. The influence of Irish on English usage in Irish English in the lexico-grammar is well documented (Shimada 2010) but is a characteristic of the speech of mostly rural populations. Likewise, New York Dutch – though spoken in the city until the 19th century – had little impact on metropolitan English. Nor does Spanish today. This is despite the fact that Spanish speakers comprise roughly 10% of the New York population. The casual observer may conclude that as succeeding generations of Spanish speakers become monolingual English speakers, the future is unstable for a robust Spanish-speaking population in New York. This is a most telling factor in bilingual society. Indeed some linguists argue that numerical superiority is more powerful than diglossic prestige, i.e., the impact of the canonical H/L relation. Hughes (1966: 275) remarks thus: "The extent of influence of a substratum language, and its survival, are nearly directly proportional to the degree of its numerical superiority or inferiority, and that all historical and linguistic developments can be satisfactorily explained on this hypothesis, without the necessity of unduly considering linguistic 'prestige' or political relationships, or any other circumstances".

The second reason for replacement is specifically diglossic. Chaucer, in particular, gradually legitimized the literary use of Middle English. This created an apparent anomaly in a multilingual situation. That is, the L variety overtook the H variety. In this case, English superseded the dominant literary languages of French and Latin. More sophisticated and seemingly more permanent, these two languages gave way to *Lingua Anglica* and became Chaucer's magnum opus *The Canterbury Tales* (1386–1400). This is an example of diglossic "leakage"; i.e., one variety takes over the functions formerly held by another variety. This signals the breakdown of a stable or "broad" diglossia (in Fasold's terminology, 1990). What is the outcome of such leakage? It will be either a mixture of the two varieties (H and L) or replacement of one language by another. The logic of leakage implies that it will be preceded by widespread bilingualism. This is the case involving the shift from German to a relatively High French variety in the *Deutschsprachige Gemeinschaft Belgiens* (German-speaking community of Wallonia, Belgium). Both languages were commonly used indiscriminately (Verdoodt 1972) with German gradually giving way to the expansion of French in some localities. By contrast, elite, educated forms of French (i.e., a standardized variety) in bilingual Quebec are predicted to become less polycentric (i.e., Canadian vernacular standard) and increasingly more like that of France and influenced by English.

6.5 Language allocation: Style and literary works

The gulf between the lexico-grammars of standard languages and their social and regional dialects poses questions about the nature of language boundaries and our characterization of them. On the scale of style, we are aware that language usage is variable. There are stylistic scales (Newmark 1988) that inform the conditions of diglossic usage in a text. At one end are prestigious, socially acceptable forms of speech and writing. At the other are styles of lower status that might be socially unacceptable. Public communication is very conscious of the need to understand such distinctions. Consider the following examples, the first five of which are taken from art galleries (Bridgestone, Ueno, Metropolitan Tokyo, Tokyo Modern, Mori) in downtown Tokyo:

1. Officialese   Baby pushchairs are categorically prohibited inside the gallery. Your kind cooperation is requested.
2. Official   Baby pushchairs are prohibited in the gallery.
3. Formal   You are requested not to bring baby strollers into the gallery.
4. Neutral   Baby pushchairs are not allowed.
5. Informal   Please do not bring baby pushchairs in here.
6. Colloquial   Don't bring that pushchair in here.
7. Slang   Get the buggy out of here, ok?
8. Vulgar   Get that damn buggy outta here.

In multilingual society, languages and language varieties look at the world differently. It is precisely their social distribution and habitation in different domains and genre that is the source of the creative impulse in multilingual/bilingual society. Whether a poet and singer in the French-speaking Canadian province of Quebec writing in English like Leonard Cohen, or a leading figure in the Yiddish literary movement in America like Isaac Bashevis Singer, the impulse towards diglossia as a common tool of literary enrichment – of the text and of the feeling of a text – is very powerful.

Writers of creative literature are well aware how the diglossic impulse influences their work. There is the example of Glasgow English in the opening of Irvine Welsh's novel *Trainspotting* (1993), which runs, "The lager's loupin. Seems tae huv gone dead flat, ken. Tastes like fuckin pish". In Emily Brontë's *Wuthering Heights*, the first sentence runs, "Tmaister's dahn' fowld. Goa rahnd by th'end u' laith, if you went tuh spake tull him". Emily's sister, Charlotte, rewrote dialogue for publication in England's south. Thomas Hardy gives numerous instances of diglossia in his novel *Tess of the d'Urbervilles* (1892). Tess's mother uses the "Wessex" (Dorset) dialect. Tess is described as speaking "two languages": a dialect at home and ordinary English with "persons of quality". Many writers have been conscious of the fundamental implications of diglossia and the metalinguistic aspects of speech.

6.6 Diglossia with bilingualism in transition

Whereas diglossia is a comparative linguistic category, a matter of the opposition between formal and informal language varieties in a community, bilingualism is the interactive capacity of two (different) languages in that community. Diglossia raises fundamental questions about the nature of language boundaries in multilingual society. The language shift that accompanies diglossia occurs over time often gradually as a language moves into one functional domain and then another. Sallabank (2014) in her studies on Channel Islands French notes that even in the 20th century Guernésiais or Guernsey French was spoken by the majority of the population for all day-to-day purposes, in a diglossic relationship with Standard French as the 'High' partner. In the present-day, French is still used for administration but the common everyday language has shifted Guernésiais (Guernsey French) to dialectal Channel Island English.

Diglossia as known in multilingual society overlaps with how it operates in the exchange of many regional and social dialects. Chambers and Trudgill note in *Dialectology* (1998: 36) that "people who are known to be *bidialectal* [i.e., those with a facility for using two dialects of the same language] do actually control the two dialects, using one of them in special circumstances, such as when visiting a speaker with a similar 'home' background, and using the other for daily social and business affairs".

Consider the following example of bidialectal usage pressed into service for specific propaganda purposes. In 1941, as German bombs were falling on London (the Blitz) and English cities causing devastation, death, and rationing, the BBC (British Broadcasting Corporation) made a decision that shook the foundations of British society. As part of an anti-Nazi propaganda strategy, it employed a Yorkshire dialect speaker Wilfred Pickles to read the news. The BBC set aside the traditional "standard" RP (Received Pronunciation) that was associated with social elite and privilege. Purportedly, the shift to dialectal English was meant to render it confusing to German listeners, i.e., more difficult for the Nazis to learn and impersonate British speakers. The result was disbelief and outrage among some listeners that a variety (RP) associated with prestige and authority (a social class) should be removed from the media (and thus the body politic) in favor of a socially lower variety. It did not feel right and was not right. This is an example of diglossia for language planning.

As social relations change, language acts as a barometer of how we manage those relations. A language, therefore, is a churning sea, reflecting social hierarchy just as, in multilingual society, rival languages and language varieties test their functional strength. Languages displace each other – "language shift" – in large and small communities. Dominant varieties win friends and influence people. They expand their role repertoires as they come to symbolize group membership. Users of a dominant variety may pursue language enforcement in the jostling classification of languages and their relative significance according to national vs. official or unofficial vs. recognized minority. Some language varieties are considered more desirable than others. These varieties are codified with orthographies and grammars. Some have the powerful backing of agencies and academies and achieve state recognition. Other codification efforts fail and sometimes there is no clear reason why (Maher 2017). Sometimes society recognizes two or more languages "as its own" – each language or language variety having its own domain and purpose. Thus, the European elites of late modernism, whether in Warsaw or Moscow, spoke (Parisian) French just as elites before them in medieval Europe communicated in Latin or Provençal or Catalan or Danish. In the 21st century of today, English appears to have taken up its role as an international status symbol, a lingua franca that presents itself as a "high" preferred form for communication in popular culture or international politics or education.

6.7 Diglossia in multilingual Japan

What is clear from an analysis of diglossia is that a speech community has a variety of repertoires related to work and play and learning. Each repertoire in the speech community possesses different combinations of situations and interlocutors, situations and interactions. There are no fully separate languages. Multilingual society comprises a mixture of situationally and functionally defined varieties: "an assembly of social styles, the argot of social group and workplace, historical continuity and change, grammars and vocabularies, and regional accents" (Maher 2017: 1). Consider the following examples of diglossia in Japan – a sociolinguistic environment that has not at all been thought by linguists (Shibatani 1990) to involve any form of diglossia. In the pre-war era, the Ainu language had already shifted to Japanese in almost all social domains. Traces of Ainu *itak* (speech) appear in family names, religious ceremony, naming, songs and dances. We glimpse the arc of language displacement in a bilingual community where forms of speech function differently in different contexts. Ainu was culturally and legally marginalized from the Meiji Period (1870s) onwards and the transmutation from ethnicity to nationality meant that the Ainu language was abandoned in favor of the new national standard, Tokyo Japanese. This involved forced assimilation to the superposed Japanese with its undisputed hegemony in all social domains. Standard Japanese (*hyojungo*) in Hokkaido is high status – compared to say, Kansai dialect in the south. Inhabitants of the north are sometimes unaware that whilst they undoubtedly read and write in Standard Japanese, in fact they speak a distinctive mainland dialect (Tohoku). This encapsulates three key dimensions of language use: degrees of status (high and low) within the same language variety, language shift in multilingual society, and the functional distribution of two languages. The Ainu language situation in the northern lands has parallels with the language situation in the far south.

In a quiet street in the Okinawan capital Naha, a woman speaks to her child in Uchinaa-Yamatoguchi, the distinctive Okinawan variety of Japanese. Symbol of ambiguous loyalty in the Ryukyu islands, this form of speech is often mistaken for Standard Japanese because the grammatical structure is very similar to Standard Japanese. It is not the same. The Okinawan Japanese variety is influenced by Ryukyuan languages or *Shima kutuba*, "Island Speech", six indigenous languages that make up the Japonic language family. It is influenced, as well, by English – the result of postwar occupation by the United States. Whilst standard Japanese is a high status form employed in public administration, education and the media, Uchinaa-Yamatoguchi is used among family and friends, for intimate and informal social relations. It is a personal problem for some young speakers like the Ryukyuan activist Shinako Oyakawa involved in language revitalization: "In Naha I became ashamed of my Uchinaa-Yamatoguchi. I thought, 'oh, I have a dialect with an accent', and I was ashamed of that back then. Then I went to the University of the Ryukyus where there were a lot of students from mainland Japan. I tried even harder to speak Japanese in the Tokyo style there, but when I found out about language revitalization in Hawai'i, I started thinking about the value of the language in Okinawa. That was a big change for me" (Heinrich, Arakaki, and Oyakawa 2015: 324). Even more isolated in the Ryukyuan social structure are the Ryukyuan languages themselves. Japan's invasion of these southern islands began in the late 19th century. This resulted in the enforced assimilation to mainland Japan (*hondo*). Heinrich (2004) has charted the narrowing of Ryukyuan language varieties to restricted functions over time. The Ryukuan languages were prohibited in most official domains such as education and the civil service. The media launched Japanese-language literacy as the only medium of communication (*Ryukyu Shimpo* established in 1893, *Okinawa Shinbun* in

1905, *Okinawa Mainichi Shinbun* 1905). Constant borrowing from Japanese resulted in penetration of Standard Japanese phonology into these languages and a definitive shift to casual speech Ryukyuan following the loss of the Ryukyuan honorific language. Detached from several social domains, the bifurcation in the functional distribution of Ryukyuan and Japanese has resulted in the unmarked use of the former language by older speakers only in casual situations.

Spoken and written language is also a complex ecology. Up until Japan's postwar period and lasting over a period of several hundred years, Japan was in a state of diglossic bilingualism: a society that has two functionally separate language codes. One variety was a highly codified complex, superposed variety, the vehicle of written literature. In Japan, this has been the H, namely Chinese, variety. In another entirely different set of circumstances, an L variety operated through spoken language and was the language of ordinary conversation. Unlike Korean or even English, the development of a writing system for Japanese did not help to stabilize one particular variety of Japanese even though Japanese syntax was employed in the earliest poems written in *Man'yogana* in the *Kojiki* and *Nihon Shoki*. The reason for this is obvious. Literacy in *kanbun* or the imported Chinese style of writing was known by only a very small minority of the elite. The rapprochement between the classical Chinese-based written form and spoken Japanese began in the mid-20th century *genbun ichi* movement.

Commonalities of diglossia are apparent in many domains of language use in Japan. The so-called *genbun ichi* movement during the Meiji period attempted to excise Japanese archaic forms from the written Japanese so that a new literary genre could emerge that was closer to the spoken, i.e., ordinary speech. This older form encompassed privileged forms of Sino-Japanese writing. Now following the incoming flood of Western influence together with increased industrialization, urban culture and increasing literacy, written language could no longer support the older form of writing and called for a new literary form. The gap between the written (H) form of Japanese and that of the spoken form of language (L) became wider and, in fact, no longer sustainable.

In the religious domain, we see a contemporary example of the stylistic difference between the (written and recited) language of *o-kyo*, recitation of the Buddhist sutra, compared, radically, with say reading aloud an email at home. The lexis and grammar and entire sound systems of the two activities diverge so dramatically that, even though both employ features of what we usually speak of as a similar system, i.e., *Nihongo*, it would be an exaggeration to refer to them as "the same language".

6.8 Diglossia and identity

Diglossia poses fundamental questions about language identity in a multilingual society. Diglossia in multilingual society frequently occurs in a diasporic setting where radically different competencies occur – monolingual to bilingual – in the heritage setting. A speaker's linguistic repertoire is typically situated "somewhere" on a continuum of speech varieties. In the Dublin or Galway communities, acrolectal Polish – standard modern Polish – is situated in literacy practices, the media and "Saturday schools" whilst low prestige varieties from regional or rural areas comprise basilectal Polish spoken at home with friends and family members. Deep descriptions of "textbook" examples of diglossia – in fact cited by Ferguson (1959) – can turn complex. In Cyprus, vernacular (regional) Cypriot Greek is commonly characterized as the L variety and Standard Modern Greek as the H variety (Arvaniti 2006). In a similar context, Karatsareas (2016) has examined the phenomenon of "transplanting diglossia" when language varieties reposition themselves in London's Greek Cypriot community: the *parikia* ('community'). Karatsareas shows that when attitudinal symmetries between Standard Greek and Cypriot Greek are transplanted to the *parikia*, the former is viewed as prestigious, correct, intelligent, attractive, whilst conversely, Cypriot Greek enjoys covert prestige as sincere, friendly, and kind, a sign of solidarity, loyalty and membership, a symbol of the migrant struggle and hardship that occasioned the migration in the first place. Yet, negative prestige typically attaches to an L variety – a robust feature of diglossia, including in the case of the London Cypriot community: "In certain cases, the use of CypGr by heritage speakers is actively discouraged by the first generation not only in the public domain but also in private domains such as the home. Active discouragement targets both lexical and grammatical variants that are traditionally associated with basilectal varieties of CypGr, and heritage language features, especially the adoption of morphologically adapted loanwords from English" (Karatsareas 2016: 1).

Given the stratificational nature of diglossia symbolized by two levels H and L, diglossia almost always involves the politics of language choice. Such choice is also dependent upon the stability of languages in a multilingual environment: language use and preference at home, work, school, changes in social networks and attitudes. For example, Matsumoto has studied, longitudinally, the changing diglossic situation in Micronesia where, in postcolonial multilingual Palau, Japanese has been replaced by English as the H language while indigenous Palauan remains the L spoken language (Matsumoto 1999, 2001). Palauan diglossia evolved in a changing multilingual society as the Japanese language first became a local vernacular and then progressively weakened over time. Matsumoto examined language abilities in the three languages (Palauan, Japanese, English) across different age groups. She indicated that Palau is probably a "temporary multilingual" society which will likely shift to a "bilingual" society (Palauan and English) after the older Japanese speakers pass away. She thus summarizes the current situation: "given that the younger generation consisted of elite monolingual English speakers and ordinary English learners, who mostly use Palauan in daily life, the direction of change in the more distant future was uncertain, with two possible scenarios: (a) Palau may remain as a bilingual society with a clear social division with only minority elite Palauans speaking English and majority ordinary islanders sticking to Palauan; or (b) there might be a further step towards an English-speaking nation, abandoning their indigenous language" (Matsumoto 2018: abstract).

6.9 Conclusion

Multilingualism places us in transcultural space. It blurs the nature of language borders. It embraces mobility and a diversity of language acts: people chatting on the street corner, singing songs in different languages, reading newspapers, novels and poetry in one or another language.

The beginning of this chapter highlighted the various functional positions that language takes in society. A language or a language variety may accrue high social status (H) or lower social status (L). A language may be a standard form and a national symbol with official status (like Irish in Ireland). Thus, as we saw, Irish is *endoglossic* – a native local vernacular – compared to English, which was historically imported and imposed, and thus, *exoglossic*.

The dynamic movement of varieties of language with different kinds of social context and status means that language in society is, indeed, always "on the move". In contemporary multilingual society, "language" is viewed as essentially a dynamic and diverse phenomenon located within (potentially bilingual) individuals and within verbal interaction. This model contrasts with the *fin de siècle* Saussurian project that attempted to describe language as a stable linguistic structure, thus providing the rationale for linguistic investigation to become "a true science" (see a similar discussion in Chapter 2, this volume). Wide-ranging criticism of this approach (Bakhtin 1986; Bourdieu 1991) centered on the overemphasis on language as a static structure. Such abstract objectivism would lead to a view of language that "takes as its point of departure the finished monologic utterance" (Volosinov 1973: 76) in order to supply "the grounds for the reification of the linguistic form" (1973: 79).

Language in multilingual society, just like money and kinship, the organization of groups, religion and other "evolutionary universals" (Parsons 1964: 339) holds together our social system. It provides a sense of identity from past to present. Biblical Hebrew and Yiddish for many Jews comprise such continuity. Standard English and Caribbean Creole for Jamaicans combine the sociocultural system of both inside (e.g., Jamaica) and outside (the world of global English). Theories of social evolution rely heavily upon what is described as integration and differentiation. Written language, for instance, is a dramatic evolutionary step because literacy embodies what Coulmas (1992: 37) terms "the adaptive capacity of social systems by advancing differentiation and specialization". Both phenomena are essential to multilingual societies. We see it in the shared use of Chinese characters (kanji) in Japan, Korea and China, which is different from the spoken vernaculars. Integration permits shared knowledge in a society where several languages co-exist. Thus, the very presence of Chinese characters permits several languages (Mandarin, Wu, and Cantonese) to co-exist as one and to be available to many speakers in different situations. It is a "common language" existing only in the written system – and this remains a quintessential case of diglossia in multilingual society.

References

Arvaniti, Amalia. 2006. Linguistic practices in Cyprus and the emergence of Cypriot Standard Greek. *San Diego Linguistic Papers* 2. 1–24.
Bakhtin, Mikail, M. 191929/1984. *Problems of Dostoevsky's poetics*. Edited by Caryl Emerson. Minneapolis: University of Minnesota Press.
Bakhtin, Mikail, M. 1986. *Speech genres and other late essays*. Translated by Vern W. McGee. Austin: University of Texas Press.
Barker, George. 1975. *Social functions of language in a Mexican-American community*. Anthropological Papers of the University of Arizona, Monograph No. 22. University of Arizona.
Bourdieu, Pierre. 1991. *Language and symbolic power*. Cambridge: Harvard University Press.
Busch, Brigitta. 2014. Building on heteroglossia and heterogeneity: The experience of a multilingual classroom. In Adrian Blackledge & Angela Creese (eds.), *Heteroglossia as practice and pedagogy*, 21–40. Dordrecht: Springer Educational Linguistics.
Chambers, Jack & Peter Trudgill. 1998. *Dialectology*. Cambridge: Cambridge University Press.
Coulmas, Florian. 1992. *Language and the economy*. Cambridge: Blackwell.
Dante Alighieri. 1996. *De vulgari eloquentia*. Edited and translated by Steven Botterill. Cambridge: Cambridge University Press.
Fasold, Ralph W. 1990. *The sociolinguistics of language*. Cambridge: Blackwell.
Feghali, Michel. 1928. *Syntaxe des parlers arabes actuels du Liban*. Paris: Geuthner.
Ferguson, Charles A. 1959. Diglossia. *Word* 15. 325–340.

Fishman, Joshua. 1967. Bilingualism with and without diglossia; diglossia with and without bilingualism. *Journal of Social Issues* 23(2). 29–38.
Fishman, Joshua. 1968. *Readings in the sociology of language*. The Hague: Mouton.
Fishman, Joshua. 1971. *Advances in the sociology of language*. The Hague: Mouton.
Furman, Louis. 1949. Changing linguistic attitudes in the Merovingian period. *Word* 5. 131–134.
Gkaragkouni, Olga-Maria. 2009. The sociolinguistic phenomenon of modern Greek diglossia: The outcome of conflicts between (H)igh and (L)ow variety and the national language question in 19th–20th c. Greece, a historico-sociolinguistic perspective. *The ITB Journal* 10(1) Article 3. 27–49.
Gumperz, John. 1967. Some remarks on regional and social language differences in India. In Anwar S. Gil (ed.), *Language in social groups: Essays by John J. Gumperz*, 24–32. Palo Alto: Stanford University Press.
Heinrich, Patrick. 2004. Language planning and language ideology in the Ryūkyū islands. *Language Policy* 3(2). 101–104.
Heinrich, Patrick, Tomoko Arakaki and Shinako Oyakawa. 2015. It's not simply about language – it's about how we want to live. In Patrick Heinrich & Mark Anderson (eds.), *Language crisis in the Ryukyu*, 322–352. Newcastle: Cambridge Scholars Publishing.
Hughes, John P. 1966. The Irish language and the brogue: A study in substratum. *Word* 22 (1–3). 259–275.
Karatsareas, P. 2016 Transplanting diglossia: Attitudes towards standard and Cypriot Greek among London's Greek Cypriot community. In *Sociolinguistics Symposium* 21 *Abstracts*. Murcia, Spain.
Kloss, Heinz. 1967. Abstand languages and ausbau languages. *Anthropological Linguistics* 9(7). 29–41.
Lipinski, Edward.1997. *Semitic languages: Outline of a comparative grammar*. Leuven: Peeters Publishers.
Maher, John. 2017. *Multilingualism*. Oxford: Oxford University Press.
Marçais, William. 1902. *Le dialecte arabe parlé à Tlemcen*. Paris: Leroux.
Matsumoto, Kazuko. 1999. The politics of language choice amongst Palauan, English and Japanese: Symbolic domination in the Republic of Palau, Micronesia. *Proceedings of the 6th Conference of the International Association for World Englishes*. Nagoya: International Association for World Englishes. 91–95.
Matsumoto, Kazuko. 2001. Multilingualism in Palau: Language contact with Japanese and English. In Thomas. E. McAuley (ed.), *Language change in East Asia*, 84–142. London: Curzon Press.
Matsumoto, Kazuko. 2018. Changing views of bilingualism in the Pacific: A restudy of postcolonial multilingual Palau after two decades. Conference Presentation Abstract. Linguapax Asia, Tsukuba University.
Newmark, Peter. 1988. *A textbook of translation*. London: Prentice Hall.
Parsons, Talcott. 1964. Evolutionary universals. *American Sociological Review* 29(3). 64–79.
Putter, Ad. 2012. Code-switching in Langland, Chaucer and the Gawain poet: Diglossia and footing. In Herbert Schendl & Laura Wright (eds.), *Code-switching in early English*, 281–302. Berlin: Mouton de Gruyter.
Rajyashree K. S. 1989. Language for survival and work in the Bombay slum of Dharavi. In Hywel Coleman (ed.), *Working with language: A multidisciplinary consideration of language use in work contexts*. 56–71. Berlin: Mouton de Gruyter.

Romaine, Suzanne. 1994. *Bilingualism*. Cambridge: Blackwell.
Rushdie, Salman. 2000 *The ground beneath her feet*. London: Picador.
Sallabank, Julia. 2014. *Attitudes to endangered languages*. Cambridge: Cambridge University Press.
Sharma, Kalpana. 2000. *Rediscovering Dharavi: A story from Asia's largest slum* Harmondsworth: Penguin Books.
Shibatani, Masayoshi. 1990. *The languages of Japan*. Cambridge: Cambridge University Press.
Stewart, William A. 1968. A sociolinguistic typology for describing national multilingualism. In Joshua Fishman (ed.), *Readings in the sociology of language*, 74–89. Berlin: Mouton.
Shimada, Tamami. 2010. *English in Ireland: Beyond similarities*. Hiroshima: Keisuisha.
Trudgill, Peter. 1997. Acts of conflicting identity: The sociolinguistics of British pop-song pronunciation. *Word* 5(2). 131–134.
Verdoodt, Albert. 1972. The differential impact of immigrant French speakers on indigenous German speakers: A case study in the light of two theories. In Joshua Fishman (ed.), *Advances in the sociology of language*, 377–385. The Hague: Mouton.
Volosinov, Valentin. 1973. *Marxism and the philosophy of language*. Cambridge: Harvard University Press.

Anat Stavans and Ronit Porat
7 Codeswitching in Multilingual Communities

7.1 Codeswitching as a trademark of multilingual societies

The term "multilingualism" is widely used to refer to proficiency in more than two languages by an individual speaker or a society. For over half a century, bilingualism was seen simply as an alternative to monolingualism and its study covered any individual or collective language situation involving more than one language. Today, however, researchers distinguish multi- from bilingualism, claiming that just as bilinguals should not be perceived as the mere sum of two monolinguals (Grosjean 2001, 2010), multilinguals are not the sum of three, four or more monolinguals. Moreover, the literature distinguishes between people who become multilingual simultaneously or consecutively, a distinction with significant implications for our understanding of the phenomenon.

Multilingualism is a dynamic phenomenon, where languages are used for different purposes with different individuals (Gumperz 1982, see also Chapter 6, this volume). Multilingualism changes over time, depending on one's linguistic needs and opportunities (Stavans and Hoffmann 2015), the speakers' knowledge and awareness or cognitive mechanisms (Dewaele 2010), and social forces. Multilingual language choices are related to linguistic accommodations, such as changing aspects of language according to the speech style of the other speaker (De Houwer 1995, 2017) or due to political factors (minority-majority language relationships, ethnic interests, attitudes towards members of the multilingual society and other members outside the community).

A common phenomenon in multilingual language choices, *codeswitching,* refers to the alternate use of two or more languages in the same utterance or conversation (Auer 2005; Montanari 2009; Poplack 1980; Quay 2001; Stavans and Swisher 2006). It is not surprising that people take advantage of the unique ability to combine elements from the languages in their linguistic repertoire (Green and Li, 2014; Muysken 2013). Just like multilingualism, codeswitching is fast becoming the norm rather than the exception. Increased migration and globalization are creating more multilingual societies. More than half of the world's population is bilingual and less than a quarter of the world's population

---

Anat Stavans and Ronit Porat, Beit Berl College, Kfar Saba, Israel

https://doi.org/10.1515/9781501507984-007

is trilingual (Grosjean 2010: 13–16; see also De Bot 1992 and statistics in Europe by European Commission 2012). From a tender age, multilinguals develop awareness of different social situations and are more sensitive and responsive to the context of communication (Stavans 1990). Codeswitchers use the different forms of language to perform sociolinguistic functions, such as role-playing, reporting what others are saying, and affiliating with a speech community to create empathy and inclusion (Barnes 2006; Lanza 1997; Montanari 2009; Quay 2001). In what follows, we present different perspectives drawing on state-of-the-art work on what makes codeswitching a multilingual's trademark. We start with definitions and theories, patterns of codeswitching, and their discursive forms and functions in different personal and social situations.

7.2 Definitions and theories

7.2.1 Codeswitching as a language contact phenomenon

Codeswitching is defined as a communication strategy typically used by multilinguals, in which they alternate between languages, in the context of a single conversation. An altered speech item is called a *switch*, and it may occur within an utterance (*intrasentential* switching), or at the end of one and the beginning of the next utterance (*intersentential* switching) (Poplack 1980). The former is also called *classic* (Myers-Scotton 1993) or *alternational* codeswitching (Muysken 2000). Other language contact terms include codemixing, borrowing, or alternation.

Not all researchers use the same terms; in particular, codeswitching, borrowing and code mixing are used interchangeably. *Borrowing* occurs when a word or short expression in one language is inserted in another while maintaining the phonology, morphology, and syntax of the original language. *Codeswitching* also occurs when fluent speakers switch languages between or within sentences but preserve the phonological and other grammatical properties of each language. Similarly, *codemixing* refers to the transfer of linguistic elements from one language to another, without conforming to the phonetic or morphological conventions of the alternate language, with the code modification occurring in the same sentence (intrasententially). Today, researchers tend to use both codeswitching and codemixing interchangeably as they stress the functional aspect of the phenomenon and consider the "switching" as evidence of a verbal skill requiring greater competence in all language repertoires (Stavans and Hoffmann 2015).

The term codeswitching was coined by Haugen (1956), who distinguished between switching, codeswitching, and integration. Here, "switching" was used to refer to the alternate use of two languages by bilinguals, and "codeswitching" to a linguistic situation where bilinguals introduced a single unassimilated word from one language into another; the third term, "integration", referred to the overlapping of two languages.

Later scholars proposed different definitions, motivated by their analyses of various codeswitched utterances from a pragmatic or grammatical approach. An influential sociocultural-linguistic approach was developed by Gumperz (1982), who introduced the terms *situational* and *metaphorical switching* to explain how setting and participants, as well as topic, affected linguistic forms and concluded that in some social situations, particular languages or dialects may be more appropriate than others. The social-psychological approach represented by Myers-Scotton's markedness model (1983, 1993, 1998) stated that each language in multilingual societies is linked with particular social roles that issue both rights but also obligations by both society and individuals. According to the model, speakers use codeswitching in an exploratory way to establish social balance when community norms are unclear as to which language is unmarked. Adopting a sociocultural approach, Heller (1992, 2007) provided explanatory and interactional understandings of codeswitching in particular social and historical settings, rather than as models for linguistic capability. Heller's research in Quebec and Ontario coined the term "economics of bilingualism", referring to codeswitching as a political strategy whereby dominant groups rely on norms of language choice to preserve symbolic control, whereas inferior groups use codeswitching to resist or redefine their political status.

In a similar vein, Rampton (1995, 1998) used the term "crossing" to refer to "the use of a language which isn't generally thought to 'belong' to the speaker" (1998: 290), that is, a type of codeswitching practiced by speakers across boundaries of ethnicity, race, or language community. Crossing is designed to achieve complex functions in everyday conversation, including the dominant outgroup's use of prestigious minority codes; pejorative secondary foreigner talk (mocking use of a foreign accent to convey distance from a particular ethnic group); or as a mitigating discourse strategy (a way to ease tension by adopting a certain stereotyped accent). Much of the described definitions have led to theoretical and other explanatory models.

7.2.2 Explanatory models

Codeswitching has been studied through the complementary lenses of socio- and psycholinguistics (Genesee 1989; Genesee and Nicoladis 2007; Green and Li 2014; MacSwan 2014; Stavans 1990, 1992), in addition to the formal linguistic perspective (MacSwan 1999; Meisel 2001; Myers-Scotton 2002). The structural approach proposed in Myers-Scotton's (1993) Matrix Language Frame model (MLF) explains intrasentential or insertional codeswitching as involving a matrix language ("base" language) and an embedded language ("contributing" language), with switches of elements of the embedded language inserted into the dominant/matrix language according to the speaker's proficiency. If speakers are proficient in the matrix language (as in classical codeswitching) "the abstract grammatical structure within a clause will come only from one of the participating languages" (Myers-Scotton and Jake 2009: 337). On the other hand, if people do not have full control of abstract grammatical forms, other participating varieties will also contribute grammatical structure. That is, there is a unique CS structure that is not sensitive to specific lexical items of a contributing language but the contributing language has a significant consequence from the outset on the syntactic structure of the CS, in that the lexical item predisposes the structure of the CS but does not constrain it (MacSwan 1999).

In contrast to the formal linguistic perspective, which considers codeswitching a product of grammatical systems and not a practice of individual speakers, psycholinguistic theories focus on the cognitive mechanisms and knowledge structures underlying language production, comprehension, and acquisition. One is Herdina and Jessner's (2002) dynamic systems theory model of multilingualism, which describes a protracted, chaotic, and highly individual course of development that cannot be described adequately from an ideal grammatical and static point of view, as it depends on social, psycholinguistic and individual factors, as well as the different contexts in which language occurs (see Chapters 13 and 15, this volume). Accordingly, each of the multilingual's language systems is an open system influenced by interdependent psychological and social factors related to language maintenance, communicative needs, and language choice, where identical incidents of language transfer can lead to different multilingual productions by the same speaker. Similarly, De Bot (1992) argues that language can be seen as a dynamic system, with a set of variables that interact over time, and based on Levelt's (1989) model, this system constitutes a language node with a monitoring function. This function provides information about the state of activation of various languages and acts as a monitoring device between the intended language and the one currently used.

Grosjean (2001) developed the notion of language mode, which concerns the variability of multilingual speech situations. Depending on the mode, the speaker can choose how many languages to activate. Thus, a bilingual may move from a monolingual speech mode when talking to a fellow monolingual and using only one language to a bilingual mode when talking to another bilingual by means of switching and borrowing. The notion of speech modes also applies to trilinguals. The language mode depends on various factors, such as the speakers' language mixing habits, the usual mode of interaction, the presence of monolinguals, the degree of formality, and the speakers' socioeconomic status. Stavans (1990, 1992, 2005; Stavans and Hoffmann 2015) incorporated these elements in the following model:

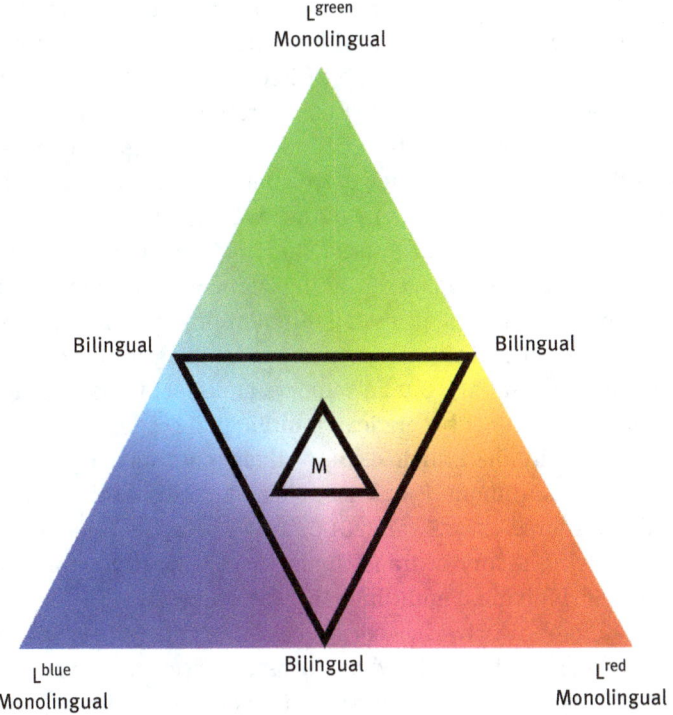

Figure 7.1: Stavans (2005) model of trilingual processing.

Maxwell's classical arrangement of colors within a triangle serves as an analogous illustration of the processing of multilingualism in general and the production of a codeswitch at the sentence or utterance level in particular. This multilingual processing originates at a monolingual point. A move along the sides of the larger triangle – the *B*ilingual area – results in a bilingual switch. A move along the sides of the inner *B*ilingual triangle results in a trilingual switch, creating the multilingual area shown in the smallest triangle. This illustrative diagram may be viewed as not only multi-layered but also specific for describing processing on the one hand and competence on the other. Processing is the distance and direction away from the monolingual vertex, whereas competence is the specific trajectory taken when the different linguistic elements are combined. The trajectory from vortex to vortex along the sides and the interior of the triangle, making a specific point in the three-dimensional triangle a possible location for a codeswitch to occur, is a result of not only sheer linguistic effects but it is also motivated and driven by communicative, social and cognitive characteristics that explain the specific loci in the triangle.

Stavans and Hoffmann (2015) extensively discuss language contact phenomena such as codeswitching in line also with sociocultural theories on codeswitching such as "translanguaging" models (Creese and Blackledge 2010; García and Li 2014), capturing the combined use of resources from different languages, with little regard for geopolitical boundaries of named languages. However, while until recently most language contact has been treated as code-switching of one kind or another, there is a need to clarify this novel perspective of translanguaging as another form of studying, understanding and interpreting language contact. García (2009: 140) explains: "Translanguaging is the act performed by bilinguals of accessing different linguistic features or various modes of what are described as autonomous languages, in order to maximize communicative potential". García's understanding of translanguaging is heavily grounded in the North American multilingual scene. Li's (2018: blog) perspective – driven by the British scene – states that translanguaging "defines language as a multilingual, multimodal, and multisensory sense- and meaning-making resource". MacSwan (2017) further proposes an alternative view of the underlying theory of translanguaging – a multilingual perspective – which accepts individual multilingualism as universal.

So, what is the difference between codeswitching and translanguaging? According to García and Lin (2016), code-switching assumes separate linguistic systems related to labeled languages as if dealing in its analysis with at least two monolingualisms. Translanguaging, on the other hand, assumes one integrated linguistic system where all " … languages are used in a dynamic and functionally integrated manner to organize and mediate mental processes in understanding, speaking, literacy, and, not least, learning" (Lewis, Jones, and Baker 2012: 1). Moreover, translanguaging is different from codeswitching not phenomenologically but theoretically in that codeswitching by and large takes a structural perspective on bilingual text or talk, whereas translanguaging focuses primarily on what speakers actually do and achieve by drawing on elements from their repertoires in situated contexts (Juffermans et al. 2014: 49). Thus both codeswitching and translanguaging wish to explain a uniquely multilingual phenomenon. However, the perspective taken is different in that codeswitching is structurally and systemically grounded in monolingual analytic paradigms of linguistic features of language systems.

Hence a new understanding of codeswitching has emerged and has taken on a more fine-tuned analysis and outlook in translanguaging. The notion of translanguaging is helpful in that it puts codeswitching firmly in its social context and emphasizes the creative abilities of multilinguals, especially creating space for multilingualism in educational contexts. Translanguaging research has indeed contributed to reconceptualizing language policy and practice in the multilingual classroom and specifically in problematizing conventional assumptions regarding language mixing in classroom settings. For instance, codeswitching is seen as instrumental in teaching and learning because it enhances learning; it welcomes multilingual children and families, and thus, it affirms the benefits of linguistic diversity – across and within communities and individuals.

However, we need bridges between linguistic, psycholinguistic and sociolinguistic analyses of codeswitching/translanguaging and a shared terminology if we are to make advances in understanding multilingual abilities (see Pavlenko 2017).

Moving outwards from the individual to the society, it is important to survey patterns of language use in different world communities in which languages are typically mixed, the social functions of such codeswitching and the social meanings it conveys, and the degree of language maintenance or language shift observed in such communities.

7.3 Patterns of language contact and their discursive functions in multilingual communities

Throughout history, the search for food, territory or trade has driven different people to settle in the same productive and accessible areas, which resulted in multilingual societies. Multilingual territories are also the result of military or religious expansions, the quest for higher education and professional opportunities overseas, and an increased recognition of minority rights and languages, all of which generate multilingual individuals and societies with new and evolving linguistic repertoires (see also the contributions in Part 1).

Usually, the statuses of specific languages and their speakers are far from balanced or equal. Motivated by nationalist or even racist ideologies, a language may be recognized as the sole official language (Spanish in Costa Rica) despite the extensive use of others. Alternatively, it may share that status with another language (English and Chinese in Hong Kong); it may be recognized as an official regional language (Basque in Spain and France); or it may be proscribed or discouraged by official sanction or restriction (Macedonian in Greece). A unique model that promotes multilingualism is provided by Singapore, where an internationalization ideology has led to adopting a non-indigenous language as the official language (English) next to three indigenous languages (Mandarin Chinese, Malay and Tamil) (see Chapter 3, this volume). This has boosted the use of codeswitching in social contexts as a communicative strategy, a device for elucidation and interpretation, and a means to establish solidarity and social bonding in multilingual discourse (Tay 1989).

Similarly, codeswitching occurs in Hong Kong, where besides the frequently studied codeswitching between Cantonese and English, trilingual codeswitching is emerging following the increasing contact with China after the decolonization and the new mainland policy of using Standard Chinese or Putonghua as the Medium of Instruction (PMI) in some primary schools (Chan 2018; see also Chapter 3, this volume). Conversely, in Dominica in the West Indies, a local, negative attitude to codeswitching is enforced where rural adults forbid children from speaking Patwa (a French-lexicon creole) in favor of acquiring English (the official language). They themselves, on the other hand, continue using Patwa for a variety of expressive functions and codeswitch regularly (Paugh 2005).

Multilingual societies provide opportunities for intense language contact causing speakers to combine languages used inside and outside the home environment. Generally, where multilingualism exists, speakers will develop cross-linguistic communication strategies such as codeswitching, which they will adopt in private as well as in public settings. The multiple discursive functions that codeswitching serves for multilingual individuals as well as societies are instrumental in establishing individual and communal identity, entitlements to rights and opportunities, fostering and enhancing multiliteracy, and promoting a country's economic and political status through multilingualism in cyberspace.

7.3.1 Codeswitching as a means to establish communal and individual identity

For bi- or trilinguals, it is normal to move between different languages, and they often fail to regard this faculty as an asset because they succumb to monolingual standards. This attitude is deeply rooted in social practices and particularly in language policies. Research shows differences between mono-, bi- and trilingual competence in flexible transition from a monolingual to a multilingual speech mode, often designed to establish identity and "belonging". Numerous studies outline trends and approaches in interpreting codeswitching as a means to create, maintain and shift individual and group identity so as to account for the reality of an "ongoing human production" where individuals have some agency to subjectively (re)create their reality" (Berger and Luckmann 1966: 192). When language(s) are concerned, switching codes can be a means through which speakers (re)construct aspects of their identities, adopting or highlighting different/partial roles that are not necessarily "dual" or contrasting as commonly believed (Auer 2005; Gumperz 1982).

The complexity of the linguistic practices of multilinguals is evident in today's postmodern societies (Giddens 1991), where speakers can negotiate/redefine their identities, or "crossover" to languages/varieties of other groups they do not ethnically belong to (Rampton 1995). The shift from the traditionally conceptualized interaction in a single language to a multilingual interaction as a norm rather than an exception acknowledges the diversity facilitated by globalization, the embracing of movement instead of stasis, and of borders instead of interiors as the underlying force behind codeswitching and identity. This outlook has motivated early research on codeswitching to focus on its systematic and rule-governed properties as a means of countering popular perceptions of bilingual speakers as cognitively deficient, if not socially belligerent. Identity, transformed through escalating contact set in motion by globalization and the transnational reconfiguration of media, migration, and markets has brought together not just languages, but also the subjectivities of the people who speak them in intensive interactions (Vu 2017). The metalinguistic awareness resulting from this intensification has been at the core of the sociocultural analysis of codeswitching.

Hall and Nilep (2015) describe four research traditions that suggest divergent theoretical perspectives on the relationship between language and identity. First, ethnography of communication in the 1960s and 70s situated codeswitching as a product of local speech community identities, in which speakers oscillated between ingroup and outgroup language varieties to establish conversational stances informed by the contrast of local vs. non-local relationships and settings. Second, language and political economy in the 1980s positioned codeswitching practices as the contrast in nation-state identities through processes of nationalism. Here codeswitching was dented by means of establishing sociolinguistic hierarchies through language standardization, often focusing on the language practices of minority speakers. Third, discursive foci in the 1990s challenged our understanding of language choice as controlled by preexisting indexical ties to identities where codeswitching was a resource of minority communities for establishing multicultural and interethnic identities. Finally, the formation of hybrid identities in this millennium focuses on codeswitching as a social byproduct of accelerated globalization. Hall and Nilep (2015) conclude that each perspective contributes to a holistic understanding of codeswitching as a social practice when languages come in contact frequently, especially through speech community identities and encounters with others which lead to the growth of local varieties and the construction of "we codes" and "they codes".

Hence, looking at codeswitching as symbolizing identities beyond the linguistic fact, Auer (2005) frames the sociolinguistic perspective on codeswitching as interaction-oriented research and the indexing of social identities in conversation. By doing this, he examines the kind of identity predicates that the alternating use of two languages can index in conversation and their relevance as an explanatory framework to multilingual pragmatics. Multilinguals do not claim co-membership simply because they speak more than one language, but rather that speaking a particular language entitles them to group membership and builds their identity (Gafaranga 2005). In some social contexts, language reflects ethno-social structures rather than creating them based on ancestry, culture, place of origin, race, etc. In this case, codeswitching within given semiotic constellations comes into play, with the ethnically "rich" language used in addition to/alternation with another language – usually the majority language – and functioning as the "seasoning" of the ethnic flavor on one's everyday language (i.e. the language of the majority, or of the receiving society in the case of immigration). Auer (2005: 409) concludes that every case of codeswitching must be viewed as a unique constellation where "[l]anguage alternation can be void of identity-relevant meaning in some contexts, and yet in others extremely rich in the identity-work it accomplishes [...] finding out for each and every case exactly what identity claims are occasioned by language alternation".

7.3.2 Codeswitching as a means of social inclusion: Recognition, rights and opportunities

Policies of social inclusion are usually conceived primarily based on economic mainstreaming considerations. As former World Bank President James Wolfensohn explains (Wolfensohn and Kircher 2005), employment is at the heart of social inclusion, but the path to individual and social wellbeing is paved not solely with employability, but also education, healthcare, and a decent standard of living, which together should lead to community participation and a sense of empowerment. Language stands at the core of this road to social inclusion and in our current context, so does multilingualism.

Multilingualism, language learning and social inclusion intersect because language mediates access to key social inclusion sites such as employment, education or health. They also intersect because the sense of belonging is negotiated through language and often tied to specific competencies, not in terms of language proficiency levels that mediate social inclusion or linguistic assimilation, but rather as the positive outcome of language practices propelled by language ideologies in particular contexts (Piller and Takahashi 2011). Therefore, language, and codeswitching in particular, should be seen as "a set of resources which circulate in unequal ways in social networks and discursive spaces, and whose meaning and value are socially constructed within the constraints of social organizational processes, under specific historical conditions" (Heller 2007: 2).

Globalization and transnational migration have made linguistic diversity a feature of many, if not all societies, and many countries are at least declaratively committed to furthering the social inclusion of the underprivileged (often seen as including most migrants). Piller (2010) claims that linguistically driven social exclusion originates from linguistic diversity, which is expected to be ironed out into linguistic assimilation before there could be social inclusion; and social exclusion is a result of a monolingual language bias towards linguistically diverse populations in need of linguistic recognition. Hence, social exclusion rather than inclusion has historical precedents. More recently, some areas in the world have become cognizant of the need and benefits of social inclusion, which they have displayed in a social agenda and public discourse that celebrate individual bi- and multilingualism and highlight the advantages of speakers of minority languages and of non-standard varieties.

Codeswitching plays an important role in social inclusion. Social legitimacy and acceptance of codeswitching requires linguistic and cultural recognition of language and linguistic traditions and of the rights to maintain, shift and use minority languages/varieties. Needless to say, codeswitchers vary in their intentionality and functionality, rather than their form, with age, socioeconomic capacity, educational background, and profession. For example, multilingual children as young as age 3;6 can use their multilingual awareness to express recognition of social inclusion, as did R (age 3;8 and trilingual in Hebrew, Russian and Spanish), who "bragged" about her multilingualism while demanding (in Hebrew) that her interlocutor stop addressing her in Spanish:

R: *Safta, tafsiki kvar ledaber besfaradit. Tedabri beiverit vezehu.*
Grandma, stop speaking in Spanish. Speak in Hebrew and that's it!
Grandmother: *R yo siempre te voy a hablar en español. Tu me puedes contestar en cualquier idioma, pero yo a tí y a tu hermano siempre les voy a hablar en español.*
R. Wliil always speak to you in Spanish. You can speak to me in any language but I will always speak to you and your brother in Spanish.
R: *Safta, at yodaat, ani yodaat ledaber basafa shel hagdolim.*
Grandma, do you know, I know (how to speak) the language of the grownups.

Grandmother:	¿De veras? A ver, ¿qué sabes decir?
	Really? Let's see, what can you say?
R:	Ani yodaat lehagid shalosh milim
	I know how to say three words
Grandmother:	A ver, ¿cuáles palabras sabes?
	Let's see which words you know?
R:	"Yes", "no", "goodbye"
Grandmother:	Aha, sí ese idioma se llama inglés.
	Oh, yes that language is called English.

For R, speaking to Grandma in and out of languages *is* the norm of communication, while at the same time she attempts not to negotiate the linguistic repertoire in which they normally engage in translanguaging and establishes social inclusion (at least in her mind) with English, "the language of the grownups".

It is unclear how and when the use of R's languages will filter into other areas of her life, especially as she grows, and these expand in terms of institutions, people, education and socialization needs. In the case of other children – first- or even second-generation immigrants who are schooled in one of their languages and who may have become bilingual or even trilingual through schooling – the situation may be very different. For them, language in the context of migration is not a one-time but rather an everyday experience, with social inclusion or exclusion hovering over every context of their lives (at home with different family members using heritage languages; at school with teachers, materials, and assessments that may exclude them, resulting in poor grades and leading to further exclusion from career opportunities; or in the playground as "immigrants" who are not "one of us"). For these children, codeswitching may not be an asset for inclusion but rather an obstacle that results in exclusion. For these children, both body and mind have migrated at a similar pace while for their parents, hearts and minds lag behind (Horenczyk 2008; Stavans 2015).

Social exclusion not rooted in the individual but rather in the monolingual bias of institutions against linguistically diverse populations has been studied and documented not only by sociolinguists, but also by human rights' movements and others. Of prevailing impact on multilingual diversity and recognition, rights and opportunities are studied in the context of education and early multilingual development (e.g., Stavans and Hoffmann 2015). Cromdal (2001a, 2001b) investigated the role of codeswitching in turn taking among bilingual kindergarteners (following Auer 1984, 1999; Gafaranga 1999; Li 1994). He showed that codeswitching and simultaneous talk were typical features of peer interaction, whereby the children diverged from the preceding language to dispute or oppose the actions of co-participants so as to take the conversational floor. Cromdal (2001b) states that when these overlaps occur as simultaneous speech, power relations between co-participants are reflected in conversational dominance characterized by explicit attempts of participants to continue the exchange without further overlap, to jointly coordinate turn-competitive moves, and to force one another to give up their turn at talk. These power struggles are resolved through the linguistic contrast created by codeswitching, which functions as a "turn security device" (Li 1994), bringing speakers to give up their turns (Auer 1984, 1995).

For nearly four decades, codeswitching has been documented in sociolinguistic, sociocultural, ethnolinguistic and socio-psychological linguistic studies as a unique multilingual practice or faculty facilitating social inclusion in terms of multilingual social recognition, entitlement to rights and equal opportunities across the lifespan and acceptability or accommodation by multilingual societies. Beyond the formal-structural linguistic studies of codeswitching and psycholinguistic studies on how, why, what and when codeswitches are used and construed, the sociolinguistic perspective of codeswitching has evolved from an analytic perspective of each separate language to the perspective of the codeswitcher's translingual repertoire. In that sense, the current perspective of codeswitching views it as a defining and empowering feature of multilinguals in different contexts and with different needs – a complex system with multiple strata of language-specific and language-universal patterns which is dynamic not only in individuals but also in society (De Bot, Lowie, and Verspoor 2007; Herdina and Jessner 2002; Jessner 2008). Individual multilinguals have changed monolingual societies, turning them into multilingual ones through codeswitching practices that have overtly or covertly propelled creativity (Kharkhurin and Li 2014), social inclusion, and recognition to different degrees in different regions. Nevertheless, codeswitching is still in the protracted process of gaining recognition in less multilingual regions of the world, and of attaining language rights and opportunities for multilinguals in schools, medical services, legal provisions, and economic opportunities.

7.3.3 Codeswitching as a means to foster and enhance multiliteracy

With the world becoming increasingly interconnected, multilingualism and diversity have turned into an everyday experience. Literacy and communicative skills are changing, as communication across real or virtual geographic boundaries generates a more transnational multilingualism, calling for multilingual education systems, in which multilingualism is no longer perceived as a deficit but as an asset (Baker 2002).

In today's world, literacy is seen more as a social practice than as a set of individual skills. According to this approach, literacy is what people do, not what they learn: "Literacy is not simply knowing how to read and write a particular script, but applying this knowledge for specific purposes in specific contexts of use" (Scribner and Cole 1981: 236). Literacy is part of a broader set of "communicative practices", which includes oral, written and visual communication; building on this, a new pedagogical approach developed in 1994 by the New London Group coined the term *multiliteracies*, a notion based on the assumption that individuals "read" the world and understand information by means other than traditional reading and writing. This multiliteracy includes different channels or modalities, such as linguistic, visual, audio, spatial, and gestural ways for creating meaning. At the core of the concept of multiliteracies is the belief that classroom instruction should be more inclusive of cultural, linguistic, communicative, and technological diversity, so that students will be able to construct knowledge from multiple sources and modes of representation and be better prepared for a successful life in a globalized world (Seel 2012). Today, more than ever, the presence of multilingual literacy practices has filtered into many walks of life, such as call centers, language specific answering services, institutional signs (Figure 7.2), commercial signs (Figure 7.3), mixed notational signs (Figure 7.4), and texts such as "em😉jis".

Literacy is described as "a dynamic, socially situated process that in contemporary contexts is often multimodal, multilingual and highly intertextual" (Duff 2010: 169). It also plays a key role in the development and preservation of culture and knowledge. In this dynamic process, policymakers are increasingly recognizing the need for educational systems that foster multilingualism and multiliteracy, not only for multilinguals but also for monolinguals

Figure 7.2: Multilingual plaque at the entrance to the offices of the Ministries of Interior and Immigrant Absorption in Rehovot, Israel, 2011 (Photo by Anat Stavans).

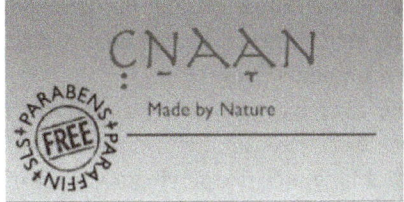

Figure 7.3: Israeli product label. Permission granted by CNAAN – Made by Nature. Note the Hebrew diacritical marks under the English capital letters CNAAN (Photo by Anat Stavans).

Figure 7.4: Sticker on the back window of car. Note the Hebrew diacritical marks under and inside the English capital letters CAPARA (Photo by Anat Stavans).

(Hélot and Ó Laoire 2011). Multilingual education typically refers to a "first language first" approach, that is, schooling which is conducted in the mother tongue and later adds other languages. On the other hand, there are multilingual classrooms that present ample and creative opportunities (not always successfully used by teachers) for effective language learning and intercultural awareness. In this dynamic setting, different linguistic resources are used by monolinguals or multilinguals to simplify communication with fellow students or teachers. Codeswitching is one of the commonly used linguistic strategies.

During the 1980s, much attention has been devoted to the study of codeswitching as a specific strategy used by foreign language teachers. This phenomenon has been the center of an ongoing debate, whether shifting between the target language (TL) and the native language (L1) during a foreign language lesson fosters or hampers language learning (Jingxia 2010; Shay 2015). Some scholars (Chaudron 1988; Lightbown 2001) argued that instruction should only be done in the target language, focusing on creating a pure foreign language setting as the exclusive linguistic model for students. Others (Levine 2003) supported codeswitching in foreign language classes, arguing that L1 can actually promote the learning of TL and serve as an effective strategy in TL instruction. In reality, however, teachers tend to codeswitch: in some cases, this is intentional and in others, it is regarded as automatic and unconscious behavior. Conscious or not, codeswitching has some basic functions which may be beneficial in language learning environments.

Flyman-Mattsson and Burenhult (1999: 25) suggest that "teachers switch code whether in teacher-led classroom discourse or in teacher-student interaction . . . . [this] may be a sophisticated language use serving a variety of pedagogical purposes". They list different functions for teachers' codeswitches: a *topic switch* function (the teacher changes language according to the topic discussed, typically observed in grammar lessons, shifting to the students' native tongue to clarify meaning and new content); an *affective* function (shifting to express emotions and create solidarity and intimacy with the students by forming a supportive language environment); and a *repetitive* function (clarify and repeat the knowledge taught in TL). Codeswitching may also encourage some negative student behavior; however, this occurs mainly when the teacher tends to repeat knowledge in L1, causing loss of interest among students who also become dependent on the explanation/translation in L1, eventually limiting their exposure to TL discourse (Tiemer 2000).

Although students are not always aware of its social and educational advantages, codeswitching has numerous beneficial functions. Eldridge (1996) lists four: *equivalence* (the student makes use of the L1 equivalent of a certain lexical item in TL allowing for the flow of communication); *floor holding* (in conversations in the TL, completely shifting to the L1 prevents a communication gap); *reiteration* (to emphasize or clarify a message in TL); and *conflict control* (avoiding a misunderstanding, especially when there is a culturally equivalent lexical or pragmatic gap between TL and L1).

The different functions of codeswitching for both teachers and students demonstrate how codeswitching is instrumental in both instruction and learning. As mentioned earlier, codeswitching may also be viewed as an example of translanguaging (MacSwan 2017). Accordingly, by shifting between languages, multilingual students are able to draw from their entire language repertoire. For example, Shlomit, a 5-year-old born in Israel to Ethiopian immigrant parents, "wrote" a letter to her teacher after her absence from class due to illness (Figure 7.5). Below is the letter written by Shlomit, which was given to the first author by her Kindergarten teacher in 2004.

When the teacher asked Shlomit to "read" her letter, she pointed at the pencil scribbles in black and read: *ani ohevet otax meod* ("I love you very much"). Then she read her name below. When the teacher asked her why she used a pencil for the letter and a yellow marker for her signature, Shlomit explained that the letter was written in Amharic (non-canonic but shape-like writing of Amharic script) but her name was in Hebrew. Here Shlomit relied on her

Figure 7.5: Shlomit's letter (given to Anat Stavans).

language repertoire to produce a preliterate form of writing and coding a message.

In an ever growing and dynamic multilingual setting, codeswitching and multiliteracy in general should be seen as an asset promoting communication, cognition and economic growth – a strategy that enables multilinguals to use all their linguistic resources to get their meaning effectively across. From the teachers' perspective, codeswitching should be viewed as a useful tool applicable in specific situations. From the students' point of view, it should be understood as a tool for cognitive development used to achieve specific communicative goals. Thus, codeswitching should not be seen as a sign of cognitive confusion, but rather as an indicator of multilingual competence.

7.3.4 Codeswitching in cyberspace

Digital communications of all kinds are still mostly textual (Coulmas 2003). The emergence, growth and spread of paralinguistic symbols to express ideas and emotions have produced ubiquitous expressions such as the acronym OMG for "Oh my God", the letter-number combination F2F for "face-to-face", or conventional symbols or numbers as substitutes for words, such as @ for "at". This trend introduces literacy as both a context-driven situated action and a socially accepted practice that involves "ways with words" (Gee 2001: 2). When writing and speaking are mediated by digital technologies, they become even more complex because they are scattered across time and space (e.g., via mails); they become essentially "language-less" (such as emoticons or emojis); and the rules governing them have evolved to generate alternative literacy practices (see also Chapter 11, this volume, for a discussion of digitally-mediated family language practices).

The use of emojis provides intriguing conceptualizations for multilingual capabilities such as codeswitching. Emojis, which visually encode emotions that in a language-grounded notation would be represented in writing, require mappings of concept to print that may involve different languages and their writing systems for a multilingual individual. These translations of ideas into a "language-less" notation system may create alternations unique to multilinguals, especially in informal, intimate writing with a multilingual cohort. Therefore, multilingual productions demonstrate different capacities than those of monolinguals when it comes to writing and other skills, and more so when a "language-less" notation system such as emojis is used to express ideas which may exist in one language and not in the other, or exist in two or three languages with slightly different connotation, usage or structural collocation. When using technologically mediated communications, multilinguals can construct a text combining the writing system (s): (a) of all languages; (b) of one language with the phonetically transcribed words of others; (c) of one language with digital symbols of the same or another (e.g. see you @ school; see you 2morrow in the Aמכללה [college]). They can also use emojis with mixed writing forms (e.g., I ♥ NY; or I ♥ the big ♥). In this sense, the written language produced by multilinguals generates affordances that are not only grounded in the written form of a specific language but also add technology-based options (Li and Storch 2017).

This is exemplified in the experiences of emergent multilinguals, especially when children have access to writing systems and to various literacy activities in both their languages. Research on emergent literacy in multilinguals has shown that these children are more likely to become biliterate rather than literate only in the dominant language: "Children alternate between the languages they use to speak, write, and listen; and they constantly code-switch throughout all their activities" (Reyes 2006: 289). The challenges of an emergent multiliterate child are that (1) languages are also represented by writing systems constituting scripts and specific orthographic information; (2) they must master different systems often consisting of different symbols; and (3) the construal of the written representation of words is represented by arbitrary symbols in different sign sequences (Hall, Cheng, and Carlson 2006; Stavans 2015). Being a language-less visual notation, emojis bring to this type of language encoding an additional layer, one that may enhance or hamper communication.

To conclude, technology-based communication has developed a "Super Text and a Meta-Language" combining "the written, oral and audio-visual modalities of human communication" into a single system that allows for open and affordable interactions in real or deferred time through the global network (Castells 1996: 328). Moreover, Castells (2000: 356–357) addresses the relation between culture and communication claiming that "culture is mediated and enacted through communication [....] cultures themselves [...] become fundamentally transformed, and will be more so over time, by the new technological system". Consequently, the encoding of ideas through language and their expression in different writing systems mean that technological development and cyber-literacy are symbiotic in that technology shapes but is also shaped by literacy practices. This symbiosis has resulted in a widespread system of notational symbols and para-lingual expressions of human emotions – such as emojis – that words fail to express in full. While this is true in monolingual communication as well, for multilinguals this adds new levels of written language complexities (having more than one language to code in writing and sometimes in different writing systems), bridging cultural and linguistic repertoires.

7.3.5 Pride and prejudice: The social meaning of codeswitches

Jane Austen's *Pride and Prejudice* explores themes of prejudice, reputation, and class. These themes from two centuries ago still prevail. The equation that prejudice in multilingualism equals pride in monolingualism and vice versa has been discussed throughout this chapter in many different ways, particularly with regard to codeswitching. The role of language as a means of communication and social interaction, a medium of education, and a vehicle for cultural expression is uncontested. For nation states, language is often regarded as a coinage of nationality, defining an ingroup and an outgroup. For the individual, countless studies have discussed how multilinguals' languages are affected by individual internal (pride) factors of identity, ethnicity, culture, migration, and livelihood. All of these affect and are affected by the external forces operating on the multilingual. Moreover, those individual internal factors may change over the lifespan when new and inevitable societal factors (pride by the majority groups, prejudice towards the minority groups) such as welfare, rights, health, education, litigation and other institutional and political forces are exerted on the multilingual individual.

The bridge between the individual and societal level is often dependent and navigated by family language policy (FLP), where explicit planning of language use among family members (King, Fogle, and Logan-Terry 2008) may provide a fertile ground for codeswitching. FLP is dynamic within a family, across time, within a geographic area, in different socioeconomic conditions, and with developing education and technologies. Evidence of FLP diversity has been documented in contrasting ideologies and management strategies influenced by different transnational experiences, competences and worldviews (Kirsch and Gogonas 2018) or a discrepancy between parents' declared commitment to L1 maintenance and their reports on actual language practice with their children (Schwartz 2008; see also Chapter 10, this volume). Such discrepancy results in different linguistic repertoires and practices that violate the maintenance or the purity of the minority/heritage language at home and often result in a shift to the majority language or in intensified intra- and intersentential codeswitching – lending further support to the claim that no FLP is resistant to the isolation of the languages (see Chapter 11, this volume, for a further discussion of this issue). Within this tension, codeswitches take on different forms for different purposes to orchestrate multilinguals' linguistic repertoire and their translanguaging.

Under these conditions, the multilingual individual must attend to three issues ingrained in the handling of linguistic pride (by the individual and its family) and linguistic prejudice (by the majority language community) with regard to the deployment of codeswitching. The first issue concerns the place and degree of language maintenance or shift in multilingual situations where codeswitching occurs. The second issue pertains to the need or wish to preserve the heritage language and culture through codeswitching. And the third issue attends to bridging the home and outside language through a family language policy.

7.4 Summary and future research

Multilingualism has always been a part of both modern and ancient traditional societies. While the social path to multilingualism has evolved into many different new societies, communities and families (following a new, global mobility that goes beyond "elite" mobility, i.e., refugees, work-migrants, ideological migration, or historical mixed language-culture population), language contact has always been a central feature. Codeswitching is the most typical linguistic phenomenon unique to multilinguals. In addition to their ability to produce and comprehend various linguistic systems, multilinguals can combine these systems in a systematic, consistent and non-random manner. The multiple definitions and interpretations of codeswitching reflect a complex multilingual competence. In this regard, more research is needed where new trends and understanding of the complexity of codeswitching consider typologically divergent languages in contact. This complexity also depends on whether multilingualism develops later in life when language acquisition has already been experienced. For these individuals, the process is substantially different compared to individuals who are multilingual from birth, and for whom two or three languages are "the" first language.

We have argued that the difference between types of multilingual competence is more than merely quantitative. There is greater complexity with the presence of three as opposed to two linguistic systems. Unlike monolinguals, multilinguals have more specific distributions of functions and uses for each of their languages than in monolingual settings. Multilinguals, even the very young, are particularly sensitive to the context of communication and responsive to the needs of their interlocutors. Therefore, the complexity of multilingual processing, competence and use as manifested in a single individual must be studied in a broader framework.

Multilingualism and codeswitching can be viewed metaphorically as the linguistic and cultural capital of an individual, community, society or nation. Languages are the currency that builds this capital – they construct the economics of communication, identity, individuals and societies. Like monetary currencies, some of them may be more or less instrumental than others in different times and places, more or less universally used. Likewise, languages can be invested in the different currencies: one may choose to invest more in a currency/language because the "interest rates" of that language may be higher in a particular context. That is why we might invest more in learning, using or expanding one or more of the currencies (languages) as opposed to the other(s). Finally, languages can be exchanged and used in tandem, and the more currencies (languages) one has as personal or sociocultural capital, the higher the "dividends". Codeswitches can offer the highest dividends in a multilingual capital economy. Unlike the past, globalization and technology have been a compelling and propelling force that enables the multilingual broker to trade profitably in the different languages in the individual and societal repertoire.

Notwithstanding, there is much more to be done in terms of research and understanding of language contact phenomena as the trademark of multilinguals from the linguistic, sociological, psychological and educational perspectives. Among the unattended issues in the research on language contact such as codeswitching, there is dire need to develop paradigms that analyze and theorize the phenomena through a multilingual lens rather than a monolingual one, especially in studies concerning multilingual processing and educational multilingualism. From a sociolinguistic perspective, a broader spread of multilingual phenomena beyond Western cultures, or the English-based multilingual world, and with languages in different modalities would not only inform us linguistically but would also enable us to ask new questions about the human capacity for multilingualism.

References

Auer, Peter. 1984. *Bilingual conversation*. Amsterdam: John Benjamins.
Auer, Peter. 1995. The pragmatics of code-switching: A sequential approach. In Lesley Milroy & Pieter Muysken (eds.), *One speaker, two languages: Cross-disciplinary perspectives on code-switching*, 115–135. Cambridge: Cambridge University Press.
Auer, Peter. 1999. From codeswitching via language mixing to fused lects: Toward a dynamic typology of bilingual speech. *International Journal of Bilingualism* 3. 309–332.
Auer, Peter. 2005. A postscript: Code-switching and social identity. *Journal of Pragmatics* 37(3). 403–410.
Baker, Colin. 2002. Bilingual education. In Robert B. Kaplan (ed.), *The Oxford handbook of applied linguistics*, 229–244. Oxford: Oxford University Press.
Barnes, Julia D. 2006. *Early trilingualism: A focus on questions*. Clevedon, UK: Multilingual Matters.
Berger, Peter. L. & Thomas Luckmann. 1966. *The social construction of reality: A treatise in the sociology of knowledge*. Garden City, NY: Anchor Books.
Castells, Manuel. 1996. *The rise of the network society* (The Information Age: Economy, Society and Culture, Volume 1). Oxford, U.K.: Blackwell.
Castells, Manuel. 2000. *The rise of the network society*, 2nd edn. Oxford, U.K.: Blackwell.
Chan, Ka Long Roy. 2018. Being a 'purist' in trilingual Hong Kong: Code-switching among Cantonese, English and Putonghua. *Linguistic Research* 35(1). 75–95.
Chaudron, Craig. 1988. *Second language classroom research on teaching and learning*. New York: Cambridge University Press.
Coulmas, Florian. 2003. *Writing systems: An introduction to their linguistic analysis*. Cambridge: Cambridge University Press.
Creese, Angela & Adrian Blackledge. 2010. Translanguaging in the bilingual classroom: A pedagogy for learning and teaching? *The Modern Language Journal* 94(1). 103–115.
Cromdal, Jakob. 2001a. Can I be with? Negotiating play entry in a bilingual school. *Journal of Pragmatics* 33(4). 515–543.
Cromdal, Jakob. 2001b. Overlap in bilingual play: Some implications of code-switching for overlap resolution. *Research on Language and Social Interaction* 34(4). 421–451.
De Bot, Kees. 1992. A bilingual production model: Levelt's 'speaking' model adapted. *Applied Linguistics* 13(1). 1–24.
De Bot, Kees, Wander Lowie & Marjolijn Verspoor. 2007. A dynamic systems theory approach to second language acquisition. *Bilingualism: Language and Cognition* 10(1). 7–21.
De Houwer, Annick. 1995. Bilingual language acquisition. In Paul Fletcher & Brian MacWhinney (eds.), *The handbook of child language*, 219–250. Oxford: Blackwell.
De Houwer, Annick. 2017. Early multilingualism and language awareness. In Jasone Cenoz, Durk Gorter & Stephen May (eds.), *Encyclopedia of language and education: Language awareness and multilingualism*, 83–97. New York: Springer.
Dewaele, Jean Marc. 2010. Multilingualism and affordances: Variation in self-perceived communicative competence and communicative anxiety in French L1, L2, L3 and L4. *IRAL: International Review of Applied Linguistics in Language Teaching* 48(2–3). 105–129.
Duff, Patricia A. 2010. Language socialization into academic discourse communities. *Annual Review of Applied Linguistics* 30. 169–192.

Eldridge, John. 1996. Code-switching in a Turkish secondary school. *ELT Journal* 50(4). 303–311.
European Commission. 2012. *Special Eurobarometer 386: Europeans and their languages report*. https://data.europa.eu/euodp/data/dataset/S1049_77_1_EBS386 (accessed 10 October 2018).
Flyman-Mattsson, Anna, & Niclas Burenhult. 1999. Code-switching in second language teaching of French. *Lund University, Dept. of Linguistics Working Papers* 47. 59–72.
Gafaranga, Joseph. 1999. Language choice as a significant aspect of talk organisation: The orderliness of language alternation. *Text* 19. 201–225.
Gafaranga, Joseph. 2005. Demythologising language alternation studies: Conversational structure vs. social structure in bilingual interaction. *Journal of Pragmatics* 37(3). 281–300.
García, Ofelia. 2009. Education, multilingualism and translanguaging in the 21st century. In Tove Skutnabb-Kangas, Robert Phillipson & Ajit K. Mohanty (eds.), *Social justice through multilingual education*, 140–158. Bristol: Multilingual Matters.
García, Ofelia & Wei Li. 2014. Translanguaging and education. In Ofelia García & Wei Li (eds.), *Translanguaging: Language, bilingualism and education*, 63–77. London: Palgrave Macmillan.
García, Ofelia & Angel M.Y. Lin. 2016. Translanguaging in bilingual education. In Ofelia García, Angel M.Y. Lin & Stephen May (eds.), *Bilingual and multilingual education*, 3rd edn., 1–14. New York: Springer.
Gee, James Paul. 2001. Reading as situated language: A sociocognitive perspective. *Journal of Adolescent & Adult Literacy* 44. 714–725.
Genesee, Fred. 1989. Early bilingual development: One language or two? *Journal of Child Language* 16. 161–179.
Genesee, Fred & Elena Nicoladis. 2007. Bilingual acquisition. In Erika Hoff & Marilyn Shatz (eds.), *Blackwell handbook of language development*, 324–342. Oxford: Blackwell.
Giddens, Anthony. 1991. *Modernity and self-identity: Self and society in the late modern age*. Stanford: Stanford University Press.
Green, David W. & Wei Li. 2014. A control process model of code-switching. *Language, Cognition and Neuroscience* 29(4). 499–511.
Grosjean, François. 2001. The bilingual's language modes. In Janet L. Nicol (ed.), *Explaining linguistics: One mind, two languages: Bilingual language processing*, 1–22. Malden: Blackwell.
Grosjean, François. 2010. *Bilingual: Life and reality*. Cambridge: Harvard University Press.
Gumperz, John. 1982. *Discourse strategies*. Cambridge: Cambridge University Press.
Hall, Joan Kelly, An Cheng & Matthew T. Carlson. 2006. Reconceptualizing multicompetence as a theory of language knowledge. *Applied Linguistics* 27(2). 220–240.
Hall, Kira & Chad Nilep. 2015. Code switching, identity, and globalization. In Deborah Tannen, Heidi E. Hamilton & Deborah Schiffrin (eds.), *The handbook of discourse analysis*, 597–619. Chichester, UK: Blackwell.
Haugen, Einar. 1956. *Bilingualism in the Americas: A bibliography and research guide*. Tuscaloosa, AL: University of Alabama Press.
Heller, Monica. 1992. The politics of codeswitching and language choice. *Journal of Multilingual & Multicultural Development* 13(1–2). 123–142.
Heller, Monica (ed.). 2007. *Bilingualism: A social approach*. Berlin: Springer.

Hélot, Christine & Muiris Ó Laoire. 2011. *Language policy for the multilingual classroom: Pedagogy of the impossible*. Clevedon, UK: Multilingual Matters.
Herdina, Philip & Ulrike Jessner. 2002. *A dynamic model of multilingualism: Perspectives of change in psycholinguistics*. Clevedon, UK: Multilingual Matters.
Horenczyk, Gabriel. 2008. Cultural identities, perceived discrimination, and adaptation: Immigrant adolescents in Israel. In Anat Stavans & Irit Kupferberg (eds.), *Studies in language and language education: Essays in honor of Elite Olshtain*, 395–411. Jerusalem: Magnes Press.
Jessner, Ulrike. 2008. A DST model of multilingualism and the role of metalinguistic awareness. *The Modern Language Journal* 92(2). 270–283.
Jingxia, Liu. 2010. Teachers' code-switching to the L1 in the EFL classroom. *The Open Applied Linguistics Journal* 3. 10–23.
Juffermans, Kasper, Jan Blommaert, Sjaak Kroon & Jinling Li. 2014. Dutch-Chinese repertoires and language ausbau in superdiversity: A view from digital media. *Discourse, Context, and Media* 4–5. 48–61.
Kharkhurin, Anatoliy & Wei Li. 2014. The role of code-switching in bilingual creativity. *International Journal of Bilingual Education and Bilingualism* 18(2). 1–17.
King, Kendall A., Lyn Fogle & Aubrey Logan-Terry. 2008. Family language policy. *Language and Linguistics Compass* 2(5). 907–922.
Kirsch, Claudine & Nikos Gogonas. 2018. Transnational experiences, language competences and worldviews: Contrasting language policies in two recently migrated Greek families in Luxembourg. *Multilingua* 37(2). 153–175.
Lanza, Elizabeth. 1997. Language contact in bilingual two-year-olds and code-switching: Language encounters of a different kind? *International Journal of Bilingualism* 1(2). 135–162.
Levelt, Willem J. M. 1989. *Speaking*. Cambridge, MA: MIT Press.
Levine, Glenn S. 2003. Student and instructor beliefs and attitudes about target language use, first language use, and anxiety: Report of a questionnaire study. *The Modern Language Journal* 87(3). 343–364.
Lewis, Gwyn, Bryn Jones & Colin Baker. 2012. Translanguaging: Developing its conceptualisation and contextualisation. *Educational Research and Evaluation* 18(7). 655–670.
Li, Mimi & Neomy Storch. 2017. Second language writing in the age of CMC: Affordances, multimodality, and collaboration. *Journal of Second Language Writing* 36. 1–5.
Li, Wei. 1994. *Three generations, two languages, one family: Language choice and language shift in a Chinese community in Britain*. Clevedon, UK: Multilingual Matters.
Li, Wei. 2018. Translanguaging and code-switching: What's the difference? *Oxford University Press Blog*. https://blog.oup.com/2018/05/translanguaging-code-switching-difference/ (accessed 14 August 2018).
Lightbown, Patsy. M. 2001. Input filters in second language acquisition. *EUROSLA Yearbook* 1(1). 79–97.
MacSwan, Jeff. 1999. *A minimalist approach to intrasentential code switching*. London: Routledge.
MacSwan, Jeff. 2014. *Grammatical theory and bilingual codeswitching*. Cambridge, MA: MIT Press.
MacSwan, Jeff. 2017. A multilingual perspective on translanguaging. *American Educational Research Journal* 54(1). 167–201.

Meisel, Jürgen M. 2001. The simultaneous acquisition of two first languages. In Jasone Cenoz & Fred Genesee (eds.), *Trends in bilingual acquisition*, 11–41. Amsterdam: John Benjamins.

Montanari, Simona. 2009. Pragmatic differentiation in early trilingual development. *Journal of Child Language* 36(3). 597–627.

Muysken, Pieter. 2000. *Bilingual speech: A typology of code-mixing*. Cambridge: Cambridge University Press.

Muysken, Pieter. 2013. Language contact outcomes as the result of bilingual optimization strategies. *Bilingualism: Language and Cognition* 16(4). 709–730.

Myers-Scotton, Carol. 1983. The negotiation of identities in conversation: A theory of markedness and code choice. *International Journal of the Sociology of Language* 44. 115–136.

Myers-Scotton, Carol. 1993. *Social motivations for codeswitching: Evidence from Africa*. Oxford: Clarendon Press.

Myers-Scotton, Carol (ed.). 1998. *Codes and consequences: Choosing linguistic varieties*. New York: Oxford University Press.

Myers-Scotton, Carol. 2002. *Contact linguistics: Bilingual encounter and grammatical outcomes*. Oxford: Oxford University Press.

Myers-Scotton, Carol & Janice L. Jake. 2009. A universal model of code-switching and bilingual language processing and production. In Barbara E. Bullock & Almeida Jacqueline Toribio (eds.), *The Cambridge handbook of linguistic code-switching* (Cambridge handbooks in linguistics), 336–357. New York: Cambridge University Press.

Paugh, Amy L. 2005. Multilingual play: Children's code-switching, role play, and agency in Dominica, West Indies. *Language in Society* 34(1). 63–86.

Pavlenko, Aneta. 2017. Superdiversity and why it isn't. In Stephan Breidbach, Lutz Kuster & Barbara Schmenkbook (eds.), *Sloganizations in language education discourse*, 142–168. Bristol, UK: Multilingual Matters.

Piller, Ingrid. 2010. Multilingualism and social exclusion. In Marilyn Martin-Jones, Adrian Blackledge & Angela Creese (eds.), *The Routledge handbook of multilingualism*, 281–296. London: Routledge.

Piller, Ingrid & Kimie Takahashi. 2011. Linguistic diversity and social inclusion. *International Journal of Bilingual Education and Bilingualism* 14(4). 371–381.

Poplack, Shana. 1980. 'Sometimes I'll start a sentence in English y termino en español': Toward a typology of code-switching. In John Amastae & Lucia Elías-Olivares (eds.), *Spanish in the United States: Sociolinguistic aspects*, 230–263. Cambridge: Cambridge University Press.

Quay, Suzanne. 2001. Managing linguistic boundaries in early trilingual development. In Jasone Cenoz & Fred Genesee (eds.), *Trends in bilingual acquisition*, 149–199. Amsterdam: John Benjamins.

Rampton, Ben. 1995. Language crossing and the problematisation of ethnicity and socialisation. *Pragmatics* 5(4). 485–513.

Rampton, Ben. 1998. Language crossing and the redefinition of reality. In Peter Auer (ed.), *Codeswitching in conversation*, 290–317. London: Routledge.

Reyes, Iliana. 2006. Exploring connections between emergent biliteracy and bilingualism. *Journal of Early Childhood Literacy* 6(3). 267–292.

Schwartz, Mila. 2008. Exploring the relationship between family language policy and heritage language knowledge among second generation Russian-Jewish immigrants in Israel. *Journal of Multilingual and Multicultural Development* 29(5). 400–418.

Scribner, Sylvia & Michael Cole. 1981. *The psychology of literacy*. Cambridge, MA: Harvard University Press.
Seel, Norbert M. 2012. *Encyclopedia of the sciences of learning*. Boston, MA: Springer.
Shay, Orit. 2015. To switch or not to switch: Code-Switching in a multilingual country. *Procedia – Social and Behavioral Sciences* 209. 462–469.
Stavans, Anat. 1990. *Codeswitching in children acquiring English, Spanish and Hebrew: A case study*. Pittsburgh, PA: University of Pittsburgh doctoral dissertation.
Stavans, Anat. 1992. Sociolinguistic factors affecting code-switches produced by trilingual children. *Language, Culture and Curriculum* 5(1). 41–53.
Stavans, Anat. 2005. Advantages and benefits trilingualism. In Irit Kupferberg & Elite Olshtain (eds.), *Discourse in education: Educational events as a field of research*, 418–449. Tel Aviv: Mofet.
Stavans, Anat. 2015. Monolingual and multilingual discrimination of written sequences' readability. *Writing Systems Research* 7(1). 108–127.
Stavans, Anat & Charlotte Hoffmann. 2015. *Multilingualism: Key topics in sociolinguistics*. Cambridge: Cambridge University Press.
Stavans, Anat & Virginia M. Swisher. 2006. Language switching as a window on trilingual acquisition. *International Journal of Multilingualism* 3(3). 193–220.
Tay, Mary W. 1989. Code switching and code mixing as a communicative strategy in multilingual discourse. *World Englishes* 8. 407–417.
Tiemer, W. 2000. *Code-switching repertoires in the language classroom: Contextualization and the enactment of shared perceptions in the talk of learners*. Edmonton, Canada: University of Alberta MA thesis.
Vu, Hai Ha. 2017. "Only when I am not ashamed of myself can I teach others": Preservice English-language teachers in Vietnam and code-switching practices. *Journal of Language, Identity & Education* 16(5). 285–298.
Wolfensohn, James David & Andrew Kircher. 2005. *Voice for the world's poor: Selected speeches and writings of World Bank president James D. Wolfensohn, 1995–2005*. Washington, DC: World Bank.

Charlotte Gooskens
8 Receptive Multilingualism

8.1 Introduction

Multilingualism is part of daily life for a large part of the world's population (see Chapters 2 through 5, this volume). For many people, multilingualism causes a communicative challenge. If speakers with different native language (L1) backgrounds want to communicate, they need to find a way to cross linguistic borders. However, language acquisition is mostly hard work. It requires mastering grammatical rules, memorizing word lists, and practicing pronunciation. Many speakers feel insecure about speaking or writing in a language that they have not mastered well. Furthermore, it is only possible for an individual to learn a limited number of languages. Many people have not learned other foreign languages up to a standard for cross-border communication. Often, the solution is to use a *lingua franca,* a language that makes communication possible between people who do not share a first language. Various lingua francas are used in different parts of the world, but English has become the global lingua franca of the 21st century. However, results of surveys (e.g., EF EPI 2017) show that people vary to a large extent in their level of English proficiency depending, for example, on gender, age, level of education and country. Many people have difficulties understanding and speaking English. Therefore, alternative modes of communication have been explored (Backus et al. 2013).

In many situations, a level of mutual understanding sufficient to exchange information can be achieved if the speakers avail themselves of what is often referred to as receptive multilingualism (RM).[1] The RM model is based on the observation that some languages are so closely related that they are mutually intelligible. In such a situation, the speakers are able to communicate rather successfully while both are using their own language. The advantage of this kind of communication is that it is easier and more efficient for most speakers to express themselves in their native language than in English or in another foreign language. The fact that both participants in a conversation can speak the language they master best, their native language, results in an inherent fairness

---
[1] Other frequently used terminology that cover approximately the same concepts are *plurilingual communication, semi-communication, intercompréhension,* and *lingua receptiva.* The choice of terminology mainly depends on the research paradigm being used.

Charlotte Gooskens, University of Groningen, Groningen, The Netherlands

https://doi.org/10.1515/9781501507984-008

and equality between speakers who both have to make an effort to understand the other language. Furthermore, language is an essential part of identity; therefore, it is important for many speakers to use their native language when communicating with others. Sometimes the motivation for engaging in RM may not be a lack of proficiency in the language of the interlocutor but rather a socio-political motivation to stress the belonging to a certain cultural or ethnic group (ethnic marking). Bilaniuk (2010) shows how speakers of Ukrainian and Russian use RM to defuse the contested issue of language choice even though they speak both languages. She notes that this kind of RM is characterized by resistance to linguistic accommodation and an attitude of purism.

Communication by means of RM typically involves languages and dialects that are genealogically related and share many grammatical, lexical and phonological features. The human language processing mechanism shows a remarkable robustness with respect to incomplete or unfamiliar information. Many possible features are not realised in a normal linguistic utterance. Usually however, understanding is not in any way hampered by this. To the listener, closely related languages and dialects show similarity with different kinds of imperfect and unfamiliar languages; therefore, speakers of languages that are mutually intelligible to various degrees can still communicate.

RM can also be used in situations where the languages are less closely related but where the interlocutors have acquired sufficient passive competence in each other's languages to be able to communicate. A distinction can be made between *inherent* and *acquired* RM (Kluge 2007). The former relies on language features that are available to interlocutors prior to language learning because of the close relationship between L1 and L2, whereas the latter presupposes some acquired knowledge and typically involves less closely related languages. The differences are gradual rather than dichotomous. Furthermore, situations where speakers use third language intervention to communicate are also considered as RM (*mediated* RM, Branets et al. 2019). An example is Estonian L1 speakers with knowledge of Russian who can understand Ukrainian (Branets et al. 2019).

For many speakers, it feels rude and impolite at first to use RM. This could be because it goes against our natural eagerness to accommodate to the speaker (Giles and Ogay 2007). However, through history, RM has been an important means of communication. For example, RM was used in face-to-face trading communication and political consultations in northern Europe between speakers of Low German and Scandinavian (Braunmüller 2007) and in the Romance language area (Blanche-Benveniste 2008) during the late Middle Ages, until nationalism and linguistic standardization and the resulting ideal of linguistic loyalty and monolingualism led to a more restricted use of this kind of communication. For many other historical situations, there is a lack of primary reports on the use of RM. We also have no information about the number of languages or the number of speakers involved in RM today. However, it can be assumed that RM was often the only possible manner of communication in the past and still is in situations where the speakers have not learned any other language than their native language or have not learned an L2 that the interlocutor can also understand.

Scandinavia provides one of the best documented examples of communication by means of inherent RM and has received the most attention from linguists (e.g. Delsing and Lundin Åkesson 2005; Schüppert 2011; Zeevaert 2004). Many people from Denmark, Sweden, and Norway favour RM above a lingua franca when talking to persons from the neighboring countries. For example, a Danish tourist visiting Sweden will often speak Danish to the Swedes he meets with the Swedes answering back in Swedish. Some research has been carried out on RM in the rest of the Germanic language area (e.g. Beerkens 2009; Gooskens et al. 2015; Ház 2005) and other Indo-European languages, in particular the Romance language area (Conti and Grin 2008; Jensen 1989) and the Slavic language area (Golubović 2016; Jágrová et al. 2019; Nábělková 2007).

Outside Europe, there was a vivid interest during the 1950s to establish the mutual intelligibility of American Indian languages (Hickerton et al. 1952; Voegelin and Harris 1951). The aim was to investigate the genealogical relationship between language varieties and to develop a single orthography for multiple closely related language varieties in the context of literacy programs (e.g. Anderson 2005; Casad 1974). More recently, there has been research on mutual intelligibility between *inter alia* Chinese dialects (Tang and Van Heuven 2009), Arabic language varieties (Čéplö et al. 2016), Finnish and Estonian (Härmävaara 2014) and Turkish and Azerbaijani (Sağın-Şimşek and Ünlü 2017). RM has also been described as a widespread mode of multilingual interaction in Australian indigenous communities (Singer and Harris 2016).

RM has received less scientific attention in other parts of the world. It is not possible to draw up a complete list of language pairs that are mutually intelligible to such an extent that they can be used for RM. To do so, we would first have to define when two language varieties are similar enough to be used for RM. Furthermore, it is unknown to what extent and between which languages RM is used worldwide. It should be noted that although research has been carried out to establish the level of mutual intelligibility between particular language pairs, it does not necessarily mean that the speakers of the involved languages actually use RM for communicative purposes. Furthermore, RM may not be used even though the linguistic preconditions are present. Quantitative data about the actual use of RM has only been collected for specific language combinations. For example, the results of a survey among 252 Dutch and German respondents who either work for governmental or civil society organizations in the Dutch-German border area (Beerkens 2009) showed that RM was said to be used at least in one situation by 27% of the respondents. RM was used less often than L1-L2 or L2-L2 combinations involving English, German and Dutch.

Whether RM is chosen as the mode of communication often depends on the individual interactants involved and the particular situation and domain in which it is used (Beerkens 2009). RM is commonly used for discourse in families where parents have different language backgrounds and inter-generationally among immigrant families. For example, the children of Turkish immigrants in Germany may speak German to the parents who then answer in Turkish (Herkenrath 2012). Such children are often productively bilingual and their choice of language may depend on various factors such as the content and context of the conversation and the presence of outsiders who may not understand one of the languages. The application of the RM mode may also depend on the language policy of particular institutions, such as educational institutions (Vetter 2012), governmental organizations (Ribbert and ten Thije 2007), the army (Berthele and Wittlin 2013), and the work place (Lüdi 2013). RM can be used for spoken as well as for written communication, but the processes leading to mutual understanding may be different. In spoken communication, the listener will mostly get only one attempt to process the input and the processing time is limited, whereas in written communication, there is no time limit and the reader can reread the message and search for additional cues in the context if necessary. On the other hand, in spoken communication there is often more interaction, and both speaker and listener can check mutual comprehension during the conversation. In most of this chapter, I will focus on spoken communication, but many aspects of RM discussed can be generalized to written communication as well.

Research on RM is interesting from a theoretical perspective. It provides a greater understanding of the robustness of the human language processing system. It may provide answers to questions of how deviant language can be before it is no longer intelligible to the listener and what factors play a role in successful communication by means of RM. Knowledge about the determinants of RM is useful for language planning at the national and international level. It is important to know how linguistic distances can be bridged. If smaller languages are to survive, it is important to understand the mechanisms involved in using one's own language for communication with speakers of other languages. RM is promoted by the European commission to increase the mobility of European citizens and to support linguistic diversity (European Commission 2007). At the level of the individual language user, engaging in RM can be seen as a way to build up broad communicative competence and cognitive linguistic flexibility (Melo-Pfeifer 2014).

8.2 How can we measure receptive multilingualism?

An important prerequisite for successful RM is that the interlocutors can understand each other's languages. Therefore, to be able to determine under what conditions RM works and what its preconditions and its limits are, we need to be able to measure mutual intelligibility. Mutual intelligibility is mostly defined as a property of a pair of languages, and in this definition, the level of mutual intelligibility is a consequence of objective lexical, phonological and grammatical similarities between the languages themselves. However, it is not a straightforward task to quantify linguistic similarity since languages may differ at all linguistic levels, and at each of the linguistic levels, languages may vary on many different parameters. For example, consonant similarities have been found to be more important for mutual intelligibility than vowel similarities (Berthele 2011), and similarities of word onsets have been found to be more important than similarities in the rest of the word (van Heuven 2008). In recent years, objective techniques for quantifying the linguistic similarity of language varieties have become more and more sophisticated (see Section 8.3). However, there is not a priori way of weighing the different linguistic dimensions in order to express how well speakers of two languages can understand each other. Furthermore, the level of mutual intelligibility is dependent on a large number of non-linguistic factors such as the background and experience of the interlocutors and their attitude towards the L2 and its speakers (see Section 8.4). For this reason, it is necessary to use behavioral tests to quantify the level of mutual intelligibility.

Ideally, we would like to be able to express how well speakers of two languages understand each other's languages by some standard measuring procedure. However, for several reasons, it is problematic to develop such a measurement. Firstly, mutual intelligibility is gradual rather than absolute, reflecting the fact that related languages are often part of a dialect continuum. It is not clear how similar two language varieties should be to be mutually intelligible and whether an intelligibility threshold can be defined. For example, how many L2 words should a listener be able to understand to engage in successful RM? Whether the exchange of information between speakers of two varieties in such a continuum is successful also depends on the purpose and the subject of a conversation. Secondly, the background and personal characteristics of participants influence how well they understand the test language (see Section 8.4) and it is impossible to select a group of participants that would be representative of all speakers of a language. When we test mutual intelligibility of two languages, we are therefore forced to test one or more specific subgroups, e.g. a specific age group, speakers from a certain geographical area and/or educational background. Thirdly, the nature and purpose of the intelligibility test will have a bearing on the results as the same participant may be more successful in one kind of test than in another.

Many different tests have been developed to test mutual intelligibility (see Gooskens 2013 for an overview). The choice of a method for measuring intelligibility depends on a number of factors such as the purpose of the measurements, available time and resources, literacy of the participants, and familiarity of the researcher with the test languages. An easy and efficient way to measure intelligibility of a language is to ask subjects to rate along a scale how well they think they understand the language at hand (opinion testing). However, a person's reported language behavior may not correspond to his or her actual language behavior. It rather provides information about people's subjective ideas about the intelligibility of languages. Therefore, most researchers prefer to test actual speech comprehension (functional testing). Examples of such tests are open questions or multiple-choice questions about a text, retelling and translation tasks, cloze tests and various kinds of behavioral or reaction time tests.

The disadvantage of functional testing is that it is generally difficult to abstract away from individual speakers and test situations. Doetjes (2007) investigated the effect of six different test types (true/false questions, multiple-choice questions, open questions, word translation, summary, and short summary) on the measurement of the intelligibility of Swedish among Danes. On average, the subjects gave the highest percentages of correct answers to the true/false questions (93%) and the lowest percentages when asked to write short summaries of a text (66%). This shows that it is not possible to give an absolute answer to the question of how well subjects understand a language. In addition, the researcher should attempt to avoid priming effects, ceiling effects, too-heavy memory load and other unwanted effects. These considerations make it rather time consuming to develop and carry out the tests.

In the context of RM, it is important to note that most methods measure the intelligibility of language A among speakers of language B. Mutual intelligibility can be measured by also testing the intelligibility of language B among speakers of language A. Speakers of language A may have more difficulty understanding language B than the other way around. By understanding the reasons for asymmetric intelligibility, we can get insight into the factors determining the level of intelligibility. Asymmetry has been observed between many language pairs, for example between Spanish and Portuguese (Jensen 1989), Dutch and Afrikaans (Gooskens and van Bezooijen 2006) and between Czech and Slovak (Nábělková 2007). The best-documented case of asymmetric intelligibility is Danish-Swedish mutual intelligibility. Danes generally understand spoken Swedish better than Swedes understand Danish (Gooskens et al. 2010; Schüppert 2011). Various linguistic and extra-linguistic factors to be discussed in detail in Sections 8.3 and 8.4 can explain these findings.

8.3 Linguistic determinants

As discussed in the introduction, a distinction can be made between inherent and acquired RM. Simons (1979: 3) defines inherent intelligibility as "Theoretical degree of understanding between dialects whose speakers have not had contact". This means that in the case of inherent RM, speakers can communicate on the basis of the linguistic overlap between their L1s. Genealogically related languages are likely to show lexical overlap; therefore, mutual intelligibility can be expected to correlate with the genealogical characterization of the languages. In addition to lexical differences, differences between languages can be found at all other linguistic levels (phonology, orthography, morphology and syntax), but some of these levels are more important for intelligibility than others (Gooskens and van Heuven 2019). Note that linguistic differences can be asymmetric and can be part of the explanation for asymmetric mutual intelligibility (see Section 8.2). For example, Danish might have two synonyms for a concept, which has only one equivalent in Swedish. An example is *rom* 'room' in Swedish and *rum* or *værelse* in Danish. A Swede will probably understand the Danish cognate word *rum* but not the non-cognate *værelse* unless he or she has somehow learned it. On the other hand, a Dane will easily understand Swedish *rom*. Phonetic, morphological and syntactic transparency may also be asymmetric. Below I will discuss linguistic factors that have been shown to play a role in the explanation of the level of mutual intelligibility between closely related languages.

8.3.1 Lexical differences

The intelligibility of words is the most important and central aspect of speech intelligibility. A listener needs to be able to recognize words to understand a message. If he has had no previous exposure to the language, he will only be able to understand words that are historically related to the corresponding words in his own language (cognates), unless he knows them from a cognate in another language that he is familiar with. Lexical differences between languages are often expressed quantitatively as the percentage of non-cognates (historically unrelated words) in the two lexicons (Séguy 1973). The percentages of non-cognates have been shown to correlate negatively with scores on tests of mutual intelligibility between closely related languages: the larger the proportion of non-cognates, the lower the intelligibility. For example, Gooskens and van Heuven (2019) found significant correlations of -.95 for 14 Germanic language combinations, -.69 for 15 Romance combinations and -.80 for 29 Slavic language combinations ($p < .01$). These results confirm the importance of lexical similarities for intelligibility, but they also show that they can only predict intelligibility to a certain extent. There are a number of explanations for this finding.

First, some non-cognate words in a text can easily be interpreted from the context or have little negative influence on intelligibility. The meaning of other words may be more difficult to predict or be more important for understanding the text. Salehi and Neysani (2017: 4) refer to such words as "critical words". It is often assumed that content words (nouns, adjectives, numerals, main verbs) are more important for intelligibility than function words (articles, conjunctions, prepositions, pronouns, auxiliaries, modals, particles, adverbs) because they express the content of the message (van Bezooijen and Gooskens 2007). The importance of content words becomes clear when looking at the vocabulary in telegrams and newspaper headlines. To express a message as shortly as possible, most function words are left out; yet it is possible to understand the message. And even within the group of content words, some words are more important than others in certain contexts. Salehi and Neysani (2017) found that Turkish listeners had more difficulties guessing the meaning of Iranian-Azerbaijani verbs and nouns than the meaning of adjectives and adverbs. They explain this by the higher semantic load of nouns and verbs. This means that it may be possible to improve lexical distance measurements as predictors of intelligibility by weighing differences in verbs and nouns more heavily than differences in function words, adjectives and adverbs.

It is often assumed that false friends, i.e. pairs of words in two language varieties that sound similar but differ in meaning, form a major problem for the mutual intelligibility of closely related languages. While non-cognates will in principle hinder intelligibility, so-called false friends may cause even larger problems because they may actually mislead the listener. In addition, listeners are less likely to use contextual cues to guess the meaning of false friends than in the case of other unknown words because they do not realize that they are non-cognates. Salehi and Neysani (2017) found that false friends have a stronger negative effect on intelligibility of Turkish among Iranian-Azerbaijani speakers than other unknown words. It should also be noted that there are words that could be considered semi-false friends. Those are words that have a broad meaning in one language and a narrow meaning in the other language, e.g. *yapmak* meaning 'to make' in Turkish and 'to bake' in Azerbajani (Salehi and Neysani 2017) or words that have several meanings and are false friends in one of these meanings, e.g. German *befestigen* meaning 'to fasten' or 'to confirm'. The Dutch equivalent *bevestigen* means 'to fasten' but does not have the meaning 'to confirm'.

8.3.2 Phonetic differences

As stated above, lexical similarities between two languages are likely to play a major role in the mutual intelligibility of two languages. However, cognates in two languages can sometimes be unrecognizable for the listener because of developments in pronunciation; therefore, phonetic similarity is likely to be an important predictor of intelligibility as well. In recent years, dialectometric methods for measuring phonetic distances objectively have been developed and refined. Even though the methods were primarily developed with the aim of characterizing dialect areas and drawing dialect maps, dialectometric measurements have also proved to be good predictors of the mutual intelligibility of closely related language varieties. The most widely used method for measuring communicatively relevant phonetic distances is the Levenshtein algorithm (Nerbonne and Heeringa 2010). Phonetic distances between two language varieties are computed for aligned cognate word pairs by computing the smallest number of string edit operations needed to convert the string of phonetic symbols in language A to the cognate string in B. Possible string operations are deletions, insertions and substitutions of symbols. The total number of points is then divided by the length of the alignment (number of alignment slots) to yield a length-normalized Levenshtein distance. The overall phonetic distance from language A to language B is the arithmetic mean of the normalized distances for all cognate word pairs. A number of investigations have found high correlations between intelligibility measurements and Levenshtein distances (Gooskens 2007). Jágrová et al. (2019) and Moberg et al. (2007) used other algorithms (adaptation surprisal and conditional entropy) that are able to capture the asymmetric mutual intelligibility found between many language pairs.

The simplest version of the Levenshtein algorithm uses binary differences between alignments; more advanced versions use graded weights that express acoustic segment distances. For example, the pair [i, o] is seen as being more different than the pair [i, ɪ]. However, for the purpose of modelling intelligibility, it is not clear how the differences should be weighted. The optimal weighing is likely to differ for each language combination and depends on predictability and generalizability of sound correspondences. Improvements of the algorithm should take into account the human decoding processes. For example, Gooskens et al. (2008) found that consonants are better predictors of the intelligibility of Scandinavian dialects among speakers of Standard Danish than vowels and that consonant substitutions are better predictors than insertions or deletions. Kürschner et al. (2008) correlated the results of an experiment on the intelligibility of 384 frequent Swedish words among Danes with eleven linguistic factors and carried out logistic regression analyses. Phonetic distances explained most of the variance. However, they also found that individual characteristics of words can influence intelligibility. Word length, different numbers of syllables in L1-L2 words pairs, Swedish sounds not used in Danish, neighborhood density, and word frequency also influenced intelligibility significantly. Gooskens et al. (2015) found that minor phonetic details that could hardly be captured by Levenshtein distances may sometimes have a major impact on the intelligibility of isolated words.

8.3.3 Morpho-syntactic differences

Previous studies of mutual intelligibility have focused largely on the role of lexical and phonetic factors. Still, there is evidence that differences in morphology and syntax might also affect the ability to comprehend a closely related language. For example, Gooskens and Van Bezooijen (2006) found that Dutch speakers tend to understand Afrikaans better than vice versa. One of the reasons for this is the simplified grammar of Afrikaans. Similarly, by means of reaction time and correctness evaluation experiments, Hilton et al. (2013) investigated whether Danes' comprehension of Norwegian sentences is impeded by certain Norwegian grammatical constructions. Their results showed that when listeners were presented with sentences with word-order and morphological differences, they needed more time to decide whether the content of the sentences was correct, and they made more mistakes. This means that morpho-syntactic differences should not be disregarded in studies of the linguistic dependencies of RM. This is confirmed by Gooskens and van Heuven (2019) who found significant correlations between syntactic distances and intelligibility ($r = .72$ for 14 Germanic language combinations, $r = .77$ for 15 Romance language combinations and $r = .53$ for 29 Slavic language combinations, $p < .01$).

8.3.4 Paralinguistic factors

In addition to linguistic factors, paralinguistic factors may also play a role in RM. Paralanguage includes pitch, volume, speech rate, modulation, and fluency.

Non-vocal phenomena such as facial expressions, eye movements, and hand gestures are often included in the list of paralinguistic factors (Lyons 1977). Little research has been carried out to experimentally test the role of paralinguistic factors for the success of RM.

It is, for example, logical to assume that high speech tempo will influence the intelligibility of a message. Speaking quickly increases the demands on the articulatory apparatus; therefore, the speaker is likely to reduce specific sound entities when speaking fast. This makes it difficult to find lexical boundaries between words, resulting in intelligibility difficulties. Furthermore, a short time frame makes it challenging for the listener to decode the message. He or she needs to decompose and process the stream of speech sounds more quickly and this is demanding for working memory. In his H & H ("hyper"- and "hypo"-articulation) theory, Lindblom (1990) argues that speakers of any language are constantly balancing between *hyperspeech*, i.e. clear articulation to maximize intelligibility in the listener, and *hypospeech*, i.e. unclear speech to minimize the articulatory effort for the speaker. Generally, these two opposing efforts lead to speech which contains a certain amount of reduction phenomena but is still fairly intelligible to the listener. The Danish language seems to be a case where speakers have a preference for hypospeech. Recent research suggests that Danish is spoken significantly faster than Norwegian and Swedish (Hilton et al. 2011) and this may be one of the reasons why Danish is difficult for Swedes to understand (Schüppert et al. 2016). Bleses et al. (2008) report a delay in vocabulary development in Danish infants and children compared to that of their peers from ten European countries and from the U.S. and Mexico. They suggest that this delay could be attributed to the high number of reduction and assimilation processes in Danish compared to other languages which makes it difficult to find lexical boundaries in the speech signal.

8.4 Extra-linguistic determinants

In the previous section, I discussed linguistic and para-linguistic differences between languages that may determine how successful RM is. However, not all speakers of the same L1 may understand an L2 equally well. The level of understanding between two interlocutors with different L1s also depends on a number of individual speaker and listener competencies and activities.

8.4.1 Personality traits

Individual personality traits identified within psychology have been shown to exercise influence on language learning; therefore, they can also be expected to play a role in RM. Examples of such traits are the ability to adapt to new situations, knowledge of the world, sociocultural resources, and cognitive resources. Only few investigations have been carried out to experimentally test the role of such individual factors for RM. Lambelet and Mauron (2017) quantified five major personality factors (neuroticism, extroversion, openness, agreeableness, and conscientiousness) by having 181 French-speaking Swiss secondary school children aged 13 to 15 years old fill out a questionnaire with 60 five-point Likert-scale questions. The children also completed four reading comprehension exercises to test their understanding of Italian and answered questions pertaining to the appreciation of the task. The results showed significant correlations between appreciation of the task and comprehension but no significant correlation between comprehension and personality traits. However, there was a clear relation between task appreciation and the personality traits "openness" and "extroversion"; therefore, the authors concluded that personality traits should not be ignored as a factor of importance for RM.

Another individual characteristic that may influence intelligibility is the age of the listener. Vanhove and Berthele (2015) had 159 German-speaking Swiss participants aged 10 to 86 translate 45 written and 45 spoken isolated Swedish words with German, English or French cognates. The results showed that in the written modality, cognate guessing skills improve throughout adulthood, while in the spoken modality, cognate guessing skills remain fairly stable between ages 20–50 but then start to decline. The authors explained the different age trends in the two modalities by a differential reliance on fluid intelligence (reasoning and problem-solving skills) and crystallized resources (in particular, L1 vocabulary knowledge). Fluid intelligence tends to increase sharply into young adulthood and then declines, while crystallized resources stay stable or even increase throughout adulthood. Vanhove and Berthele (2015) found crystallized knowledge to be a stronger predictor of written cognate guessing success, whereas fluid intelligence is the most important predictor in the spoken modality. As possible explanations for these results, they suggest that it may be more cognitively challenging to compare spoken phonemes across languages than letters and graphemes and that it may be the time pressure associated with auditory stimulus presentation that causes the difference.

8.4.2 Attitudes

There are large inter-individual differences in attitudes towards RM as a mode of communication and towards the language and country of the speakers of other languages. Such attitudes may affect the willingness and motivation to understand an L2 speaker (Lambelet and Mauron 2017). Negative attitudes or social stigmas attached to languages are often seen as a potential obstruction for successful communication between speakers of different languages. If people do not have the will to try to understand each other, linguistic similarity between languages is of little help. Inhabitants from neighboring countries often have an ambivalent attitude towards each other. For example, it has repeatedly been suggested that the asymmetric intelligibility between Swedes and Danes can be traced back to the less positive attitudes among Swedes towards the Danish language, culture, and people than the other way around. Significant correlations between attitude and intelligibility have been found (Delsing and Lundin Åkesson 2005). However, it is difficult to establish whether negative attitudes are a result of poor intelligibility, or whether poor intelligibility is a result of negative attitudes, caused by some other factor.

Various sources of attitudes towards languages can be distinguished. Giles et al. (1975) formulated two hypotheses, termed the imposed-norm hypothesis and the inherent-value hypothesis. The imposed-norm hypothesis stresses the importance of non-linguistic factors such as social connotations and cultural norms. A language variety would be considered attractive when its speakers are socially privileged. This would explain why English listeners locate Received Pronunciation (RP or BBC English) at the top of the aesthetic hierarchy, regional English accents in the middle, and urban English accents at the bottom (e.g., Trudgill and Giles 1978). RP would be placed at the top because of cultural prestige, whereas regional accents are judged more positively than urban accents because the former are associated with a more attractive lifestyle and environmental setting. The inherent-value hypothesis claims that language attitudes are (at least partly) triggered by qualities that are intrinsic in language. It argues that some languages (or language varieties) are intrinsically more esthetically pleasing than other languages due to their sound characteristics.

It is not a straightforward task to measure language attitudes. This may be part of the explanation for the weak relation between intelligibility and attitude found in previous research. Direct questioning may elicit opinions that are different from subconsciously held language attitudes (cf. Kristiansen 2009). Evaluations of recordings of languages may be affected by individual speaker characteristics such as voice quality, mean pitch level and intonation (e.g. Zuckerman and Driver 1989). A way to collect less consciously held attitudes and neutralize the influence of voice characteristics on esthetic judgments is to use the "matched-guise" technique. A matched-guise test consists of lexically identical speech samples from a balanced bilingual speaker (i.e., a bilingual with equally high proficiency levels in both languages). The recordings of the bilingual are played interspersed with other recordings (distracters) to avoid listeners being aware of hearing the same speaker twice. Listeners are then asked to evaluate the speakers that they are hearing for different personality traits such as kindness, richness and beauty. Since the two varieties spoken by the bilingual are in fact produced by the same speaker, language usage is the only feature between the two recordings that differs. This matched-guise technique was first used for the investigations of language attitudes in the French-English bilingual setting in Quebec, Canada (Lambert et al. 1960). The results showed that the way participants judged personality traits of the bilingual speaker were strongly influenced by the language spoken. Both English and French-speaking participants rated the speaker more positively on status and solidarity traits when he spoke English, which is believed to reflect the English language's higher status in Quebec.

8.4.3 Exposure

An important factor in explaining the level of intelligibility of a closely related language is the nature and amount of previous exposure to the language. The more exposure listeners have had to a language, the more likely they are to understand it. Previous research (e.g., Golubović 2016; Hedquist 1985) has shown that in the case of closely related languages, only a short language course that makes speakers conscious of the most important differences and similarities between their native language and the language of the speaker can improve receptive proficiency considerably.

Similarly, the amount of exposure to the language of the speaker outside the classroom has been shown to correlate positively with intelligibility and may be part of the explanation for the asymmetric intelligibility between Swedish and Danish. Generally, Danes are more often confronted with Swedish, for example through the media and on vacation, than the other way around (Jørgensen and Kärrlander 2001). Through exposure, the participant will get used to the sounds of the language and how these sounds correspond to those in his own language. He or she is also likely to learn some of the vocabulary.

Exposure can be measured and quantified in various ways. The most straightforward way is to ask participants to indicate on a scale how often they are exposed to the language, for example by reading books and newspapers, watching television, meeting speakers in person, etc. (Delsing and Lundin Åkesson 2005; Gooskens and van Heuven 2019). Second, participants are likely to be more exposed to varieties spoken in geographically close places than to more remote varieties. Geographical distances can therefore be used to predict intelligibility. Distances can be measured as straight-line distances in kilometers ("as the crow flies") or as travel distances (Gooskens 2005). Finally, exposure can be measured by calculating percentages of non-cognates that the listener can understand. The assumption is that a listener will only be able to understand a non-cognate if he or she has had some exposure to the language variety, so participants with little exposure to a language are expected to translate fewer non-cognates correctly than listeners with a lot of previous exposure (Gooskens and Schneider 2019).

8.4.4 Literacy

Orthographical knowledge may play a role in the intelligibility of a closely related language in the spoken form. This may be at least part of the explanation for the asymmetric mutual intelligibility between Danish and Swedish as can be illustrated by the following example. Literate Danes confronted with the Swedish word *land* /land/ 'country' can probably use their orthographic knowledge to match this word to their native correspondent *land* /lan$^?$/. On the other hand, this is not the case for Swedes listening to the Danish word because of the absence of the phoneme /d/, which is present in Swedish pronunciation as well as orthography. Gooskens and Doetjes (2009) showed that there are more Swedish words that Danes can understand by means of the orthography in the corresponding Danish cognates than Danish words that Swedes can use their orthography to recognize. This difference can be explained by the fact that spoken Swedish is close to both written Swedish and written Danish, whereas spoken Danish has changed rapidly during the last century and has undergone a number of reduction processes that are not reflected in the orthographic system. This means that Danes can often understand spoken Swedish due to its close similarity to written Danish, while Swedes get less help from written Swedish when understanding spoken Danish. Schüppert (2011) used event-related brain potentials (ERPs) to collect evidence that online activation of L1 orthography enhances word recognition among literate speakers of Danish who are exposed to samples of spoken Swedish. On the basis of these investigations, it can be concluded that Danish listeners indeed seem to make more use of the additional information that the L1 orthography can provide when listening to Swedish than Swedes when listening to Danish.

8.4.5 Plurilingual resources

It can be assumed that listeners can understand a closely related language because of its linguistic overlap with the native language (see Section 8.3). However, most listeners have knowledge of more languages or dialects than their own L1. Often, this knowledge can also be used to understand the closely related language. Listeners may understand some non-cognate words because they are loanwords from a language they are familiar with. For example, Danish has German loanwords that are not found in Dutch. Most Dutch people learn some German at school and can use this knowledge to understand some Danish words borrowed from German but without a Dutch cognate. Speakers of Dutch might, for example, be able to correctly translate the Danish word *bogstav* 'letter' into the Dutch non-cognate *letter* through the L2 German cognate *Buchstabe* (Swarte et al. 2015). The EuroCom project (e.g., Hufeisen and Marx 2007; Chapter 4, this volume) is based on the principle that learners of a new language can be trained to use their knowledge of a related, formerly learned language during language comprehension.

When listeners are multilingual, they can use several languages when trying to understand an unknown related language. The languages are interrelated in the mind of the listener in a complex and dynamic way, and a number of factors determines which languages are activated and how. Mieszkowska and Otwinowska (2015) provide an overview of such factors. For example, recently and frequently activated languages tend to be more easily activated than less recently and infrequently activated languages; languages that are perceived to be linguistically close are more easily activated; if the degree of proficiency in a language is high, it is more likely to be activated. Multilingual listeners tend to have a higher level of metalinguistic awareness and are better able to use crosslinguistic similarity to understand a language (see also Chapter 15, this volume).

8.4.6 Strategies

As in all kinds of interaction, participants in RM need to master interaction strategies to cope with and prevent misunderstandings. Depending on their proficiency levels, both speakers and hearers can employ various strategies. Many interaction strategies have been described by discourse analytical experts for communication between L1s or L2s and various taxonomies have been proposed within second language acquisition studies. Van Mulken and Hendriks (2015) base their taxonomy of RM and English as a Lingua Franca communication strategies on some of these studies. They make a distinction between five groups of strategies: showing communicative vulnerability (asking for help, signaling uncertainty), offering help, compensatory strategies (describing, code-switching), meta-discursive strategies (discussing task fulfilment), and paralinguistic strategies. They found that different written communication modes (RM, Lingua Franca, L2-L1) are characterized by a preference for particular strategies. In the case of the RM interactions that they set up for their investigation, participants often resorted to paralinguistic strategies. The authors explain that speakers do not need to focus on resolving lexical deficiencies when using their native language and therefore, feel free to add evaluative cues to the conversation. Maybe for the same reason, metacommunication is the second common strategy used in RM interactions.

Braunmüller (2006) and Zeevaert (2004), summarized in Beerkens (2009), make a distinction between hearer strategies and speaker strategies. If the speaker is monolingual, he can only adapt his language according to his knowledge about his own language and communication with other L1 speakers. He may, for example, speak slowly and reformulate sentences. He may also avoid using words he knows to be difficult in his own language. Such words may in fact be a cognate in the language of the listener and therefore actually could have helped to improve mutual intelligibility. A speaker with knowledge of the language of the listener can use additional strategies to reach mutual understanding, such as using particular words from the language of the listener that he knows to be cognates in the two languages and avoiding non-cognates. The hearer on the other side can make clear when he does not understand the speaker and can provide feedback to show he has understood (back-channeling). On the basis of his observations, Braunmüller (2006), cited in Beerkens (2009: 28), formulates the following advice for interaction by means of RM: "don't speak too fast", "avoid certain words", "articulate clearly", "repeat", "explain", and "ask if something is not understood".

Another set of strategies are of a more linguistic nature. Berthele (2011) shows that interlocutors can use their linguistic knowledge to guess the meaning of cognates in a related but unknown language (inferencing strategies). The competences for good guessing capacities that he mentions are the ability to make a flexible and selective comparison of features and patterns, focusing on consonants and neglecting or systematically varying the vowels, and the ability to use contextual information to make decisions. Furthermore, the interlocutors should know when to stop searching in order not to waste time.

8.5 RM and language policy

The use of RM as a means of communication depends to a large extent on the linguistic overlap between the languages involved and on the backgrounds of the interlocutors. However, language policy at different levels within governmental and civil society is also an important factor that determines when RM is supported and encouraged. In Scandinavia, RM has traditionally been the default communication mode among the speakers of the closely related Scandinavian languages (Danish, Swedish and Norwegian). Speakers of the Scandinavian languages are strongly encouraged by the Scandinavian authorities to use their own language rather than a lingua franca such as English when communicating with other Scandinavians because this can function as a means to unite the Northern countries politically, culturally, and economically (*Deklaration om nordisk språkpolitik* 2006). In other language constellations that may have the same linguistic basis for communicating by means of RM, this possibility is less widely applied. For example, Beerkens (2009) notes that even though the linguistic distance between Dutch and German is small enough for RM to be used as a means of communication, this language mode is not very well-known for this language constellation. At the European level, RM has been acknowledged as a means of communication that can support language diversity and maintenance and improve communication among the speakers of the large number of languages spoken in Europe (European Commission 2007). Many initiatives have been made to develop didactic programs for speakers to learn RM in different language constellations (see section 8.5.1). Such initiatives and a language policy that is supportive of RM are important for the successful use of RM because they can make speakers conscious about the possibility of communicating by means of RM and introduce it for communication at a larger scale.

8.5.1 Acquisition

Worldwide, there are many language combinations that are mutually intelligible to such an extent that the speakers can engage in RM without any prior training. However, even though communication between related languages is often possible at a basic level, in many cases where speakers have to exchange information about abstract, formal, and less familiar topics, successful receptive multilingual communication often requires some training. In various parts of Europe, educational programs have been developed to teach receptive multilingualism (e.g., the GalaNet and GalaPro,[2] EuroCom,[3] Linee[4] and Dylan[5] projects; see also Chapter 4, this volume) but only little research has been conducted to investigate the effects of these programs. In contrast with traditional language acquisition, the speaker only needs to focus on understanding the L2, and the more challenging language production plays no role. In traditional foreign language acquisition studies, most attention has been paid to the productive aspects of the L2, and the L2 is often very different from the L1. In the case of RM, learners need to develop receptive strategies and discover that they can profit from their own language when trying to crack the L2 code; it is not necessary for them to actively acquire grammatical constructions, words and pronunciation.

Receptive competence can be improved by explicit instruction and focused attention to specific communicatively relevant linguistic similarities and differences between the L1 and the L2. Extensive discussions are found in the literature about the use of focusing on form in language teaching (Doughty 2003). An important assumption underlying explicit instruction is awareness-raising leading to metalinguistic awareness (Schmidt 2001). Due to metalinguistic awareness, learners are assumed to be able to "notice the gap" between features in the input and the learner's own actual performance and this is a necessary step in language acquisition (Schmidt 2001). Frameworks discussed by, for example, Swain (1998) are relevant for the construction of tasks to be used to develop receptive multilingualism. In such tasks, the learners' attention is drawn to lexical and phonetic/orthographic differences between L1 and L2 in order to enhance learners' intelligibility of related languages and to develop meta-linguistic awareness.

Previous studies have shown that for the acquisition of an active command of an L2, explicit instruction (tutored input with instruction and feedback) is more effective than implicit instruction without specific instruction or feedback (Spada and Tomita 2010). The situation in the case of receptive multilingualism may be different from a situation where a less closely related or unrelated language must be learned, since listeners may more easily be able to infer correspondences with their native language from untutored input than in a situation where the languages are incomprehensible for the learner.

---

2 http://www.aidenligne-francais-universite.auf.org/spip.php?page=sommaire_galpro_galnet
3 http://www.eurocomprehension.eu/
4 https://cordis.europa.eu/publication/rcn/11712_en.html
5 http://www.dylan-project.org/

8.6 Conclusion

There is a large number of interacting linguistic and extra-linguistic factors that should be taken into consideration when explaining or predicting how well speakers of two languages can communicate in the RM mode. RM has been suggested as a valuable addition to other modes of communication for crossing language barriers. However, more knowledge and awareness both among linguists and language professionals and among language users and policy makers are needed for this manner of communication to be more widely accepted and used.

References

Anderson, Heidi. 2005. *Intelligibility testing (RTT) between Mendankwe and Nkwen*. Dallas, Texas: Summer Institute of Linguistics.

Backus, Ad, Durk Gorter, Karlfried Knapp, Rosita Schjerve-Rindler & Jos Swanenberg. 2013. Inclusive multilingualism: Concept, modes and implications. *European Journal of Applied Linguistics* 1(2). 1–37.

Beerkens, Roos. 2009. *Receptive multilingualism as a language mode in the Dutch-German border area*. Münster: Westfälischen Wilhelms-Universität.

Berthele, Raphael. 2011. On abduction in receptive multilingualism. Evidence from cognate guessing tasks. *Applied Linguistics Review* 2. 191–220.

Berthele, Raphael & Gabriele Wittlin. 2013. Receptive multilingualism in the Swiss Army. *International Journal of Multilingualism* 10(2). 181–195.

Bezooijen, Renée van & Charlotte Gooskens. 2007. Interlingual text comprehension: Linguistic and extralinguistic determinants. In Jan D. ten Thije & Ludger Zeevaert (eds.), *Receptive multilingualism and intercultural communication: Linguistic analyses, language policies and didactic concepts*, 249–264. Amsterdam: John Benjamins.

Bilaniuk, Laada. 2010. Language in the balance: The politics of non-accommodation on bilingual Ukrainian-Russian television shows. *International Journal of the Sociology of Language* 201. 105–133.

Blanche-Benveniste, Claire. 2008. Comment retrouver l'expérience des anciens voyageurs en terres de langues romanes? In Virginie Conti & François Grin (eds.), *S'entendre entre langues voisines: Vers l'intercompréhension*, 33–51. Chêne-Bourg: Georg.

Bleses, Dorthe, Werner Vach, Marlene Slott, Sonja Wehberg, Pia Thomsen, Thomas O. Madsen & Hans Basbøll. 2008. Early vocabulary development in Danish and other languages: A CDI based comparison. *Journal of Child Language* 35. 619–650.

Branets Anna, Daria Bahtina & Anna Verschik. 2019. Mediated receptive multilingualism: Estonian-Russian-Ukrainian case study. *Linguistic Approaches to Bilingualism*. https://www.jbe-platform.com/content/journals/10.1075/lab.17079.ver (accessed 18 May 2019).

Braunmüller, Kurt. 2006. Vorbild Skandinavien? Zur Relevanz der rezeptiven Mehrsprachigkeit in Europa. In Konrad Ehlich & Antonie Hornung (eds.), *Praxen der Mehrsprachigkeit*, 11–31. Münster: Waxmann Verlag.

Braunmüller, Kurt. 2007. Receptive multilingualism in northern Europe in the Middle Ages. In Jan ten Thije & Ludger Zeevaert (eds.), *Receptive multilingualism: Linguistic analyses, language policies and didactic concepts*. Amsterdam: John Benjamins.

Casad, Eugene H. 1974. *Dialect intelligibility testing*. Norman: Summer Institute of Linguistics of the University of Oklahoma.

Čéplö, Slavomír, Ján Bátora, Adam Benkato, Jiří Milička, Christophe Pereira & Petr Zemánek. 2016. Mutual intelligibility of spoken Maltese, Libyan Arabic, and Tunisian Arabic functionally tested: A pilot study. *Folia Linguistica* 50(2). 583–628.

Conti, Virginie & François Grin. 2008. *S'entendre entre langues voisines: Vers l'intercompréhension*. Chêne-Bourg: Georg.

Deklaration om nordisk språkpolitik [Declaration on Nordic language policy]. 2006. Copenhagen: Nordiska ministerådet.

Delsing, Lars-Olof & Katarina Lundin Åkesson. 2005. *Håller språket ihop Norden? En forskningsrapport om ungdomars förståelse av danska, svenska och norska* [Does the language keep together the Nordic countries? A research report of mutual comprehension between young speakers of Danish, Swedish and Norwegian]. Copenhagen: Nordic Council of Ministers.

Doetjes, Gerald. 2007. Understanding differences in inter-Scandinavian language understanding. In Jan D. Ten Thije & Ludger Zeevaert (eds.), *Receptive multilingualism. Linguistic analyses, language policies and didactic concepts*, 217–230. Amsterdam: John Benjamins.

Doughty, Catherine J. 2003. Instructed SLA: Constraints, compensation, and enhancement. In Catherine J. Doughty & Michael H. Long (eds.), *The handbook of second language acquisition*, 256–310. Oxford: Blackwell.

EF EPI. 2017. EF English Proficiency Index. http://www.ef.nl/epi/ (accessed 18 May 2019).

European Commission. 2007. *Final report High Level Group on Multilingualism*. Luxembourg: Office for Official Publications of the European Communities.

Giles, Howard, Richard Y. Bourhis & Ann Davies. 1975. Prestige speech styles: The imposed norm and inherent value hypotheses. In William C. McCormack & Stephen A. Wurm (eds.), *Language in anthropology. IV: Language in many ways*, 589–596. The Hague: Mouton.

Giles, Howard & Tania Ogay. 2007. Communication Accommodation Theory. In Bryan B. Whaley & Wendy Samter (eds.), *Explaining communication: Contemporary theories and exemplars*, 293–310. Mahwah, NJ: Lawrence Erlbaum.

Golubović, Jelena. 2016. *Mutual intelligibility in the Slavic language area*. Doctoral dissertation. Groningen: University of Groningen.

Gooskens, Charlotte. 2005. Travel time as a predictor of linguistic distance. *Dialectologia et Geolinguistica* 13(13). 38–62.

Gooskens, Charlotte. 2007. The contribution of linguistic factors to the intelligibility of closely related languages. *Journal of Multilingual and Multicultural Development* 28(6). 445–467.

Gooskens, Charlotte. 2013. Experimental methods for measuring intelligibility of closely related language varieties. In Robert Bayley, Richard Cameron & Ceil Lucas (eds.), *The Oxford handbook of sociolinguistics*, 195–213. Oxford: Oxford University Press.

Gooskens, Charlotte & Renée van Bezooijen. 2006. Mutual comprehensibility of written Afrikaans and Dutch: symmetrical or asymmetrical? *Literary and Linguistic Computing* 23. 543–557.

Gooskens, Charlotte & Gerald Doetjes. 2009. Skriftsprogets rolle i den dansk-svenske talesprogsforståelse [The role of orthography in the Danish-Swedish spoken language comprehension]. *Språk och Stil* 19. 105–123.

Gooskens, Charlotte & Vincent J. van Heuven. 2017. Measuring cross-linguistic intelligibility in the Germanic, Romance and Slavic language groups. *Speech Communication* 89. 25–36.

Gooskens, Charlotte & Vincent J. van Heuven. 2019. How well can intelligibility of closely related languages in Europe be predicted by linguistic and non-linguistic variables? *Linguistic Approaches to Bilingualism*. www.jbe-platform.com/content/journals/10.1075/lab.17084.goo (accessed 18 May 2019).

Gooskens, Charlotte & Cindy Schneider. 2019. Linguistic and non-linguistic factors affecting intelligibility across closely related varieties in Pentecost Island, Vanuatu. *Dialectologia* 23. 59–84.

Gooskens, Charlotte & Femke Swarte. 2017. Linguistic and extra-linguistic predictors of mutual intelligibility between Germanic languages. *Nordic Journal of Linguistics* 40(2). 123–147.

Gooskens, Charlotte, Renée van Bezooijen & Vincent van Heuven. 2015. Mutual intelligibility of Dutch-German cognates by children: The devil is in the detail. *Linguistics* 53(2). 255–283.

Gooskens, Charlotte, Wilbert Heeringa & Karin Beijering. 2008. Phonetic and lexical predictors of intelligibility. *International Journal of Humanities and Arts Computing* 2 (1–2). 63–81.

Gooskens, Charlotte, Vincent J. van Heuven, Renée van Bezooijen & Jos J. A. Pacilly. 2010. Is spoken Danish less intelligible than Swedish? *Speech Communication* 52(11–12). 1022–1037.

Härmävaara, Hanna-Ilona. 2014. Facilitating mutual understanding in everyday interaction between Finns and Estonians. *Applied Linguistics Review* 5(1). 211–245.

Ház, Eva. 2005. *Deutsche und Niederländer. Untersuchungen zur Möglichkeit einer unmittelbaren Verständigung*. Hamburg: Kovač.

Hedquist, Rolf. 1985. *Nederländares förståelse av danka och svenska. En språkpedagogisk undersökning med utnyttjande av likheterna mellan språken* [The comprehension of Danish and Swedish among Dutchmen. A language pedagogical investigation using the similarities between the languages]. Umeå: Institutionerna för Fonetik och Nordiska Språk, Umeå Universitet.

Herkenrath, Annette. 2012. Receptive multilingualism in an immigrant constellation: Examples from Turkish-German children's language. *International Journal of Bilingualism* 16(3). 287–314.

Heuven, Vincent J. van. 2008. Making sense of strange sounds: (Mutual) intelligibility of related language varieties. A Review. *International Journal of Humanities and Arts Computing* 2(1–2). 39–62.

Hickerton, Harold, Glen D. Turner & Nancy P. Hickerton. 1952. Testing procedures for estimation transfer of information among Iroquois dialects and languages. *International Journal of American Linguistics* 18. 1–8.

Hilton, Nanna H., Charlotte Gooskens & Anja Schüppert. 2013. The influence of non-native morphosyntax on the intelligibility of a closely related language. *Lingua* 137(4). 1–18.

Hilton, Nanna H., Anja Schüppert & Charlotte Gooskens. 2011. Syllable reduction and articulation rates in Danish, Norwegian and Swedish. *Nordic Journal of Linguistics* 34(2). 215–237.

Hufeisen, Britta & Nicole Marx. 2007. How can DaFnE and EuroComGerm contribute to the concept of receptive multilingualism? Theoretical and practical considerations. In Jan D. ten Thije & Ludger Zeevaert (eds.), *Receptive Multilingualism*, 307–321. Amsterdam, Philadelphia: John Benjamins.

Jágrová, Klára, Tania Avgustinova, Irina Stenger & Andrea Fischer. 2019. Language models, surprisal and fantasy in Slavic intercomprehension. *Computer Speech and Language* 53. 242–275.

Jensen, John B. 1989. On the mutual intelligibility of Spanish and Portuguese. *Hispania* 72(4). 848–852.

Jørgensen, Nils & Eva Kärrlander. 2001. *Grannspraksförståelse i Öresundsregionen år 2000. Gymnasisters hörförståelse* [The comprehension of neighboring languages in the Öresund area in 2000. The comprehension of spoken language among secondary school children]. Lund: University of Lund.

Kluge, Angela. 2007. *"Sorry, could you repeat that, please?!" – Where does one language end and the next begin?* Jakarta: SIL International-Indonesia.

Kristiansen, Tore. 2009. The macro-level social meanings of late-modern Danish accents. *Acta Linguistica Hafniensia* 41. 167–192.

Kürschner, Sebastian, Charlotte Gooskens & Renée van Bezooijen. 2008. Linguistic determinants of the intelligibility of Swedish words among Danes. *International Journal of Humanities and Arts Computing* 2(1–2). 83–100.

Lambelet, Amelia & Pierre-Yves Mauron. 2017. Receptive multilingualism at school: An uneven playing ground? *International Journal of Bilingual Education and Bilingualism* 20(7). 854–867.

Lambert, Wallace E., R. C. Hodgson, Robert D. Gardner & Samuel Fillenbaum. 1960. Evaluational reactions to spoken languages. *The Journal of Abnormal and Social Psychology* 60(1). 44–51.

Lindblom, Björn. 1990. Explaining phonetic variation: A sketch of the H & H theory. In William Hardcastle & Alain Marchal (eds.), *Speech production and speech modeling*, 403–439. Dordrecht: Kluwer.

Lüdi, Georges. 2013. Receptive multilingualism as a strategy for sharing mutual linguistic resources in the workplace in a Swiss context. *International Journal of Multilingualism* 10 (2). 140–158.

Lyons, John. 1977. *Semantics*. Cambridge: Cambridge University Press.

Melo-Pfeifer, Silvia. 2014. Intercomprehension between Romance languages and the role of English: a study of multilingual chat rooms. *International Journal of Multilingualism* 11(1). 120–137.

Mieszkowska, Karolina & Agnieszka Otwinowska. 2015. Is A2 in German better than B2 in French when reading Danish? The role of prior language knowledge when faced with an unknown language. In Gessica De Angelis, Ulrike Jessner & Marijana Kresić (eds.), *Crosslinguistic influence and crosslinguistic interaction in multilingual language learning*, 213–234. London: Bloomsbury Academic.

Moberg, Jens, Charlotte Gooskens, John Nerbonne & Nathan Vaillette. 2007. Conditional entropy measures intelligibility among related languages. In Peter Dirix, Ineke Schuurman, Vincent Vandeghinste & Frank Van Eynde (eds.), *Computational Linguistics in the Netherlands 2006: Selected papers from the 17th CLIN Meeting*, 51–66. Utrecht: LOT.

Mulken, Margo van & Berna Hendriks. 2015. Your language or mine? Or English as a lingua franca? Comparing effectiveness in English as a lingua franca and L1–L2 interactions:

Implications for corporate language policies. *Journal of Multilingual and Multicultural Development* 36(4). 404–422.

Nábělková, Mira. 2007. Closely-related languages in contact: Czech, Slovak, "Czechoslovak". *International Journal of the Sociology of Language* 183. 53–73.

Nerbonne, John & Wilbert Heeringa. 2010. Measuring dialect differences. In Jürgen E. Schmidt & Peter Auer (eds.), *Language and space: Theories and methods*, 550–567. Berlin: Mouton De Gruyter.

Ribbert, Anne & Jan D. Ten Thije. 2007. Receptive multilingualism in Dutch-German intercultural team cooperation. In Jan D. Ten Thije & Ludger Zeevaert (eds.), *Receptive multilingualism: Linguistic analyses, language policies and didactic concepts*, 73–101. Amsterdam: Benjamins.

Sağın-Şimşek, Çiğdem & Elena A. Ünlü. 2017. A hearer-based analysis of Turkish-Azerbaijani receptive multilingual communication. *International Journal of Bilingualism*. https://doi.org/10.1177/1367006917703457 (accessed 18 May 2019).

Salehi, Mohammad & Aydin Neysani. 2017. Receptive intelligibility of Turkish to Iranian-Azerbaijani speakers. *Cogent Education* 4 (1). https://doi.org/10.1080/2331186X.2017.1326653 (accessed 18 May 2019).

Schmidt, Richard. 2001. Attention. In Peter Robinson (ed.), *Cognition and second language instruction*, 3–32. Cambridge: Cambridge University Press.

Schüppert, Anja. 2011. *Origin of asymmetry: Mutual intelligibility of spoken Danish and Swedish*. Groningen: University of Groningen dissertation.

Schüppert, Anja, Nanna H. Hilton & Charlotte Gooskens. 2016. Why is Danish so difficult to understand for fellow Scandinavians? *Speech Communication* 79. 47–60.

Séguy, Jean. 1973. La dialectométrie dans l'atlas linguistique de Gascogne. *Revue de Linguistique Romane* (37). 1–24.

Simons, Gary F. 1979. *Language variation and limits to communication*. Ithaca, NY: Department of Modern Languages and Linguistics, Cornell University.

Singer, Ruth & Salome Harris. 2016. What practices and ideologies support small-scale multilingualism? A case study of Warruwi community, northern Australia. *International Journal of the Sociology of Language* 241. 163–208.

Spada, Nina & Yasuyo Tomita. 2010. Interactions between type of instruction and type of language feature: A meta-analysis. *Language Learning* 60. 263–308.

Swain, Merrill. 1998. Focus on form through conscious reflection. In Catherine J. Doughty & Jessica Williams (eds.), *Focus on form in classroom second language acquisition*, 64–81. New York: Cambridge University Press.

Swarte, Femke, Anja Schüppert & Charlotte Gooskens. 2015. Does German help speakers of Dutch to understand written and spoken Danish words? –The role of second language knowledge in decoding an unknown but related language. In Gessica De Angelis, Ulrike Jessner & Marijana Kresić (eds.), *Crosslinguistic influence and crosslinguistic interaction in multilingual language learning*, 173–197. London: Bloomsbury Publishing.

Tang, Chaoju & Vincent J. van Heuven. 2009. Mutual intelligibility of Chinese dialects experimentally tested. *Lingua* 119(5). 709–732.

Trudgill, Peter & Howard Giles. 1978. Sociolinguistics and linguistic value judgments: Correctness, adequacy, and aesthetics. In Frank Coppieters & Didier L. Goyvaerts (eds.), *Functional studies in language and literature*, 167–190. Gent: Story-Scientia.

Vanhove, Jan & Raphael Berthele. 2015. The lifespan development of cognate guessing skills in an unknown related language. *International Review of Applied Linguistics in Language Teaching* 53(1). 1–38.

Vetter, Eva. 2012. Exploiting receptive multilingualism in institutional language learning: The case of Italian in the Austrian secondary school system. *International Journal of Bilingualism* 16(3). 348–365.

Voegelin, Charles F. & Zellig S. Harris. 1951. Methods for determining intelligibility among dialects of natural languages. *Proceedings of the American Philosophical Society* 45. 322–329.

Zeevaert, Ludger. 2004. *Interskandinavische Kommunikation. Strategien zur Etablierung von Verständigung zwischen Skandinaviern im Diskurs*. Hamburg: Dr. Kovač.

Zuckerman, Miron & Robert E. Driver. 1989. What sounds beautiful is good: The vocal attractiveness stereotype. *Journal of Nonverbal Behavior* 13(2). 67–82.

Deborah Chen Pichler, Wanette Reynolds
and Jeffrey Levi Palmer

9 Multilingualism in Signing Communities

9.1 Introduction

This chapter examines the diverse language practices of individuals raised in signing communities, focusing on children from families that use at least one natural sign language. These individuals may be Deaf or hearing; the latter are often referred to as Codas (Children of Deaf Adults) or, when emphasizing the minor status of young individuals, Kodas (Kids of Deaf Adults). In terms of child language acquisition, research so far has demonstrated that children who have access to a natural sign language from birth achieve the classic developmental milestones (e.g., onset of babbling, first words, first 50 words, first-word combinations) on a timeline that is strikingly similar to that of hearing children acquiring a spoken language from birth (Meier and Newport 1990). However, the complex issues of multilingualism discussed in this volume exist in signing communities just as they do in spoken language communities, including migration patterns of multilingual families, geographic proximity to international borders, and maintenance of family culture.

The impact of multilingualism on language acquisition is further complicated by issues related to accessibility and modality. Deaf children vary widely in the degree to which they can hear, so their access to spoken languages varies accordingly. Their access to natural sign language(s) also varies, depending on when (or whether) their parents expose them to fluent signed input. These variations in access to spoken and signed languages in turn affect how Deaf people use those languages in their own production, which in turn affect the language input that they provide to their own Deaf and Koda children. Finally, multilingual interactions may be *unimodal*, occurring in a single modality, or *bimodal*, involving both signed and spoken language(s). Multilingualism in Deaf and Koda children's language use is thus characterized by highly complex interactions of many features, some of which are unique to signing communities. The question of how these interactions shape language development has traditionally been approached from the perspectives of linguistics and language acquisition, but

---

Deborah Chen Pichler, Gallaudet University, Washington (DC), U.S.A.
Wanette Reynolds, California State University, Long Beach (CA), U.S.A.
Jeffrey Levi Palmer, National Deaf Center on Postsecondary Outcomes at the University of Texas, Austin (TX), U.S.A.

https://doi.org/10.1515/9781501507984-009

recently, inquiries from a variety of other fields have also yielded groundbreaking insights, some of which we highlight in this chapter.

Although multilingualism is a defining feature of many signing communities, it is only now being recognized as such. The preponderance of existing research on language acquisition in signing communities focuses on bilingualism, either in terms of sign+print bilingualism or sign+spoken bilingualism. The latter is known as *bimodal bilingualism* and has emerged as a very productive research domain in recent years. This chapter thus makes frequent mention of empirical findings about bimodal bilingual acquisition, which we extend whenever possible to multilingual contexts. We include numerous examples of bilingual and multilingual utterances by children exposed from birth to one or more sign languages at home; some of these examples highlight potential *modality effects*, or phenomena that are unique to contexts involving signed languages.

9.2 Background information

Sign languages generally arise among low incidence deaf communities. The Ethnologue (www.ethnologue.com), a listing of every known living language, lists 143 sign languages as of July 2019. However, this number may underestimate the actual total, depending on where one draws the line between "languages" and "dialects"; as is the case for spoken languages (see Chapter 2, this volume), sign languages with large numbers of users dispersed across wide geographical areas (e.g., Chinese Sign Language) or those in countries with historically de-centralized systems of government and education (e.g., Italian Sign Language) display regional variation that may not be mutually comprehensible across signers from different parts of the country. Natural sign languages develop spontaneously within Deaf communities and are distinct from the ambient spoken languages used in the surrounding hearing communities. However, language contact provides rich possibilities for contact phenomena across languages and modalities, discussed later in this chapter.

Transmission of sign languages follows unusual patterns due to the fact that the vast majority of deaf children (over 95% in the U.S., according to Mitchell and Karchmer 2004) are born to hearing parents who do not sign. Most of these children are educated following the oral philosophy, which focuses on development of listening (to the extent possible) and speaking to the exclusion of any natural sign language. In contrast, the incidence of hearing children born to Deaf parents is quite high, over 80% in the U.S. (Mitchell et al. 2006). As Compton (2014) points out, this means that in the United States the majority of American Sign Language (ASL) native signers are not Deaf (and the majority of Deaf signers are not native signers). Even among Deaf native signing children (those with Deaf parents), an increasing number receive cochlear implants early enough to allow early bilingual acquisition of a spoken language in addition to their home sign language. These Deaf children of Deaf parents, who use cochlear implants (*DDCI* for short), develop language in similar ways to Codas (Davidson et al. 2014; Palmer 2015). We therefore group both populations in the category of native signer bimodal bilinguals.

9.3 Many different types of signing bilinguals and multilinguals

Bilinguals in signing communities exhibit proficiency in a sign language and varying degrees of proficiency in the ambient spoken language, determined by the complex factors outlined in the previous section. Signing communities actively promote bilingualism, since literacy in the dominant spoken/written language plays a crucial role in Deaf individuals' access to education, employment and civic integration. Accordingly, the World Deaf Federation recognizes bilingualism as a fundamental human right for the education of deaf children (World Deaf Federation 2016). Signing communities typically emerge in contexts with a pre-existing spoken language community, giving rise to expected pairings of an indigenous sign language and its ambient spoken language. In Table 9.1, the four most commonly distinguished types of sign language bilinguals in North America are presented. *Native Deaf bilinguals* acquire sign language in the home and literacy in the ambient spoken language (through print

Table 9.1: Types of bilinguals in sign communities.

Bilingual Signer Type	Home Language(s)	Language of the General Community	Language in School
Native Deaf Bilingual	ASL	written English	ASL, written(/spoken) English
Native Bimodal Bilingual	ASL	English	English
Nonnative Deaf Bilingual	English	written English	(ASL), written(/spoken) English
Nonnative Bimodal Bilingual	English	English	(ASL), English

and sign language fingerspelling) from the environment and at school. *Native bimodal bilinguals* simultaneously acquire the spoken and signed languages either as hearing signers with Deaf parents (e.g., K/Codas) or as DDCI. As mentioned earlier, this group of native bilinguals account for the smallest segment of the signing community, the largest number of bilinguals being nonnative sign language users, both Deaf and hearing. *Nonnative Deaf bilinguals* are born to hearing nonsigning parents and often do not receive regular exposure to a sign language until later in life. Finally, *Nonnative bimodal bilinguals* are monolingual users of a spoken language who learn a sign language as a second language (also referred to as *second modality L2* or *M2L2 learners*).[1]

While ensuring early and unfettered first language exposure for deaf children remains a crucial issue (Humphries et al. 2012), awareness of multilingualism in the sign community is attracting growing interest. Pizzo (2016) uses Gallaudet Research Institute data (2009–2010) to estimate that up to 35% of school-aged deaf children are multilingual in the United States. As in other multilingual communities, members of signing communities acquire more than two languages in a variety of contexts and due to varying circumstances. Table 9.2 lists a sampling of common signing community multilinguals with native sign language exposure. The multilingual types are divided into two general categories: *Deaf Multilinguals* and *Bimodal Multilinguals*. Ostensibly, there is little difference between the two groups other than a distinction between the acquisition of spoken language by eye (writing and reading) and the ability to perceive and acquire spoken languages by ear. This distinction is based on well-documented differences between literacy development and natural language acquisition (Cormier et al. 2012; Padden and Ramsey 2000). Table 9.2 illustrates common subtypes that exist among Deaf multilinguals and bimodal multilinguals. The table is not meant to be exhaustive but rather demonstrates the complex linguistic diversity of signing communities that emerges once we take multilingualism into full consideration. Immigrants and their children (i.e., heritage signers, discussed in section 9.4.3) make up a majority of the Deaf multilinguals, although Deaf students may also acquire foreign spoken languages and sign languages through formal coursework (Ammons 1988; Kontra, Kata, and Piniel 2015). Some bimodal multilinguals immigrate to the United States with their parents and learn the sign language and spoken language of their new homeland. Second-generation immigrants may learn more than one sign language

---

[1] This chapter focuses on child and adult native signers, and as such, will not discuss hearing signers who learn one or more sign languages as a second language. However, the M2L2 signer population is growing quickly and exhibit many of the multilingual phenomena we discuss in this chapter. Readers interested in M2L2 sign language acquisition are referred to Chen Pichler and Koulidobrova (2015), Koulidobrova and Palmer (2015), and Woll (2012).

Table 9.2: Examples of native-signing multilinguals.

Bilingual Type	Home Language(s)	Language of the General Community	Language in School
Deaf Multilingual			
Deaf immigrant to US	Korean Sign Language, written Korean	written Korean	Korean Sign Language, written Korean, ASL, written English
Deaf heritage signer in US	ASL, Japanese Sign Language	written English	ASL, written English
Deaf language learner in US	ASL	written English	ASL, written English, written Spanish (and/or Lengua de Signos Española or LSE)
Bimodal Multilingual			
Coda or DDCI immigrant	Lengua de Señas Mexicana (LSM), Spanish, ASL	Spanish, English	Spanish, English
Coda or DDCI heritage signer	Russian Sign Language, ASL	English	English
Coda or DDCI heritage signer and heritage speaker	ASL, English, Spanish	English	Spanish
Coda or DDCI language learner	ASL, English, Mandarin Chinese	English	English

in the home or receive early exposure to two spoken languages in addition to native sign exposure in the home; both groups are classified as multilingual heritage signers.

9.4 Multidisciplinary insights on bimodal bilingualism

As is demonstrated from Tables 9.1 and 9.2, the variety of multilingual contexts in signing communities is dauntingly complex, and the multilingual, multimodal mixing that occurs in those contexts has consequently evaded systematic investigation until very recently. Bimodal mixing in particular has emerged as a major topic of interest; speakers are normally under physical constraints that prevent them from articulating content from two languages simultaneously (i.e. humans have only one tongue), but this physical constraint is suspended in bimodal mixing, where both signed and spoken (or mouthed) content can be articulated at the same time. This critical difference between unimodal spoken language bilinguals and bimodal signed + spoken bilinguals has far-reaching consequences for how human languages are organized in the mind, acquired, processed, and lost, and how multiple languages interact across modalities. Researchers have approached these questions from a number of different angles. In the next section, we overview some of the findings that have been reported so far, focusing on the perspectives from linguistics, psycholinguistics/cognitive neurolinguistics, and child language acquisition, currently the three most prolific domains in bimodal bilingual research.

9.4.1 Linguistics: Defining different code-mixing behaviors in the signing community

The phenomenon of bimodal bilingualism under its current definition as bilingualism in a signed language and a spoken language[2] came to the attention of most linguistics researchers through influential publications introducing the general public to the concept of Deaf and Coda cultural identities and the central role of natural sign languages for both identities (e.g., Lane, Hoffmeister, and Bahan 1996; Padden and Humphries 1990; Preston 1995). Over the course of interviewing 150 adult hearing children of deaf parents in the late 1980s, Preston (1995) often encountered a "hybrid language" that was part ASL, part English, which "mirrored [the] bilingual and bicultural heritage" of Codas. Bishop and Hicks (2005) explored the unique cross-linguistic mixing phenomena observed among adult Codas, situating them in the complex sociolinguistic context that Codas inhabit at the intersection of Deaf and hearing cultures. They focused primarily on *Coda-talk*

---

2 We should note the sporadic and now largely defunct use in the past of "bimodal bilingualism" to refer to (a) text+sign bilingualism (for those considering written language as its own modality) and (b) speech+sign bilingualism for Deaf students in educational programs espousing the Total Communication philosophy (strongly associated with Simultaneous Communication or Signed English, in which the grammaticality of the signed portion is degraded). Since the mid-2000s, both of these usages have faded, but they still persist in older publications that remain in circulation.

or *Coda speak*, first described by Lucas and Valli (1992) as "spoken English words produced with ASL syntactic structure, what might be called 'spoken ASL'" (1992: 114). Bishop and Hicks (2005) extended Coda-talk to include spoken, spoken and signed, and written production; some representative examples are given in Table 9.3.

Table 9.3: Examples of Coda-talk from Bishop and Hicks (2005: 205–211).

	Coda-talk examples	English equivalent and explanation
Written English with omitted arguments, morphology and function words	He not even wince. I finally find.	'He didn't even wince.' 'I finally found it.'
Lexical innovations playing on English glosses for ASL signs	You think me furniture?	'You think I'm nothing?' (Plays on the similarity of ASL signs NOTHING and FURNITURE)
Expressions mimicking forms used by Deaf parents	Allaboo! King Burger	'I love you!' (simultaneously signed and spoken in deaf voice) 'Burger King' (a word reversal common among Deaf signers)

Bishop and Hicks (2005) argued that regardless of the modality (or modalities) of the expressions in Table 9.3, they all reflect "a conscious and purposeful commitment to spoken ASL" that is the hallmark of Coda-talk (2005: 215). Other sociolinguistics researchers have also noted the role of Coda-talk as an ingroup cultural identifier used only among Codas (Bishop 2010), and often in private; for instance, the mimicking of Deaf people's distinct vocal patterns through deaf voice is normally considered rude and offensive, especially if produced by someone who is not Coda.

While Coda-talk has so far been studied only among adult Codas, similar constructions have been noted from young Kodas, who sometimes produce speech, with or without accompanying signing, that reflects ASL grammar. Example (1) is a speech-only utterance by a Koda participant in our research program, *Development of Bimodal Bilingualism* (Lillo-Martin, Quadros, and Chen Pichler 2016). This utterance, produced when the child was unable to separate two fused pieces of playdoh, features a null subject in preverbal position and a sentence-final copy of the (null) subject, in pronoun form. Such a construction is ill-formed in spoken English, but well-formed and quite frequent in ASL.

(1) *Stuck it. Stuck it.*
 'It's stuck. It's stuck.'
 (Young bimodal bilingual Coda-talk, Ben 2;3)

At the other end of the spectrum are utterances in which signs are produced in English word order, sometimes incorporating invented signs to represent affixes common in spoken English. This type of signing is variously labeled as *Simultaneous Communication, Signing Exact English* or *Manually Coded English,* and can also be thought of as a category of language mixing between English and ASL, albeit this mixing can be so English-dominant as to render the signed component largely unintelligible to Deaf viewers (Tevenal and Villanueva 2009).

In addition to signing in English word order or speaking in ASL word order, code-mixing in the context of bimodal bilingualism also allows *code-switching,* in the familiar sense of the term, wherein an individual switches between only speaking or only signing. However, multiple researchers have reported that although Codas sometimes engage in code-switching between their spoken and signed languages (e.g., switching from ASL only to spoken English only, or vice versa), they are much more likely to *code-blend,* producing a bimodal utterance in which spoken and signed elements are produced simultaneously (Emmorey et al. 2008 for ASL/English).

Of all bimodal bilingual phenomena, code-blending has attracted perhaps the most intense research attention. Many analyses have focused on the anatomy of code-blending, structural patterns that distinguish different types of code-blended utterances, and contexts that trigger each one. Code-blending typologies differ but linguistic analyses generally fall into one of two basic approaches. The first, common in earlier research that focused on Deaf rather than Coda or DDCI signers, regards mixed utterances as part of a contact variety of signing, an ASL-English pidgin (Lucas and Valli 1992). Under this view, code-mixed utterances are governed by grammatical rules specific to a "third grammar" (e.g. Poplack 1980), distinct from either ASL or English grammar.

Other linguists reject positing a third grammar as both unnecessary and theoretically undesirable, arguing that the grammatical rules governing code-mixing should be derivable from nothing more than the interacting grammars of the participant languages (e.g. MacSwan 2000). Researchers with this perspective often identify either the signed language or the spoken language as the matrix language of a mixed utterance (c.f. Myers Scotton 2001), into which elements of the auxiliary language are inserted, as in Example (2). Sometimes no matrix language can be identified, and the message of the utterance appears to be distributed in a complementary fashion across both modalities, as in (3). And yet other times, the message essentially appears twice, once in each modality, as in (4) (in code-blended examples, signed glosses are printed in CAPITAL LETTERS. Spoken words appear directly below the signs they accompany, in *italics*; if speech is in a language other than English, English glosses are provided immediately below, also in italics. Finally, the translation for the combined code-blend is given in 'quotes'.

(2) English base ASL code-blend (adapted from Emmorey et al. 2008: 48)
 ASL: SIGN
 English: *She didn't even sign until fourteen.*
 'She didn't even sign until (she was) fourteen (years old).'

(3) Complementary Italian Sign Language (LIS)-Italian code-blend (adapted from Bishop, Hicks, Bertone, and Sala 2006: 96)
 LIS: (MY)-ENTIRE-FACE
 Italian: *Ero viola.*
 (I) was purple [black and blue]
 'My entire face was black and blue.'

(4) Fully bimodal ASL-English code-blend (adapted from Emmorey et al. 2008: 48)
 ASL: NOT THINK REALLY LIVE
 English: *I don't think he would really live.*
 'I don't think he would really live.'

For the most part, signed and spoken content of adult code-blended utterances is *congruent* and *temporally coordinated*; that is, co-occurring signing and speech generally express equivalent information. This is not to say that code-blended content is always congruent. Bimodal bilinguals whose signed and spoken languages differ more strikingly in word order than do ASL and English encounter frequent opportunities for *incongruent* or *mismatched code-blending*. Example (5) from Italian Sign Language (LIS, an SOV language) code-blended with spoken Italian (an SVO language) is one such case, as the meaning of the first and last signs do not match that of the speech with which they are aligned.

(5) Incongruent/mismatched LIS-Italian code-blend (adapted from Branchini and Donati 2016: 11)
 LIS: FROG   EAT   WHAT
 Italian: *Cosa ha mangiato la rana*
 What have.3SG eat.PRTC the frog
 'What did the frog eat?'

Even among ASL-English Codas, Quadros, Lillo-Martin, and Chen Pichler (2015) noted that children produced more mismatched code-blends than adults, as well as more cases of repetitions and self-corrections, indications that although congruent code-blending is favored, temporal coordination of bimodal material requires time to develop. However, in all cases, the combined signed and spoken content expresses a single proposition, even in incongruent cases, consistent with assumptions that the human language computational system only outputs one proposition at a time, even when that proposition appears in two modalities simultaneously.

This assumption forms the basis of the *Language Synthesis Model*, one of several theoretical models of the human language capacity recently proposed to account for code-blending and other bimodal bilingual mixing phenomena. The technical details of this model are beyond the scope of this chapter (interested readers are referred to Lillo-Martin, Quadros, and Chen Pichler 2016), but in brief, it proposes that acquiring a language involves acquiring a set of syntactic features (abstract morphemes) for that language that exist independently of the phonological forms (words) that match or "check" those features. Multilinguals possess one set of features and phonological forms for each of their languages, and these elements can interact, creating mixed structures. The same set of features in a given derivation can be checked by phonological forms from a sign language, a spoken language, or both simultaneously as long as no features of the signed form clash with those of the co-occurring spoken form. Although the language synthesis model is still a work in progress, it approaches the challenges posed by bimodal mixing head-on and embodies a new awareness among sign language researchers that any theoretical model we propose for the human language capacity must be able to accommodate multilingual mixing, regardless of modality.

9.4.2 Psycholinguistics and cognitive neuroscience

Investigations of bimodal bilingualism from the psycholinguistic perspective have yielded important insights related to language processing, control and other cognitive functions in the bilingual brain. Much of the psycholinguistic research on adult Codas is relevant to the proposal that both of a bilingual's languages remain active at all times (Kroll, Bobb, and Wodnieka 2006), such that when a bilingual wants to use only language A, language B must be inhibited or suppressed, and vice versa (Green 1998). Switching between languages incurs a cognitive cost, and unimodal spoken language bilinguals show a greater switching cost when switching into their dominant language than when switching into their weaker language, because a dominant language must be more strongly suppressed to prevent interference when speaking the weaker language (Meuter and Allport 1999).

Unlike unimodal bilinguals, bimodal bilinguals have the option of not inhibiting either language, since they can code-blend, yet they still exhibit asymmetrical switching costs. English-dominant adult Codas studied by Emmorey et al. (2008) code-blended often, but strongly preferred either continuous bimodal production or single-sign code blends, consisting of a one-sign-long blend in otherwise spoken English utterances. Both options involve full activation of English and either full or partial activation of ASL, the weaker language. No single-word code-blends occurred, according to Emmorey et al. (2008), because English-dominant Codas must firmly suppress English in order to produce well-formed ASL.

Interestingly, Codas' reduced requirement to inhibit one language or another may mean that some aspects of the much-touted "bilingual advantage in cognitive control" (Bialystok et al. 2009) do not occur for bimodal bilinguals. Emmorey et al. (2008) reported that adult Codas scored lower than unimodal bilinguals and no higher than monolingual hearing controls on a task of executive control. This result has been widely interpreted as evidence that the enhanced bilingual cognitive control develops in part due to frequent monitoring of which language to use with different people and, accordingly, repeated inhibition of one or the other language. However, further exploration of bimodal bilinguals in this area is needed to confirm the accuracy of this proposal.

Finally, the high frequency of code-blending observed among adult Codas also suggests that lexical retrieval in two languages at once incurs less cognitive cost than inhibiting one language. Emmorey, Petrich, and Gollan (2012) confirmed this hypothesis through tests in which adult Codas named pictures in ASL only, English only, or ASL-English code-blends. Response times in the code-blended condition were no slower than in the ASL only condition, and adding English also had a facilitative effect when naming low-frequency signs that are normally difficult to retrieve. Similarly, processing studies have demonstrated cross-language activation of ASL by Deaf ASL-English bilinguals engaged in an English-only task in which they must judge whether pairs of English words were semantically related. Morford et al. (2011) reported that Deaf adults showed interference from the ASL translation equivalents of the English words they were judging. These and other psycholinguistic studies clearly demonstrate that the cross-language activation observed for unimodal bilinguals also occurs for bimodal bilinguals, despite the fact that words in different modalities share no phonological overlap. This outcome challenges standing assumptions based on unimodal spoken language bilingualism, according to which cross-language activation depends on similarities in phonological form between equivalent words in the two languages.

9.4.3 Child language acquisition: Insights made possible by bimodal bilingual data

Language acquisition researchers studying bimodal bilingualism ask how typical bilingual developmental patterns are affected when the child's languages occupy different modalities. When differences arise, they sometimes reveal errors in our previous assumptions that are difficult to see from unimodal bilingual data alone. One classic example of this is Pettito et al. (2001), a study of Canadian Kodas that challenged the claim that bilingual babies are "confused" by exposure to two languages at once and are delayed in achieving early developmental milestones compared to monolingual children. Furthermore, the apparent paucity of translation equivalents in young bilingual speech led to speculation that bilingual children do not differentiate the vocabulary or grammatical rules of their two languages before the age of 3;0 (Volterra and Taeschner 1978). Petitto et al. (2001) argued that existing studies of bilinguals underestimated children's early vocabulary size by discarding a high number of "neutrals" (p. 13) or words which the researcher is unable to attribute to one language or the other, perhaps because the target forms in the child's two languages sound similar, and/or because the child is not yet able to articulate those target words accurately. By examining the early lexical development of three Kodas learning Québec Sign Language (LSQ) and French, Petitto et al. (2001) eliminated the problem of neutrals and found that the Kodas achieved their first word, first two-word combinations and first fifty words at ages comparable to monolingual norms. Translation equivalents between LSQ and French also accounted for 40–51% of the youngest Kodas' acquired signs. Together these results suggest that language input in two languages does not confuse bilingual children or delay their vocabulary development, although the presence of neutrals in unimodal bilingual data may depress figures for total vocabulary and translation equivalents. Bimodal bilinguals offer a way to eliminate neutrals, resulting in more accurate findings.

Bimodal bilingual children are often surrounded by a mix of hearing and Deaf people, and like their unimodal bilingual counterparts, they learn fairly quickly to determine the appropriate language to use with various interlocutors. Griffith (1985) describes a Koda engaging in "mode-finding" with an unfamiliar interlocutor as early as 20 months, which she describes as alternatively addressing the stranger in ASL alone, code-blended ASL and English, and English alone to determine, by the stranger's response, which "mode" was the right one. Lillo-Martin et al. (2014) also report differentiation of language choice by American and Brazilian Kodas between ages 1;4 and 3;6, with all children producing more spoken language with hearing interlocutors and more sign language with Deaf interlocutors. However, they engaged in code-blending much more often when addressing Deaf adults than when addressing hearing adults (also reported for Finnish Kodas by Kanto, Laasko, and Huttunen 2017). This pattern is initially perplexing, unless the Kodas' voicing is for their own benefit rather than that of their interlocutors, as suggested by Petroj, Guerrera, and Davidson (2014). This may indicate that these Kodas, who are dominant in their spoken language like the adult Codas discussed in the previous section, also resort to code-blending as a strategy for easing the cognitive costs of fully suppressing English when they sign. Because ASL is a weaker language for them, it is more easily suppressed when speaking English, and code-blending is not necessary.

With regard to language mixing, bimodal bilingual children resemble their adult counterparts in strongly preferring code-blending over code-switching (e.g. van den Bogaerde 2000 for Sign Language of the Netherlands/Dutch; Petitto et al. 2001 for LSQ/French; Chen Pichler and Quinn 2008 for ASL/English; Kanto, Laasko, and Huttunen 2017 for Finnish Sign Language/Finnish). Because of the prevalence of code-mixing by adults (both hearing and Deaf), it is possible that bimodal bilingual children's use of code-blending reflects that of their input. This possibility was investigated by van den Bogaerde and Baker (2008) through a longitudinal study of Kodas in the Netherlands ranging in age from 2;11 to 6;0. They found that the children's use of Dutch-only, Sign Language of the Netherlands (NGT)-only and code-blended utterances partially matched their Deaf mothers' use but was also variously affected by the children's proficiency in Dutch and NGT and their changing preferences for each language. Additionally, the Koda participant whose Deaf mother was the least tolerant of being addressed in Dutch-only was the most consistent of the Koda participants in using either NGT-only or code-blending with his mother. Van den Bogaerde and Baker (2008) suggest that the strictness with which Deaf parents expect their children to sign may ultimately be the best predictor of language choice among young bimodal bilinguals (see also Chapter 10, this volume).

Most bimodal bilingual children are integrated into the majority spoken language environment by age 5;0, when they enter school. Accordingly, many become dominant in their spoken language around this time, exerting noticeable effects on their sign language development. Lillo-Martin, Quadros, and Chen Pichler (2016) report several syntactic domains in which American and Brazilian

Koda and DDCI children diverged from patterns previously reported for Deaf children (without cochlear implants). For instance, ASL and Libras (Brazilian Sign Language) allow Wh-elements in initial, final and doubled positions, and Wh-questions elicited from Deaf children between ages 4;0–6;0 include all of these variants (Lillo-Martin 2000). American and Brazilian Kodas spontaneously produced varied word order for Wh-questions around 2;0 (Quadros, Lillo-Martin, and Chen Pichler 2013), but when they were tested between ages 4;0–6;0, they produced almost exclusively Wh-initial constructions, the primary word order for Wh-questions in both English and Brazilian Portuguese.

Similarly, Palmer (2015) found that by 23 months, ASL-English bimodal bilinguals developed Subject-Verb (SV) and Verb-Object (VO) word orders in their spontaneous ASL production. These orders are consistent with the basic word order (SVO) for both ASL and English. However, by 40 months, bimodal bilinguals had still not developed productive use of VS and OV orders, noncanonical word orders that are grammatical in ASL and used productively by Deaf children (without implants) by 30 months (Chen Pichler 2001). Developmental differences between young bimodal bilingual children and Deaf comparison groups also manifest at the discourse level, affecting subject referent tracking patterns in ASL narratives. Reynolds (2016) elicited narratives from six bimodal bilinguals at ages 5;2–6;9, and again at 6;7–8;2. The results showed an increasing dependence on overt forms for referent maintenance and reintroduction, diverging from their age-matched Deaf counterparts.

Many ASL developmental patterns of bimodal bilinguals dominant in their spoken language call to mind similar patterns reported for heritage speakers' development of their home language (Benmamoun, Montrul, and Polinsky 2013). An emerging literature on *heritage signers* identifies developmental patterns for some aspects of sign language grammar that appear to diverge from those reported for Deaf children from Deaf families who do not have access to spoken language through cochlear implants (Chen Pichler et al. 2017; Chen Pichler, Lillo-Martin, and Palmer 2018; Palmer 2015; Reynolds 2018). This line of investigation is still in its infancy but highlights the importance of understanding how variation in the input affects ultimate attainment for heritage language users, regardless of modality.

9.5 Extensions into multilingualism

Multilingualism in signing communities is a new field of investigation comprising several lines of research that are still largely autonomous. These include studies of Deaf communities in contact where more than one sign language coexist (e.g., Quinto-Pozos and Adam 2015); studies of *cross-signing*, documenting *ad hoc* communication strategies used between signers without a common sign language (e.g., Byun et al. 2018); and *translanguaging* in contexts of Deaf education (e.g. Swanwick 2017). Although researchers in these domains may not reference each other yet, many of their findings are highly relevant for each other, as we hope to demonstrate by grouping them together in this chapter. Note that in some of the studies reviewed below, researchers refer to "bilinguals" and "bilingualism" rather than "multilinguals" and "multilingualism". The former usage is common in studies of signers who know more than one sign language, reflecting a focus of those studies on the interaction between those sign languages. Of course, signers who know more than one sign language invariably also know at least one spoken language, which exerts an influence even in signed-only utterances (in the form of fingerspelled words, borrowings of lexical items, calques, etc.). The term "signing bilingual" in this context can thus be understood to refer to multilinguals.

9.5.1 Multilingualism among signing communities in contact

The popularity of bimodal bilingualism as a topic of research has given the impression that there are two distinct kinds of bilingualism: unimodal, of the traditionally studied spoken language type, and bimodal, strongly associated with signing and modality effects. Unimodal bilingualism in two sign languages is overlooked in this dichotomy, yet it is precisely this variety of bilingualism that can best answer some of the most interesting questions raised by bimodal bilingualism research (Chen Pichler, Koulidobrova, and Palmer, in press). Many of the novel insights from bimodal bilingualism stem from the involvement of a sign language, creating the possibility for simultaneous articulation of two languages across different modalities. That option seems unavailable in unimodal signed bilingualism (although theoretically, the presence of paired articulators, the hands, still leaves open the possibility of co-articulation of two different sign languages). This raises the interesting question of whether unimodal sign language bilinguals pattern like unimodal spoken language bilinguals in domains where bimodal bilinguals differ, for instance in frequency of code-switching or concomitant advantages in tasks of cognitive control.

Investigation of unimodal bilingual code-switching patterns exists from communities where two sign languages have been in sustained contact. These include Australian Sign Language (Auslan)/Australian Irish Sign Language (AISL) in parts of Australia where several schools for the deaf taught in AISL

(Adam 2012) and Mexican Sign Language (LSM)/ASL along the US-Mexico border (Quinto-Pozos 2000). Research on these signing populations has identified *code-switch insertions* and several types of *reiterative code-switches*. Example (6) from Adam (2012) features two AISL signs, WARATAH and WHEN, inserted into an Auslan structure. AISL was used at the school for the Deaf in Waratah which may have prompted the signer's switch to the AISL forms. Code-switch insertions comprised the majority of code-switching types in the Auslan-AISL data, mostly involving inserted AISL, reflecting Auslan dominance for Australian unimodal bilingual signers. (Note: the notation IX represents pointing, directed towards the referent or location specified in parentheses).

(6) Auslan-AISL code-switch insertions (adapted from Quinto-Pozos and Adam 2015: 44)
IX(self) GO T-O WARATAH(AISL) AGE WHEN(AISL) FIVE-YEARS-OLD
'I started school at Waratah when I was 5 years old.'

Example (7) illustrates reiterative code-switching at the lexical level, characterized by presentation of a lexical item in one sign language (in this case TOMATO in ASL) followed by the same lexical item in a different sign language (TOMATO in LSM).

(7) Lexical reiteration ASL-LSM code-switch (adapted from Quinto-Pozos and Adam 2015: 43)
IX(listing on non-dominant hand) TOMATO TOMATO(LSM) ADD-INGREDIENTS MIX gesture(good)
'(and then you take) tomatoes and you add them to the other ingredients and mix everything together. It's great.'

Both of the code-switching patterns in (6) and (7) are familiar from spoken language bilingualism, suggesting that code-switching behavior may be one domain for which unimodal bilinguals pattern similarly, regardless of modality.

There are two aspects of unimodal sign bilingual data reported so far that appear strikingly different from either bimodal or unimodal speech bilingual data. The first is a very high incidence of ambiguous or shared lexical forms across the two sign languages, reported by both Quinto-Pozos (2000) and Zeshan and Panda (2015). Zeshan and Panda examine bilingual Burundi Sign Language (BuSL)/Indian Sign Language (ISL) data from Deaf Burundian students living in India. BuSL and ISL are genetically unrelated and have no previous history of sustained contact, yet Zeshan and Panda (2015) report that only about a third of their data could be unambiguously identified as belonging to BuSL or ISL. Upon closer inspection, a large number of the ambiguous/shared forms were index points, highly iconic classifier constructions and directional signs that occur with high frequency in most sign languages. Even after these forms were excluded from analysis, however, shared forms still comprised 38–46% of the data and were frequently interspersed among clearly ISL or BuSL signs, as exemplified in (8). The result is a high density of switching within a single utterance, making it impossible in many cases to identify a base language.

(8) ISL-BuSL code-switch (shared items are affixed with the subscript label (S)) (adapted from Zeshan and Panda 2015: 117)
IX(3fs)$_{(S)}$ LIKE$_{(BuSL)}$ NONE$_{(S)}$ / IX(3pl)$_{(S)}$ SOLVE$_{(S)}$ DIFFICULT+$_{(ISL)}$ DIFFICULT$_{(BuSL)}$
'She did not like India. To resolve this with all of them was very difficult.'

The degree of lexical overlap and resulting density of code-switching in the BuSL/ISL data set seem much higher than what is typical for either bimodal bilingual or unimodal spoken bilingual code-switching, but only investigations of other sign bilingual cases can determine if these patterns are unique characteristics of unimodal sign bilingualism.

Finally, Adam (2012) documents a psycholinguistic finding among Irish Sign Language (Irish SL)-British Sign Language (BSL) bilinguals that suggests a possible divergence from unimodal spoken bilingual patterns. Deaf bilinguals viewed a series of pictures and were instructed to produce the sign for each picture, using BSL for those outlined in red, and Irish SL for those outlined in blue. Response times revealed a switching cost, which was decreased on items for which the Irish SL and BSL signs are phonologically similar (i.e., overlapping in one or more of the following: handshape, location or movement of the sign). This facilitative effect of phonological overlap has been noted for both unimodal spoken and bimodal bilinguals. However, an unexpected finding was that switching costs for the Irish SL/BSL bilinguals were not asymmetrical, despite the fact that all participants were Irish SL dominant, having learned BSL as an L2. Many factors could potentially affect switching costs, including length of language experience, degree of genetic relatedness between languages, and the presence of a community of proficient sign bilinguals (reducing the cognitive burden required for monitoring appropriate language choice). Adam (2012) concedes that the absence of asymmetric switching costs in his data may reflect some yet unidentified feature of the Deaf bilinguals he tested, but it may also point to an unexpected modality effect unique to unimodal sign bilinguals.

9.5.2 Multilingualism among individual signers in contact

Deaf communities have a long history of international gatherings for sports competitions and cultural events. At these events, signers frequently find themselves communicating with signers from other countries, with whom they do not share any common sign language. These are prime situations for complex multilingual meaning negotiation that Byun et al. (2018) term *cross-signing*. Cross-signing involves "a relatively rich and structured grammar" based on features common to many sign language grammars, such as pointing conventions, meaningful use of space, nonmanual marking to indicate topicalization, focus, and contrast, etc. This shared grammar is paired with "a severely impoverished lexicon" that must be supplemented by lexical items negotiated on the spot (Allsop, Woll, and Brauti 1995: 187). Skilled multilingual signers accomplish this negotiation with impressive efficiency, using visually-oriented strategies that are just beginning to be documented.

Communication breakdowns are inevitable during cross-signing, but Byun et al. (2018) document the remarkable speed with which some Deaf signers are able to repair these breakdowns. Figure 9.1 shows an NGT signer (C) conversing with a KSL (Korean Sign Language) signer (A) for the first time.

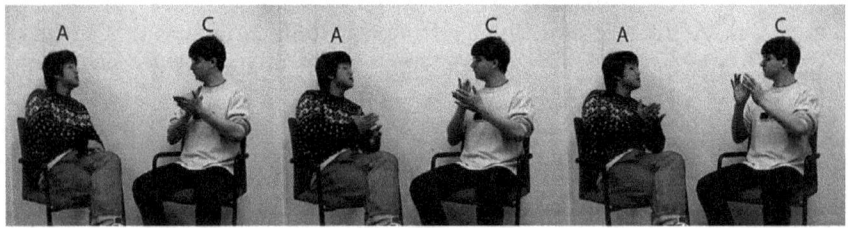

Figure 9.1: Fast track repair of conversational breakdown with try marking (Byun et al. 2018:15, reprinted with permission).

In the first panel, signer C introduces the NGT sign for INTERPRETER, but does so with what Byun et al. (2018) call a *try marker*: he holds the sign for an extra beat and maintains steady eye gaze, signaling that he recognizes this sign may not be familiar to signer A. Indeed, signer A begins to copy the sign, an indication that he has not understood it, but before he even finishes, signer C switches to the ASL sign for INTERPRETER, and the communication breakdown is repaired. Byun et al. (2018) found that breakdowns involving try markers were consistently repaired more quickly than those without try markers. Crucially, strategies like try marking depend on multilingual experience; in Figure 9.1, signer C not only had sufficient cross-sign language awareness to suspect that the NGT sign for INTERPRETER (common throughout European sign languages) might not be recognized by a Korean signer, he was also able to produce an alternative in ASL, a signed lingua franca. These skills are also among those mentioned by McKee and Napier (2002) as essential for interpreters using International Sign (IS), regarded by many as a more equitable solution than choosing an existing sign language to serve as lingua franca for communicating at international Deaf gatherings. Effective IS interpreters "must also possess the linguistic flexibility and imagination to think beyond known lexicon and improvise with productive sign and gesture resources to express meaning in unconventionalized, yet characteristically 'Deaf' ways" (McKee and Napier 2002: 51).

9.5.3 Translanguaging in signing communities

The same "Deaf ways" of making meaning that are emphasized for skilled cross-signing and IS interpreting are also emerging as a central foundation for translanguaging in signing communities. Translanguaging had its beginnings in the field of bilingual education, as a practice that encourages students to use their full communicative repertoire for learning and recognizing the highly individual and creative ways that bilingual and multilingual people make meaning. In the field of Deaf education, translanguaging approaches are growing in popularity in countries like Sweden and the U.K., where an influx of immigration has led to highly multilingual Deaf classrooms. In these "super-diverse" situations, teachers are using translanguaging techniques to leverage newly arrived Deaf students' varying knowledge of their home languages (spoken or signed), global languages like English, and the local signed and spoken languages (Allard and Chen Pichler to appear).

Translanguaging is not a haphazard mixing of languages, but rather an intentional practice that adheres to certain best practices. Visually-oriented practices and proficiency in at least one signed language are emerging as critical features of effective translanguaging in the Deaf context. Holmström and Schönström (2018) describe the translanguaging practices of one Deaf university lecturer's skillful integration of Swedish Sign Language (SSL), English and Swedish mouthing, fingerspelling of English and Swedish words, and printed English and Swedish text over the course of a single lecture (Figure 9.2).

Importantly, the lecture maintains equal accessibility for Deaf and hearing students, since any Swedish or English content is rendered visible through mouthing and fingerspelling, two mechanisms "native" to natural sign languages.

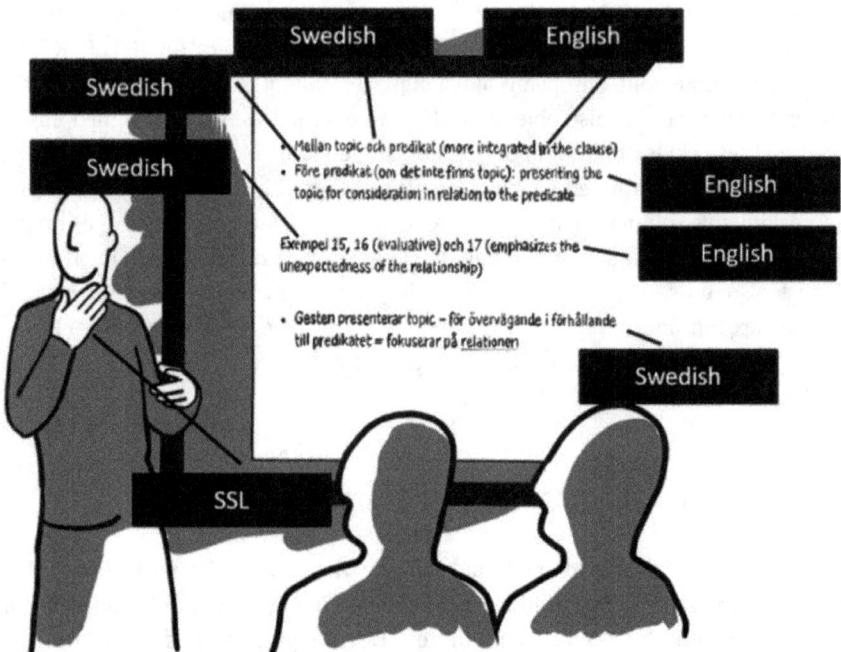

Figure 9.2: Multilingual translanguaging in a Deaf lecture (Holmström and Schönström 2018: 10, reprinted with permission).

9.6 Multilingual child signers

Signing populations today are increasingly globalized and mobile, leading to richly multilingual communities featuring unexpected combinations of signed and spoken languages (Hiddinga and Crasborn 2011). Children growing up in these communities display varying proficiency in multiple signed and spoken languages, and the concepts of language synthesis, cross-signing, heritage language and translanguaging all offer important tools for investigating development in these multimodal multilingual contexts. We end this chapter with a brief summary of the only systematic research on multilingual signing children that we are currently aware of (Vere 2014), supplemented with examples of signing children's multimodal linguistic combinations that still await scientific investigation.

Vere (2014) conducted a longitudinal case study of a Koda child from 2;9–3;10 learning English, Maltese, and Maltese Sign Language (Maltese SL) from his Deaf parents. Vere describes the child's use of code-blending to serve a variety of purposes, sometimes with concurrent code-switching between English and Maltese, as in (9).

(9) Bimodal trilingual English-Maltese code-switch and partial Maltese Sign Language code-blend [2;9] (Maltese content is marked with a subscript "M".) (Adapted from Vere 2014: 88)
Maltese SL: KBIR
big
Speech: This big a vapur$_{(M)}$
'This is a big ship.'

The child is aware of the various language preferences of his interlocutors, and code-blending allows him "to satisfy all conversational partners in a multilingual conversation" (p. 111). At age 3;4, he is also observed code-blending an iconic gesture with exaggerated mouthing of a spoken Maltese word *sigar* 'tree' as a strategy to fill a lexical gap in his developing Maltese SL lexicon. Based on these preliminary observations, bimodal trilingual L1 development bears many resemblances to what has been reported for bimodal bilingual children, but naturally, much more research on other language combinations is needed.

Examples (10) and (11) present a sample of spontaneously produced trilingual code-mixing that we have encountered in casual interactions with multilingual signing children. Bai (age 8;6), a Deaf Cantonese, English and ASL multilingual, primarily uses ASL for communication but also speaks some English and Cantonese. In (10) he produces a fully bimodal code-blend where each signed constituent has a co-occurring spoken language element, and also performs a code-switch from English to Cantonese.

(10) Bimodal trilingual English-Cantonese code-switch and full ASL code-blend [Bai 8;6] (Cantonese content is marked with a subscript "C".)
ASL: IX(self) LOVE GRANDMOTHER
Speech: I love 婆婆 (pópo)$_{(C)}$
Grandmother
'I love (my) grandma.'

Similarly, in (11) Sia (age 3;0), a hearing English, Spanish and ASL multilingual, produces a trilingual simultaneous code-blend and code-switch involving all three languages.

(11) Bimodal trilingual English-Spanish code-switch and partial ASL code-blend [Sia 3;0] (Spanish content is marked with a subscript "S".)
ASL: DARK
Speech: After dark I need una₍s₎   light flash.
                         INDF.ART.F.SG
'After (it gets) dark I need a flashlight.'

The gender feature of the Spanish indefinite article *una* matches the gender feature of the Spanish translation equivalent of *flashlight* (*linterna*), a phenomenon that has been well-documented for unimodal Spanish-English bilinguals (Liceras et al. 2008). Furthermore, Sia's word order choice in *light flash* shows influence from the ASL sequence LIGHT FLASH, or alternatively, from Spanish word order if she has analyzed *flash* as an adjective modifying *light*. This is a particularly fascinating example of the many options for simultaneous code-switching, code-blending and other language synthesis that are already produced by multilingual signing children at young ages.

9.7 Future directions and importance of continued research

The field of multilingualism in signing communities is still brand new, presenting countless directions for promising future research. For linguists and psycholinguists, the central question of how modality affects familiar patterns of language acquisition, interaction, processing, etc. remains a major line of inquiry that requires many more studies of signing bilinguals and multilinguals from a variety of backgrounds. In light of the novel discoveries related to bimodal bilingualism in recent years, unimodal sign bilingualism seems a particularly promising test case for distinguishing effects of sign languages from effects of bimodality. Broadening our focus from bilingualism to multilingualism also opens the door to complex new types of blending and switching that have not been considered before, presenting challenging but valuable opportunities to refine theoretical models that account for language mixing.

The study of multilingual signers' linguistic development benefits immensely from the current explosion of research on translanguaging and heritage languages. Both disciplines advocate a highly individualized, nuanced view of language acquisition in which a language does not need to be fully mastered before it can be considered an active part of an individual's multilingual repertoire. Language mixing is viewed not as a sign of disorder but as a natural consequence of multilingualism, and in some cases, even a mark of linguistic prowess. This perspective is especially validating for users of vulnerable minority languages with limited recognition, a category that still includes all sign languages. At the same time, ongoing research of K/Codas and DDCI as heritage signers can foster development of resources tailored to the distinct needs of heritage signers (e.g., special heritage signer schools or sign language curricula), thereby supporting continued development of their sign language skills.

Finally, recognizing the multilingual nature of signing communities has many important practical applications, too. Professionals in the fields of interpretation, education, speech-language pathology, etc. currently operate according to models that greatly underestimate, or worse, disregard the linguistic diversity of the signing communities they serve. This approach undermines the effectiveness of their services and perpetuates a system of social inequality that privileges those who have access to majority languages. Committing to systematic study of multilingual signers is to finally acknowledge their existence, a move that will greatly enrich both the scientific community and signing communities everywhere.

References

Adam, Robert. 2012. *Unimodal bilingualism in the deaf community: Contact between dialects of BSL and ISL in Australia and the United Kingdom*. London, UK: University College London dissertation.

Allard, Karin & Deborah Chen Pichler. 2018. Multi-modal visually-oriented translanguaging among Deaf signers. *Translation and Translanguaging in Multilingual Contexts* 4(3). 384–404.

Allsop, Lorna, Bencie Woll & John Martin Brauti. 1994. International Sign: The creation of an international deaf community and sign language. In Heleen Bos & Trade Schermer (eds.), *Sign Language research*, 171–188. Hamburg: Signum.

Ammons, Donalda K. 1988. *Instructional guide for foreign language instruction with deaf and hard-of-hearing*. Washington DC: Gallaudet University Press.

Benmamoun, Elabbas, Silvina Montrul & Maria Polinsky. 2013. Heritage languages and their speakers: Opportunities and challenges for linguistics. *Theoretical Linguistics* 39(3–4). 129–81.

Bialystok, Ellen, Fergus I.M. Craik, David W. Green & Tamar H. Gollan. 2009. Bilingual minds. *Psychological Science in the Public Interest* 10(3). 89–129.

Bishop, Michelle & Sherry Hicks. 2005. Orange eyes: Bimodal bilingualism in hearing adults from deaf families. *Sign Language Studies* 5(2). 188–230.

Bishop, Michele. 2010. Happen can't hear: An analysis of code-blends in hearing, native signers of American Sign Language. *Sign Language Studies* 11(2). 205–240.

Bishop, Michele & Sherry L. Hicks. 2008. *Hearing, mother father deaf: Hearing people in deaf families*. Washington DC: Gallaudet University Press.

Bishop, Michele, Sherry L. Hicks, Antonella Bertone & Rita Sala. 2006. Capitalizing on simultaneity: Features of bimodal bilingualism in hearing Italian native signers. In Ceil Lucas (ed.), *Multilingualism and sign languages: From the Great Plains to Australia*, 79–118. Washington, DC: Gallaudet University Press.

Bogaerde, Beppie van den. 2000. *Input and interaction in deaf families*. Utrecht, Netherlands: University of Amsterdam.

Bogaerde, Beppie van den & Anne E. Baker. 2008. Bimodal language acquisition in Kodas. In Michele Bishop & Sherry L. Hicks (eds.), *Hearing, mother father deaf*, 99–131. Washington DC: Gallaudet University Press.

Byun, Kang-Suk, Connie De Vos, Anastasia Bradford, Ulrike Zeshan & Stephen C. Levinson. 2018. First encounters: Repair sequences in cross-signing. *Topics in Cognitive Science, Special Issue on Miscommunication* 10(2). https://doi.org/10.1111/tops.12303

Chen Pichler, Deborah. 2001. *Word variation and acquisition in American Sign Language*. Storrs: University of Connecticut dissertation.

Chen Pichler, Deborah & Helen Koulidobrova. 2015. Acquisition of sign language as a second language. In Marc Marschark & Patricia Elizabeth Spencer (eds.), *The Oxford handbook of deaf studies in language: Research, policy, and practice*, 218–230. New York: Oxford University Press.

Chen Pichler, Helen Koulidobrova & Jeffrey Levi Palmer. In press. Modality (in-)dependent second language learning. In Ritsuko Kikusawa & Fumiya Sano (eds.), *Minpaku Sign Language Studies 1 (Senri Ethnological Studies)*.

Chen Pichler, Deborah, Diane Lillo-Martin & Jeffrey Levi Palmer. 2018. A short introduction to heritage signers. *Sign Language Studies* 18(3). 309–327.

Chen Pichler, Deborah, Wanette Reynolds, Jeffrey Levi Palmer, Ronice Muller de Quadros, Viola L. Kozak & Diane Lillo-Martin. 2017. Heritage signers: Bimodal bilingual children from deaf families. In Jiyoung Choi, Hamida Demirdache, Oana Lungu & Laurence Voeltzel (eds.), *Language acquisition at the interfaces: Proceedings of GALA 2015*, 247–269. Newcastle upon Tyne, UK: Cambridge Scholars Publishing.

Compton, Sarah. 2014. American Sign Language as a heritage language. In Terrence G. Wiley, Joy Kreeft Peyton, Donna Christian, Sarah Catherine K. Moore & Na Liu (eds.), *Handbook of heritage, community, and Native American languages in the United States: Research, policy, and educational practice*, 272–288. London: Routledge.

Cormier, Kearsy, Adam Schembri, David Vinson & Elani Orfanidou. 2012. First language acquisition differs from second language acquisition in prelingually deaf signers: Evidence from sensitivity to grammaticality judgement in British Sign Language. *Cognition* 124(1). 50–65.

Davidson, Kathryn, Diane Lillo-Martin & Deborah Chen Pichler. 2014. Spoken English language development among native signing children with cochlear implants. *The Journal of Deaf Studies and Deaf Education* 19(2). 238–250.

Dijkstra, Ton & Walter J.B. van Heuven. 2002. The architecture of the bilingual word recognition system: From identification to decision. *Bilingualism: Language and Cognition* 5(3). 175–197.

Emmorey, Karen, Jennifer Petrich & Tamar H. Gollan. 2012. Bilingual processing of ASL–English code-blends: The consequences of accessing two lexical representations simultaneously. *Journal of Memory and Language* 67(1). 199–210.

Branchini, Chiara & Caterina Donati. 2016. Assessing lexicalism through bimodal eyes. *Glossa* 1(1). 1–30.

Emmorey, Karen, Helsa B. Borinstein, Robin Thompson & Tamar H. Gollan. 2008. Bimodal bilingualism. *Bilingualism: Language and cognition* 11(1). 43–61.
Ethnologue. https://www.ethnologue.com/subgroups/sign-language (accessed 24 May, 2018).
Green, David W. 1998. Mental control of the bilingual lexico-semantic system. *Bilingualism: Language and Cognition* 1(2). 67–81.
Griffith, Penny L. 1985. Mode-switching & mode-finding in a hearing child of deaf parents. *Sign Language Studies* 48(1). 195–222.
Hiddinga, Anja & Onno Crasborn. 2011. Signed languages and globalization. *Language in Society* 40(4). 483–505.
Holmström, Ingela & Krister Schönström. 2018. Deaf lecturers' translanguaging in a higher education setting. A multimodal multilingual perspective. *Applied Linguistics Review* 9(1). 90–111.
Humphries, Tom, Poorna Kushalnagar, Gaurav Mathur, Donna Jo Napoli, Carol Padden, Christian Rathmann & Scott R. Smith. 2012. Language acquisition for deaf children: Reducing the harms of zero tolerance to the use of alternative approaches. *Harm Reduction Journal* 9(16). 1–9.
Kanto, Laura, Marja-Leena Laakso & Kerttu Huttunen. 2017. Use of code-mixing by young hearing children of Deaf parents. *Bilingualism: Language and Cognition* 20(5). 947–964.
Kontra, Edit. H., Kata Csizér & Katalin Piniel. 2015. The challenge for deaf and hard-of-hearing students to learn foreign languages in special needs schools. *European Journal of Special Needs Education* 30(2). 141–155.
Koulidobrova, Helen & Jeffrey Levi Palmer. 2015. *Whaddayaknow: Effects of exposure to a sign language on seeing another one*. New Britain, CT: Central Connecticut State University unpublished manuscript.
Kroll, Judith F., Susan C. Bobb & Zofia Wodnieka. 2006. Language selectivity is the exception, not the rule: Arguments against a fixed locus of language selection in bilingual speech. *Bilingualism* 9(2). 119–135.
Lane, Harlan, Robert Hoffmeister & Benjamin Bahan. 1996. *A journey into the Deaf-world*. San Diego, CA: DawnSignPress.
Liceras Juana, Raquel Fernàndez Fuertes, Susana Perales, Rocìo Pèrez-Tattam & Kenton Todd Spradlin. 2008. Gender and gender agreement in bilingual native and non-native grammars: A view from child and adult functional-lexical mixings. *Lingua* 118(6). 827–51.
Lillo-Martin, Diane, Ronice Muller de Quadros & Deborah Chen Pichler. 2016. The development of bimodal bilingualism. *Linguistic Approaches to Bilingualism* 6(6). 719–755.
Lillo-Martin, Diane, Ronice Muller de Quadros, Deborah Chen Pichler & Zoe Fieldsteel. 2014. Language choice in bimodal bilingual development. *Frontiers in Psychology* 5(1163). 1–15.
Lucas, Ceil & Clayton Valli. 1992. *Language contact in the American deaf community*. San Diego, CA: Academic Press.
Mayberry, Rachel I. & Elizabeth Lock. 2003. Age constraints on first versus second language acquisition: Evidence for linguistic plasticity and epigenesis. *Brain and Language* 87(3). 369–384.
McKee, Rachel & Jemina Napier. 2002. Interpreting into International Sign Pidgin: An analysis. *Sign Language & Linguistics* 5(1). 27–54.
Meier, Richard & Elissa Newport. 1990. Out of the hands of babes: On a possible sign advantage in language acquisition. *Language 66(1)*. 1–23.
Meuter, Renata F.I. & Alan Allport.1999. Bilingual language switching in naming: Asymmetrical costs of language selection. *Journal of Memory and Language* 40(1). 25–40.

Mitchell, Ross E. & Michael A. Karchmer. 2004. Chasing the mythical ten percent: Parental hearing status of deaf and hard of hearing students in the United States. *Sign Language Studies* 4(2). 138–163.

Mitchell, Ross E., Travas A. Young, Bellamie Bachleda, & Michael A. Karchmer. 2006. How many people use ASL in the United States? Why estimates need updating. *Sign Language Studies* 6(3). 306–335.

Morford, Jill P., Erin Wilkinson, Agnes Villwock, Pilar Piñar & Judith F. Kroll. 2011. When deaf signers read English: Do written words activate their sign translations? *Cognition* 118(2). 286–292.

Myers-Scotton, Carol. 2001. The matrix language frame model: Development and responses. In Rodolfo Jacobson (ed.), *Codeswitching Worldwide II*. 23–58. Berlin & New York: Mouton de Gruyter.

Padden, Carol & Tom Humphries. 1990. *Deaf in America*. Cambridge: Harvard University Press.

Padden, Carol & Claire Ramsey. 2000. American Sign Language and reading ability in deaf children. In Charlene Chamberlain, Jill P. Morford & Rachel I. Mayberry (eds.), *Language acquisition by eye*, 65–89. Mahwah, NJ: Lawrence Erlbaum Associates.

Palmer, Jeffrey Levi. 2015. *ASL word order development in bimodal bilingual children: Early syntax of hearing and cochlear-implanted deaf children from signing families*. Washington, DC: Gallaudet University dissertation.

Petitto, Laura Ann, Marina Katerelos, Bronna G. Levy, Kristine Gauna, Karine Tetreault & Vittoria Ferraro. 2001. Bilingual signed and spoken language acquisition from birth: Implications for the mechanisms underlying early bilingual language acquisition. *Journal of Child Language* 28(2). 453–496.

Pizzo, Lianna. 2016. d/Deaf and hard of hearing multilingual learners: The development of communication and language. *American Annals of the Deaf* 161(1). 17–32.

Poplack, Shana. 1980. Sometimes I'll start a sentence in Spanish y termino en espanol: Toward a typology of code-switching. *Linguistics* 18. 581–618.

Preston, Paul. 1995. *Mother father deaf: Living between sound and silence*. Cambridge, MA: Harvard University Press.

Preston, Paul. 2008. Foreword. In Michele Bishop & Sherry L. Hicks (eds.), *Hearing, mother father deaf*, ix-xiii. Washington, DC: Gallaudet University Press.

Quadros, Ronice Muller de, Diane Lillo-Martin & Deborah Chen Pichler. 2013. Early effects of bilingualism on WH-question structures: Insight from sign-speech bilingualism. In Stavroula Stavrakaki, Marina Lalioti & Polyxeni Konstantinopoulou (eds.), *Proceedings of GALA 2011*, 300–308. Newcastle upon Tyne: Cambridge Scholars Press.

Quadros, Ronice Muller de, Diane Lillo-Martin & Deborah Chen Pichler. 2015. Acquisition of sign language as a second language. In Marc Marschark & Patricia Elizabeth Spencer (eds.), *The Oxford handbook of deaf studies in language: Research, policy, and practice*, 181–196. New York: Oxford University Press.

Quinto-Pozos, David. 2000. *Contact between Mexican sign language and American sign language in two Texas border areas*. Austin, TX: University of Texas at Austin doctoral dissertation.

Quinto-Pozos, David & Robert Adam. 2015. Sign languages in contact. In Adam C. Schembri & Ceil Lucas (eds.), *Sociolinguistics and deaf communities*, 29–60. Cambridge: Cambridge University Press.

Reynolds, Wanette. 2016. *Early bimodal bilingual development of ASL narrative referent cohesion*. Washington, DC: Gallaudet University dissertation.

Reynolds, Wanette. 2018. Young bimodal bilingual development of referent tracking in signed narratives: Further justification of heritage signer status. *Sign Language Studies* 18(3). 328–354.

Shantie, Courtney & Robert J. Hoffmeister. 2000. Why schools for deaf children should hire deaf teachers: A preschool issue. *Journal of Education* 182(3). 37–47.

Swanwick, Ruth. 2017. Translanguaging, learning and teaching in deaf education. *International Journal of Multilingualism* 14(3). 233–249.

Tevenal, Stephanie & Miako Villanueva. 2009. Are you getting the message? The effects of SimCom on the message received by deaf, hard of hearing, and hearing students. *Sign Language Studies* 9(3). 266–286.

Tomasello, Michael. 2003. *Constructing a language: A usage-based theory of language acquisition*. Cambridge, MA: Harvard University Press.

Vere, Alison. 2014. *Bimodal trilingual language acquisition: A case study looking at the linguistic development of a hearing child with deaf parents*. Malta: University of Malta MA thesis.

Volterra, Virginia & Traute Taeschner. 1978. The acquisition and development of language by bilingual children. *Journal of Child Language 5(2)*. 311–326.

Woll, Bencie. 2012. Second language acquisition of sign language. In Carol A. Chapelle (ed.), *The encyclopedia of applied linguistics*. Oxford: Wiley-Blackwell. http://onlinelibrary.wiley.com/doi/10.1002/9781405198431.wbeal1050/abstract (accessed 24 May, 2018).

Zeshan, Ulrike. 2015. "Making meaning": Communication between sign language users without a shared language. *Cognitive Linguistics* 26(2). 211–260.

Zeshan, Ulrike & Sibaji Panda. 2015. Two languages at hand: Code-switching in bilingual deaf signers. *Sign Language and Linguistics* 18(1). 90–131.

Zeshan, Ulrike & Sibaji Panda. 2017. Sign-speaking: The structure of simultaneous bimodal utterances. *Applied Linguistics Review* 9(1). 1–34.

Part III: Individual Multilingualism: From Development to Loss

Suzanne Quay and Sarah Chevalier
10 Fostering Multilingualism in Childhood

10.1 Introduction

The use of two or more languages and language choice within the home has increasingly been framed within the field of family language policy (FLP; see Chapter 11, this volume, for further discussion). Most parents, however, do not consciously set out to raise multilingual children but do so due to personal circumstances and the political and sociolinguistic environments where they live (Caldas 2012). If parents *do* have a particular FLP, it is often not founded on empirical research, contrary to the expectations of King and Fogle (2006). The parents they interviewed who strategically planned language outcomes for their children did so based on information from the popular press, the experiences of other extended family members or friends, and especially, on their own personal experiences with languages rather than on academic research. Barron-Hauwaert (2004) also found that most parents in her study consulted bilingual advice books that were not necessarily empirically-based sources to inform their child-rearing practices. This chapter focuses on what data-driven research (as discussed in Quay 2011a) can tell us about the processes and challenges involved in raising young children with two or more languages before they enter formal education at age five. Once children start attending school, teachers and peers tend to have a stronger influence on children's language choice (see also Chapter 12, this volume). But before then, parents have a certain amount of control over their children's language development through caregiver-child interactions and particular discourse patterns that ensure adequate exposure to input from different languages. This chapter discusses, in addition, research on the role played by other family members like siblings and grandparents, as well as others in their community. A further exploration of socio-political, cultural, contextual and child-internal (e.g., personality) factors can reveal how such factors affect the variability children display in multilingual attainment.

Suzanne Quay, International Christian University, Tokyo, Japan
Sarah Chevalier, University of Zurich, Zurich, Switzerland

10.2 Parental language choice in the early years

Parents' influence on language development starts with their own language repertoires, which may consist of one or more native languages, as well as languages acquired later in life. Parents may or may not have mastered the majority language, and may want or need to use a lingua franca as their couple language. Braun and Cline (2014) interviewed 35 trilingual families in England and 35 in Germany. They found three main types of parents where: (1) each parent has a different mother tongue, with neither speaking the societal language natively; (2) one or both are bilingual, with the societal language possibly being one of their languages; and (3) one or both are trilingual, again with the societal language possibly being one of their languages. This study found that the first type of parents, with different native languages that were not the same as the societal language, were more successful at raising trilingual children than the bilingual (type 2) and trilingual (type 3) parents, many of whom had the societal language in their repertoire. Thus, if the majority language is less likely to be spoken in the home, a child is more likely to acquire the minority languages of the parents.

Without a doubt, most parents of potentially multilingual children are faced with language choices; these may appear to be self-evident for some and less so for others. For example, it was obvious for a Swedish-American couple living in German-speaking Switzerland that each parent should speak their one and only native language to their children (Chevalier 2015; type 1 parents as above). However, for a couple consisting of a Polish-Swiss mother and an Egyptian father, also living in German-speaking Switzerland, this choice was not obvious at all. Since English was their only shared language, they not only communicated in English with each other, but also with their son (Chevalier 2016). Thus, decisions concerning which languages to use from parental repertoires play a crucial role in a child's multilingual language development.

10.2.1 The OPOL approach

A common choice of parents is to follow the "one person one language" (OPOL) approach, as in the example of the Swedish-American family above. In the fifteen studies of trilingualism reviewed in Chevalier (2015), it could be seen that the children whose parents followed OPOL were more likely to become actively multilingual than those whose parents did not. When OPOL was not followed, usually the societal language took over and the children stopped speaking one or more parental languages. Braun and Cline (2010) found that an important factor in the success of maintaining OPOL in trilingual families was whether parents had one different native language from each other or not, which was also different from the societal language (i.e. type 1 as described earlier). They found that among 24 such families, 19 were able to maintain the strategy of OPOL. However, in the other 46 families, in which one or both parents were bi- or multilingual (whether their native languages included the societal language or not), only three families managed to maintain OPOL. In all the other cases, the societal language was used partially or fully (Braun and Cline 2010: 119, Table 6).

While the strategy of each parent consistently speaking his/her native language to the child can play an important role in fostering the minority languages, this does not mean OPOL will automatically result in active multilingualism. Depending on other factors, such as the interactional style of the parents (see section 10.2.3), which may not provide children with adequate exposure or require them to speak in a minority language, OPOL may only lead to receptive multilingualism (e.g., Chevalier 2015; Döpke 1992; Quay 2001). On the other hand, more flexible language input patterns than OPOL can also result in active multilingualism (see sections 10.2.2 and 10.4).

10.2.2 Other parental language use patterns in the home

In De Houwer's (2004) large-scale survey in Flanders of 244 trilingual families, various input patterns were correlated with active versus passive trilingualism. In these families, the primary-school aged children had bilingual exposure to two minority languages in the home (although in some families the societal language, Dutch, was also spoken). Forty-two percent of the children in the survey were considered to be actively trilingual by parents who indicated that their children spoke the two minority languages at home (all the children would also have spoken Dutch in school). Of relevance is the finding that when both parents spoke the same two minority languages at home, the children had almost an equally good chance of becoming actively trilingual as not. Thus, we see that a non-OPOL strategy (when both parents speak the same two minority languages X and Y) also has a reasonable chance of resulting in active multilingualism. De Houwer (2004: 132) speculates that this situation gives children "more balanced and varied opportunities to learn and use these languages than children whose parents speak different languages"; moreover, parents who speak the same two languages may "project a more similar linguistic identity than those who do not," which may in turn encourage the use of the home languages.

Hélot (1988) reports on two trilingual families in Ireland where neither followed OPOL, but both had actively trilingual children. In both families, French was the mother's native language and Irish the father's. In Family 1, the parental input patterns and the children's language choices changed according to location. In Dublin, where they lived, the mother spoke to the children in French and occasionally English, while the father addressed the children mainly in English and sometimes in Irish. The children attended an English-medium school. The parents spoke mainly English to each other, and the children spoke mainly English to both parents. In France, however, when the family visited the children's grandparents, the children spoke to their mother in French. During summer in the Gaeltacht, the father spoke Irish rather than English to his children, who in turn responded to him in Irish. There being no English exposure at all, the children also responded to their mother in French, and spoke both Irish and French to each other. Thus, in the case of this family, mainly receptive multilingualism in one location turned into productive multilingualism in different language environments. In Family 2, French was the home language, spoken by both parents as well as the siblings among themselves. Since the family had opted for Irish-medium schooling, Irish and English were automatically taken care of by the environment.

Curdt-Christiansen (2009) also found that the external environment can provide input for additional languages to flourish in her qualitative study of ten Chinese immigrant families in Montreal. The parents in all ten families spoke Chinese in the home but they raised French-English-Chinese trilingual children in a French-speaking province of Canada, a country where English is a majority and prestigious language. Dagenais (2003) also reports on how parents in 12 immigrant families with diverse origins were raising multilingual children in Vancouver in an English-speaking province of Canada by choosing to enroll their children in French immersion schools. All families spoke English and one or more home languages such as Spanish, French, Mandarin, Cantonese, Korean, Punjabi, Gujarati, Urdu and Hindi. Their children, with the addition of French at school in officially bilingual Canada, could thus gain another language as capital. These families, according to Dagenais, ultimately saw multilingualism as an investment with economic benefits in the future for their children and used their environment to take advantage of this possibility.

In another Canadian study, Slavkov (2017) found 42% (coincidentally, the same percentage as De Houwer 2004) of the children he surveyed in Ontario, Canada, to be active multilinguals out of the 170 exposed to English (majority language), French (minority language), and numerous other languages spoken by immigrant or indigenous residents. His results on actively multilingual children are from two types of families: (1) where two family members speak two different minority languages at home, and (2) when both parents speak one heritage language (not French) at home while their children attend French immersion or Francophone schools and are exposed to English from the social environment or within French immersion programs. Slavkov (2017: 385) points out that "heritage language speaking families seem to have an advantage because their children have a chance of becoming multilingual if they add both of Canada's official languages to the language already spoken at home," as earlier found by Curdt-Christiansen (2009) and Dagenais (2003). His survey revealed that the likelihood of children becoming multilingual is also due to parental communication in a minority language. He states that the choice of the language of communication between parents is an opportunity to provide extra input and potential modeling of home languages for children. The choice of French as the language of schooling for children also contributes to positive multilingual outcomes in the Canadian setting. In addition, Ontario, unlike other Canadian provinces, subsidizes heritage-language programs held on weekends that contribute to children's success in becoming active multilinguals. Slavkov (2017: 392) explains that "parents who send their children to such classes on weekends" and "enrol their children in French programmes for the regular weekday schooling" demonstrate positive attitudes and commitment to multilingualism that in itself contributes to their children's positive outcomes. This study concludes that "Heritage language through FLP, French-language instruction as a school choice, and English through community interactions (and also at school since English classes are included in all French medium instruction)" (Slavkov 2017: 394) can strategically increase multilingual outcomes in Canada.

10.2.3 Parental discourse styles

Considerable evidence exists showing that parental discourse styles have an impact on children's multilingual language acquisition. Lanza (2007) describes her concept of a continuum of parental discourse strategies, a tool with which to analyze how parent-child interactions in bilingual families foster, or prevent, the development of a child's two languages. She demonstrates that parents can create a context in which a child is socialized into speaking the parental language (or not) by how parents respond when their child uses a language not being used by the parent.

In the following, we briefly outline Lanza's (2007) five parental discourse strategies, from the most to the least constraining. When a child uses the nonparental language, a parent may attempt to get the child to speak their language by indicating a lack of comprehension of the child's utterance ("minimal grasp"). Alternatively, a parent may reformulate the utterance in the parental language in a questioning tone ("expressed guess"), so the child has to confirm (or disconfirm). While an expressed guess shows to the child that the parent has understood (thus indicating that it is possible for the child to speak the non-parental language and be understood), the repair sequence nevertheless hinders the flow of conversation. The child must answer a question about language (and hopefully use this as a cue to change language as well) before the topic can be pursued. In the middle of the continuum is "adult repetition"; here the adult provides a translation in the parental language, but, unlike with the expressed guess, the child does not have to confirm. Nevertheless, this strategy provides the child with the appropriate vocabulary, and children sometimes also repeat the vocabulary given (Chevalier 2015; Lanza 2007). By contrast, a child will not feel constrained to speak the parental language if the parent responds to the use of another language by "moving on" – that is, by simply continuing the conversation; indeed, if moving on is the usual response to the non-use of a parental language, then "dual-lingual" interactions, in which parties speak different languages to each other, may become the norm (discussed further in section 10.4). The strongest signal to a child that he/she does not need to speak the parental language is when the parent actually switches to the language the child has been using ("code-switching").

The value of this discourse continuum has been attested in explaining bilingual (e.g. Juan-Garau and Pérez-Vidal 2001; Kasuya 1998; Lanza [1997] 2004; Mishina-Mori 2011) as well as trilingual (e.g. Chevalier 2015; Montanari 2009; Nibun and Wigglesworth 2014; Quay 2012) production in various studies. In Chevalier (2015), for example, the use of these parental discourse strategies is the most important explanation for one child's production of her aunt's language compared to her lack of production of her paternal language. When the child, Lina (aged 2;1–3;1), spoke the societal language, Swiss German, to her French-speaking father, the most common response of the father was simply to carry on with the conversation ("move on"). On the other hand, when Lina spoke Swiss German to her American aunt, the aunt often supplied her with the English vocabulary ("adult repetition") or, if the aunt believed the child already knew the word, indicated that Lina should produce English by asking "what?" ("minimal grasp"), or simply telling the child to translate.

Although the trilingual mothers in Quay (2012) both used similar discourse strategies that encouraged their children between ages 1;1 and 2;1 to use the societal language, Japanese, in the home context (more "move on" than the other strategies and some "code-switching"), the outcome was notably different for their respective child. In one family, the child, Xiaoxiao, who heard Chinese from her mother, English from her father and Japanese at a community-based daycare center she entered at age 0;5, became an active trilingual. In the other family, the child, Freddy, exposed to English from his mother, German from his father and Japanese at daycare from age 0;11, was a passive or receptive trilingual speaking mainly Japanese ("active" versus "passive" pertains here to two children who are in the early stages of developing their languages and does not signify an endpoint to their (in)ability to produce the three languages they heard). The implication of Xiaoxiao's case is that parental discourse strategies encouraging bilingual contexts in the home do not necessarily prevent active multilingualism. Although many studies have found parental discourse strategies to be important in fostering active bi- and trilingualism, there are other variables that might be at play, for example, individual child factors such as gender, personality, language aptitude, and preference as well as family dynamics (discussed further in 10.4).

An example of parents adapting their discourse strategies according to the extent to which they believe a child is capable of producing a minority language can be seen in Juan-Garau and Pérez-Vidal (2001). The family in this study lived in Spain; the mother spoke Catalan to their son, Andreu, and the father English. Until Andreu was three years old, the father mainly made use of the "move on" strategy, but also provided vocabulary via "adult repetition". Around age three, the father felt Andreu had enough knowledge of English to produce it more. He used a very child-friendly and effective way to insist on English, by making use of two puppets that, he told the three-year-old, could only understand English ("minimal grasp" strategy). Andreu's production of English with his father showed a considerable increase from this period on.

It can be seen that if children do not feel constrained to use a particular language by their adult interlocutors, they may well produce (more of) the language they are strongest in (usually the societal one, as Lina and Freddy did) to the detriment of their other language(s). However, depending on other factors, a lack of constraint does not necessarily mean that multilingualism will not develop, as seen with Xiaoxiao. Insisting strategies can moreover be introduced at a later stage, and in a highly sensitive manner, as shown by the father of Andreu.

10.3 Quantity of input

In the case of a child being raised multilingually, there are two main issues concerning the quantity of parental/caregiver input. One is the minimum amount of input in any single language needed to acquire it, and the other is how the proportion of input in the different languages affects multilingual development.

Concerning the minimum quantity of input, evidence from Quay (2008: 30) reveals that minority language input of only one-fifth of the total language input can result in "the development and maintenance of [...] skills" in that language. As described previously, Xiaoxiao (1;10–2;4) was growing up with Chinese (maternal language), English (paternal language) and Japanese (societal language). Her parents estimated that Xiaoxiao was exposed to English maximally only 20% of the time. Further, her father did not insist on the child speaking English, but accepted her utterances in all three languages. Despite these circumstances, Xiaoxiao spoke more English with her father than any other language (45% of her utterances). This, however, does not imply that one-fifth of total language input in a particular language is adequate for long-term active trilingualism for a general population, as this is a case study of one child until age 2;4 only. The factors that may have influenced Xiaoxiao's production of English are the close relationship shared by father and daughter, as well as the sociable and accommodating nature of the child (Quay 2008: 30). The fact that English was the main language of communication between the parents may also have played a role (cf. Slavkov 2017 in section 10.2.2 on the importance of parents' use of a minority language with each other).

A similar situation can be observed in Chevalier (2015) with Elliot (2;1–3;1), who was being raised in French-speaking Switzerland with French (daycare), English (maternal language) and Swiss German (paternal language). The father worked in another part of the country and was only at home on weekends (although the Swiss German-speaking grandmother visited for several days once a month). Exposure to Swiss German was thus not daily and was considerably less than exposure to his other two languages. Nevertheless, Elliot produced Swiss German with his father most of the time (92% of utterances, excluding incomprehensible and mixed utterances). Reasons can be found in the father's lively and didactic style of interaction (as pointed out also by Döpke 1992 regarding how interactional styles are related to language maintenance) and reinforcement from the paternal grandmother and other Swiss German speakers. While Elliot's Swiss German was not of the same level of proficiency as his English and French, he did use it addressee-appropriately. Thus, it can be seen that a language can be acquired even with a relatively small proportion of input as long as other supporting factors exist.

With regard to the overall proportion of input in different languages, it can be observed that children growing up multilingually are rarely exposed to their different languages equally. While balanced input is not necessary for multilingual language acquisition, a large proportion of input in the majority language is also not conducive to the development of the other languages. Thus Elliot, who had more exposure to his mother's language (English) than to the majority language (French), was an active trilingual while Lina, who had considerable exposure to the majority language both inside and outside the home, was not (Chevalier 2015). Indeed, as discussed in section 10.2, the lack of parental talk in the majority language at home has been attested as an important factor in children becoming actively multilingual. In De Houwer's (2004) survey, among those families in which the societal language was not spoken by parents at home, three-quarters of the children were actively trilingual. Keeping the majority language out of the home means a greater proportion of exposure to the minority languages and correlates with a greater likelihood of active multilingualism.

10.4 Other factors affecting language outcome in the home

As discussed thus far, children experience differences in language input depending on parental language use patterns, socio-interactional strategies and the relative and absolute frequencies of input for each language (see also Unsworth 2013). This leads to the variability we see in the degree of multilingual abilities, with stronger and weaker languages in children's linguistic repertoires.

Besides child-external factors, child-internal factors also contribute to individual variation in multilingual development. Factors such as language aptitude, gender and personality – typically discussed in the context of second language (L2) acquisition – as well as preference can lead to different language outcomes for children exposed to multiple languages. Through a battery of tests in English, Paradis (2011) found memory and analytic reasoning components of language aptitude to be a major source of individual differences in minority language children acquiring English as an L2 in Canada, as was found in previous research on other child L2 populations. A striking finding of her study was that child-internal factors pertaining to language aptitude such as "cognitive maturity, verbal working memory, analytic reasoning and the presence of an established linguistic system" (Paradis 2011: 233) had a larger impact on the variance of individual outcome than child-external factors like input quality and quantity.

The literature on gender differences in language development indicates that girls tend to acquire language more rapidly than boys in the first two years of life but that child sex as an influential factor on language development lessens considerably during the preschool years (Barbu et al. 2015 for a review). Personality differences can also have an impact, as a child who is sociable and eager to please others (as Xiaoxiao in Quay 2008) is more likely to accommodate to the language used by interlocutors than a child who is strong-willed, self-motivated and inner-directed.

Children's preference and choice of the dominant language (as Freddy did in Quay 2001), on the other hand, can lead to dual-lingual practices as described by Nakamura (2018). Smith-Christmas (2016) believes that caregivers who participate in such dual-lingual interactions are following a "stand-your-ground" approach to their children's receptive bilingualism. She gives the example of a grandmother in a Gaelic-speaking family who continued to speak Gaelic to her grandson, David, who only responded in English, and would not code-switch even when the child requested her to do so. David and others like him may be content to be passive bilinguals speaking only one of their languages since communication difficulties do not arise in this dual-lingual context (cf. Nakamura 2018). As argued in Quay (2001), passive bi/trilingual children have the potential for active multilingualism later in life. Smith-Christmas (2016) reports that even David, who participated in predominantly dual-lingual conversations where he spoke mainly English, did produce utterances in Gaelic when it served his purpose to obtain something he wanted, to get someone's attention or to mitigate an argument or admonishment.

Although the literature suggests that it is important for parents and caregivers not to give up speaking a home language in spite of children's resistance to responding in that same language, De Houwer (2015) has argued that such dual-lingual interactions may not reflect "harmonious" bilingual development – that is, the use of two (or more) languages is no longer a positive experience for the family – and may lead instead to parents feeling guilty, embarrassed or having a sense of failure regarding their children's passive bilingualism. According to De Houwer (2017), this is a threat to their socio-emotional well-being. Kopeliovich (2013) describes the Russian-Hebrew development of four siblings from birth to late childhood and reports that the parents felt they had to accommodate their children's language preference with the birth of each child for the sake of family harmony (to be "happylingual"). The parents changed their policy of using only Russian in their home in Israel once the second child, three years younger than the first, was born. With the birth of each sibling, the older ones preferred to use Hebrew among themselves and to their younger siblings.

Oftentimes, children need to draw on their whole repertoires while their multilingual abilities emerge and even parents espousing the OPOL approach do not always limit themselves to their chosen language to communicate with their children. Danjo (2015) advocates flexible multilingual practices rather than the OPOL approach. That is, she believes that parents do not need to view their own inconsistencies in adhering to their OPOL policy when they mix languages as a "failure" (and therefore, "non-harmonious" bilingual development) but as a useful resource for multilingual childrearing from a much wider social perspective. Her study explored the language practices of eight Japanese mothers married to

English spouses in the United Kingdom who were following the OPOL approach with their pre- and early-school age children (3;0–8;0). Three of the eight mothers shifted from a strict OPOL practice to a more relaxed approach allowing for multilingual practices which Danjo has termed "translingual", where multilingual speakers create and use the linguistic resources available to them according to their purposes and intentions in socially situated contexts. Slavkov (2017: 387) also found that 43% of 170 children exposed to two or more languages in his survey were exposed to a "Mixed" home language use model where at least one parent did not adhere strictly to a single language when communicating with the child. Unfortunately, he does not indicate how many of these children were successful at becoming active multilinguals among the 42% who did.

Such strategic and creative employment of linguistic resources by parents who accept this practice undermines, according to Danjo, the monolingualist dogmas that OPOL is reliant on (that is, the strict separation of two or more "named" languages and the attribution of each "language" to different parental roles). "Translanguaging", while encompassing "code-switching", differs from it by moving away from attention to the traditional concept of language as a solid systemic unit to the use of a multilingual speaker's full linguistic repertoire beyond the socially and politically defined boundaries of named languages (see García and Li 2014; also Chapter 7, this volume, for more about translanguaging). In a family home context, family members are constantly negotiating their language use. The children in these situations, according to Gyogi (2015), are exercising their "agency" when they contest, negotiate or redefine their mothers' monolingual practices through their own flexible use of two home languages (see also Chapter 11, this volume). One example of the difficulties of language separation from Danjo's data involves the use of English loan words in Japanese (i.e., *katakana* pronunciation when foreign words are pronounced according to the Japanese phonological system) by a four-year-old boy, Ken, with his mother. Although there is no plural ending in Japanese as in English, the boy refers to *aisukurimu**zu*** for "ice creams" (bold indicates the plural ending) instead of *aisukurimu*. His mother not only repeats his utterance without correcting him but also goes on to create her own *katakana* pronunciation for "cake" as *keiku* instead of the usual *keiki* (Danjo 2015: 193–195). These two examples are typical of translingual practices because they show a combination of features from both languages that defies separation into two separate languages. One interesting point that Danjo (2015: 200) raises is that a shift from "pretended monolingualism" by the Japanese mothers who were following strictly the OPOL approach allowed them to challenge the idea that language should always be taught by native speakers, presenting themselves instead as models of multilinguals.

While these practices may promote harmonious development, whether they foster or prevent active multilingualism is unclear from studies like Danjo (2015), Gyogi (2015) and Slavkov (2017). It does appear, though, that while OPOL and strict language separation are common and useful early on because they help children to acquire more than one language, once children are older and proficient in all their languages, it becomes less of an issue to use translanguaging since switching languages when one is proficient in all of them would not prevent active multilingualism and does ensure harmonious multilingual development.

10.5 Diversity of language contact and exposure

10.5.1 Interactions with other family members

Parents are not the only ones who can provide language input and affect multilingual childrearing. Fukuda (2017) found that the OPOL strategy only worked when parents had a single child, but not when they had more than one child. In sibling communication, 55% of the 36 children in her study communicated with their siblings in both the home language (Japanese) and the school/societal language (Catalan) while the rest used just the societal language. Older siblings tend to bring the societal language into the home. Bridges and Hoff (2014) report that older siblings used the societal language to talk to toddlers under age 2;6 in the United States. Thus, toddlers with older school-aged siblings became more advanced in the societal language, English, while those without such siblings were more advanced in the home language, Spanish. The presence of school-aged older siblings also increased the mothers' use of the societal language with their toddlers. In contrast, Kennedy and Romo (2013) describe a case where the parents were successful in explicitly asking an older child to help transmit the minority language to a younger sibling.

Braun (2012) found that monolingual grandparents in families where the mother and father each spoke a different minority language (type 1) were more successful than bilingual grandparents (in types 2 and 3 families, as defined in section 10.2) in helping to pass on their native languages and cultures to grandchildren. Bilingual grandparents tended not to provide the minority language support expected by parents raising multilingual children because they would choose to use the more prestigious societal language (particularly English). Nevertheless, grandparents can be important minority language resources as in Montanari's (2009) study of the language development of a young child growing up with Tagalog, Spanish and English in the United States. The child's maternal grandparents supplemented her exposure to Tagalog from her mother while her paternal grandmother provided additional Spanish input with her father, thus supporting both home languages. In a study of a preschooler, Quay (2013) further shows how a code-switching grandmother helped her grandson between ages three and five to shift dominance from the home language, Chinese, to the societal language, English, in preparation for formal schooling in the Canadian context. In this case, the grandmother decided not to follow the parents' FLP to expose the child mainly to the home language before the start of school because she feared that her grandson would be at a disadvantage when he entered kindergarten. The grandparents in these studies all had an impact on their grandchildren's multilingualism, either by fostering it as in Montanari (2009) or not doing so, as exemplified by the bilingual grandparents who decided not to follow parents' FLPs in Braun (2012) and Quay (2013) (see also Chapter 11, this volume, on digitally mediated transnational communication with grandparents).

10.5.2 Communities of practice

The larger speech community outside the home (Quay 2011b) also affects language use as children can invite more input in the societal language by using it more often themselves. Similarly, the language environment of the child outside the family can also indirectly influence parental language use. Prevoo et al. (2011) showed that Turkish immigrant mothers in the Netherlands increased their use of Dutch while addressing their toddlers when these children began attending a playgroup or daycare center, especially when the families lived in predominantly Dutch neighborhoods. As environmental contacts and children's own language preferences have a strong impact on parental language, Prevoo et al. (2011: 574) warn that parents need to be made aware of this finding to "find an appropriate balance between the use of the ethnic and the host language".

Studies in which children became actively bi/multilingual attest to the importance of the children having a variety of contacts in the minority language (s). Exposure to different minority language interlocutors is the main focus of an investigation of Japanese heritage language maintenance in Australia. Oriyama (2016: 291) examines the extent to which membership in a "heritage language community of practice" is influential on heritage language maintenance. She defines such communities as:

> socially and closely networked H[eritage] L[anguage] groups with common ideology: values, attitudes, norms, knowledge, and goals (e.g., HL development and maintenance,

pursuing interest in HL culture) who regularly and actively contribute to, and engage in, shared practices and learning to achieve their goals, often through HL community schools and associations.

She compared two groups of five Japanese-English bilingual children who attended a weekend Japanese school. The families of one group matched the criteria of a "heritage language community of practice", the mothers sharing resources and their children becoming friends and participating in various activities together, all the while communicating in Japanese. The families of the second group did not meet beyond the weekend school, and their children communicated with each other in English. All the children of the first group still communicated with their parents in Japanese as adults, while three of those in the second group had shifted to English (despite high maintenance of Japanese on the part of the Japanese-speaking parents).

In Chevalier (2015), one child, Elliot, became actively trilingual while the other child, Lina, did not. While living in French-speaking Switzerland with his English mother and German Swiss father, Elliot had a variety of contacts in Swiss German – not only his paternal grandmother, a regular babysitter with whom he frequently spent holidays in German-speaking Switzerland without his parents, but also his father's Swiss German-speaking friends. Many of his parents' friends also spoke English, as did people in their expatriate neighborhood. His older brother attended an international school, and Elliot was therefore aware that entire communities of Swiss German and English speakers existed. Since some of the people were close family members, friends or neighbors with whom he interacted regularly, he would have felt part of these communities. Lina, however, did not belong to a community of speakers in either of her minority languages and was highly dominant in Swiss German, using this language with her English-speaking aunt about half of the time and with her French-speaking father most of the time. In contrast, throughout the study, Elliot spoke all three languages addressee-appropriately.

Just as heritage language communities within the country of residence positively influence the maintenance of minority languages, actually spending time in the heritage country also plays an important role (Festman, Poarch, and Dewaele 2017; Kazzazi 2011). Dewaele, whose daughter was growing up in London with Belgian parents (Dutch-speaking mother, French-speaking father), writes that on holidays in Belgium, Livia had exposure to other native speakers of Dutch and French, both family members and friends. The children she played with were generally monolingual speakers of Dutch; in this environment, the child managed to avoid her usual code-switching into English and produce only Dutch. Kazzazi (2011: 69), whose son was being raised trilingually in Germany, attributes the child's greater linguistic development in Farsi (paternal language) compared to English (maternal language) to "strong[er] input through regular longer visits to Iran and frequent contact with a social network of Iranian friends and family in Germany" (the extended family as a "community of practice" is discussed further in Chapter 11, this volume). Thus, we see that a variety of contacts in a minority language, and especially children being made to feel that they belong to a community of speakers of that language, supports multilingual development.

10.5.3 The role of media and literacy

Spontaneous, unmediated speech is not the only means by which small children experience language. Many young children are further exposed to language through electronic media (radio, television, internet) and printed sources (books read aloud to them), which also increases the quality of their input. Bellay (2016) investigated the influence of songs, rhymes, stories and children's television in the language production of four siblings acquiring French and English simultaneously. She postulates that such input is particularly important for the acquisition of the minority language, since it provides a rich source of linguistic material from which children can acquire greater knowledge of that language. The study provides evidence of how children make considerable use of vocabulary and phrases from "musical, audio-visual, poetic and narrative input" (Bellay 2016: 149), language forms to which they are not necessarily exposed in conversation with their parents. Nevertheless, Slavkov (2017: 389) found that in spite of parental focus on minority language maintenance, "126 (79%) of the children who watch TV or play video games do so either exclusively or primarily in [the majority language] English," which may in part explain why multilingual childrearing is not always successful despite parents' best efforts.

For the later development of literacy skills, pre-literacy practices such as joint storybook reading in the early years have been found to be an influential form of language exposure (Wood 2002). Literacy skills in the minority languages, in turn, play a role in the development and maintenance of these languages more generally. In Oriyama's (2016) study described above, the mothers in the first group did not just rely on the community school to teach literacy skills. Rather, individual parents fostered literacy in various ways, for example, teaching a child the number of *kanji* (Chinese characters) needed to read a newspaper or reading to a child daily in Japanese. This resulted in their bilingual children growing up in Australia using Japanese for private reading. Slavkov (2017), however, found that although the families in Canada were strongly committed to minority language transmission and maintenance, more parents read to their children in English only or mainly (N=90) than in a minority language (N=65). Such practices can undoubtedly hamper multilingual outcomes as Slavkov (2017: 391) found that the "presence of some reading or writing skills in a minority language strongly increased the probability (91%) of a child being multilingual, as compared to a child acquiring literacy only in the majority language" (probability percentage from logistic regression models done in that study).

10.6 Societal attitudes

Inevitably, young children are also exposed to and affected by socio-political factors. In the early years, it is their parents who may be influenced by societal attitudes towards particular languages. Nevertheless, children soon become aware of the value of certain languages over others when they participate more in the community outside their home (Quay 2011b). As already suggested in the discussion of bilingual grandparents who did not comply with parental language policies, the status of a language is an important variable in whether or not the language is transmitted to the next generation. This is true both for entire communities (e.g., Ferguson 2006) as well as for individual families (Chevalier 2016). When parents and grandparents do use their heritage languages, the task of fostering them may be easier or more difficult depending on the status of these languages.

10.6.1 The hegemony of English

The particular position of English today often plays a role for parents in multilingual families, even among those who neither live in anglophone countries nor speak English as a native language. Yamamoto (2008) compared language use and perceptions of bilingualism in 118 Japanese-English (i.e., anglophone) and 34 Japanese-Filipino bilingual families in Japan. The most common pattern for non-Japanese parents whose native language was English and their children was the exclusive use of English, whereas for the Filipino parents and children, it was Japanese. With respect to perceptions of bilingualism, Yamamoto found notable differences between the two groups. Among the parents in the Japanese-English set, almost all felt that their bilingualism was perceived very or somewhat positively. However, among the Japanese-Filipino set, less than half of the respondents thought that their bilingualism was perceived so positively. One Japanese-Filipino respondent laments: "I think only English has a good impression to the Japanese" (Yamamoto 2008: 143).

A further consequence of the global prestige of English is that the maintenance of a minority language in an anglophone country can be challenging. Braun and Cline (2014) observed that parents seemed to find it harder to maintain trilingualism in England than in Germany. Among the families in England, young children were often sent to nurseries or playgroups in order to acquire English if it was not used in the home. Consequently, many children began to prefer speaking English, "even to their parents" (Braun and Cline 2014: 91). In Germany, 20 out of the 35 families sent their children to international nurseries or schools with English medium instruction (Braun and Cline 2010) because of the perceived economic value of English. In this situation, a trilingual upbringing may only be the outcome of parents adding non-native English via the choice of a bilingual or English language pre-school or school (Braun and Cline 2014; Chevalier 2016).

Further evidence of the importance of English in multilingual families is that English is frequently chosen as a lingua franca among mixed-language couples without a common native language. The consequence of parents' speaking English primarily or exclusively to each other when it is the majority language, however, is the lower chance of raising multilingual children (Slavkov 2017). In addition, in parent-child interactions, sometimes one or more native languages are dropped in favor of English (Chevalier 2016; Yamamoto 2008). In Chevalier's (2016) study of 35 multilingual families in Switzerland, two bilingual mothers chose not to speak either of their native languages (Swiss German-Italian and Swiss German-Polish) to their children but opted for English instead.

Nevertheless, research shows that for parents with an "impact belief", namely a belief "that the language environment matters and can be manipulated" (De Houwer 2009: 96), it is possible to counter the hegemony of English. For example, Silva-Corvalàn (2014: 30) reports on a bilingual English-Spanish family in California where Spanish tends to have low prestige, but where Spanish was "valued and respected" (2014: 30) in the family itself. The children developed a positive attitude towards the language despite the higher status of English.

10.6.2 The status or prestige of languages

Fukuda (2017) explored language use in Catalonia where two languages of different status, Catalan and Spanish, exist in a bilingual society. She focused on 29 cross-linguistic couples with one Japanese spouse to determine how they were able to maintain the socially "weaker" language, Catalan, along with a minority language, Japanese, in the face of the prestigious language, Spanish. Although she found that parents communicated with each other in Spanish and that the Japanese spouse was more likely to use Japanese and Spanish with their children, such use of Spanish did not affect the use of the two minority languages, Japanese and Catalan, at home – that is, children still used predominantly Japanese with the Japanese-speaking parent and Catalan with the Catalan-speaking parent (note, though, that the data were collected through parental self-reports rather than empirically). She attributes this finding to three factors: (1) the acceptance of Spanish as the dominant language of the country, and because Catalonia is a bilingual society, the resulting attitude of the families that three languages can coexist in their daily life; (2) the parents' "generous attitude towards children's use of the local language with heritage language parents" (Fukuda 2017: 415); and (3) the association of the minority language, Japanese, with economic power as well as cultural trendiness, resulting in a positive attitude that helps it "survive the complex reality of Catalonia" (Fukuda 2017: 415).

In sum, raising actively multilingual children can be more challenging when the children are acquiring languages that are not highly valued in society. The importance of this factor should not be underestimated.

10.7 Conclusion and future research

In summary, a certain level of success in raising multilingual children has been found in three different contexts: (1) when parents each choose to use a different native language at home with their children (OPOL), both of which are different from the societal language, (2) when parents both use the same two minority home languages at home and their children are exposed to a third language in society, and (3) when they live in bilingual communities supporting two societal languages and use another heritage language at home (Section 10.2). For all three situations, multilingual outcomes are related to the quantity (10.3) and quality of input (parental discourse styles in 10.2). Quality of input can also be increased by exposing children to native-speaking family and friends in the community or abroad, through reading books and story-telling in different languages, and engaging in other media like music and television (10.5). The research indicates that besides family beliefs and the social context, societal attitudes towards the status and benefits of particular languages (10.6) greatly affect linguistic outcomes. These outcomes are also dependent on child-internal factors – as seen in children's behavior or agency based on their experiences, linguistic opportunities, strengths and abilities – which have been found to be a major source of individual variation in multilingual development (10.4).

When children start attending school, they tend to learn the majority language, especially when it is also the school language; thus special attention needs to be given to the quality and quantity of exposure to minority languages at this time. Once parents have decided to raise multilingual children, they must also find a balance between "harmonious" development and staying on course with "impact beliefs" – a fine line to manage when children reject one or more home languages in favor of a societal one.

Early successful multilingualism before children enter school and society is no guarantee of later multilingualism when family-external influences on communication and language learning become more prevalent. This is an unavoidable challenge that all parents must face. Some are able to overcome this by choosing bilingual education options for their children. But as Barron-Hauwaert (2004) found, most (92% of the 98 bilingual families in her study) send their children to monolingual majority language schools. When bilingual options *are* chosen, there is evidence of success. As Slavkov (2017) and others before him have found in Canadian settings, children growing up with two or more languages in Canada were more likely to develop as multilingual individuals when their parents chose to send them to French language schools that also provided majority language classes in English. In addition, families in Ontario often took advantage of the availability of publicly funded heritage language weekend classes not available in other Canadian provinces to ensure literacy development in all languages.

The research reviewed shows that multilingual childrearing can be successful although not for all families in spite of a strong desire to make it so. We need more studies of different types of families in different environmental contexts, as mobility and "transnationalism" have become prevalent aspects of 21st century language contact. Besides the fact that one or more individuals in families are now making transnational moves and leaving behind parts of the nuclear and extended family (Hirsch and Lee 2018; Chapter 11, this volume), Fogle and King (2017: 90) also point out that "transnational adoption, same-sex parent families, single-parent families, and grandparents as primary caregiver" are increasing in society and changing family structures. As most studies have focused on child-external input factors (namely, parental and caregiver language choices and discourse styles), more research is also needed on child-internal factors – currently discussed mainly in the context of L2 acquisition (Paradis 2011) rather than for child multilingualism. How do internal factors such as personality, language aptitude and language preferences lead to variable multilingual outcomes? How do they correlate with external factors?

More studies focusing on families raising multilingual children are needed to help us unpack the complex relationships between home, environmental, societal and individual child factors and the development and maintenance of childhood multilingualism. Such research in the future can help us better understand the different pathways in the route towards optimal multilingual outcomes.

References

Barbu, Stéphanie, Aurélie Nardy, Jean-Pierre Chevrot, Bahia Guellaï, Ludivine Glas, Jacques Juhel & Alban Lemasson. 2015. Sex differences in language across early childhood: Family socioeconomic status does not impact boys and girls equally. *Frontiers in Psychology* 6(1874). http://doi.org/10.3389/fpsyg.2015.01874 (accessed July 5, 2018).

Barron-Hauwaert, Suzanne. 2004. *Language strategies for bilingual families: The one-parent-one-language approach*. Clevedon: Multilingual Matters.

Bellay, Catrin. 2016. Musical, audio-visual, poetic, and narrative input: A longitudinal case study of French-English bilingual first language acquisition. In Monika Reif & Justyna A. Robinson (eds.), *Cognitive perspectives on bilingualism*, 149–182. Boston & Berlin: Walter de Gruyter.

Braun, Andreas. 2012. Language maintenance in trilingual families – a focus on grandparents. *International Journal of Multilingualism* 9(4). 423–436.

Braun, Andreas & Tony Cline. 2010. Trilingual families in mainly monolingual societies: Working towards a typology. *International Journal of Multilingualism* 7(2). 110–127.

Braun, Andreas & Tony Cline. 2014. *Language strategies for trilingual families: Parents' perspectives*. Bristol: Multilingual Matters.

Bridges, Kelly & Erika Hoff. 2014. Older sibling influences on the language environment and language development of toddlers in bilingual homes. *Applied Psycholinguistics* 35(2). 225–241.

Caldas, Stephen. 2012. Language policy in the family. In Bernard Spolsky (ed.), *The Cambridge handbook of language policy*, 351–373. Cambridge: Cambridge University Press.

Chevalier, Sarah. 2015. *Trilingual language acquisition: Contextual factors influencing active trilingualism in early childhood*. Amsterdam & Philadelphia: John Benjamins.

Chevalier, Sarah. 2016. The value of English in multilingual families. In Martin Leer & Genoveva Puskas (eds.), *Economies of English* (SPELL Swiss Papers in English Language and Literature 33), 97–116. Tübingen: Narr Francke Attempto Verlag.

Curdt-Christiansen, Xiao Lan. 2009. Invisible and visible language planning: Ideological factors in the family language policy of Chinese immigrant families in Quebec. *Language Policy* 8(4). 351–375.

Dagenais, Diane. 2003. Accessing imagined communities through multilingualism and immersion education. *Journal of Language, Identity, and Education* 2(4). 269–283.

Danjo, Chisato. 2015. *A critical ethnographic inquiry into the negotiation of language practices among Japanese multilingual families in the UK: Discourse, language use and perceptions in the hoshuko and the family home*. Newcastle upon Tyne: Northumbria University doctoral thesis. http://nrl.northumbria.ac.uk/27269/ (accessed 19 January 2018).

De Houwer, Annick. 2004. Trilingual input and children's language use in trilingual families in Flanders. In Charlotte Hoffmann & Jehannes Ytsma (eds.), *Trilingualism in family, school and community* (Bilingual Education and Bilingualism), 118–135. Clevedon: Multilingual Matters.
De Houwer, Annick. 2009. *Bilingual first language acquisition*. Bristol: Multilingual Matters.
De Houwer, Annick. 2015. Harmonious bilingual development: Young families' well-being in language contact situations. *International Journal of Bilingualism* 19(2). 169–184.
De Houwer, Annick. 2017. Minority language parenting in Europe and children's well-being. In Natasha Cabrera & Birgit Leyendecker (eds.), *Handbook on positive development of minority children and youth*, 231–246. Cham, Switzerland: Springer.
Döpke, Susanne. 1992. *One parent one language: An interactional approach*. Amsterdam & Philadelphia: John Benjamins.
Ferguson, Gibson. 2006. *Language planning and education*. Edinburgh: Edinburgh University Press.
Festman, Julia, Gregory J. Poarch & Jean-Marc Dewaele. 2017. *Raising multilingual children*. Bristol & Blue Ridge Summit, PA: Multilingual Matters.
Fogle, Lyn & Kendall King. 2017. Bi- and multilingual family language socialization. In Patricia Duff & Stephen May (eds.), *Language socialization* (Encyclopedia of Language and Education), 79–95. Cham, Switzerland: Springer.
Fukuda, Makiko. 2017. Language use in the context of double minority: The case of Japanese-Catalan/Spanish families in Catalonia. *International Journal of Multilingualism* 14(4). 401–418.
García, Ofelia & Wei Li. 2014. *Translanguaging: Language, bilingualism, and education*. New York: Palgrave MacMillan.
Gyogi, Eiko. 2015. Children's agency in language choice: A case study of two Japanese-English bilingual children in London. *International Journal of Bilingual Education and Bilingualism* 18(6). 749–764.
Hélot, Christine. 1988. Bringing up children in English, French and Irish: Two case studies. *Language, Culture and Curriculum* 1(3). 281–287.
Hirsch, Tijana & Jin Sook Lee. 2018. Understanding the complexities of transnational family language policy. *Journal of Multilingual and Multicultural Development*. https://doi.org/10.1080/01434632.2018.1454454 (accessed 24 March 2018).
Juan-Garau, Maria & Carmen Pérez-Vidal. 2001. Mixing and pragmatic parental strategies in early bilingual acquisition. *Journal of Child Language* 28. 59–86.
Kasuya, Hiroko. 1998. Determinants of language choice in bilingual children: The role of input. *International Journal of Bilingualism* 2(3). 327–346.
Kazzazi, Kerstin. 2011. *Ich brauche mix-cough*: Cross-linguistic influence involving German, English and Farsi. *International Journal of Multilingualism* 8(1). 63–79.
Kennedy, Kimberley & Harriet Romo. 2013. "All colors and hues": An autoethnography of a multiethnic family's strategies for bilingualism and multiculturalism. *Family Relations* 62. 109–124.
King, Kendall A. & Lyn Fogle. 2006. Bilingual parenting as good parenting: Parents' perspectives on family language policy for additive bilingualism. *International Journal of Bilingual Education and Bilingualism* 9(6). 695–712.
Kopeliovich, Shulamit. 2013. Happylingual: A family project for enhancing and balancing multilingual development. In Mila Schwartz & Anna Verschik (eds.), *Successful family language policy: Parents, children and educators in interaction* (Multilingual Education 7), 249–275. Dordrecht: Springer.

Lanza, Elizabeth. 2004 [1997]. *Language mixing in infant bilingualism: A sociolinguistic perspective*, 2nd edn. Oxford: Oxford University Press.

Lanza, Elizabeth. 2007. Multilingualism in the family. In Peter Auer & Wei Li (eds.), *Handbook of multilingualism and multilingual communication* (Handbooks of Applied Linguistics 5), 45–68. Berlin & New York: Mouton de Gruyter.

Mishina-Mori, Satomi. 2011. A longitudinal analysis of language choice in bilingual children: The role of parental input and interaction. *Journal of Pragmatics* 43(13). 3122–3138.

Montanari, Simona. 2009. Pragmatic differentiation in early trilingual development. *Journal of Child Language* 36(3). 597–627.

Nakamura, Janice. 2018. Parents' use of discourse strategies in dual-lingual interactions with receptive bilingual children. In Elena Babatsouli (ed.), *Crosslinguistic research in monolingual and bilingual speech*, 181–200. Chania, Greece: Institute of Monolingual and Bilingual Speech.

Nibun, Yukari & Gillian Wigglesworth. 2014. Early pragmatic differentiation in Japanese and German: A case study of a developing trilingual child in Australia. *International Journal of Multilingualism* 11(1). 76–96.

Oriyama, Kaya. 2016. Community of practice and family language policy: Maintaining heritage Japanese in Sydney – ten years later. *International Multilingual Research Journal* 10(4). 289–307.

Paradis, Johanne. 2011. Individual differences in child English second language acquisition: Comparing child-internal and child-external factors. *Linguistic Approaches to Bilingualism* 1(3). 213–237.

Prevoo, Mariëlle, Judi Mesman, Marinus van IJzendoorn & Suzanne Pieper. 2011. Bilingual toddlers reap the language they sow: Ethnic minority toddlers' childcare attendance increases maternal host language use. *Journal of Multilingual and Multicultural Development* 32(6). 561–576.

Quay, Suzanne. 2001. Managing linguistic boundaries in early trilingual development. In Jasone Cenoz & Fred Genesee (eds.), *Trends in bilingual acquisition* (Trends in Language Acquisition Research 1), 149–199. Amsterdam & Philadelphia: John Benjamins.

Quay, Suzanne. 2008. Dinner conversations with a trilingual two-year-old: Language socialization in a multilingual context. *First Language* 28(1). 5–33.

Quay, Suzanne (ed.). 2011a. Trilingual children in the making: Data-driven insights. [Special issue]. *International Journal of Multilingualism* 8(1).

Quay, Suzanne. 2011b. Trilingual toddlers at daycare centres: The role of caregivers and peers in language development. *International Journal of Multilingualism* 8(1). 22–41.

Quay, Suzanne. 2012. Discourse practices of trilingual mothers: Effects on minority home language development in Japan. *International Journal of Bilingual Education and Bilingualism* 15(4). 435–453.

Quay, Suzanne. 2013. Shifting dominance through language mixing: Caregiver input and a preschooler's bilingual discourse. Paper presented at the International Symposium on Bilingualism 9, Nanyang Technological University, Singapore, June 10–13.

Silva-Corvalán, Carmen. 2014. *Bilingual language acquisition: Spanish and English in the first six years*. Cambridge: Cambridge University Press.

Slavkov, Nikolay. 2017. Family language policy and school language choice: Pathways to bilingualism and multilingualism in a Canadian context. *International Journal of Multilingualism* 14(4). 378–400.

Smith-Christmas, Cassie. 2016. *Family language policy: Maintaining an endangered language in the home*. Basingstoke, UK: Palgrave MacMillan.
Unsworth, Sharon. 2013. Current issues in multilingual first language acquisition. *Annual Review of Applied Linguistics* 33. 21–50.
Wood, Clare. 2002. Parent-child pre-school activities can affect the development of literacy skills. *Journal of Research in Reading* 25(3). 241–258.
Yamamoto, Masayo. 2008. Language use in interlingual families: Do different languages make a difference? *International Journal of Sociology of Language* 189. 133–148.

Elizabeth Lanza and Kristin Vold Lexander
11 Family Language Practices in Multilingual Transcultural Families

11.1 Introduction

With intensified transnational migration in recent years, raising children with more than one language has become an increasingly widespread phenomenon as people cross borders, integrate into new cultural and linguistic landscapes, form intermarriages and partnerships, and create multilingual families (Curdt-Christiansen and Lanza 2018b; Lanza and Li 2016). While this phenomenon is relatively new in a European and North American context, in a global context, such socio-cultural patterns are not, when we take southern experiences of multilingualism, mobility and diversity into account (cf. Comaroff and Comaroff 2012). The linguistic anthropological research on language socialization has indeed had a global reach in its investigations of how children are socialized in and through language ever since the seminal works of Elinor Ochs and Bambi Schieffelin (see the review in Ochs and Schieffelin 2011). However, the study of multilingualism in the family has, despite earlier sociolinguistic contributions (e.g., Döpke 1992, Lanza [1997] 2004), only come to the fore the past ten years through the burgeoning field of family language policy (FLP), the aim of which is to investigate language planning in relation to language use and literacy practices within home domains and among family members (King, Fogle and Logan-Terry 2008). While not all studies targeting language practices in multilingual transcultural families actually define themselves as studies of FLP, this approach has indeed been a catalyst promoting the sociolinguistic inquiry of family language policies and practices in multilingual families, with the term "family language policy" having been first used by Luykx (2003). FLP has indeed become an umbrella term for encompassing research on both interactional language practices and more conscious language planning in multilingual transcultural families.

Anchored in the field of language policy, the original focus in FLP was on explicit and overt planning and the decision-making processes families undergo in regards to language use in the home. Inspired by Spolsky's (2003) model of language policy, the focus has been on language ideologies, language practices

---

Elizabeth Lanza and Kristin Vold Lexander, Center for Multilingualism in Society across the Lifespan (MultiLing), University of Oslo, Oslo, Norway

https://doi.org/10.1515/9781501507984-011

and language management in the family. Spolsky (2012) himself refers to the family as "the critical domain" of language policy. Various questions underlie this enterprise of studying multilingual families' language policy such as what language conditions provide affordances and constraints for multilingual development, and what measures parents should take to ensure desirable multilingual outcomes. Explicit deliberate language planning strategies in the home are, as pointed out by Curdt-Christiansen and Lanza (2018b: 124), " ... often motivated by parents' past experiences and future aspirations for their children's language development. They consist of various approaches that parents use to enrich their children's language experiences and their linguistic repertoires, including the 'one parent, one language' (OPOL) strategy; one language on certain days; minority language only at home (hot-house approach) and mixed language strategies, or 'translanguaging' ... ". Hence policies play out in practices (cf. Van Mensel 2018; see also Chapter 10, this volume). In line with contemporary language policy research (cf. Hult and Johnson 2015), current approaches to FLP also investigate implicit and covert aspects of language planning (Curdt-Christiansen 2013), for example, underlying language ideologies, through the study of family language practices in multilingual transcultural families. Indeed what families say they do and what they actually do can be at odds (Curdt-Christiansen 2016; Palviainen and Boyd 2013), and thus warrants investigation. Such an approach can not only provide insights into language learning and use but also to larger questions of heritage language maintenance and shift in multilingual families and communities.

FLP builds ostensibly on previous scholarship. In an article on FLP and bilingual parenting, King and Fogle (2013: 172) point out the links between studies of child language acquisition and early second language learning and bilingualism with the field of language policy, emphasizing that "FLP examines language policy in relation to language use and language choice within the home among family members". While more psycholinguistics-oriented investigations of bilingualism have targeted what is referred to as "input" and its impact on the child's acquisition of more than one language (Lanza 2017), "the emphasis of FLP is on the balance between and use of languages within the family unit. Thus, FLP addresses child language learning and use as functions of parental ideologies, decision-making and strategies concerning languages and literacies, as well as the broader social and cultural context of family life" (King and Fogle 2013: 172).

In this chapter, we discuss the state-of-the-art research on language practices in multilingual transcultural families in terms of multilingual families' practices and ideologies, and how social and cultural contexts may impact on these practices and policies. In the following, we first address various approaches to studying multilingual families and theoretical underpinnings or perspectives involved in these approaches (section 11.2). Subsequently, we give an overview of current studies of family language practices in multilingual transcultural families, first with a focus on spoken interactions in the family (11.3). Given the ever-increasing role of technology in communication, we then address digitally mediated family interactions (11.4), an important aspect of FLP that is receiving increasing attention in current research. Lastly (in 11.5), we conclude and propose directions for further research.

11.2 Theoretical perspectives in studying the (multilingual) family

In any study of family language practices, an important question to address is how one may define *family*. Studies of FLP have not just considered families as households in which children learn more than one language; they also investigate how families construct their identities and define themselves by and through their linguistic practices (King and Lanza 2019b), and with digitally mediated communication, the scope of "family" to be considered is indeed quite large (see also Coetzee 2018; Ruby 2012 for the notion of family). Such a social constructionist theoretical anchoring weighs heavily in current sociolinguistic scholarship addressing multilingual family language use. King (2016), in her commentary to a special issue on multilingual transcultural families (Lanza and Li 2016), highlights the turn in FLP studies to include a more diverse range of family types, languages, and contexts and points out the increasing focus on globally dispersed, transnational, multilingual populations. This opens up the way for understanding how multilingual transcultural families construct their identities through language both locally and globally. Current FLP research is highly influenced by two broad processes of change in more recent approaches to sociolinguistic research on multilingualism, as articulated by Martin-Jones and Martin (2017). These concern: (1) "broad epistemological shifts in the field of sociolinguistics to ethnographic and critical approaches"; and (2) "increasing focus on the study of the social, cultural and linguistic changes ushered in by globalization" (Martin-Jones and Martin 2017: 1). In this regard, we may highlight in particular the affordances of new communication technologies and their impact on family language practices (cf. 11.4), as well as political and economic changes across the globe.

The study of family language practices in FLP studies with its sociolinguistic basis builds on language policy, language maintenance and shift studies, and language socialization. Each of these has a distinct theoretical and methodological origin and focus stemming from the sociology of language and anthropology. Ochs and Schieffelin (2011: 1) state that " ... the study of language socialization examines how children and other novices apprehend and enact 'the context of situation' in relation to the 'context of culture'. In so doing, language socialization research integrates discourse and ethnographic methods to capture the social structurings and cultural interpretations of semiotic forms, practices, and ideologies that inform novices' practical engagements with others". Language socialization is an interactional process and studying this requires analysis over time through ethnographic methods in order to unveil the impact of cultural beliefs and child-rearing on language development and use. FLP approaches may, for example, study how the One Person – One Language (OPOL) policy is actually practiced in interaction (cf. Lanza [1997] 2004). Fogle and King (2017: 14) highlight: "The study of bi- and multilingual family language socialization has provided important insights into the ways in which language ideologies, practices, and management in the family connect with societal language maintenance and shift, children's educational experiences, and the construction of identity and belonging in post-industrial, globalizing, and transnational contexts". Borrowing from Wenger (1998), Lanza (2007: 47) has called the family a "community of practice", a social unit that has its own norms for speaking, acting and believing and hence provides a focus on praxis, the cornerstone for language socialization.

Finally, we may also conceive of the family as a *space*. As space theorists have argued, space is constantly negotiated between a variety of social actors with different discursive power, material constraints, and spatial practices (Cresswell 2014; Lefebvre 1991; Massey 2005). In Western scholarship, the family has been a major social institution, considered the most private space we can experience in our everyday life, and indeed in sociolinguistic inquiry, family has traditionally been considered a private domain (Fishman 1965). Dagenais (2009: 39) points out that, historically, the family has moved from being more public to more private while in fact the "public-private duality that is so characteristic of modern life did not exist in traditional societies". The family as a space for language learning and use was highlighted by Canagarajah (2013: 221): "Space doesn't emerge as determining the status of migrants. Migrants enjoy agency to negotiate the differing scales and indexical orders to their advantage and reconstruct space. They make spaces for their places, voices and norms as they contest dominant language ideologies and orders". Purkarthofer (2019) points out that the family can be a "safe" space; through language use and everyday actions, spatial practices can contribute to the construction of (safe) spaces, and make them recognizable to speakers, particularly important for children.

With the advent of technological advancements, the public-private dichotomy has indeed become blurred. The notion of the family as a private space has been challenged by the mediatization of migrant families and the public viewpoints imposing cultural assimilation concerning not only lifestyle but also what language is to be spoken in the home (Lanza in press). Digital language practices in the home and multilingual families' engagement with online platforms and fora deserve more attention. In 11.4 below, we focus on digitally mediated practices among family members. First, however, we turn to current research on spoken non-digital interactional practices in multilingual families.

11.3 Spoken language practices in multilingual transcultural families

The growing interest in family language policies and practices is demonstrated in an increasing number of publications, including several books. Fogle's (2012) in-depth study examined how Russian-speaking adoptees in three US families actively shaped opportunities for language learning and identity construction in everyday interactions, thereby exerting speaker agency, despite the fact that their adoptive parents did not speak their language when they joined their home. Schwartz and Verschik (2013) edited the first volume to explore the link between family language policy, practice and management in light of state and community language policy in more than 20 ethno-linguistic communities worldwide. Smith-Christmas' (2016) monograph on maintaining an endangered language in the home is the first full-length ethnographic study of FLP – an eight-year study of a family on the Isle of Skye, Scotland. It provides micro-level interactional analyses shedding light on why the children in the family do not often speak Gaelic, despite the adults' best efforts to use the language with them, as well as the children's attendance at a Gaelic immersion school. Macalister and Mirvahedi (2017) present a collection of case studies from across the globe, illustrating opportunities, challenges and consequences that families face in language maintenance and language learning in the home.

These contributions illustrate on the whole the myriad of methods used in research to document family language practices/policies: large scale language use surveys, online questionnaires, interviews, focus group conversations, ethnography, diaries, and interactional analyses of video recordings – both quantitative and qualitative methods. Special issues of international journals

(*International Journal of Bilingualism, International Journal of Multilingualism, Journal of Multilingual and Multicultural Development* and *Multilingua*), have also focused on family language practices (Curdt-Christiansen and Lanza 2018a; King and Lanza 2019a; Lanza and Curdt-Christiansen 2018; Lanza and Li 2016; Li 2012). Several themes arise in the current literature on family language practices and we examine the most topical below.

11.3.1 Agency in family language practices

While language socialization research has emphasized adult caregivers' roles in nurturing young children in the family and society as they become full-fledged members of their culture, studies of multilingual families have also highlighted the agency of children in negotiating their language learning environment. As noted above, Fogle (2012) illustrated this in adoptive families. Drawing on conversation analysis and extending Lanza [1997] (2004), Gafaranga (2010) carefully illustrates through minute interactional analyses how children assume agency in instigating language shift in the Rwandan community in Brussels where language shift is purported to be in progress from Kinyarwanda-French bilingualism to French monolingualism. The children were active actors in the socialization process and, moreover, were blamed for this impending shift. However, as Gafaranga points out, the adults were also guilty as they too contributed to the language shift through their responses to the children when the children used their preferred language, French. Kheirkhah (2016a,b) combine family language policy with a language socialization approach, examining family interactions in five bi/multilingual Iranian families in Sweden. The analysis is of video-recordings of the families' everyday interactions and includes interviews and observations. Considering children's active role in family interactions, Kheirkhan explores parents' heritage language maintenance practices and children's responses to these practices. In addition, Kheirkhan and Cekaite (2017) examine siblings' contributions to family language choices and practices, adding a much needed dimension to studies of family language practices.

Purkarthofer (2019) addressed young parents' projected view of child agency in regard to their imagined family language policy and social space. She critically examined the language expectations of three multilingual couples, each with a different language background and varied experiences of migration – and each of whom was expecting, or had just had, their first child. Using innovative speaker-centered qualitative methods, including language portraits, biographic narratives and Lego blocks to construct a home, she analyzed (real and imagined) constructed spaces of interaction. The analysis indicates the parents' construction of the child as a multilingual self with agency, although potentially influenced by the parents. The multimodal data provided a window into the future parents' negotiation of language policy. Obojska and Purkarthofer (2018) examined agency in transnational families in Norway using language portraits and semi-structured interviews, revealing how family members perceive and construct their agency in language learning, maintenance, and management. The importance of individual agency in the management of minority languages is underscored in Nandi's (2018) study of parents as stakeholders in urban Galician homes. As he concludes, "Their under-the-radar participation in LPP [Language Policy and Planning] may appear extremely intermittent and ad hoc, but their individual language management and practice, taken together, can have a significant impact in their immediate society's language behaviour" (Nandi 2018: 221).

11.3.2 Literacy development in heritage language maintenance

Spoken family language practices are a central element to children's literacy development. Stavans (2012) investigated home literacy among 60 Ethiopian families living in Israel and revealed certain patterns shaped by internal and external forces in parent-child interactions. The findings indicate that the parents preferred certain extended discourses, the form and function of which coincided with those needed for better scholastic literacy. Ethiopian parents were shown to prefer oral, not written discourse as the anchor for their literacy-driven parent-child interactions in the home. Stavans' study underscores the necessity to take home language practices into account in school literacy development. Song's (2016) study of four Korean bilingual children in home literacy events in the US also emphasizes the importance of taking family literacy practices into account in school environments. Building on research on translanguaging practices in classrooms (e.g., García 2009), she investigated through participant observation, video recordings, and field notes how the children's families used their two languages in order to support their heritage language development in literacy events. Findings revealed that " ... translanguaging practices not only foster children's learning of their two languages, but they are also as a vehicle for bilingual children to expand and enrich their learning in both academic and non-academic settings as they clarify meaning and enhance their understanding ... " (Song 2016: 102).

Family language practices in relation to heritage language literacy were studied by Curdt-Christiansen and La Morgia (2018). They drew on a sample of 66 families, each with at least one child between 2 and 8, with all children learning/speaking English along with their heritage language – either Chinese, Italian or Urdu. Through different data sources including questionnaires, overviews of literacy resources and activities in both heritage languages and English, as well as interviews with the parents, they found that there were interesting differences among the various language groups not only in their family language practices but also in their attitudes to home language literacy and their practice of it. These results corroborate earlier results by Curdt-Christiansen (2016) and De Houwer (2007). Parents' use of the heritage language between themselves and with their children increased the chances for the child to use the heritage language (see also Chapter 10, this volume). However, English literacy skills were given more attention than heritage language literacy skills across all three groups.

11.3.3 Family language practices and affective dimensions

Language and emotion in multilingualism has been studied extensively (cf. Dewaele 2013). Pavlenko (2004) addressed the issue of emotions and language choice in the family through quantitative and qualitative analyses of responses to a carefully designed web questionnaire. Through this work, she could add perceived language emotionality and cross-linguistic differences in affective repertoires to the list of factors influencing parental language choice in bi- and multilingual families. Interestingly, Pavlenko's study called into question the popular belief that a speaker's first language is the language of emotion while other languages are one of distance or detachment.

Tannenbaum (2012) draws attention to family language policies and language practices as being affected by and affecting emotional issues and psychological dimensions that are seldom acknowledged as playing an important role in the analysis of FLP. As indicated in the title of her article, she calls FLP a "form of coping or defense mechanism". Recent work has looked at affective dimensions of interaction. Smith-Christmas (2018) focuses on the affective dimensions of FLP and demonstrates how the very same child-centered discourse style used by a grandmother as a means to encourage her grandchildren to use their minority language – Scottish Gaelic – can have different results (positive and negative) among siblings. Smith-Christmas illustrates the reflexive nature of FLP in terms of emotional affect, linguistic input and language shift. Zhu and Li (2016) argue for the need to examine how family members experience multilingualism and their strategies to deal with the challenges of multilingualism, as opposed to focusing on overall patterns of language maintenance and shift. Building on data collected from a sociolinguistic ethnography of three multilingual and transnational families from China in Britain, they show how these family members' lived experiences affect how they perceive social relations and social structures, and how this affects their own identity constructions and aspirations (cf. also Kirsch and Gogonas 2018). In an ethnographic study of two multilingual migrant families from Timor-Leste living in Northern Ireland, da Costa Cabral (2018) reveals the parents' beliefs and values regarding the languages in their communicative repertoire – Tetum, Portuguese and Indonesian – related to differences in their lived experiences. Once they moved to Northern Ireland, however, these parents' language ideologies became closely linked with their aspirations for their children, and they actively encouraged them to learn and use English.

11.4 Family interactions – digitally mediated language practices

New information and communication technologies are crucial for transnational families, or *stretched families* (Porter et al. 2018), to stay in touch across borders, to exchange information and for practices of mobile intimacy (Hjorth 2011) or virtual intimacies (Wilding 2006). Access is facilitated through lower cost, and the availability of user-friendly means of communication invites a wider range of kin to become involved in transnational communication. Also research on multilingual families is increasingly interested in the connection between language use and media use, that is, how families are constructed through multilingual language practices "in contexts of transmigration, social media and technology saturation, and hypermobility" (King and Lanza 2019b: 718). However, this interest has so far not led to a substantial body of research on how language use in interpersonal mediated communication affects family language policy and practices in transcultural families. In this section, we will present and discuss research on the relation between digital interaction, identity, and heritage language use; studies of modality and language use; and informal learning through interpersonal digitally mediated communication.

11.4.1 Digital interaction, identity and heritage language use

Digital aspects of communication are sometimes cited in FLP studies (e.g., Haque 2012), and we also find references to the importance of family interaction in studies of migrants' media use within other fields, in particular in educational research (Marrapodi 2016; Rydin and Sjöberg 2008; Szecsi and Szilagyi 2012). Cuban (2014) found that transnational families built new vocabularies and interaction styles, including non-verbal means, for their emotions in digital communication and thereby managed family relationships as well as a changing sense of selves, while Rydin and Sjöberg (2008) consider the internet as a communicative space for identity construction for diaspora families in Sweden.

Also media studies and digital anthropology have taken an interest in the transnational family to study how media use shapes the migration experience and how it is fundamental for the management of relationships. Already at the turn of the millennium, Miller and Slater (2000) identified a transition from what they call *diaspora family* to *internet family* in the Trinidadian context. As most Trinidadian families have at least one nuclear family member living abroad, the internet has been crucial in offering the possibility for these transnational families to stay in closer, more intimate and more frequent contact. Some twelve years later, as mediated communication has diversified, from the phone calls, emails and chat that the *internet family* relied upon into a range of communicational tools, Madianou and Miller (2012) introduced the concept of *polymedia* to study how the availability of various communicational tools leads to usages that impact on how relationships are managed and experienced. There are also various ways in which media choices have consequences for language use, like the choice of modality. Yoon (2018), for instance, finds that young Korean Canadians consider the messaging app Kakaotalk as a type of identity badge, as it is predominantly used by Koreans in Korea and overseas. The choice of using Kakaotalk thus implies language choice and choice of background of potential interlocutors.

Several studies show how digital communication is important for identity construction and performance among young immigrants (Lam 2014; Lee 2006) as the young have been leading the way, and much of their interaction is intra-generational (e.g., Yoon 2018). However, also their parents, uncles, aunts, and grandparents have started using the communicational tools available (Dyers 2014; Ivan and Hebblethwaite 2016). As language use with friends differs from language use with family (see e.g., Lasekan 2018 on language choice on Facebook), increased digitally mediated interaction with family members may be important for migrants' linguistic identity: migrant families in Sweden find that just to have and use the possibility of chatting in one's mother tongue is more important than the actual content of the interaction online (Rydin and Sjöberg 2008), and young urban Senegalese say that their migrant relatives wish to use their first language when they interact with them digitally because they miss it (Lexander 2011b).

In his study of FLP in migrant families from India living in Europe, Haque (2012) points out three uses of Indian languages: (1) trips back home, (2) phone calls and (3) internet-based contact with people in India. The trips back home are evidently limited, and phone calls are expensive; internet thus becomes an important space for assuring the frequency in the use of these languages. Haque further finds that the families use not only the Indian languages, but diverse languages online and in text-messages on the mobile phone; mediated communication thus enhances multilingual practices. In their autoethnographic study of their immigrant families in the USA, Szecsi and Szilagyi (2012) investigated the children's and adolescents' development and maintenance of the heritage language, Hungarian, in digital interaction. They point out that the three arenas for heritage language use identified by Haque (2012) are related: the trips back home and the mediated communication mutually reinforce the effect of one another. After a trip to the country of origin, the adolescents increased their email and Facebook communication with contacts in Hungary, while technology use bridges the time between the visits. Through interviewing each other and their family members, the researchers also reveal digitally mediated strategies like "Grandma-TV" and other efforts from the adults to enhance the children's use of Hungarian in both spoken and written communication. Szecsi and Szilagyi (2012: 271) find that the regular use of various media technologies positively affects the children's heritage language skills, but that the outcome relies on the adults' "creative and dedicated participation". This participation is important both for the younger and the older children, and ranges from the grandmother reading stories and singing to infants via Skype to the parents buying a Hungarian keyboard for the adolescents and correcting their email spelling upon their request. King-O'Riain (2015) studied long Skype sessions in transnational families in Ireland. Through what the researcher calls "streaming their emotions into each other's lives" (2015: 268), one of the goals for the grandparents was to maintain the grandchild's ability to converse in Italian. This takes place not only through direct conversations, but during long sessions where the grandparents for instance watch their grandchild watch TV, asking him for translations to Italian. Taken together, these studies show that digital interaction in the heritage language(s) is an arena for identity construction and expression in the family context.

11.4.2 Modalities and linguistic repertoires

Some heritage languages are mostly used in spoken communication; two aspects are of importance for the use of these languages in digitally mediated interaction: (1) the polymedia environment (Madianou and Miller 2012) allows for both spoken and written communication, and (2) languages that are mostly used in spoken communication also enter the written domain through the digital (Deumert 2014; Kouassi and Hurst-Harosh 2018), especially in interpersonal and informal communication. In addition to this, the mobile and Web 2.0 media practices create new spectres of mobile intimacy, and the choice of media reflects these various forms of affection. For instance, voice may be used in intimate relationships, especially within the family, while texting is used in distant relations (Hjorth 2011).

The choice of a medium may imply a choice of modality (like phone calls for speech or SMS for writing), but many media offer both spoken and written interaction, in addition to the exchange of videos and pictures (e.g., WhatsApp). Some languages are preferred in written communication and some in voice messages and phone calls, so that the user's choice of media and modality influences language choice. In Senegal, for instance, French is the official language and language of instruction in school, while the national languages, local languages, are dominant in spoken communication. These mode-and-language boundaries are blurred in informal digital communication, as national languages are used to write text messages, to chat and write informal emails, and often writers mix languages, in particular, the majority language Wolof and French (Lexander 2011a, 2018). The Senegalese transnational family makes up an interesting case for the study of multilingual digital interaction, as its repertoire consists of the dominant language(s) in the country of residence and several languages from their country of origin: Wolof, the dominant spoken language; French, the official language and language of instruction; possibly other Senegalese languages; Arabic; and sometimes English.

In a study of digital communication in four Norwegian families with Senegalese background, Androutsopoulos and Lexander (2018) use ethnographic interviews, interactional data collection (spoken and written), media diaries, and observation to look at language use with various media in different modalities. The findings show that the families mostly use Norwegian when they text each other within the nuclear family in Norway, while the use of Senegalese languages depends to a large extent on communication with relatives and other contacts in Senegal or in the Senegalese diaspora. With the diversity of apps for spoken and written communication, the participants stay in touch with a range of family members of different generations, close and more distant, and the variation with regards to media and interlocutors coincides with linguistic diversity. With grandparents, the children usually speak through phone calls (via WhatsApp or other applications), in Wolof or in another Senegalese language, either because the grandparents do not speak French, or because they request it, thus implementing some kind of family language policy from far away. With cousins and other peers, the interaction is more multilingual, and the interactional data show that it comprises both Senegalese languages, English, French, and Arabic. While the migrant families spend most of their time in settings dominated by Norwegian language, the digitally mediated interaction offers a space for multilingual communication in which heritage languages may be used and cultivated "to practice language for authentic purposes" (Lee 2006: 98; Szecsi and Szilagyi 2012: 273). In these families, digital communication thus seems to play an important role in counteracting language shift. Another important practice in this vein is informal heritage language learning.

11.4.3 Informal language learning

The transnational family can be considered a mobile learning community, "caring and language sharing" (Cuban 2014: 748), and a couple of studies have looked at language learning in digital communication in the family. Cuban focuses on the entire range of learning that can take place via Information and Communication Technology (ICT), and also reveals interesting aspects of language learning. She classifies phone calls within the family as "socio-cognitive exchanges that included teaching and sharing new languages and how to code-switch" as the Filipino-migrant workers "transitioned their families from American English (which they learned in school in the Philippines) to a regional English dialect, and back and forth between Taglish, Tagalog and English" (Cuban 2014: 748). This way, they advocate multilingual family language practices, while also policing them: some exclude Taglish (a mix of Tagalog and English) because it does not promote what they consider to be proper speaking of the language. The Filipino migrants engage with their families in digital literacies through texting, for example, teaching new acronyms (Cuban 2014). Despite such examples of learning, the fear of texting as destructive for literacy skills is also found in transnational families. In Wilding's (2006) study covering a range of countries, some participants worried about the informal character of email communication, stating that they would lose their language skills over time. Lee's (2006: 107) participants, however, found that they had improved their Korean oral skills through reading "the phonetic ways that people write online". The lack of pressure to produce correct spelling online gave these Korean learners a space to experiment with and engage in literacy practices in the language.

The Arabic-speaking mothers in Al-Salmi and Smith's (2015) study only started using digital devices when they migrated to the USA. When their children entered school, the use of the computer and the internet increased: Google Translate is used to translate between Arabic and English, and the mothers create email addresses to be able to follow their children's progress in school on certain websites. Through improving their English digital literacy, the mothers find that they also improve their spoken command of the language. At the same time, the mothers help their children expand their skills in Arabic, as they assist them, for instance when they post responses on Facebook. Online encounters are spontaneous unplanned instances of learning Arabic literacy for the children, encouraged by the mother; the mother encourages the children to talk to their grandmother who again encourages them to talk in Arabic and asks them for the meaning of the English words that they use.

Other studies have observed literacy learning in digital family communication, not only *in* interpersonal digital interaction, but also *around* the computer or mobile phone. In Lasekan's (2018) study of multilingual Indian students' use of language on Facebook with family members, one respondent claims that he uses English on Facebook with his younger siblings to improve their skills in the language and corrects them if they make grammatical mistakes. Kheirkhah and Cekaite (2017) observed how older siblings in Iranian migrant families in Sweden help the younger with Swedish literacy through using the cell phone calendar.

Intergenerational communication between grandparent and grandchild as they sit by the computer together is the focus in Parven's (2016) and Kenner et al.'s (2008) studies. Parven (2016) describes how a seven-year-old child from a Bengali-speaking family in Northern England learns Qur'anic literacy from his grandmother. As he searches religious texts in Arabic, a language that he does not speak but that his grandmother knows from her religious education, he uses English, a language that the grandmother does not speak, and Bengali, that they both speak. Multilingual speech is hence intermingled with digital literacy activities in two different scripts, Roman and Arabic, as the child searches for the English translation of the Arabic text and for YouTube videos where the text is recited under his grandmother's guidance. A similar interchange of knowledge and skills between generations around literacy, language and ICT is investigated in the Kenner et al. (2008) study of Sylheti/Bengali-speaking families in East London. Bengali is used for the spoken exchange between grandmother and grandchild, as they talk about what they are doing with the computer, with the reading and writing on the screen taking place in English.

In Palviainen's (2018a, 2018b) study, interaction and meta-interaction go hand in hand as children in single-parent families interact with the second parent. In one family, the child, aged 4;5, lives with her mother in Finland, while her father lives in a different country. When interacting via computer-mediated video calls on FaceTime, the father uses English and Dutch and the daughter English and Finnish, asking her mother for help with translations from Finnish to English. The choice of video calls is important, as the father does not speak Finnish and relies on facial expressions to understand his daughter. The communication between father and daughter depends heavily on the mother, as she both facilitates the technical aspects and provides translations when needed. Through this role, she appears as a key person for the daughter's informal learning of English in language practices with her father.

A more indirect facilitation of language learning by parents is discussed by Aarset (2015), who found that some Norwegian-Pakistani families preferred Skype Qur'an courses by Pakistani teachers for their children, instead of sending them to a local mosque. Even though the goal was to learn the Arabic alphabet and to read the Qur'an, the parents were happy that their offspring also practiced Urdu, the language of instruction in these courses. Norwegian-Senegalese families also consciously exploit mediated interaction as a means for learning languages (Androutsopoulos and Lexander 2018). In one family, the husband and wife texted each other in Norwegian, even though Wolof is their main language of spoken communication with each other and they were both schooled in French. The father explained this choice of language for texting by his desire to improve his wife's Norwegian skills. Similar practices were found in the other families in this study, be it to learn better Norwegian, French, English or Wolof.

A rich and varied use of digital space as an arena for language learning can thus be observed in multilingual transcultural families. Multilingualism and language mixing, digital literacy and speech, and both heritage languages and languages in the country of residence are exploited in this informal learning. However, even though the technology is more user-friendly and often demands less sophisticated digital literacy, there are still challenges to transnational communication. According to Kang (2012), women of the older generation found themselves gradually silenced from the communication of Chinese migrants in London because of their lack of digital literacy. In their study of Indian migrants in Cambodia, Kaur and Shruti (2016) found that since the migrants had bought their mobile phones in the country of residence, they did not have Hindi keypads, and only a few of them had the English competence necessary to send text messages. The phones were, therefore, mostly used for incoming calls, whereby the migrants would go to an internet café and make Skype or Yahoo calls with the help of the staff (Kaur and Shruti 2016: 80), thus reducing their own control over the communication. These are, however, examples of challenges that may be overcome as technology continues to develop and gradually becomes more accessible.

11.5 Conclusion

The research reviewed in this chapter covers a wide overview of family language practices both in the home and digitally across other contexts. Studies of family language practices have drawn on a multitude of methods, and new technologies will continue to offer further platforms for research. Issues addressed include practices and policies in language shift and revitalization situations, sociopsychological issues such as emotions and aspirations in family language use and identity constructions, home language literacy, agency in interaction, and informal language learning. While many studies build on reported language practices, more empirical work is needed on family interactions including work on translanguaging and code-switching. Moreover, as the family figures in the political spotlight in issues of culture and integration, we need to unveil the political dimensions impacting on family language practices.

Digital family language practices include both practices in and around media: family members communicate with each other via different media, making use of a range of digital tools, like instant messaging, video calls, email, and SMS. They also interact face-to-face around a smartphone or a computer, and parents facilitate their children's digital interaction in specific languages with specific interlocutors, as well as their pedagogical use of digital media. In fact, parents' facilitation of interaction is often crucial, but even young children show agency in these practices and adolescents also communicate independently with relatives in the home country. These digital family language practices often involve translanguaging, and sometimes comprise not only diverse languages, but also different scripts.

Diverse methods are applied to study digitally mediated interaction in the family. Most studies are qualitative and make use of ethnographic tools like observation, ethnographic interviews, extended case method, autoethnography, and mixed methods approach including the analysis of digital interaction. The studies are often exploratory, also with regards to methods. In Palviainen's study (2018a, 2018b), the combination of interviews, observation and transcription of interactions and a media diary written by the mother adds several perspectives to the analysis, while Szecsi and Szilagyi's (2012) autoethnography leads to reflections on how and why transnational families communicate. Digitally mediated family interaction holds great promise for the development of new methodologies for studying language practices in the family.

While the impetus to work on FLP was to address the influence of conscious language planning on language development in children acquiring more than one language at home, recent work has expanded this scope. Moreover, as King and Lanza (2019b: 722) point out, these studies are " … characterized by research questions that examine language as a means through which multilingual adults and children define themselves and their families; by a focus on globally dispersed, transnational or multilingual populations beyond the traditional, two-parent family; and by research methods that attend to meaning-making in interaction and as well as the broader context". The launch of FLP as a field of study has also had an effect on the study of bilingual/multilingual first language acquisition (BFLA). As noted by Quay and Montanari (2016: 37), "The trend to study BFLA as part of FLP is expected to increase awareness that the varied learning environments in which bilingual children are raised in the home in the early years and outside the home in child care facilities and educational institutions strongly affect their language and academic learning". Interdisciplinary approaches to studying children's language development and family language practices are indeed necessary.

The way forward needs to seriously address the growing use of digitally mediated communication, as investigated in other research fields that highlight the transnational family in a nexus of social media. In digitally mediated language practices, the importance of the extended family was illustrated although the very notion of family was broadened in the case of family language practices in a South African township context, as illustrated in Coetzee (2018). While the focus in FLP research is often on the parent-children relationship, research on spoken and digitally mediated interaction shows that communication with cousins and grandparents is important as well. Through the use of affective technologies to talk about their daily lives, family members can be considered to reproduce the family dinner table (Cuban 2014), which is an important arena for family language policy research (see e.g., Said and Zhu 2017). Greater emphasis in FLP studies on actual family language practices in multilingual transcultural families, both digital and non-digital, will provide insight into important current questions in FLP such as how families make sense of multilingualism across generations, how language is woven into family dynamics, and how families make decisions about language (King and Lanza 2019b).

Acknowledgements: This work was partly supported by the Research Council of Norway through its Centres of Excellence funding scheme, project number 223265.

References

Aarset, Monica Five. 2015. Transnational practices and local lives. Qur'an courses via Skype in Norwegian-Pakistani families. *Identities* 23(4). 438–453.

Al-Salmi, Laila & Patrick Smith. 2015. Arab immigrant mothers parenting their way into digital biliteracy. *Literacy in Composition Studies* 3. 48–66.

Androutsopoulos, Jannis & Kristin V. Lexander. 2018. Modalities of language and media choice: transnational communicative repertoires of Senegalese families in Norway. Paper presented at TLANG Seminar Language, Social Media and Migration, University of Birmingham, 2 February.

Canagarajah, Suresh. 2013. Agency and power in intercultural communication: Negotiating English in translocal spaces. *Language and Intercultural Communication* 13(2). 202–224.

Coetzee, Frieda. 2018. "Hy leer dit nie hier nie" ('He doesn't learn it here'): Talking about children's swearing in extended families in multilingual South Africa. *International Journal of Multilingualism* 15(3). 291–305.

Comaroff, Jean & John L. Comaroff. 2012. Theory from the South: Or, how Euro-America is evolving toward Africa. *Anthropological Forum: A Journal of Social Anthropology and Comparative Sociology* 22 (2). 113 –131.

Cresswell, Tim. 2014. *Place: An introduction*, 2nd edn. Malden, MA: Wiley.

Cuban, Sondra. 2014. Transnational families, ICTs and mobile learning. *International Journal of Lifelong Learning* 33(6). 737–754.

Curdt-Christiansen, Xiao Lan (ed.). 2013. Family language policy. [Special Issue]. *Language Policy* 12.

Curdt-Christiansen, Xiao Lan. 2016. Conflicting language ideologies and contradictory language practices in Singaporean multilingual families. *Journal of Multilingual and Multicultural Development* 37(7). 694–709.

Curdt-Christiansen, Xiao Lan & Francesca La Morgia. 2018. Managing heritage language development: Opportunities and challenges for Chinese, Italian and Pakistani Urdu-speaking families in the UK. *Multilingua* 37(2): 177–200.

Curdt-Christiansen, Xiao Lan & Elizabeth Lanza (eds.). 2018a. Multilingual family language management: Efforts, measures and choices. [Special issue]. *Multilingua* 37 (2).

Curdt-Christiansen, Xiao Lan & Elizabeth Lanza. 2018b. Language management in multilingual families: Efforts, measures and challenges. *Multilingua* 37(2). 123–130.

da Costa Cabral, Ildegrada. 2018. From Dili to Dungannon: An ethnographic study of two multilingual migrant families from Timor-Leste. *International Journal of Multilingualism* 15(3). 276–290.

Dagenais, Daniel. 2009. *The (un)making of the modern family*. Vancouver: University of British Columbia Press. Translated by Jane Brierley. Originally published as *La fin de la famille moderne: Signification des transformations contemporaines de la famille.* Presses de l'Université de Laval, 2000.

De Houwer, Annick. 2007. Parental language input patterns and children's bilingual use. *Applied Psycholinguistics* 27. 411–424.

Deumert, Ana. 2014. *Sociolinguistics of mobile communication.* Edinburgh: Edinburgh University Press.

Dewaele, Jean-Marc. 2013. *Emotions in multiple languages.* Basingstoke, UK: Palgrave Macmillan.

Döpke, Susanne. 1992. *One Parent – One Language. An interactional approach.* Amsterdam: Benjamins.

Dyers, Charlyn. 2014. Texting literacies as social practices among older women. *Per Linguam* 30(1). 1–17.

Fishman, Joshua. 1965. Who speaks what language to whom and when? *La Linguistique* 1(2). 67–88.

Fogle, Lyn Wright. 2012. *Second language socialization and learner agency: Talk in three adoptive families.* Bristol: Multilingual Matters.

Fogle, Lyn Wright & Kendall King. 2017. Bi- and multilingual family language socialization. In Patsy A. Duff & Stephen May (eds.), *Language socialization* (Encyclopedia of Language and Education), 79–95. Cham, Switzerland: Springer.

Gafaranga, Joseph. 2010. Medium request: Talking language shift into being. *Language in Society* 39. 241–270.

García, Ofelia. 2009. *Bilingual education in the 21st century: A global perspective.* Malden, MA: Wiley-Blackwell.

Haque, Shahzaman. 2012. *Étude de cas sociolinguistique et ethnographique de quatre familles indiennes immigrants en Europe: Pratiques langagières et politiques linguistiques nationales et familiales.* Grenoble: Université de Grenoble doctoral dissertation.

Hjorth, Larissa. 2011. Mobile specters of intimacy: A case study of women and mobile intimacy. In Rich Ling & Scott W. Campbell (eds.), *Mobile communication. Bringing us together and tearing us apart,* 37–60. New Brunswick & London: Transaction Publishers.

Hult, Francis & David Johnson. 2015. *Research methods in language policy and planning: A practical guide.* Malden, MA: Wiley.

Ivan, Loredana & Shannon Hebblethwaite. 2016. Grannies on the net: Grandmothers' experiences of Facebook in family communication. *Romanian Journal of Communication and Public Relations* 18(1). 11–25.

Kang, Tingyu. 2012. Gendered media, changing intimacy: Internet-mediated transnational communication in the family sphere. *Media, Culture and Society* 34(2). 146–161.

Kaur, Ravinder & Ishita Shruti. 2016. Mobile technology and "doing family" in a global world: Indian migrants in Cambodia. In Sun Sun Lim (ed.), *Mobile communication and the family* (Mobile communication in Asia: Local insights, global implications), 73–91. Dordrecht: Springer.

Kenner, Charmian, Mahera Ruby, John Jessel, Eve E. Gregory & Tahera Arju. 2008. Intergenerational learning events around the computer: A site for linguistic and cultural exchange. *Language and Education* 22(4). 298–319.

Kheirkhah, Mina. 2016a. *From family language practices to family language policies: Children as socializing agents.* Linköping, Sweden: Linköping University dissertation.

Kheirkhah, Mina. 2016b. Language choice negotiations in parent-child interaction: Family language policy as a collaborative achievement. In Jaspal Naveel Singh, Argyro Kantara & Dorottya Cserző (eds.), *Downscaling cultures: Revisiting intercultural communication*, 228–251. Cambridge: Cambridge Scholars.

Kheirkhah, Mina & Asta Cekaite. 2017. Siblings as language socialization agents in bilingual families. *International Multilingual Research* 12(4). 255–272.

King, Kendall. 2016. Language policy, multilingual encounters, and transnational families. *Journal of Multilingual and Multicultural Development* 7(7). 726–733.

King, Kendall & Lyn Fogle. 2013. Family language policy and bilingual parenting. *Language Teaching* 46 (2). 172–194.

King, Kendall, Lyn Fogle & Aubrey Logan-Terry. 2008. Family language policy. *Language and Linguistics Compass* 2(5). 907–922.

King, Kendall & Elizabeth Lanza (eds.). 2019a. Ideology, agency and imagination in multilingual families. [Special issue]. *International Journal of Bilingualism* 23(3).

King, Kendall & Elizabeth Lanza. 2019b. Ideology, agency and imagination in multilingual families: An introduction. *International Journal of Bilingualism* 23(3). 717–723.

King-O'Riain, Rebecca C. 2015. Emotional streaming and transconnectivity: Skype and emotion practices in transnational families in Ireland. *Global Networks* 15. 256–273.

Kirsch, Claudine & Nikolaos Gogonas. 2018. Transnational experiences, language competences and worldviews: Contrasting language policies in two recently migrated Greek families in Luxembourg. *Multilingua* 37(2). 153–175.

Kouassi Roland Raoul & Ellen Hurst-Harosh. 2018. Social media as an extension of, and negotiation of space for, a community of practice: A comparison of Nouchi and Tsotsitaal. In Ellen Hurst-Harosh & Fridah Kanana Erastus (eds.), *African youth languages*, 75–101. Cham, Switzerland: Palgrave Macmillan & Springer Nature.

Lam, Wan Shun Eva. 2014. Literacy and capital in immigrant youths' online networks across countries. *Learning, Media and Technology* 39(4). 488–506.

Lanza, Elizabeth. 2004 [1997]. *Language mixing in infant bilingualism: A sociolinguistic perspective*, 2nd edn. Oxford: Oxford University Press.

Lanza, Elizabeth. 2007. Multilingualism and the family. In Peter Auer & Wei Li (eds.), *Handbook of multilingualism and multilingual communication*, 45–67. Berlin: Mouton de Gruyter.

Lanza, Elizabeth. 2017. The multilingual child and the family: Input, practices and policies. Keynote address at the International Symposium on Bilingualism, Limerick, Ireland, 11–15 June 2017.

Lanza, Elizabeth. In press. Urban multilingualism and family language policy. In Giuditta Caliendo, Rudi Janssens, Stef Slembrouck & Piet Van Avermaet (eds.), *Urban multilingualism in Europe. Bridging the gap between language policies and language practices*. Berlin: Mouton De Gruyter.

Lanza, Elizabeth & Xiao Lan Curdt-Christiansen (eds.). 2018. Multilingual families. Aspirations and challenges. [Special issue]. *International Journal of Multilingualism* 15 (3).

Lanza, Elizabeth & Wei Li. 2016 (eds.). Multilingual encounters in transcultural families. [Special Issue]. *Journal of Multilingual and Multicultural Development* 7(7).

Lasekan, Olusjiji A. 2018. Multilinguals' choice of language with families, friends and acquaintances during online and offline interaction. *Language Art* 3(1). 85–96.

Lee, Jin Sook. 2006. Exploring the relationship between electronic literacy and heritage language maintenance. *Language Learning and Technology* 10(2). 93–113.

Lefebvre, H. 1991. *The production of space*. Malden, MA: Blackwell.
Lexander, Kristin Vold. 2011a. Texting and African languages literacy. *New Media and Society* 13(3). 427–443.
Lexander, Kristin Vold. 2011b. *Pratiques de l'écrit électronique: Alternances codiques et choix de langue dans les SMS, les courriels et les conversations de la messagerie instantanée des étudiants de Dakar, Sénégal*. Oslo: University of Oslo dissertation.
Lexander, Kristin Vold. 2018. Nuancing the jaxase. Young and urban texting in Senegal. In Cecelia Cutler & Unn Røyneland (eds.), *Analyzing multilingual youth practices in computer mediated communication (CMC)*, 68–86. Cambridge: Cambridge University Press.
Li, Wei (ed.). 2012. Family language policy in multilingual transnational families and beyond. [Special issue]. *Journal of Multilingual and Multicultural Development* 33(1).
Luykx, Aurolyn. (2003). Weaving languages together: Family language policy and gender socialization in bilingual Aymara households. In Robert Bayley & Sandra Schecter (eds.), *Language socialization in bilingual and multilingual societies*, 10–25. Clevedon: Multilingual Matters.
Macalister, John & Seyed Hadi Mirvahedi (eds.). 2017. *Family language policies in a multilingual world: Opportunities, challenges, and consequences*. London: Routledge.
Madianou, Mirca & Daniel Miller. 2012. *Migration and new media. Transnational families and polymedia*. London: Routledge.
Marrapodi, Maryann. 2016. Transmedia meets the digital divide: Adapting transmedia approaches to reach underserved Hispanic families. *Journal of Children and Media* 10(2). 276–284.
Martin-Jones, Marilyn & Deidre Martin (eds.). 2017. *Researching multilingualism: Critical and ethnographic perspectives*. London: Routledge.
Massey, Doreen. 2005. *For space*. London: Sage.
Miller, Daniel & Don Slater. 2000. *The internet: An ethnographic approach*. Oxford & New York: Berg.
Nandi, Anik. 2018. Parents as stakeholders: Language management in urban Galician homes. *Multilingua* 37(2). 201–223.
Obojska, Maria & Judith Purkarthofer. 2018. 'And all of a sudden, it became my rescue': Language and agency in transnational families in Norway. *International Journal of Multilingualism* 15(3). 249–261.
Ochs, Elinor & Bambi Schieffelin. 2011. The theory of language socialization. In Alessandro Duranti, Elinor Ochs & Bambi Schieffelin (eds.), *The handbook of language socialization*, 1–21. Malden, MA: Wiley-Blackwell.
Palviainen, Åsa. 2018a. Family language policy among single-parent families in the digital age. Paper presented at the Conference of the American Association for Applied Linguistics (AAAL), Chicago, 23–27 March.
Palviainen, Åsa. 2018b. Doing transnational parenthood in the digital age. Do languages matter? Paper presented at Language, Identity and Education in Multilingual Contexts, University of Dublin, 1–3 February.
Palviainen, Åsa & Sally Boyd. 2013. Unity in discourse, diversity in practice: The one person one language policy in bilingual families. In Mila Schwartz & Anna Verschik (eds.), *Successful family language policy*, 223–248. Dordrecht: Springer.

Parven, Akhter. 2016. A young child's intergenerational practices through the use of visual screen-based multimodal communication to acquire Qur'anic literacy. *Language and Education* 30(6). 500–518.

Pavlenko, Aneta. 2004. "Stop doing that, ia komu skazala!": Language choice and emotions in parent-child communication. *Journal of Multilingual and Multicultural Development* 25(2). 179–203.

Porter, Gina, Kate Hampshire, Albert Abane, Alister Munthali, Elsbeth Robson, Augustine Tanle, Samuel Owusu, Ariane de Lannoy & Andisiwe Bango. 2018. Connecting with home, keeping in touch: Physical and virtual mobility across stretched families in sub-Saharan Africa. *Africa* 88(2). 404–424.

Purkarthofer, Judith. 2019. Building expectations: Imagining family language policy and heteroglossic social spaces. *International Journal of Bilingualism* 23(3). 724–739.

Quay, Suzanne & Simona Montanari. 2016. Early bilingualism: From differentiation to the impact of family language practices. In Elena Nicoladis & Simona Montanari (eds.), *Lifespan perspectives on bilingualism*, 23–42. Washington, D.C. & Berlin: American Psychological Association & De Gruyter Mouton.

Ruby, Mahera. 2012. The role of a grandmother in maintaining Bangla with her granddaughter in East London. *Journal of Multilingual and Multicultural Development* 33(1). 67–83.

Rydin, Ingegerd & Ulrika Sjöberg. 2008. Internet as a communicative space for identity construction among migrant families in Sweden. In Ingegerd Rydin & Ulrika Sjöberg (eds.), *Mediated crossroads: Identity, youth culture and ethnicity. Theoretical and methodological challenges*, 193–214. Göteborg: Nordicom.

Said, Fatma & Hua Zhu. 2017. No, no Maama! Say 'Shaatir ya Ouledee Shaatir'! Children's agency in language use and socialization. *International Journal of Bilingualism*. https://doi.org/10.1177/1367006916684919 (accessed 20 June 2018).

Schwartz, Mila & Anna Verschik (eds.). 2013. *Successful family language policy*. Dordrecht: Springer.

Smith-Christmas, Cassie. 2016. *Family language policy. Maintaining an endangered language in the home*. Basingstoke: Palgrave Macmillan.

Smith-Christmas, Cassie. 2018. 'One *cas*, two *cas*': Exploring the affective dimensions of family language policy. *Multilingua* 37(2). 131–152.

Song, Kwangok. 2016. "Okay, I will say in Korean and then in American": Translanguaging practices in bilingual homes. *Journal of Early Childhood Literacy* 16(1). 84–106.

Spolsky, Bernard. 2003. *Language policy*. Cambridge: Cambridge University Press.

Spolsky, Bernard. 2012. Family language policy – the critical domain. *Journal of Multilingual and Multicultural Development* 33(1). 3–11.

Stavans, Anat. 2012. Language policy and literacy practices in the family: The case of Ethiopian parental narrative input. *Journal of Multilingual and Multicultural Development* 33(1). 13–33.

Szecsi, Tunde & Janka Szilagyi. 2012. Immigrant Hungarian families' perceptions of new media technologies in the transmission of heritage language and culture. *Language, Culture and Curriculum* 25(3). 265–281.

Tannenbaum, Michal. 2012. Family language policy as a form of coping or defence mechanism. *Journal of Multilingual and Multicultural Development* 33(1). 57–66.

Van Mensel, Luk. 2018. 'Quiere *koffie?*' The multilingual familylect of transcultural families. *International Journal of Multilingualism* 15(3). 233–248.

Wenger, Etienne. 1998. *Communities of practice: Learning, meaning, and identity*. Cambridge: Cambridge University Press.
Wilding, Raelene. 2006. 'Virtual' intimacies? Families communicating across international contexts. *Global Networks* 6(2). 125–142.
Yoon, Kyong. 2018. Multicultural digital media practices of 1.5-generation Korean immigrants in Canada. *Asian and Pacific Migration Journal* 27(2). 148–165.
Zhu, Hua & Wei Li. 2016. Transnational experience, aspiration and family language policy. *Journal of Multilingual and Multicultural Development* 37(7). 655–666.

Xiao-lei Wang
12 Multilingualism through Schooling

Multilingual acquisition can occur at different ages, in different settings, under various circumstances, and for different purposes. Some multilinguals acquire their multiple languages in the home context during early years and continue to develop one or all of these languages in the school environment. Other multilinguals obtain more than one language early in life and begin to learn an *additional language* or *languages* (AL henceforth for singular and plural) when they enter school. Still others learn an AL much later in life. This chapter focuses on how typically-developing children and adolescents who have already developed foundations in two or more languages in the home and community environment acquire an AL in the school setting by building upon their previous linguistic experiences and use the AL to learn subject content and develop literacy skills.

The chapter begins with an overview of the complexity of acquiring an AL in the school context for multilinguals. It follows with a discussion on the common mechanisms multilingual children employ in approaching AL learning. It concludes with the characteristics demonstrated by AL learners in the phonological, lexical-semantic, morphosyntactic, pragmatic, literacy, and figurative language domains while they learn different subjects in classrooms.

Since very little is known about longitudinal normative development among multilingual AL learners (especially those entering school with two or more languages), three factors need to be considered when interpreting the information provided in this chapter. First, much information presented is inferred from studies on learners acquiring a L2 or L3 in school. Second, many research findings in the current literature are not conclusive or even contradictory as a result of various complex issues related to multilingual participants, such as their languages, age of exposure to each language, and family socioeconomic background. Third, multilingual AL learners are heterogeneous in their linguistic and early literacy abilities as well as their cultural and socioeconomic experiences.

Xiao-lei Wang, Adelphi University, Garden City (NY), U.S.A.

https://doi.org/10.1515/9781501507984-012

12.1 Complexity of AL acquisition for multilinguals in the school environment

Adding an AL to multilinguals' existing language repertoires not only widens their linguistic capacity quantitatively but also qualitatively. Given that the AL acquisition process for multilingual learners in the school environment is profoundly different from the one in the home context and that their academic success depends heavily on their AL and literacy abilities, several complexities of AL acquisition are discussed below. Due to space limitations, other intricacies such as motivation, gender, identity, and individual factors are omitted.

12.1.1 Differences in the acquisition process

The essential distinction in language acquisition between home and school lies in the fact that the foundation for first language acquisition (L1) early in life in the home setting is universal grammar (Chomsky 1980), whereas the underpinning for AL acquisition in the school environment is L1 knowledge as well as other compounding factors, such as age, language typologies, cultures, socioeconomic background, identity, affects, attitude, and motivation (Hoff 2009; Wang 2015a). Because many multilingual children have been exposed to more than one L1 or L2 in the home environment before schooling, *previous languages* (hereafter PL for singular and plural) is used in this chapter to refer to their different L1s and/or L2s.

Moreover, multilinguals' PL input from parents in the home environment is usually contextual, situational, and informal. The major modality of input is oral. Language use is mainly focused on daily and situational communication. However, AL input from teachers in the school setting is often decontextualized, intentional, and formal.

Furthermore, the complexity in learning an AL in the school setting is exacerbated by the fact that, while many of the AL-learning-multilinguals are still developing their PL, they are beginning to acquire an AL that needs to be developed at a high level to assure academic success (Collier 1995). In other words, these learners need to acquire an academic language in the AL that is different from their everyday PL in the areas of word selection, formality, sentence construction, and discourse patterns (Gottlieb and Ernst-Slavit 2014).

12.1.2 Brain capacity

Multilinguals' PL acquisition early in life at home is generally a result of exposure to a large amount of unmodified linguistic input from the surrounding environment. However, as the brain matures, its ability to process input in this manner invariably declines. Consequently, learners in the school context may need to rely on different cognitive processes to acquire an AL (Ellis 2008). Research suggests that the brain's capacity to acquire a language may be qualitatively different before and after age 5 and that the optimum language-learning window may begin to close between the ages of 5 and 10 (e.g., Newport, Bavelier, and Neville 2001). It becomes increasingly difficult for an individual to achieve native competence in a new language beyond puberty. For instance, the timing in achieving native-like phonology is crucial; even a delay of a few years in childhood can lead to irreversible changes (Norrman and Bylund 2016). This phenomenon is often referred to as the critical period (CP) in language acquisition. Typically, CP gradually phases out in the age range of 7–10 (Meisel 2006). Since multilingual children usually receive formal schooling and learn an AL at or after age 5, their brain changes may influence how they acquire the AL.

However, the CP in later language acquisition remains a controversial topic. Some researchers have proposed a model called the Multiple Critical Period Effects (MCPE), which posits a system of a nested series of optimal periods that are inter-dependent and have overlapping timelines. In this model, language acquisition begins with the categorization of acoustic and phonetic stimuli, which then trigger a cascade of optimal periods across different domains of language. The optimal periods for higher order domains, such as grammar and reading, are partially dependent upon fundamental phonological ability. The closing of the optimal period for the higher-order domains thus occurs later than those related to phonology. Consequently, declines in plasticity begin sooner in phonological domains (i.e., speech perception and production) than in grammar (e.g., Abrahamsson and Hyltenstam 2009). Thus, it is possible that some multilingual children who learn an AL in the school environment can still develop native-like proficiency in the new language.

Moreover, learning an AL after the critical period may also have some advantages. Comparing with younger learners (e.g., in early and middle childhood) who may have a better chance of achieving native competence, older learners (e.g., in adolescence) may have stronger cognitive skills such as better memory and metalinguistic abilities (Jia and Fuse 2007). In fact, research shows that older AL learners performed (at least, on tests) better in suprasegmental phonology or prosodic properties (rhythm, tone, pitch, stress, intonation, and length), in syntax (e.g., Long 1990), and in learning speed (Jia and Fuse 2007).

12.1.3 Language typology and psychotypology

The similarities or differences between learners' PL and AL typologies (classification of languages according to their structural characteristics, such as phonological systems, writing systems, and word order) are important in AL acquisition (e.g., Cenoz 2001). When the PL and AL typologies are close, AL acquisition is easier for learners than when the PL and AL typologies are distant (Ute et al. 2014). For example, L1 speakers of English (a satellite-framed language in which information about a path of movement is expressed outside the verb by an adverbial particle, such as "The ball rolled *out* of the box") learning Czech and German (also satellite-framed languages) produce more target-like verbs than learners whose L1 is Spanish (a verb-framed language in which information about a path of movement is expressed in a verb, such as "La pelota *salió* de la caja").

However, not only do the actual PL and AL typologies play a role in AL acquisition, but also *psychotypology* (the degree of similarity and difference between the languages perceived by learners and what the languages mean to them) is determinant of AL learning (Cenoz, Hufeisen, and Jessner 2001). When learners perceive the AL to be closer to their PL, their perception can be a facilitative factor for AL learning. For example, a study has shown that Turkish-German bilinguals learning English as L3 made use of German grammatical rules in their English productions rather than Turkish ones because they perceived German as having more common features with English than Turkish (Cedden and Şimşek 2014; see Chapter 14, this volume, for a more in-depth review).

12.2 Common mechanisms used in approaching AL acquisition

Multilinguals tend to employ several mechanisms in the AL learning process as a result of their exposure to multiple languages.

12.2.1 Cross-linguistic transfer

One of the most commonly observed phenomena in learning an AL is transfer, which broadly refers to conveying linguistic knowledge from one language to another. Initially, the directionality of transfer may be from the PL to the AL. However, as language learners gain more exposure to the AL and become more proficient in it, the directionality can also occur from the AL to the PL.

When transfer facilitates the AL acquisition process, it is called positive transfer and when it hinders AL learning, it is termed as negative transfer. Transfer is not always automatic. Two factors must be at play for transfer to occur. First, the language skills in one language can only be transferred to another if there is sufficient exposure to that language and the motivation to learn it (Cummins 1981). Second, some skills can be transferred across languages, whereas others are language-specific. For instance, AL learners who can detect and manipulate sounds in one of their languages should also be able to detect and manipulate those same sounds in their AL. However, some areas such as vocabulary knowledge (aside from cognates) are language-specific and solely related to the quality and quantity of input received in the AL (e.g., Gottardo and Mueller 2009). See Chapter 15, this volume, for a more in-depth discussion of cross-linguistic transfer.

12.2.2 Metalinguistic awareness

Another frequently observed mechanism used by multilinguals in learning an AL is their metalinguistic ability. Despite inconsistent research findings, it has been recognized that multilingual children tend to have a metalinguistic advantage compared to their monolingual peers as an effect of the exposure to more than one language early in life. This advantage often extends to learning an AL. Multilinguals' explicit knowledge about language leads them to attend and reflect upon features of languages (Bialystok and Martin 2004). Research shows that both more proficient multilinguals and less proficient multilinguals outperformed monolinguals in some metalinguistic tasks such as attention control tasks; however, only the more proficient multilinguals outperformed monolinguals in cognitive tasks (Bialystok 1988). Moreover, research suggests that reading proficiency in multilinguals' PL such as L1 and L2 can facilitate their L3 reading proficiency, largely because the metalinguistic awareness abilities they developed in the PL allow them to compare and contrast the respective grammars (Rauch, Naumann, and Jude 2012, discussed further in Chapter 15, this volume).

12.2.3 Translanguaging

The third noticeable tactic that multilingual learners use to approach AL learning is translanguaging. Translanguaging is defined as a process where multilinguals draw upon their different linguistic, cognitive and semiotic resources to make meaning and make sense. In practicing translanguaging, multilinguals "transgress" the boundaries between named languages (such as English, Chinese, Arabic) and their use conventionally (Li 2018). Some researchers see translanguaging practice as dynamic, effective and functional (Lewis, Jones, and Baker 2012) while others see it as the ability to mediate complex social and cognitive activities through strategic employment of multiple semiotic resources to act, to know, and to be (García and Li 2014; Chapter 7, this volume). Taken together, translanguaging is multilingual speakers' own mental grammar that has been developed in social interaction with others (García and Li 2014) and it reflects their unique communicative mechanism that they use to think and communicate.

12.3 Characteristics of multilingual AL acquisition in the school context

Operating with the above-mentioned strategies, multilingual AL learners may demonstrate the following characteristics in phonological, lexical-semantic, morphosyntactic, pragmatic, literacy, and figurative language learning. Since the topic of this chapter is AL acquisition in the school context, developmental characteristics are focused on middle childhood (ages 5–11) and adolescence (ages 12–18) as most children around the world receive formal education during these age ranges.

12.3.1 Phonological development

Research has shown that multilingual AL learners generally have comparable phonological acquisition milestones to those of monolingual peers acquiring the same language (Lim, Wells, and Howard 2015). However, they also exhibit some distinct phonological developmental characteristics.

12.3.1.1 Accent and pronunciation

As discussed previously, phonology seems to be particularly susceptible to timing. The age of AL acquisition plays a crucial role in the quality and accuracy of accent and pronunciation. Typically, the later learners are exposed to the AL, the less accurate they are in articulating some paralinguistic elements, such as prosody, intonation, stress, and tones. With increased age of acquisition, the phonological features of learners' PL may increasingly interfere with the ones in the AL. For example, a Japanese L1 child who is learning English as an AL may have difficulty in distinguishing between /r/ and /l/, because there is only one alveolar liquid in Japanese (a sound represented in English transcription of Japanese as /r/), while the English phonological system has two alveolar liquids, /r/ and /l/ (Wang 2015a). Usually, learners with a more phonologically marked (or complex) PL structure than the AL will have an easier time learning the AL structure than a speaker whose PL is less marked. For instance, a speaker whose L1 is English will have no difficulty in producing German words where there is no contrast in final position. On the other hand, a German L1 speaker learning English will have to learn how to make a contrast in final position (*tab* vs *tap*; a more marked structure than in German) and can be expected to make articulation errors (Gass and Selinker 2001).

Usually, a PL accent tends to interfere with the AL accent. However, it can also go the other way, that is, cross-linguistic interactions may not be "heard" in multilingual speakers early on although they may be revealed by acoustic analyses. In their study of two Italian-Spanish-English trilingual sisters, Mayr and Montanari (2015) found that cross-linguistic interactions in the girls' consonant productions, which differed from language to language, were not evident to "the naked ear" but were seen only through acoustic analyses. Moreover, the phonological interferences of multilinguals may present themselves at different developmental stages depending on the intensity of linguistic exposure to the ambient languages. For instance, longitudinal observations of two multilingual siblings by Wang (2008 and 2015b) revealed that one of the children's home languages, Chinese, went through some changes as a result of more exposure to English in the school environment. In particular, the children began to show some signs of problems in pronouncing the third tone (the falling-rising tone), although not to the degree of unintelligibility. It has been suggested that Chinese tones are especially fragile for children learning Chinese in an English-speaking environment (Erbaugh 1992).

Overall, the impact of cross-linguistic influence on accent in middle childhood is less strong than during adolescence. Many multilingual children who acquire an AL in middle childhood can still develop a native-like or near native accent in the AL.

However, if an AL is acquired during the adolescent period (ages between 11–18), the accent may be more pronounced. For example, adolescents who are learning English as an AL may have difficulties with English word-final consonant clusters such as *fifth* and *fists* (Gass and Selinker 2001). Also, some AL learners tend to use epenthesis (insert a sound in words). For example, when pronouncing the English word *floor*, Iraqi-Arabic AL speakers tend to pronounce it as *filoor* and Egyptian-Arabic speakers tend to say it as *ifloor* (Gass and Selinker 2001). Sometimes AL learners may delete or add sounds to the AL. Using English as an AL again as an example, Korean L1 learners tend to add a final sound to the English word *sack* /sæke/. It is also usually difficult for AL learners to combine sounds as native English speakers, such as *I'm gonna wriDa leDer* ('I am going to write a letter'). Similarly, it is harder for French-as-an-AL learners to articulate the liaisons accurately.

Besides the age factor in accent and pronunciation, Flege, Munro, and Mackay (1995) identified five additional areas that can influence the degree of accent and pronunciation of older AL learners (e.g., adolescents). The first area is AL learners' sound perception. Some may fail to accurately perceive phonetic details in the AL. The second area can be attributed to learners' incentive to pronounce sounds in the AL exactly, if articulatory errors do not impede their communication. The third area can be individual differences. The fourth reason can also be how language learners want to identify themselves with the AL; some AL learners may not want to sound like a native speaker of a language they are learning and prefer to keep their accent deliberately in order to retain their self-respect or to gain the approval of their peers (Sung 2013). Finally, AL learners' phonetic input can influence their accent. In fact, the input frequency heard by language learners is more important, among all other factors, in terms of accent and pronunciation.

12.3.1.2 Phonological awareness

Phonological awareness (PA) belongs to the area of metalinguistic awareness that refers to the ability to recognize differences and similarities in the sounds of different languages rather than their meaning. PA has been shown to be a strong predictor of word reading skills in alphabetic languages such as English (e.g., Gottardo 2002). In general, multilingual learners with more than one alphabetical language tend to demonstrate advantages in PA. However, such advantage may depend on learners' proficiency in the PL and AL. It is likely that a greater PA advantage is only observed for children who have high proficiency in their respective languages (e.g., Bialystok, Luk, and Kwan 2005) or who have reached a threshold proficiency level in their respective languages (Cummins 1979) after longer exposure to the AL. For example, in a longitudinal study (Grades 3–4) comparing French monolingual children with French-speaking children learning Occitan (a French regional language), Laurent and Martinot (2010) found that the bilingual advantage in phonological awareness only appeared in Grade 4 (i.e., after five consecutive years of classes) when the children reached high proficiency in both languages.

12.3.2 Lexical and semantic development

In general, it is rare for multilinguals to have equivalent lexical knowledge in their different languages. As a matter of fact, the lexical development of multilinguals is typically language-specific; that is, AL learners' vocabulary knowledge seems to be mostly associated with other aspects of the AL but not with vocabulary knowledge in PL. For instance, Lindsey, Manis, and Balley (2003) found that multilingual English (AL) – Spanish (L1) children's English expressive vocabulary was strongly associated with their English letter-word identification abilities, while Spanish expressive vocabulary predicted Spanish letter-word identification abilities. That is, these children's English vocabulary did not predict their Spanish letter-word identification abilities, and their Spanish vocabulary did not affect their English letter-word identification abilities. Similarly, Páez, Tabor, and López (2007) found that children with higher vocabulary skills in their AL (English) had lower lexical abilities in their L1 (Spanish) and vice versa.

The PL lexicon may influence learners' AL lexical organization, access to word meanings, and vocabulary selection (Tabors, Páez, and López 2003). For example, in Chinese, the word *cup* (杯子) is used to refer to all containers for drinking liquids, whereas the word *cup* in English is used for drinking liquids such as coffee or tea and the word *glass* is used for drinking liquids such as wine and juice. A Chinese L1 learner of English is likely to use *cup* for wine instead of *glass* (Li and Zhu 2013). Similarly, AL speakers may misuse words that are superficially similar. For instance, a Spanish PL speaker used *suburbio* ('slum quarter') for *suburbs* in English (AL).

When AL learners enter school, there may be discrepancies in their lexical knowledge in the PL and AL. For example, a learner may know many words related to math in his/her AL and many words related to daily life in his/her PL. This is called distributed characteristic of multilingual word learning (Oller 2005). AL learners' PL vocabulary may stagnate when entering school. A rapid growth in AL vocabulary and stabilization of the PL vocabulary have often been observed (De Houwer 2009; Wang 2008). Unless children continue to receive enriched input in PL, they will make vocabulary gains in AL but not in PL.

Vocabulary discrepancies are also evident in AL learners' receptive and expressive lexicons. It has been suggested that vocabulary growth may be seen in comprehension (receptive lexicon) before production (expressive lexicon). A discrepancy between receptive and expressive vocabulary growth has been commonly reported in monolingual lexical acquisition (Bates, Bretherton, and Snyder 1988) as well as in children who are exposed to more than one language. Barnett et al. (2007) examined the vocabulary growth of 147 preschool children who were learning English as an AL following one year of attendance in Head

Start. The children demonstrated significant gains in receptive vocabulary on a standardized measure but did not demonstrate comparable gains in expressive vocabulary. This asymmetry of vocabulary development has also been noted by other studies in the past, which found greater initial linguistic crossover from PL to the AL for receptive tasks than for expressive tasks. Production tasks in the AL require more lexical experience and prolonged lexical acquisition (Magiste 1979).

However, multilingualism does have positive effects on the overall process of lexical acquisition. Recent research comparing monolingual children and multilingual children in the classroom setting suggests that multilingual children outperformed monolingual children on a word learning task where they had to map novel words onto familiar referents, i.e., pictures of animals. However, when the word learning task involved mapping novel words onto unfamiliar referents (i.e., pictures of aliens), multilinguals and monolinguals performed identically (Kaushanskaya, Gross, and Buac 2014, discussed further in Chapter 14, this volume).

12.3.2.1 Lexical mixing and semantic transfer

Although Cross-Linguistic Mixing (CLM) can affect different AL components, the lexicon is the most affected area. Initially, learners may use the PL lexicon in the AL. As they become more proficient, AL words also frequently appear in their PL. A longitudinal study by Wang and Bernas (under review) suggests that multilinguals' use of lexical mixing is, for the most time, not random or just a strategy to compensate vocabulary deficiency. It serves many important communicative functions for multilinguals. First, the lexical mixing produced by the children in the study was functional from the very beginning and became increasingly dynamic over the years. Second, it had distinct developmental characteristics: an instrumental function was more noticeable in early childhood; representational and heuristic functions were more visible in middle childhood; and interactional, personal, regulatory, and divertive functions were more prominent in adolescence. Third, multilinguals progressively interweaved more than one function in one single mixing through phonological manipulation and nonverbal cues to achieve different communicative purposes and negotiate their multilingual and multicultural identities. Overall, the multilingual participants in the study were able to use lexical mixing to capitalize their multilingual resources to leverage their intents in a socially intelligent way and maximize their communicative potential. See Chapter 7, this volume, for a more in-depth discussion of CLM.

Moreover, AL learners may also exhibit semantic transfer as a result of false friends (words that have common etymology but now have different meanings). A case in point is the Spanish word *embarazada* ('pregnant') and the English word *embarrassed* (Brown and Attardo 2008).

12.3.2.2 Emotion and emotion-laden words

Emotion words (words directly referring to particular affective states such as "scared" and "anxious") and emotion-laden words (words that do not refer to emotions directly but instead express emotion, such as "loser," or elicit emotions from interlocutors, such as "malignancy,") are represented, processed, and recalled differently from concrete words (e.g., "cup" or "chair") and abstract words (e.g., "myth" or "emancipation") (e.g., Altarriba and Bauer 2004). Some researchers suggest that emotion words and emotion-laden words should be separated as a distinct class of words because they are more deeply encoded in speakers' L1 and depend more on context availability than other types of words (e.g., Pavlenko 2008).

AL learners, especially those who are exposed to an AL later in upper grades, are often hindered by their limited emotion and emotion-laden words in the AL, especially when they need to express anger and frustration (Pavlenko 2008). This is because a language acquired early in life (i.e., L1) is more emotional than an AL learned later. At an early age, the development of the L1 linguistic system coincides with the development of concepts and emotional regulation. In the process of affective socialization in young children's L1, some words become stimuli for positive or negative arousal. However, when learning an AL at a later age (such as during adolescence), learners need to develop such responses anew in the AL. The school environment where most adolescents spend a substantial amount of time daily may not necessarily offer the same opportunities for affective linguistic conditioning as the environment where L1 is learned in childhood. Because adolescent AL learners' conceptual system and emotion regulation system may have already reached a more or less stable state, many emotion and emotion-laden words in the AL may not trigger their personal and affective associations or sensory representations (Pavlenko 2008). Thus, many adolescent AL learners are likely to experience difficulty in expressing emotion-related vocabulary.

12.3.3 Morphosyntactic development

Morphosyntactic development in AL learners is complex. On the one hand, early language acquisition theories suggest that the process of acquiring grammatical morphemes is similar in L1 or AL learners (e.g., Gass and Selinker 2001). On the other hand, depending on the learners' L1 backgrounds, the AL morphology may show different characteristics. For example, when expressing time in English, inflectional morphology is used (e.g., adding suffixes, -ed and -ing). In Chinese, however, there is no system of grammatical morphology for tense. Instead, temporal adverbs such as 左天 ('yesterday'), 今天 ('today'), and 明天 ('tomorrow') are used to indicate the time in the past, present, and future (Li 2013). It is possible that Chinese L1 learners of English may have difficulties in learning the morphological rules related to temporal reference. Likewise, these learners may also have difficulties in several morphosyntactic areas such as passive voice, adverbial conjuncts, regular and irregular past tense, third-person singular, progressive aspect -ing, copula be, and auxiliary do. Even though these areas can be taught, adolescent AL learners of English may not always produce them correctly in spontaneous speech and writing. In general, if the learners' PL is closer to the AL, acquisition will be facilitated, and if their PL is distant from the AL, learners may have more difficulties in mastering AL morphosyntactic features.

12.3.4 Pragmatic development

Pragmatic skills are critical for building peer relationships and making academic progress in the school environment. Moreover, the process of acquiring an AL is not only a linguistic issue, but also a cultural one. Using the AL properly in the right situation, to the right person, and for the right purpose (cultural pragmatic acquisition) is particularly challenging for AL learners, especially in the areas of apologizing, thanking, face-saving, conventions, and the cooperative strategy (people cooperate to achieve mutual conversation ends). For example, Japanese learners of English may express gratitude by saying, "I am sorry," a direct transfer from *Sumimasen* (which conveys a sense of gratitude, especially to persons with higher status) (Brown 2000). The cooperative strategy is the most difficult for AL learners to master. In different cultures, there are different styles of communication and different ways in which men and women use language to communicate. For instance, among the Carib Indians in the Lesser Antilles, males and females must use entirely different syntactic and phonological variations. Similarly, Japanese women's language and men's language are differentiated by formal (syntactic) variations, intonation patterns, and nonverbal expression (Brown 2000). It is not an easy task for AL learners (especially adolescents) to master the pragmatic aspects of the AL because learners may not know the idiomatic expressions or cultural norms in the AL, or they may transfer their PL rules and conventions to the AL.

There are two commonly occurring pragmatic failures among AL learners: pragma- linguistic failure and sociopragmatic failure. Pragmalinguistic failure occurs when the pragmatics used by AL learners is systematically different from the one used by native speakers of the target language or when speech act strategies are inappropriately transferred from PL to the AL. Pragmalinguistic failure can be illustrated by the example of transferring the Russian word конечно ('of course') in place of да ('yes') in English as in "Are you coming to the party?" "Of course". When конечно is transferred into English in this way, it may be interpreted as a peremptory response or even as an insult, as if the first speaker is asking a question that is stupid to ask or to which the answer is self-evident. Sociopragmatic failure refers to different communication practices based on different cultural beliefs in social interaction. For instance, a Russian speaker asks an American for a cigarette on the assumption that Americans share cigarettes with strangers as in Russia (Baba 2010).

12.3.5 Narrative and literacy development

12.3.5.1 Narratives in the AL

A close relationship between narrative skills and literacy is well-documented. Depending on children's age, AL learners' narrative development may fall into two categories. For those children who are at the beginning of elementary grades, their AL narrative development may be similar to their native-speaking peers. Like their peers, AL learners at the beginning of schooling are in the process of developing their narrative abilities. Although AL learners tend to underachieve in AL vocabulary and morphosyntactic comprehension compared with their monolingual peers, they do equally well in the macro-structure narrative complexity (Bonifacci et al. 2018), as well as narrative production and comprehension (Boerma et al. 2016).

Nevertheless, if learners who have already developed a narrative structure in their PL learn AL in the mid or late elementary school years, their narrative structure may exhibit different characteristics as suggested in previous studies. The question is whether these later AL learners' narrative differences only show in some narrative domains or whether they demonstrate a completely different narrative process. A study by Viberg (2001) suggests that the multilingual Swedish-Finnish children tended to provide more detailed and concrete narrative versions in both of their languages than monolingual children. However, these children provided a similar narrative structure in both of their languages.

12.3.5.2 Universal and language-specific factors in literacy development

The language-universal theory suggests that specific cognitive and linguistic processes are related across languages and are basic to reading in any language (Geva and Siegel 2000). Some language-general linguistic knowledge such as phonological awareness might need to be acquired only once while acquiring PL literacy, whereas other processes might need to be acquired for each language (Durgunoğlu 2002). For other areas, such as semantic processing, PL and AL skills are likely separate (Cobo-Lewis et al. 2002). Grammatical knowledge is likely to be related across languages if the grammatical structures are formed in similar ways, and unrelated if the structures are unique to the PL or AL and require experience with the given language (Gottardo 2002).

Thus, the PL and AL might provide unique and different contributions to reading development. For example, the script and phonology of the PL and the AL can explain the relationships between reading and oral language in the PL and AL (e.g., Geva and Siegel 2000). The degree of similarity between the PL and AL phonology will affect language-specific phonological representations (see Eckman 2004 for a review) and written language acquisition (Wade-Woolley and Geva 2000). In addition, the syllabic structure of the language can have an impact on the ways speakers segment their language (Ziegler and Goswami 2005). For example, English is characterized by complex syllable onsets and syllable boundaries that are unclear (Álvarez, Carreiras, and Taft 2001). These properties might make speakers more sensitive to onset-rime segments (DeCara and Goswami 2003). Spanish has a simpler syllabic structure with consistent and easy-to-determine syllable boundaries (Bradley, Sanchez-Casas, and Garcia-Albea 1993). Therefore, the syllable might be a more psychologically salient sub-lexical unit in Spanish (Álvarez, Carreiras, and Perea 2004).

In addition to the phonological properties of the PL and AL, differences in the ways languages map print to speech might affect the relationships between PL and AL reading skills (Ziegler and Goswami 2005). A PL with a shallow orthography (a writing system that has direct spelling-sound correspondences) is likely to facilitate AL reading to a greater extent than a PL with a deep orthography (a writing system that does not have a one-to-one correspondence between sounds (phonemes) and the letters (graphemes) that represent them) (e.g., Gottardo et al. 2001).

Further, a study by Kahn-Horwitz, Schwartz, and Share (2011) examined the impact of Russian and Hebrew literacy on English orthographic knowledge needed for spelling and decoding among fifth graders. They compared the performance of three groups: Russian-Hebrew-speaking emerging triliterates, Russian-Hebrew-speaking emerging biliterates who were not literate in

Russian (but only in Hebrew), and Hebrew-speaking emerging biliterates. Because of the similarities between Russian and English orthographies, Russian-Hebrew-speaking emerging triliterates outperformed both other groups on spelling and decoding of short vowels and consonant clusters. However, all three groups experienced difficulty with spelling and decoding the digraph *th* as well as the split digraph (silent e). Even the Russian-Hebrew-speaking emerging triliterates did not achieve anywhere close to ceiling results for either spelling or decoding of short vowels after 3 years of English literacy instruction. This result clearly reflects the challenges presented by English orthography.

In her analyses of writing in schools, Christie, Derewianka, and Hylands (2010) found that children writing in English as an L1 begin to learn to expand the nominal group structure at around the age of seven and, as they mature, they increase the resources available to them for nominal group expansion. Christie and colleagues explain that such a facility assists in the building of the lexical density that marks mature written language. Coffin (2006) shows that texts produced by AL learners at later points in school differ considerably from those written by younger learners; the differences in their texts include increased nominalization and generalization/abstraction created through complexity within the nominal group. Research suggests that pedagogical intervention, specific instruction, and sufficient input (Marfin Uriz and Whittaker 2005), as well as more cognitively demanding tasks, do help AL learners improve their writing.

Literacy activities or performances are never pure linguistic events. Instead, they are always organized on the basis of the integration of a learner's cultural beliefs and values. In literacy practices, AL learners will always incorporate their cultural values, beliefs, emotions, practices, identity, and resources into the organization of literacy activities. In other words, when different cultural and linguistic systems interact, learners rarely simply replace one linguistic system with the other; in fact, their literacy activities tend to reflect the integration of more than one system. The creative forms of literacy practices that learners draw from their existing pool of languages and literacy practices in their homes, schools, and communities that blend familiar practices with new forms are called syncretic literacy (e.g., Curdt-Christiansen 2013). A growing body of research has suggested that syncretic literacy is a common practice in classrooms among children and adolescents who are exposed to more than one linguistic system and culture (Souto-Manning 2013).

12.3.6 AL figurative language development

Figurative language is a general term for linguistic expressions, such as metaphors, idioms, similes, proverbs, humor, jokes, hyperbole, irony, and proverbs. The interpretation of figurative language is nonliteral, where the meaning of the expression as a whole cannot be computed directly from the meaning of its constituents (Vulchanova et al. 2015). Many factors (such as cognitive, semantic, pragmatic, metalinguistic knowledge, and literacy of a speaker) are at play in appreciating and producing figurative language.

It typically takes a long time for a speaker in any language to become more proficient in figurative language comprehension and use. It is not until age 10 that most children have the true ability to interpret metaphors (Hoff 2009). Similarly, children start to appreciate and use context in idiom comprehension at about age 9 (Laval 2003) with a peak at around 11 years old (Vulchanova et al. 2015). But, it is during adolescence that the understanding of figurative language becomes reliable. There is a U-shaped curve in the production of figurative language. During early childhood, preschoolers are commonly observed using imaginative expressions such as "The faucet is crying" and "Pretend the headlights are eyes". During middle childhood, the use of imaginative expressions decreases, but the expressions increase again during adolescence (Nippold 2007).

Depending on AL learners' prior knowledge of figurative language in their PL, adolescent AL learners already possess a rich idiomatic knowledge base in their PL in addition to their cognitive advancement. They are able to detect idioms in readings with ease. However, they may not be able to understand and interpret AL figurative meanings right away. They may first use a literal interpretation, and after that fails, they may begin to try other strategies. AL learners' ability to make sense of figurative language largely depends on their mastery of the AL. Research suggests that AL learners use cues to understand and interpret figurative language such as vivid phrasal idioms in addition to the pragmatic system that they employ in order to construct the appropriate cultural meaning of a given idiom in the AL. Idiomatic understanding in an AL is a continuous and interactive/integrative process. AL learners transact and produce meaning from a text and from what they bring to the dynamic act of reading by way of their prior personal and cultural background knowledge, experience, interests, values, and societal paradigms (Liontas 2002).

12.4 Summary

This chapter has briefly touched upon the complexity of multilingual children learning an AL in the school environment and the typical mechanisms they use to acquire the AL. Characteristics demonstrated in various aspects of AL attainment were also addressed to shed light on how multilingual learners develop the AL while learning different subjects. As our world becomes increasingly globalized, more children enter classrooms with more than one language. Thus, longitudinal research in the school context is critically needed to help us better understand how educational systems can ensure the sustainability of multilingual development.

References

Abrahamsson, Niclas & Kenneth Hyltenstam. 2009. Age of onset and nativelikeness in a second language: Listener perception versus linguistic scrutiny. *Language Learning* 59. 249–306.

Altarriba, Jeanette & Lisa M. Bauer. 2004. The distinctiveness of emotion concepts: A comparison between emotion, abstract, and concrete words. *American Journal of Psychology* 117. 389–410.

Álvarez, Carlos J., Manuel Carreiras & Manuel Perea. 2004. Are syllables phonological units in visual word recognition? *Language and Cognitive Process* 19(3). 427–452.

Álvarez, Carlos J., Manuel Carreiras & Marcus Taft. 2001. Syllables and morphemes: Contrasting frequency effects in Spanish. *Journal of Experimental Psychology: Learning, Memory, and Cognition* 27(2). 545–555.

Baba, Junko. 2010. Interlanguage pragmatics study of indirect complaint among Japanese ESL learners. *Sino-US English Teaching* 12. 23–32.

Barnett, Steven W., Donald Yarosz, Jessica Thomas, Kwanghee Jung & Dulce Blanco. 2007. Two-way and monolingual English immersion in preschool education: An experimental comparison. *Early Childhood Research Quarterly* 22(3). 277–293.

Bates, Elizabeth, Inge Bretherton & Lynn Snyder. 1988. *From first words to grammar: Individual differences and dissociable mechanisms*. Cambridge: Cambridge University Press.

Bialystok, Ellen. 1988. Levels of bilingualism and levels of linguistic awareness. *Developmental Psychology* 24(4). 560–567.

Bialystok, Ellen & Michelle M. Martin. 2004. Attention and inhibition in bilingual children: Evidence from the dimensional change card sort task. *Developmental Science* 7(3). 325–339.

Bialystok, Ellen, Gigi Luk & Ernest Kwan. 2005. Bilingualism, biliteracy, and learning to read: Interactions among languages and writing systems. *Scientific Studies of Reading* 9. 43–61.

Boerma, Tessel, Paul Leseman, Mona Timmermeister, Frank Wijnen & Elma Blom. 2016. Narrative abilities of monolingual and bilingual children with and without language impairment: Implications for clinical practice. *International Journal of Communication Disorder* 51(6). 626–638.

Bonifacci, Paola, Margherita Barbieri, Marta Tomassini & Maja Roch. 2018. In few words: Linguistic gap but adequate narrative structure in preschool bilingual children. *Journal of Child Language* 45(1). 120–147.

Bradley, Dianne C., Rosa M. Sanchez-Casas & José E. Garcia-Albea. 1993. The status of the syllable in the perception of Spanish and English. *Language and Cognitive Processes* 8(2). 197–233.

Brown, H. Douglas. 2000. *Principles of language learning and teaching*. White Plains: Pearson Education.

Brown, Steven & Attardo Salvatore. 2008. *Understanding language structure, interaction, and variation: An introduction to applied linguistics and sociolinguistics for nonspecialists*. Michigan: University of Michigan Press.

Cedden, Gulay & Çiğdem Sağin Şimşek. 2014. The impact of a third language on executive control processes. *International Journal of Bilingualism* 18(6). 558–569.

Cenoz, Jasone. 2001. The effect of linguistic distance, L2 status and age on cross-linguistic influence in third language acquisition. In Jasone Cenoz, Britta Hufeisen & Ulrike Jessner (eds.), *Cross-linguistic influence in third language acquisition: Psycholinguistic perspectives*, 8–20. Clevedon: Multilingual Matters.

Cenoz, Jasone, Britta Hufeisen & Ulrike Jessner (eds.). 2001. *Cross-linguistic influence in third language acquisition: Psycholinguistic perspectives*. Clevedon: Multilingual Matters.

Chomsky, Noam A. 1980. Rules and representations. *Behavioral and Brain Sciences* 3(127). 1–16.

Christie, Frances, Beverly Derewianka & K. Hylands. 2010. School discourse: Learning to write across the years of schooling (Continuum Discourse). *Journal of Adolescent and Adult Literacy* 54(1). 74–77.

Cobo-Lewis, Alan, Barbara Z. Pearson, Rebecca E. Eilers & Vivian C. Umbel. 2002. Effects of bilingualism and bilingual education on oral and written Spanish skills: A multifactor study of standardized test outcomes. In Kimbrough Oller & Rebecca Eilers (eds.), *Language and literacy in bilingual children*, 98–117. Clevedon, UK: Multilingual Matters.

Coffin, Caroline. 2006. *Historical discourse: The language of time, cause and evaluation*. London, UK: Continuum.

Collier, Virginia. P. 1995. Acquiring a second language for school. *Directions in Language & Education* 1(4). 3–12.

Cummins, James. 1979. Linguistic interdependence and the educational development of bilingual children. *Review of Educational Research* 49. 222–251.

Cummins, James. 1981. The role of primary language development in promoting educational success for language minority students. In California State Department of Education (eds.), *Schooling and language minority students: A theoretical framework*, 3–49. Los Angeles: Evaluation, Dissemination, and Assessment Center, California State University, Los Angeles.

Curdt-Christiansen, Xiao L. 2013. Implicit learning and imperceptible influence: Syncretic literacy of multilingual Chinese children. *Journal of Early Childhood Literacy* 13(3). 348–370.

De Cara, Bruno & Usha Goswami. 2003. Phonological neighborhood density: Effects in a rhyme awareness task in five-year-old children. *Journal of Child Language* 30(3). 695–710.

De Houwer, Annick. 2009. *An introduction to bilingual development*. Bristol: Multilingual Matters.

Durgunoğlu, Aydin Yücesan. 2002. Cross-linguistic transfer in literacy development and implications for language learners. *Annals of Dyslexia* 52. 189–204.
Eckman, Fred. R. 2004. From phonemic differences to constraint rankings: Research on second language phonology. *Studies in Second Language Acquisition* 26(4). 513–549.
Ellis, Rod. (2008). *The study of second language acquisition*. Oxford: Oxford University Press.
Erbaugh, Mary. S. 1992. The acquisition of Mandarin. In Dan Isaac Slobin (ed.), *The crosslinguistic study of language acquisition volume 3*, 373–455. Hillsdale: Lawrence Erlbaum.
Flege, James Emil, Murray J Munro, & Ian R. A. Mackay. 1995. Effects of age of second language learning on the production of English consonants. *Speech Communication* 16. 1–26.
García, Ofelia & Wei Li. 2014. *Translanguaging: Language, bilingualism, and education*. London: Palgrave Macmillan.
Gass, Susan M. & Larry Selinker. 2001. *Second language acquisition, an introductory course*. Mahwah, NJ: Lawrence Erlbaum Associates.
Geva, Esther & Linda Siegel. 2000. Orthographic and cognitive factors in the concurrent development of basic reading skills in two languages. *Reading and Writing* 12. 1–30.
Gottardo, Alexandra. 2002. The relationship between language and reading skills in bilingual Spanish-English speakers. *Topics in Language Disorders* 22(5). 46–70.
Gottardo, Alexandra & Julie Mueller. 2009. Are first- and second-language factors related in predicting second-language reading comprehension? A study of Spanish-speaking children acquiring English as a second language from first to second grade. *Journal of Educational Psychology* 101. 330–344.
Gottardo, Alexandra, Bernice Yan, Linda S. Siegel & Lesley Wade-Woolley. 2001. Factors related to English reading performance in children with Chinese as a first language: More evidence of cross-language transfer of phonological processing. *Journal of Educational Psychology* 93 (3). 530–542.
Gottlieb, Margo & Gisela Ernest-Slavit. 2014. *Academic language in diverse classrooms: Definitions and contexts*. Thousand Oaks, CA: Corwin Press.
Hoff, Erika. 2009. *Language development*. Belmont, CA: Wadsworth.
Jia, Gisela and Akiko Fuse. 2007. Acquisition of English grammatical morphology by native Mandarin-speaking children and adolescents: Age-related differences. *Journal of Speech, Language, and Hearing Research* 50. 1280–1299.
Kahn-Horwitz, Janina, Mila Schwartz & David Share. 2011. Acquiring the complex English orthography: A triliteracy advantage? *Journal of Research in Reading* 34(1). 136–156.
Kaushanskaya, Margarita, Megan Gross & Milijana Buac. 2014. Effects of classroom bilingualism on task-shifting, verbal memory, and word learning in children. *Developmental Science* 17(4). 564–583.
Laurent, Angélique & Clara Martinot. 2010. Bilingualism and phonological awareness: The case of bilingual (French-Occitan) children. *Reading and Writing* 23. 435–452.
Laval, Virginie. 2003. Idiom comprehension and metapragmatic knowledge in French children. *Journal of Pragmatics* 35. 723–739.
Lewis, Gwyn, Bryn Jones & Colin Baker. 2012. Translanguaging: Developing its conceptualization and contextualization. *Educational Research and Evaluation* 18(7). 655–670.
Li, Ping. 2013. Successive language acquisition. In François Grosjean and Ping Li (eds.), *The psycholinguistics of bilingualism*, 157–194. Oxford, UK: Wiley-Blackwell.

Li, Wei. 2018. Translanguaging as a practical theory of language. *Applied Linguistics* 39(1). 9–30.
Li, Wei & Hua Zhu. 2013. Translanguaging identities and ideologies: Creating transnational space through flexible multilingual practices amongst Chinese university students in the UK. *Applied Linguistics* 34 (5). 516–535.
Lim, Hui W., Bill Wells & Sara Howard. 2015. Rate of multilingual phonological acquisition: Evidence from a cross-sectional study of English-Mandarin-Malay. *Clinical Linguistics and Phonetics* 29(11). 793–811.
Lindsay, Kim A., Franklin R. Marnis & Caroline E. Balley. 2003. Prediction of first-grade reading in Spanish-speaking English-language learners. *Journal of Educational Psychology* 95(3). 482–494.
Liontas, John I. 2002. Exploring second language learners' notions of idiomaticity. *System* 30(3). 289–313.
Long, Michael. 1990. Maturational constraints on language development. *Studies in Second Language Acquisition* 12. 251–258.
Magiste, Edith. 1979. The competing linguistic systems of the multilingual: A developmental study of decoding and encoding processes. *Journal of Verbal Learning and Verbal Behavior* 18. 79–89.
Martîn Úriz, Ana Maria & Rachel Whittaker. 2005. *La composición como comunicación: Una experiencia en las aulas de lengua inglesa de bachillerato* (Colección Estudios). Madrid, Spain: UAM Ediciones.
Mayr, Robert & Simona Montanari. 2015. Cross-linguistic interaction in trilingual phonological development: The role of the input in the acquisition of the voicing contrast. *Journal of Child Language* 42(5). 1006–1035.
Meisel, Jürgen M. 2006. The bilingual child. In Tej K. Bhatia and William C. Ritchie (eds.), *The handbook of bilingualism*, 91–144. Oxford & New York: Blackwell.
Newport, Elissa L., Daphne Bavelier & Helen J. Neville. 2001. Critical thinking about critical periods: Perspectives on a critical period for language acquisition. In Emmanuel Dupoux (ed.), *Language, brain and cognitive development: Essays in honor of Jacques Mehler*, 481–502. Cambridge, MA: MIT Press.
Nippold, Marilyn A. 2007. *Later language development: School-age children, adolescents, and young adults*. Austin, TX: Pro-ed.
Norrman, Gunnar & Emanuel Bylund. 2016. The irreversibility of sensitive period effects in language development: Evidence from second language acquisition in international adoptees. *Developmental Science* 19 (3). 513–520.
Oller, D. Kimbrough. 2005. The distributed characteristic in bilingual learning. In James Cohen, Kara T. McAlister, Kellie Rolstad & Jeff MacSwan (eds.), *Proceedings of the 4th International Symposium on Bilingualism*, 1744–1749. Somerville, MA: Cascadilla Press.
Páez, Mariela M., O Patton Tabor & Lisa M. López. 2007. Dual language and literacy development of Spanish-speaking preschool children. *Applied Developmental Psychology* 28(2). 85–102.
Pavlenko, Aneta. 2008. Emotion and emotion-laden words in the bilingual lexicon. *Bilingualism: Language and Cognition* 11. 147–164.
Rauch, Dominique P., Johannes Naumann & Nina Jude. 2012. Metalinguistic awareness mediates effects of full biliteracy on third-language reading proficiency in Turkish German bilinguals. *International Journal of Bilingualism* 16(4). 402–418.

Souto-Manning, Mariana. 2013. On children as syncretic natives: Disrupting and moving beyond normative binaries. *Journal of Early Childhood Literacy* 13(3). 371–394.

Sung, Chit Cheung Matthew. 2013. English as a lingua franca and English language teaching: A way forward. *ELT Journal* 67(3). 350–353.

Tabors, Patton O., Mariela Páez & Lisa López. 2003. Dual language abilities of bilingual four-year-olds: Initial findings from the early childhood study of language and literacy development of Spanish-speaking children. *NABE Journal of Research and Practice* 1. 70–91.

Ute, Romer, Matthew Brook O'Donnell & Nick Ellis. 2014. Second language learner knowledge of verb-argument constructions: Effects of language transfer and typology. *The Modern Language Journal* 98(4). 952–975.

Viberg, Ake. 2001. Age-related and L2-related features in bilingual narrative development in Sweden. In Ludo Verhoeven and Sven Strömqvist (eds.), *Narrative development in a multilingual context*, 87–128. Amsterdam, Netherlands: John Benjamins.

Vulchanova Mila, Joel Talcott, Valentin Vulchanov, Margarita Stankova & Hendrik Eshuis. 2015. Morphology in autism spectrum disorders: Local processing bias and language. *Cognitive Neuropsychology* 29. 584–600.

Wade-Woolley, Lesly & Esther Geva. 2000. Processing novel phonemic contrasts in the acquisition of L2 word reading. *Scientific Studies of Reading* 4(4). 295–311.

Wang, Xiao-lei. 2008. *Growing up with three languages: Birth to eleven*. Bristol, UK: Multilingual Matters, Ltd.

Wang, Xiao-lei. 2015a. *Understanding language and literacy development: Diverse learners in the classroom*. Boston, MA: Wiley-Blackwell publisher.

Wang, Xiao-lei. 2015b. *Maintaining three languages: The teenage years*. Bristol, UK: Multilingual Matters.

Wang, Xiao-lei & Ronan Bernas. (under review). The art of mixing: A longitudinal study of trilingual siblings' pragmatic competency from a functional perspective. *International Journal of Multilingualism*.

Ziegler, Johannes C. & Usha Goswarmi. 2005. Reading acquisition, developmental dyslexia, and skilled reading across languages: A psycholinguistic grain size theory. *Psychological Bulletin* 131(1). 3–29.

Ulrike Jessner and Manon Megens
13 Language Attrition in Multilinguals

13.1 Introduction

During recent years, research interest in the contact between more than two languages has increased. Consequently, attitudes have changed from negative to seemingly embracing a higher level of awareness of the complexity and dynamics of multilingualism. Over the last 20 years, research on multilingualism and third or additional language acquisition has progressively intensified. One of the main goals has been to describe multilingual phenomena in order to investigate differences and similarities between second and third language acquisition. Multilinguals, however, not only acquire or learn languages, but also experience language attrition over time with ongoing changes in dominance, proficiency, and linguistic skills in each and all of their languages. To date, language attrition in multilinguals remains under-researched, and research on the attrition of more than one language within the individual is virtually non-existent.

The present chapter deals with attrition in multilinguals from a dynamics and complexity systems (DSCT) perspective, in particular from the perspective of the Dynamic Model of Multilingualism (DMM; Herdina and Jessner 2002). Multilingualism and multilingual development in the present chapter refer to the use and development of more than two languages. This means that a difference is made between bilingualism and multilingualism because of the quantitative distinction between these two and the greater complexity and diversity of the factors involved in the development and use of three or more languages.

We will first give an overview of the field and study of language attrition, dealing with definitions and theories used to conceptualize the phenomenon and the most important factors that (might) influence the attrition process. Since research on language attrition to date mainly takes a bilingual approach and studies language attrition in bilinguals, we will then present a multilingual holistic approach to language attrition, discussing the dynamics and complexity of multilingual development, language attrition, and language maintenance (effort) in multilingual systems. In support of the crucial role that language attrition plays in the dynamic and complex process of multilingual development, we will follow with an overview of attrition studies, focusing particularly on research involving more than two languages. A conclusion and outlook will be presented at the end of the chapter.

Ulrike Jessner, Universität Innsbruck, Innsbruck, Austria & University of Pannonia, Veszprém, Hungary
Manon Megens, Universität Innsbruck, Innsbruck, Austria

https://doi.org/10.1515/9781501507984-013

13.2 The study of language attrition: historical and current perspectives

13.2.1 Definitions

Language attrition has been defined as the "non-pathological decrease in proficiency in a language that has previously been acquired by an individual" (Köpke and Schmid 2004: 5). The study of this phenomenon gained momentum in the years following a conference organized at the University of Pennsylvania in 1980 (Bardovi-Harlig and Stringer 2010). The major contributions to this conference were then edited by Lambert and Freed (1982) into a volume entitled *The Loss of Language Skills*. As the use of the term "loss" in the title indicates, this conference covered a broader spectrum of phenomena than what is described as attrition by Köpke and Schmid (2004). In fact, language attrition research has historically been aligned with research on other types of language loss. These include pathological language loss (aphasia) as well as intergenerational language loss or shift of language skills in speech communities, which is often termed "language shift". Therefore, the addition of the adjective "non-pathological" and the focus placed on the individual in Köpke and Schmid's (2004) definition stands to reason in order to separate the object under investigation from other phenomena it used to be aligned with.

Ecke (2004: 322) defines language attrition along similar lines, describing it as "the decline of any language (L1 or L2), skill or portion thereof in a healthy individual speaker." The latter definition rightly underlines that the term attrition does not necessarily denote a decrease in global language proficiency; instead, attrition may only affect certain language skills, and even those only partly. In any case, these processes all lead to a "reduction or simplification of language systems and/or the impairment of access to them, [which] is assumed to be a normal, often inevitable aspect of language development in the lifespan of a bi- or multilingual speaker" (Ecke and Hall 2013: 735).

13.2.2 Theories on language attrition

As becomes evident from above, research on attrition stresses that linguistic knowledge is not necessarily fully lost from memory, nor that it is irretrievably covered up and obliterated completely by more newly acquired knowledge. Instead, knowledge that is rarely or not used becomes less interconnected and therefore more difficult to access for the language user. To account for this notion, several scholars, in particular from the psycholinguistic branch of attrition research, draw attention to theories and hypotheses of related disciplines, for instance, the neurolinguistic Activation Threshold Hypothesis (ATH) by Paradis (2004) or the Savings Hypothesis/Paradigm as discussed by de Bot, Martens and Stoessel (2004). The "retrieval slowdown and failure theory" and the "interference theory", two theories of forgetting, have also been discussed in this context (for more on theories of forgetting and language attrition, see Ecke 2004).

Other linguistic, psycholinguistic and sociolinguistic theories and hypotheses within attrition research, again, are often borrowed from related fields and disciplines (for detailed overviews of different theories, see e.g., Bardovi-Harlig and Stringer 2010; Köpke 2007). It should be noted, however, that most attrition research to date has not been based on theoretical-probing studies but rather on investigations focused on descriptive data and on the factors that influence language attrition.

13.2.3 Factors influencing language attrition

In her theoretical article, Köpke (2007) enumerates a variety of factors that influence language attrition. She discusses four brain mechanisms (biological factors) that attrition seems to be dependent upon, namely plasticity (closely linked to the age factor), activation (thresholds), inhibition, and emotional implications, i.e., subcortical involvement (Köpke 2007: 10–15). These mechanisms, according to Köpke (2007: 15), "seem also to be reflected in the cognitive processes implied in language attrition," such as memory, aptitude, literacy, and task dependency. Attrition, though clearly defined as an individual phenomenon (see section 13.2.1), is closely related to social aspects of language use, i.e., external factors, too. Influencing external factors are language contact and use, the cultural context, and attitudinal factors such as motivation, as discussed by Köpke (2007: 22–26), but also the acquisition setting, the educational level, and the nature of instruction (for a detailed discussion of external factors in L1 and L2 attrition research and studies, see also Bardovi-Harlig and Stringer 2010).

Generally, it has been assumed that language disuse is the primary factor governing language attrition (e.g., Herdina and Jessner 2002; Köpke 2007; Schmid 2007). Intuitively, this seems to make sense, but more current research has failed to find strong empirical evidence for the prediction that language disuse will lead to language attrition. While Köpke (1999) and Hulsen (2000), for instance, reported on a positive correlation between infrequent use and attrition, Schmid (2007: 150) concludes that "while there clearly is an attrition effect, the amount of use of the L1 in daily life does not seem to have any predictive power for this effect". Both Köpke (2007) and Schmid (2007) argue that it is not enough to consider the frequency of language contact and use only and emphasize that one has to look at its quality in addition. It will make a difference whether a person only engages in activities that employ receptive skills or if s/he actually speaks or writes in this language (Köpke 2007: 23). Based on Grosjean's (2001) Language Mode Continuum, Schmid (2007: 139–141) further distinguishes between five types of language use among emigrants and stresses that these types place different demands on the activation or inhibition levels, respectively, of the L1 and the L2. For this reason, she stresses that the different types of language mode, i.e., types of language contact and use, "should not be lumped together under the common factor 'L1 contact' in attrition studies" (Schmid 2007: 141).

Finally, "language contact and use" also means contact with and use of other languages. With respect to language attrition, however, research on the influence of contact with and use of another (foreign) language is a quite recent phenomenon, and the influence of two or more other (foreign) languages, as in multilingualism, is still in its infancy.

13.3 Approaching a holistic bilingual view on language attrition

While language attrition has been studied for a long time as a process largely divorced from other linguistic developmental processes without taking into account the use of and contact with other languages, in the first years of the new millennium, it became widely recognized that language attrition "usually proceeds in the context of broader changes to the linguistic system, for example as a result of the simultaneous acquisition of another language" (Opitz 2013: 702). As De Bot and Hulsen (2002: 262) point out, "[l]anguages are never lost in isolation, and L1 attrition typically comes as a by-product of language contact, particularly in migrant settings". Also, Schmid (2007: 151) elaborates that "the findings from [her] investigation suggest that it is relatively meaningless to study the attrition and use of only one of a bilingual's languages in isolation, and exclude the development and use of the other [and that the] results suggest a delicate balance of the two language systems and their activation, inhibition, and accessibility". These and other such observations have led to the integration of the notion of "multi-competence", which has been defined as "the knowledge of more than one language in the same mind" (Cook 2003: 2–3) and, more recently, as "the overall systems of a mind or a community that uses more than one language" (Cook 2016: 2), and to dynamic views of bi-/multilingual development within language attrition research (e.g., De Bot 2007; Herdina and Jessner 2002; Jessner 2003). Recent research (e.g., Opitz 2013; Schmid and Köpke 2017; Seton and Schmid 2016) takes this holistic view on language attrition.

It should be noted, however, that most researchers who take a holistic approach study language attrition in bilinguals. While some researchers might even apply the term "multilingualism" or "multilinguals" (e.g., Schmid 2013) to their work, they study language attrition in one of a bilingual's two languages or language development in two languages (one attrition, one acquisition). In other words, they do not differentiate between bilingualism and multilingualism. Their focus of research is on a maximum of two languages or language systems in interaction. From our research perspective, these researchers are taking a bilingual holistic approach to language attrition and not a multilingual holistic approach, as will be discussed in the following section.

13.4 A multilingual holistic approach to language attrition

13.4.1 The dynamics and complexity of multilingual development in multilingual systems

More recent work in second language acquisition and/or development (SLA/SLD), and particularly in the fields of multilingualism and third or additional language acquisition (TLA), has increasingly adopted a more complex and dynamic approach based on either Dynamic Systems Theory (DST) or Complexity Theory (CT) or both (e.g., Jessner 2008; Larsen-Freeman and Cameron 2008). Within this approach, language is conceived as a complex dynamic system, and language development is seen as being shaped by "interrelated patterns of experience, social interaction and cognitive processes" ('Five Graces Group' 2009: 2). The Dynamic Model of Multilingualism (DMM) by Herdina and Jessner (2002) was the first published monograph to address the application of dynamic systems and/or complexity theory (DSCT) to multilingualism, i.e., in multilingual development and use.

In the past decades, research into language acquisition and development, in particular in the fields of SLA and TLA, has moved away from seeing these processes as an ordered sequence of individual steps towards an (idealized) end-state (i.e. native-speaker-like competence). In such (linear) reductionist models, a certain amount of input is often assumed to result in a proportionate degree of growth; moreover, such traditional models look at growth or increase but do not account for or simply ignore decline or attrition. In the DMM, however, language development is not seen as a linear process; instead it is "made of non-linear and reversible processes: that is, development refers to both acquisition and attrition" (Jessner, Megens, and Graus 2016: 196), and attrition is thus an integral and normal part of (multilingual) language development itself (Jessner 2003, 2008). An individual's communicative needs, or rather *perceived* communicative needs, are seen as the central factor behind language development: "Language change in the individual results from adjusting one's language system(s) to one's communicative needs" (Herdina and Jessner 2002: 74). From this it becomes clear that the description of individual multilingual development, that is, contact with more than two languages during the life-span, has to take changes in multilingual proficiency into account. Figure 13.1 (based on Herdina and Jessner 2002: 124, fig. 29b) models the development of a multilingual system; that is, it shows how a trilingual learner develops language proficiency in more than two languages during a certain period of time. While the primary language system remains dominant during this time, the simultaneously acquired secondary system undergoes development – it declines. The development of the third, tertiary language system is dependent on the development of the other two language systems.

As pointed out by Herdina and Jessner (2002: 88–89), the graphs used in the DMM "simply relate language learning to time needed and predict the modifications in expected language growth due to the effect of certain factors assumed to affect multilinguals and ignore the fact that the level of achievement is heterogenous even in monolinguals, let alone multilinguals". Yet, this figure illustrates well how language systems develop, i.e., both grow and decline, in a non-linear manner.

Languages within the individual are not seen as separate from each other; rather, in the DMM, the multilingual language system is a complex dynamic system which consists of other nested systems (i.e., the language systems LS1, LS2, LS3, etc.), all of which are in constant interaction with each other and within the multilingual system and with the environment (i.e., between the individual and society) in ongoing processes of change and development. In other words, language systems are interconnected and interdependent, "and it would therefore not make sense to look at the systems in terms of isolated development" (Herdina and Jessner 2002: 92).

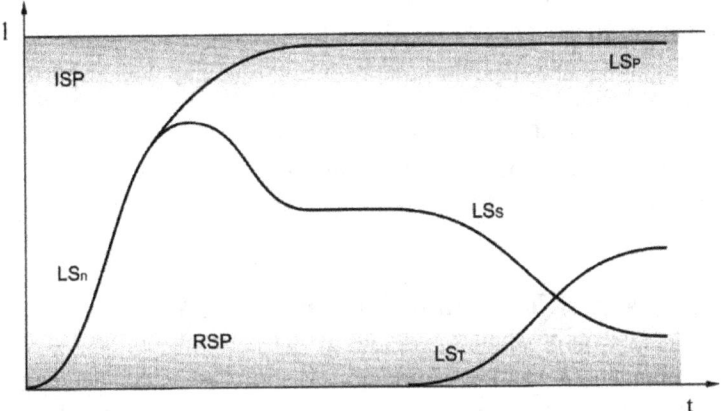

Figure 13.1: Learner multilingualism: overall development (Herdina and Jessner 2002: 124, reprinted with permission) LSn = prior language system(s); LSp = primary language system; LSs = secondary language system; LSt = tertiary language system; ISP = ideal native speaker proficiency; RSP = rudimentary speaker proficiency; t = time; l = language level.

The necessity of adopting a multilingual holistic perspective is determined not only by the complex crosslinguistic interactions (CLINs) of the multilingual system due to contact with different language speakers and languages and, thus, interdependent with the multilingual's perceived communicative needs, but also by the change of quality of the multilingual mind that arises from them. The system as a whole develops properties that its individual parts do not, and these emergent properties, collectively referred to in the DMM as the M-factor or M-effect, refer "to proficiency skills as developed in the multilingual speakers [and] include skills in language learning, language management and language maintenance" (Herdina and Jessner 2002: 131). The new qualities that emerge, such as an enhanced level of multilingual awareness including "at least two dimensions of awareness in the form of crosslinguistic and metalinguistic awareness" (Jessner, Megens and Graus, 2016: 208), distinguish multilinguals from bilinguals and, of course, from their monolingual counterparts (Jessner 2018; Megens 2011). CLIN phenomena thus work on both the linguistic and the cognitive level of multilingual development and use and refer to the language systems as well as to increased multilingual awareness and metacognitive skills in multilinguals (Jessner, Megens, and Graus 2016; for a detailed discussion of the phenomena touched upon above, see Chapter 15, this volume).

Precisely because the dynamic complex multilingual system and its emergent properties are in a constant process of adaptation and (internal) reorganization, it has a sensitive dependence on initial conditions – "another key feature of complex systems inherent to multilingualism" (Jessner 2018: 34) – such as the different ways of learning (i.e., naturalistic and/or instructed and formal language learning) and the proficiency in a given language at the onset of non-use in the context of multilingual development/attrition (Megens 2019).

13.4.2 Language attrition in multilingual systems

One of the main tenets of a DSCT perspective concerns language development as consisting of processes of language growth and language attrition. In the DMM, Herdina and Jessner (2002) pinpoint language loss as one of the key aspects of the development of multilingual systems. According to Fase, Jaspaert, and Kroon (1992: 9),

> [f]rom a psycholinguistic point of view, the pattern of language loss may offer insights into the structure of the linguistic system. In much the same way as language acquisition is believed to be governed by general principles of language and language ability, patterns of language loss are believed to offer a similar view of language, be it from the other end. [...] [T]he explanation for systematicity in both fields raises similar questions: the universality of the process, the role of interlinguistic versus intralinguistic factors in the explanation of the process, the degree to which competence and/or performance is involved. [...] In another sense, language loss relates closely to research in language variation and language change.

The DMM regards language attrition as something natural that can be observed in all forms of language development and use, and in both non-native and native speakers, and describes the process itself as one of "gradual decay in time" (Jessner 2003: 237–239). Furthermore, it points out two general theories of forgetting which may be applied to research on language attrition:
1. Theory of forgetting as a gradual process of information decay: here the attrition is seen to pertain to the time component, i.e., "the longer the phase between learning and forgetting, the more difficult or less likely the particular recall of an item of information will be", and
2. Cognitive interference theory: here, "the access to information is reduced because old information is covered up by new [one and so] the linguistic knowledge relevant to the language systems is interpreted as competing for memory space and recall as known from cognitive linguistics research" (Herdina and Jessner 2002: 94–95).

Herdina and Jessner (2002) state that due to its dynamic nature, language attrition is inevitably linked to language maintenance. According to the DMM, the reason for language attrition is a lack of language maintenance effort (LME; see below). Since the multilingual's time and energy are naturally limited and the lack of "refreshment" of what is already known leads to an adaptation of the system, it gradually starts eroding and the language loss curve (see Figure 13.1) appears. At first, language attrition goes almost unnoticed owing to the fact that the system is able "to absorb the effect of decreasing language use by internal adjustments which are not perceived by the outward observer" (Herdina and Jessner 2002: 97). The multilingual individual might, for example, use fewer synonyms or less elaborated structures during this stage. After this initial phase, the gradual loss curve suddenly drops dramatically. Herdina and Jessner (2002: 105) explain the decrease in the (idealized) inverted sine curve as follows:

> One of the reasons for the sharp decline after a more gradual initial deterioration can be found in the self-reinforcing processes entailed in language loss: for example, loss of language competence will lead to a reduction in use, as the command of the language is more difficult to maintain and the risk of exposure by goofing and resulting stigmatization is greater and naturally avoided.

Here the importance of individual (social, psycholinguistic and cognitive) factors in language attrition becomes apparent. Additionally, the DMM poses that a heightened monitoring effort and metalinguistic abilities could also counteract a reduced system (Herdina and Jessner 2002: 115–116; see Megens 2019).

13.4.3 Language maintenance (effort) in multilingual systems

The development of any language system, and of a multilingual system in particular, requires effort, regardless of whether this endeavor is conscious and intentional (e.g., as in school language learners) or less deliberate (as in a natural acquisition context). Yet, it is often neglected in language acquisition and development research that effort is also necessary in maintaining language proficiency that was already achieved. As De Bot (2004: 234) relates:

> [...] the average multilingual is faced with the fact that all those languages in the system need maintenance and advanced use to keep them. The discussion on retention of new languages to the system is not about how much memory space we have to store language material, since there probably is no real limit there, but about the time and resources needed to keep all parts of the system in the foreground of processing.

Throwing a brief glance at terminology, Hyltenstam and Stroud (1996: 568), for instance, do not use the terms "retention" and "maintenance" synonymously. In contrast to De Bot (2004), they differentiate between language retention as "the individual ability to keep up a language system" on the one side, and language maintenance with regard to social aspects (e.g., "a speech community tries to continue to use its traditional language although threatened by language shift to the dominant language of the community") on the other side (Hyltenstam and Stroud 1996: 568). The DMM does not make this distinction but uses only "language maintenance" as a general term and, according to the model, the "language maintenance effort" (LME) can be seen as composed of or dependent on:

1. The language use factor: (re)activation and renewal of various parts of the linguistic system/subsystem(s) e.g. through actual use of the language in communication or otherwise,
2. "[T]he language awareness factor: a factorial specification of what has been discussed as metalinguistic awareness" (Herdina and Jessner 2002: 106).

It should be noted here that in everyday situations, LME does not need to take place deliberately and does not always occur consciously, as it does in a classroom or in an explicit situation when the speaker is purposely pursuing communicative situations in any given language. LME may also happen incidentally, without volition: incidental exposure to the language or thinking in or about language and reflecting on learning and maintenance processes constitute LME too.

If LME is the mainstay of maintaining the stability of a language system, it logically follows that its absence can be considered as the core of attrition (de Bot 2004). Deficient LME can even go so far as to lead to a displacement of one language system by another. A less drastic outcome is a change of dominance within the system. Yet, wanting to maintain three or more languages at a similar (dominance) level, i.e. wanting to counteract the "complex process of competition between existing and developing psycholinguistic systems for limited resources [is very] strenuous" (Jessner 2003: 241) and requires a disproportionally larger effort than keeping just one or two language systems stable.

LME, thus, is particularly relevant in multilinguals and its importance becomes evident when investigating multilingual systems, where multiple subsystems compete both for limited cognitive capacities in terms of on-line processing, recall or working memory, and for time and resources in terms of LME. The larger the number of these competing systems in continuous contact and interaction, the greater the changes within the multilingual systems will be, influencing the proficiency in the respective language system(s), which is additionally interdependent on the transformations in the (perceived) communicative needs in the environment (Megens 2019). While during these processes some language systems may be maintained or stabilized, others may gradually attrite (Herdina and Jessner 2013).

The dynamics and complexity of all the CLINs within the multilingual systems makes evident why the theoretical basis for the research carried out on multilingual development in general, and language attrition in multilinguals in particular, is provided by the DMM, which relates "variables and phenomena, such as language acquisition, language maintenance effort, transfer/interference, and loss of languages to each other" (Ecke 2004: 326). This multilingual holistic approach, as discussed above, allows us to study "language attrition in multilinguals" (*multilinguals* "forgetting" any of their three or more languages) and "multilingual attrition" (multilinguals "forgetting" two or more of their *languages*) (Megens and Jessner 2016).

13.5 Studies on language attrition in multilinguals

Since language attrition emerged as an independent field of research, most studies have examined the attrition of the L1 in an L2 environment, i.e., the attrition of bilingual immigrants' first or native language (for an extensive overview of L1 attrition in an L2 context up to 2015, see Schmid, 2016). Within the field of attrition research this type of attrition is distinguished from research on the attrition of languages learned or acquired later in life (Megens 2011). In research on L2 attrition, or better, attrition in languages that are not the L1, there is often little or no systematic differentiation between different types (i.e., second, third or even further/additional [foreign] languages). The amount and quality of input in, exposure and contact to, and use of a language learned in an explicit, formal, instructed-learning setting, however, will generally differ substantially from – and thus present a fundamental difference in terms of initial conditions with – situations where a language is (also) learned and used in a more implicit, naturalistic way, as it often takes place in immersion or migration contexts. Within the broader category of what we will term "non-L1 attrition", we therefore distinguish "foreign language (FL) attrition", which focuses on those languages (L2, L3, L4, … Ln) that have been acquired in an institutional formal learning setting but do not form a significant part of the learner's everyday life outside this context.

To date, only a small number of studies on language attrition have included participants who are multilingual, namely Cohen (1989), Weltens (1989), Grendel (1993), Nakuma (1997), Mehotcheva (2010) and the LAILA and LAILA-BICs project studies (2011–2016, further described in 13.5.2). With the exception of Cohen (1989), all these studies investigated foreign language attrition. To our knowledge, only the LAILA and LAILA-BICs studies have analyzed multilingual attrition, that is, taking more than one of the multilingual's attriting language systems into account. In the following section, these studies and selected findings will be outlined and linked to other studies within the field as well as to the multilingual holistic approach to language attrition in multilinguals, described in the previous sections.

13.5.1 Language attrition studies with multilingual subjects

Cohen (1989) investigated the retention of productive lexical knowledge in two English-Hebrew bilingual children (age 9 and 13) who had acquired Portuguese as an L3 during a one-year stay in Brazil. A picture-based storytelling task uncovered attrition in productive lexical knowledge (particularly nouns) of both children nine months after leaving Brazil. The younger sibling gradually started using shorter and fewer t-units (independent clause with whatever dependent clauses, phrases and words) per utterance and attrited proportionately more nouns than words from other word classes unlike the older sibling. Cohen (1989) found that the children could still identify most of the words in question in an oral recognition task, leading him to conclude that "these words were not lost from memory but that the memory links were increasingly blocked [...] preventing the production of the desired word" (Cohen 1989: 147). Olshtain (1986) found similar results when using, among other tasks, the same story-telling tasks as Cohen (1989) to examine the attrition of English as a second language in L1-Hebrew children aged 5–14. The children had learned English during a prolonged stay (minimum 2 years) in an English-speaking environment and were tested immediately and six months after their return to Israel. The language samples elicited by oral and written tests showed considerable lexical loss for the younger group and that lexical attrition was far less pronounced within the older group, though there were signs of early attrition such as retrieval difficulties and transfer errors. Olshtain (1986) ascribes the difference between the two groups to the fact that the older ones were literate and thus able to stay in contact with English via reading.

Weltens (1989) investigated foreign language attrition during a longer period of non-use. The study focused on the attrition of French (L3, L4 or L5) among 150 Dutch L1 secondary school graduates, two and four years after the end of formal instruction. A combination of a longitudinal and cross-sectional design and a variety of receptive tests were used. Additionally, the researcher collected self-report data with the help of a questionnaire. The test results yielded only very little attrition in the lexical and in the grammatical area. With listening and reading skills, there was even a gain. Furthermore, there was no difference found between the two training levels. Weltens (1989) partly ascribed the small amount of attrition to the lack of time-pressure during the tests. This was also confirmed by the participants in the self-report questionnaire who had the impression of having "lost" fairly more than what the tests actually indicated. However, this did not fully explain the results. Weltens, van Els and Schils (1989: 214), referring to Weltens' (1989) study, supposed that either further academic training and/or the learning of other foreign languages was beneficial to the retention of French. The importance of the influence of additional further language learning is emphasized in the DMM which attributes catalyzing effects to multiple language acquisition. Responsible for this is the M-factor, mainly constituted of metalinguistic awareness (see Chapter 15, this volume). From a DMM point of view, Weltens, van Els and Schils' (1989) assumption and Weltens' (1989) results in general could therefore be seen as an indicator of the beneficial effects of metalinguistic awareness on language attrition (Megens 2019). Apart from this outcome, Weltens' (1989) study confirmed Bahrick's (1984) finding that attrition seems to be independent of the training level.

Bahrick (1984) studied over 500 individuals in the USA, of whom we assume many to have been multilinguals. Their instruction in Spanish had occurred from one to fifty years prior to being tested. Their initial proficiency (measured as "level of training" or the number of Spanish courses taken in high school and college) did not make a difference: during the first five years, the "total amount of content to be forgotten [was] relatively constant" across the groups, but this amount "becomes a progressively smaller portion of total knowledge with the higher levels of training" (Bahrick 1984: 116). This still left those with higher initial proficiency with a greater proportion of knowledge, meaning that the higher the training level, the greater the amount of content likely to be retained. Moreover, Bahrick (1984) reports that the grades received in the courses were valid predictors of performance even several decades after training had ceased. As grades can, to some degree, be considered as an indicator of language proficiency, these findings indicate that higher proficiency is associated with better retention. Bahrick (1984: 16) also remarks that attrition affected "smaller portions of recognition vocabulary than of recall vocabulary," assuming that productive skills are more vulnerable to attrition than receptive ones. The results furthermore show that after an initial period of fairly sharp decrease, which lasts about three to six years, the language knowledge remains remarkably stable for almost twenty-five years or even longer. In this case, Bahrick (1984: 111–114) speaks of "permastore content". De Bot and Clyne (1989: 167) examined the same phenomenon of "critical threshold" after which there is (almost) no attrition in their longitudinal study with Dutch-English bilinguals (or multilinguals). From a DMM perspective, this threshold phenomenon describes a typical chaotic state where the balance or the equilibrium is redressed after some time.

Grendel (1993) used Weltens' (1989) study design to again investigate the attrition of French (L3, L4 or L5) among Dutch learners and, like Weltens, focused on receptive skills only. She, however, decided to use a lexical decision paradigm; that is, a time limit for completing the test was set. Despite a four-year span during which French was not used by the participants, Grendel (1993) found no signs of attrition either. For this reason, Weltens and Grendel (1993: 154) concluded that "future studies of language attrition should focus on language production".

In contrast to the studies discussed so far, Nakuma (1997) focused primarily on communicative rather than on linguistic competence in his pilot study with thirteen Spanish L3 subjects. Nakuma (1997: 233) uses the term L3 as "a convenient shortcut for the more accurate description language-beyond-the-second-language". For some of the subjects, Spanish might therefore have actually been the L4, L5, L*n*. The subjects who were all from Ghana, spoke at least one of the indigenous Ghanaian languages as well as the official language English and had all graduated from the same Ghanaian university with Spanish as their major. The thirteen participants were divided into three groups. The first consisted of those who were professionally using Spanish in North America at the time of the study. The second group had stayed in Ghana after their graduation and had not been in contact with the language since then. Both of these groups had graduated ten years before. The third group, in contrast, was made up of recent graduates whose speech data was used to establish the control baseline competence level against which the communicative competence of the "regular users" and "non-users" was measured. The results revealed a quite significant loss of communicative competence by the second group of non-users. They were approximately "2 ½ times less competent ten years after graduation than the recent graduates" (Nakuma 1997: 219). The first group, in contrast, had gained 3.6% in communicative competence over the decade since their graduation. These findings show once again the dynamisms of a multilingual system at work and the language maintenance (effort) (LME) required.

Like Nakuma, Mehotcheva (2010) also examined foreign language attrition of Spanish in multilinguals. Her participant sample consisted of 51 Dutch L1 and German L1 university students in their twenties who had participated in a study abroad program in Spain between four and twelve months. All of them had between two and as many as seven foreign languages in their repertoire, Spanish being the L5 for most of them. The substantial differences in time since the end of the study abroad program allowed for attrition to be studied by comparing three attriting groups to a baseline group as well as by studying the longitudinal data of five participants over the span of a year, thus combining cross-sectional and longitudinal examinations. Mehotcheva (2010) found attrition signs in the longitudinal as well as in the cross-sectional data sets, though less evident in the latter, with attrition being more visible in those who had been away from Spain for a longer time. Additionally, test results showed that initial proficiency was "the most salient predictor of language retention with high proficiency at onset leading to better retention of the language" (Mehotcheva 2010: 154).

The importance of initial proficiency for attrition was also found in Xu's (2010) study on the attrition and retention of school-learned English in Chinese and Dutch university students. Although there is no evidence of more than two languages in the repertoires of the students in the study, two different populations of English learners are compared. Xu (2010) investigated the effect of attained proficiency, language contact and use, and language attitude in two different environments, two years after instructed English learning ended. Attrition was observed in both participant groups, but while the Chinese participants showed deterioration across all four skills (reading, writing, listening and speaking), the Dutch students' attrition could only be detected for their writing skills. It was found that language contact did not predict performance, which, according to Xu (2010), demonstrated that the different contexts had no effect on attrition. Xu (2010) furthermore found that both initial proficiency and language attitudes influenced attrition. However, while initial proficiency was a strong influencing factor for both groups, the effect of language attitudes was only significant for the Chinese learners.

13.5.2 Multilingual attrition in multilinguals

The LAILA (Linguistic awareness in language attrition) and LAILA-BICs (bilingual context) longitudinal studies (both headed by Jessner) were carried out in Tyrol (Austria) and South Tyrol (Italy) between 2011 and 2016 to investigate the development of language skills and metalinguistic abilities in 700 young multilingual adults and to connect these with language attrition processes. More precisely, LAILA and LAILA-BICs studied how skills in school-learned foreign languages (English, Italian, French, Spanish) and meta-/multilingual awareness developed over a period of approximately 18 months of reduced or non-use after learning ceased with the participants' graduation from upper secondary education. All participants had been learning at least two foreign languages at test-time 1 (TT1), with English being the first foreign language (FL1) for most participants. Unlike previous studies on foreign language attrition which typically looked at the development of one language in isolation, LAILA and LAILA-BICS took a multilingual approach informed by the DMM and explored development in all the foreign languages a participant had learned, thus investigating the development of not one but several languages in interaction. The aim of both project studies was to establish a stronger connection between research on language attrition, multilingualism/third language acquisition and meta-/multilingual awareness.

Attrition of linguistic skills was found in both LAILA and LAILA-BICs. However, while signs of attrition have been unquestionably proven for French in both LAILA and LAILA-BICs and for Italian in LAILA, English proficiency in both studies and Italian proficiency in the LAILA-BICS study had improved at test-time 2 (TT2; Jessner and Megens 2016; Török 2017). Török (2017: 196) reflects that "While it is evident why this is the case for the LAILA-BICs participants, given the fact that Italian is the official language of their home country (Italy) and every further type of schooling and most jobs would involve a rather high proficiency in Italian [...], it is rather challenging to postulate why the LAILA participants got better" in their English proficiency and skills.

Although evidence exists in both studies that linguistic skills decreased by TT2, results from the Llama-test, a language aptitude test (Meara 2005), showed a significant increase in students' metalinguistic awareness (MLA) at TT2 (Jessner, 2019). This had already been anticipated after the piloting which had shown a strong increase of crosslinguistic interactions (CLINs) and the use of supporter languages for crosslinguistic consultation, hinting at crosslinguistic awareness (XLA) to be at work, and that MLA remained stable or even improved for most of the participants while attrition took place (Betsch 2011; Megens 2011).

In a LAILA study focusing on attrition in Italian as a third language in the participating Austrian schools (Jessner et al. 2018), minor language attrition was detected in a written task in the use of articles, adjectives and subject-verb-agreement but lexical complexity of written production in Italian after a period of non-use in one-third of the cases had actually increased in TT2. A closer look at information provided in the questionnaires on how students had spent their time during TT1 and TT2 showed that a third of the students had either learned other languages or increased their level of proficiency in Italian and/or English between testing times.

The results are supported by another LAILA study on foreign language attrition in 114 randomly chosen learners (including 20 from the Italian study)

(Jessner, Oberhofer, and Megens, submitted), in which another set of spontaneous oral production tasks was explored. In contrast to their FL1 English where nearly no attrition had been found on all measures of lexical diversity and fluency, two-thirds of the learners showed a significant decrease in the occurrence of self-corrections in their FL2 (Italian and/or French), while one-third had improved significantly on tokens and filled pauses and therefore also showed improvement of fluency.

As discussed by the DMM, language development and use are dependent on the communicative environment and the resulting frequency of productive and/or receptive exchanges in a specific language; i.e., every instance of use activates a particular language system and its subsystems. Yet, and most importantly, at the same time, because of multidirectional crosslinguistic interactions (CLINs) within the complex multilingual system, but also owing to CLIN processes (e.g., cross-linguistic consultation), other language systems and/or subsystems are activated too. From all these CLINs, interdependent with external and individual factors, new properties, in particular metalinguistic and crosslinguistic awareness (MLA and XLA), emerge or in the case of experienced multilinguals become enhanced (Megens 2019). As already shown in other studies (see Jessner, Megens and Graus 2016), MLA and XLA, which form part of a multilingual's metacognitive strategies, can help to cope with "knowledge gaps" due to attrition, reduced access, or if confronted with a new or additional "unknown" language (see Chapter 15, this volume). Please note that research so far has only dealt with certain – often related – languages, but according to the DMM, it is assumed that other language combinations would further support the hypotheses.

13.6 Conclusion and outlook

Throughout the past 35 years, different studies on language attrition with a variety of languages in contact have been carried out, most dealing with L1 attrition. Different theories and hypotheses have been tested and a series of biological, cognitive and external factors, first and foremost "language contact and use" (on a linguistic level), have been found to be influential factors.

Studying language attrition in multilinguals is highly complex since multilingual development and attrition merge many aspects of different language systems and cognitive performance. While eliciting information and drawing patterns and conclusions is easier with two language systems, comparing different findings in research that examines more than two language systems is more challenging due to the complex crosslinguistic interactions and emergent properties such as metalinguistic awareness.

One of the most important contribution that studies on language attrition in multilinguals can make to our understanding of multilingual development is that such development is neither linear nor unidirectional and that it forms part of normal language development. Complexity, fluency and (thus) proficiency in all of a multilingual's languages, the effort to maintain (LME) all languages, language contact and use (both on a linguistic and on a cognitive level), and so on, change and vary throughout a multilingual's lifespan, and these developments again are influenced by many complex crosslinguistic interactions and are paramount to the multilingual's perceived communicative needs (Megens 2019).

Future research should consider multilingualism studies as a research area in its own right, creating its own research framework that accounts for the dynamic and complex nature of multilingual development. For us, the holistic multilingual approach, that is, a DSCT perspective from the stance of the DMM (Herdina and Jessner 2002), as presented in this chapter, presents such a research framework. Accordingly, for us, any study of multilingual development or of language attrition in multilinguals can be considered incomplete if it merely looks at changes in one of the multilingual's languages in isolation. For bilinguals, it is already the case that development of two languages (one attrition, one acquisition) has been investigated, but where multilinguals are concerned, the study of (development with) attrition of two or more languages has, so far, been largely neglected. We suggest that a holistic multilingual approach is needed in order to move forward our understanding of multilingual development and use. In addition, a perspective that takes into account not only linguistic processes but also (meta)cognitive ones will shed more light on our understanding of the complexity and dynamics of language attrition processes.

As discussed in this chapter, metalinguistic and crosslinguistic awareness (MLA and XLA), which form part of a multilingual's metacognitive strategies, can help to cope with "knowledge gaps" due to language attrition. Accordingly, training in and an explicit focus on MLA and XLA, i.e., making learners aware of their own metacognitive knowledge (Jessner 2006: 128) and encouraging them to use the languages with a variety of people and in different contexts during and after institutional language learning (Allgäuer-Hackl and Megens, in preparation; Jessner, Allgäuer-Hackl, and Hofer 2016), may facilitate language maintenance (effort) and counteract (multilingual) language attrition processes.

References

Allgäuer-Hackl, Elisabeth & Manon Megens. (in preparation). An applied perspective on multicompetence and plurilingual proficiency approaches to foreign language learning and teaching. In Anna Krulatz, Georgios Neokleous & Anne Dahl (eds.), *Theoretical and applied perspectives on teaching foreign languages in multilingual settings*. Bristol: Multilingual Matters.

Bahrick, Harry P. 1984. Fifty years of second language attrition: Implications for programmatic research. *The Modern Language Journal* 68(2). 105–118.

Bardovi-Harlig, Kathleen & David Stringer. 2010. Variables in second language attrition: Advancing the state of the art. *Studies in Second Language Acquisition* 32(1). 1–45.

Betsch, Jeanette. 2011. *L2 and L3 attrition after four months?: The role of metalinguistic awareness and implications for teaching*. Innsbruck: University of Innsbruck MA thesis.

Cohen, Andrew D. 1989. Attrition in the productive lexicon of two Portuguese third language speakers. *Studies in Second Language Acquisition* 11(2). 135–149.

Cook, Vivian J. (ed.). 2003. *Effects of the second language on the first*. Clevedon: Multilingual Matters.

Cook, Vivian J. 2016. Premises of multi-competence. In Vivian J. Cook & Wei Li (eds.), *The Cambridge handbook of linguistic multi-competence*, 1–25. Cambridge: Cambridge University Press.

De Bot, Kees. 2004. The multilingual lexicon: Modelling selection and control. *International Journal of Multilingualism* 1(1). 17–32.

De Bot, Kees. 2007. Dynamic systems theory, lifespan development and language attrition. In Barbara Köpke, Monika S. Schmid, Merel Keijzer & Susan Dostert (eds.), *Language attrition: Theoretical perspectives* (Studies in Bilingualism 33), 53–68. Amsterdam & Philadelphia: John Benjamins.

De Bot, Kees & Michael Clyne. 1989. Language reversion revisited. *Studies in Second Language Acquisition* 11(2). 167–177.

De Bot, Kees & Madeleine Hulsen. 2002. Language attrition: Test, self-assessments and perceptions. In Vivian Cook (ed.), *Portraits of the L2 user*, 253–274. Clevedon: Multilingual Matters.

De Bot, Kees, Vanessa Martens & Saskia Stoessel. 2004. Finding residual lexical knowledge: The "Savings" approach to testing vocabulary. *International Journal of Bilingualism* 8(3). 373–382.

Ecke, Peter. 2004. Language attrition and theories of forgetting: A cross-disciplinary review. *International Journal of Bilingualism* 8(3). 321–354.

Ecke, Peter & Christopher J. Hall. 2013. Tracking tip-of-the-tongue states in a multilingual speaker: Evidence of attrition or instability in lexical systems? *International Journal of Bilingualism* 17(6). 734–751.

Fase, Willem, Koen Jaspaert & Sjaak Kroon. 1992. Maintenance and loss of minority languages: Introductory remarks. In Willem Fase, Koen Jaspaert & Sjaak Kroon (eds.), *Maintenance and loss of minority languages* (Studies in Bilingualism 1), 3–13. Amsterdam & Philadelphia: John Benjamins.

'Five Graces Group', Clay Beckner, Richard Blythe, Joan Bybee, Morton H. Christiansen, William Croft, Nick C. Ellis, John Holland, Jinyun Ke, Diane Larsen-Freeman & Tom

Schoenemann. 2009. Language is a complex adaptive system: Position paper. *Language Learning* 59. 1–26.

Grendel, Marjon. 1993. *Verlies en herstel van lexicale kennis* [Attrition and recovery of lexical knowledge]. Nijmegen: University of Nijmegen dissertation.

Grosjean, François. 2001. The bilingual's language modes. In Janet L. Nicol (ed.), *One mind, two languages: Bilingual language processing*, 1–22. Oxford: Blackwell.

Herdina, Philip & Ulrike Jessner. 2002. *A dynamic model of multilingualism: Perspectives of change in psycholinguistics*. Clevedon: Multilingual Matters.

Herdina, Philip & Ulrike Jessner. 2013. The implications of language attrition for dynamic systems theory: Next steps and consequences. *International Journal of Bilingualism* 17 (6). 752–756.

Hulsen, Madeleine E. H. 2000. *Language loss and processing: Three generations of Dutch migrants in New Zealand*. Nijmegen: Catholic University of Nijmegen dissertation.

Hyltenstam, Kenneth & Christopher Stroud. 1996. Language maintenance. In Hans Goebl, Peter H. Nelde, Zdeněk Starý & Wolfgang Wölck (eds.), *Kontaklinguistik* 1, 567–578. Berlin: De Gruyter.

Jessner, Ulrike. 2003. A dynamic approach to language attrition in multilinguals. In Vivian Cook (ed.), *Effects of the second language on the first*, 234–247. Clevedon: Multilingual Matters.

Jessner, Ulrike. 2006. *Linguistic awareness in multilinguals: English as a third language*. Edinburgh: Edinburgh University Press.

Jessner, Ulrike. 2008. A DST model of multilingualism and the role of metalinguistic awareness. *Modern Language Journal* 92(2). 270–284.

Jessner, Ulrike. 2018. Metacognition in multilingual learning. A DMM perspective. In Åsta Haukås, Camilla Bjørke & Magne Dypedahl (eds.), *Metacognition in language learning and teaching*, 31–47. London: Routledge.

Jessner, Ulrike. 2019. Metalinguistic awareness and multilingual development. In Jeroen Darquennes, Joe Salmons & Wim Vandenbussche (eds.), *Handbook of language contact*, 221–232. New York: Mouton de Gruyter.

Jessner, Ulrike & Manon Megens. 2016. Multilingual awareness in processes of language attrition. Paper presented at the 3rd International Conference on Language Attrition (ICLA3), University of Essex, 5–7 July.

Jessner, Ulrike, Elisabeth Allgäuer-Hackl & Barbara Hofer. 2016. Emerging multilingual awareness in educational contexts: From theory to practice. *The Canadian Modern Language Review* 72(2). 157–182.

Jessner, Ulrike, Manon Megens & Stefanie Graus. 2016. Crosslinguistic influence in third language acquisition. In Rosa Alonso Alonso (ed.), *Crosslinguistic influence in second language acquisition*, 193–124. Clevedon: Multilingual Matters.

Jessner, Ulrike, Kathrin Oberhofer & Manon Megens. (submitted). The attrition of school-learned foreign languages: A multilingual perspective. *Applied Psycholinguistics*.

Jessner, Ulrike, Claudia Pellegrini, Claudia Cossarini, Valentina Török & Judith Santer. 2018. Lexical processing and attrition processes in L3 production. *Rivista di Psicolinguistica Applicata* 2. 17–36.

Köpke, Barbara. 1999. *L'attrition de la première langue chez le bilingue tardif: Implications pour l'étude psycholinguistique du bilinguisme*. Toulouse: University of Toulouse dissertation.

Köpke, Barbara. 2007. Language attrition at the crossroads of brain, mind, and society. In Barbara Köpke, Monika S. Schmid, Merel Keijzer & Susan Dostert (eds.), *Language attrition: Theoretical perspectives* (Studies in Bilingualism 33), 9–38. Amsterdam & Philadelphia: John Benjamins.

Köpke, Barbara, & Monika S. Schmid. 2004. Language attrition: The next phase. In Monika S. Schmid, Barbara Köpke, Merel Keijzer, & Lina Weilemar (eds.), *First language attrition: Interdisciplinary perspectives on methodological issues* (Studies of Bilingualism 28), 1–43. Amsterdam & Philadelphia: John Benjamins.

Lambert, Richard D. & Barbara F. Freed (eds.). 1982. *The loss of language skills*. Rowley: Newbury House.

Larsen-Freeman, Diane & Lynne Cameron. 2008. *Complex systems and applied linguistics*. Oxford: Oxford University Press.

Meara, Paul. 2005. *Llama language aptitude tests*. Swansea: Lognostics.

Megens, Manon. 2011. *Language attrition after four months of non-use?: Emergence of lexical attrition in the English L2 oral production of multilingual learners*. Innsbruck: University of Innsbruck MA thesis.

Megens, Manon. 2019. *Foreign language attrition, crosslinguistic interaction and crosslinguistic awareness in multilingual young adults*. Innsbruck: University of Innsbruck dissertation.

Megens, Manon & Ulrike Jessner. 2016. Multilingual awareness in processes of language attrition. Paper presented at the Association for Language Awareness (ALA) Conference 2016: Languages for life: Educational, Professional and Social Context. Vienna University of Economics and Business, 19–22 July.

Mehotcheva, Teodora. 2010. *After the fiesta is over: Foreign language attrition of Spanish in Dutch and German Erasmus students*. Groningen: University of Groningen dissertation.

Nakuma, Constancio. 1997. A method for measuring the attrition of communicative competence: A pilot study with Spanish L3 subjects. *Applied Psycholinguistics* 18(2). 219–235.

Olshtain, Elite. 1986. The attrition of English as a second language. In Bert Weltens, Kees de Bot & Theo van Els (eds.), *Language attrition in progress* (Studies on Language Acquisition 2), 187–204. Dordrecht: Foris.

Opitz, Conny. 2013. A dynamic perspective on late bilinguals' linguistic development in an L2 environment. *International Journal of Bilingualism* 17(6). 701–715.

Paradis, Michel. 2004. *A neurolinguistic theory of bilingualism*. Amsterdam & Philadelphia: John Benjamins.

Schmid, Monika S. 2007. The role of L1 use for L1 attrition. In Barbara Köpke, Monika S. Schmid, Merel Keijzer & Susan Dostert (eds.), *Language attrition: Theoretical perspectives* (Studies in Bilingualism 33), 135–168. Amsterdam & Philadelphia: John Benjamins.

Schmid, Monika S. 2013. Attrition and multilingualism. In Carol A. Chapelle (ed.), *The encyclopedia of applied linguistics*, 281–290. Oxford: Blackwell.

Schmid, Monika S. 2016. First language attrition. *Language Teaching* 49(2). 186–212.

Seton, Bregtje & Monika S. Schmid. 2016. Language attrition and multicompetence. In Vivian J. Cook & Wei Li (eds.), *The Cambridge handbook of linguistic multicompetence*, 338–354. Cambridge: Cambridge University Press.

Schmid, Monika S. & Barbara Köpke. 2017. The relevance of first language attrition to theories of bilingual development. *Linguistic Approaches to Bilingualism* 7 (6).637–667.

Török, Valentina K. 2017. *Approaching the M(ultilingualism)-factor: On the development of strategic processing in multilinguals*. Innsbruck: University of Innsbruck dissertation.

Weltens, Bert. 1989. *The attrition of French as a foreign language* (Studies on Language Acquisition 6). Dordrecht: Foris.

Weltens, Bert & Marjon Grendel. 1993. Attrition of vocabulary knowledge. In Robert Schreuder & Bert Weltens (eds.), *The bilingual lexicon* (Studies in Bilingualism 6), 135–156. Amsterdam & Philadelphia: John Benjamins.

Weltens, Bert, Theo van Els & Erik Schils. 1989. The long-term retention of French by Dutch students. *Studies in Second Language Acquisition* 11(2). 205–216.

Xu, Xiaoyan. 2010. *English language attrition and retention in Chinese and Dutch university students*. Groningen: University of Groningen dissertation.

Part IV: **Differences between Bilingualism and Multilingualism**

Simona Montanari
14 Facilitated Language Learning in Multilinguals

14.1 Introduction

Research in the last three decades suggests that multilingualism is associated with a variety of advantages both in the cognitive domain, where knowing more than one language has been linked to better executive function including higher selective attention and inhibitory control (Bialystok and Barac 2013), and in the linguistic domain, where speakers of multiple languages display greater metalinguistic awareness and develop this awareness at an earlier age than monolinguals (see Chapter 15, this volume, for a review). It has been argued that such cognitive and linguistic advantages result in facilitated novel language learning in speakers who already know two languages as compared to monolingual learners. Indeed, when learning a new language, multilinguals are typically better than learners who have only had experience with one language (for reviews see Cenoz 2013; Hirosh and Degani 2018). Research has found evidence of facilitated novel language learning among multilinguals both in the areas typically assessed in the foreign language classroom – listening, speaking, reading and writing – and in the different language domains, including phonetics and phonology, vocabulary, grammar, and literacy. In the next sections I will first review early studies on novel language learning in multilinguals, which have focused on the acquisition of a third language (L3) in the classroom. The following section presents more recent research, which has turned to novel language learning among environment-based multilinguals, that is, individuals who have learned multiple languages naturally and not only as a result of formal teaching. Finally, the last section examines the factors that might make multilinguals better language learners, in particular, the direct and indirect effects of multilingualism on the acquisition of new languages.

14.2 Early studies: L3 learning in the classroom

Early studies that compared novel language learning among monolinguals and multilinguals focused on L2 or L3 acquisition in the classroom. Most of

---

Simona Montanari, California State University, Los Angeles (CA), U.S.A.

https://doi.org/10.1515/9781501507984-014

these investigations involved students educated bilingually in Canada and Spain and focused on their attainment in core foreign language components, that is, listening, speaking, reading, writing. Bild and Swain (1989) and Swain et al. (1990), for instance, compared the level of French proficiency attained by English-speaking monolingual and bilingual students (with different language backgrounds) controlling for different variables including sex, age, school achievement, parental education and occupation, and English and French proficiency. The results indicated a strong advantage in the learning of French as L3 for bilingual students, irrespective of the linguistic relatedness between French and the languages the bilinguals knew. Similar findings were reported by Cenoz and Valencia (1994) in the Basque Country, who found that bilingualism significantly improved different measures of English L3 achievement among Basque-Spanish bilingual students as compared to monolinguals. Lasagabaster (2000) and Sanz (2000) replicated Cenoz and Valencia's (1994) findings in other regions of Spain, concluding that bilinguals who live in additive bilingual environments and speak, besides the majority language, a minority language with official status in the community (as the bilingual students in Spain) obtain higher levels of proficiency in an L3 as compared to monolinguals.

However, some studies conducted with bilingual immigrant children in other regions of Europe in the same years failed to find a multilingual advantage in novel language learning. For instance, Jaspaert and Lemmens (1990), who studied French monolinguals and Italian-French immigrant children learning Dutch as an L3 in Belgium, found no significant differences in the children's attainment in Dutch. Similarly, Sanders and Meijers (1995) reported no differences in the acquisition of English as an L3 between immigrant Turkish- or Arabic-Dutch bilingual learners and monolingual Dutch learners in the Netherlands. Also in the context of Sweden, no differences were found in English L3 proficiency between monolingual and bilingual students (Balke-Aurell and Lindblad 1982). Overall, these mixed findings were interpreted as stemming from contextual variables such as socioeconomic and socio-educational status. As put by Cenoz (2008: 220):

> The results concerning general aspects of proficiency indicate that bilingualism has a positive effect on third language acquisition when L3 acquisition takes place in additive contexts and bilinguals have acquired literacy skills in both their languages ... However, bilingualism does not always result in more efficient third language learning because socioeconomic and socioeducational variables can also play an important role. In fact, the sociolinguistic context in which the research takes place is very important, and third language acquisition is a complex phenomenon affected by a large number of individual and contextual factors.

14.3 Recent studies: Novel language learning by environment-based multilinguals

More recent studies have examined novel language learning not by classroom-based multilinguals, individuals who have learned their L3 through formal instruction, but by environment-based multilinguals, that is, individuals who have learned their languages through informal interactions in the environment. It has been argued indeed that the superior performance observed for experienced (i.e. bilingual) versus inexperienced (i.e. monolingual) language learners could have resulted from a transfer of learning strategies developed in the classroom, and not from bilingualism per se. Although most studies have focused on vocabulary learning, research has also been conducted in other language domains including phonetics and phonology, grammar, and literacy. In this section, I will review these studies as well as the possible interpretations of their findings.

14.3.1 Phonetics and phonology

The majority of research on facilitated novel language learning by environment-based multilinguals has examined vocabulary acquisition. A few studies, nonetheless, have also explored this issue with respect to phonetic discrimination and phonological learning, yielding mixed results. An early study by Rabinovitch and Parver (1966) (as reported by Antoniou et al. 2015) found that bilingual children had an advantage when discriminating non-native Russian contrasts as opposed to monolinguals. Similarly, Cohen, Tucker, and Lambert (1967) reported better perception and production of non-native initial phoneme sequences in bilingual than in monolingual children. Enomoto (1994) also found an advantage for multilinguals over monolinguals with respect to the discrimination of Japanese singleton versus geminate stops. Overall, these findings were interpreted as evidence that more extensive language learning experience enhances perceptual sensitivity. In particular, L3 language learners may have a larger repertoire of articulatory gestures and increased perceptual knowledge than L2 speakers; they may also have more phonological awareness and cognitive flexibility, which might promote their acquisition of the sound systems of additional languages (Gut 2010).

However, other studies have failed to find an advantage among multilinguals in the perception of non-native sounds. For example, Davine, Tucker, and Lambert (1971), who compared third- and fourth-grade students who were receiving monolingual and bilingual instruction, revealed no significant differences between monolingual and bilingual children with respect to their ability to discriminate phoneme sequences. Similarly, Werker (1986), who investigated the perceptual ability of monolinguals and multilinguals to discriminate a Salish and a Hindi contrast, found equal performance for the two groups, concluding that general multilingual experience does not help maintain the perceptual flexibility required to discriminate phonetic contrasts in a new language.

Recent research has shown that the benefit of language experience on phonetic/phonological learning may only be seen by using more sophisticated methods and paradigms. Trembley and Sabourin (2012), for instance, examined the pre- and post-training discrimination of a non-native contrast in English monolinguals, English-French bilinguals, and multilinguals. The findings revealed no difference among the groups before training. However, bilinguals and multilinguals' performance improved with training. Moreover, comparisons at post-test showed a significant advantage for multilinguals over the monolingual participants. The results were interpreted as evidence that multilinguals and bilinguals have enhanced speech perception abilities compared to monolinguals, but these might be due to superior learning abilities.

Furthermore, Trembley (2010), who used both behavioral and neurophysiological methods to examine the same issue, found that while behavioral data showed only a post-training bilingual advantage, neurophysiological data from event-related potentials (ERPs), which reflect electric brain responses to stimuli, demonstrated a facilitative effect for language experience both before and after training. Therefore, it is possible that the mixed results obtained in past studies may derive from the fact that behavioral methods are simply not sophisticated enough to detect differences between monolinguals and multilinguals. Neurophysiological methods, on the other hand, are more objective than other types of measures influenced by voluntary processes and thus may be potentially more informative of a multilingual advantage in novel phonetic discrimination.

In addition, it has been argued that non-native phonetic learning may be facilitated not only by previous linguistic experience but by a variety of other factors, including language relatedness and sound difficulty. Antoniou et al. (2015) tested adults' learning of novel phonetic contrasts (from an artificial language) modifying their difficulty level and degree of similarity to contrasts in the subjects' native languages. In a first experiment, where English monolinguals were compared to Mandarin-English bilinguals on their ability to discriminate Mandarin-like (retroflex) and English-like (fricative voicing) phonetic contrasts, the bilinguals did better than monolinguals on both types of contrasts. In addition, both groups did better with the learning of the easier retroflex contrasts. In the second experiment, which also included Korean-English bilinguals and also tested the acquisition of Korean-like phonetic contrasts (lenition), both bilingual groups outperformed English monolinguals on the learning of the Mandarin-like contrasts. However, only the Korean-English bilinguals showed an advantage in the discrimination of the more difficult Korean-like (lenition) phonetic contrasts. The results were interpreted as evidence that, relative to monolinguals, bilinguals show a general advantage in novel phonetic learning when contrasts are universally easy. However, phonetic similarity to L1 facilitates the learning of universally difficult contrasts.

To summarize, extant research suggests that there may be a bilingual advantage in novel phonetic/phonological learning, but this is mediated by the difficulty of novel sounds and by the similarity of these sounds to those in the languages already known (discussed further in section 14.4).

14.3.2 Word learning in children and adults

A large body of research has explored whether multilingualism is associated with facilitated learning of novel words both in children and in adults. Novel word learning in young children has been typically investigated in the context of the mutual exclusivity assumption. This assumption, initially postulated for monolingual learners, posits that by 16–18 months of age, children assume that there are one-to-one relations between linguistic forms and their meanings; that is, children assign a new word they hear to an unknown referent rather than to one for which they already have a label (Markman 1990). Studies have therefore examined whether children growing up with more than one language are more flexible in following this assumption when learning new words and whether this flexibility can result in facilitated novel word learning.

Byers-Heinlein and Werker (2013) specifically investigated whether infants' knowledge of translation equivalents (words with the same meaning across languages) affected their use of the mutual exclusivity assumption while learning new words. Seventeen-/eighteen-month-old English-Chinese bilingual infants were compared to monolingual English-speaking infants in a disambiguation task that required them to associate a novel label to either a novel or a familiar item. The results showed that bilingual infants who understood fewer translation equivalents preferred novel items – and hence applied the mutual exclusivity assumption – to a larger extent than other bilingual children who knew many translation equivalents. These results suggest that the specific experience of having multiple labels for the same referent directly influences how children learn new words. Thus, multilingualism appears to influence the principles that guide and constrain early word learning.

A subsequent study found that while young bilingual preschoolers may still rely on mutual exclusivity when learning new words, such reliance decreases with age and with accumulated vocabulary knowledge. Kalashnikova, Mattock, and Monaghan (2014) investigated differences between monolingual and bilingual children in their acceptance of two novel labels for a single, unfamiliar referent. Three-to-five-year-old children completed two tasks where successful word learning depended on either the use of the mutual exclusivity assumption or the acceptance of two labels for the same referent. The results showed that while all children resorted to the mutual exclusivity assumption early on, older bilinguals were better able than older monolinguals to assign two novel words to a single unfamiliar referent, that is, to learn new words. These results suggest that reduced reliance on the mutual exclusivity assumption emerges once children have had enough experience with learning translation equivalents and, overall, that multiple language experience facilitates novel word learning.

Kaushanskaya, Gross, and Buac (2014) asked whether reduced reliance on mutual exclusivity is evident even in classroom bilinguals who have had more limited experience in two languages. In particular, the authors compared 5-to-7-year-old monolingual English-speaking children to native-English peers who had been learning Spanish for two years in a dual language program. The children were asked to assign a novel word to either an unfamiliar referent for which no word existed (such as a type of alien) or to a familiar referent for which a word was already known (such as an animal). While the monolingual and bilingual children did not differ on non-linguistic task-shifting and verbal short-term memory measures, the classroom-based bilinguals showed superior word learning performance. However, the bilingual advantage was found only for familiar referents, suggesting that this advantage exists only in learning situations that are similar to those previously experienced. That is, extensive practice with mapping new labels to known referents in the classroom allows classroom bilinguals to directly transfer this experience to a new learning situation.

While Kaushanskaya, Gross, and Buac (2014) attributed the bilingual advantage to the overlap between prior experience and the learning situation, Yoshida et al. (2011) interpreted facilitated word learning in multilinguals as originating from increased executive (i.e., attentional) control. The authors compared the performance of 3-year-old vocabulary-matched bilinguals and monolinguals in an artificial adjective-learning task as well as in a non-linguistic task that measured attentional control. The results showed again a bilingual advantage in children's ability to not only learn novel adjectives but also in the attentional control task. The authors argued that learning novel adjectives depends on attentional control because children must inhibit the typical tendency to interpret novel labels as nouns (e.g., Markman 1990). Indeed, children's performance in the two tasks was positively correlated, suggesting that better attentional control may also result in superior word learning performance.

Overall, these studies confirm a multilingual advantage in novel word learning not only for environment-based but also for classroom-based multilingual children. This advantage has been attributed to the overlap between previous experiences and the novel learning task, and thus to the transfer of learning strategies across situations, and to the increased executive control abilities brought about by multilingualism.

As with children, research with adults has revealed facilitated vocabulary learning among multilinguals, with the advantage increasing with the number of languages spoken. A seminal study by Papagno and Vallar (1995) compared multilinguals (speakers of Italian and two or three other languages) to bilinguals on the acquisition of Russian non-native words as well as on a paired associate learning task where the participants had to learn the pairing of two Italian words. The results showed that while the two groups did not differ in the paired associate learning task, the multilinguals had a superior level of performance than the bilinguals in learning new Russian words. The authors concluded that multilingualism results in a novel word learning advantage that is possibly due to superior phonological memory. Indeed, multilinguals showed significantly higher digit span performance and did better than bilinguals in a non-word repetition task, and their phonological memory as assessed by these tasks was significantly and positively correlated with their acquisition of non-native Russian words.

Papagno and Vallar's (1995) study fueled a wealth of research on novel word learning in speakers of a different number of languages. A few of these studies focused on the acquisition of words in real non-native languages (van Hell and Candia Mahn 1997 in Spanish or Dutch; Keshavarz and Astaneh 2004 in English), also documenting a multilingual advantage. Nonetheless, more recent investigations turned to the impact of language experience on novel word learning using artificial languages. In two seminal (2009) studies, Kaushanskaya and Marian provided additional evidence of a multilingual advantage in novel word learning, showing, however, that this advantage might not derive from increased phonological short-term memory.

In particular, Kaushanskaya and Marian (2009a) compared environment-based English-Spanish bilinguals to English monolinguals on the acquisition of artificially constructed novel words accompanied by English translations. The words were learned in two conditions: in the first, the subjects heard the new word and saw its English translation; in the second condition, the subjects heard the new word but also saw its form spelled using English orthography together with its translation. Thus, in the second condition, the novel words overlapped with English orthographically (they were spelled using the Roman alphabet as in English) but diverged from English phonologically (i.e., they were based on different sets of phonemes than in English). The results documented superior performance for the bilinguals in both conditions, despite the fact that the two groups demonstrated similar phonological short-term memory. In the second condition, the orthographic information presented during learning, which was based on English orthography, interfered with encoding of novel words in monolinguals but not in bilinguals. The authors interpreted this finding as evidence that prior exposure to more than one language exposes the learner to competition between phonology and orthography, reducing interference in subsequent learning situations and facilitating novel language learning.

In a follow-up study, Kaushanskaya and Marian (2009b) showed that the multilingual word learning advantage does not originate from prior experience with mapping competing phonologies into a single orthographic system. For instance, a comparison of monolingual English speakers, early English-Spanish bilinguals, and early English-Mandarin bilinguals showed that both bilingual groups outperformed the monolingual group in novel language learning. Since English and Mandarin have different orthographies, these findings suggest that multilingualism facilitates the acquisition of new words irrespective of the degree of overlap between writing systems. The authors speculated that early experience with two phonological systems might lead to a richer and more flexible phonological system and hence to more efficient encoding of unfamiliar phonological information.

Other recent investigations that have documented a multilingual advantage in vocabulary learning have attributed it to other factors. For instance, Kaushanskaya and Rechtzigel (2012) argued that it is increased experience with associating two labels with the same concept, and thus a wider activation of the lexical-semantic system (which involves activation of two lexical-semantic networks for bilinguals) that facilitates word learning. The study, which compared bilinguals to monolinguals' acquisition of new words paired with concrete or abstract English translations, found indeed a multilingual advantage only for words paired with concrete concepts. The authors speculated that translation equivalents associated with concrete referents enjoy a larger semantic overlap across languages and cause more activation of the bilingual's lexical-semantic network than equivalents associated with abstract concepts. Thus, it is the organization and activation patterns of the lexical-semantic network that may promote word learning in multilinguals.

Furthermore, in a later study, Kaushanskaya, Yoo, and Van Hecke (2013) showed that the multilingual advantage in word learning may derive from the transfer of previously-developed learning strategies (as also argued for children,

Kaushanskaya, Gross, and Buac 2014). The research, which compared English native speakers with different degrees of Spanish proficiency on the acquisition of phonologically familiar or unfamiliar novel words paired with either familiar or unfamiliar referents, found that native English speakers with higher levels of Spanish experience did better than less experienced Spanish learners only when phonologically unfamiliar novel words were paired with familiar referents. As in Kaushanskaya, Gross, and Buac (2014), these findings were interpreted as evidence that not only full bilingualism but also experience with a foreign language can facilitate novel word learning, but only in situations that have been experienced before, such as when mapping phonologically unfamiliar words to known concepts as in the foreign language classroom. Therefore, as argued for children, the degree of overlap between the learning situation and the speakers' prior learning experience is largely responsible for the bilingual advantage in vocabulary learning.

Finally, studies that have found a multilingual advantage in adult word learning have also attributed it to enhanced cognitive control abilities, similar to what has been documented during development (Yoshida et al. 2011). Bartolotti and Marian (2012) examined the effect of bilingualism on the ability to control native-language interference by comparing monolinguals and bilinguals on the acquisition of an artificial language designed to elicit between-language competition. Using eye-tracking and mouse-tracking to measure cross-language interference during a spoken comprehension task after the learning of the new language, the study found that monolinguals looked more, and for a longer period of time, at cross-language competitors than bilinguals. Similarly, their mouse movements were more attracted to native language competitors than bilinguals, who instead attended to competitors and control items to a similar extent. The authors speculated that bilinguals manage cross-linguistic interference more effectively than monolinguals. Thus, experience with more than one language, which involves the parallel activation of multiple language systems, may improve the ability to suppress competition from known languages, facilitating novel language learning.

To summarize, the adult literature on vocabulary learning suggests a robust multilingual advantage. As with children, this advantage could be due to a variety of factors, including increased phonological short-term memory (Papagno and Vallar 1995), a richer and more flexible phonological system (Kaushanskaya and Marian 2009a, 2009b), a wider activation of the lexical-semantic system (Kaushanskaya and Rechtzigel 2012), the direct transfer of prior learning strategies and experiences (Kaushanskaya, Yoo, and Van Hecke 2013), or enhanced language management abilities (Bartolotti and Marian 2012).

14.3.3 Grammar

Research that has compared grammatical/syntactic learning in multilinguals as compared to monolinguals has been surprisingly scarce. In addition, the few studies that have examined this issue have employed different methodologies and populations; they have adopted opposing theoretical perspectives, and they have been more interested in the impact of known languages on the acquisition of additional syntactic systems in terms of cross-linguistic influence rather than in terms of monolingual-multilingual differences.

Early investigations were laboratory studies with artificial linguistic systems that found greater flexibility in multilingual learners than monolinguals in the use of learning strategies (Nation and McLaughlin 1986; Nayak et al. 1990). In particular, Nation and McLaughlin (1986) compared monolinguals, bilinguals, and multilinguals on their learning of a system of consonant letter strings, the structure of which was determined by a set of rules. The participants were visually exposed to these strings with either no instructions (implicit condition) or by being told that the system followed specific rules which they had to discover (explicit condition). A grammaticality judgment test after training revealed that while all subjects performed similarly in the explicit condition, the multilinguals showed superior performance than both the bilinguals and monolinguals in finding the rules that determined the structure of the letter strings in the implicit condition. In a following study, Nayak et al. (1990) similarly found that multilinguals outperformed monolinguals when having to identify the word order rules in an artificial language in which words were depicted as specific geometric figures. In both studies, the authors concluded that multilinguals have an advantage for grammar learning over monolinguals because they have increased grammatical sensitivity and might be better able to allocate processing resources to learn syntactic rules.

A few year later, Klein (1995) compared grammatical learning in monolinguals and multilinguals in the context of a generative comparison between L2 and L3 acquisition. The study tested both English lexical learning (mastery of specific verbs and their prepositional complements) and syntactic learning (preposition stranding) in students learning English as either their L2, L3 or L4 in the U.S. The results showed that the multilingual students outperformed L2 learners in both English constructions, clearly revealing a multilingual advantage in the acquisition of additional syntactic systems. The author attributed the findings to multilinguals' increased metalinguistic skills, enhanced lexical knowledge, and less conservative learning strategies. Experience with multiple languages might indeed promote the use of specific learning strategies that free up cognitive resources to process other aspects of the input (as argued by

Nation and McLaughlin 1986 and Nayak et al. 1990), thereby accelerating the acquisition of additional grammatical systems. Indeed, this was Kemp's (2007) speculation when interpreting the findings of her study on multilinguals' grammatical learning strategies. While the author did not compare multilinguals and monolinguals' performance while learning novel grammar, Kemp (2007) asked 144 multilinguals speaking between 2 to 12 languages to reflect on and report the strategies they employed while learning and using the grammatical rules of new languages. The study found that multilinguals applied more grammar-learning strategies and became faster at learning grammar the more languages they knew, even when those languages were not typologically related. These results were interpreted as evidence that multilingualism may promote the automatization of these strategies, facilitating the learning of additional grammatical systems and languages.

Interestingly, recent research suggests that the multilingual advantage in grammatical learning persists even in old age. Cox (2017) tested English-Spanish older bilinguals (all > 60 years old) and English monolinguals on their learning of basic Latin morphosyntax with or without explicit instruction (i.e., grammatical explanations). Four aspects of learning were assessed: written sentence interpretation, auditory sentence interpretation, grammaticality judgment, and written sentence production. The results showed that the bilinguals did better than the monolinguals on all sentence interpretation tasks in both conditions. In addition, for grammaticality judgment and written sentence production, the bilinguals in the explicit instruction condition tended to outperform the monolinguals in the implicit instruction condition, although the two groups performed the same when they received grammatical explanations. Overall, the findings were interpreted as evidence of superior learning of additional grammars in bilinguals compared to monolinguals, at least under some conditions.

It is possible that one of these conditions is literacy rather than explicit instruction or oral bilingual abilities. Indeed, most studies that have examined novel grammatical learning in multilinguals as compared to monolinguals have typically included participants who were not only bilingual but also biliterate. Sanz (2000), who compared Catalan-Spanish biliterate bilinguals to Spanish monolinguals on tests of English grammar and vocabulary in the context of classroom-based L3 acquisition in Spain, found better L3 performance for the bilingual/biliterate group. However, her later study (Sanz 2007), which focused on the role of oral and written proficiency in bilinguals' two languages in predicting L3 learning, found that grammatical abilities were correlated with balanced biliteracy skills but not with oral bilingual abilities. In other words, it was the ability to read and write in two languages – but not to speak them – that facilitated novel syntactic learning. Other studies have shown that multiliteracy facilitates syntactic learning in additional languages (Abu-Rabia and Sanitsky 2010). However, few investigations have specifically looked at the direct link between multilingualism alone (and not multiliteracy) and grammatical learning in L2 and L3 because bilingual participants have also been typically biliterate.

Rather than investigating the role of oral multilingualism on novel grammatical learning, many studies have focused on the role of previous linguistic knowledge on the acquisition of new morphosyntactic systems. For instance, Leung (2005) compared the acquisition of articles in French by two groups of speakers of article-less languages: the first group included Chinese-L1 speakers who also knew English as L2; the second group comprised of monolingual Vietnamese speakers. The participants were tested on the use of articles in obligatory contexts and the appropriate use of definiteness when needed. The results showed that Chinese learners did better than the Vietnamese learners in both aspects, despite the fact that both groups spoke languages without articles and definiteness. The author interpreted the results as strong evidence of a multilingual advantage in novel grammatical learning rooted in the knowledge of earlier acquired language systems. Unlike in L2 acquisition, where influence from a previously acquired language can only come from L1, cross-linguistic influence in L3 acquisition can occur from the L1 or from the L2 or from both L1 and L2, possibly adding to the repertoire of syntactic rules and constructions that can be successfully used in L3.

It is specifically in the direction of cross-linguistic influence that much research on L3 grammatical learning has turned to (see Chapter 15, this volume, for a detailed review). While this research has not directly examined monolingual-multilingual differences in the learning of additional morphosyntactic systems, its focus on the role of language typology on the acquisition of L3 morphosyntax has revealed important insights into the multilingual advantage debate. Rothman and colleagues, for instance, have conducted extensive work that has shown that the learning of L3 morphosyntax is strongly influenced by the (psycho)typology of previously learned languages. Rothman and Cabrelli Amaro (2010), in particular, compared bilinguals (both with L1 English and L2 advanced Spanish) and monolinguals (L1 English) on their performance with null/overt subjects and pronouns in non-native Italian or French. The results showed that the L3 learners performed differently than their L2 counterparts because they transferred the null-subject properties of Spanish, their L2, on the acquisition of the new language. In the case of Italian, such transfer facilitated acquisition – and bilinguals outperformed monolinguals – because Italian is a null-subject language as Spanish. However, in the case of French, such transfer did not accelerate learning because French is a non-null-subject language as English. These results point to the complex relationship between multilingualism and the acquisition of new morphosyntactic systems and to the strong influence of the (psycho)typology of previously learned languages on novel language learning.

Recent research has also shown, as in the area of phonetics/phonology, that the benefit of language experience on novel grammatical learning may only be seen when using paradigms that examine the neural correlates of language processing such as event-related potential (ERP) measures. ERPs can reveal qualitative differences in how linguistic information is processed, including in the processing of lexical and grammatical features of an L2, that may not be evident when using behavioral paradigms. Indeed, Grey et al. (2017), who used both behavioral and neurophysiological methods to examine pre- and post-practice syntactic processing in an artificial language in monolinguals and multilinguals, found that while behavioral measures failed to reveal differences between the two groups, Chinese-English bilinguals displayed distinct ERP patterns than monolinguals. In particular, at limited proficiency, only the bilinguals showed a P600 – a neural correlate of native syntactic processing – in response to word order violations. At high proficiency, both groups showed P600s for word order violations; however, the monolinguals also showed a neural pattern – anterior positivity – not typically attested in native syntactic processing. The authors interpreted these findings as evidence that bilinguals process novel languages differently than monolinguals; specifically, they may more rapidly develop the neural processes found in native speakers of languages – even without showing significantly better performance in behavioral tasks.

To summarize, research conducted so far in the area of novel grammatical learning among multilinguals is limited and diverse in methods, approaches, and interpretations. While the extant studies suggest a multilingual advantage in the acquisition of additional morphosyntactic systems, the same investigations point to the importance of other variables, including language relatedness and literacy, that have a profound effect on the mastery of new grammars and new languages. In addition, as also argued in section 14.3.1, recent research points to the need for new methodological approaches – such as neurophysiological measures – to better understand the effects of multilingualism on novel grammatical learning (discussed further in section 14.4).

14.3.4 Literacy

The role of multilingualism on learning to read and write in additional languages has been studied extensively, especially in the context of the foreign language classroom. As reviewed in section 14.2, early studies, conducted in Canada and in Spain, reported a positive influence of bilingualism on L3 reading and writing, especially in contexts of additive bilingualism, where the bilinguals spoke languages with official status in the community. More recent studies, conducted in different realities that also tend to support bilingualism, have also confirmed the role of multilingualism on literacy development in additional languages. For example, in the context of Switzerland, Romansch-German bilingual eighth-graders were found to have overall higher competencies in French (including reading and translation) than German-speaking monolinguals (Brohy 2001). Similarly, in Australia, secondary school students who were bilingual were more effective learners of community languages such as Greek or Spanish than monolingual students (Clyne, Hunt, and Isaakidis 2004). Similar findings were obtained in Iran, where Turkish-Persian bilinguals received higher English reading comprehension scores than Persian monolinguals (Modirkhamene 2006). Finally, Mady (2014), in a study assessing French proficiency in the Canadian context among monolinguals, Canadian-born bilinguals, and bilingual immigrants who arrived in Canada during elementary school, found that both bilingual groups outperformed the monolinguals on writing. As researchers in other language domains, these studies' authors have attributed the multilingual advantage in novel literacy learning to the interdependence between languages and writing systems (Modirkhamene 2006), to increased metalinguistic awareness in multilinguals (Clyne, Hunt, and Isaakidis 2004), and to a more general interest in and positive attitudes towards languages in multiple language users (Brohy 2001; Clyne, Hunt, and Isaakidis 2004).

It has been pointed out, however, that the positive effects of bilingualism on literacy learning in additional languages may be mediated by socio-psychological and socio-cultural factors as well. Indeed, Mady (2014) found that only the immigrant bilingual group showed an advantage in reading French, while no difference was found between the Canadian-born bilinguals and the monolinguals. Multiple linear regression analyses revealed that the immigrant group's advantages did not derive from proficiency in L1 or English, motivation, attitude, metalinguistic awareness, or strategy use. Rather, it was socio-psychological variables such as the immigrants' willingness to communicate in and lower anxiety towards French that were predictive of higher reading proficiency in that language. In other words, it was the immigration experience coupled with daily use of an L2 (English) that lowered the immigrant bilinguals' fear and facilitated their readiness to learn and use a new language.

Evidence that socio-cultural factors may mediate the extent to which bilingualism facilitates novel literacy learning comes from studies of bilingual immigrants in socio-political contexts that are not supportive of bilingualism. These studies have either failed to find differences between monolinguals and bilinguals or have even documented lower performance among bilingual students. For example, Schoonen et al. (2002), who focused on written English proficiency by immigrants who were bilingual in their L1 and Dutch (L2) and Dutch monolinguals in the Netherlands, found no significant differences between the two groups. Moreover, Van Gelderen et al. (2003), who studied English acquisition in the same population, found that bilingual immigrant students performed worse on reading proficiency and sentence verification tests than the monolingual Dutch students. Thus, like those European studies conducted in the 1990s with immigrant children (see section 14.2), some research conducted in subtractive bilingual environments where bilinguals' L1 has low status has failed to find evidence of a bilingual advantage in L3 acquisition. Van Gelderen and colleagues speculated that the bilingual advantage in novel literacy learning might not be rooted in oral bilingualism but rather in the ability to read and write in more than one language. That is, experience with multiliteracy may result in a more flexible orthographic system that promotes more efficient learning of new writing systems and conventions to represent spoken language. On the other hand, experience with two oral languages, while it might help some aspects of L3 acquisition, might not necessarily confer superior decoding, reading, spelling and writing skills in a new language.

A series of studies that compared the influence of biliteracy versus oral bilingualism on L3 literacy development were recently conducted by Schwartz and colleagues (Kahn-Horwitz et al. 2014; Kahn-Horwitz, Schwartz, and Share 2011; Schwartz et al. 2007; Schwartz, Kahn-Horwitz, and Share 2014). All studies were conducted in Israel and involved immigrant 8-to-11-year-old students who were either only bilingual or both bilingual and biliterate in Hebrew and their first language (Russian or Arabic). In general, the results of these studies demonstrated that biliterate bilinguals outperformed monoliterate bilinguals, and these, in turn, outperformed monolingual students on a number of English literacy measures, including phoneme deletion and analysis, decoding, and spelling (Kahn-Horwitz, Schwartz, and Share 2011; Schwartz et al. 2007). In addition, biliterate bilinguals also showed superior self-teaching of English orthographic conventions (Schwartz, Kahn-Horwitz, and Share 2014). These results were confirmed by Abu Rabia and Sanitsky (2010), who also documented stronger word reading, spelling, and reading comprehension skills in English among bilingual and biliterate Russian/Hebrew bilingual sixth graders as compared to Hebrew monolinguals. Overall, these findings were interpreted as evidence that multiliteracy aids in the process of developing literacy skills in a new language because decoding, reading, spelling and writing abilities transfer and can be applied across languages. The transfer occurs even when languages have different orthographies, as in the case of Russian and English. The authors speculated that Russian literacy skills promote the development of English reading because the alphabets of both languages are based on similar orthographic principles – a fully-fledged alphabet with letters representing consonants and vowels, unlike Hebrew which has a consonantal orthography where vowels are not represented by letters.

Thus, the question remains whether the bilingual advantage in novel literacy development exists even when there is no overlap between the conventions of the known writing systems and those of the novel one. Kahn-Horwitz et al. (2014) specifically investigated English decoding and spelling by Hebrew monolingual and multilingual 10-year-old students who spoke Circassian as L1 and were also literate in Hebrew and Arabic. As expected, the multilingual/multi-literate children outperformed the Hebrew monolinguals in decoding and spelling target English orthographic conventions. However, there were no significant differences between the two groups in decoding and spelling the silent ⟨e⟩, an orthographic feature that does not exist in either the Arabic or Hebrew writing system. The authors interpreted this finding as suggesting that phonemes and orthographic characteristics that exist in known writing systems facilitate the learning of orthographic conventions in a new language. However, multiliteracy alone does not aid in the process of learning novel orthographic features to which the learner has never been exposed before.

In conclusion, it appears that multilingualism facilitates literacy development in additional languages but only to the extent that multilingualism is associated with other characteristics, in particular, specific socio-psychological variables (such as low anxiety and willingness to communicate in the new language), an additive bilingual environment that promotes and values multiple languages, multiliteracy, and overlap between known and novel writing systems.

14.4 Direct and indirect effects of multilingualism on novel language learning

The studies reviewed so far indicate a general multilingual advantage in novel language learning in different language domains, in particular, phonetics/phonology, vocabulary, grammar and literacy. Hirosh and Degani (2018) have proposed a model to account for the direct and indirect effects of multilingualism that might facilitate novel language learning (see Figure 14.1). As can be seen, direct effects include skills that "transfer 'as is' from prior experience to the learning situation" (2018: 893). These processes include both the transfer of knowledge – sound contrasts, articulatory gestures, lexical patterns, syntactic

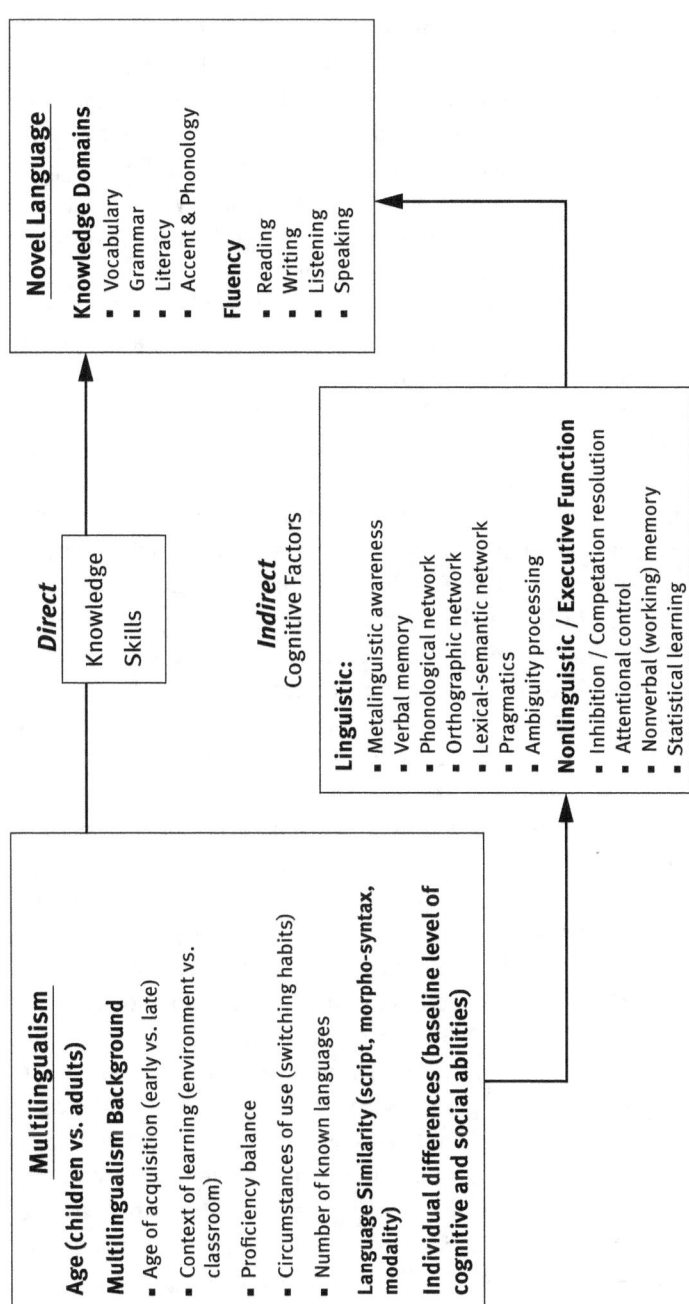

Figure 14.1: Theoretical framework for the influence of multilingualism on novel language learning (Hirosh and Degani 2018, reprinted with permission).

rules and constructions, and orthographic conventions – from previously learned languages to the new language as well as the use of learning strategies and skills developed from prior language learning experiences in the new situation. Indirect effects, on the other hand, are those that originate from the cognitive and social abilities of the learner which have changed following prior language learning. When faced with a new language, learners will make use of these enhanced cognitive and social abilities to acquire it in a process that is indirectly influenced but also facilitated by these abilities.

Many of the studies reviewed in this chapter provide evidence of the facilitating effects of the direct transfer of knowledge and skills from a previously learned language to a novel one. In the area of phonetics/phonology, for instance, Antoniou et al. (2015) found that only Korean-English bilinguals – and not Chinese-English bilinguals – outperformed monolinguals on the discrimination of universally-difficult Korean-like contrasts, a result that suggests that the bilingual advantage originated from the direct transfer of a known phonetic contrast. Similarly, the post-training multilingual advantage on contrast discrimination found by Trembley and Sabourin (2012) was interpreted as the direct result of extensive experience with learning new sounds, a learning situation that is familiar to multilinguals. In the area of word learning, the multilingual advantage found in studies of both adults and children (Byers-Heinlein and Werker, 2013; Kaushanskaya, Gross, and Buac 2014; Kaushanskaya, Yoo, and Van Hecke 2013) has similarly been interpreted as stemming from the direct transfer of the experience of mapping two labels to one referent. That is, extensive practice with learning and using translation equivalents allows bilinguals to directly transfer this experience to a new learning situation, improving novel word learning by virtue of direct implementation of prior learning strategies. The same has been argued in studies that have documented a multilingual advantage in the area of grammar. Multilinguals have indeed been argued to have a larger repertoire of syntactic rules and constructions (Leung 2005) and grammatical learning strategies (Kemp 2007) that can be directly transferred when learning a new language, facilitating the acquisition of its grammatical system. Finally, evidence of higher literacy learning in multilinguals as compared to monolinguals has also been interpreted as suggesting that it is the direct overlap between the orthographic characteristics of known writing systems and those of the novel language that facilitates the acquisition of novel orthographic conventions. Thus, accumulated recent research in different areas of language learning suggests that prior knowledge of multiple languages directly contributes to and facilitates the acquisition of new languages.

At the same time, recent research also suggests that multilingualism may further exert an indirect effect on language learning by virtue of changes that have occurred in the social and cognitive abilities of the learner following previous language learning experiences. For example, multilingualism may bring about changes to the cognitive linguistic system (Grey et al. 2017) and to statistical learning mechanisms, enhancing phonological memory (Papagno and Vallar 1995; Trembley and Sabourin 2012), increasing the flexibility of the phonological system (Kaushanskaya and Marian 2009b), expanding the lexical-semantic network (Kaushanskaya and Rechtzigel 2012), improving metalinguistic skills and overall learning strategies (Klein 1995; Nation and McLaughlin 1986; Nayak et al. 1990; see also Chapter 15, this volume), and enhancing cognitive control abilities (Bartolotti and Marian 2012; Yoshida et al. 2011). Multilingualism may also alter the learners' social abilities, lowering their anxiety and increasing their willingness to communicate in a new language (Mady 2014). The abilities conferred by multilingualism can be linguistic or nonlinguistic in nature (see Figure 14.1) but they both operate indirectly to promote language learning.

It is important to note, however, as argued by Hirosh and Degani (2018), that these direct and indirect effects of multilingualism do not operate independently on novel language learning; rather they are mediated by the characteristics of the learner and of the languages involved. Indeed, as shown in Figure 14.1, direct and indirect forces may play a different role in child and adult learners, in classroom- and environment-based multilinguals, in proficient and more limited learners, in literate and oral speakers of multiple languages, and in additive and subtractive bilingual environments. For example, classroom bilinguals may be facilitated in novel word learning only in situations that have been practiced before, such as when mapping phonologically unfamiliar words to known concepts, as they can directly transfer their prior learning experience to the new learning situation (Kaushanskaya, Yoo, and Van Hecke 2013). On the other hand, environment-based bilinguals might show facilitation in novel word learning due to the indirect cognitive changes – i.e. increased attentional control abilities – that have occurred following their life-long use of two languages and of translation equivalents (Bartolotti and Marian 2012; Yoshida et al. 2011). Similarly, biliteracy may enhance the learning of novel orthographic conventions because the characteristics of the two known writing systems can be directly transferred to the new learning task (Abu Rabia and Sanitsky 2010; Kahn-Horwitz, Schwartz, and Share 2011; Schwartz et al. 2007). However, oral multilingualism may also facilitate literacy learning in a more indirect manner, by increasing metalinguistic awareness and positive attitudes towards languages and language learning (Brohy 2001; Clyne, Hunt, and Isaakidis 2004).

At the extreme, multilingualism can directly and indirectly benefit novel language learning in environments that support, value, and promote the use of multiple languages (Bild and Swain 1989; Cenoz and Valencia 1994; Lasagabaster 2000; Sanz 2000; Swain et al. 1990). However, in subtractive bilingual environments, these positive influences may be suppressed or "masked" by socioeconomic and socioeducational variables – such as low SES and limited education – that work against multilingualism (Jaspaert and Lemmens 1990; Sanders and Meijers 1995; Schoonen et al. 2002; Van Gelderen et al. 2003). Indeed, when such SES factors are controlled for, bilinguals continue to outperform monolinguals in novel language learning, confirming the benefits of multiple language knowledge when encountering a new language. A recent study by Hopp et al. (2019) supports this hypothesis. The authors compared English L3 learning (vocabulary and grammar) in 200 3rd and 4th graders who were either German monolingual or bilingual in German and a heritage language. The study found that while the bilingual group scored lower than the monolingual group overall when group means were compared, there were significant advantages for bilingual students in English vocabulary and grammar once social background factors were controlled for. Thus, it is possible that previous studies that failed to find a bilingual advantage in bilingual immigrant populations either did not control or controlled only a subset of background variables in group comparisons, masking bilingual performance advantages in novel language learning.

The direct and indirect effects of multilingualism on novel language learning are not only mediated by the characteristics of the learner but also of the languages involved. For example, when languages share a high degree of similarity, learners are more likely to directly transfer knowledge and skills from a known language to a novel one, aiding its acquisition process. For instance, Korean-English bilinguals outperformed monolinguals and Chinese-English bilinguals on the discrimination of Korean-like contrasts, suggesting that phonetic contrast similarity facilitated novel language learning (Antoniou et al. 2015). Similarly, in the area of literacy, many studies have documented the facilitative effects of orthographic similarity in the acquisition of novel orthographic conventions (Abu Rabia and Sanitsky 2010; Kahn-Horwitz, Schwartz, and Share 2011; Schwartz et al. 2007). On the other hand, it is possible that when languages are less related, multilingualism still benefits novel language learning but in a more indirect way. Indeed, knowledge of highly unrelated languages may result in stronger inhibition of one language when using the other (Van Assche, Duyck, and Gollan 2013), increasing cognitive control abilities and the potential indirect influences of multilingualism on novel language learning. Conversely, knowledge of closely-related languages may promote more parallel language activation, altering the organization of the linguistic and cognitive system and increasing opportunities for direct transfer.

14.5 Conclusion and future research

In conclusion, this chapter has reviewed extant research on the effects of multilingualism on the acquisition of new languages, focusing on the learning of phonetics/phonology, vocabulary, grammar, and literacy. In general, this research suggests that multilinguals are typically better than learners who have only had experience with one language when learning new sound contrasts and words and novel grammatical systems and orthographic conventions. It was proposed that this multilingual advantage derives from the direct and indirect influences of multilingualism on novel language learning. Direct influences include the direct transfer of knowledge and skills from known languages and previous learning experiences to the novel language and learning task; indirect influences derive from the changes to the general cognitive and linguistic abilities of the learner that have occurred because of multilingualism. Such direct and indirect influences do not operate independently but rather they are mediated by the characteristics of the learner – age, context of learning, proficiency and literacy level – and by the degree of similarity of the languages involved.

While evidence that multilingualism facilitates the acquisition of new languages is robust, more research is needed to elucidate the relative contribution of direct and indirect influences on language learning in different domains. For example, evidence in phonetics/phonology is limited and the latest studies have shown complex patterns. For example, both the Chinese-English and Korean-English bilinguals in Antoniou et al. (2015) outperformed monolinguals on the learning of universally-easy Chinese-like contrasts, although only the Korean-English bilinguals did better than monolinguals in the learning of universally difficult Korean-like contrasts. Therefore, it is possible that the direct and indirect forces behind the multilingual advantage operate differently depending on the complexity of the learning task. When learning is easy (e.g., as in the case of the Chinese-like contrasts), the advantage may be rooted in the indirect changes to the cognitive linguistic system brought about by multilingualism. Yet, when learning is difficult, enhanced cognitive abilities might not be sufficient to produce an advantage, and multilinguals may show superior performance than monolinguals only through direct transfer of specific knowledge and experiences (Hirosh and Degani 2018).

Also, future studies on the contribution of multilingualism on novel language learning should alter the characteristics of the learners involved to truly understand how these mediate the multilingual advantage. Indeed, with the exception of research on vocabulary learning which has included children and adults and compared classroom- with environment-based multilinguals, studies in other language domains have been limited to only adults (phonology, grammar) or primarily school-age children (literacy) and to environment-based multilinguals. Likewise, the role of bi- or multi-literacy in the acquisition of a new language must be further investigated because its specific contribution to novel phonological, lexical, morphosyntactic and literacy learning is not well understood. Most importantly, since contradicting results regarding the multilingual advantage have come from studies in subtractive bilingual environments, it is imperative that future studies examine whether socioeconomic and socioeducational variables such as low SES and limited education truly suppress or mask the positive influences that multilingualism can have on novel language learning. Cummins's threshold hypothesis (1976, 1991) posited that bilingualism results in cognitive advantages when the L1 is valued and the acquisition of an L2 does not result in the loss of L1 but rather in high levels of bilingual proficiency. In this case, such cognitive benefits can be expected to also facilitate the acquisition of a new language. On the other hand, in environments where the L1 is not valued and learners develop L2 at the expense of L1, limited bilingual proficiency may result in lack of cognitive benefits or even in cognitive disadvantages, with no or negative effects on novel language learning. However, is this the case in all language domains? Why are advantages sometimes reported even in the case of subtractive environments? Did previous studies that failed to find a bilingual advantage in bilingual immigrant populations not control or only control for a subset of background variables in group comparisons, masking bilingual performance advantages in novel language learning?

Finally, studies in the areas of phonetics/phonology and grammar have shown that monolingual-multilingual differences in novel language learning are often masked by behavioral paradigms that might not be sophisticated enough to capture patterns of language processing in mono- and multilingual speakers (Grey et al. 2017; Trembley 2010). Therefore, future research should make use of neurophysiological methods such as ERPs that reflect electric brain responses to stimuli. These methods are more objective than other types of measures influenced by voluntary processes and thus may be potentially more informative of a multilingual advantage in novel language learning. Indeed, Trembley (2010) and Grey et al. (2017) found that while behavioral measures failed to reveal differences between monolingual and multilingual learners, ERPs demonstrated a facilitative effect of language experience on contrast discrimination (Trembley 2010) and grammatical processing (Grey et al. 2017). Therefore, future studies should make use of new methodologies and paradigms that reveal the neural correlates of language learning and combine them with behavioral methods to obtain a more complete picture of how previous language experience shapes language processing and cognition. These studies could shed new light on the differences between monolinguals and multilinguals in the acquisition of new languages and uncover the underlying mechanisms by which multilingualism directly and indirectly affects language learning.

References

Abu-Rabia, Salim & Ekaterina Sanitsky. 2010. Advantages of bilinguals over monolinguals in learning a third language. *Bilingual Research Journal* 33(2). 173–199.
Antoniou, Mark, Eric Liang, Mark Ettlinger & Patrick C. M. Wong. 2015. The bilingual advantage in phonetic learning. *Bilingualism: Language and Cognition* 18(4). 683–695.
Balke-Aurell, Gudrun & Torsten Lindblad. 1982. *Immigrant children and their languages*. Gothenburg: Department of Education Research, University of Gothenburg.
Bartolotti, James & Viorica Marian. 2012. Language learning and control in monolinguals and bilinguals. *Cognitive Science* 36. 1129–1147.
Bild, Eva Rebecca & Merrill Swain. 1989. Minority language students in a French immersion programme: Their French proficiency. *Journal of Multilingual and Multicultural Development* 10. 255–274.
Brohy, Claudine. 2001. Generic and/or specific advantages of bilingualism in a dynamic plurilingual situation: The case of French as official L3 in the school of Samedan (Switzerland). *International Journal of Bilingual Education and Bilingualism* 4(1). 38–49.
Bialystok, Ellen & Raluca Barac. 2013. Cognitive effects. In François Grosjean & Ping Li (eds.), *The psycholinguistics of bilingualism*, 192–213. Chichester, UK: Wiley-Blackwell.
Byers-Heinlein, Krista & Janet F. Werker. 2013. Lexicon structure and the disambiguation of novel words: Evidence from bilingual infants. *Cognition* 128. 407–416.
Cenoz, Jasone. 2008. The acquisition of additional languages. *Estudios de Lingüística Inglesa Aplicada* 8. 219–224.
Cenoz, Jasone. 2013. The influence of bilingualism on third language acquisition. Focus on multilingualism. *Language Teaching* 46(1). 71–86.
Cenoz, Jasone & Jose F. Valencia. 1994. Additive trilingualism: Evidence from the Basque Country. *Applied Psycholinguistics* 15. 195–207.
Clyne, Michael, Claudia Rossi Hunt & Tina Isaakidis. 2004. Learning a community language as a third language. *The International Journal of Multilingualism* 1. 33–52.
Cohen, Stephen P., G. Richard Tucker & Wallace E. Lambert. 1967. The comparative skills of monolinguals and bilinguals in perceiving phoneme sequences. *Language and Speech* 10. 159–168.
Cox, Jessica G. 2017. Explicit instruction, bilingualism, and the older adult learner. *Studies in Second Language Acquisition* 39. 29–58.
Cummins, James. 1976. The influence of bilingualism on cognitive growth. *Working Papers on Bilingualism* 9. 1–43.
Cummins, Jim. 1991. Interdependence of first and second language proficiency. In Ellen Bialystok (ed.), *Language processing in bilingual children*, 70–89. Cambridge, U.K.: Cambridge University Press.
Davine, M., G. Richard Tucker & Wallace E. Lambert. 1971. The perception of phoneme sequences by monolingual and bilingual elementary school children. *Canadian Journal of Behavioral Science* 3. 72–76.

Enomoto, Kayoko. 1994. L2 perceptual acquisition: The effect of multilingual linguistic experience on the perception of a "less novel" contrast. *Edinburgh Working Papers in Applied Linguistics* 5. 15–29.

Grey, Sarah, Cristina Sanz, Kara Morgan-Short & Michael T. Ullman. 2017. Bilingual and monolingual adults learning an additional language: ERPs reveal differences in syntactic processing. *Bilingualism: Language and Cognition* 21(5). 970–994.

Gut, Ulrike. 2010. Cross-linguistic influence in L3 phonological acquisition. *International Journal of Multilingualism* 7(1). 19–38.

Hell, Janet G. van & Andrea Candia Mahn. 1997. Keyword mnemonics versus rote rehearsal in learning concrete and abstract foreign words by experienced and inexperienced foreign language learners. *Language Learning* 47. 507–546.

Hirosh, Zoya & Tamar Degani. 2018. Direct and indirect effects of multilingualism on novel language learning: An integrative review. *Psychonomic Bulletin and Review* 25(3). 892–916.

Hopp, Holger, Markus Vogelbacher, Teresa Kieseier & Dieter Thoma. 2019. Bilingual advantages in early foreign language learning: Effects of the minority and the majority language. *Learning and Instruction* 61. 99–110.

Jaspaert, Koen & Gertrud Lemmens. 1990. Linguistic evaluation of Dutch as a third language. In Michael Byram & Johan Leman (eds.), *Bicultural and trilingual education: The Foyer model in Brussels*, 30–56. Clevedon: Multilingual Matters.

Kahn-Horwitz, Janina, Mila Schwartz & David Share. 2011. Acquiring the complex English orthography: A triliteracy advantage? *Journal of Research in Reading* 34. 136–156.

Kahn-Horwitz, Janina, Sara Kuash, Raphiq Ibrahim & Mila Schwartz. 2014. How do previously acquired languages affect acquisition of English as a foreign language: The case of Circassian. *Written Language & Literacy* 17. 40–61.

Kalashnikova, Margarita, Karen Mattock & Padraic Monaghan. 2014. The effects of linguistic experience on the flexible use of mutual exclusivity in word learning. *Bilingualism: Language and Cognition* 18. 626–638.

Kaushanskaya, Margarita & Viorica Marian. 2009a. Bilingualism reduces native-language interference during novel-word learning. *Journal of Experimental Psychology: Learning, Memory, and Cognition* 35. 829–835.

Kaushanskaya, Margarita & Viorica Marian. 2009b. The bilingual advantage in novel word learning. *Psychonomic Bulletin & Review* 16. 705–710.

Kaushanskaya, Margarita & Katrina Rechtzigel. 2012. Concreteness effects in bilingual and monolingual word learning. *Psychonomic Bulletin & Review* 19. 935–941.

Kaushanskaya, Margarita, Megan Gross & Milijana Buac. 2014. Effects of classroom bilingualism on task-shifting, verbal memory, and word learning in children. *Developmental Science* 17. 564–583.

Kaushanskaya, Margarita, Jeewon Yoo, & Stephanie Van Hecke, S. 2013. Word learning in adults with second language experience: Effects of phonological and referent familiarity. *Journal of Speech, Language, and Hearing Research* 56. 667–678.

Kemp, Charlotte. 2007. Strategic processing in grammar learning: Do multilinguals use more strategies? *International Journal of Multilingualism* 4. 241–261.

Keshavarz, Mohammad Hossein & Hamideh Astaneh. 2004. The impact of biliguality on the learning of English vocabulary as a foreign language (L3). *International Journal of Bilingual Education and Bilingualism* 7. 295–302.

Klein, Elaine C. 1995. Second versus third language acquisition: Is there a difference? *Language Learning* 45. 419–465.

Lasagabaster, David. 2000. Three languages and three linguistic models in the Basque educational system. In Jasone Cenoz & Ulrike Jessner (eds.), *English in Europe: The acquisition of a third language*, 179–197. Clevedon: Multilingual Matters.

Leung, Yan-Kit Ingrid. 2005. L2 vs L3 initial state: A comparative study of the acquisition of French DPs by Vietnamese monolinguals and Chinese-English bilinguals. *Bilingualism: Language and Cognition* 8. 39–61.

Mady, Callie. 2014. Learning French as a second official language in Canada: Comparing monolingual and bilingual students at Grade 6. *International Journal of Bilingual Education and Bilingualism* 1. 330–344.

Markman, Ellen M. 1990. Constraints children place on word meanings. *Cognitive Science* 14. 57–77.

Modirkhamene, Sima. 2006. The reading achievement of third language versus second language learners of English in relation to the inter-dependence hypothesis. *International Journal of Multilingualism* 3. 280–295.

Nation, Robert & Barry McLaughlin. 1986. Novices and experts: An information processing approach to the "good language learner" problem. *Applied Psycholinguistics* 7. 41–56.

Nayak, Nandini, Nina Hansen, Nancy Krueger & Barry McLaughlin. 1990. Language-learning strategies in monolingual and multilingual adults. *Language Learning* 40. 221–244.

Papagno, Costanza & Giuseppe Vallar. 1995. Verbal short-term memory and vocabulary learning in polyglots. *The Quarterly Journal of Experimental Psychology Section A* 48. 98–107.

Rabinovitch, M. S. & L. M. Parver. 1966. Auditory discrimination in monolinguals and poliglots. Paper presented at the meeting of the Canadian Psychological Association, Montreal, Canada.

Rothman, Jason & Jennifer Cabrelli Amaro. 2010. What variables condition syntactic transfer? A look at the L3 initial state. *Second Language Research* 26. 189–218.

Sanders, Marianne & Guust Meijers. 1995. English as L3 in the elementary school. *ITL International Journal of Applied Linguistics* 107/108. 59–78.

Sanz, Cristina. 2000. Bilingual education enhances third language acquisition: Evidence from Catalonia. *Applied Psycholinguistics* 21. 23–44.

Sanz, Cristina. 2007. Predicting enhanced L3 learning in bilingual contexts: The role of biliteracy. In Carmen Pérez-Vidal, María Juan-Garau & Aurora Bel (eds.), *A portrait of the young in the new multilingual Spain*, 220–240. Buffalo: Multilingual Matters.

Schoonen, Rob, Amos van Gelderen, Kees de Glopper, Jan Hulstijn, Patrick Snellings, Annegien Simis & Marie Stevenson. 2002. Linguistic knowledge, metacognitive knowledge and retrieval speed in L1, L2 and EFL writing. In Sarah Ransdell & Marie-Laure Barbier (eds.), *New directions for research in L2 writing*, 101–122. Dordrecht: Kluwer Academic Publishers.

Schwartz, Mila, Janina Kahn-Horwitz & David L. Share. 2014. Orthographic learning and self-teaching in a bilingual and biliterate context. *Journal of Experimental Child Psychology* 117. 45–58.

Schwartz, Mila, Esther Geva, David L. Share & Mark Leikin. 2007. Learning to read in English as third language: The cross-linguistic transfer of phonological processing skills. *Written Language and Literacy* 10. 25–52.

Swain, Merrill, Sharon Lapkin, Norman Rowen & Doug Hart. 1990. The role of mother tongue literacy in third language learning. *Language, Culture and Curriculum* 3. 65–81.

Trembley, Marie-Claude. 2010. *Comparing the perceptual abilities of monolinguals, bilinguals and multilinguals: A combined behavioural and event-related potential experiment.* Ottawa, Canada: University of Ottawa doctoral dissertation.

Trembley, Marie-Claude & Laura L. Sabourin. 2012. Comparing behavioral discrimination and learning abilities in monolinguals, bilinguals and multilinguals. *The Journal of the Acoustical Society of America* 132. 3465–3474.

Van Assche, Eva, Wouter Duyck & Tamar H. Gollan. 2013. Whole-language and item-specific control in bilingual language production. *Journal of Experimental Psychology: Learning, Memory, and Cognition* 39(6). 1781–1792.

Van Gelderen, Amos, Rob Schoonen, Kees De Glopper, Jan Hulstijn, Patrick Snellings, Annegien Simis & Marie Stevenson. 2003. Roles of linguistic knowledge, metacognitive knowledge and processing speed in L3, L2 and L1 reading comprehension: A structural equation modeling approach. *International Journal of Bilingualism* 7. 7–25.

Werker, Janet F. 1986. The effect of multilingualism on phonetic perceptual flexibility. *Applied Psycholinguistics* 7. 141–156.

Yoshida, Hanako, Duc N. Tran, Viridiana Benitez & Megumi Kuwabara. 2011. Inhibition and adjective learning in bilingual and monolingual children. *Frontiers in Psychology* 2. Article 210. https://doi.org/10.3389/fpsyg.2011.00210

Elisabeth Allgäuer-Hackl and Ulrike Jessner
15 Cross-linguistic Interaction and Multilingual Awareness

15.1 Introduction

The present chapter deals with language contact phenomena in relation to multilingual awareness, an umbrella term including metalinguistic and cross-linguistic awareness, from a dynamic and complexity systems (DSCT) point of view, in particular from the stance of the Dynamic Model of Multilingualism (DMM; Herdina and Jessner 2002). The first part gives an overview of the main concepts used in research on the interaction of the languages in a person's mind and discusses cross-linguistic influence (CLI) and cross-linguistic interaction (CLIN) in more detail. The section that follows is dedicated to studies on metalinguistic and cross-linguistic awareness in multilinguals, highlighting the differences between monolingualism, bilingualism, and multilingualism. Enhanced multilingual awareness on the part of learners, which can be linked not only to their prior experience as multilingual learners but also to their knowledge of different linguistic systems and of how these interact, can lead to more successful language learning. It may also support multilinguals' efforts to compensate for the effects of attrition more easily and effectively.

The second part of the chapter reflects our main research focus, namely the role of metalinguistic and cross-linguistic awareness in multilingual development and the multilingual system, both interpreted from a DSCT perspective but also from other theoretical backgrounds whenever deemed necessary. Multilingualism and multiple language learning refer to the use and learning of more than two languages. The terms include simultaneous as well as consecutive processes of acquisition of three or more languages. That is, a difference is made between SLA/bilingualism and TLA/trilingualism since the initial conditions in L3 learning differ from those an L2 learner encounters. For a number of researchers, including the authors of the present chapter, however, the study of multilingualism provides a new theoretical lens for *all* language acquisition processes including L1 acquisition (cf. Flynn, Foley, and Vinnitskaya 2004; Herdina and Jessner 2002).

Elisabeth Allgäuer-Hackl, Universität Innsbruck, Innsbruck, Austria
Ulrike Jessner, Universität Innsbruck, Innsbruck, Austria & University of Pannonia, Veszprém, Hungary

15.2 Contact phenomena in the multilingual mind

Up to the 1960s, languages were perceived as separated, competing for cognitive resources, space and identity in a bilingual person's brain or mind, an idea visualized through the balloon picture (e.g., Baker 2011). Many studies on language contact phenomena such as transfer and interference in bilinguals still reflect the presupposition that languages are stored in separate compartments (Cook 2016: 25). From a DSCT perspective, however, multilingual development is dynamic and complex and includes language growth as well as attrition. The language systems interact with each other and within the multilingual system in a process that changes the system and the subsystems continually and leads to emergent properties in the multilingual mind. Additionally, there is also constant interaction between the individual and the societal level. Therefore, considerable individual differences can be expected to exist within a group of learners.

The following subsections deal with different types of relationships that have been proposed between multiple languages in the multilingual mind such as those investigated in research on transfer/interference, cross-linguistic influence (CLI), cross-linguistic interaction (CLIN), as well as code-switching.

15.2.1 Transfer and interference

The transfer of knowledge is an important part of all learning processes: "In the case of languages, transfer [...] consists of using an element of one language in another" (Lüdi & Py 2009: 155). In SLA research, transfer usually refers to the influence of previous language knowledge on *acquisition*, not on the speech processes (cf. Cook 2016: 27). Above all in educational contexts, positive transfer is differentiated from negative interference. While transfer may not be detectable (e.g., in the case of genetically close languages), interference in this connection denotes visible products of transfer processes or, in other words, non-correct output in the target language and serves as an explanation for deficiencies in language learners and bi-/multilinguals. For Odlin (2016: 6), the distinction between positive transfer and negative interference "does suggest an eventual effect of behaviourist psychology" on SLA research.

Cook (2016) discusses the term in connection with multi-competence and defines transfer as one possible relationship between the languages in the mind of a speaker. For Herdina and Jessner (2002: 28), transfer can be observed in all (linguistic) systems and subsystems, can take any direction and can lead to diverse outcomes. Since it is a dynamic process, psychological studies on what motivates learners to see languages as related and to transfer knowledge from one to the other language should complement psycholinguistic studies of transfer. Thus, the DMM distinguishes between (spontaneous) production processes or speech processes during which languages might interfere with each other in the moment of speaking and the transfer of structures that has a lasting effect on a given language (e.g. fossilization). DSCT-based multilingualism research discusses transfer in connection with the wider phenomena of CLI and CLIN, which are outlined in the following subsections.

15.2.2 Cross-linguistic influence (CLI)

CLI, a concept defined by Kellerman and Sharwood-Smith in 1986, denotes the influence that linguistic systems exert on each other and includes phenomena such as transfer, interference, borrowing, and avoidance. Odlin (2016), however, points out that the notion of *influence* is not entirely clear and subject to more research.

Up to the 1980s, CLI was mainly interpreted as transfer from the L1 to the other languages. Since then, research has provided evidence that in bilinguals or L2 learners, CLI is bidirectional; i.e., influence happens in two possible directions (cf. Cook 2003, 2016). Pavlenko and Jarvis (2002), for example, studied the influence of L1 Russian on L2 English and vice versa and discovered that the use of the L2 also started to shape L1 written productions.

15.2.2.1 CLI in multilinguals

Research on transfer in SLA has a long tradition, but the body of research on CLI within TLA has also grown considerably over the last years. Since complexity increases with each language added, CLI in TLA is different from CLI in SLA. The contact between, for example, three language systems is much more complex than between two, as "apart from the bidirectional relationship between L1 and L2, L3 can influence L1 and vice versa and L2 and L3 can also influence each other" (Herdina and Jessner 2002: 66). Consequently, CLI in multilinguals is multidirectional, meaning that all language systems influence each other and this influence can take any direction. Additionally, two or more languages can influence one target language, a phenomenon that De Angelis (2007) termed *combined* CLI. De Angelis, Jessner and Kresic (2015: 1) describe CLI in multilinguals as a dynamic phenomenon that is "determined and defined by the amount and type of language knowledge held in the mind, and by the use that multilinguals make of such knowledge in production and comprehension". From a DSCT point of view, the influence that language systems exert on each other due to their interaction is cumulative and often unpredictable (cf. Herdina and Jessner 2002; cf. Flynn et al. 2004 on syntactic development).

15.2.2.2 CLI factors in L3 acquisition

According to Hammarberg (2001: 21–41), several criteria are influential in the relationship between languages in L3 production such as typological and cultural similarity, level of proficiency, recency of use, and L2 status. Typology plays an important role in CLI phenomena (e.g., Cenoz 2003a) and remains a dominant topic within research on syntax (e.g., Rothman 2011). But also psychotypology (Kellerman 1995), which reflects the learners' perception of similarities between languages even if they are factually not similar (cf. Zawadzka 2011), has been defined as a robust predictor of CLI (cf. De Angelis et al. 2015: 2). According to Cenoz (2001), typology may be decisive in the case of bilinguals whose typologically related L1 may play a specific role as a supporter language in L3 learning. Multilingualism research has also raised the question of the level of proficiency in the non-native languages that is necessary for transfer to occur (e.g., De Angelis 2007). Some researchers have added context as an influential factor (Cenoz, Hufeisen, and Jessner 2001: 2; De Angelis 2007), while others have focused on external factors such as the interlocutor's role in language mixing in production (e.g., Cenoz, Hufeisen, and Jessner 2003). A concise overview of research into these and other factors can be found in De Angelis, Jessner, and Kresic (2015: Chapter 1).

15.2.2.3 What is transferred?

Phenomena of CLI have been identified at all linguistic levels (cf. De Angelis and Dewaele 2011: viii) even though there are considerably more studies on syntactic than on morphological/phonological transfer. Several studies have dealt with lexical transfer and the mental lexicon in L3 production (e.g., Ecke 2001; Herwig 2001), while others with the transfer of specific structures or lexical units (e.g., Cenoz 2001; Williams and Hammerberg 1998). Phonological CLI, with a focus on specific areas of phonological transfer, has been the focus of recent studies (Gut 2010; Marx and Mehlhorn 2010; Mayr and Montanari 2015; Wrembel 2010). In addition, some researchers have explored issues of CLI and metalinguistic awareness (e.g., Jessner, Megens, and Graus 2016).

15.2.2.4 On the L2 status

Another discussion refers to the role of the L1 as opposed to that of the L2 in multilingual CLI. Proponents of L1 transfer hypotheses assume a decisive influence of the L1, while L2 transfer hypotheses assign a special role to the second (often foreign) language for L3/Ln acquisition. Many TLA studies show a particular role of the L2, above all in connection with syntactic development. Learners typically transfer linguistic and language learning knowledge from their L2 to their L3, for instance when the L2 is typologically related to the L3 (see De Angelis, Jessner, and Kresic 2015 for an overview). Another explanation for the special status of the L2 in TLA is the foreign language effect as learners tend to transfer from the foreign language most recently learned (e.g., Bardel and Falk 2007; Bono 2011).

Similarly, in their investigation of L3 use, De Angelis and Selinker (2001: 51) introduced the concept of interlanguage transfer. They hold that activation occurs across language systems, and these compete for selection. Phonological criteria seem to be important, meaning that in this process, foreign languages win over the L1 in multilingual CLI, since, as the researchers believe, "there is a potential cognitive mode called 'talk foreign' or 'foreign language mode' [...] that eases the path of interlanguage transfer" (De Angelis and Selinker 2001: 51).

Many studies reveal the differing roles of L1 and L2 when used as supporter languages in L3 acquisition. Hammarberg (2001) and Jessner (2006) discovered that learners activate all their languages during L3 production and that the languages involved play different roles. Hammarberg (2001: 25) found a "characteristic division of roles" in the oral Swedish productions of polyglot researcher Sarah Williams between the English L1 and German L2 at different linguistic levels (lexicon, pronunciation, morphology etc.). Language switches into English were more frequent than into German, above all at the beginning, while the learner relied more heavily on German as a supplier language for word constructions (Hammarberg 2001: 31).

In their Cumulative Enhancement Model, Flynn et al. (2004) argue that the L1 does not play a special role, but that all languages influence the target language (cf. De Angelis, Jessner, and Kresic 2015: 2). Vanhove and Berthele (2015) investigated CLI in connection with cognate guessing and found that the L1 is used together with non-native languages; i.e., all previously known languages play a role in this type of task.

15.2.2.5 Complexity of interaction of factors

Cenoz (2001) investigated the role of language typology, L2 status, and age in Basque-Spanish bilingual school children (grades 2, 6 and 9) learning English as an L3. Generally speaking, older learners presented more instances of CLI than younger learners despite higher English proficiency. Transfer mostly occurred from Spanish to English, even in bilingual Basque-Spanish students. Consequently, linguistic distance seems to play a role, but also psychotypology, as the author points out. Apart from language typology, the different status of Spanish (the majority language) and Basque (the minority language) in the specific (socio)linguistic context further influenced the choices the students made, highlighting the complexity of research on CLI in trilinguals.

Many studies have focused on typology and psychotypology such as Ecke (2001), who highlights the role of psychotypology in learners of L3 German and the prominent role of the L2 (English). Ringbom's (2001) research on lexical transfer confirms the different roles that the L1 and the L2 play in transfer processes in L3 English and supports the significance of typology, which, however, is reduced in the case of transfer of meaning (as opposed to transfer of form). Psychotypology also seems to play a role in Zawadzka's (2011) study on learners' self-perceived transfer bases between their target language Polish and previously learned languages (German, English, Latin, French), and in Lindquist's (2015) research on the role of psychotypology and CLI in young Swedish learners of French as L3.

Typology or language distance may refer not to the languages per se but to different subsystems. In Sanchez (2011), the influence of L3 German on the L4 English of Spanish-Catalan bilingual primary school learners was analyzed in an area where German is relatively distant from all the other languages involved, namely with respect to verb placement and syntax. Results provided strong evidence for the activation of L3 German in L4 initial English productions. That is, typological distance between German and English in connection with verb placement did not discourage transfer from German to English. Or, in other words, typological closeness between Spanish and Catalan (L1s) on the one hand and English on the other in this particular syntactic field did not encourage transfer between these languages. The factor that seemed to be stronger than typology was L2 status, which denotes the influence of a non-native language (German) in TLA (L4 English in this study).

A study carried out by Gibson, Hufeisen, and Libben (2001) on German prepositional verbs compared learners of German as an L2 with those who studied German as an L3 or L4. Expectations that another foreign language (English) acquired before German would facilitate the acquisition of prepositional verbs were not fulfilled, as L3/L4 learners did not outperform L2 learners on the task. The typological similarity of German and English, for instance, did not help learners in this specific task. Furthermore, the L1 (a variety of languages) did not have any decisive influence on the production of German verbs.

Most TLA studies deal with the transfer of structures from previously learned languages to a new target language, while research interest in transfer from a new to a known language is a more recent phenomenon. The transfer of L3 German onto L2 English was investigated by Cheung, Matthews, and Tsang (2011: 54) in a study involving L1 Cantonese speakers, which focused on the transfer of tense/aspect in connection with the (present) perfect tense in the two Indo-European languages. Learners with L3 German used non-target sentences in their English productions to a much higher degree than learners with other third languages, and their judgments of present perfect/past sentences showed a higher acceptability rate of non-target sentences than the control group's judgments. Thus, the results provide strong evidence for CLI from German L3 to English L2. The reasons proposed by the researchers for CLI are the typology of the two languages and the recency of use/acquisition.

The role of the non-native language German in decoding the unknown language Danish in L1 Dutch speakers was investigated by Swarte, Schüppert, and Gooskens (2015). They found certain evidence for the *foreign language mode* factor (see section 15.2.2.4.), but also for the significance of German proficiency in translating German-Danish cognates. In a similar vein, the impact of proficiency in a non-native language (L2 English, L3 German or French) when processing an unknown language (Danish) turned out to be higher than that of language typology in a Polish study carried out by Mieszkowska and Otwinowska (2015). Furthermore, the use of English as a language of testing seemed to motivate learners to use this language as a source of transfer.

Recapitulating, language typology, perceived language distance or psychotypology, recency of acquisition and use, frequency of use or of certain structures (cf. Jarvis and Pavlenko 2008), the level of proficiency in the target language, and the foreign language effect have been identified as the main factors that interact and influence the activation of previously learned languages in the acquisition and use of a further language (cf. De Angelis 2007; see also Chapter 14, this volume).

15.2.3 Cross-linguistic interaction (CLIN)

15.2.3.1 Definition
There is a range of phenomena that Herdina and Jessner (2002: 29) define as cross-linguistic interaction or CLIN. Jessner (2008: 275) describes CLIN in multilinguals as

an umbrella term, including not only transfer and interference, but also codeswitching and borrowing. Furthermore, it is also meant to cover another set of phenomena, including the cognitive effects of multilingual development. These are nonpredictable dynamic effects that determine the development of the systems themselves.

Thus, CLIN phenomena work on both the linguistic and the cognitive level of multilingual learning and use and are part of multilingual proficiency (Herdina and Jessner 2002). They also refer to increased metalinguistic awareness and metacognitive skills in multilinguals (cf. Jessner, Megens, and Graus 2016). CLIN may have both a retarding and/or an accelerating effect on language development in general and on cross-linguistic awareness in particular since it is assumed to initiate "autocatalytic developments observed in multilingual speakers" (Herdina and Jessner 2002: 107).

15.2.3.2 Multilingual CLIN processes in literacy development

In her study on cross-lexical search in German-Italian bilingual students learning English as an L3, which aimed at exploring "the relationship between cross-linguistic interaction and linguistic awareness in the use of multilingual compensatory strategies," Jessner (2006: 87) provides a detailed analysis of the differing roles that German and Italian play in her subjects' written productions in English using introspection in the form of Think Aloud Protocols (TAP). The activation of both languages in the production of English shows cross-lexical consultation between the three languages, for instance when cognates were involved. In the case of lexical deficits, the two languages played different roles, which depended on language proficiency, recency of use, and typology.

Cenoz and Gorter (2011) looked at the written productions of Basque-Spanish-English trilingual students in Basque schools where Basque is used as a medium of instruction. The participants were asked to write a composition based on differing pictures in each of their three languages on different days. The correlations between the scores obtained in the three languages for the dimensions of content, organization, grammar, vocabulary and mechanics were calculated. The results showed that most of the correlations were significant, indicating that the dimensions across languages are interrelated and that "multilingual speakers share some skills across their different languages" (2011: 362). Interdependence was also found for general writing skills. Cenoz and Gorter (2011: 365) conclude that their analyses "point in the same direction, suggesting that there is an underlying common multilingual strategy that is then produced in three languages".

De Angelis and Jessner (2012) applied a dynamic systems approach to their investigation of trilingual writing (L1 Italian, L2 German and L3 English) of 8th graders in the bilingual South Tyrolean context. The main DSCT tenets that provided the basis for the study were the interaction of language systems, the interdependence of language development and use, and the assumption of qualitative changes in the overall multilingual system. Data analysis included measures of fluency, proficiency levels in the non-native languages, and measures of association between proficiency levels and school grades. The results showed a significant correlation between the length of L1 Italian texts and the proficiency levels in German; a strong positive correlation was found between fluency in L2 German production and the grades in English and between L3 English fluency and L2 German proficiency. Moreover, results revealed that all languages depended on each other.

Stavans (2015) carried out a study on the development of multilingual pre-literacy in young children who were exposed to English and Arabic writing systems in their surroundings, and who were compared to children living in Hebrew monolingual environments. Mono- and multilingual children differed from each other in several ways, but the most striking difference was found in the explanations the multilingual children gave when judging the (non-)readability of sequences of signs. Stavans (2015) draws attention to the dynamic interaction between the multilingual linguistic landscape and the processes of understanding writing systems before formal schooling.

Summarizing, we can state that studies into multilingual literacy have shown that there is an interplay between writing processes in the various languages which might be comparable to the common underlying proficiency (CUP) introduced by Cummins (cf. Baker and Hornberger 2001) but should also be interpreted as part of the M(ultilingualism)-Factor.

15.2.4 Code-switching

Code-switching, which denotes the alternation of at least two languages or language varieties in an utterance or interaction, is another language contact phenomenon. Code-switching has been studied as a social as well as a linguistic phenomenon. It is more or less acceptable depending on the context and has a variety of aims and purposes (cf. Baker 2011: 108–110; for more details on this linguistic behavior, see Chapter 7, this volume).

15.3 Multilingual awareness (MLA)

Metalinguistic (MeLA) and cross-linguistic awareness (XLA) are the two components of multilingual awareness that interact in the multilingual mind, and the levels of awareness exert influence on the organization of the multilingual mental lexicon. The acronym MLA refers to multilingual awareness as an umbrella term that also includes multilanguage aptitude (MuLA). These concepts are seen as related. Aptitude does not constitute an innate property but an "emergent property of multilingual systems" (Herdina and Jessner 2002: 117).

The following section provides an overview of concepts related to metalinguistic and cross-linguistic awareness as defined within the DMM paradigm (Herdina and Jessner 2002; Jessner 2019).

15.3.1 Metalinguistic awareness (MeLA)

A number of scholars have investigated the concept of metalinguistic awareness in monolinguals, contributing to the present understanding of MeLA. Malakoff and Hakuta (1991: 147), for example, define MeLA as the ability to "step back from the comprehension or production of an utterance in order to consider the linguistic form and structure underlying the meaning of the utterance". Metalinguistic awareness in multilinguals has been defined in a variety of ways, for example as the ability to focus on language, play with and manipulate language, switch between form, function and meaning, reflect on and manipulate the rules of a language, and use the corresponding metalanguage (Jessner 2006; Jessner 2008; Simard and Gutiérrez 2018). MeLA can also be regarded as one aspect of Cognitive Academic Language Proficiency (cf. Baker and Hornberger 2001: 110ff).

Monolinguals, above all those who work with language, develop metalinguistic awareness. A number of studies, however, have shown that bilinguals display a heightened awareness of the forms, meanings, and rules of a language (De Angelis 2007: 121–122); i.e., they develop enhanced metalinguistic awareness in specific areas (cf. Jessner 2019). In multilinguals, MeLA is again different in quality. It is defined as one of the most important factors that contribute to an increased ability of multilinguals to learn languages (cf. Cenoz 2003b; see also Chapter 14, this volume). Thomas (1988), one of the first scholars to link metalinguistic awareness with multilingualism, claimed that learners who have received formal instruction in their L2 are better learners of an L3 (cf. De Angelis 2007: 122). Gibson and Hufeisen (2011: 83) looked into the MeLA of students with advanced English as Ln and found that more foreign language experience "translates into more efficient linguistic abilities at the grammatical level". MeLA in multilinguals has been defined as an emergent property of the multilingual system or mind, since multilingual learners develop skills such as language learning, language management, and language maintenance skills that are linked to metalinguistic awareness and to a new quality in language learning. MeLA is further connected with cognitive advantages such as creativity and flexibility (e.g., Kharkhurin 2012), with enhanced social skills and with increased flexibility to switch and adapt strategies (e.g., Kemp 2007).

MeLA is or may be connected with metalanguage or metalinguistic expressions that learners use while commenting on the tasks given. These have been studied in connection with language switches (Hammarberg 2001; Williams and Hammarberg 1998) or language learning in formal education (cf. Jessner 2005: 57–58). Jessner investigated the use of metalinguistic questions and comments made by students while they were searching for appropriate expressions in their L3, and defined them "as evidence of the multilingual speakers reflecting upon language and languages" (Jessner 2005: 59). This work ties in with Woll (2018: 14), who, studying the reflexive and applied dimensions of MeLA, explored the role of MeLA in the lexical transfer from English L2 to German L3 in French-speaking Canadians by means of introspective verbal data and found that "higher levels of MLA [referring to metalinguistic awareness here] in terms of an explicit analysis of cross-linguistic correspondences, really did seem to impact transfer rates". A detailed analysis of the participants' verbalizations revealed different levels of awareness of the underlying rules even if the corresponding metalinguistic terminology was not known, which led Woll (2018: 14) to conclude that "awareness at the level of understanding can occur in the absence of metalinguistic terms".

15.3.2 Cross-linguistic awareness (XLA)

An emergent property that is closely interwoven with MeLA is cross-linguistic awareness (XLA), which can be defined as the awareness of the interaction between the languages in a multilingual's mind.

In her language biography, Todeva (2009: 53ff) describes how a high level of MeLA, and, more importantly, XLA, facilitated her learning of additional languages. Her examples stem from morphology (Greek and Latin suffixes or prefixes), describing how, with the help of these structures, she discovered cross-linguistic similarities (for instance, suffixes such as *-ment/-mente* or *-ción/-tion*). This can be interpreted as one concrete example of cross-linguistic awareness mediated through metalinguistic awareness; i.e., metalinguistic awareness makes objectification possible.

MeLA in general and XLA in particular act as a catalyst in TLA. Based on Jessner's (2006: 116) South Tyrol study, XLA is described as "(a) tacit awareness shown by the use of cognates in the supporter languages [...] and (b) explicit awareness in the case of switches that are introduced by meta-language". However, both properties interact and are "difficult to disentangle". Consequently, XLA is seen as one aspect of multilingual awareness rather than as an independent phenomenon. As James (1996: 143; italics in original) points out, the *"language transfer* issue of classical Contrastive Analysis becomes a new issue of *metalinguistic transfer* – its relationship to cross-linguistic awareness".

The facilitative effect of MeLA combined with XLA on language learning has been found in a number of studies (see also Chapter 14, this volume). According to Ó Laoire (2005: 48), studies of L3 learning (in Ireland)

> corroborate the assumption that the beneficial effects of metalinguistic awareness are increased if systematic or deliberate linkages are forged between learners' previous language learning experiences and their experience of learning the target L3/L4.

James (1996: 143) remarks that bilinguals exploit the differences between the languages to their advantage due to their enhanced XLA. The author concludes that "what bilinguals do socially and spontaneously" (1996: 144) should be introduced in the classroom as a systematic way of looking at language, since language learners have to be shown how to do this. In a similar way, the studies carried out by members of the "Dynamics of multilingualism with English" (DyME) research group at Innsbruck University (www.dyme.uibk.ac.at), which focuses on the nature of cross-linguistic interaction and multilingual awareness, suggest that applying to the classroom what experienced multilinguals do, namely using explicit comparisons, contrasting the languages, and raising the learners' awareness of commonalities and differences between their L1 and/or their foreign languages, may be a successful strategy to enhance learners' MeLA/XLA (cf. also Hornberger 2003; Ringbom 2005; Woll 2018).

15.3.3 Multilingual awareness (MLA) and the M-factor

The M-factor as an emergent property of the multilingual mind denotes the characteristics that multilingual speakers develop due to the constant interaction (CLIN) of several languages in their mind. Emergent phenomena in multilinguals are specific skills that comprise metalinguistic and metacognitive skills, but also certain social skills such as communicative sensitivity and pragmatic flexibility. They develop in unpredictable ways, and they differ from the properties displayed by the subsystems, i.e., single languages. The M-factor is described as a "dispositional effect which will have a priming or catalytic effect in TLA" (Herdina and Jessner 2002: 129–130). It might be called M-effect since it is difficult to decide whether it constitutes a precondition or a result of multilingualism. The M-effect refers to skills in multilingual speakers that "include skills in language learning, language management and language maintenance" (Herdina and Jessner 2002: 131). L3 learners display higher language learning skills than second language learners. Their language management skills can be defined as "the multilingual art of balancing communicative requirements with language resources" (Herdina and Jessner 2002: 131). Language maintenance refers to the effort needed to counteract language attrition. These skills are a crucial aspect of language acquisition that should receive more attention both in research and in the classroom.

The M-factor or M-effect has two main components, namely multilingual awareness (MLA) and an enhanced multilingual monitor (EMM), as illustrated in Figure 15.1. MLA consists of metalinguistic and cross-linguistic awareness, as already stated, as well as language learning awareness.

The M-factor, a function of the number of languages in a multilingual system and of their interaction (CLIN), expresses the difference in skills between monolingual and bi- or multilingual speakers when learning an L3 (Herdina and Jessner 2002: 130). The M-factor can thus be seen as a measure of the advantages that bi- and multilinguals have over monolinguals since the underlying assumption is that well-developed bi-/multilingual systems have components that are not present in monolingual systems or that are qualitatively different from those developed in monolingual systems (cf. Bono and Stratilaki 2009; Jessner 2008; Jessner 2016).

In DMM, multilingual awareness has been identified as *the* key factor of multilingual learning. It has a catalytic effect on further language learning (l) over time (t), leading to an improved learning curve, which is illustrated in Figure 15.2 taking the example of the development of a third language system or LS3.

Multilingual/metalinguistic awareness and abilities influence and facilitate L3 acquisition and learning, as a number of scholars have shown (e.g., Gibson and Hufeisen 2003; Hufeisen 2003; Jessner 2006; Meißner 2002; see also Chapter 14, this volume), and language maintenance (Herdina and Jessner 2000; see also Chapter 13, this volume). The level of multilingual/metalinguistic awareness and skills seems to increase with the number of languages involved.

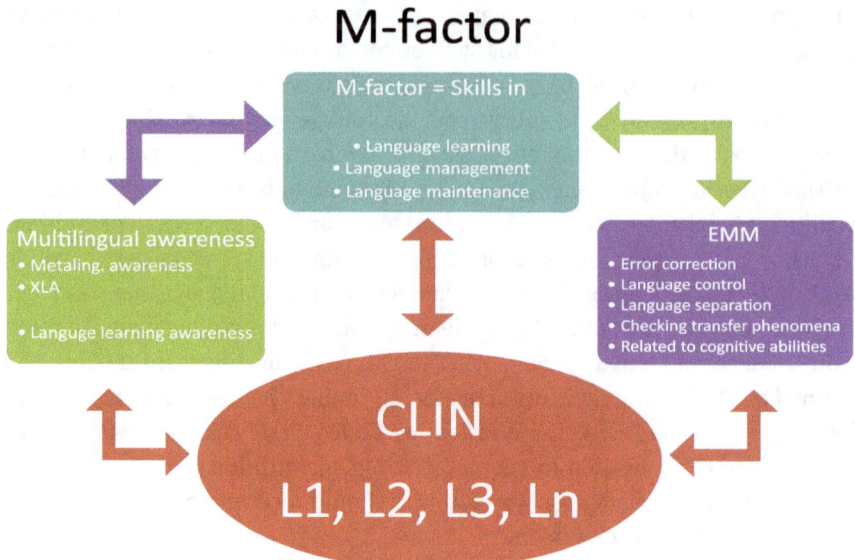

Figure 15.1: The M-factor as an emergent property of the multilingual mind (Allgäuer-Hackl 2017: 148, reprinted with permission).

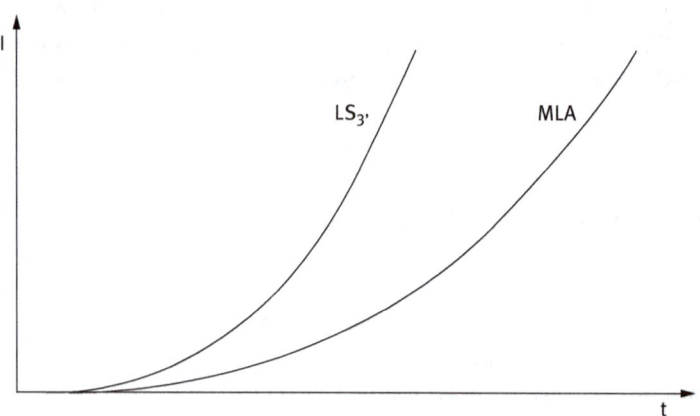

Figure 15.2: The catalytic effect of MLA on the development of LS3. MLA = multilingual awareness; LS3 = third language system; t = time; l = language level (adapted from Herdina and Jessner 2002: 117, reprinted with permission).

15.3.4 Testing multilingual awareness

A variety of test designs have been used and reported about in the literature on MLA, and they include various aspects such as grammatical metalinguistic awareness, pragmatic awareness, phonological awareness and morphological awareness. The following overview focuses on test designs used in the context of the "Dynamics of multilingualism with English" (DyME) research group on MeLA/XLA (see Section 15.3.3).

Pinto, Titone, and Trusso (1999) investigated MeLA in (monolingual) children, adolescents and adults and developed one of the most comprehensive test batteries for the three age groups, the Metalinguistic Abilities Test (MAT). The MAT I asks children, for instance, to carry out word order corrections, evaluate word length, and identify words, numbers and rhyme. For the MAT II, participants have to analyze the linguistic problems posed (semantic and grammatical relations; synonymy, ambiguity, and anomaly) and provide an explanation. In the MAT III, respondents are assessed on their ability to identify and correct errors of a morphosyntactic nature (linguistic tasks) and on the justification of their solutions (metalinguistic tasks). Additionally, they are tested on their understanding of figurative language. The tests have mainly been used to assess MeLA in native speakers of Italian, English, and Spanish; in the meantime, the MAT II and the MAT III have been translated into German (cf. Jessner, Hofer, and Pinto 2015a; Jessner et al. 2015b) and used in bilingual contexts in South Tyrol.

In the Metalinguistic Knowledge Test (MKT), an adaptation of a test developed by Alderson et al. (1997, as cited in Elder 2009), participants are given ungrammatical sentences in which the erroneous part is underlined, plus multiple-choice options that give (correct and incorrect) explanations for the rule which is being violated. According to Elder (2009: 117), the test measures passive metalinguistic knowledge, since learners do not have to actively verbalize rules.

Decoding or learning an unknown language is a further test format used in studies on MeLA. In Kemp (2007), the multilingual subjects were better at learning Basque than the monolinguals based on a higher level of grammatical metalinguistic awareness. Fehling (2008) included grammatical and morphological inferencing tasks (Swedish plural forms; Spanish and Swedish morphology) in her tests on MeLA. Another widely used method is that of grammaticality judgment tests. While studies on SLA mainly use grammaticality judgment tests to investigate MeLA, research into multilingualism covers a broader range of skills related to metalinguistic awareness, e.g., communicative sensibility, creativity, and flexibility.

Qualitative research employs Think Aloud Protocols (TAP) with introspective and/or retrospective comments to elicit information on processes involved in cross-linguistic word retrieval or text comprehension tasks (cf. Jessner 2006; Jessner and Török 2017). In her introspective study on lexical search in L3 production, Jessner (2006) also found that XLA and MeLA, tested in the form of explicit meta-language, exerted influence on the activation of the individual languages in the multilingual mental lexicon (see also Jessner, Megens, and Graus 2016). According to Woll (2018), introspective verbal data collected through TAPs complement findings based on language-inherent characteristics of CLI.

15.3.5 Studying multilingual awareness from a DMM perspective

15.3.5.1 Multilingual learning in institutional contexts

As pointed out above, members of the DyME group at Innsbruck University (www.dyme.uibk.ac.at) carried out a number of studies that focused on the nature of cross-linguistic interaction and multilingual awareness. Results consistently showed that experienced multilingual learners are specific language learners with a significant advantage in the development of multilingual/metalinguistic skills in comparison with less experienced learners/users.

Hofer (2015) studied the development of MeLA/XLA in 8- and 9-year-old primary school students in South Tyrol comparing pupils in what the researcher calls a "trilingual branch" with Italian and German as languages of instruction and English as L3 with pupils in a traditional setting, i.e. with Italian as the language of instruction and German plus English as additional languages. The trilingual branch in one school additionally offered a *Riflessione Lingua* ('reflection on language') class. All children's language proficiency was assessed in the three languages, and MeLA was tested using a shortened version of the MAT-2 (Pinto, Titone, and Trusso 1999). The results revealed a clear advantage for the children taught trilingually, who outperformed the control group by a significant margin in all language proficiency and MeLA tests. An equal number of hours in Italian and German in addition to systematic reference to language forms and structures in all three languages served to reinforce the trilingual pupils' multilingual awareness. This ties in with the notions of emergent properties and qualitative changes in trained multilinguals (cf. Hofer and Jessner 2019).

Another study on the development of MeLA/XLA in an Austrian vocational college carried out by Allgäuer-Hackl (2017) focused on emergent multilingual awareness among students who studied four languages at school, comparing those who additionally participated in a multilingual training class ("Multilingual Seminar" [MS]) with a control group who received no additional training. The research examined whether this type of training positively influenced multilingual awareness. The tasks to be carried out in the test related to metalinguistic awareness, cross-linguistic awareness, linguistic awareness, and language learning awareness (Jessner, Hofer, and Pinto 2015a; Jessner et al. 2015b; Pinto, Titone, and Trusso 1999). The study revealed that multilingual awareness training and multiple language use had a significant positive influence on the metalinguistic knowledge and skills the students needed for the analysis of an unknown language. Students in the MS group significantly outscored those in the control group on measures of (grammatical) metalinguistic awareness. The results thus point to an emerging quality in those students who participated in the training and highlight the different quality of language learning skills found in experienced multilinguals as compared to beginners (Cenoz 2003b). The three XLA tasks included in the MeLA test, by contrast, produced mixed results. MS participants, however, outscored the non-participants in one of the XLA tasks and displayed a broader range of word/text comprehension strategies than the control group. The MS group further scored significantly higher when the overall test results were compared. In addition to this, the MS participants displayed an enhanced self-reported awareness of language learning strategies and multilingual awareness. The findings of the present study substantiate the claim that multiple language use and MeLA/XLA training as offered in the MS contribute to enhanced multilingual awareness in its broadest sense (see also Haukås, Bjørke, and Dypedahl 2018).

15.3.5.2 Multilingual strategies as emergent properties in experienced multilinguals

Multilingual acquisition processes are considered to be supported by synergetic effects that emerge in experienced multilingual learners due to the enhanced (meta)linguistic and metacognitive knowledge which they accumulate. Results from two large-scale studies carried out at Innsbruck University (for a more detailed discussion, see Chapter 13, this volume) provide extensive proof of such emergent properties in multilinguals when dealing with an unknown foreign language, Rumanian. The participants' heightened MLA was evidenced through their use of supporter languages, which was based on (psycho)typology and grammatical awareness. The strategies that multilinguals used differed from those of both monolinguals and bilinguals, and to a certain extent also from those of less experienced multilingual language learners, not only in terms of quantity, but also with respect to their quality (cf. Jessner and Török 2017; cf. Kemp 2007).

From a DMM perspective, MeLA and XLA, which form part of multilinguals' strategies in L3 learning, can help overcome lack of knowledge in the case of reduced access to a language or confrontation with an unknown language. Furthermore, as indicated above, it has become evident that MLA as developed in multilingual learners and users adds to the quality of heightened awareness in strategy building in connection with problem solving and decision making.

Within the scope of the same unknown language task, Pargger (2013) compared German-speaking high school students who had been in contact with English and Italian as school subjects with a second group of students who had also been taught Latin. Think Aloud Protocols (TAPs) were used and, additionally, retrospective logs were compiled. The analysis of the records and logs revealed that both groups displayed a very high level of MLA; the learners of Latin, however, adopted a clearer analytical approach and used strategies based on solid linguistic principles, while the learners without Latin relied more on guesses. It seems that learners of Latin are more accustomed to analyzing and objectifying language and to reflecting on multilingual strategies than their peers who have had no Latin instruction. Although the former used their Latin knowledge relatively rarely in their cross-linguistic search, they showed a high level of MeLA and XLA by extensively applying successful problem-solving strategies while taking advantage of the interaction between their language systems. The results of the study make clear that experience with Latin led to qualitative differences in the use of cross-linguistic problem-solving strategies. Evidence for the positive effect of Latin in multilingual language learning from this and other studies (e.g., Siebel 2017) supports the claim for "multilingualism with Latin" (see Jessner, Török, and Pellegrini 2018), i.e., for curricula that include Latin to support the teaching and learning of multiple languages in European schools.

Dahm (2015: 43) further investigated the development of metacognitive strategies in young French students with English as an L2 who were successively confronted with three unknown languages (Dutch, Italian, and Finnish) through the PAUL (Pluralistic Approaches to Unknown Languages) approach. The overall experiment included semantic, syntactic and phonological activities. An analysis of the meta-semantic task – three short texts in the three languages mentioned above – showed that students developed certain cognitive strategies (e.g. comparing, translating, inferencing) and were able to transfer these successfully from one PAUL session to another. Dahm (2015), however, points out that for transfer to L2 English to happen, explicit instruction has to take place that bridges the gap between the PAUL tasks and the tasks in English.

15.4 Outlook: Multilingual awareness as an emergent factor in multilingual development

The research presented in the first part of this chapter deals with language contact phenomena in multilinguals, in particular with cross-linguistic influence (CLI) and cross-linguistic interaction (CLIN). The second part focuses on multilingual awareness (MLA), an umbrella term for metalinguistic and cross-linguistic awareness, from a DSCT/DMM stance. In this connection, the authors argue that MLA has to be regarded as a key factor in multilingual learning, maintenance and management processes. In order to support this claim, a number of studies carried out within a DMM context have been presented to highlight the crucial role of MLA in multiple language learning and use.

MeLA is increased in those monolinguals who work with language, and it has been shown to be enhanced in bilinguals when compared to monolinguals (cf. Bialystok 2005, 2009; De Angelis 2007). TLA research, for example, has provided ample evidence for the catalytic effect of MeLA on L3 learning (Cenoz 2003b; Herdina and Jessner, 2002: 116–117).

Multiple language learning and use, by contrast, is characterized by highly complex interactions between the various languages, which are additionally influenced by a variety of external factors, leading to emergent qualities in the overall system described as the M-factor (Herdina and Jessner 2002). The complex interplay of more than two languages in the multilingual brain results in a *multilingual advantage*, a unique state that can be related to multilingual awareness, i.e., metalinguistic and cross-linguistic awareness, emerging cognitive factors (cf. Cook 2016), and increased creativity (e.g., Kharkurin 2012). That is, MLA as an emergent property of the multilingual system differs from MLA in bilinguals, and there is an additional difference between more and less experienced multilinguals as a number of studies presented in this chapter have shown (Allgäuer-Hackl 2017; Aronin and Jessner 2015; Hofer 2015).

Future research should consider multilingualism studies as a research area in its own right, creating its own research framework that accounts for the dynamic and complex nature of CLIN in multilinguals. Within this framework, studies on MLA in connection with language learning and language maintenance strategies constitute one important focus since multilingual awareness plays a role in both processes. Furthermore, more qualitative research into the relationship between CLIN and MLA in multilingual comprehension and production is necessary to better understand how MLA works. A third research interest to be pursued in this connection is the enhanced strategic processing in experienced multilingual language learners as proof of the M-factor.

References

Allgäuer-Hackl, Elisabeth. 2017. *The development of metalinguistic awareness in multilingual learners. How effective is multilingual training in the classroom?* Innsbruck: University of Innsbruck dissertation.

Aronin, Larissa & Ulrike Jessner. 2015. Understanding current multilingualism: What can the butterfly tell us? In Ulrike Jessner & Claire Kramsch (eds.), *The multilingual challenge: Cross-disciplinary perspectives*, 271–291. Berlin & New York: Mouton de Gruyter.

Baker, Colin. 2011. *Foundations of bilingualism and bilingual education*. Clevedon: Multilingual Matters.

Baker, Colin & Nancy Hornberger. 2001. *An introductory reader to the writings of Jim Cummins*. Clevedon: Multilingual Matters.

Bardel, Camilla & Ylva Falk. 2007. The role of the second language in third language acquisition: The case of Germanic syntax. *Second Language Research* 23(4). 459–484.

Bialystok, Ellen. 2005. Consequences of bilingualism for cognitive development. In Judith F. Kroll & Annette M. B. De Groot (eds.), *Handbook of bilingualism: Psycholinguistic approaches*, 417–432. Oxford: Oxford UP.

Bialystok, Ellen. 2009. Bilingualism: The good, the bad, and the indifferent. *Bilingualism: Language and Cognition* 12(1). 3–11.

Bono, Mariana. 2011. Crosslinguistic interaction and metalinguistic awareness in third language acquisition. In Gessica De Angelis & Jean-Marc Dewaele (eds.), *New trends in crosslinguistic influence and multilingualism research*, 25–52. Bristol: Multilingual Matters.

Bono, Mariana & Sofia Stratilaki. 2009. The M-factor, a bilingual asset for plurilinguals? Learners' representations, discourse strategies and third language acquisition in institutional contexts. *International Journal of Multilingualism* 6(2). 207–227.

Cenoz, Jasone. 2001. The effect of linguistic distance, L2 status and age on cross-linguistic influence in third language acquisition. In Jasone Cenoz, Britta Hufeisen & Ulrike Jessner (eds.), *Cross-linguistic influence in third language acquisition: Psycholinguistic perspectives*, 8–20. Clevedon: Multilingual Matters.

Cenoz, Jasone. 2003a. The role of typology in the organization of the multilingual lexicon. In Jasone Cenoz, Britta Hufeisen & Ulrike Jessner (eds.), *The multilingual lexicon*, 103–116. Dordrecht: Kluwer Academic Publishers.

Cenoz, Jasone. 2003b. The additive effect of bilingualism on third language acquisition: A review. *The International Journal of Bilingualism: Cross-Disciplinary, Cross-Linguistic Studies of Language Behavior* 7(1). 71–87.

Cenoz, Jasone & Durk Gorter. 2011. Focus on multilingualism: A study of trilingual writing. *The Modern Language Journal* 95(3). 356–369.

Cenoz, Jasone, Britta Hufeisen & Ulrike Jessner. (eds.) 2001. *Cross-linguistic influence in third language acquisition: psycholinguistic perspectives*. Clevedon: Multilingual Matters.

Cenoz, Jasone, Britta Hufeisen & Ulrike Jessner. 2003. Why investigate the multilingual lexicon? In Jasone Cenoz, Britta Hufeisen & Ulrike Jessner (eds.), *The multilingual lexicon*, 1–9. Dordrecht: Kluwer Academic Publishers.

Cheung, Anna, Stephen Matthews & Wai Lan Tsang. 2011. Transfer from L3 German to L2 English in the domain of tense/aspect. In Gessica De Angelis & Jean-Marc Dewaele (eds.), *New trends in crosslinguistic influence and multilingualism research*, 53–73. Bristol: Multilingual Matters.

Cook, Vivian (ed.). 2003. *Effects of the second language on the first*. Clevedon: Multilingual Matters.

Cook, Vivian. 2016. Transfer and the relationships between the languages of multicompetence. In Rosa Alonso Alonso (ed.), *Crosslinguistic influence in second language acquisition*, 24–37. Bristol: Multilingual Matters.

Dahm, Rebecca. 2015. Developing cognitive strategies through pluralistic approaches. In Gessica De Angelis, Ulrike Jessner & Marijana Kresic (eds.), *Crosslinguistic influence and crosslinguistic interaction in multilingual language learning*, 43–70. London: Bloomsbury.

De Angelis, Gessica. 2007. *Third or additional language learning*. Clevedon: Multilingual Matters.

De Angelis, Gessica & Jean-Marc Dewaele. 2011. *New trends in crosslinguistic influence and multilingualism research*. Bristol: Multilingual Matters.

De Angelis, Gessica & Ulrike Jessner. 2012. Writing across languages in a bilingual context: A dynamic systems theory perspective. In Rosa Manchon (ed.), *L2 writing development: Multiple perspectives*, 47–68. Berlin & New York: Mouton de Gruyter.

De Angelis, Gessica & Larry Selinker. 2001. Interlanguage transfer and competing linguistic systems in the multilingual mind. In Jasone Cenoz, Britta Hufeisen & Ulrike Jessner (eds.), *Cross-linguistic influence in third language acquisition: Psycholinguistic perspectives*, 42–58. Clevedon: Multilingual Matters.

De Angelis, Gessica, Ulrike Jessner & Marijana Kresic (eds.). 2015. *Crosslinguistic influence and crosslinguistic interaction in multilingual language learning*. London: Bloomsbury.

Ecke, Peter. 2001. Lexical retrieval in a third language: Evidence from errors and tip- of-the-tongue states. In Jasone Cenoz, Britta Hufeisen & Ulrike Jessner (eds.), *Cross-linguistic influence in third language acquisition: Psycholinguistic perspectives*, 90–114. Clevedon: Multilingual Matters.

Elder, Catherine. 2009. Validating a test of metalinguistic knowledge. In Rod Ellis, Shawn Loewen, Catherine Elder, Rosemary Erlam, Jenefer Philp & Hayo Reinders (eds.), *Implicit and explicit knowledge in second language learning, testing and teaching*, 113–138. Bristol: Multilingual Matters.

Fehling, Sylvia. 2008. *Language awareness und bilingualer Unterricht* (Series Language culture literacy 1). Frankfurt & Main: Peter Lang.

Flynn, Suzanne, Claire Foley & Inna Vinnitskaya. 2004. The Cumulative-Enhancement Model for language acquisition: Comparing adults' and children's patterns of development in first, second and third language acquisition of relative clauses. *International Journal of Multilingualism* 1(1). 3–16.

Gibson, Martha & Britta Hufeisen. 2003. Investigating the role of prior foreign language knowledge: Translating from an unknown into a known foreign language. In Jasone Cenoz, Britta Hufeisen & Ulrike Jessner (eds.), *The multilingual lexicon*. Dordrecht: Kluwer, 87–102.

Gibson, Martha & Britta Hufeisen 2011. Perception of preposition errors in semantically correct versus erroneous contexts by multilingual advanced English as a Foreign Language learners: Measuring metalinguistic awareness. In Gessica De Angelis & Jean-Marc Dewaele (eds.), *New trends in crosslinguistic influence and multilingualism research*, 74–85. Bristol: Multilingual Matters.

Gibson, Martha, Britta Hufeisen & Garry Libben 2001. Learners of German as an L3 and their production of German prepositional verbs. In Jasone Cenoz, Britta Hufeisen & Ulrike Jessner (eds.), *Cross-linguistic influence in third language acquisition: Psycholinguistic perspectives*, 138–148. Clevedon: Multilingual Matters.

Gombert, Jean, E. 1992. *Metalinguistic development*. New York, London: Harvester-Wheatsheaf.

Gut, Ulrike. 2010. Cross-linguistic influence in L3 phonological acquisition. *International Journal of Multilingualism* 7(1). 19–38.

Hammarberg, Björn. 2001. Roles of L1 and L2 in L3 production and acquisition. In Jasone Cenoz, Britta Hufeisen & Ulrike Jessner (eds.), *Cross-linguistic influence in third language acquisition: Psycholinguistic perspectives*, 21–41. Clevedon: Multilingual Matters.

Haukås, Åsta, Camilla Bjørke & Magne Dypedahl (eds.). 2018. *Metacognition in language learning*. London: Routledge (OA).

Herdina, Philip & Ulrike Jessner. 2000. The dynamics of third language acquisition. In Jasone Cenoz & Ulrike Jessner (eds.), *English in Europe: The acquisition of a third language*, 84–98. Clevedon: Multilingual Matters.

Herdina, Philip & Ulrike Jessner. 2002. *A dynamic model of multilingualism: Perspectives of change in psycholinguistics*. Clevedon: Multilingual Matters.

Herwig, Anna. 2001. Plurilingual lexical organisation: Evidence from lexical processing in L1-L2-L3-L4 translation. In Jasone Cenoz, Britta Hufeisen & Ulrike Jessner (eds.), *Cross-linguistic influence in third language acquisition: Psycholinguistic perspectives*, 115–137. Clevedon: Multilingual Matters.

Hofer, Barbara. 2015. *On the dynamics of early multilingualism: A psycholinguistic study*. (Trends in applied linguistics 13). Berlin & Boston: De Gruyter.

Hofer, Barbara & Ulrike Jessner. 2019. Multilingualism at the primary level in South Tyrol: How does multilingual education affect young learners' metalinguistic awareness and proficiency in L1, L2 and L3? *The Language Learning Journal* 47(1). 76–87.

Hornberger, Nancy H. (ed.). 2003. *Continua of biliteracy: An ecological framework for educational policy, research and practice in multilingual settings*. Clevedon: Multilingual Matters.

Hufeisen, Britta. 2003. Muttersprache Französisch – Erste Fremdsprache Englisch – Zweite Fremdsprache Deutsch: Sprachen lernen gegeneinander oder besser miteinander? In Franz-Joseph Meißner & Ilse Picaper (eds.), *Mehrsprachigkeitsdidaktik zwischen Frankreich, Belgien und Deutschland*, 49–61. Tübingen: Gunter Narr.

James, Carl. 1996. A cross-linguistic approach to language awareness. *Language Awareness* 5(3–4). 138–148.

Jarvis, Scott & Aneta, Pavlenko. 2008. *Crosslinguistic influence in language and cognition*. New York: Routledge.

Jessner, Ulrike. 2005. Expanding scopes and building bridges: Learning and teaching English as a third language. In Claus Gnutzmann & Frauke Intemann (eds.), *The globalisation of English and the English language classroom*, 231–244. Tübingen: Narr.

Jessner, Ulrike. 2006. *Linguistic awareness in multilinguals: English as a third language*. Edinburgh: Edinburgh University Press.

Jessner, Ulrike. 2008. A DST model of multilingualism and the role of metalinguistic awareness. *Modern Language Journal* 92(2). 270–284.

Jessner, Ulrike. 2016. Multicompetence approaches to language proficiency development in multilingual education. In Ofelia García & Angel Lin (eds.), *Encyclopedia of language and education* (Bilingual Programs Vol. 5), 161–173. New York: Springer.

Jessner, Ulrike. (2019). Metalinguistic awareness and multilingual development. In Jeroen Darquennes, Joe Salmons & Wim Vandenbussche (eds.), *Handbook of language contact*, 221–232. New York: Mouton de Gruyter.

Jessner, Ulrike & Valentina Török. 2017. Strategies in multilingual learning: Opening new research avenues. In Judit Navracsics & Simone Pfenninger (eds.), *Implications for the future: Applied linguistics perspectives*, 192–211. Bristol: Multilingual Matters.

Jessner, Ulrike, Barbara Hofer & Maria A. Pinto. 2015a. *MKT Metalinguistischer Kompetenztest, Teil 2*. Innsbruck: Universitätsverlag Studia.

Jessner, Ulrike, Manon Megens & Stefanie Graus. 2016. Crosslinguistic influence in third language acquisition. In Rosa Alonso Alonso (ed.), *Crosslinguistic influence in second language acquisition*, 193–124. Clevedon: Multilingual Matters.

Jessner, Ulrike, Valentina Török & Claudia Pellegrini. 2018. The role of Latin in multilingual learners' strategies. *Langscape* 1. 85–102.

Jessner, Ulrike, Claudia Pellegrini, Verena Moroder, Barbara Hofer & Maria A. Pinto. 2015b. *MKT Metalinguistischer Kompetenztest, Teil 3*. Innsbruck: Universitätsverlag Studia.

Kellerman, Eric. 1995. Crosslinguistic influence: Transfer to nowhere? *Annual Review of Applied Linguistics* 15. 125–150.

Kellerman, Eric & Michael Sharwood-Smith. (eds.). 1986. *Crosslinguistic influence and second language acquisition*. Oxford: Pergamon Press.

Kemp, Charlotte. 2007. Strategic processing in grammar learning: Do multilinguals use more strategies? *International Journal of Multilingualism* 4. 241–61.

Kharkhurin, Anatoliy V. 2012. *Multilingualism and creativity*. Bristol: Multilingual Matters.

Lindquist, Christina. 2015. Do learners transfer from the language they perceive as most closely related to the L3? The role of psychotypology for lexical and grammatical crosslinguistic influence in French L3. In Gessica De Angelis, Ulrike Jessner & Marijana Kresic (eds.), *Crosslinguistic influence and crosslinguistic interaction in multilingual language learning*, 231–252. London & New York: Bloomsbury.

Lüdi, Georges & Bernard Py. 2009. To be or not to be ... a plurilingual speaker. *International Journal of Multilingualism* 6(2). 154–167.

Malakoff, Marguerite & Kenji Hakuta. 1991. Translation skill and metalinguistic awareness in bilinguals. In Ellen Bialystok (ed.), *Language processing in bilingual children*, 141–166. Cambridge & New York: Cambridge University Press.

Marx, Nicole & Grit Mehlhorn. 2010. Pushing the positive: Encouraging phonological transfer from L2 to L3. *International Journal of Multilingualism* 7(1). 4–18.

Mayr, Robert & Simona Montanari. 2015. Cross-linguistic interaction in trilingual phonological development: The role of the input in the acquisition of the voicing contrast. *Journal of Child Language* 42(5). 1006–1035.

Meißner, Franz-Joseph. 2002. Transfer aus der Sicht der Mehrsprachigkeitsdidaktik. In Armin Wolff & Martin Lange (eds.), *Europäisches Jahr der Sprachen: Mehrsprachigkeit in Europa* (Materialien DaF 65), 128–142. Regensburg: Verlag.

Mieszkowska, Karolina & Agnieszka Otwinowska. 2015. Is A2 in German better than B2 in French when reading Danish? The role of prior language knowledge when faced with an unknown language. In Gessica De Angelis Ulrike Jessner & Marijana Kresic (eds.), *Crosslinguistic influence and crosslinguistic interaction in multilingual language learning*, 199–230. London: Bloomsbury.

Odlin, Terence. 2016. Was there really ever a contrastive analysis hypothesis? In Rosa Alonso Alonso (ed.), *Crosslinguistic influence in second language acquisition*, 1–23. Clevedon: Multilingual Matters.

Ó Laoire, Muiris. 2005. L1, L2 and L3 teaching in Ireland: Towards a common curriculum. In Britta Hufeisen & Madeline Lutjeharms (eds.), *Gesamtsprachencurriculum, Integrierte Sprachendidaktik, Common Curriculum*, 45–50. Tübingen: Narr.

Pargger, Katharina. 2013. *The impact of metalinguistic awareness on multilingual learners exploring foreign languages in the classroom: The role of Latin in crosslinguistic search*. Innsbruck: University of Innsbruck diploma thesis.

Pavlenko, Aneta & Scott Jarvis. 2002. Bidirectional transfer. *Applied Linguistics* 23. 190–214.

Pinto, Maria A., Renzo Titone & Francesca Trusso. 1999. *Metalinguistic awareness: Theory, development and measurement instruments*. Pisa: Istituti Editoriali e Poligrafici Internazionali.

Ringbom, Håkan. 2001. Lexical transfer in L3 production. In Jasone Cenoz, Britta Hufeisen & Ulrike Jessner (eds.), *Cross-linguistic influence in third language acquisition: Psycholinguistic perspectives*, 59–68. Clevedon: Multilingual Matters.

Ringbom, Håkan. 2005. L2-transfer in third language acquisition. In Britta Hufeisen & Robert J. Fouser (eds.), *Introductory readings in L3 (Tertiärsprachen. Drei- und Mehrsprachigkeit)*, 71–82. Tübingen: Stauffenburg.

Rothman, Jason. 2011. L3 syntactic transfer selectivity and typological determinacy: The typological primacy model. *Second Language Research* 27(1). 107–217.

Sanchez, Laura. 2011. "Luisa and Pedrito's Dog will the Breakfast Eat": Interlanguage transfer and the role of the second language factor. In Gessica De Angelis & Jean-Marc Dewaele (eds.), *New trends in crosslinguistic influence and multilingualism research*, 86–104. Bristol: Multilingual Matters.

Siebel, Katrin. 2017. *Mehrsprachigkeit und Lateinunterricht: Überlegungen zum lateinischen Lernwortschatz*. Göttingen: V&R Unipress.

Simard, Daphnée & Xavier Gutiérrez. 2018. The study of metalinguistic constructs in second language acquisition research. In Peter Garrett & Josep M. Cots (eds.), *The Routledge handbook of language awareness*, 205–221. London: Routledge.

Stavans, Anat. 2015. "If you know Amharic, you can read this": Emergent literacy in multilingual pre-reading children. In Gessica De Angelis, Ulrike Jessner & Marijana Kresic (eds.), *Crosslinguistic influence and crosslinguistic interaction in multilingual language learning*, 149–172. London: Bloomsbury.

Swarte, Femke, Anja Schüppert & Charlotte Gooskens. 2015. Does German help speakers of Dutch to understand written and spoken Danish words? The role of non-native language knowledge in decoding an unknown but related language. In Gessica De Angelis, Ulrike Jessner & Marijana Kresic (eds.), *Crosslinguistic influence and crosslinguistic interaction in multilingual language learning*, 173–198. London: Bloomsbury.

Thomas, Jaqueline. 1988. The role played by metalinguistic awareness in second and third language learning. *Journal of Multilingual and Multicultural Development* 9(3). 235–246.

Todeva, Elka. 2009. Multilingualism as a kaleidoscopic experience: The mini universes within. In Elka Todeva & Jasone Cenoz (eds.), *The multiple realities of multilingualism: Personal narratives and researchers' perspectives*, 53–74. Berlin: Mouton de Gruyter.

Vanhove, Jan & Raphael Berthele. 2015. Item-related determinants of cognate guessing in multilinguals. In Gessica De Angelis, Ulrike Jessner & Marijana Kresic (eds.), *Crosslinguistic influence and crosslinguistic interaction in multilingual language learning*, 71–94. London: Bloomsbury.

Williams, Sarah & Björn Hammarberg. 1998. Language switches in L3 production: Implications for a polyglot speaking model. *Applied Linguistics* 19(3). 295–333.

Woll, Nina. 2018. Investigating dimensions of metalinguistic awareness. What think-aloud protocols revealed about the cognitive processes involved in positive transfer from L2 to L3. *Language Awareness* 27(1–2). 167–185.

Wrembel, Magdalena. 2010. L2-accented speech in L3 production. *International Journal of Multilingualism* 7(1). 75–90.

Zawadzka, Agnieszka. 2011. Transfer aus vorgelernten Sprachen als Lernerleichterung im schulischen Unterricht: Polnisch als dritte Fremdsprache? Zum (möglichen) Umgang mit sprachlichem Vorwissen. In Rupprecht S. Baur & Britta Hufeisen (eds.), *"Vieles ist sehr ähnlich". Individuelle und gesellschaftliche Mehrsprachigkeit als bildungspolitische Aufgabe*. (Multilingualism and Multiple Language Acquisition and Learning, 6), 7–29. Baltmannsweiler: Schneider Hohengehren.

Dorit Segal, Gitit Kavé, Mira Goral and Tamar H. Gollan

16 Multilingualism and Cognitive Benefits in Aging

16.1 Introduction

The increased number of older people across the world has led many scientists to search for protective factors against the deleterious effects of cognitive aging (Bak 2016). Several studies have shown that higher levels of education, and especially literacy levels, improve memory and executive functioning in old age (e.g., Albert et al. 1995; Barnes et al. 2004; Manly et al. 2005). Similarly, childhood intelligence level, more complex lifetime occupation (Finkel et al. 2009), and mentally stimulating leisure activities (Valenzuela and Sachdev 2006) improve cognitive performance in old age. The assumption is that intellectual engagement and mental effort create *cognitive reserve*, which may delay the onset of cognitive decline, slow its progress, or alleviate its manifestations (Richards and Deary 2005; Stern 2002). Several studies have suggested that bilingual language use has a similar effect. Indeed, it has been found that bilingualism is associated with cognitive advantages on non-linguistic tasks in old age (e.g., Bialystok, Craik, and Ryan 2006; Bialystok et al. 2004; but see Lehtonen et al. 2018; Paap, Johnson, and Sawi 2015). Bilingualism has also been associated with a delay of up to four years in the onset of dementia (e.g., Alladi et al. 2013; Bialystok, Craik, and Freedman 2007; Bialystok et al. 2014; Craik, Bialystok, and Freedman 2010; Schweizer et al. 2012; Woumans et al. 2015).

16.2 Bilingualism and cognitive performance in old age

Bilingual language use may benefit cognitive performance because it forces speakers not only to select between within-language competitors, just as monolingual speakers do, but also to select between translation equivalent competitors, to

---
Dorit Segal, Tamar H. Gollan, University of California, San Diego (CA), U.S.A.
Gitit Kavé, The Open University, Ra'anana, Israel
Mira Goral, Lehman College and the Graduate Center of CUNY, New York (NY), U.S.A. & Multiling, Center for Multilingualism in Society across the Lifespan, University of Oslo, Oslo, Norway

https://doi.org/10.1515/9781501507984-016

switch between their languages, and to monitor which language is used in what context. Thus, bilingual speakers have to choose between multiple competing alternatives both within and across languages, and to switch between lexicons and grammatical structures. They repeatedly decide whether to constrain their communication to one language or use both languages in a single conversation, or even in a single sentence. This experience in bilingual language use was shown to improve cognitive functions, especially in older adults. For example, Bialystok et al. (2004) found that bilingualism was associated with better inhibition (smaller Simon effects), and the effect was larger in older adults. They compared performance on a task that required participants to press a left key when seeing a blue square and a right key when seeing a red square. On half the trials the square appeared on the same side as the associated response key (congruent condition) and on the other half the square appeared on the opposite side (incongruent condition). Responses to congruent items were generally faster than responses to incongruent items. Importantly, the incongruent items were less disruptive for both middle aged and older bilinguals relative to monolinguals of the same age. Note, however, that several studies failed to replicate these results. For example, Kirk et al. (2014) found no group differences in either the magnitude of the Simon interference effect or in global reaction times (see also reviews by Lehtonen, et al., 2018; Paap, Johnson, and Sawi, 2015).

In recent years, studies have shown that specific aspects of language use, such as the frequency of use or the relative proficiency in one language versus the other, are the source of cognitive advantages. For example, Goral, Campanelli, and Spiro (2015) found differences in inhibition between balanced bilinguals who used their two languages equally often and dominant bilinguals who used primarily one language although they knew another. Dominant bilinguals showed no age-related inhibition decline, as measured by the Simon test, whereas balanced bilinguals demonstrated a greater Simon effect with increasing age. The authors suggested that dominant bilinguals invest more effort in inhibiting the more proficient language, while balanced bilinguals have achieved greater independence of the two languages, thus exercising inhibition less regularly. However, Bogulski et al. (2015) found that full bilinguals outperformed monolinguals on memory tasks, and that individuals who were fluent in a second language and then stopped using it (i.e., lapsed bilinguals) performed somewhere between them. Therefore, the studies described above are inconclusive as to whether more second language use (Bogulski et al. 2015) or less second language use (Goral et al. 2015) is related to more advantageous cognitive performance. Yet, both studies show that specific characteristics of bilingualism might affect performance, as well as the subsequent effect on cognitive aging.

The extent of language switching practices has also been shown to be especially critical for cognitive performance (for a review see Yang, Hartanto, and Yang 2016). For example, Prior and Gollan (2011) showed that bilinguals who reported frequent language switching demonstrated a lower cost of task-switching relative to bilinguals who reported infrequent switching. Verreyt et al. (2016) found that bilingual speakers who switched languages frequently had better executive control (i.e., smaller congruency effects) than did bilinguals with similar language proficiency who did not switch as often. Furthermore, Hofweber, Marinis, and Treffers-Daller (2016) demonstrated that the type of code switching that bilinguals used affected inhibitory advantages on a condition that required more conflict-monitoring in a flanker task (i.e., a task that requires focus of attention in the presence of visual distraction). These studies suggest that language switching enhances cognitive performance by making speakers practice monitoring and inhibition mechanisms. Other studies revealed important differences between intended and unintended switches, with the latter reflecting greater susceptibility to cross-language interference and revealing weaker monitoring abilities. For example, Festman, Rodriguez-Fornells, and Münte (2010) asked bilingual participants to name pictures in German or in Russian in a fixed order (two pictures in German followed by two pictures in Russian). Bilinguals who often named pictures in the wrong language (unintended intrusions) also performed worse on tasks of executive functioning (see also Gollan, Sandoval, and Salmon 2011). As these studies suggest, specific characteristics of the bilingual experience, such as language switching, might be responsible for the improvement in cognitive performance and for the delay in cognitive aging that have been associated with bilingualism.

16.3 Multilingualism and cognitive performance in old age

If using two languages enhances cognitive abilities and provides cognitive reserve, using more than two languages may magnify these effects even further. Indeed, several studies have found that the number of languages that a person speaks predicts cognitive functioning in old age. For example, Kavé et al. (2008) analyzed data from a sample of 814 older people in Israel, which was stratified by age group (75–79 years, 80–84 years, 85–89 years, 90–94 years), and by country of birth (Israel, Europe or America, Asia or Africa). Data collection involved three interviews across 12 years. Participants reported speaking two, three, or more than three languages, and those who knew more languages performed best on a cognitive-screening test that assessed time orientation, memory, and concentration. Furthermore, the number of languages predicted cognitive status beyond other demographic variables, such as age, gender, place of birth, age at immigration, and education level. The same effect of number of languages was also found for a subset of individuals with no formal education at all. In a later study, Chertkow et al. (2010) examined files of 632 Canadian individuals who received a diagnosis of probable Alzheimer's disease (AD) and found that speaking two or more languages delayed diagnosis by five years, especially in immigrants. Perquin et al. (2013) tested 232 older adults (mean age = 73) in Luxembourg where there are three official languages. Relative to bilinguals, individuals who used more than two languages were three times less likely to demonstrate a decline in memory or in other cognitive abilities. Pot, Keijzer, and de Bot (2018) examined 387 older adults in the Netherlands who spoke several dialects or several different languages. They found that the number of dialects and languages that a person reported knowing was not related to smaller flanker effects. However, proficiency and frequency of use of the second and third languages in different social contexts predicted the size of the flanker effect. These studies suggest that the use of several languages, in different contexts, can affect performance on nonlinguistic cognitive tests, and that testing multilingual speakers can broaden our understanding of the effects of language use on cognition beyond the demonstrated effect of bilingualism. Nevertheless, there are currently relatively few studies of multilingualism in old age, and the roles of the different multilingual variables are not well understood.

16.3.1 Challenges to research on multilingualism and aging

This scarcity of research on multilingualism and cognitive performance in old age is likely related to the difficulty in defining and measuring multilingualism and to the heterogeneity of this construct. For example, studies of bilingualism often determine language proficiency by asking participants to self-rate their language proficiency or by presenting them with parallel versions of a test that should be performed in each of their languages (Gollan et al. 2011). Comparing two languages through such methods is relatively straightforward, but the same is not true when more languages are involved. While it is fairly easy to find bilinguals who speak the same two languages, it is much harder to recruit participants who speak the same three or four languages, and to test all participants with an equivalent task. Therefore, studies of multilingual speakers often use self-reported language proficiency, even though this method has been shown to be less accurate than objective measures (Tomoschuk, Ferreira, and Gollan 2018).

Moreover, multilingual speakers are quite diverse in their education and literacy levels, two factors that have been shown to be critical when looking for bilingual advantages (Gollan et al. 2011; Zahodne et al. 2014). Indeed, bilingualism is often correlated with education level, and this correlation can be even stronger in multilingual participants, since some speakers acquire their first one or two languages informally but their other languages through formal instruction. For instance, Ihle et al. (2016) examined over 2500 adults (ages 65–101), and found that the number of languages that participants spoke did not predict their processing speed and cognitive flexibility beyond education level. However, these results contrast with earlier findings in which the number of languages contributed to cognitive performance beyond the effect of education (i.e., Kavé et al. 2008). Another challenge in studies of older multilingual speakers is the question of literacy (Kemp 2009). It is very common for multilingual speakers to be literate in only one or two of the languages that they speak, and literacy has been shown to affect cognitive performance (e.g., Barnes et al. 2004; Scribner and Cole 1981; Chapter 14, this volume).

Thus, it might be necessary to match groups in terms of education, and to also control for lifestyle, socio-economic status, IQ, gender, and age (e.g., de Bruin, Bak, and Della Sala 2015; Gathercole et al. 2014; Paap and Greenberg 2013; Zahodne et al. 2014) before we can tell whether multilingual language use in fact improves cognitive performance. Yet, it is difficult to apply such an approach to the study of multilingualism in old age, primarily because any group of multilingual speakers is quite diverse in language background and experience. For example, the participants in Kavé et al.'s (2008) study spoke 35 different languages, and those who immigrated to Israel, where they learned the language in which the interview was conducted, varied greatly in country of origin and age of immigration. This heterogeneity limits our understanding of how the type of language, the age of acquisition of the languages that a person speaks, or the frequency of language switching, among other factors, might mediate the association between the number of languages and cognitive functioning in old age. We note that another possible challenge to the study of the benefits of multilingualism in old age is the fact that many multilingual speakers change their patterns of language use and language proficiency across their lifespan, and it is often difficult for them to provide a reliable report of some of these critical variables.

Thus, although there are studies that show that multilingualism benefits cognitive performance in aging, these studies have mainly focused on short screening tests (Kavé et al. 2008) or on the possible delay in dementia onset (e.g., Chertkow et al. 2010), with only few investigations of the effects of multilingualism on tasks of memory or inhibitory control (Ihle et al. 2016; Pot, Keijzer, and de Bot 2018). In addition, the few studies of multilingualism in old age have rarely investigated the effects of individual differences in language use on the presumed benefit of multilingualism. It remains to be seen whether the same individual differences that have been identified in research on bilingualism also play an important role in mediating the multilingualism effect. Despite the "noise" inherent in studying heterogeneous groups of participants, such individual differences must be acknowledged and directly examined within a multilingual sample.

16.4 A preliminary study of the effects of multilingualism on cognitive performance in aging

To examine whether multilingualism mediates the effects of age on cognitive performance, we conducted a preliminary study with a heterogeneous sample of monolingual, bilingual, and multilingual adults spanning a wide age range. We examined how variables that have been found to mediate the bilingual effect might associate with the effects of multilingualism. We focused on age of language acquisition, level of language proficiency, frequency of language use, and switching habits, and analyzed their impact on cognitive performance. Specifically, we asked whether the number of languages that a person knows and the proficiency in these languages would add to the prediction of cognitive performance beyond the effects of education and age.

16.4.1 Participants

We recruited 198 participants between age 22 and age 90 (M = 51, SD = 17) to complete an online survey. Snowball sampling was used to recruit participants primarily in Israel, among Israelis living in English-speaking countries (the US, Canada, Australia, and Great Britain), or among their non-Israeli acquaintances. Eighteen participants who did not complete critical parts of the questionnaire (e.g., age) were excluded from the sample. For participants who filled out the questionnaire in more than one session (N = 30), only the first session was included in the analysis to eliminate possible practice effects. Table 16.1 shows the language characteristics of the final sample (N = 180). Thirty-one participants

Table 16.1: Means and standard deviations of background variables.

	Youngest (ages 22–39) n = 55 70% female			Middle age (ages 40–59) n = 72 65% female			Oldest (ages 60–90) n = 53 65% female			Comparison of the three age groups		
	M	SD	n	M	SD	n	M	SD	n	F	p	Effect size (η^2)
Age	31.96	4.88	55	50.36	5.50	72	71.96	7.27	53	619.28	<.001	.88
Education	17.40	2.67	55	17.40	2.67	72	16.91	3.13	53	.39	.68	.00
Number of Languages	2.28	.86	53	2.32	.98	71	2.27	1.05	52	.05	.953	.00
Language Switch [a]	2.52	1.25	48	2.75	1.23	57	2.36	1.33	44	1.22	.298	.02
L1 self-rating [b]	6.84	.48	49	6.70	.66	57	6.37	.84	41	5.65	.004	.07
L1 AoA [c]	1.00	2.29	49	1.80	4.97	57	5.00	6.64	42	8.46	<.001	.11
L2 self-rating [b]	5.13	1.14	47	5.11	1.29	54	4.49	1.42	35	3.14	.047	.05
L2 AoA [c]	7.03	3.53	47	9.48	6.94	52	10.04	4.86	36	3.88	.023	.06
L3+L4 self-rating [d]	2.52	.25	15	2.95	.22	31	3.45	.29	20	2.72	.073	.08
L3+L4 AoA [e]	12.8	6.71	15	17.94	13.25	31	12.70	17.18	20	1.21	.304	.04

[a] Frequency of language switching was rated on a scale of 1 (do not switch at all) to 5 (switch most of the time).
[b] Average of self-rating of proficiency across modalities (speaking, understanding, reading, and writing), with 1 corresponding to "almost not at all" and 7 to "like a native speaker" in most proficient language.
[c] Age of Acquisition.
[d] Average of L3 and L4 self-ratings. [e] Average of L3 and L4 AoA.

reported knowing one language, 71 participants reported knowing two languages, 43 participants reported knowing three languages, and 24 participants reported knowing four languages. The remaining participants (N = 11) could not be classified as monolingual, bilingual, or multilingual, because they did not report the number of languages that they knew. These participants were included only in analyses that did not investigate the effects of multilingualism (e.g., analyses of aging effects). Seventy percent of the sample reported living in Israel, 20% reported living in the U.S., 6% reported living in Canada, and the remaining participants reported living elsewhere. Thirty percent of the participants were immigrants (i.e., did not live in the country in which they were born), and education levels varied from 10 to 28 years. The dominant or the second-most dominant languages were mostly Hebrew (73% and 12%, respectively) or English (23% and 70%, respectively), and the third language was more varied (31% French, 15% Spanish, 13% English, 12% German, 9% Arabic, and lower percentages for several other languages). There were no clear patterns regarding the fourth language, and there were almost as many different fourth languages as there were participants who reported speaking them.

16.4.2 Procedure and materials

Demographic questions. At the beginning of the survey, participants were asked to report their age and level of education, as well as the country in which they lived, the country in which they were born, and their age of immigration (if applicable).

Language Background. Participants were asked to report their language history (for example, which language was learned first and which language was spoken at home while growing up). In reference to each language that they knew, starting from the most dominant one, participants were asked to report how old they were when they first started learning that language, in which environment they learned that language (family, school, work, other), and how proficient they were in speaking, understanding, reading, and writing in that language on a scale of 1 to 7 (1 – very poor, 2 – poor, 3 – basic, 4 – good, 5 – very good, 6 – excellent, 7 – like a native speaker). Participants were also asked whether they switched languages when speaking to other people who spoke the same languages, and how often they did so (1 – no, 2 – hardly, 3 – some, 4 – often, 5 – most of the time). The language history questionnaire was very detailed in order to reflect the multilingual experience as accurately as possible. However, to reduce the number of comparisons, we focused on variables that were shown to be significant in the literature. We thus analyzed the number of languages that the person reported knowing, language proficiency (self-rated proficiency in each language), age of acquisition of each language, and the frequency of language switching.

The survey included several cognitive tasks as follows:

Naming and memory. We selected 12 black and white drawings whose names varied in frequency (barrel, curtain, drum, fish, glass, hammer, hand, nest, peacock, ruler, table, and tree). Each item has the same number of syllables in both Hebrew and English.

First, participants studied items for later recall through semantic classification. Each item was presented on the screen with no time limitation and participants were asked to press YES if it was man-made (7 items) or NO if it was not (5 items). The next item was presented after a decision was made. Classification began with two examples (i.e., house, apple), and the order of experimental items was randomly determined for each participant.

Second, participants were asked to name items in their dominant language. They were told that they would see the same drawings again, and that they were to type the name of the drawing in one word. They were asked to use their best language and work as quickly as possible. Each item was presented on the screen separately with no time limitation. The order of items was randomly determined for each participant. We analyzed the number of pictures that were named correctly (range 1–12), and this naming score served as a language proficiency measure. The naming score also contributed to classification of language dominance (see below).

Third, immediate recall was examined. Immediately following the naming task, participants were presented with 12 empty slots and were asked to write down as many names of drawings as they could remember. The instructions did not refer to the language in which naming should be done. We analyzed the number of recalled items (range 1–12).

Fourth, delayed recall was examined. Following all tasks and demographic questions, participants were again presented with 12 empty slots and were asked to write down as many names of drawings as they could remember. Again, there was no mention of which language should be used to name the pictures. We analyzed the number of recalled items (range 1–12), as well as the percent of items remembered on the delayed recall task relative to those recalled on the immediate recall task (percent savings).

Fifth, naming in other languages was examined. After the delayed recall task, participants were asked if they spoke any other languages. If they answered YES, they were told that they would see the same drawings that they saw at the beginning of the study. They were asked to name them in another language from the one that they just used. It was possible to skip an item if naming failed. The same procedure was repeated for each language that the participant reported using, up to three additional languages beyond the most dominant language. The order of items was randomly determined for each participant and for each language. We analyzed the number of pictures that were named correctly (range 1–12) in each language.

Automatic and controlled attention. We used two tasks that measured selective attention to stimuli presented among different (automatic) or same (controlled) distracters (as in Ruff, Evans, and Light 1986). To test automatic detection, we presented the digits 3 and 8 among upper case letters. The array consisted of ten 3s and ten 8s, as well as 80 letters. Participants were told that they would see a string of digits and letters for a limited time, and their task was to count all the 3s and 8s as quickly as possible, and then type the number that they managed to count. Each array was presented for 10 seconds. The trial began with an example in which there were four target digits and six letters. To test controlled detection, we presented the digits 3 and 8 among other digits. The array consisted of ten 3s and ten 8s, as well as 80 other digits. Instructions were the same as in the automatic detection task, and there was an example trial with five target digits and five other digits. We analyzed the number of digits typed for automatic detection and the number of digits typed for controlled detection (with a range of 1–20 in each).

Flanker task. Following Fan et al. (2002), we created 16 congruent trials (five arrows facing the same direction), 16 incongruent trials (five arrows in which the middle arrow faced the opposite direction from the other four arrows), and 16 neutral trials (middle arrow facing either right or left, with two straight lines on each side). In each condition, half of the target (middle) arrows pointed right and half pointed left. Participants were told that if the middle arrow was pointing to the right, they were to mouse-click on a circle on the right side of the screen, and if the middle arrow was pointing to the left, they should click on a circle on the left side of the screen. Each set was presented for 2 seconds. The order of the trials was randomly determined for each participant. The task began with two neutral practice trials, with feedback on those trials, and then five mixed practice trials with no feedback. We analyzed four measures: reaction times (RTs) for congruent trials, RTs for incongruent trials, RTs for neutral trials, and the flanker effect, calculated for each participant as the average RT on incongruent trials minus the average RT on neutral trials.

16.4.3 Results

We divided the sample into three age groups: youngest (ages 20–39), middle aged (ages 40–59), and oldest adults (ages 60+), and compared their education level, number of languages, frequency of language switching, self-rated proficiency and age of acquisition (AoA) in each language. In cases of discrepancy between self-ratings and naming scores, language dominance (the strongest and the second strongest language) was classified according to the objectively measured picture naming scores (following Tomoschuk, Ferreira, and Gollan 2018). If naming scores were missing, the strongest language was classified according to self-ratings. We had more proficiency data (self-ratings or naming scores) for the language reported as strongest than for the first acquired language. Therefore, in all subsequent analyses we define L1 as the most dominant language rather than as the language that was acquired first. Note that for 13% of the participants, the strongest language was different from the language that they reported acquiring first. Moreover, since we had relatively few reports of third and fourth language measures, the self-ratings and naming scores of the third and fourth languages were combined to a single measure (L3-L4 combined score). The combined naming score was the sum of L3 and L4 naming scores, and the combined self-ratings and AoA scores were their averages. For example, the combined naming score of a participant who named 6 pictures in the third language and 4 pictures in the fourth language was 10, while the combined self-rating score of a participant who rated L3 as 4 and L4 as 2, was 3 (summing instead of averaging the self-rating scores of L3 and L4 did not affect the results reported below).

Analyses of variance (ANOVA) showed significant differences among the three age groups in self-rating of language proficiency and in age of acquisition of the most dominant language and the second-most dominant language (see Table 16.1). A comparison of the youngest and oldest adults revealed that the oldest adults reported acquiring their strongest and second-most strongest language later in life than did the younger adults, $t(49) = -3.72$, $p < .001$, and $t(81) = -3.27$, $p = .002$, respectively. In addition, the oldest adults rated their proficiency in their first and second-most dominant language as lower compared to the youngest participants, $t(62) = 3.15$, $p = .003$, and $t(80) = 2.25$, $p = .027$, respectively, and rated their proficiency in their third and fourth languages as higher than did the youngest adults, $t(33) = -2.36$, $p = .024$. There were no other differences between the three age groups or between the youngest and the oldest adults (all $ps \geq .495$).

Next, we looked at the effects of age on all cognitive measures in the different domains. We analyzed these effects with a series of ANOVAs that were conducted separately for each cognitive measure. As can be seen in Table 16.2, age effects were found for picture naming in the dominant language, for immediate and delayed recall, and for automatic and controlled detection (but note that age effects in controlled detection would not be significant when correcting the p value for the number of comparisons within a domain – in this case, controlled and automatic detection). Thus, older adults named and recalled fewer pictures, and detected fewer digits on the selective attention task. The effect of age was seen for reaction times on the flanker task only when comparing the youngest and the oldest groups, $t\,(68) = -2.47$, $p = .016$. All other comparisons of cognitive measures across the three age groups or between the youngest and the oldest participants were not significant (all $ps \geq .138$).

Figure 16.1 presents the correlation between the number of languages and percent savings (e.g., delayed recall divided by immediate recall), as well as the correlation between language switching and percent savings within the oldest group (N = 53, age 60–90). In addition, the figure presents the correlation between age of acquisition of the second most-dominant language and flanker effect in error rates in this group. To examine the contribution of the language background variables to the prediction of cognitive performance, regressions were conducted for the entire sample together and then for the oldest group alone. In each regression we entered education in the first step to account for the possible contribution of education to cognitive performance, then age, and then the relevant language background variable (e.g., number of languages, frequency of language switching, self-rated proficiency of second, third and fourth languages, and their age of acquisition). Analyses of the entire sample showed that education accounted for 5% of the variance in automatic detection, age accounted for an additional 15.4% of the variance beyond education, and the number of languages added 4% beyond education and age. For controlled detection, age predicted 4.1% of the variance, and self-rating of the second-most dominant language predicted an additional 3.5%. No other variables in any of the cognitive measures explained an additional share of the variance beyond education and age.

When running the regressions for the oldest adults alone, the reported number of languages added 9.8% to the prediction of the percent of items remembered on the delayed recall task relative to those recalled on the immediate recall task (percent savings), and the same was true for language switching, which also explained 9.8% of the variance in percent savings. Moreover, the age of acquisition of the second-most dominant language explained 19% of the variance in error rates on the flanker task (see Table 16.3 for all significant regression models). No other variables contributed to the prediction of cognitive measures within the oldest group beyond the effects of education and age.

Table 16.2: Means, standard deviations and group comparisons of cognitive measures.

	Youngest n = 55			Middle age n = 72			Oldest n = 53			Comparison of the three age groups		
	M	SD	n	M	SD	n	M	SD	n	F	p	Effect size (η^2)
L1 naming [a]	11.94	.31	50	11.94	.24	67	11.71	.54	49	6.36	.002	.07
L2 naming	10.41	2.28	32	10.63	1.84	38	10.22	1.85	27	.34	.713	.01
L3+L4 naming	7.00	3.46	3	9.23	5.79	13	9.33	5.24	9	.35	.706	.03
Immediate Recall [b]	75.63	10.57	53	69.95	12.72	71	67.95	14.14	52	5.37	.005	.06
Delayed Recall [b]	71.01	11.78	48	66.07	13.09	56	64.53	16.48	43	2.82	.063	.04
Percent Saving [c]	94.26	14.05	48	95.61	13.25	56	94.46	15.37	42	.14	.870	.002
Automatic Detection [b]	85.60	15.83	50	78.55	19.80	62	64.88	24.80	43	12.45	<.001	.14
Controlled Detection [b]	68.60	18.79	50	64.67	19.83	60	57.70	22.53	37	3.12	.047	.04
Flanker Congruent [d]	844	201	41	944	167	55	1015	211	29	7.24	.001	.11
Flanker Incongruent	893	198	41	1022	170	55	1121	196	29	13.37	.001	.18
Flanker Neutral	819	192	41	922	188	55	980	213	29	6.27	.003	.09
Flanker Effect [e]	74	103	41	101	128	55	141	126	29	2.71	.071	.04

[a] The highest possible naming score is 12.
[b] Results are presented as percentages.
[c] Delayed recall divided by immediate recall; results are presented as percentages.
[d] Reaction times (RT) in milliseconds.
[e] RT for the incongruent condition minus RT for the neutral condition.

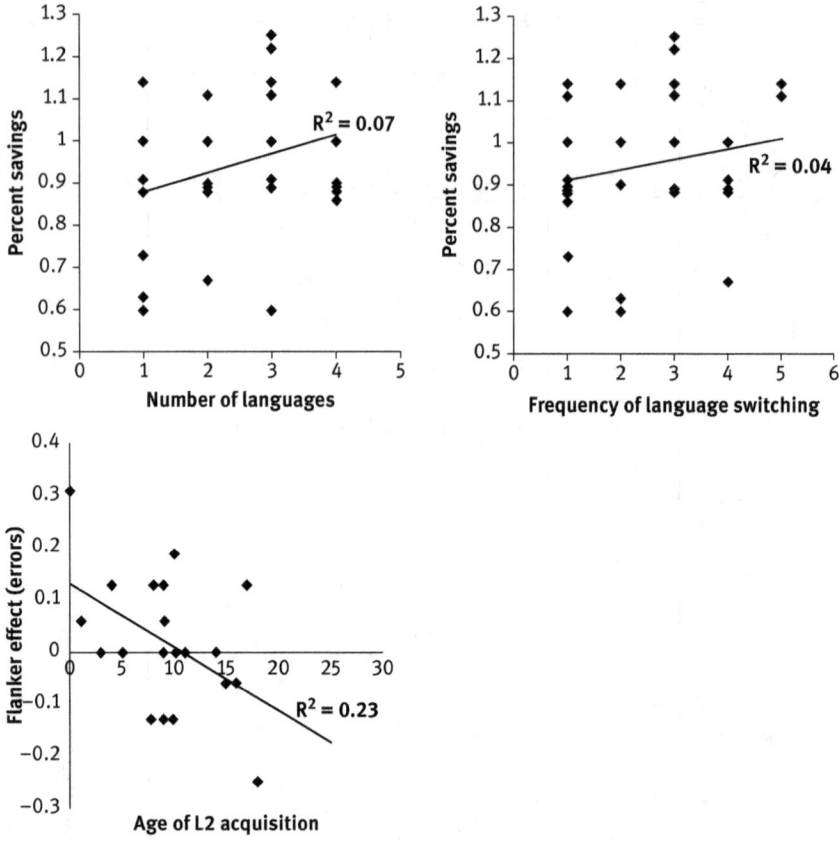

Figure 16.1: The correlation (and the trend line with R squared value) between percent savings and both the number of languages (left panel) and the frequency of language switching (right panel), and both the correlation (and trend lines) between age of L2 acquisition and flanker effect in error rates (lower panel) in the oldest group (N = 53).

16.4.4 Summary of main findings

We examined the performance of 180 adults between the ages of 22 and 90 and found robust aging effects. These effects were found despite having a very heterogeneous sample in terms of language history and use, and presumably also in terms of familiarity with computerized tasks. Furthermore, the effects were found despite the fact that data collection was done online, from various devices, and under uncontrolled conditions (e.g., varied level of internet connection). Relative to younger adults, older adults named fewer pictures in their dominant language,

Table 16.3: Regression analyses predicting cognitive measures with education, age, and linguistic background variables in the oldest group.

Dependent variable	Predictor	R² Change	F Change	df	p	β	Sig. β
Percent savings [a]	Education	.14	6.59	1,40	.014	−.44	.005
	Age	.02	.92	1,39	.345	−.18	.242
	Number of languages	.098	5.06	1,38	.030	.33	.030
	Language switching	.098	5.01	1,38	.031	.32	.031
Flanker effect (errors) [b]	Education	.086	2.06	1,22	.165	−.03	.880
	Age	.035	.84	1,21	369	.26	.202
	AoA Second language	.190	5.50	1,20	.029	−.48	.029

[a] The percent of items remembered on the delayed recall task relative to those recalled on the immediate recall task.
[b] Percent errors in the incongruent condition minus percent errors in the neutral condition.

retrieved fewer items on the immediate recall task, detected fewer digits on the automatic and controlled detection tasks, and exhibited larger flanker effects. The effect of age was found both when the three groups were compared to each other using age as a discrete variable, and in regression analyses in which age was entered as a continuous variable. These results are consistent with the literature on cognitive aging (e.g., Burke and Shafto 2008; Salthouse 2016) in demonstrating the deleterious effects of aging on specific aspects of cognition. They also show that the tasks that we selected were sensitive to aging effects and could thus be used to study the effects of language experience on cognitive performance.

In comparison to the robust aging effects, the effect of the number of languages on cognitive performance was much more subtle. The hierarchical regression analyses revealed that the number of languages that a person speaks explained a significant but small share of the variance in selective attention (automatic detection) beyond the effects of education and age. Moreover, self-rated proficiency in the second-most dominant language explained some of the variance in the controlled detection task. When the analysis focused on the oldest group alone, the number of languages, as well as the frequency of language switching, explained about 10% of the variance in memory function (percent savings) beyond the effects of education and age. In addition, the age of acquisition of the second-most dominant language contributed almost

20% to the prediction of the error rates on the flanker task. Thus, although not all aspects of language use affected all cognitive domains, and despite the great variability in participants' language backgrounds, we found that language use added to the prediction of several cognitive measures.

16.5 Discussion and implications of the study to research on multilingualism and aging

Our findings are consistent with the results reported by Kavé et al. (2008) whose study showed that the number of languages added to the prediction of cognitive state beyond the effects of other demographic variables. They also support Pot, Keijzer, and de Bot's (2018) findings that language proficiency and language usage in different social contexts predict the flanker effect beyond the contribution of age, gender, income, and education, although the mere number of languages was not a sensitive enough predictor of cognitive performance in their study. Furthermore, the current results corroborate the results of studies that found memory advantages in bilinguals compared to monolinguals (e.g., Schroeder and Marian 2012; Wodniecka et al. 2010). For example, Wodniecka et al. (2010) found that older (but not younger) bilingual adults who had acquired a second language later in life were better than age-matched monolingual adults in memory functions. Specifically, they were better at recollection (retrieving contextual information) of non-verbal information, which according to the authors, required executive control. Wodniecka et al. suggested that the use of two languages, rather than their age of acquisition, was critical for bilingual advantages. Similarly, Schroeder and Marian (2012) found bilingual effects on episodic memory and ascribed these effects to earlier bilingualism and to better inhibitory control. In contrast, Fernandes et al. (2007) found no such advantage in older bilinguals who were asked to recall words rather than pictures. Our results suggest that multilingualism is associated with better memory and attention functions, supporting studies that documented a connection between the number of languages and the age of dementia onset (e.g., Chertkow et al. 2010; Perquin et al. 2013).

Even though multilingualism can be confounded with level of education, since some languages might have been acquired through formal education, and some well-educated individuals might have been encouraged to learn more languages as part of their schooling, the present findings suggest that multilingualism predicts cognitive performance above and beyond education level. Yet, while it is reasonable to tease apart the effect of multilingualism and education, we did not analyze the effects of the number of languages that a person knows beyond other variables of language use. Thus, we examined whether the number of languages that a person knows affected cognitive performance beyond education and age, but not whether it affected performance separately from the effects of frequent language switching, self-rated proficiency, or age of acquisition of each language. Such analyses are problematic because these variables are all interdependent, with any attempt to separate them being somewhat artificial and possibly obscuring the actual effect. For example, Zahodne et al. (2014) examined the effect of bilingualism on cognitive decline in more than 1000 Spanish-English bilinguals in 18–24 month intervals for up to 23 years. They found that bilingualism was related to higher initial scores on cognitive tests and to higher educational attainment, but it was not independently associated with rates of cognitive decline or with dementia conversion when country of origin, gender, education, time spent in the United States, recruitment cohort, and age at enrollment were entered as covariates. These variables are not independent of language use; therefore, treating them as covariates, instead of studying their relationship to cognitive decline, might have led to misleading conclusions in that study.

We note that people who report knowing several languages may differ in the frequency of their language switching, in the level of proficiency in each of their languages, and/or in the age of acquisition of each language. In principle, people who speak more languages have more opportunities to switch between languages than either monolinguals or bilinguals, especially if people around them speak all their other languages. In our data, the frequency of language switching was associated with improved memory functions (percent savings) beyond education and age. While language switching can be viewed as the most obvious byproduct of multilingualism, it can also be the case that language switching *is* the source of cognitive reserve, and multilingualism simply provides the opportunity to switch. Although we did not include an objective language switching measure and used self-ratings instead, several studies that used a similar approach found an association between self-perceived language tendencies and more objective measures of cognitive control. For example, our results correspond with Prior and Gollan's (2011) findings of better task switching in bilinguals who reported switching languages frequently compared to those who reported switching languages less often. They are also in line with the findings reported by Hofweber et al. (2016) and Rodriguez-Fornells et al. (2012) who demonstrated that acceptability ratings of different types of code switching and reported frequency of code switching were associated with conflict monitoring advantages on a flanker task and inhibitory advantages in a stop-signal task, respectively. Interestingly, in the present study both the number of languages and the frequency of switching were related to better memory functions, a cognitive ability that had not been so clearly associated with language use. It is difficult to determine whether better memory leads to better language learning (Papagno and Vallar 1995), or whether the frequent practice of conflict monitoring improves memory functions (Hussey et al. 2017). In either case, these associations might suggest that certain aspects of multilingualism contribute to cognitive reserve.

Other than switching, age of acquisition might have a critical effect on cognitive performance, especially since multilingual individuals acquire their languages at different ages. For example, a trilingual who acquired all three languages as a child might benefit more from multilingualism than a trilingual who acquired one language in early childhood and the other two as an adult. Early benefits might be related to greater neural plasticity in children than in older age (e.g., Johnson and Newport 1989) or to a longer period of practicing multiple language monitoring. On the other hand, it is also possible that acquiring a third language later in life would be associated with greater effort, which creates greater cognitive stimulation, and ultimately increases the benefits of multilingualism in older age (e.g., Costa and Santesteban 2004; Goral et al. 2015; Whalley et al. 2004). Our findings in this regard are puzzling since later age of acquisition of the second-most dominant language was associated with lower error rates in the incongruent compared to the congruent condition on the flanker task (see lower panel of Figure 16.1). Therefore, both our results and the present state of research in the field do not yet clarify the association between the age of language acquisition and cognitive benefits in older age. It is possible that the multilingualism advantage might arise only in the context of a certain combination of the different variables that we examined, yet to be defined.

Notably, in the current study, the number of languages and the extent of language switching had a greater predictive value among the oldest adults than in the larger sample, supporting the finding that the benefit of bilingualism has been more consistently reported in older than in younger adults (e.g., Gold et al. 2013; Valian 2015; but see Lethonen et al., 2018 and Paap et al. 2014). Furthermore, in the current study we did not compare monolinguals or bilinguals to multilingual speakers, and instead treated language knowledge as a continuum, as we did with the other background measures. While most research on the bilingual advantage sampled carefully selected bilinguals who were often almost equally proficient in their two languages, multilingualism comes in many different shapes and forms, precluding reliance on such strict selection criteria. The majority of the current sample reported knowing two languages. However, participants were not necessarily balanced bilinguals, as their self-ratings of L1 were higher than their self-ratings of L2. In addition, participants were not necessarily using all languages on a daily basis or for the same purposes (e.g., speaking Hebrew at home, writing in English for work, or vice versa). It remains to be seen which of the multitude of individual differences that we targeted matters more for cognitive benefits in older age.

16.6 Conclusion

It is most likely impossible to determine whether multilingualism is the result or the cause of better cognitive performance, especially since individuals who become multilingual later in life might have different baseline characteristics from those who remain monolingual or bilingual (the "reverse causality" problem). In other words, it might not be multilingualism that leads to later-life cognitive differences but rather cognitive differences that lead to multilingualism. However, the same methodological problem is true for other factors related to cognitive reserve, such as education level or complex occupation. We cannot determine whether innate cognitive abilities lead people to pursue more education, to engage in more demanding cognitive activities, or to acquire more languages, or whether these characteristics improve their cognitive abilities.

As our literature review suggests and as our preliminary attempt at data exploration shows, the study of multilingualism and aging requires a careful consideration of a variety of individual differences in order to map the possible benefits that the relevant variables might provide to cognitive performance in old age. Challenges include the difficulty in determining some people's first language, as well as the difficulty in resolving mismatches between one's first acquired language, one's most proficient language, and one's most used language. Other challenges pertain to the need for objective measures of language proficiency and of language switching. Despite these challenges, we believe that instead of attempting to minimize individual differences in order to reduce "noise", these differences should be acknowledged and their effect should be better investigated.

Lastly, we note that the effects that were obtained in our preliminary study were small, especially in light of the multiple comparisons that are inevitable when trying to study a complex phenomenon such as multilingualism with variables that are by nature related and therefore non-separable. Moreover, our results are somewhat surprising since bilingualism and multilingualism have been shown to affect monitoring behaviors (e.g., task switching, attention, and inhibition) more often than they have been shown to affect memory functions, whereas the most robust results in the current preliminary study associated multilingualism with memory (percent savings), which did not show any aging effects. Therefore, our results need to be interpreted with caution. Nevertheless, the data collected here were obtained within a matter of weeks and by word of mouth (with no formal advertising), overcoming many of the difficulties in recruiting older multilingual participants. Using a similar approach of online data collection to recruit a much larger sample or using a more conservative data collection method (e.g., interviews and objective measures of switching behaviors and switching types) can move the field forward. Access to heterogeneous participant samples can reveal the effects of specific individual differences on the degree and types of multilingual advantages. Such an approach can improve our understanding of the ways in which multilingualism may benefit cognitive performance in aging.

References

Albert, Marilyn S., Kenneth Jones, Cary R. Savage, Lisa Berkman, Teresa Seeman, Dan Blazer & John W. Rowe. 1995. Predictors of cognitive change in older persons: MacArthur studies of successful aging. *Psychology and Aging* 10(4). 578–589.

Alladi, Suvarna, Thomas H. Bak, Vasanta Duggirala, Bapiraju Surampudi, Mekala Shailaja, Anuj K. Shukla, Jaydip R. Chaudhuri & Subhash Kaul. 2013. Bilingualism delays age at onset of dementia, independent of education and immigration status. *Neurology* 81. 1–7.

Bak, Thomas H. 2016. The impact of bilingualism on cognitive ageing and dementia. *Linguistic Approaches to Bilingualism* 6(1). 205–226.

Barnes, Deborah E., Ira B. Tager, William A. Satariano & Kristine Yaffe. 2004. The relationship between literacy and cognition in well-educated elders. *Journal of Gerontology: Medical Sciences* 59(4). 390–395.

Bialystok, Ellen, Fergus I. Craik & Morris Freedman. 2007. Bilingualism as a protection against the onset of symptoms of dementia. *Neuropsychologia* 45(2). 459–464.

Bialystok, Ellen, Fergus. I. Craik & Jennifer Ryan. 2006. Executive control in a modified antisaccade task: Effects of aging and bilingualism. *Journal of Experimental Psychology: Learning, Memory, and Cognition* 32(6). 1341–1354.

Bialystok, Ellen, Fergus. I. Craik, Raymond Klein & Mythili Viswanathan. 2004. Bilingualism, aging, and cognitive control: Evidence from the Simon task. *Psychology and Aging* 19(2). 290–303.

Bialystok, Ellen, Fergus I. Craik, Malcolm A. Binns, Lynn Ossher & Morris Freedman. 2014. Effects of bilingualism on the age of onset and progression of MCI and AD: Evidence from executive function tests. *Neuropsychology* 28(2). 290–304.

Bogulski, Cari A., Michael Rakoczy, Michelle Goodman & Ellen Bialystok. 2015. Executive control in fluent and lapsed bilinguals. *Bilingualism: Language and Cognition*, 18(3). 561–567.

Bruin, Angela de, Thomas H. Bak & Sergio Della Sala. (2015). Examining the effects of active versus inactive bilingualism on executive control in a carefully matched non-immigrant sample. *Journal of Memory and Language* 85. 15–26.

Burke, Deborah M. & Meredith A. Shafto. 2008. Language and aging. In Timothy A. Salthouse (ed.), *The handbook of aging and cognition*, 373–443. New York: Psychology Press.

Chertkow, Howard, Victor Whitehead, Natalie Phillips, Christina Wolfson, Julie Atherton & Howard Bergman. 2010. Multilingualism (but not always bilingualism) delays the onset of Alzheimer disease: Evidence from a bilingual community. *Alzheimer Disease & Associated Disorders* 24(2). 118–125.

Costa, Albert & Mikel Santesteban. 2004. Lexical access in bilingual speech production: Evidence from language switching in highly proficient bilinguals and L2 learners. *Journal of Memory and Language* 50(4). 491–511.

Craik, Fergus I. M., Ellen Bialystok & Morris Freedman. 2010. Delaying the onset of Alzheimer disease: Bilingualism as a form of cognitive reserve. *Neurology* 75(19). 1726–1729.

Fan, Jin, Bruce D. McCandliss, Tobias Sommer, Amir Raz & Michael I. Posner. 2002. Testing the efficiency and independence of attentional networks. *Journal of Cognitive Neuroscience* 14(3). 340–347.

Fernandes, Myra A., Fergus I. M. Craik, Ellen Bialystok & Sharyn Kreuger. 2007. Effects of bilingualism, aging, and semantic relatedness on memory under divided attention. *Canadian Journal of Experimental Psychology/Revue Canadienne de Psychologie Expérimentale* 61(2). 128–141.

Festman, Julia, Antoni Rodriguez-Fornells & Thomas F. Münte. 2010. Individual differences in control of language interference in late bilinguals are mainly related to general executive abilities. *Behavioral and Brain Functions* 6(1). 5–17.

Finkel, Deborah, Ross Andel, Margaret Gatz & Nancy L. Pedersen. 2009. The role of occupational complexity in trajectories of cognitive aging before and after retirement. *Psychology and Aging* 24(3). 563–573.

Gathercole, Virginia C., Enlli M. Thomas, Ivan Kennedy, Cynog Prys, Nia Young, Nestor Viñas Guasch, Emily J. Roberts, Emma K. Hughes & Leah Jones. 2014. Does language dominance affect cognitive performance in bilinguals? Lifespan evidence from preschoolers through older adults on card sorting, Simon, and metalinguistic tasks. *Frontiers in Psychology* 5. Article 11. doi: 10.3389/fpsyg.2014.00011

Gold, Brian T., Chobok Kim, Nathan F. Johnson, Richard J. Kriscio & Charles D. Smith. 2013. Lifelong bilingualism maintains neural efficiency for cognitive control in aging. *Journal of Neuroscience* 33(2). 387–396.

Gollan, Tamar H., Tiffany Sandoval & David P. Salmon. 2011. Cross-language intrusion errors in aging bilinguals reveal the link between executive control and language selection. *Psychological Science* 22(9). 1155–1164.

Gollan, Tamar H., David P. Salmon, Rosa I. Montoya & Douglas R. Galasko. 2011. Degree of bilingualism predicts age of diagnosis of Alzheimer's disease in low-education but not in highly educated Hispanics. *Neuropsychologia* 49(14). 3826–3830.

Goral, Mira, Luca Campanelli & Avron Spiro. 2015. Language dominance and inhibition abilities in bilingual older adults. *Bilingualism: Language and Cognition* 18(1). 79–89.

Hofweber, Julia, Theodoros Marinis & Jeanine Treffers-Daller. 2016. Effects of dense code-switching on executive control. *Linguistic Approaches to Bilingualism* 6(5). 648–668.

Hussey, Erika K., Isaiah J. Harbison, Susan E. Teubner-Rhodes, Alan Mishler, Kayla Velnoskey & Jared M. Novick. 2017. Memory and language improvements following cognitive control training. *Journal of Experimental Psychology: Learning, Memory, and Cognition* 43(1). 23–58.

Ihle, Andreas, Michel Oris, Delphine Fagot & Matthias Kliegel. 2016. The relation of the number of languages spoken to performance in different cognitive abilities in old age. *Journal of Clinical and Experimental Neuropsychology* 38(10). 1103–1114.

Johnson, Jacqueline S. & Elissa L. Newport. 1989. Critical period effects in second language learning: The influence of maturational state on the acquisition of English as a second language. *Cognitive Psychology* 21(1). 60–99.

Kavé, Gitit, Nitza Eyal, Aviva Shorek & Jiska Cohen-Mansfield. 2008. Multilingualism and cognitive state in the oldest old. *Psychology and Aging* 23(1). 70–78.

Kemp, Charlotte. 2009. Defining multilingualism. In Larissa Aronin & Britta Hufeisen (eds.), *The exploration of multilingualism: Development of research on L3, multilingualism and multiple language acquisition*, 11–26. Amsterdam/Philadelphia: John Benjamins Publishing Company.

Kirk, Neil W., Linda Fiala, Kenneth C. Scott-Brown & Vera Kempe. 2014. No evidence for reduced Simon cost in elderly bilinguals and bidialectals. *Journal of Cognitive Psychology* 26(6). 640–648.

Lehtonen, Minna, Anna Soveri, Aini Laine, Janica Järvenpää, Angela de Bruin & Jan Antfolk. 2018. Is bilingualism associated with enhanced executive functioning in adults? A meta-analytic review. *Psychological Bulletin* 144(4). 394–425.

Manly, Jennifer J., Nicole Schupf, Ming X. Tang & Yaakov Stern. 2005. Cognitive decline and literacy among ethnically diverse elders. *Journal of Geriatric Psychiatry and Neurology* 18(4). 213–217.

Paap, Kenneth R. & Zachary I. Greenberg. 2013. There is no coherent evidence for a bilingual advantage in executive processing. *Cognitive Psychology* 66(2). 232–258.

Paap, Kenneth R., Hunter A. Johnson & Oliver Sawi. 2015. Bilingual advantages in executive functioning either do not exist or are restricted to very specific and undetermined circumstances. *Cortex* 69. 265–278.

Paap, Kenneth R., Oliver M. Sawi, Chirag Dalibar, Jack Darrow & Hunter A. Johnson. 2014. The brain mechanisms underlying the cognitive benefits of bilingualism may be extraordinarily difficult to discover. *AIMS Neuroscience* 1(3). 245–256.

Papagno, Costanza & Giuseppe Vallar. 1995. Verbal short-term memory and vocabulary learning in polyglots. *The Quarterly Journal of Experimental Psychology Section A* 48(1). 98–107.

Perquin, Magali, Michel Vaillant, Anne M. Schuller, Jessica Pastore, Jean F. Dartigues, Marie-Lise Lair, Nico Diederich & MemoVie Group. 2013. Lifelong exposure to multilingualism: New evidence to support cognitive reserve hypothesis. *PloS One 8* (4).e62030. doi: 10.1371/journal.pone.0062030

Pot, Anna, Merel Keijzer & Kees de Bot. 2018. Intensity of multilingual language use predicts cognitive performance in some multilingual older adults. *Brain Sciences* 8 (5).Article 92. doi: 10.3390/brainsci8050092

Prior, Anat & Tamar H. Gollan. 2011. Good language-switchers are good task-switchers: Evidence from Spanish-English and Mandarin-English bilinguals. *Journal of the International Neuropsychological Society* 17(4). 682–691.

Richards, Marcus & Ian J. Deary. 2005. A life course approach to cognitive reserve: A model for cognitive aging and development? *Annals of Neurology* 58(4). 617–622.

Rodriguez-Fornells, Antoni, Ulrike M. Kramer, Urbano Lorenzo-Seva, Julia Festman & Thomas F. Münte. 2012. Self-assessment of individual differences in language switching. *Frontiers in Psychology 2*. Article 388. doi.org/10.3389/fpsyg.2011.00388

Ruff, Ronald M., Randall W. Evans & Rudolph H. Light. 1986. Automatic detection vs. controlled search: A paper-and-pencil approach. *Perceptual and Motor Skills* 62(2). 407–416.

Salthouse, Timothy A. 2016. *Theoretical perspectives on cognitive aging*. New York: Psychology Press.

Schroeder, Scott R. & Viorica Marian. 2012. A bilingual advantage for episodic memory in older adults. *Journal of Cognitive Psychology* 24(5). 591–601.

Schweizer, Tom A., Jenna Ware, Corinne E. Fischer, Fergus. I. M. Craik & Ellen Bialystok. 2012. Bilingualism as a contributor to cognitive reserve: Evidence from brain atrophy in Alzheimer's disease. *Cortex* 48(8). 991–996.

Scribner, Sylvia & Michael Cole. 1981. Unpacking literacy. In Marcia Farr Whiteman. (ed.), *Writing: The nature, development, and teaching of written communication*, 71–87. New York: Routledge.

Stern, Yaakov. 2002. What is cognitive reserve? Theory and research application of the reserve concept. *Journal of the International Neuropsychological Society* 8(3). 448–460.

Tomoschuk, Brendan, Victor S. Ferreira & Tamar H. Gollan. 2018. When a seven is not a seven: Self-ratings of bilingual language proficiency differ between and within language populations. *Bilingualism: Language and Cognition* 22(3). 516–536.

Valenzuela, Michael J. & Perminder Sachdev. 2006. Brain reserve and dementia: A systematic review. *Psychological Medicine* 36(4). 441–454.

Valian, Virginia. 2015. Bilingualism and cognition. *Bilingualism: Language and Cognition* 18(1). 3–24.

Verreyt, Nele, Evy Woumans, Davy Vandelanotte, Arnaud Szmalec & Wouter Duyck. 2016. The influence of language-switching experience on the bilingual executive control advantage. *Bilingualism: Language and Cognition* 19(1). 181–190.

Whalley, Lawrence J., Ian J. Deary, Charlotte L. Appleton & John M. Starr. 2004. Cognitive reserve and the neurobiology of cognitive aging. *Ageing Research Reviews* 3(4). 369–382.

Wodniecka, Zofia, Fergus I. M. Craik, Lin Luo & Ellen Bialystok. 2010. Does bilingualism help memory? Competing effects of verbal ability and executive control. *International Journal of Bilingual Education and Bilingualism* 13(5). 575–595.

Woumans, Evy, Patrick Santens, Anne Sieben, Jan Versijpt, Michael Stevens & Wouter Duyck. 2015. Bilingualism delays clinical manifestation of Alzheimer's disease. *Bilingualism: Language and Cognition* 18(3). 568–574.

Yang, Hwajin, Andree Hartanto & Sujin Yang. 2016. The complex nature of bilinguals' language usage modulates task-switching outcomes. *Frontiers in Psychology* 7. Article 560. doi: 10.3389/fpsyg.2016.00560

Zahodne, Laura B., Peter W. Schofield, Meagan T. Farrell, Yaakov Stern & Jennifer J. Manly. 2014. Bilingualism does not alter cognitive decline or dementia risk among Spanish-speaking immigrants. *Neuropsychology* 28(2). 238–246.

Iris M. Strangmann, Stanley Chen and Loraine K. Obler

17 Multilingual Language Processing and the Multilingual Brain

17.1 Introduction

Different life experiences can alter your brain. For example, London taxi drivers have a bigger hippocampus compared to non-taxi drivers as the result of studying for the taxi license (Maguire, Woollet, and Spiers 2006). Here we review studies that examine what multilingualism does to the brain. Although research on the multilingual brain has grown considerably in recent decades, much is still unknown, as most studies focus on bilingualism rather than multilingualism. This chapter focuses on the effects of multilingualism on the brain, but we also discuss bilingual studies to give a more complete picture of what speaking more than one language can do to the brain. Our discussion starts by reviewing studies that examine the neural representation and language processing of multilingualism and relevant modulating factors. Then, we turn to studies examining the neural underpinnings of language control.

17.2 Neural representation of language

The goal of neurolinguistics is to create a model of speech and language for both comprehension and production that is theoretically sound and biologically based in the human brain (e.g., Hickok and Poeppel 2004). Studies examining language in the brain date from the late 19th century. Seminal work by Broca, Wernicke, Lichtheim and other researchers led to a straightforward, left-lateralized model of language: Broca's area for speaking, Wernicke's area for understanding, and the arcuate fasciculus that connects the two (reviewed, e.g., by Geschwind 1970). Within the field of neurolinguistics, there is consensus that this "Classic Model" is outdated for several reasons. It not only lacks anatomical specificity but also focuses on cortical structures, featuring only a single pathway (e.g., Poeppel et al. 2012; Tremblay and Dick 2016). Current findings on language in the brain indicate a complex network involving both hemispheres with various cortical areas, subcortical structures, and multiple neural

---

Iris M. Strangmann, Stanley Chen and Loraine K. Obler, The Graduate Center, City University of New York, New York (NY), U.S.A.

pathways connecting the areas (for a relatively current picture see, e.g., Price 2012).

The critical question in most studies examining the neurobiology of multilingualism is to what extent our current understanding of language processing in monolinguals needs to be modified to account for more than one language in the same brain. How do the regions and networks underlying a person's two or more languages overlap and/or diverge in terms of supporting several languages? Is the general region the same one that supports monolinguals' sole language? In general, studies examining the neural correlates of language demonstrate a substantial overlap between *monolingual* and *bilingual* language representation, with some separate (language-specific) regions and networks (for meta-analyses see Indefrey 2006 or Wong, Yin, and O'Brien 2016; for reviews see Costa and Sebastián-Gallés 2014; Higby, Kim, and Obler 2013; Perfetti and Harris 2013). The overlapping activation has led some researchers to coin the terms "Universal Language Network" (Wong et al. 2016) and "Convergence Hypothesis" (Green 2003), both indicating that similar neural networks are involved in language acquisition and processing, regardless of the number of languages the brain has to accommodate (Costa and Sebastián-Gallés 2014).

The network that is hypothesized to overlap between languages incorporates various regions across the cortex. Processing phonology involves Heschl's gyrus (HG) for auditory input, together with the superior temporal gyrus (STG), inferior frontal gyrus (IFG), and inferior parietal cortex (IPC). Lexical semantics involves multiple regions in the temporal lobe, such as the middle temporal gyrus (MTg), the temporal pole (T.pole), the supramarginal gyrus (SMG), and the anterior inferior frontal cortex (aIFC). Syntax has been associated with the pars opercularis (pOp), pars triangularis (pTr), and the posterior superior temporal gyrus (pSTG). Often, researchers refer to the entire "language" area by using the term peri-sylvian region (see Figure 17.1. for these cortical areas).

In terms of differences between monolinguals and bilinguals, some studies have found greater bilateral hemispheric involvement for bilinguals, as opposed to monolinguals (e.g., Hull and Vaid 2006, 2007; Park, Badzakova-Trajkov, and Waldie 2012; Połczyńska, Japardi, and Bookheimer 2017; Román et al. 2015). Additionally, several studies have found structural changes in the brain with respect to increased gray matter density and white matter integrity (Klein et al. 2014; Li, Legault, and Litcofsky 2014; Stein et al. 2012; for a review see Stein et al. 2014). Lastly, the degree of neural overlap may depend on the linguistic component under study. Differences in function, structure, and connectivity are more reliably found in the regions of phonological processing in contrast to morphosyntax and lexical semantics, respectively (for a review see Wong, Yin, and O'Brien 2016).

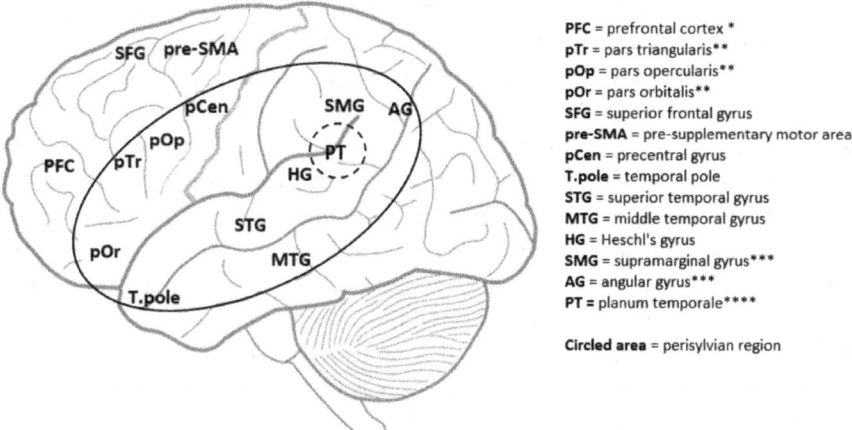

Figure 17.1: Representation of the left hemisphere of the brain with several cortical regions, see text for which regions are hypothesized to be shared between languages. *PFC includes Brodmann's Areas 46 and 9, ** pTr, pOp, and pOr are all part of the inferior frontal cortex (IFC), *** SMG and AG are both part of the inferior parietal cortex (IPC), **** PT is dashed here as it is below the cortical view.

17.2.1 Factors influencing language representation

A complicating factor in examining the neural representation of language in multilinguals is that additional language acquisition (of a second or more languages) can occur in various contexts, at different rates and times across the lifespan. Several factors influence the neural correlates of language representation, including, but not limited to: (a) Age of Acquisition; (b) proficiency; (c) language use; and (d) language distance. We briefly address each of these factors below.

There is currently no consensus in the literature on what is early or late regarding Age of Acquisition. Generally, exposure to two or more languages before the age of three to six years of life has been described as early (e.g., Meisel 2004) whether the two languages are simultaneously (e.g., Połczyńska et al. 2016) or sequentially acquired (e.g., Mohades et al. 2015). Late acquisition, by contrast, can be after age seven (e.g., Silverberg and Samuel 2004), or beginning in puberty going into adulthood (e.g., Montrul and Foote 2012). The exact effect of Age of Acquisition remains inconclusive, but several studies have found more functional and anatomical overlap between languages in early as opposed to late acquirers (Cherodath and Singh 2015; Dehaene et al. 1997; Kim et al. 1997; Perani et al. 1996; Saur et al. 2009; Ullman 2001). This would mean that the earlier one acquires an additional language, the more overlap it shares with the first language. This contrasts to late acquisition where the second language would, for example, be processed in more distinct areas, relative to the first language.

Additionally, some functional studies have reported more activation in later as opposed to earlier acquisition (e.g., Hernandez, Hofmann, and Kotz 2007; Wartenburger et al. 2003). However, more activation is not necessarily indicative of more effort. An unresolved issue in the study of neurolinguistics is whether more activation is seen for better-mastered materials, as in this study, or less activation is shown because automatically processed materials require fewer resources. Liu and Cao (2016) conducted a meta-analysis and found that most studies reported more activation in the left SFG for late bilinguals during L2 processing compared to L1 processing; nonetheless, early bilinguals demonstrated greater activation in the left fusiform gyrus during L1 processing as compared to late bilinguals. Furthermore, although the authors did not specifically plan to assess the effects of multilingualism, several of their participants spoke more than two languages. For those participants, activation was greater in the pars triangularis, insula, and planum temporale (see Figure 17.1.).

With respect to proficiency, several studies found positive correlations with overlap, where the higher the L2 proficiency, the more overlap between L1 and L2 in terms of neural correlates (e.g., Abutalebi et al. 2007; Gandour et al. 2007; Hull and Vaid 2007; Perani et al. 1998). Some of this divergent cortical activation has been associated with increased cognitive demands (Abutalebi et al. 2009; Briellmann et al. 2004; Golestani et al. 2006). In other words, the greater activation found in less proficient multilinguals might not be indicative of language processing, but rather of cognitive effort associated with lower proficiency. Additionally, these findings are supported by studies using electroencephalography (EEG) that found no significant differences in processing the L2 vs. L1 in late L2 learners during morphosyntactic tasks (Morgan-Short et al. 2012a; Morgan-Short et al. 2012b; Rossi et al. 2006). However, it should be noted that, when examining proficiency, most researchers rely on participants' self-report as opposed to measuring proficiency in a more objective way. Self-report has been shown by some studies to be an unreliable indicator of proficiency (e.g., Hakuta and D'Andrea 1992), although others have indicated no significant differences between self-report and other (objective) measures (Gollan et al. 2012).

Currently, more attention has been devoted to language use as opposed to the traditional factors, such as proficiency and Age of Acquisition (de Bruin and Della Sala 2016), though the importance of language use was mentioned early on in the bilingual aphasia literature (e.g., Pitres 1895). More recently, Green and Abutalebi (2013) put forward the *Adaptive Control Hypothesis*. In their proposal, the authors hypothesize that the actual language use – either mostly single-use, dual-use, or dense code-switching – will differentially affect language control processes. Few studies have examined the effect of daily exposure on the neural underpinnings of language, though one study by Tu and colleagues (2015) demonstrated differential activation after changing exposure within a short time window. The authors carefully selected a group of Cantonese-Mandarin bilinguals (who had similar proficiency in both languages) and scanned them while having 50/50 daily exposure to both of their two languages, and again after a 30-day vacation period where exposure changed to 90/10 (L1/L2, respectively). Participants demonstrated varied activation at the two scanning times depending on language and exposure in the left pars opercularis and other regions associated with language control, like the left ACC and left caudate nucleus. This study provides strong evidence for brain plasticity even after short-term exposure (30 days) and emphasizes the need to take more dynamic variables, such as exposure and use, into account when examining multilingualism.

Lastly, we briefly address the variable of language distance. Findings from studying bilinguals with two structurally distant languages or contrasting monolingual groups speaking distant languages have pointed in a similar direction. Generally, the assumption is that similar languages will be more similarly represented in the brain (i.e., in the course of learning them, participants will assimilate the new language to the prior language), whereas languages that differ will be organized less similarly (i.e., the brain will accommodate them such that cortical representation of L2 differs somewhat from that of L1). For example, Kochunov and colleagues found structural anatomical differences between English-speaking Caucasians and Chinese-speaking Asians in gyri in the frontal, temporal, and parietal lobes (Kochunov et al. 2003). Moreover, Liu and Cao (2016) found an effect of orthographic transparency in their meta-analysis such that the bilateral auditory cortex and right precentral gyrus were more involved during L2 processing when the L1 was orthographically more transparent (e.g., Finnish). The authors interpreted this result as an indication of greater involvement in the phonological and sensorimotor regions. This contrasts with L2 speakers whose L1 is orthographically less transparent (e.g., unvowelled Hebrew). As indicated by Liu and Cao's meta-analysis, Hebrew speakers' left frontal cortex was more involved, arguably due to the assumption of arbitrary mapping between the orthographic and phonological representations. Other studies have found support for an effect of language distance by directly contrasting word processing in Chinese characters versus in alphabetic scripts (Cao et al. 2014; for a review see Perfetti and Harris 2013) or word order (Saur et al. 2009). Finding effects of language distance on cerebral representation could have consequences for generalizability across studies involving different languages, where some may be more typologically similar than others.

17.2.2 Studies on three or more languages

Few studies have examined the neural correlates of multilingualism as opposed to bilingualism. Yetkin et al. (1996) conducted a covert word fluency task using fMRI with five multilinguals who had different language backgrounds. Participants were proficient in two of their languages but less proficient ("non-fluent") in their third. In general, activation overlapped for all three languages in the frontal, fronto-parietal, and parietal regions. However, this seemed to be modulated by the degree of proficiency, such that the least proficient language elicited the most activation, whereas no significant difference in activation was found between the two proficient languages.

Two other studies have found support for this result, in that activation depends on proficiency. Vingerhoets et al. (2003) examined Dutch-French-English trilinguals in three different covert tasks: word fluency, picture naming, and reading for comprehension. Generally, activation overlapped for the different languages, but these areas (e.g., inferior frontal cortex and middle temporal gyrus) were recruited more extensively in the non-native (less proficient) languages in contrast to the native language. Similarly, Videsott et al. (2010) found effects of proficiency in a relatively homogenous group of trilinguals, who acquired Ladin as the L1, Italian as the L2 around the age of 3, and English as the L3 during puberty. Covert multilingual word production activated a network of areas associated with picture naming (e.g., the occipital lobe and the hippocampus). However, the proficient languages recruited the right prefrontal cortex more than the less proficient language did (i.e., English). This may seem contradictory, given the results of Vingerhoets et al. (2003), where more activation was found for less proficient languages; however, as previously indicated, an unresolved issue in neurolinguistics is how to interpret such relative activation.

Another study examining quadrilinguals found that all four languages activated convergent brain areas during a covert verb generation task (Briellmann et al. 2004), in which participants were asked to covertly generate a verb (e.g., *swim*) that matched the visually presented noun (e.g., *fish*). This activation correlated negatively with proficiency such that the lower proficiency language demonstrated the greatest activation in contrast to languages with higher proficiency. Briellmann and colleagues found no effect of Age of Acquisition, but also did not specifically manipulate this variable. Indeed, the age difference between participants in terms of late and early was small. Two out of the six participants had actually become dominant in a language other than their native one. However, for these subjects there was little difference in the amount of activation among the four languages compared to resting state.

Other studies did specifically examine Age of Acquisition in multilinguals. A study by Bloch et al. (2009) examined the effect of the Age of L2 Acquisition in 44 multilingual participants with various language backgrounds. Participants either acquired their L1 and L2 simultaneously, sequentially, or late (i.e., after the age of 9). Moreover, all participants were proficient in a later acquired third language. Although all languages demonstrated considerable overlap, participants who acquired their L2 late showed more variability in terms of the degree of activation in their languages. The authors argue that a monolingual upbringing might result in a language network that is less able to accommodate later learned languages than the language network of a person who is multilingual in early childhood. This effectively is a Critical Period position, suggesting decline for native-like language representation of the L2 (and any additional languages).

Bloch et al.'s (2009) findings are supported by a study by Wattendorf et al. (2014). Wattendorf and colleagues examined Age of Acquisition in multilingual participants from various languages, dividing them into early (before age three) and late (after age nine) acquirers. Overall, proficiency was high, yet somewhat lower for L3 in contrast to L2 in both early and late multilinguals. The authors found an effect of Age of Acquisition, such that late multilinguals (who acquired multiple languages after the age of nine) demonstrated higher activity in the left posterior superior temporal gyrus (pSTG) in contrast to early multilinguals while covertly generating sentences in their respective languages. Moreover, early multilinguals showed higher neural activity in the prefrontal and subcortical areas in contrast to late multilinguals. The authors hypothesize that this finding might result from the late multilinguals requiring a higher degree of control during phonological processing. By contrast, early multilinguals establish distinct phonological representations early in life; hence, less control is required.

In sum, the few studies that have examined multilingualism specifically, as opposed to bilingualism, tend to align with the greater body of research on bilingualism. In general, most functional imaging studies demonstrate a common language network in the peri-sylvian neural substrate. Similarly to bilingualism research, multilingual studies found effects of both Age of Acquisition and proficiency. Moreover, some of the divergent activation found in the different languages of multilinguals is explained by different degrees of proficiency, suggesting that the processes of weaker languages might be more cognitively demanding.

17.2.3 Electric stimulation mapping studies

To this point, our discussion on language representation has mainly focused on methods examining multilingualism functionally or structurally (using fMRI, MRI, or DTI). In this section, we briefly turn to a different method: Electric Stimulation Mapping (ESM), which puts forward strong evidence for somewhat distinct, language-specific regions in traditional language areas of the brain. ESM is typically applied to patients during brain surgery because they either have a tumor and/or are epileptic. The goal of ESM is to localize and preserve brain areas that are critical for behavioral performance (e.g., language production/comprehension). Typically, a part of the skull is temporarily removed through a craniotomy. The size of the craniotomy varies, depending on (e.g.) the location and size of the tumor. Subsequently, the different exposed cortical regions are stimulated while the patient is engaged in a language task. Critical regions for language are localized when language processing is disrupted at the behavioral level in that the patient cannot perform on a given language task (see, e.g., Obler and Gjerlow 1999).

Ojemann and Whitaker (1978) were the first to use ESM with a focus on bilinguals. They found both shared and separate areas in two bilingual patients. The separate areas were located in the frontal and parietal regions. Their findings are supported by several other studies using ESM on bilinguals (e.g., Rapport, Tan, and Whitaker 1983; Serafini et al. 2008; Walker, Quiñones-Hinojosa, and Berger 2004; for a partial review see Giussani et al. 2007). Disparities were found such that some studies showed similar but separate cortical surface areas for the two languages next to overlapping regions (Roux et al. 2004; Roux and Trémoulet 2002). Interestingly, Roux and colleagues (2004) also found task-specific and language-specific areas. For example, reading was only disrupted in one but not in the other language. Others have found a greater representation of L2 in terms of cortical surface areas (Cervenka et al. 2011) or a larger amount of language-specific sites as well as unshared language areas in eight out of 22 patients (Lucas, McKhann, and Ojemann 2004). Thus, ESM studies examining bilinguals have all found both shared and separate language areas but mainly differ in the amount of cortical surface devoted to an individual's languages and in the extent to which the area is language-specific.

To the best of our knowledge, there are four studies that have used ESM on multilingual patients. Bello and colleagues (2006) used ESM in the left frontal lobe on seven late, yet highly proficient, multilingual patients. Cortical sites critical to naming and counting tasks were reliably found in five out of seven patients, in both shared and separate areas. Contradicting Cervenka et al.'s (2011) study, Bello and colleagues found a greater cortical representation for L1 compared to the other languages. A potential explanation for this difference is that Cervenka and colleagues used electrocorticography, which measures neural activity using electrodes without electric stimulation. Additionally, Bello et al. (2006) found that L1 cortical sites were always distinct, whereas overlap was found in languages that were acquired later. Moreover, the authors stimulated subcortical structures and identified language-specific white matter fiber tracts in some patients. This finding deviates from that of a study by Lubrano et al. (2012), in which the authors found shared white-matter tracts when assessing one patient's L1 and the late acquired L3 (L2 was not assessed in this study because it was of lesser importance to the patient's daily life). In terms of cortical representation, Lubrano and colleagues (2012) identified both shared and separate areas in the left inferior frontal cortex, whereas left dorsolateral prefrontal cortex was associated with language switching. The rest of the brain was not examined due to craniotomy being limited to the left frontal region of the brain.

Two recent ESM studies on multilingual participants also demonstrate substantial variability in terms of cortical representation. Połczyńska et al. (2016) examined language representation in a highly proficient quadrilingual.[1] Only few cortical areas were shared by all four languages, all located around the perisylvian (language) region. Interestingly, Połczyńska et al. (2016) did not find an effect of language similarity; although highly similar, German and Swiss-German were represented somewhat differently at the cortical level and also differed in their functional impairments. This idiosyncratic organization is supported by a study with 13 proficient multilinguals with various language backgrounds (Fernández-Coello et al. 2016). Albeit the findings indicate both shared and separate areas, the authors also claim an effect of Age of Acquisition such that early-acquired languages (before age seven) had a broader cortical representation in contrast to later-acquired languages (after age seven). Also, cortical areas overlapped significantly more for early-acquired languages than later-acquired languages. The early-acquired languages were mostly represented within the perisylvian region, which led the authors to hypothesize that only early-acquired languages might map onto classic language regions.

It is difficult to reconcile the ESM findings with the other neurolinguistic data on bilingualism and multilingualism. As described earlier, evidence from functional neuroimaging studies seems to point to a substantial common neural network, with some separate language-specific areas. Some of this activity takes place outside of the perisylvian region, for example, in the dorsolateral prefrontal cortex, which is thought to be indicative of cognitive effort as opposed to language processing *per se*. Moreover, as pointed out by Wong and Liu (2015), language-specific functional activation is more reliably found for phonological

---

[1] The patient's L1 was Swiss-German and they learned French (L2) around the age of five. Around puberty, the patient acquired both English (L3) and German (L4).

processing than in other language faculties. However, this specific result also contradicts ESM findings where all studies find distinct language areas, despite using tasks that are not specifically associated with phonological processing alone (e.g., picture naming or counting).

What can explain the different findings between ESM and neuroimaging studies? One possibility is that the presence of tumors or epilepsy substantially alters an individual's neural representation of language. Indeed, there is some evidence that the brain demonstrates plasticity throughout life; for example, neural circuits can be modified even after short-term exposure to an L2 (e.g., Tu et al. 2015), and slow-growing tumors do reorganize language such that it appears typical for an extended period. However, it seems unlikely that the presence of, for instance, a tumor would substantially modify the cortical representation of all the languages of a multilingual, specifically leading to more distinct language-specific areas than healthy multilinguals show. A more likely explanation lies in the better spatial resolution of ESM compared to imaging from hemodynamic data (i.e., blood oxygen flow used in fMRI studies), as de Bot and Jaensch (2015: 139) report as a result from a discussion with Indefrey and Paradis in 2012. In this view, fMRI would not be able to differentiate between the language-specific neural circuits that are recruited during language processing due to its coarser level of resolution. As pointed out by Indefrey, ESM data can also demonstrate shared language areas when they employ a coarser-than-usual level of resolution. In any case, with respect to the organization and representation of multilingualism compared to bilingualism, the ESM results converge on finding both shared and separate language areas in cortical representation.

17.3 The multilingual challenge

Studies examining multilingualism tend to agree on the concept of a "shared semantic store" (see French and Jacquet 2004, for a review on models of bilingual memory). This means that multilinguals access the same semantic system independently of the language they are using. Moreover, the field is converging on the notion of non-selective access (e.g., Thierry and Wu 2007, cf. Costa et al. 2017) as the default. This means that with few exceptions (Kroll 2006), multilinguals would have access to all of their lexicons at any given time.

Logically, a shared semantic store and non-selective access lead to a challenge: How do multilinguals select the right words for the interlocutors they are addressing at any given time? In many interactional contexts, there is a strict target language. Deviating from the target language can lead to breakdowns in communication. However, we know that multilinguals select the words from the right language virtually all the time, typically with minimal intrusions from the other languages (e.g., Poplack, 1980). So how do they do it? This led researchers to examine the neural underpinnings of language control.

17.3.1 Language control

The efficient use of language requires a certain level of control that allows the speaker to select preferred words and suppress others. This is true for both monolinguals and multilinguals; however, we assume that multilinguals face a greater challenge due to the issues described above. Recently, the inherent interference of bi-/multilingualism has attracted attention with respect to cognitive functioning. Using more than one language could enhance cognitive control performance, such that bi-/multilinguals outperform monolinguals on cognitive (executive) tasks (for a review see Bialystok et al. 2009; for a more in-depth discussion, see Chapter 16, this volume).

However, the supporting evidence is variable as recent comparisons have yielded no differences between bilinguals and monolinguals (for reviews, see De Bruin, Treccani, and Della Sala 2015; Duñabeitia and Carreiras 2015; Lehtonen et al. 2018). Regardless of whether one agrees that there is a "bilingual advantage", managing more than one language requires some degree of control. This section focuses on those control processes and their neural representation.

17.3.2 Cortico-subcortical network and language control

One of the most detailed proposals on the neural correlates of language control is by Abutalebi and Green (2007, 2016; Green and Abutalebi 2013). Focused on production, the authors describe speech regions together with regions responsible for language control. As shown in Figure 17.2., this model involves a cortico-subcortical network, involving the prefrontal cortex (PFC; including the inferior frontal gyrus, IFG), pre-supplementary motor area (pre-SMA), anterior cingulate cortex (ACC), inferior parietal lobules (supramarginal gyrus, SMG, and angular gyrus), subcortical structures, and the cerebellum. Moreover, there is a strong focus on language use, such that Green and Abutalebi (2013) propose that different interactional contexts modify the requirements placed on control processes. Their *Adaptive Control Hypothesis* (Green and Abutalebi 2013) differentiates among three language-use contexts: (a) single-language; (b) dual-language; and (c) dense code-switching.

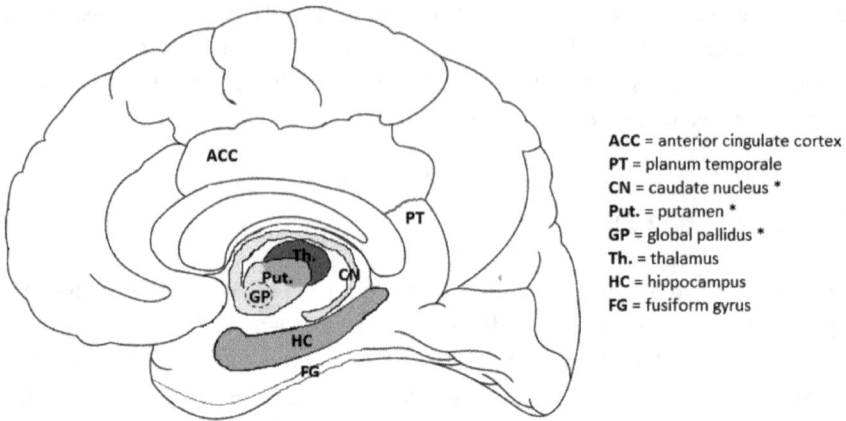

Figure 17.2: Representation of a medial view of the right hemisphere of the brain with the subcortical structures exposed, see text for which regions are hypothesized to be shared between languages. * CN, Put, and GP are part of the basal ganglia. In this view the GP is behind the CN.

The single-language context describes settings where one language is used with designated individuals while a different language is used in a different setting with other individuals. For example, one may use different languages at the workplace and at home. In this context, multilingual users are rarely required to switch between their languages. This contrasts to the dual-language context, where switching can occur between conversations. Consider, for example, a home situation where the parents are bilingual, but their children are relatively monolingual. Among themselves, the parents could speak language A, but when they turn to their children, they will address them in language B. The third setting, dense code-switching, describes a situation where speakers frequently switch languages, even within an utterance. In this context, several people in a conversation are proficient in multiple languages, which licenses switching among them.

Abutalebi and Green (2013) propose that these different interactional contexts place different demands on the control system. They describe eight different control processes that are taxed differently depending on the type of setting. Some of the control processes are more devoted to selecting and maintaining one language, such as interference suppression, which would be critical to multilinguals who mainly operate in single- and dual-language contexts where switching is dispreferred or dysfunctional. However, dense-code switching would demand less control because multiple languages are licensed. At the same time, in dense code-switchers, the general speech planning mechanism (called opportunistic planning) would be heavily taxed, for example, monitoring when a code-switch can occur within an utterance, such that the words of one language obey the syntactic frame of another.

These interactional settings and the different demands they place on the control processes would be reflected in the neural correlates of control. Green and Abutalebi (2013) propose that single and dual-language contexts extensively engage the inferior frontal and parietal cortices (bilaterally), the anterior cingulate cortex, the pre-supplementary motor area, the basal ganglia, and the thalamus (see Figure 17.2. for a representation of the relevant subcortical areas). This is due to the situational setting (i.e., dual-language and single-language contexts) requiring speakers to engage in extensive goal maintenance, conflict monitoring, and interference suppression (Abutalebi and Green 2016). Dense code-switching, on the other hand, would also involve this network, but to a lesser extent. Here, the opportunistic planning process is of importance, which would draw on the connection between the cerebellum and the left-prefrontal cortex (Abutalebi and Green 2016).

A critical question is to what extent this network is modulated by the same factors that modulate language representation. For example, de Bruin et al. (2014) conducted a language-switching study using picture naming in trilinguals. The results indicated activation of the right inferior frontal gyrus (rIFG) and the pre-supplementary motor area (pre-SMA) when participants were switching from their dominant L1 (Dutch) to their less-dominant, yet proficient L2 (English) and L3 (German) in contrast to non-switching. Interestingly, this difference in activation was not significant when participants switched to their L1 from their L2 or L3. This evidence aligns with proposals that hypothesize that inhibitory control is the crux to language switching (e.g., Green 1998) and that proficiency modulates the language control network. Tu et al. (2015) also showed that changing language exposure from 50/50 (L1, L2) to predominantly L1 for only 30 days changed the activation in the left pars opercularis and other regions associated with language control (e.g., the left anterior cingulate cortex and the left caudate nucleus). Thus, it seems that at least some of the factors known to influence language representation affect the cortico-subcortical network responsible for language control.

To neutralize possible effects of proficiency and to seek the most extreme version of language control, some studies have sought to test language control in simultaneous interpreters (SI). SIs have to process incoming auditory input in one language and simultaneously convert that to a different one, retrieving the correct lexical semantics and syntactic frames. This requires not only mastering the two or more languages, but also a high degree of language control.

Studies focusing on SIs have found the pars opercularis, pars triangularis, and subcortical regions to be affected by their unique training. A study by Elmer (2016), for example, revealed activation in the pars triangularis in five SIs during L2 to L1 translation, using both group and single-subject analyses. Elmer reports that the other regions of the control network demonstrated strong interindividual variability, whereas the pars triangularis was consistently activated. In a different study, Elmer, Hänggi, and Jäncke (2014) found structural differences, such that SIs had reduced grey matter volume in several areas amongst the bilateral pars triangularis, the left pars opercularis, and the left supramarginal gyrus. Some studies using a typical population have also tied the left pars opercularis to language control, demonstrating greater activation in bilinguals in contrast to monolinguals (Parker Jones et al. 2012).

Studies indicating the crucial role of subcortical structures in language switching mainly involve the basal ganglia. Hervais-Adelman, Moser-Mercer, and Golestani (2015) conducted a longitudinal study using fMRI, scanning SIs before and after their 15-month training program. SIs demonstrated reduced recruitment in the right caudate nucleus during simultaneous interpretation in post-training compared to pre-training scanning. The authors hypothesize that this reduced recruitment is indicative of emerging expertise, indicating that some tasks become more automatic with practice. Several other studies have found differential activity in the caudate nucleus during language switching (Crinion et al. 2006; Garbin et al. 2010; Luk et al. 2012).

The role of subcortical structures (i.e., the basal ganglia and the thalamus) in language control is further supported by evidence from the aphasia literature. Several studies have reported pathological code-mixing as a result of lesions or hemorrhages to the left caudate nucleus (Abutalebi, Miozzo, and Cappa 2000), the global pallidus and putamen (Abutalebi et al. 2009), and the left thalamus (Mariën et al. 2005).

Virtually all of the studies discussed above tested SIs – and, often, patients with aphasia – in only two languages and are unspecific to what extent their participants might be proficient in additional languages. Therefore, it is an open question to what extent speaking more than two languages modifies the control processes. However, the few studies that were explicitly on multilinguals (e.g., de Bruin et al. 2014) found activation in the same areas associated with language switching as in bilinguals. One can hypothesize that under the *Adaptive Control Hypothesis*, the situation of dense-code switching involving three or more languages would be rare. In that sense, multilingualism might not differ much from bilingualism (but see Chapter 9, this volume, to see how studying bimodal multilingualism can potentially assess this issue better). However, if the number of competitors (e.g., lexical items) is related to the amount of interference, one can imagine that differences could be detected between multilinguals versus bilinguals.

In sum, the current work on the neural representation of language control involves a network with cortical structures involving the prefrontal cortex, the inferior frontal gyrus (including the pars opercularis, pars triangularis, and pars orbitalis), the pre-supplementary motor area, the anterior cingulate cortex, and the inferior parietal lobules (including the supramarginal gyrus and the angular gyrus). Moreover, it is clear there are subcortical structures involved as well, such as the basal ganglia (including the caudate nucleus and the putamen) and the cerebellum.

17.4 Conclusion

It is clear that broadly considered, a Universal Language Network exists as Wong, Yin, and O'Brien (2016) argued. The perisylvian "language area" of the left hemisphere of the brain is primarily responsible for one language in the monolingual, two in the bilingual, and all languages in the multilingual. Within this perisylvian language region, the imaging data suggests there are regions of overlap, more so than separate language-specific regions. However, the electrical-stimulation (ESM) studies, on the whole, report more separation than the imaging studies do, which, we suggest, is because they record from finer-grained regions of the brain.

Complementing the language regions involved in bilingual and, presumably, multilingual processing are the control regions that include pre-frontal, caudate, and ACC areas as well as the perisylvian inferior parietal lobe. Related processes of control must operate in monolinguals as well, in making decisions to employ different speech registers (e.g., when speaking to one's boss or child). However, it seems that in bi-/multilinguals – especially those who switch languages in daily life – the cognitive control system is enhanced. This "bilingual advantage" has been associated with spared or enhanced abilities of bi-/multilinguals even on non-verbal tasks that require resistance to interference and inhibition, although controversies remain regarding this view.

Cutting across these generalizations are the individual differences in brain organization and functioning in adulthood that arise from Age of Acquisition and proficiency achieved in each language a participant knows (and presumably, though less studied from a 21st century neuro perspective, from manner of acquisition). As a rule, it appears that more overlap is seen for individuals who learned two or more languages earlier. Activation is often greater in later learners and those who are less proficient in the tested language, but – as the meta-analysis of Liu and Cao (2016) points out – this is not necessarily the case. The outstanding question regarding the meaning of activation may account – at least in part – for contradictory findings in the neurolinguistic literature whereby greater expertise across a number of activities can be linked either to more or less brain activation when they are performed.

With respect to possible distinctions in the organization and processing of languages between bilinguals and multilinguals, there is only a small literature at this time, and studies examining the neural representation of bilingualism versus multilingualism are even more limited. The current multilingualism studies seem to align with the greater body of work on bilingualism, indicating a common language network that is modulated by known factors, such as proficiency and exposure. However, as with bilingual ESM studies, multilingual ESM studies, as compared to multilingual fMRI studies, more often find separate language areas contiguous with shared ones due to their narrower levels of measurement.

In sum, there are some perisylvian regions of the left hemisphere that seem to be particularly dedicated to language learning, whether for a mere single language or for more, at any age. The brain's plasticity may decline, such that the ability to easily pick up aspects of a new language drops off after some point in the first two decades of life, depending on which aspect of language one considers. Nevertheless, language practices appear to take advantage of (or build on) some degree of brain plasticity well into later adulthood, reflecting the interactive patterns mostly used in daily life.

Acknowledgments: Thanks are due to Taryn Malcolm and Aviva Lerman for their help in constructing the figures.

References

Abutalebi, Jubin & David Green. 2007. Bilingual language production: The neurocognition of language representation and control. *Journal of Neurolinguistics* 20(3). 242–275.
Abutalebi, Jubin & David W. Green. 2016. Neuroimaging of language control in bilinguals: Neural adaptation and reserve. *Bilingualism: Language and Cognition* 19(4). 689–698.
Abutalebi, Jubin, Antonio Miozzo & Stefano F. Cappa. 2000. Do subcortical structures control 'language selection' in polyglots? Evidence from pathological language mixing. *Neurocase* 6(1). 51–56.
Abutalebi, Jubin, Pasquale Anthony Della Rosa, Marco Tettamanti, David W. Green & Stefano F. Cappa. 2009. Bilingual aphasia and language control: A follow-up fMRI and intrinsic connectivity study. *Brain and Language* 109(2–3). 141–156.

Abutalebi, Jubin, Jean-Marie Annoni, Ivan Zimine, Alan J. Pegna, Mohamed L. Seghier, Hannelore Lee-Jahnke, Francois Lazeyras, Stefano F. Cappa & Asaid Khateb. 2007. Language control and lexical competition in bilinguals: An event-related fMRI study. *Cerebral Cortex* 18(7). 1496–1505.

Bello, Lorenzo, Francesco Acerbi, Carlo Giussani, Pietro Baratta, Paolo Taccone, Valeria Songa, Marica Fava, Nino Stocchetti, Costanza Papagno & Sergio M. Gaini. 2006. Intraoperative language localization in multilingual patients with gliomas. *Neurosurgery* 59(1). 115–125.

Bialystok, Ellen, Fergus I. M. Craik, David W. Green & Tamar H. Gollan. 2009. Bilingual minds. *Psychological Science in the Public Interest* 10. 89–129.

Bloch, Constantine, Anelis Kaiser, Esther Kuenzli, Daniela Zappatore, Sven Haller, Rita Franceschini, Georges Luedi, Ernst-Wilhelm Radue & Cordula Nitsch. 2009. The age of second language acquisition determines the variability in activation elicited by narration in three languages in Broca's and Wernicke's area. *Neuropsychologia* 47(3). 625–633.

Bot, Kees de & Carol Jaensch. 2015. What is special about L3 processing? *Bilingualism: Language and Cognition* 18 (2).130–144.

Briellmann, Regula S., Michael M. Saling, Ailie B. Connell, Anthony B. Waites, David F. Abbott & Graeme D. Jackson. 2004. A high-field functional MRI study of quadri-lingual subjects. *Brain and Language* 89(3). 531–542.

Bruin, Angela de & Sergio Della Sala. 2016. The importance of language use when studying the neuroanatomical basis of bilingualism. *Language, Cognition and Neuroscience* 31(3). 335–339.

Bruin, Angela de, Barbara Treccani & Sergio Della Sala. 2015. Cognitive advantage in bilingualism: An example of publication bias? *Psychological Science* 26(1). 99–107.

Bruin, Angela de, Ardi Roelofs, Ton Dijkstra & Ian FitzPatrick. 2014. Domain-general inhibition areas of the brain are involved in language switching: FMRI evidence from trilingual speakers. *NeuroImage* 90. 348–359.

Cao, Fan, Say Kim, Yanni Liu & Li Liu. 2014. Similarities and differences in brain activation and functional connectivitiy in first and second language reading: Evidence from Chinese learners of English. *Neuropsychologia* 63. 275–284.

Cervenka, Mackenzie C., Dana Boatman-Reich, Julianna Ward, Piotr J. Franaszczuk & Nathan Ecrone. 2011. Language mapping in multilingual patients: Electrocorticography and cortical stimulation during naming. *Frontiers in Human Neuroscience* 5. Article 13. doi:10.3389/fnhum.2011.00013

Chertkow, Howard, Victor Whitehead, Natalie Phillips, Christina Wolfson, Julie Atherton & Howard Bergman. 2010. Multilingualism (but not always bilingualism) delays the onset of Alzheimer disease: Evidence from a bilingual community. *Alzheimer Disease and Associated Disorders* 24(2). 118–125.

Costa, Albert & Nuria Sebastián-Gallés. 2014. How does the bilingual experience sculpt the brain? *Nature Reviews Neuroscience* 15(5). 336–345.

Costa, Albert, Mario Pannunzi, Gustavo Deco & Martin J. Pickering. 2017. Do bilinguals automatically activate their native language when they are not using it? *Cognitive Science* 41(6). 1629–1644.

Cherodath, Sarika & Nandini Chatterjee Singh. 2015. The influence of orthographic depth on reading networks in simultaneous biliterate children. *Brain and Language* 143. 42–51.

Crinion, Jenny, Robert Turner, Alice Grogan, Takashi Hanakawa, Uta Noppeney, Joseph T. Devlin, Toshihiko Aso, Shinichi Urayama, Hidenao Fukuyama, Kath Stockton, Keiko Usui, David W. Green & Cathy J. Price. 2006. Language control in the bilingual brain. *Science* 312(5779). 1537–1540.

Dehaene, Stanislas, Emmanuel Dupoux, Jacques Mehler, Laurent Cohen, Eraldo Paulesu, Daniela Perani, Pierre-François van de Moortele, Stephane Lehericy & Denis Le Bihan. 1997. Anatomical variability in the cortical representation of first and second language. *Neuroreport* 8(17). 3809–3815.

Duñabeitia, Jon Andoni & Manuel Carreiras. 2015. The bilingual advantage: Acta est fabula? *Cortex* 73. 371–372.

Elmer, Stefan. 2016. Broca pars triangularis constitutes a "hub" of the language-control network during simultaneous language translation. *Frontiers in Human Neuroscience* 10. Article 491. doi: 10.3389/fnhum.2016.00491

Elmer, Stefan, Jurgen Hänggi & Lutz Jäncke. 2014. Processing demands upon cognitive, linguistic, and articulatory functions promote grey matter plasticity in the adult multilingual brain: Insights from simultaneous interpreters. *Cortex* 54. 179–189.

Fernández-Coello, Alejandro, Viktoria Havas, Montserrat Juncadella, Joanna Sierpowska, Antoni Rodríguez-Fornells & Andreu Gabarrós. 2016. Age of language acquisition and cortical language organization in multilingual patients undergoing awake brain mapping. *Journal of Neurosurgery* 126(6). 1912–1923.

French, Robert M. & Maud Jacquet. 2004. Understanding bilingual memory: Models and data. *Trends in Cognitive Sciences* 8(2). 87–93.

Gandour, Jackson, Yunxia Tong, Thomas Talavage, Donald Wong, Mario Dzemidzic, Yisheng Xu, Xiaojian Li & Mark Lowe. 2007. Neural basis of first and second language processing of sentence-level linguistic prosody. *Human Brain Mapping* 28(2). 94–108.

Garbin, Gabrielle, Ana Sanjuan, Cristina Forn, Juan Carlos Bustamante, Aina Rodríguez-Pujadas, Vicente Belloch, M. Hernandez, Albert Costa & César Ávila. 2010. Bridging language and attention: Brain basis of the impact of bilingualism on cognitive control. *NeuroImage* 53(4). 1272–1278.

Geschwind, Norman. 1970. The organization of language and the brain. *Science* 170(3961). 940–944.

Giussani, Carlo, Franck-Emmanuel Roux, Vincent Lubrano, Sergio M. Gaini & Lorenzo Bello. 2007. Review of language organisation in bilingual patients: What can we learn from direct brain mapping? *Acta Neurochirurgica* 149(11). 1109–1116.

Green, David W. 1998. Mental control of the bilingual lexico-semantic system. *Bilingualism: Language and Cognition* 1(2). 67–81.

Green, David W. 2003. The neural basis of the lexicon and the grammar in L2 acquisition. In Roeland van Hout, Aafke Hulk, Folkert Kuiken & Richard Towell (eds.), *The interface between syntax and the lexicon in second language acquisition*. Amsterdam: John Benjamins.

Green, David W. & Jubin Abutalebi. 2013. Language control in bilinguals: The adaptive control hypothesis. *Journal of Cognitive Psychology* 25(5). 515–530.

Gollan, Tamar H., Gali Weissberger, Elin Runnqvist, Rosa I. Montoya & Cynthia M. Cera. 2012. Self-ratings of spoken language dominance: A Multilingual Naming Test (MINT) and preliminary norms for young and aging Spanish-English bilinguals. *Bilingualism: Language and Cognition* 15(3). 594–615.

Golestani, Narly, F.-Xavier Alario, Sebastien Meriaux, Denis Le Bihan, Stanislas Dehaene & Christophe Pallier. 2006. Syntax production in bilinguals. *Neuropsychologia* 44(7). 1029–1040.
Kenji, Hakuta & Daniel d'Andrea. 1992. Some properties of bilingual maintenance and loss in Mexican background high-school students. *Applied Linguistics* 13(1). 72–99.
Hartshorne, Joshua K., Joshua B. Tenenbaum & Steven Pinker. 2018. A critical period for second language acquisition: Evidence from 2/3 million English speakers. *Cognition* 177. 263–277.
Hernandez, Arturo E., Juliane Hofmann & Sonja A. Kotz. 2007. Age of acquisition modulates neural activity for both regular and irregular syntactic functions. *NeuroImage* 36(3). 912–923.
Hervais-Adelman, Alexis, Barbara Moser-Mercer & Narly Golestani. 2015. Brain functional plasticity associated with the emergence of expertise in extreme language control. *NeuroImage* 114. 264–274.
Higby, Eve, Jungna Kim & Loraine K. Obler. 2013. Multilingualism and the brain. *Annual Review of Applied Linguistics* 33. 68–101.
Hull, Rachel & Jyotsna Vaid. 2006. Laterality and language experience. *Laterality* 11(5). 436–464.
Hull, Rachel & Jyotsna Vaid. 2007. Bilingual language lateralization: A meta-analytic tale of two hemispheres. *Neuropsychologia* 45(9). 1987–2008.
Indefrey, Peter. 2006. A meta-analysis of hemodynamic studies on first and second language processing: Which suggested differences can we trust and what do they mean? *Language Learning* 56 (s1). 279–304.
Kim, Karl H. S., Norman R. Relkin, Kyoung-Min Lee & Joy Hirsch. 1997. Distinct cortical areas associated with native and second languages. *Nature* 388(6638). 171–174.
Klein, Denise, Kevin Mok, Jen-Kai Chen & Kate E. Watkins. 2014. Age of language learning shapes brain structure: A cortical thickness study of bilingual and monolingual individuals. *Brain and Language* 131. 20–24.
Kochunov, Peter, Peter Fox, Jack Lancaster, Li-Hai Tan, Katrin Amunts, Karl Zilles, John Mazziotta & Jia-Hong Gao. 2003. Localized morphological brain differences between English-speaking Caucasians and Chinese-speaking Asians: New evidence of anatomical plasticity. *Neuroreport* 14(7). 961–964.
Kroll, Judith F., Susan C. Bobb & Zofia Wodniecka. 2006. Language selectivity is the exception, not the rule: Arguments against a fixed locus of language selection in bilingual speech. *Bilingualism: Language and Cognition* 9(2). 119–135.
Lehtonen, Minna, Anna Soveri, Aini Laine, Janica Järvenpää, Angela de Bruin & Jan Antfolk. 2018. Is bilingualism associated with enhanced executive functioning in adults? A meta-analytic review. *Psychological Bulletin* 144(4). 394–425.
Li, Ping, Jennifer Legault & Kaitlyn A. Litcofsky. 2014. Neuroplasticity as a function of second language learning: Anatomical changes in the human brain. *Cortex* 58. 301–324.
Liu, Hengshuang & Fan Cao. 2016. L1 and L2 processing in the bilingual brain: A meta-analysis of neuroimaging studies. *Brain and Language* 159. 60–73.
Lubrano, Vincent, Katia Prod'homme, Jean-François Démonet & Barbara Köpke. 2012. Language monitoring in multilingual patients undergoing awake craniotomy: A case study of a German-English-French trilingual patient with a WHO grade II glioma. *Journal of Neurolinguistics* 25(6). 567–578.

Lucas, Timothy H., Guy M. McKhann & George A. Ojemann. 2004. Functional separation of languages in the bilingual brain: A comparison of electrical stimulation language mapping in 25 bilingual patients and 117 monolingual control patients. *Journal of Neurosurgery* 101(3). 449–457.

Luk, Gigi, David W. Green, Jubin Abutalebi & Cheryl Grady. 2012. Cognitive control for language switching in bilinguals: A quantitative meta-analysis of functional neuroimaging studies. *Language and Cognitive Processes* 27(10). 1479–1488.

Maguire, Eleanor A., Katherine Woollett & Hugo J. Spiers. 2006. London taxi drivers and bus drivers: A structural MRI and neuropsychological analysis. *Hippocampus* 16(12). 1091–1101.

Mariën, Peter, Jubin Abutalebi, Sebastiaan Engelborghs & Peter P. De Deyn. 2005. Pathophysiology of language switching and mixing in an early bilingual child with subcortical aphasia. *Neurocase* 11(6). 385–398.

Meisel, Jurgen M. 2004. The bilingual child. In Tej K. Bhatia & William C. Ritchie (eds.), *The handbook of bilingualism* (Blackwell Handbooks in Linguistics), 91–113. Malden, MA: Blackwell Publishing Ltd.

Mohades, Seyede Ghazel, Peter Van Schuerbeek, Yves Rosseel, Piet Van De Craen, Robert Luypaert & Chris Baeken. 2015. White-matter development is different in bilingual and monolingual children: A longitudinal DTI study. *PLoS One* 10 (2).e0117968.

Montrul, Silvina & Rebecca Foote. 2012. Age of acquisition interactions in bilingual lexical access: A study of the weaker language of L2 learners and heritage speakers. *International Journal of Bilingualism* 18(3). 274–303.

Morgan-Short, Kara, Ingrid Finger, Sarah Grey & Michael T. Ullman. 2012a. Second language processing shows increased native-like neural responses after months of no exposure. *PLoS One* 7(3). doi: e32974.

Morgan-Short, Kara, Karsten Steinhauer, Cristina Sanz & Michael T. Ullman. 2012b. Explicit and implicit second language training differentially affect the achievement of native-like brain activation patterns. *Journal of Cognitive Neuroscience* 24(4). 933–947.

Obler, Loraine & Kris Gjerlow. 1999. *Language and the brain*. Cambridge: Cambridge University Press.

Ojemann, George A. & Harry A. Whitaker. 1978. Language localization and variability. *Brain and Language* 6(2). 239–260.

Park, Haeme R., Gjurgjica Badzakova-Trajkov & Karen E. Waldie. 2012. Language lateralisation in late proficient bilinguals: A lexical decision fMRI study. *Neuropsychologia* 50(5). 688–695.

Parker Jones, Ōiwi, David W. Green, Alice Grogan, Christos Pliatsikas, Konstantinos Filippopolitis, Nilufa Ali, Hwee Ling Lee, Sue Ramsden, Karine Gazarian, Susan Prejawa, Mohamed L. Seghier & Cathy J. Price. 2012. Where, when and why brain activation differs for bilinguals and monolinguals during picture naming and reading aloud. *Cerebral Cortex* 22(4). 892–902.

Perani, Daniela, Stanislas Dehaene, Franco Grassi, Laurent Cohen, Stefano F. Cappa, Emmanuel Dupoux, Ferruccio Fazio & Jacques Mehler. 1996. Brain processing of native and foreign languages. *NeuroReport-International Journal for Rapid Communications of Research in Neuroscience* 7(15). 2439–2444.

Perani, Daniela, Eraldo Paulesu, Nuria Sebastian Galles, Emmanuel Dupoux, Stanislas Dehaene, Valentino Bettinardi, Stefano F. Cappa, Ferruccio Fazio & Jacques Mehler. 1998.

The bilingual brain: Proficiency and age of acquisition of the second language. *Brain: A Journal of Neurology* 121(10). 1841–1852.

Perfetti, Charles A. & Lindsay N. Harris. 2013. Universal reading processes are modulated by language and writing system. *Language Learning and Development* 9(4). 296–316.

Pitres, Albert. 1895. Etude sur l'aphasie chez les polyglottes. *Revue de médicine* 15. 873–899.

Poeppel, David & Gregory Hickok. 2004. Towards a new functional anatomy of language. *Cognition* 92(4). 1–12.

Poeppel, David, Karen Emmorey, Gregory Hickok & Liina Pylkkänen. 2012. Towards a new neurobiology of language. *Journal of Neuroscience* 32(41). 14125–14131.

Połczyńska, Monika M., Kevin Japardi & Susan Y. Bookheimer. 2017. Lateralizing language function with pre-operative functional magnetic resonance imaging in early proficient bilingual patients. *Brain and Language* 170. 1–11.

Połczyńska, Monika M., Christopher F. A. Benjamin, Kevin Japardi, Andrew Frew & Susan Y. Bookheimer. 2016. Language system organization in a quadrilingual with a brain tumor: Implications for understanding of the language network. *Neuropsychologia* 86. 167–175.

Poplack, Shana. 1980. "Sometimes I'll start a sentence in Spanish y termino en español": Toward a typology of code-switching. *Linguistics* 18(7). 581–618.

Price, Cathy J. 2010. The anatomy of language: A review of 100 fMRI studies published in 2009. *Annals of the New York Academy of Sciences* 1191(1). 62–88.

Price, Cathy J. 2012. A review and synthesis of the first 20 years of PET and fMRI studies of heard speech, spoken language and reading. *Neuroimage* 62(2). 816–847.

Rapport, Richard L., Chong Tin Tan & Harry A. Whitaker. 1983. Language function and dysfunction among Chinese-and English-speaking polyglots: Cortical stimulation, Wada testing, and clinical studies. *Brain and Language* 18(2). 342–366.

Román, Patricia, Julio González, Noelia Ventura-Campos, Aina Rodríguez-Pujadas, Ana Sanjuán & César Ávila. 2015. Neural differences between monolinguals and early bilinguals in their native language during comprehension. *Brain and Language* 150. 80–89.

Rossi, Sonja, Manfred F. Gugler, Angela D. Friederici & Anja Hahne. 2006. The impact of proficiency on syntactic second-language processing of German and Italian: Evidence from event-related potentials. *Journal of Cognitive Neuroscience* 18(12). 2030–2048.

Roux, Franck-Emmanuel & Michel Trémoulet. 2002. Organization of language areas in bilingual patients: A cortical stimulation study. *Journal of Neurosurgery* 97(4). 857–864.

Roux, Franck-Emmanuel, Vincent Lubrano, Valérie Lauwers-Cances, Michel Trémoulet, Christopher R. Mascott & Jean-François Démonet. 2004. Intra-operative mapping of cortical areas involved in reading in mono-and bilingual patients. *Brain* 127(8). 1796–1810.

Saur, Dorothee, Annette Baumgaertner, Anja Moehring, Christian Büchel, Matthias Bonnesen, Michael Rose, Mariachristina Musso & Jurgen M. Meisel. 2009. Word order processing in the bilingual brain. *Neuropsychologia* 47(1). 158–168.

Schweizer, Tom A., Jenna Ware, Corinne E. Fischer, Fergus I. M. Craik & Ellen Bialystok. 2012. Bilingualism as a contributor to cognitive reserve: Evidence from brain atrophy in Alzheimer's disease. *Cortex* 48(8). 991–996.

Sebastian, Rajani, Angela R. Laird & Swathi Kiran. 2011. Meta-analysis of the neural representation of first language and second language. *Applied Psycholinguistics* 32(4). 799–819.

Serafini, Sandra, Sridharan Gururangan, Allan Friedman & Michael Haglund. 2008. Identification of distinct and overlapping cortical areas for bilingual naming and reading using cortical stimulation. *Journal of Neurosurgery* 1(3). 247–254.

Silverberg, Stu & Arthur Samuel. 2004. The effect of age of second language acquisition on the representation and processing of second language words. *Journal of Memory and Language* 51(3). 381–398.

Stein, Maria, Carmen Winkler, Anelis Kaiser & Thomas Dierks. 2014. Structural brain changes related to bilingualism: Does immersion make a difference? *Frontiers in Psychology* 5. Article 1116. doi:10.3389/fpsyg.2014.01116

Stein, Maria, Andrea Federspiel, Thomas Koenig, Miranka Wirth, Werner Strik, Roland Wiest, Daniel Brandeis & Thomas Dierks. 2012. Structural plasticity in the language system related to increased second language proficiency. *Cortex* 48(4). 458–465.

Thierry, Guillaume & Yan Jing Wu. 2007. Brain potentials reveal unconscious translation during foreign-language comprehension. *Proceedings of the National Academy of Sciences,* 104(30). 12530–12535.

Tremblay, Pascale & Anthony Steven Dick. 2016. Broca and Wernicke are dead, or moving past the classic model of language neurobiology. *Brain and Language* 162. 60–71.

Tu, Liu, Junjing Wang, Jubin Abutalebi, Bo Jiang, Ximin Pan, Meng Li, Wei Gao, Yuchen Yang, Bishan Liang, Zhi Lu & Ruiwang Huang. 2015. Language exposure induced neuroplasticity in the bilingual brain: A follow-up fMRI study. *Cortex* 64. 8–19.

Ullman, Michael T. 2001. The neural basis of lexicon and grammar in first and second language: The declarative/procedural model. *Bilingualism: Language and Cognition* 4(2). 105–122.

Videsott, Gerda, Barbel Herrnberger, Klaus Hoenig, Edgar Schilly, Jo Grothe, Werner Wiater, Manfred Spitzer & Markus Kiefer. 2010. Speaking in multiple languages: Neural correlates of language proficiency in multilingual word production. *Brain and Language* 113(3). 103–112.

Vingerhoets, Guy, John Van Borsel, Cathelijne Tesink, Maurits van Den Noort, Karel Deblaere, Ruth Seurinck, Pieter Vandemaele & Eric Achten. 2003. Multilingualism: An fMRI study. *NeuroImage* 20(4). 2181–2196.

Walker, John A., Alfredo Quiñones-Hinojosa & Mitchel S. Berger. 2004. Intraoperative speech mapping in 17 bilingual patients undergoing resection of a mass lesion. *Neurosurgery* 54(1). 113–118.

Wartenburger, Isabell, Hauke R. Heekeren, Jubin Abutalebi, Stefano F. Cappa, Arno Villringer & Daniela Perani. 2003. Early setting of grammatical processing in the bilingual brain. *Neuron* 37(1). 159–170.

Wattendorf, Elise, Julia Festman, Birgit Westermann, Ursula Keil, Daniela Zappatore, Rita Franceschini, Georges Luedi, Ernst-Wilhelm Radue, Thomas F. Munte, Gunter Rager & Cordula Nitsch. 2014. Early bilingualism influences early and subsequently later acquired languages in cortical regions representing control functions. *International Journal of Bilingualism* 18(1). 48–66.

Wong, Becky, Bin Yin & Beth O'Brien. 2016. Neurolinguistics: Structure, function, and connectivity in the bilingual brain. *BioMed Research International* 2016. Article ID 7069274. doi.org/10.1155/2016/7069274

Yetkin, Oguz F., Zerrin Yetkin, Victor M. Haughton & Robert W. Cox. 1996. Use of functional MR to map language in multilingual volunteers. *American Journal of Neuroradiology* 17(3). 473–477.

Simona Montanari and Suzanne Quay
18 Conclusion and Directions for Future Research

The last twenty years have witnessed a surge in the number of studies that examine the acquisition, use, and unlearning of more than two languages. While multilingualism remains understudied and at times misunderstood, this volume has attempted to review the latest research on how societies and individuals learn and manage multiple languages in different communities, across different modalities, at distinct life stages, and in varied socio-political contexts.

18.1 Expanding the geography and accounts of multilingualism

One of the emerging themes from this volume is that multilingualism is intrinsic to many societies and perhaps more prevalent than monolingualism or bilingualism *per se* in many regions around the world. The contributions in the first section have indeed highlighted the countless and usually intertwined circumstances that have turned monolingual or bilingual societies into multilingual ones. Some of these circumstances are historical – as is the case of colonialism in North Africa (Ech-Charfi, Chapter 2) or Southeast Asia (Ng and Cavallaro, Chapter 3); some are political, as with Singapore's internationalization ideology that made a non-indigenous language, English, the official language and inter-ethnic lingua franca of the country (Ng and Cavallaro, Chapter 3). Yet at other times, education has been the driving force behind the creation of multilingual speakers – as in Europe (Bartelheimer, Hufeisen and Montanari, Chapter 4) and Canada (Wright and Chan, Chapter 5); or migration, which has brought millions of immigrants from the world's poor regions to wealthier Europe (Bartelheimer, Hufeisen and Montanari, Chapter 4) and North America (Wright and Chan, Chapter 5), increasing linguistic and cultural diversity in traditionally monolingual or bilingual countries. These

Simona Montanari, California State University, Los Angeles (CA), U.S.A.
Suzanne Quay, International Christian University, Tokyo, Japan

examples suggest that multilingualism results from a wider variety of social, cultural and economic forces than bilingualism, and accounts of this heterogeneity are even more complex than in the case of bilingual populations.

Despite the prevalence of multilingualism in many diverse world regions, research on multilingualism remains geographically limited, and includes primarily middle-class multilinguals from Europe and North America. Although we have attempted to involve contributors from as many different parts of the world and encouraged them to consider relevant findings on multilingualism from Africa, Asia, and Latin America, few have been able to do so simply because this research does not exist. This is unfortunate because it means that what is known about multilingualism is mostly based on research involving individuals from middle or upper socioeconomic backgrounds in Western cultures, speaking only a few of multilinguals' possible language combinations, and operating in contexts that exert a social pressure to conform to monolingual expectations. Since social and cultural variables strongly condition multilingual outcomes, it is thus imperative that more studies are conducted in socio-political and socio-linguistic realities in which multilingualism is natural and seen as *the norm*, as in India, Africa, and certain areas of Asia (Bhatia and Ritchie 2012). Studies in these areas – where bilingual and multilingual individuals outnumber monolinguals – may reveal intriguing patterns of language development, use, and attrition and may uncover cognitive, emotional, and academic advantages (or disadvantages) different from those documented so far. This geographically-broader research would also allow the study of multilingualism in the context of languages that are typologically different from those studied so far, revealing new types and degrees of cross-linguistic interactions than those documented in the current research.

By expanding the geography of multilingualism research, future studies and theoretical interpretations can also move away from long-established definitions of "language" and traditional accounts of language use put forward by a Western monoglossic ideology that holds the idealized notions of monolingualism and nativeness as gold standards. Surveying the heterogeneous nature of multilingual interactions, the contributions in this volume have indeed put into question traditional notions and accounts of multilingual use such as diglossia (Ech-Charfi, Chapter 2; Maher, Chapter 6), code-switching (Stavans and Porat, Chapter 7; Chen Pichler, Reynolds and Palmer, Chapter 9), or even multilingualism conceived as two interlocutors' speaking different languages to each other (Gooskens, Chapter 8). In the context of North Africa, for example, Ech-Charfi (Chapter 2) laments that, besides imposing their languages, the colonial powers brought to the region the same notion of "language" – and the European discourse about language and nation – with consequences that are still visible today in the lack of recognition of local French varieties, in the use of the term "diglossia" to differentiate the use of Literary Arabic from colloquial Arabic or of "Berber" to refer to the heterogeneous linguistic landscape that characterizes the indigenous populations of the region.

Therefore, this volume's contributions emphasize that new models of language learning, processing, use, and attrition in multilinguals are needed to accommodate the complex and dynamic nature of the multilingual system, a system in which different languages interact with each other in a process that continually changes the system and leads to emergent properties in the multilingual mind (Jessner and Megens, Chapter 13; Allgäuer-Hackl and Jessner, Chapter 15). This is indeed the perspective proposed by Jessner and colleagues who examine multilingualism from a dynamic and complexity systems point of view, in particular from the stance of the Dynamic Model of Multilingualism (Herdina and Jessner 2002). According to this approach, and as highlighted in other contributions, any study of multilingualism – or of multilingual development or language attrition in multilinguals – is incomplete if one considers only one of the multilingual's languages in isolation. This is because multilingual development is neither linear nor unidirectional but rather characterized by changes, throughout the lifespan, in fluency and proficiency in each language, in the effort to maintain each language, in the degree(s) of language contact and use, and in the many complex cross-linguistic interactions. Jessner and colleagues (Chapter 13; Chapter 15) particularly lament that while the study of bilingualism has taken into account the two languages of bilinguals (one being developed and the other undergoing attrition), the study of multilingualism that considers all of the multilinguals' languages remains underresearched and virtually in its infancy. Thus, the authors advocate for a holistic multilingual approach that takes into consideration not only linguistic processes but also (meta)cognitive ones such as metalinguistic and crosslinguistic awareness (Chapter 15).

We praise Jessner and colleagues for advancing a theory of multilingualism that moves beyond static descriptions and captures the fluctuating nature of linguistic knowledge across the lifespan. At the same time, in order to advance not only a dynamic, integrated, and holistic but also a "universal" understanding of multilingualism, we call for an increase in language diversity (beyond Germanic and Romance languages) in the studies framed within this perspective. Only by expanding the geography of multilingual studies can we indeed truly break away from the Euro-centric monolingual ideology that has framed studies of multilingualism so far.

18.2 Learning and unlearning multiple languages in the family and educational context

At the individual level, the contributions in this volume have shown that languages can be learned and unlearned quickly across the lifespan due to child-internal and external factors (Quay and Chevalier, Chapter 10), family language policies in the early years (Lanza and Lexander, Chapter 11) and educational policies in the school years (Wang, Chapter 12; Jessner and Megens, Chapter 13). Moving beyond language socialization research, which has traditionally emphasized adult caregivers' roles in young children's socialization process, Quay and Chevalier (Chapter 10) and Lanza and Lexander (Chapter 11) highlight the agency of children in negotiating their language learning environment, at times promoting their own multilingualism, at times instigating language shift within the family. Gooskens (Chapter 8) points out that receptive multilingualism can also be seen in the discourse of families when children speak the societal language while their parents respond in the heritage language (also termed "dual-lingual" interactions in Quay and Chevalier, Chapter 10). Quay and Chevalier (Chapter 10) further address the need to revisit the traditional, monolingualist dogmas of the "one-person-one-language approach" and consider more flexible multilingual practices when raising multilingual children because only the latter may ensure harmonious multilingual development. Similarly, Lanza and Lexander (Chapter 11) set the study of the language and literacy practices of multilingual families within the new, burgeoning field of Family Language Policy, which examines language "as a means through which multilingual adults and children define themselves and their families," with "a focus on globally dispersed, transnational or multilingual populations beyond the traditional, two-parent family," and with "research methods that attend to meaning-making in interaction and as well as the broader context" (King and Lanza 2019: 722).

The family context is particularly important for multilingual development in the early years, notably also for deaf and hearing children of signing Deaf parents (Chen Pichler, Reynolds, and Palmer, Chapter 9). However, it is the school context that can significantly foster (or hamper) multilingualism in middle and late childhood. For instance, as pointed out above, children in North Africa (Ech-Charfi, Chapter 2), Southeast Asia (Ng and Cavallaro, Chapter 3), Europe (Bartelheimer, Hufeisen and Montanari, Chapter 4), and Canada (Wright and Chan, Chapter 5) become proficient in multiple languages thanks to educational policies. Children who are already proficient in two or more home or heritage languages may also learn the society's language or additional languages at school (Chen Pichler, Reynolds, and Palmer, Chapter 9; Wang, Chapter 12). However, this process is more challenging than the natural language learning experience that occurs early on at home because it is decontextualized, intentional, and formal. At the same time, because multilingual students' academic success heavily depends on their literacy abilities in the school (i.e., societal) language(s), educational systems often fail to sustain their students' multilingual development, especially in traditionally monolingual contexts that are not supportive of multilingualism. This may result in educational systems favoring only the societal language (Wang, Chapter 12) or more marketable foreign languages such as English (Ng and Cavallaro, Chapter 3; Bartelheimer, Hufeisen and Montanari, Chapter 4) with the consequence of language attrition in one or more of the multilingual's languages (Jessner and Megens, Chapter 13) or even language shift within a country (Ng and Cavallaro, Chapter 3).

Thus, another emerging theme in this volume is the hegemony of majority languages, and especially of English, in the raising and education of multilingual children. In the home context, parents in mixed-language couples who choose English as a lingua franca lower their chances of raising multilingual children, and in anglophone countries, the overall maintenance of minority languages is seriously challenged (Quay and Chevalier, Chapter 10). In the educational context, introducing English too early in the curriculum and favoring it over other languages may ultimately result in the loss of multilingualism in less marketable languages (Ng and Cavallaro, Chapter 3; Bartelheimer, Hufeisen and Montanari, Chapter 4). English has even become a "high" preferred form for communication in popular culture (e.g., music) and international politics (Maher, Chapter 6), and it has been adopted as the official language and interethnic lingua franca even in countries in which it is non-indigenous (i.e., Singapore, Ng and Cavallaro, Chapter 3). Hufeisen (personal communication) further laments the pressure to publish in English in the academic context and the resulting lack of or disinterest in publications in languages other than English, which, as she puts, is ultimately "highly destructive to a vivid multilingual world". Hence, there is need to not only expand the geography of multilingualism research as argued above but also to advocate for the preservation and study of linguistic diversity. To this end, adopting a European Commission's (2007) initiative, Gooskens (Chapter 8) proposes to focus on one extreme of the multilingual language use continuum – receptive multilingualism. Indeed, this form of language use has the potential to not only reveal the remarkable robustness of speakers' language processing mechanisms, communicative competence, and cognitive/linguistic flexibility but also to maintain linguistic diversity and ensure the survival of "smaller" or less marketable languages while increasing individuals' mobility. Similarly, more research is needed in "cross-signing", when signers who do not share a common sign language nevertheless negotiate meaning by using visually-oriented strategies (Chen Pichler, Reynolds, and Palmer, Chapter 9).

18.3 Common themes and new insights

The world is becoming increasingly more multilingual as more individuals move around it with rising interconnectivity. Indeed, migration, globalization and the information technology revolution are the threads in the early 21st century that have brought together opportunities and challenges for communicating and learning in new environments, both real and online. The age of social media and the Internet forces us to study multilingualism from a new perspective. Of particular relevance are thus Lanza and Lexander's sections (in Chapter 11) on digitally mediated language practices, a new modality that allows families "to stretch" and stay in touch, exchange information across borders, and practice mobile or virtual "intimacy" (Hjorth 2011). This body of work moves beyond traditional examinations of language and literacy practices within families to include new technologies that modify interaction styles and add non-verbal means to express emotions (such as the use of emojis), thereby managing family relationships in new ways, changing sense of selves, and constructing new identities. The importance to examine language use in cyberspace is also highlighted by Stavans and Porat (Chapter 7: 139), who show that when "writing and speaking are mediated by digital technologies, they become even more complex because they are scattered across time and space (e.g., via mails); they become essentially 'language-less' (such as emoticons or emojis); and the rules governing them have evolved to generate alternative literacy practices". Thus, together with the study of traditional spoken interactions, the study of digitally mediated interactions should be pursued in future research because it provides new insights into how languages are combined to create meaning, how they are woven into family dynamics and across generations, and how they contribute to identity and identity development.

The use of new technologies, media, and modalities is part and parcel of communication in the multilingual world that was highlighted throughout this volume and that should be subject to future study. Communication via multiple modalities is particularly displayed in the population that Chen Pichler, Reynolds, and Palmer feature in Chapter 9 – namely, Codas or Children of Deaf Adults, who have natural sign languages from birth along with spoken languages (bimodality) in their repertoire. Like multilingual communities and families in

Part 1 and in Chapters 10 (Quay and Chevalier) and 11 (Lanza and Lexander), this population also experiences issues related to migration, geographic proximity to international borders, and determination to maintain family culture. At the same time, multilingual signing communities make use of language practices that are more complex and diverse than in the case of two spoken languages because they involve two different modalities. Indeed, it is precisely when signed and spoken content is articulated simultaneously (i.e., code-blending) that language boundaries dissolve and traditional accounts of language use and mixing fail. The issue of code-blending is relevant to the discussion of translanguaging in other chapters as well, which explore a multilingual use of language that goes beyond named languages to encompass the dynamic nature of human meaning-making and of languaging. For example, Stavans and Porat (Chapter 7) advocate for moving beyond studying code-switching from a structural perspective that examines the mixing of separate linguistic systems related to labeled languages to embrace this practice as "a multilingual, multimodal, and multisensory sense- and meaning-making resource" (Li 2018: blog).

At a time of increasing hybridization when there are fewer boundaries between spoken and sign languages, between written and aural/audio-visual texts, between real and virtual worlds, and between languages and identities, examples abound throughout this volume of translanguaging not only from an educational perspective (Stavans and Porat, Chapter 7, Chen Pichler, Reynolds, and Palmer, Chapter 9, and Wang, Chapter 12) but also in discourse (Chapters 7 and 9 again, Quay and Chevalier, Chapter 10, and Lanza and Lexander, Chapter 11). As a pedagogical approach, translanguaging refers to specific teaching strategies that emphasize the dynamic use of multiple languages to foster learning (Allgäuer-Hackl and Jessner, Chapter 15) and to affirm the value and multiplicity of linguistic diversity across and within communities and individuals (Stavans and Porat, Chapter 7). Spontaneous translanguaging, on the other hand, refers to multilingual practices in discourse, which offer more learning opportunities and space to negotiate social identities and meaning. Therefore, in a way, as shown in Chapter 6 (Maher), even monolingual individuals who use different varieties (written as well as spoken) of a named language – and not just those who speak different named languages – can practice translanguaging. As put by MacSwan (2017: 188), "[w]e are all multilinguals in the sense that we each use different ways of talking in different social contexts". Although no explicit reference to the theme of translanguaging is made, Chapter 14 (Montanari) also offers examples of a transfer of knowledge from earlier learned languages, akin to using all of one's resources, to facilitate learning a new language in a new situation. Likewise, Chapter 15 (Allgäuer-Hackl and Jessner) shows that it is precisely the enhanced (meta)linguistic and metacognitive knowledge that multilinguals have accumulated through their use of "all their linguistic resources" that makes them efficient language learners. These examples from a wide range of spheres vividly demonstrate the dynamic nature of the multilingual phenomena as further expounded in Chapter 13 (Jessner and Megens) and Chapter 15 (Allgäuer-Hackl and Jessner) on cross-linguistic influence and interaction in the multilingual mind.

Language differences can be conceptualized according to the structural or linguistic patterns evidenced by speakers (Stavans and Porat, Chapter 7; Gooskens, Chapter 8; Chen Pichler, Reynolds, and Palmer, Chapter 9; Wang, Chapter 12; Montanari, Chapters 14) or to the political identifications of languages (contributions in Part 1). In proposing a "multilingual perspective on translanguaging", MacSwan (2017) advocates that the political use of language names can and should be distinguished from the social and structural idealizations used to study linguistic diversity. Only in this way can translanguaging support not only a heteroglossic language ideology but also traditional basic scientific research on codeswitching, mother tongues, and language rights, thus bridging the linguistic aspect with contributions to language ideology, policy, and pedagogy. The themes of diglossia, codeswitching and translanguaging as multilingual practices have raised fundamental questions about the nature of language boundaries in multilingual society that we have only just started to traverse. The dynamics of language choice in individuals and as used in educational institutions, cities, nations, and cyberspace are undergoing changes as a result of cultural, political and economic forces. The value of multilingualism to the individual and to society can be seen in this volume by the transformative effect that multilingualism has on language learning, its impact on the structures of education, society, culture, family and national policies, and even on cognitive and brain functions (Segal et al., Chapter 16; Strangmann, Chen, and Obler, Chapter 17).

Another common theme that appears in this volume is that of multilingual literacy (i.e., reading and writing in different languages). It is of significant importance for a variety of reasons. Multilingual children and adults who are literate use this skill to maintain their languages (Quay and Chevalier, Chapter 10; Wang, Chapter 12), particularly for heritage language maintenance through digital literacy (Lanza and Lexander, Chapter 11). A writing system can also be a lingua franca or common language not only between the Deaf and non-signing interlocutors (Chen Pichler, Reynolds, and Palmer, Chapter 9) but also for the hearing (Maher, Chapter 6; Gooskens, Chapter 8). For example, the shared use of Chinese characters in much of East Asia and parts of Southeast Asia (Maher, Chapter 6) comprises shared knowledge between different languages and cultures and enhances the co-existence of the people using this writing system. Orthographical knowledge as part of literacy skills also facilitates the learning of new languages (Montanari, Chapter 14). Furthermore, orthographical knowledge helps increase intelligibility between speakers of Scandinavian languages (Gooskens, Chapter 8) and reading comprehension among speakers of different Germanic languages (Bartelheimer, Hufeisen and Montanari, Chapter 4). Indeed, literacy skills have also been shown to affect cognitive performance in old age by improving memory and executive functioning (Segal et al., Chapter 16).

Multilingual literacy, moreover, plays a key role in the development of culture and knowledge (Stavans and Porat, Chapter 7); that is, it helps individuals construct knowledge from multiple sources and promote cultural and communicative diversity. In classrooms where students are exposed to more than one linguistic system and culture, learners can draw from their existing pool of languages and literacy practices to blend familiar practices with new forms, called "syncretic" literacy (Wang, Chapter 12). Allgäuer-Hackl and Jessner (Chapter 15) argue that while multilingual literacy involves a common underlying proficiency between writing processes in the various languages, cross-linguistic interaction also affects it.

18.4 Multilingualism as opposed to bilingualism

The last significant theme that emerges from this volume's contributions – particularly those in the final section – focuses on what makes multilingualism unique with respect to bilingualism, a contentious issue in contemporary research. Indeed, despite years of progress marked by an increasing recognition of the importance of studying the acquisition and use of "more than one language", multilingualism – in the sense of learning and speaking not just two but "multiple languages" – is often dismissed by bilingualism researchers as a simple variant of bilingualism (de Bot and Jaensch 2015). Yet, this volume makes clear that multilingualism should rather be studied in its own right as further evidence of the human potential and capacity for language. For instance, the learning, processing and use of multiple languages in the mind results in the development of components in multilingual systems that are not present in or are qualitatively different from those developed in bilingual systems (Jessner and Megens, Chapter 13; Allgäuer-Hackl and Jessner, Chapter 15). These include skills in language learning, management and maintenance that result in more complex cross-linguistic interactions and increased multilingual awareness than in bilinguals due to all language systems influencing each other in any direction (Jessner and Megens, Chapter 13; Allgäuer-Hackl and Jessner,

Chapter 15). Interaction between multiple language systems coupled with increased metalinguistic and cross-linguistic awareness facilitate novel language learning in multilinguals (Montanari, Chapter 14) and may lead to better cognitive performance in older multilinguals as opposed to bilinguals or monolinguals (Segal et al., Chapter 16). Thus, despite the fact that similar variables impact bilingualism and multilingualism, multilingualism cannot be equated to bilingualism because of the increasingly dynamic, multidimensional, and heterogeneous complexity that derive from the learning, processing, use, and unlearning "of more than two languages", across different modalities, at distinct life stages, and in varied contexts.

Of course the question remains as to why, while linguistic and psycholinguistic studies suggest differences in the processing of a third compared to a first or second language, neurolinguistic research shows that generally the same areas of the brain – and the same cognitive mechanisms – are activated during language use in proficient multilinguals (Strangmann, Chen, and Obler, Chapter 17). De Bot and Jaensch (2015), for instance, question the notion of languages as separate entities in the brain and posit a more dynamic perspective that focuses on "overall" language development and processing over time. The very limited literature that compares the organization and processing of languages in speakers of multiple languages also indicates a common language network for bilinguals and multilinguals that is modulated by factors such as age of acquisition, proficiency, and language use (Strangmann, Chen, and Obler, Chapter 17).

However, simply because neurolinguistics studies show the same areas of the brain activated in bilingual and multilingual processing does not imply that the processes are the same. In other words, although specific areas of the left hemisphere have evolved to better process transient stimuli that require high temporal resolution such as language (be it the first, second or third) (Zatorre, Belin, and Penhune 2002), the processes might be qualitatively different when a third or fourth language is involved as opposed to a second, especially given that age of acquisition, proficiency and language use will be different. Furthermore, bilingual neurolinguistics research has suffered from serious methodological shortcomings. First, most of the "bilingual" subjects in these studies have been European university students who are actually multilingual – and not just bilingual – for socio-political and educational reasons. Second, the majority of these investigations has used neuroimaging techniques, which have a coarse level of resolution and are thus unable to differentiate between the language-specific neuronal circuits that are recruited during language processing (de Bot and Jaensch 2015). On the other hand, more recent multilingual electrical-stimulation studies, which record from finer-grained regions of the brain, more often find separate language areas for L1, L2, and L3 contiguous with shared ones due to their narrower levels of measurement (Strangmann, Chen, and Obler, Chapter 17). Thus, the conclusions we can draw as to differences in the neural organization of two vs. three or more languages are limited because research in this area is virtually in its infancy and there are many outstanding questions regarding the interpretation of language-related neural data. It goes without saying that, while we know humans have the neurocognitive capacity to learn multiple languages when the sociopolitical and sociolinguistic conditions permit, much work needs to be done in the future to examine the neural correlates of different languages in multilingual speakers.

18.5 Conclusion

Taken together, the contributions in this volume and the questions they raise highlight the complexity of multilingualism, the diversity of multilingual interactions for signers and speakers, the distinct paths in the learning, use and unlearning of multiple languages, and crucial differences between bilingualism and multilingualism. One of the strengths and distinguishing features of this volume is that it brings together researchers from a range of different subjects, from education, linguistics (applied, psycho-, socio-) to cognitive psychology and neuroscience. The multidisciplinary nature of this volume is meant to help students and scholars studying different areas of multilingualism become more aware of work in other domains – from sociopolitical and sociolinguistic forces pertaining to mobility and transnationalization to diverse approaches to language learning and language use.

It is hoped that future research will advance a dynamic, integrated and holistic view of multilingualism, extending studies to areas where multilingualism is the norm and where typologically distant languages are learned, used in different ways and across different modalities, or lost across the lifespan. Only such investigations can truly advance language-related research and move away from the idealized notions of monolingualism and nativeness put forward by the Euro-centric monoglossic ideology that has characterized the study of multilingualism so far. Future research can hopefully demonstrate how languages can help us respond to the key issues of our times. While some new paths are opening up, we are well aware that the journey started in this volume may not be straightforward, as we seek to better understand the complexity inherent in multilingualism while embracing the opportunities it offers and the challenges it poses.

References

Bhatia, Tej K. & William C. Ritchie (eds.). 2012. *The handbook of bilingualism and multilingualism*, 2nd edn. Malden, MA: Blackwell Publishing.

Bot, Kees de & Carol Jaensch. 2015. What is special about L3 processing? *Bilingualism: Language and Cognition* 18(2). 130–144.

European Commission. 2007. *Final report high level group on multilingualism*. Luxembourg: Office for Official Publications of the European Communities.

Herdina, Philip & Ulrike Jessner. 2002. *A dynamic model of multilingualism: Perspectives of change in psycholinguistics*. Clevedon: Multilingual Matters.

Hjorth, Larissa. 2011. Mobile specters of intimacy: A case study of women and mobile intimacy. In Rich Ling & Scott W. Campbell (eds.), *Mobile communication. Bringing us together and tearing us apart*, 37–60. New Brunswick & London: Transaction Publishers.

King, Kendall & Elizabeth Lanza. 2019. Ideology, agency and imagination in multilingual families: An introduction. *International Journal of Bilingualism* 23(3). 717–723.

Li, Wei. 2018. Translanguaging and code-switching: What's the difference? *Oxford University Press Blog*. https://blog.oup.com/2018/05/translanguaging-code-switching-difference/ (accessed 13 February 2019).

MacSwan, Jeff. 2017. A multilingual perspective on translanguaging. *American Educational Research Journal* 54(1). 167–201.

Zatorre, Robert J., Pascal Belin, and Virginia Penhune. 2002. Structure and function of auditory cortex: Music and speech. *Trends in Cognitive Sciences* 6. 37–46.

Index of Key Words

accent 7, 109, 114, 115, 125, 161, 258–260, 326
acquisition 166–167, 254–263, 391, 405–406
– L2 167, 213, 222, 223, 254, 275, 277, 279, 308–313, 320, 325, 329–331, 364, 381
– L3 186–188, 275, 290, 299–300, 308–313, 325, 328–331, 337, 381
advantage(s) 123, 133, 185, 257, 260, 299–320, 336, 337, 340, 343, 351, 353, 355, 366, 368, 370, 385, 389
– bilingual 185, 260, 302–304, 307, 313–316, 318, 320, 355, 366, 368, 385, 389
– multilingual 300, 302, 305–312, 314, 316, 319, 320, 343, 370
agency 215, 222, 232–235, 244, 400
aging 2, 3, 351–370
attitude(s) 130, 150, 153, 161, 221, 222, 254, 289, 312
attrition 1, 275–292, 325, 326, 337, 398, 399, 401
– foreign language 286, 288, 290
– multilingual 285, 286, 289–291
awareness 124, 131, 133, 164, 167, 178, 257, 266, 281, 284, 287, 289, 299, 301, 312, 315, 317, 325–344, 399, 405–406
– cross(-)linguistic (XLA) 290–292, 334–336, 339–342
– metalinguistic (MeLA) 334–344
– multilingual (MLA) 290–292, 334–344
– phonological (PA) 260

bicultural 180
bilingual(ism) 1, 38, 93, 105–107, 110, 113–114, 123, 125, 176–177, 179–191, 196, 214, 220–221, 230, 234, 275, 279, 300, 307, 312–313, 320, 325, 351–356, 366–369, 375, 380–381, 383–384, 388, 390, 397–399, 405–407
– bimodal 175, 176–191, 195–196, 388, 402
– signing 177–179, 189, 196
– unimodal 185–186, 189–190
borrowing 13, 116, 124, 126, 189, 232, 327, 332

brain 163, 184, 255, 277, 302, 320, 326, 343, 375–390, 404, 406–407

child(-) 175, 180, 186–188, 230
– external 213, 223
– internal 205, 213, 222
– language learning 223, 230, 232, 234, 400
– multilingual(ism) 129, 133, 194–196, 205, 206, 208, 214, 216, 219, 221–224, 253–255, 257, 259, 262, 269, 305, 333, 400, 401, 404
cochlear implant(s) (CI) 177, 188
Codas/Kodas 175, 181, 186–188
– Coda speak 181
– Coda-talk 180–182
code-blend(ing) 182–185, 187, 195–196, 403
code(-)mixing 39, 180–184, 187, 195, 388
– Manually Coded English 182
– Signing Exact English 182
– Simultaneous Communication 180, 182
code(-)switch(ing) 105, 107, 128, 140, 165, 182, 187, 189–191, 195–196, 210, 214, 215, 217, 218, 241, 244, 326, 333, 378, 385–387, 403. *See also* switching
– alternational 124
– function(s) 124, 130–133, 135, 138
– intersentential 124, 142
– intrasentential 124, 126
cognitive 66, 123, 126, 128, 131, 139, 152, 160, 180, 184–186, 189, 213, 241, 255, 257, 258, 266–268, 277, 279, 281–284, 291, 292, 299, 301, 307, 308, 315–320, 326, 329, 332, 334–335, 337, 341–343, 351–370, 378, 381, 383, 385, 389, 398, 399, 401, 403–408
– ability/ies 307, 317–319, 354, 368, 369
– benefits 320, 351–370
– differences 369
– functions 184, 352, 353, 355, 385
– performance 3, 291, 351–356, 362, 365–370, 405, 406
– reserve 351, 353, 367, 368, 369
– tests 354, 367
colonialism 3, 27, 45, 397

Common European Framework of References for Languages (CEFR) 67, 68
communication 14–16, 20, 30–32, 42, 53, 57, 61–64, 67, 96, 112, 114, 115, 124, 130, 131, 134–141, 143, 149–152, 161, 164–166, 168, 180, 182, 189, 192, 195, 209, 212, 214, 216, 217, 223, 231, 237–245, 254, 260, 264, 265, 284, 352, 385, 401, 402
– intergenerational 242
Complexity Theory (CT) 279
Content and Language(s) Integrated Learning (CLIL) 65–66
critical period (CP) 255, 381
cross(-)linguistic 2, 149, 180, 221, 236, 256–257, 259, 262, 291, 307, 308, 310, 325–344, 398, 399, 404
– awareness 325, 332, 334–337, 341, 343, 406
– influence (CLI) 259, 308, 310, 325–331, 340, 343, 404
– interactions (CLIN) 2, 259, 281, 291, 325–344, 398, 399, 405
– mixing (CLM) 180, 262
– transfer 256, 257
cross-signing 189, 192, 193, 194, 401

DDCI (Deaf children of Deaf parents, who use cochlear implants) 177–179, 182, 188, 197
Deaf 175–182, 185–195, 400, 402, 404
development 3, 11, 12, 14, 15, 17, 27, 31, 37, 41, 54, 55, 59, 69, 70, 90, 92, 94, 96, 108, 111, 116, 126, 134, 136, 139, 141, 157, 159, 175, 176, 178, 181, 186–188, 194–197, 205, 206, 209, 211–214, 216, 219, 223, 224, 230, 232, 234–236, 239, 245, 253, 258–268, 275, 276, 278–283, 285, 289–292, 307, 312–314, 325, 326, 328, 329, 332–333, 337, 338, 340–344, 398–402, 405, 406
– figurative language 268
– harmonious 216, 223
– language 54, 175, 187, 205, 206, 213, 216, 230, 232, 235, 245, 268, 276, 279, 280, 282, 291, 292, 332, 333, 334, 398, 406
– lexical 186, 261
– literacy 178, 223, 235–236, 265–267, 312–314, 332–333
– morphosyntactic 263–264
– multilingual 92, 96, 134, 211, 213, 216, 219, 223, 230, 269, 275, 279–282, 285, 291, 292, 325, 326, 343–344, 399, 400, 401
– narrative 265
– phonological 258–260
– pragmatic 264–265
dialect(s) 7, 12, 13, 15–22, 23, 42, 52, 57, 58, 61, 62, 91, 92, 103, 107, 108, 112, 113, 115, 125, 150, 151, 153, 155, 157, 158, 164, 176, 241, 354
digital(ly) 3, 139, 140, 217, 231, 233, 237–245, 402, 404
– communication 139, 238, 240, 241
– interaction 233, 237–240, 242, 244
– mediated 3, 139, 217, 231, 233, 237–245, 402
– tools 244
diglossia/diglossic 2, 3, 12–14, 103–119, 398, 399, 404
discourse 7, 10, 11, 14, 15, 17–19, 22, 24, 62, 67, 105, 125, 130, 133, 138, 152, 164, 188, 205, 209–211, 222, 223, 232, 235, 236, 254, 398, 400, 403
– continuum 210
– patterns 205, 254
– strategies 209, 210, 211
– style(s) 209–211, 222, 223, 236
dominance 2, 29, 30, 41, 59, 135, 190, 217, 275, 284, 359, 361
dual-lingual 210, 214, 400
Dynamic Model of Multilingualism (DMM) 275, 279–285, 287, 288, 290–292, 325, 327, 334, 337, 340–343, 399
Dynamic Systems and/or Complexity Theory (DSCT) 275, 279, 282, 292, 325–328, 333, 343
Dynamic Systems Theory (DST) 126, 279

education(al) 2–4, 10, 14, 18, 28–38, 40, 41, 55, 58–60, 63, 66, 67, 69–71, 77, 80, 83, 86–96, 106, 107, 114, 115, 129, 132, 133, 134, 136–138, 141, 143, 149, 152,

154, 166, 176, 177, 180, 189, 193, 197, 205, 223, 232, 238, 242, 245, 258, 269, 277, 290, 300, 318, 320, 326, 335, 351, 354–358, 361, 362, 365, 366, 367, 369, 397, 400–404, 406, 407
– bilingual 88–91, 94, 95, 193, 223
endoglossic 104, 118
ERP (Event-Related Potential) 302, 311
ESM (Electric Stimulation Mapping) 381–384, 389, 390
exoglossic 104, 118
exposure 91, 138, 155, 162–163, 178, 179, 186, 205, 207, 208, 212, 213, 216–220, 223, 253, 255, 256, 257, 259, 260, 284, 285, 306, 377, 379, 384, 387, 390

family/families 2–4, 32, 33, 42, 60, 84, 95, 103, 104, 105, 107, 114, 115, 117, 129, 134, 139, 141, 142, 152, 175, 188, 205–211, 213–224, 229–245, 253, 400–404
– diaspora 238
– internet 238
– transcultural 2, 3, 229–245
family language policy (FLP) 141, 142, 205, 209, 217, 229–233, 234, 236–239, 241, 245, 400

global/globalization 2, 3, 28, 36, 45, 51, 67, 68, 88, 106, 119, 123, 131, 133, 140, 142, 143, 149, 193, 221, 229, 231, 276, 352, 388, 402
grandparents 104, 205, 208, 216, 217, 220, 223, 238, 239, 241, 242, 245

heritage 84, 88, 91–96, 117, 134, 142, 178–180, 188, 194, 196, 197, 208, 209, 217, 218, 220, 222, 223, 230, 234, 235–241, 243, 318, 400, 404
– language(s) 88, 91–96, 117, 134, 142, 188, 194, 196, 208, 209, 217, 218, 220, 222, 223, 230, 234–241, 243, 318, 400, 404
– learner(s) 92, 95
– signer(s) 178, 179, 188, 197
hybridization 403

identity/identities 16, 17, 20, 28, 30, 35, 38, 41, 42, 44, 52, 56, 62, 68, 117–119, 130–132, 141, 143, 150, 180, 207, 231–233, 237–239, 244, 254, 262, 267, 326, 402, 403
ideology/ideologies 7–24, 129, 130, 133, 141, 142, 229, 230, 232, 237, 397–399, 404, 407
– assimilation 133
– exclusion 133
– impact beliefs 221, 223
– inclusion 132–135
immigrant(s) 35, 59, 60, 61, 70, 77, 78, 80–84, 86, 91, 93, 94, 134, 152, 178, 208, 238, 312, 313, 354, 358, 397
immigration 29, 59, 60, 77, 78, 80–82, 86–89, 95, 96, 193, 312, 354, 355, 358
indigenous 8, 34, 35, 37–39, 77, 87, 93–96, 115, 117, 118, 130, 177, 208, 399
Information and Communication Technology (ICT) 241, 242
input 31, 152, 167, 175, 186, 187, 188, 205, 207–209, 211–213, 216, 217, 219, 222, 223, 230, 237, 254, 255, 257, 260, 261, 267, 280, 285, 308, 376, 387
intelligibility 8, 16, 21, 22, 151, 153–163, 165, 167, 405
interference 185, 259, 285, 306, 307, 326–327, 353, 385, 386, 387, 389
interlanguage 10, 329

knowledge 2, 14, 24, 37, 68, 119, 123, 126, 136, 150, 163–165, 193, 211, 219, 242, 256, 257, 261, 266, 268, 276, 279, 282, 286–288, 303, 304, 310, 316, 318, 325–329, 339, 341, 342, 368, 382, 399, 403–405
– metacognitive 292, 341, 403
– metalinguistic 268, 339, 341

LAILA (linguistic awareness in language attrition) 286, 289, 290
language(s) 1–4, 7–24, 27–45, 51–70, 77–80, 82–96, 103–119, 123–143, 149–167, 175–180, 182–197, 205–223, 229–245, 253–261, 263–268, 275–292,

299–321, 325–337, 339–342, 351–356, 358–362, 375–390, 397–407
– additional (AL) 2, 57, 65, 208, 253–268, 275, 279, 301, 310, 311, 312, 314, 335, 340, 360, 377, 388, 400
– attitude(s) 32, 38, 161, 162, 289 (see also attitude)
– choice 59, 117, 125, 126, 131, 150, 187, 205–211, 223, 230, 234, 236, 238, 240, 404
– contact 39, 42, 110, 124–125, 128–143, 176, 216–220, 223, 277, 278, 289, 292, 325, 326, 333, 343, 399
– control 375, 378, 379, 385–389
– development 54, 175, 187, 205, 206, 213, 216, 230, 232, 235, 245, 268, 276, 279, 280, 282, 291, 292, 332, 333, 398, 406
– distance/distant 8, 330, 331, 377, 379, 407
– dual 89, 90–92, 304, 385, 386, 387
– foreign (FL) 7, 9–11, 16, 51–53, 55, 56, 63–68, 88, 91, 95, 137, 149, 167, 278, 287, 289, 290, 299, 300, 307, 311, 329, 330, 334, 336, 341, 401
– heritage 88, 91, 92, 94–96, 117, 134, 142, 188, 194, 196, 208, 209, 217, 218, 220, 222, 223, 230, 234–241, 243, 318, 400, 404
– home 2, 32, 33, 60, 68, 78–80, 82, 90, 188, 193, 207, 208, 209, 214, 215, 216, 217, 222, 223, 235, 236, 244, 259
– hybrid 180
– immigrant 52, 59–62, 68, 85, 92–94, 96
– indigenous 34, 37, 38, 77, 87, 95, 115, 118, 130
– maintenance 37, 126, 129, 142, 212, 217, 219, 230–237, 275, 281, 283–285, 288, 292, 335, 337, 343, 404
– majority 60, 132, 142, 197, 206, 208, 212, 213, 220, 221, 223, 240, 300, 330, 401
– minority 37, 38, 52, 58–59, 62, 86, 110, 133, 197, 206, 207, 208, 209, 211–213, 216–223, 230, 235, 236, 300, 330, 401
– mixing 110, 127, 129, 182, 187, 196, 243, 328
– mode 126, 127, 166, 278

– native 38, 87, 89, 91, 137, 149–151, 162, 164, 165, 167, 206, 207, 216, 220, 221, 222, 285, 302, 307, 380
– official 18, 22, 28, 29, 31, 34, 35, 41, 42, 52–56, 61, 62, 77, 82, 85, 87, 92, 93, 96, 104, 105, 129, 130, 209, 240, 288, 290, 354, 397, 401
– planning 27, 114, 152, 229, 230, 245
– policy/policies 28, 29, 31, 35, 42, 51, 52, 53, 61, 63, 66, 68, 70, 86, 87, 93, 94, 129, 130, 152, 166–167, 220, 229–231, 233–236
– practice(s) 2, 104, 131, 133, 175, 214, 229–245, 390, 402, 403
– previous (PL) 3, 254–257, 259, 261, 262, 264–266, 268, 317, 320, 326
– processing 2, 184, 311, 320, 375–390, 401, 406
– proficiency 59, 79, 133, 276, 280, 283, 287, 332, 340, 353–356, 359, 361, 366, 369
– representation 376, 377–379, 381, 383, 387
– shift 37, 44, 94, 110–111, 113–115, 129, 234, 237, 241, 244, 276, 284, 400, 401
– sign 94, 175–178, 180, 184, 187–193, 196, 197, 402, 403
– signed 175, 176, 178, 180, 182, 193
– socialization 229, 232, 234, 400
– societal 59, 206, 207, 210, 212, 213, 216, 217, 222, 232, 400, 401
– spoken 2, 3, 28, 30–32, 84, 116, 175, 176–180, 182–190, 193–195, 233–237, 240, 313, 402–403
– target 65, 69, 92, 137, 265, 326, 327, 329–331, 384
– usage/use 2, 28, 29, 38, 43, 45, 108, 112, 115, 116, 117, 129, 132, 138, 141, 162, 175, 207–209, 213, 215, 217, 220, 221, 229–233, 237, 238–240, 254, 277, 278, 283, 341, 351, 352, 354–356, 366, 367, 368, 377, 378, 385, 398, 401, 402, 403, 406
– world 90, 91
language learning 2, 10, 53, 61, 63, 66, 68, 132, 137, 138, 150, 160, 223, 230, 232–234, 235, 241–244, 258, 281, 282,

287, 292, 299–321, 325, 329, 335, 336, 337, 341, 342, 343, 368, 390, 399–401, 404–407
– facilitated 299–321
– novel 53, 299–314, 317, 318, 319, 320, 406
lingua franca 21, 28, 30, 33, 37, 38, 41, 44, 108, 114, 149, 151, 164, 165, 166, 193, 206, 221, 397, 401, 404
linguistic 1, 2, 7–14, 16, 18, 19, 21, 24, 27, 28, 34, 44, 52–54, 59, 60, 62–64, 66, 69, 77, 85, 86–95, 103, 105, 110, 111, 113, 117, 118, 123–126, 128, 129, 131–137, 139, 141–143, 149–153, 155–167, 175, 178, 180–184, 193, 194, 196, 197, 207, 213, 215, 219, 222, 229–231, 237, 238, 240–241, 253, 254, 257, 259, 263, 264, 266, 267, 268, 275, 276, 277, 278, 281, 288, 290, 292, 299, 300, 302, 303, 308, 310, 311, 317, 318, 328, 330, 333, 335, 339, 341, 376, 397, 399, 401, 403, 404, 405
literacy 3, 69, 110, 115, 116, 117, 119, 128, 135, 136, 139–141, 151, 154, 163, 177, 178, 219–220, 223, 229, 235–236, 241–243, 253, 254, 258, 265–267, 277, 301, 309, 311–314, 316–320, 332–333, 351, 355, 400–402, 404, 405
– biliteracy 32, 309, 313, 317
– digital 242, 243, 404
– home 235
– learning 242, 312, 313, 316, 317, 320
– multilingual 52, 332, 337, 340–341, 343 (*see also* multiliteracy)
– syncretic 267, 405
literate 13, 16, 140, 163, 266, 286, 314, 317, 355, 404
– biliterates 31, 32, 140, 266, 267, 309, 310, 313
– triliterates 266, 267
LME (language maintenance effort) 283–285, 288

media 10, 17, 31, 32, 44, 58, 103, 105, 107, 113, 115, 117, 131, 162, 219–220, 237–241, 244, 245, 402
metalinguistic 17, 113, 131, 164, 167, 255, 257, 260, 268, 281, 283, 287, 289, 290,

291, 292, 299, 308, 312, 317, 325, 329, 332, 334–336, 337, 339, 340, 341, 343, 399, 406
migrant(s) 60, 69, 70, 81, 82, 117, 232, 233, 238, 239, 241, 242, 243, 244, 278
migration 3, 4, 51, 59, 110, 117, 123, 131, 133, 134, 141, 142, 175, 229, 229, 234, 238, 285, 397, 402, 403
mobility 30, 32, 35, 37, 41, 118, 142, 152, 223, 229, 237, 401, 407
– elite 142
– global 142
– hypermobility 237
modality/modalities 136, 140, 143, 160, 175, 176, 180, 181, 182, 184, 186, 188, 189, 190, 191, 196, 237, 238, 240–241, 254, 397, 402, 403, 406
– bimodality 196, 402
– effects 176, 189
mode-finding 186
monoglossic 398, 407
monolingual(ism) 7, 28, 29, 41, 52, 55, 111, 117, 118, 123, 126, 127, 128, 130, 133–137, 140, 141, 143, 150, 165, 178, 185, 186, 216, 218, 223, 234, 257, 258, 261, 262, 265, 280, 281, 299–314, 316, 318, 325, 333, 334, 337, 339, 342, 343, 351, 352, 356, 358, 366, 367, 368, 376, 378, 379, 381, 385, 386, 388, 397, 398, 401, 403, 406
multi-competence 278, 326
multidisciplinary 1–4, 179–188
multilingual 1–4, 7–24, 27–45, 51–71, 77–96, 103–119, 123–143, 149–168, 175–197, 205–224, 229–245, 253–269, 275–292, 299–321, 325–344, 351–370, 375–390, 397–408
– child(ren) 3, 129, 133, 194, 205, 206, 208, 214, 216, 219, 221–224, 253–255, 257, 259, 262, 269, 305, 333, 400, 401, 404
– classrooms 129, 137
– education 80, 91, 92, 94, 95, 136, 137
– language use 4, 355, 401
– learners 92, 254, 257, 260, 269, 308, 320, 325, 335, 340–342

– participants 253, 262, 355, 370, 381, 383
multilingual(s)
– bimodal 178, 388
– Deaf 178, 179
– Emergent 140, 341
multilingualism 1–4, 7–24, 27–45, 51–71, 77–96, 149–168, 175–197, 205–224, 253–269, 351–370, 375, 376, 378–381, 383–385, 388, 390, 397–408
– active 206–217, 222
– childhood 3, 205–224
– national 52, 54, 56, 57
– passive 207, 214, 339
– receptive 3, 149, 153–155, 166, 167, 207, 208, 400, 401
– regional 52, 54, 57
multiliteracy/multiliteracies 130, 135, 136, 139, 310, 313, 314
multimodal 95, 128, 136, 179, 194, 235, 403
mutually intelligible 2, 57, 149–151, 153, 166

native 11, 13, 20, 24, 37, 38, 40, 60, 87, 89, 90, 91, 104, 137, 149–151, 162, 164, 167, 177, 178, 193, 206, 207, 215, 216, 218, 220–222, 255, 259, 260, 265, 280, 282, 285, 302, 304, 305, 307, 311, 339, 358, 380, 381
neurobiology 376
neuroimaging 2, 383, 384, 406
neurolinguistic(s) 1, 2, 180, 277, 375, 378, 380, 383, 390, 406
neuroscience 184, 407
non(-)native 11, 178, 221, 282, 301, 302, 305, 310, 328–331, 333, 380

OPOL (one person one language) 206, 207, 214–216, 222, 230, 232, 400

para(-)linguistic 139, 141, 158, 159, 165, 258
peer(s) 32, 94, 134, 159, 205, 241, 257, 258, 260, 264, 265, 304, 342
personality 160, 162, 205, 211, 213, 223
plurilingual(ism) 52, 53, 61, 68, 70, 77, 83, 86, 87, 91, 95, 96, 149, 164

prestige 10, 28, 31, 33, 35, 45, 107, 111, 113, 117, 161, 221
proficiency 10, 11, 14, 30, 32, 36–38, 57, 59, 60, 79, 80, 83, 88–91, 123, 126, 133, 149, 150, 162, 164, 177, 187, 193, 194, 212, 255, 257, 260, 275, 276, 280–285, 287, 289, 290, 292, 300, 307, 309, 311–313, 319, 320, 328, 330–334, 340, 352–359, 361, 362, 365–367, 377–381, 387, 389, 390, 399, 405, 406
psycholinguistic 1, 2, 53, 125, 126, 129, 135, 180, 184, 185, 191, 230, 277, 282–284, 327, 406
psychotypology 256, 328, 330, 331

receptive 3, 149–168, 207, 208, 210, 214, 261, 262, 278, 287, 288, 291, 400, 401
receptive multilingualism (RM) 3, 149–168, 207, 208, 400, 401
– acquired 150, 155
– inherent 150, 155
refugee(s) 59, 60, 69–71, 81, 82, 91, 142

sibling(s) 205, 208, 214, 216, 219, 234, 236, 242, 259, 286
sign(ing) 2, 37, 53, 58, 68, 110, 117, 136, 139, 140, 175–197, 259, 286, 288–290, 333, 400–404
– bimodal 2, 180
– unimodal 189–191, 196
SLA (second language acquisition) 1, 52, 164, 279, 325–327, 329
strategy/strategies 9, 20, 33, 64, 113, 124, 125, 130, 137, 139, 141, 164, 165, 167, 187, 189, 192, 195, 205, 207, 209–211, 213, 215, 216, 230, 237, 239, 258, 262, 264, 265, 268, 291, 292, 301, 305–309, 312, 316, 317, 332, 335, 336, 341–343, 402, 403
switching 104, 124, 184, 185, 191, 196, 216, 353, 355, 356, 359, 361, 362, 365, 367–370, 383, 386–388
– language 216, 353, 355, 359, 361, 362, 365, 367–369, 383, 387, 388

- metaphorical 125
- situational 125

technology 36, 140, 141, 143, 231, 237, 239, 243, 244, 402
- digital 139
- information 402
TLA (third or additional language acquisition) 275, 279, 325, 327, 329–331, 336, 337, 343
transcultural 2, 3, 118, 229–231, 233, 237, 242, 245
transfer 3, 124, 126, 256, 257, 262, 264, 265, 285, 286, 301, 304–307, 310, 313, 314, 316–319, 326–332, 335, 336, 342, 343, 403
- cross(-)linguistic 256, 257
- interlanguage 329
- negative 257

- positive 257, 326
- semantic 262
translanguaging 128, 129, 134, 138, 142, 189, 193, 194, 196, 215, 216, 230, 235, 244, 257, 258, 403, 404
trilingual(ism) 28, 31, 32, 44, 52, 53, 57, 91, 92, 124, 127, 130, 133, 134, 195, 206–208, 210–214, 218, 221, 259, 280, 325, 330, 332, 340, 368, 380, 387
- active 210, 212
- passive 207, 214
- receptive 210, 211
typology 256, 310, 311, 328, 330–332, 342

vernacular 33–36, 38, 40–44, 92, 104–106, 108, 109, 111, 117–119
vocabulary 64, 156, 159, 160, 162, 186, 210, 211, 219, 257, 261–263, 265, 287, 299, 301, 304–307, 309, 314, 318, 319, 332

Index of Languages / Language Families

Afrikaans 154, 158
Ainu 114, 115
American Indian languages 151
American Sign Language (ASL) 94, 177, 179–190, 192, 193, 195, 196
Arabic 7, 10–18, 36, 40, 52, 59, 60, 69, 70, 79, 82, 83, 85, 91, 94, 95, 105, 106, 110, 151, 240–243, 258, 259, 300, 313, 314, 333, 358, 399
Armenian 60, 84
Australian Irish Sign Language (AISL) 189, 190
Australian Sign Language (Auslan) 189, 190
Austronesian 34
Azerbaijani/Azerbajani 151, 156, 157

Basque 52, 58, 59, 62, 130, 300, 330, 332, 339
Bengali 34, 60, 242
Berber 7, 17, 19–24, 59, 399
Bosnian 54
Breton 52, 58, 59
British Sign Language (BSL) 191
Burundi Sign Language (BuSL) 190, 191

Cantonese 28–34, 44, 82–86, 119, 130, 195, 208, 331, 379
Caribbean Creole 119
Catalan 54, 58, 114, 211, 216, 221, 222, 309, 330
Chinese 27–36, 38–45, 61, 79, 84, 85, 91, 92, 116, 119, 129, 130, 151, 208, 210, 212, 217, 219, 236, 243, 258, 259, 261, 264, 289, 303, 310, 311, 316, 319, 379, 404
Chinese Sign Language 176
Circassian 314
Cree 93, 95
Croatian 54
Czech 51, 154, 256

Danish 52, 57, 61, 64, 114, 151, 154, 155, 158, 159, 161–164, 166, 331

Dutch 27, 33, 45, 53–55, 62, 107, 111, 151, 152, 154, 157, 158, 164, 166, 187, 207, 217, 218, 243, 287, 288, 289, 300, 305, 313, 331, 342, 380, 387

English 8–11, 27–45, 51, 53, 55–57, 60–65, 67–71, 77, 79, 80, 82–96, 103–106, 108–119, 129, 130, 134, 137, 143, 149, 152, 160–162, 164, 166, 177, 179–188, 193–196, 206, 208–223, 236, 237, 240–243, 256, 258–261, 263–267, 286, 288–291, 300, 302–314, 316, 318, 319, 327, 329–336, 339, 340, 342, 343, 356, 358, 359, 367, 369, 379, 380, 387, 397, 401
Estonian 150, 151

Farsi 61, 83, 84, 86, 219
Filipino/Pilipino 61, 83, 84, 86, 220, 221, 241
Finnish 63, 109, 151, 187, 243, 265, 342, 379
Finnish Sign Language 187
Flemish 55, 107
Foochow 34
French 9–11, 17–20, 23, 27, 45, 51–58, 61–63, 65, 68, 77, 79, 82–86, 91, 93–96, 105, 107, 109, 110–114, 130, 160, 162, 186–187, 207–212, 218, 219, 223, 234, 240, 241, 243, 260, 286–291, 300, 302, 310, 312, 330, 331, 335, 342, 358, 380, 383, 384, 399

Gaelic 111, 214, 233, 236
Galician 58, 235
German 12, 15, 18, 51–57, 59, 61–66, 68–70, 77, 79, 81, 82, 88, 91, 94, 106–107, 109, 111, 113, 150–152, 156–158, 160, 164, 166, 206, 210, 212, 218, 219, 221, 256, 259, 288, 312, 318, 329–335, 339–342, 353, 358, 383, 387, 399, 405
Ghanaian languages 288
Greek 20, 85, 105, 106, 117, 312, 335
Gujarati 34, 109, 110, 208

https://doi.org/10.1515/9781501507984-020

Haitian 79, 91, 106
Hakka 34
Hebrew 84, 94–95, 105, 119, 133, 137–138, 214, 266–267, 286, 313, 314, 333, 358–359, 369, 379
Hindi 34, 107, 110, 208, 243, 302
Hokkien 34, 42
Hungarian 51, 63, 239

Indian languages 34, 43, 151, 239
Indian Sign Language (ISL) 190–191
Indo-European languages 80, 151, 331
Indonesian 237
International Sign (IS) 193
Inuktitut 93
Irish 104, 110–111, 118, 189, 191, 207–208
Irish Sign Language (Irish SL) 189, 191
Israel 136–138, 214, 235, 286, 313, 351, 353, 355, 356, 358
Italian 9, 10, 11, 53, 56, 61, 82, 83, 85, 86, 106, 107, 160, 176, 183, 221, 236, 239, 259, 289, 290, 291, 300, 305, 310, 332, 333, 339, 340, 342, 380
Italian Sign Language 176, 183

Japanese 27, 85, 88, 114, 115–118, 120, 179, 210–212, 214–222, 259, 264, 301

Kashubian 103–104
Khmer 34, 85, 95
Kinyarwanda 234
Korean 79, 84–86, 116, 179, 192–193, 208, 235, 238, 241, 260, 302–303, 316, 318, 319

Latin 20, 77, 105–108, 111, 114, 309, 330, 335, 342, 398
Libras (Brazilian Sign Langauge) 188
Luxembourgish 53, 56, 57, 62, 63

Malay 28, 34–44, 130
Malayalam 34, 110
Maltese 194–195
Maltese Sign Language (Maltese SL) 194–195

Mandarin 28–34, 36, 38, 42, 43–45, 82–86, 91, 92, 94
Marathi 109–110
Mexican Sign Language (LSM) 179, 190
Mon-Khmer 34

The Netherlands 54, 59, 82, 187, 217, 300, 313, 354
Norwegian 53, 57, 64, 65, 158, 159, 166, 240, 241, 243

Occitan 58, 59, 260
Ojibway 93

Pacific Islander languages 80
Palauan 117–118
Panjabi/Punjabi 60, 83
Patwa 130
Persian 82–86, 312
Polish 61, 81, 103–104, 117, 206, 221, 330–331
Portuguese 33, 85–86, 154, 188, 237, 286
Provençal 14
Putonghua 30–31, 130

Québec Sign Language (LSQ) 186–187

Rhaeto-Romance 53, 56
Romance 53, 56, 150–151, 156, 158, 399
Romani/Sinte 60
Romansch 312
Russian 59, 79, 81–84, 88, 91, 133, 150, 179, 214, 233, 265–267, 301, 305, 313–314, 327, 353
Ryukyuan languages 115

Scandinavian 3, 8, 63, 64, 150, 158, 166, 405
Serbian 54
Serbo-Croatian 54
Sign Language of the Netherlands (NGT) 187, 192–193
Slovak 154
Somali 60
Sorbian 52, 62

Spanish 9–11, 58, 61, 63, 79–80, 82–86, 89–92, 95, 106, 108, 109, 111, 129, 133, 154, 179, 195–196, 208, 216–217, 221–222, 256, 259, 261, 263, 266, 287–289, 300, 304–307, 309–312, 330, 332, 339, 358, 367
Swedish 64–65, 109, 151, 154–155, 158–160, 162–163, 166, 193, 206, 242, 265, 329, 330, 339
Swedish Sign Language (SSL) 193
Switzerland 12, 53–56, 70, 106, 206, 212, 218, 221, 312
Sylheti 242

Tagalog 79, 82–86, 217, 241
Taglish 241

Tamil 34, 36, 38, 40–43, 85–86, 110, 130
Telugu 34
Teochew 34
Tetum 237
Turkish 52, 59, 60–62, 151–152, 156–157, 217, 256, 300, 312

Urdu 60, 77, 82–83, 85–86, 107, 109, 110, 208, 236, 243

Welsh 110, 112
Wolof 240–241, 243

Yiddish 105, 112, 119

Index of Countries and Continents

Afghanistan 60
Africa 8, 353, 398
Algeria 9, 10, 18, 19, 21–23
Americas 77, 78
Asia 8, 27, 77, 78, 82, 109, 353, 398
Australia 151, 189, 217, 219, 312, 356
Austria 59, 66, 68, 77, 289

Balearic Islands 58
Basque Country 58, 300
Belgium 52–57, 59, 62, 106, 107, 111, 218, 300
Bermuda 82
Britain 9, 28, 87, 105, 237, 356
British Isles 81, 82

Cambodia 82, 84, 243
Canada 1, 3, 77, 81–83, 85–87, 92–96, 162, 208, 209, 213, 219, 223, 300, 311, 312, 356, 358, 397, 400
Caribbean 82, 119
Catalonia 58, 221, 222
China 27, 28, 30–32, 39, 78, 82, 119, 130, 237
Costa Rica 129
Cuba 78, 106
Cyprus 117

Denmark 57, 151
Dominican Republic 78

Egypt 9, 13
El Salvador 78
England 45, 105, 110, 112, 206, 221
Estonia 58, 66
Europe 1, 3, 51–71, 81, 108, 109, 114, 124, 151, 166, 239, 300, 353, 397, 398, 400
European Union/EU 52, 60–63

Flanders 54, 55, 207
France 9, 51, 52, 58, 59, 63, 81, 82, 109, 111, 130, 208

Galicia 58
Germany 52, 59, 61, 62, 63, 66, 69, 77, 81, 82, 152, 206, 219, 221

Ghana 288
Great Britain 256
Greece 12, 82, 130
Guatemala 78

Haiti 12, 82, 91, 106, 107
Hong Kong 3, 27–33, 39, 44, 45, 82, 129, 130
Hungary 77, 239

India 3, 10, 11, 27, 78, 82, 84, 85, 109, 190, 191, 239, 398
Indonesia 27, 45
Iran 82, 219, 312
Ireland 3, 52, 55, 66, 77, 103, 104, 110, 118, 207, 237, 239, 336
Israel 138, 214, 235, 286, 313, 353, 355, 356, 358
Italy 9, 58, 60, 61, 77, 82, 85, 289, 290

Jamaica 82, 119
Japan 3, 82, 114–116, 119, 220

Korea 27, 78, 82, 85, 119, 238

Labuan islands 33
Laos 82
Latin America 77, 398
Libya 9, 10
Luxembourg 53, 56, 57, 63, 354

Malacca 33, 40
Malaysia 3, 27–45
Mauritania 9
Mexico 78, 82, 159, 190
Middle East 15, 17, 60, 91, 106
Morocco 9, 10, 17–23

North Africa 1, 3, 7–24, 397, 398, 400
North America 1, 77–96, 128, 177, 229, 288, 397, 398
Northern Ireland 237
Norway 53, 57, 63, 70, 151, 235, 240, 246

Oceania 81

https://doi.org/10.1515/9781501507984-021

Pakistan 82
Palau 117, 118
Penang 33, 40
Philippines 27, 78, 82, 241
Poland 62, 77, 82, 85
Portugal 82, 85

Romania 58, 82

Scandinavia 81, 82, 151, 166
Scotland 233
Senegal 240
Singapore 3, 27–45, 397, 401
Somalia 60
South Africa 245
Southeast Asia 1, 27–45, 81, 397, 400, 404
Spain 9, 54, 58, 59, 62, 63, 130, 211, 289, 300, 309, 312
Sweden 59, 63, 151, 193, 234, 238, 242, 300

Switzerland 12, 53–56, 70, 107, 206, 212, 218, 221, 312

Taiwan 27, 30
Timor-Leste 237
Trinidad and Tobago 82
Tunisia 9, 10, 110

United Kingdom (UK) 59, 60, 62, 63, 77, 82, 215
United States (US) 1, 3, 77, 78–83, 87, 88, 91, 95, 96, 115, 176, 178, 216, 217, 367

Vietnam 27, 45, 78, 82

Wales 110
Wallonia 54, 55, 111
West Indies 130

Yugoslavia 8, 54, 82

www.ingramcontent.com/pod-product-compliance
Lightning Source LLC
Chambersburg PA
CBHW051554230426
43668CB00013B/1843